A New History of German Cinema

Screen Cultures: German Film and the Visual

Series Editors:
Gerd Gemünden (*Dartmouth College*)
Johannes von Moltke (*University of Michigan*)

A New History of German Cinema

Edited by
Jennifer M. Kapczynski &
Michael D. Richardson

CAMDEN HOUSE
Rochester, New York

Copyright © 2012 by the Editors and Contributors

All Rights Reserved. Except as permitted under current legislation, no part of this work may be photocopied, stored in a retrieval system, published, performed in public, adapted, broadcast, transmitted, recorded, or reproduced in any form or by any means, without the prior permission of the copyright owner.

First published 2012 by Camden House
Transferred to digital printing 2013
Reprinted in paperback 2014

Camden House is an imprint of Boydell & Brewer Inc.
668 Mt. Hope Avenue, Rochester, NY 14620, USA
www.camden-house.com
and of Boydell & Brewer Limited
PO Box 9, Woodbridge, Suffolk IP12 3DF, UK
www.boydellandbrewer.com

Paperback ISBN-13: 978-1-57113-595-7
Paperback ISBN-10: 1-57113-595-2
Hardcover ISBN-13: 978-1-57113-490-5
Hardcover ISBN-10: 1-57113-490-5

Library of Congress Cataloging-in-Publication Data

A new history of German cinema / edited by Jennifer M. Kapczynski & Michael D. Richardson.
  p. cm. — (Screen cultures: German film and the visual)
Includes bibliographical references and index.
ISBN 978-1-57113-490-5 (hardcover : alk. paper) —
ISBN 1-57113-490-5 (hardcover : alk. paper)
 1. Motion pictures—Germany—History—20th century. 2. Motion pictures—Germany—History—21st century. I. Kapczynski, Jennifer M., 1972– II. Richardson, Michael David, 1970– III. Title.

PN1993.5.G3N485 2012
791.430943—dc23

2012008162

This publication is printed on acid-free paper.
Printed in the United States of America.

for Tate and Max, respectively

Contents

Acknowledgments   xvii

An Introduction to *A New History of German Cinema*: 1932   1
   Jennifer M. Kapczynski & Michael D. Richardson

Selected Bibliography • Introduction   11

Part I: 1895–1918   13

Selected Bibliography • 1895–1918   20

1 November 1895: Premiere of Wintergarten Program Highlights
   Transitional Nature of Early Film Technology   23
   Janelle Blankenship

22 September 1907: Sigmund Freud Is Attracted to the
   Movies but Feels Lonely in the Crowd   31
   Tan Waelchli

Spring 1911: At Munich's Frankfurter Hof a Comedy
   Team Is Born   37
   Christian Rogowski

27 May 1911: Asta Nielsen Secures Unprecedented
   Artistic Control   44
   Heide Schlüpmann

18 December 1913: *Atlantis* Triggers Controversy about
   Sinking of Culture   51
   Deniz Göktürk

21 January 1914: Premiere of *Die Firma heiratet* Inaugurates
   Fashion Farce   57
   Mila Ganeva

Part II: 1918–1932   63

Selected Bibliography • 1918–1932   70

6 March 1920: Chinese Students Raise Charges of Racism against *Die Herrin der Welt*   73
Tobias Nagl

23 May 1920: *Das Cabinet des Dr. Caligari* Brings Aesthetic Modernism to the Fairground   80
Paul Dobryden

15 October 1920: Ernst Lubitsch Fuels Debate over Tears in the Cinema   86
Michael Wedel

4 March 1921: With *Das Floss der Toten*, the Dead Come Back to Town   93
Philipp Stiasny

1 April 1921: Walther Ruttmann's *Lichtspiel: Opus 1* Shapes Culture of Abstract Filmmaking   98
Gregory Zinman

27 May 1921: *Scherben* Seeks Cinematic Equivalent of Theatrical Intimacy   105
Patrick Vonderau

14 September 1922: Schüfftan Process Reconciles Artistic Craftsmanship with Demands of Entertainment Industry   111
Katharina Loew

13 October 1922: Alexander Kolowrat-Krakowsky Sets Course of Austrian (Inter)National Film   117
Robert von Dassanowsky

29 November 1923: Karl Grune's *Die Straße* Inaugurates "Street Film," Foreshadows Film Noir   124
Anton Kaes

31 January 1924: Premiere of *Orlacs Hände* Marks Beginning of the End of Expressionism   129
Paul Coates

14 February 1924: *Die Nibelungen* Premieres,
   Foregrounds "Germanness" 136
   Adeline Mueller

10 May 1924: *Der Berg des Schicksals* Inaugurates the Genre
   of the "Mountain Film" 142
   Kamaal Haque

23 December 1924: *Der letzte Mann* Explores Limits of
   Modern Community 148
   Robert Schechtman

16 March 1925: *Wege zu Kraft und Schönheit* Educates
   Audiences in the Art of Nudity 153
   Britta Herdegen

3 May 1925: French and German Avant-Garde Converge
   at *Der absolute Film* 160
   Joel Westerdale

10 January 1927: Brigitte Helm Embodies Ambivalence
   of the New Woman 167
   Valerie Weinstein

17 June 1927: Amateur Film League Aids Invention of
   Film Culture 173
   Martina Roepke

16 December 1927: Debut of *Familientag im Hause Prellstein*
   Provokes Debate about Jewish Identity in Popular Cinema 178
   Daniel H. Magilow

31 January 1929: Limits on Racial Border-Crossing
   Exposed in *Piccadilly* 185
   Cynthia Walk

29 May 1929: Oscar for Emil Jannings Highlights Exchange
   between German and American Film Industries 191
   Gerd Gemünden

3 June 1929: Lloyd Bacon's *The Singing Fool* Triggers
   Debate about Sound Film 197
   Lutz Koepnick

4 February 1930: *Menschen am Sonntag* Provides New Model
of Cinematic Realism   202
Noah Isenberg

13 June 1930: *Weekend* Broadcast Tests Centrality of
Image in Cinema   208
Brian Hanrahan

17 October 1930: Bertolt Brecht's *Threepenny Opera* Lawsuit
Identifies Contradiction between Individual Creativity
and Collective Production in Cinema   213
Marc Silberman

11 December 1930: Ban of *All Quiet on the Western Front*
Highlights Tensions over Sound Technology   219
Dayton Henderson

11 May 1931: With Premiere of *M*, a Gala Hit Becomes a
Cultural Controversy   227
Sara F. Hall

Part III: 1933–1945   233

Selected Bibliography • 1933–1945   240

28 March 1933: Goebbels's Kaiserhof Speech Reveals Tension
between National and International Aims of Nazi Cinema   243
Laura Heins

29 February 1935: *Der alte und der junge König* Instrumentalizes
Myth of Prussian Nationalism   249
Martina G. Lüke

28 March 1935: Premiere of *Triumph des Willens* Presents
Fascism as Unifier of Communal Will   255
Michael Cowan & Kai Sicks

19 June 1935: Celebration of Lilian Harvey's Return Belies
Ideological Incongruence in Nazi Entertainment Films   262
Antje Ascheid

30 August 1936: Luis Trenker Tries but Fails to Sidestep
Nazi *Filmpolitik* 268
Carola Daffner

30 December 1940: Von Borsody's *Wunschkonzert* Mobilizes
Melodrama for Total War 275
Jaimey Fisher

18 February 1941: *The Devil and Daniel Webster* Puts American
Politics on Trial 282
Simon Richter

28 May 1942: Bertolt Brecht and Fritz Lang Write a
Hollywood Screenplay 288
Jonathan Skolnik

3 September 1942: With Venice Premiere of *Die goldene Stadt*,
Veit Harlan Enters Debate on Color Cinema 294
Russell A. Alt

18 January 1943: Bateson Analysis of *Hitlerjunge Quex* Stressses
Value of Film as Key to National Culture 300
Gary L. Baker

Part IV: 1945–1961 305

Selected Bibliography • 1945–1961 311

18 May 1945: *Welt im Film* Newsreels, Rubble Films Model
"Cool Conduct" 314
Wilfried Wilms

22 March 1946: Screenings of *Die Todesmühlen* Spark Controversy
over German Readiness to Confront Nazi Crimes 321
Ulrike Weckel

16 August 1949: Ilse Kubaschewski Founds Gloria-Filmverleih,
Sets the Course of Popular West German Film 328
Hester Baer

16 February 1952: Peter Lorre Leaves Germany Again 335
Gerd Gemünden

13 January 1954: Preminger's Dual-Language *The Moon Is Blue* (1953) and *Die Jungfrau auf dem Dach* (1954) Seek Glocal Success — 341
Christine Haase

9 March 1954: *Ernst Thälmann — Sohn seiner Klasse* Marks High Point of Socialist Realism — 347
Hunter Bivens

22 December 1955: *Sissi* Trilogy Bridges Hapsburg to Hollywood through Hybrid Blend of Film Genres — 353
David Bathrick

2 February 1956: In Letter to Enno Patalas, Siegfried Kracauer Advocates a Socio-Aesthetic Approach to Film — 359
Johannes von Moltke

21 June and 30 August 1957: *Jonas* and *Berlin — Ecke Schönhauser* Link Urban Reconstruction to National Cinema in Both West and East — 365
Bastian Heinsohn

19 September 1958: Douglas Sirk's *A Time to Love and a Time to Die* Tests Limits of Postwar Feeling — 372
Jennifer M. Kapczynski

4 September 1959: *Der Frosch mit der Maske* Moves Popular Cinema from Idyllic Pastures to Crime-Infested City Streets — 378
Tassilo Schneider

Part V: 1962–1976 — 385

Selected Bibliography • 1962–1976 — 392

28 February 1962: Oberhausen Manifesto Creates Founding Myth for New German Cinema — 394
Eric Rentschler

1 February 1968: *Herstellung eines Molotow-Cocktails* Promotes Film as a Tool for Political Violence — 400
Tilman Baumgärtel

1 February 1968: Konrad Wolf's *Ich war neunzehn* Evokes an
East German Nation in Transition 405
Larson Powell

7 April 1968: Straub, Huillet, and Fassbinder Share the
Stage at Munich's Action-Theater 411
Barton Byg

23 June 1968: Alexander Kluge Egged in Berlin, Months
Later Awarded Gold Lion in Venice 417
Richard Langston

Fall 1968: Expulsion of Thomas Brasch from GDR Film
School Signals Fate of East German '68ers 423
Katie Trumpener

30 June 1970: A Faltering Berlinale Founders on *o.k.* Controversy 430
Kris Vander Lugt

29 February 1972: With *Die Angst des Tormanns beim Elfmeter*
New German Cinema Learns to Read 436
Brad Prager

24 June 1974: Launching of *Frauen und Film* Creates Lasting
Forum for Feminist Film Writing and Practice 443
Annette Brauerhoch

Part VI: 1977–1989 449

Selected Bibliography • 1977–1989 455

20 June 1977: DEFA's Biggest Star, Manfred Krug,
Leaves the GDR 458
John Griffith Urang

27 October 1977: *Deutschland im Herbst* Equivocates on RAF
and Marks End Stage of Radical Filmmaking 464
Jennifer Marston William

22 January 1979: West German Broadcast of *Holocaust* Draws
Critical Fire and Record Audiences 470
Erin McGlothlin

20 August 1981: R. W. Fassbinder's *Lola* Revisits Kracauer
to Critique Adenauer Period 476
Brigitte Peucker

6 August 1984: *Heimat* Celebrated as "European Requiem
for the Little People" 483
Rachel Palfreyman

8 June 1986: Farocki's *Wie man sieht* Urges New Ways of Seeing 490
Michael Cowan

2 February 1988: Last Generation of DEFA Directors
Calls in Vain for Reform 497
Reinhild Steingröver

Part VII: 1990–2011 503

Selected Bibliography • 1990–2011 509

23 July 1991: ZDF Broadcast of *Ostkreuz* Initiates Darker
Reckoning with the *Wende* 512
Mattias Frey

16 May 1992: Marlene Dietrich's Berlin Burial Links
Postunification Germany with Weimar Republic's
Internationalism 518
Barbara Kosta

25 August 1992: *Ostalgie* Provides Pushback against Western
Views on the East German Collapse 524
Roger F. Cook

10 August 1994: One Month after Founding of X-Filme,
Filmboard Berlin-Brandenburg Paves Way for New
Productions in the Capital 530
Brigitta B. Wagner

2 November 1995: *Neurosia* Embodies Seventy-Five Years of
Queer Film History 537
Randall Halle

31 December 1995: *Der bewegte Mann* Sells 6.5 Million Tickets
to Mark Peak of New German Comedy 543
David N. Coury

10 February 1999: Berlinale Premiere of Four Turkish-German
Films Signals New Chapter in Cinematic Diversity 548
Andrea Reimann

30 April 1999: Werner Herzog's "Minnesota Declaration"
Performs Critique of Documentary Cinema 553
Eric Ames

13 May 1999: Germany's Best Fiend, Klaus Kinski,
Remembered at Cannes 559
Will Lehman

19 May 2000: With *Code Inconnu* Haneke Asserts Cinema's
Centrality to Public Sphere 565
Monica Filimon

21 October 2001: Television Provides Platform for Record
Box-Office Success of *Der Schuh des Manitu* 572
Sebastian Heiduschke

16 October 2003: Chancellor Gerhard Schröder Sheds
Tears — Again — at Premiere of *Das Wunder von Bern* 578
Cornelius Partsch

14 February 2004: Golden Bear for *Gegen die Wand* Affirms
Fatih Akın as Germany's Preeminent Transnational Director 583
Barbara Mennel

8 September 2004: *Der Untergang* Offers Palatable Authenticity 589
Michael D. Richardson

22 October 2005: Winner of Hessian Film Award *Fremde Haut*
Queers Dual Binaries of Sexual and National Identity 596
Faye Stewart

22 January 2007: Film Establishment Attacks "Berlin School" as
Wrong Kind of National Cinema 602
Marco Abel

25 February 2007: *Das Leben der Anderen* Follows Blueprint
for Foreign-Language Oscar Success 609
Paul Cooke

6 December 2007: Indie Film *Für den unbekannten Hund* Seeks
Space for Marginalized Male Heroism 615
Patricia Anne Simpson

11 February 2008: Ulrike Ottinger's *Prater* Wins German
Critics' Award for Best Documentary Yet Highlights the
Director's Ties to Both Fiction and Nonfiction Film 622
Nora M. Alter

Epilogue: The Many Lives of Contemporary German Cinema 629
Jennifer M. Kapczynski & Michael D. Richardson

Notes on the Contributors 637

Index of Subjects 645

Index of Names 651

Index of Film Titles 664

Acknowledgments

A GREAT MANY PEOPLE have contributed to the realization of this book. First, we owe a tremendous debt to our series editors, Gerd Gemünden and Johannes von Moltke, and press editor Jim Walker, who first understood our vision of the project and who have been tireless in their assistance, encouragement, and patience. No less important were Anton Kaes and Eric Rentschler, who continue to inspire us through their own writing and their exceptional record as mentors in the field of German film studies. Their long-standing series of summer German Film Institute workshops provide a model of collaborative scholarly inquiry, and it is no accident that this anthology was conceived at one such gathering. Although this book is dedicated to our two children, since they pay a particular price for their parents' academic work, *A New History of German Cinema* also stands as a tribute to Rick's and Tony's enduring labor to build and support an academic network of film scholars.

Closer to home, our own departments — at Washington University in St. Louis, the Department of Germanic Languages and Literatures, and at Ithaca College, the Department of Modern Languages and Literatures — have offered superb intellectual support and companionship, not to mention several co-contributors, for which we are very grateful. Our respective administrations have continued to support our fields in difficult economic times, and we are thankful for their strong commitment to the humanities and our departments. Special thanks are owed to Russell Alt for research support and to Karin Breuer and Warren Rosenblum for their assistance in the final stages of the editing process. Our families — nuclear, extended, and elective — have given us invaluable support and diversion, for which we owe them more than we can express adequately in any single acknowledgement.

An Introduction to *A New History of German Cinema*: 1932

Jennifer M. Kapczynski and Michael D. Richardson

IT SEEMS ONLY FITTING that the introduction to an event-centered history of German cinema would itself begin with a date. In this case, we shall consider a year wholly emblematic of the intentions of this project yet otherwise unrepresented in this volume: 1932. At first glance, the selection of this year may appear obvious. It fell, of course, at a particularly dire moment in German history: on the eve of the country's descent into National Socialism and an era that would irrevocably mark contemporary German politics, society, and culture. It was also in many respects a banner year for the German film industry — a moment that generated a complex constellation of triumphs, failures, and false starts, some (but not all) of which may be explained by the larger sociopolitical context. Taking the measure of this single annum, we stand to gain a new appreciation not only for the intensely contradictory impulses of German film culture in a time of overweening political turmoil, but also for the simultaneous imbrication and relative independence of film history and political history. The year 1932 further offers a marker of history's nonsynchronicity, providing a fixed point from which we might observe not only outcomes, but also alternative trajectories — that is, the culmination of longer trends in German film history, their inception, and their concurrence.

Most haunting now when we look back at 1932 are the signs of fascism's rise, and with it, a film culture that cultivated visions of national elevation. The year saw the premiere of both Leni Riefenstahl's mystical mountain film *Das blaue Licht* (*The Blue Light*) and Luis Trenker's *Der Rebell* (*The Rebel*), as well as an array of National Socialist documentary shorts recording Hitler's speeches and Stahlhelm paramilitary parades. It was the year that a seventeen-year-old Herbert Reinecker joined the Hitler Youth and from there began a lifelong career as a screenwriter, first working for various National Socialist propaganda organs and later finding employment in the postwar West German radio and film industry. But 1932 was also a year in which critical, avant-garde art was still, at least briefly, possible. *Kuhle Wampe oder: Wem gehört die Welt* (*Kuhle Wampe, or Who Owns The World?*) premiered, and experimental filmmaker

Oskar Fischinger showed his cinematic sound-experiment *Experimente mit synthetischem Ton — Tönende Ornamente* (Experiments with synthetic sound: sounding ornaments). Other projects from the political and aesthetic Left were shut down: arrested during filming, documentarian Ella Bergmann-Michel broke off shooting her piece on the Frankfurt elections of that year, *Wahlkampf 1932 (Letzte Wahl)* (Election campaign 1932 [Final vote]), and because the authorities destroyed a portion of her footage, her final film exists now only as a fragment. Future director of DEFA (Deutsche Film-Aktiengesellschaft, East Germany's state-owned film company) Peter Pewas was a fledgling filmmaker in 1932 when he was arrested and German police confiscated his material for a documentary project about Alexanderplatz. Although as these aborted projects suggest, German cinema was about to take a near fatal turn into cinematic nationalism, 1932 still afforded some opportunity for international exchange. Just months before appearing in all three (German, English, and French) versions of *Ein blonder Traum* (*A Blonde's Dream*), actress Lilian Harvey went under contract with American studio 20th Century Fox, while cinematographer Richard Angst traveled to Greenland under contract with Universal to shoot both the English and German-language versions of *SOS Iceberg*, directed by Tay Garnett and Arnold Fanck respectively.

However tempting it may be to read 1932 retroactively through the lens of 1933 and beyond, a closer look at the year suggests the importance of the moment as one in which alternatives, if quickly fading, nevertheless remained available. To be sure, the forced exodus of Jewish and leftist filmmakers was already beginning: *Mädchen in Uniform* (1931) director Leonine Sagan emigrated to England in 1932, while avant-garde filmmaker Hans Richter traveled to Leningrad, just one stop in a peripatetic exile that extended from the Soviet Union to America. Although Karl Grune would release his short film *Heimkehr* (Homecoming) in 1932, by the next year he, too, would be in exile. Working conditions grew all but impossible for those who remained: operetta librettist Friedrich Hollaender's revue "Es war einmal" (Once upon a time) premiered but quickly closed after Nazi agitators disrupted performances. Hollaender turned to film directing, shooting *Ich und die Kaiserin* (*The Empress and I*) with Lilian Harvey, but one week after its 1933 premiere Ufa (Universum Film A.G.) began dismissing all Jewish personnel. For those artists not threatened on the basis of their ethnic or political affiliations, 1932 was a date that still offered a choice. Some of the events of that year indicated the future to come — Marlene Dietrich, already an American film star by that time, made her final visit to Germany before siding wholly with her adoptive country during the Second World War, while Gustaf Gründgens, playing Mephisto in Lothar Müthels's production of *Faust* in his first role after moving to the Preußisches Staatstheater, channeled the Faustian bargain he would soon make. But other events offered far less indication of what lay ahead. In 1932, a year before his own exile would begin, Max Ophüls directed *Liebelei*, based on the play by Arthur Schnitzler. One of his lead actors was Wolfgang Liebeneiner — future production head at Ufa (1942–45), Reich Film Academy instructor, and a prominent director during both the Nazi and postwar eras. Rudolf Meinert's 1932 Napoleonic occupation epic *Die elf Schill'schen Offiziere* (Schill's eleven officers) featured none other than Veit Harlan. While Harlan would go on to direct perhaps the most notorious antisemitic film of the Nazi era, *Jud Süß* (*Jew Süss*, 1940), along with numerous nationalistic dramas starring his spouse, Kristina Söderbaum, Meinert fled Germany following the National Socialist rise to power, and although the precise date and circumstances of the director's death remain obscure, according to some accounts he was murdered in the Majdanek death camp.

Still other events of 1932 resist explanation according to the prevailing political climate, and instead require institutional and medium-specific elucidation. In the realm of technological advancements, the Agfa Company released an early version of Germany's first color film stock, naming it Agfacolor. While the look of Agfacolor would substantially shape the aesthetics of National Socialist and postwar cinema in both East and West, the product was intended to compete with US-powerhouse Technicolor. That same year, the American Kodak Corporation introduced Super-8, inaugurating an international revolution in amateur filmmaking. Rudolf Arnheim published his defense of cinematic art, *Film als Kunst* (*Film as Art*), and the practice of film historiography received a boost when the Deutsches Museum in Munich acquired part of film pioneer Oskar Messter's collection of early film reels and equipment. Although the silent era had begun to wane several years earlier with the advent of sound film technology, the fate in 1932 of two of the period's greatest stars suggests that this year marked its definitive conclusion: Asta Nielsen filmed what would be her first sound film and her last film, *Unmögliche Liebe* (*Crown of Thorns*), and Henny Porten, after overspending on the filming of *Luise, Königin von Preußen* (*Luise, Queen of Prussia*), was forced to declare her production company bankrupt. These endings were also coupled with a number of beginnings. The year 1932 marked the birth of a host of famous and lesser-known figures who would shape the future of German cinema: directors Alexander Kluge, Edgar Reitz, and Frank Beyer; critic Ulrich Gregor; cameraman Roland Dressel; and actors Johanna Matz, Christiane Maybach, Alfred Edel, Helmut Griem, and Michael Max Degen, to name just a few.

This story of a year suggests the ways in which 1932 was both ordinary and exceptional: a moment in time that provides a window on a larger swath of film history and of German cultural history more generally, and a year that, like many others, illustrates the ways in which German cinema has been shaped by and helped to shape national and international history. It also suggests the meaningful nature of the "moment" itself, as that small lens through which greater vistas open up to view. Precisely this recognition informs the logic and structure of this volume, and is the reason that this is "an" but not "the" introduction for a volume we have titled not "The" but rather "A" *New History of German Cinema*. Our book seeks to highlight this history's multiple trajectories and associations by presenting a range of cinematic "events," whether at the level of the individual film, the individual artist, or cinematic institutions, and to explore how these moments in cinematic history relate to their larger social, political, and cultural contexts — whether by dint of their emblematic quality or because they buck the trends of their time. In the spirit of the Foucauldian notion of "eventalization," as that which breaches the self-evidence of historical continuities, this volume hopes to inspire new understandings of German film history through the surprising affinities and disjunctures that arise when we examine it not as an overarching narrative, but rather as a series of small moments, each of which holds the potential to illuminate something larger about the history and future of German cinema.

In compiling the essays for this book, we have sought further to take a broad view of the event as such. While some of the moments cataloged here, like the founding of the Gloria-Filmverleih (1949) or the signing of the Oberhausen Manifesto (1962), mark obvious sea changes in film history, others, such as the premiere of Karl Grune's *Die Straße* (1924) or the box office success of *Der bewegte Mann* (1995), achieve their relevance for the way in which they stand in for larger aesthetic tendencies, shifts, or contributions. Certain events, such as the premiere of the chamber play film *Scherben* (1921), are known but beg for a new appreciation, while others, for example the formation of the Amateur Film League (1927), reveal themselves as important precisely for the way in which they have, until now, remained lost or underappreciated in scholarly memory. Still others, like the doomed call for reform by East German directors (1988) or the lackluster premiere of Sirk's *A Time to Love and a Time to Die* (1958), represent paradigmatic cases of bad historical timing, as events that went unappreciated in their own day and that gain their significance only in retrospect. What links all of these events, whether they constitute sea changes, countercurrents, or minor ripples that resonate gently but inexorably, is their usefulness for engendering a reflection on the state of German cinema and the larger cultural context from which it has emerged over the course of more than a century.

As our brief discussion of 1932 makes evident, even such a sizeable volume as ours cannot offer a complete account. Indeed, where it concerns historiography, the very claim of comprehensiveness, of totality, fails to acknowledge the essentially subjective and contingent nature of such an endeavor — the fact that any history is defined as much by what it excludes as includes, and itself must inevitably bear the imprint of its own moment of production. Moreover, it is not only a question of defining a particular context as a single, linear trajectory: the same moment in time and place can lead to films very different in nature and meaning. Just as the significance of an individual film and its relation to a historical moment cannot be exhausted in a single reading, the longevity of cinematic works — which not only premiere but also enjoy runs in movie theaters, and which often experience an extended life in audiences' memories and in the digital forms that have proliferated in our modern age — necessitates a consideration of their meaning across time. Thus Valentina Vitali characterizes context in terms of a "force field, in which multiple and contradictory temporalities and forces operate simultaneously."[1] And yet, as Barbara Klinger has argued, the impossibility of comprehensiveness should not lead to its dismissal: the pursuit of a *histoire totale* for cinematic history enables film scholars to go beyond established lines of demarcation and open themselves up to new methods and perspectives.[2] Klinger contends that, in order to study films, scholars must approach them both synchronically (i.e., how they construct meaning within the particular moment of their appearance, the circumstances of their production, distribution, and exhibition) as well as diachronically (i.e., how, over time, these meanings shift and transform, as social and political contexts, circumstances of exhibition, even technological delivery methods, change).

This volume attempts to engage with both the synchronic and diachronic approaches. Individually, many of the essays focus on the synchronic; when juxtaposed with other moments, the diachronic comes to the fore. While many of the entries offer close readings of individual films or film genres, others rely on an analysis of the elements of a work's production or reception to account for the process by which a particular event generated meaning. Many of the essays included here take the moment of a film's release as the seminal occasion for its historical contribution. This is a consequence of the particular historical approach of this volume, with its inclination to view the cultural and sociopolitical moment of a work's creation as central to its meaning. While this focus yields rich rewards, such as when it leads researchers back into the archives to uncover lost layers of a film's or an artist's origins, it also reveals the potential limits of any event-based history, which in emphasizing the importance of a particular instance in the life of a work, an actor, or a director, may attend less closely to the sum total of their accrued interventions or interpretations. Yet numerous other essays in this volume pursue precisely a diachronic approach. Thus the very first entry, about the 1895 Wintergarten premiere of the Skladanowsky films, connects the story of German cinema's earliest days to the revival and rewriting of that narrative under National Socialism. In other cases this diachronic history is apparent in how, or rather when, a particular event appears in this volume. At first glance, one may wonder why the event chosen to discuss Marlene Dietrich's performances is her 1992 funeral in Berlin instead of a more obvious choice such as the premiere of *Der blaue Engel* (*The Blue Angel*, 1930), or why an essay on *Hitlerjunge Quex* focuses on an analysis of the film that appeared some ten years after its 1933 premiere. In both cases these moments were chosen precisely because this temporal deferral serves to free these works from their standard interpretations and enable fresh readings.

We have sought to take a broad view of the concept of *German* cinema here. To be sure, the concept of a national cinema has become increasingly problematic, as traditional modes of definition — where a film is made, who financed it, which language is spoken in the film — have been complicated by an increasingly global film industry and the demands that films appeal to audiences beyond national boundaries. So, too, have definitions of national cinema that restrict it to a country's high-cultural "art films" given way to a broader understanding of the role that popular film has played in the shaping of national identity. Even those definitions of national cinema that seek to use consumption (i.e., reception), rather than production, all too often rely on a constructed, homogeneous notion of national identity (à la Benedict Anderson) — one that represses domestic contradictions and highlights national difference.[3]

Imaginary or not, however, to suggest that the notion of German cinema can be dismissed entirely fails to recognize the central role that it has played in representing, shaping, and interpreting German history and culture. Thus, while the concept of a "German" national cinema should be construed as shifting and porous, it nevertheless provides a critical starting point for the study of that set of people, films, and events that have defined German cinematic history up to this point. There is an inherent, unresolvable, but also useful tension in the definition of national cinema between the manner in which films may articulate a national identity and the manner in which that identity is actually constructed by audiences in their engagement with national and international films. In keeping with the state of the field, our volume inevitably leans heavily toward those films created within the historical political boundaries of the nation, but we have also taken pains to take notice of filmic events that highlight moments of international influence and exchange, that acknowledge the significance of German filmmakers working outside of Germany, and that address the contributions of German-language cinema more generally.

A further hallmark of this volume's pursuit is its approach to the existing film canon. The form through which we have chosen to engage in film historiography — eventalization — opens itself up to charges of incompleteness in a way that other methodologies do not. While the essays included have been selected to offer a good measure of temporal and topical spread, this book places greater emphasis elsewhere, on the rewards yielded through the juxtaposition of famous and unknown stories and an attention to a range of cinematic events. Taken as a whole, this collection seeks to offer a dynamic view of German film history, one that pursues the multiple, intersecting narratives that comprise it, even at the cost of omitting well-known works or figures. This is not born out of an aim to dismantle the canon, to dismiss those works that have had a lasting impact on the history of German cinema, or to construct a wholly alternate set of seminal moments; rather, through the constellation of events we have assembled here, we hope to encourage readers to rethink preconceived notions about how the canon has been and continues to be constructed and understood. It is our hope that we may hereby complement existing research and inspire future exploration into German cinema's multidirectional histories.

It is this approach to the canon that most sets apart *A New History of German Cinema* from existing comprehensive volumes on German film history, which have tended either to offer overarching narratives that, by their nature, can grant only little attention to the individual film, or to organize themselves around a familiar list of standard works. Our volume is intended neither as rejoinder nor as rebuke to these earlier publications. Indeed, we maintain that *A New History of German Cinema*, with its presentation of multiple narratives of cinema history, may be best appreciated in dialogue with those existing histories of German film that take a more holistic approach. Hans Helmut Prinzler's *Chronik des deutschen Films* remains an invaluable resource for key names, dates, and filmographies. Sabine Hake's *German National Cinema* provides a richly detailed account of German cinema that illuminates the central role that film has played not just in reflecting, but also in shaping the history of Germany in the twentieth and now twenty-first centuries. *The German Cinema* book, edited by Erica Carter, Tim Bergfelder, and Deniz Göktürk, addresses both traditional and previously underappreciated aspects of the cinema, with a particular emphasis on genres and stars. Most recently, in *A Critical History of German Film*, Stephen Brockmann situates readings of seminal works within a broader discussion of German cinematic history. This volume has profited immeasurably from the insights of these and myriad other scholars. As Robert Sklar has argued, the practice of film historiography is fundamentally dialogic: "Historical discourse is constantly being transformed through historians' commentaries and critiques on the work of other past and present historians."[4] *A New History of German Cinema* seeks to follow the lead of earlier research while also carving out room for new approaches and probing the very meaning of film history itself— striving to elucidate its less obvious connections and to pursue those moments of collusion and contradiction that mark any historical moment.

From a methodological standpoint, *A New History of German Cinema* resonates with other recent reevaluations of literary historiography. Clearly, *A New History of German Literature* (along with similar volumes that have followed in its wake, such as *A New Literary History of America* and the *Yale Companion to Jewish Writing and Thought in German Culture*) served as a fruitful model. Structured as they are around key dates, these works, their success, and the absence of such a work for German cinema, convinced us of the contribution to be made by a similar volume treating film history.

In the case of *A New History of German Cinema*, each essay takes a particular date as its starting point and expounds on its significance for German film history. Although these essays are organized chronologically, the volume does not present them as a continuous narrative, but rather seeks to provide an understanding of the history of German film as a series of events and interventions. Cross-references included at the close of each entry link individual entries with additional suggested readings, encouraging readers not only to pursue familiar trajectories in the development of German film, but also to trace particular figures and motifs across genres and historical periods. In order to avoid a heavy, encyclopedic tone to the essays, footnotes within the individual pieces have been limited to archival references or directly referenced primary and secondary sources. The goal here is not simply to provide a summary of existing scholarship. In some cases, scholarship on the event in question has become, by virtue of its interpretive influence, part of film history itself, and must be acknowledged in the essay; in general, however, these entries eschew such references in favor of a fresh perspective on the moments that have shaped German cinema.

While this volume reflects our wariness regarding conventional efforts at periodization, we are nevertheless cognizant of its value as one interpretive tool and remain committed to a belief in the broader importance of historical context for understanding any singular event. To that end, we have organized the essays into seven time periods. Each section is prefaced by a short introduction that offers a larger historical and film historical framework intended to illuminate the essays within it, and to offer students as well as the casual reader a "setting" for the individual texts and figures under investigation. These divisions should not be regarded as absolute, but rather as a gesture of practicality. While one aim of this volume is to highlight international connections within cinema, given that it is German cinematic history that remains the focus of our work, we have limited ourselves in these introductions to a discussion of German history and included references to international contexts as they bear directly on German film. To encourage readers to look beyond the divisions of period, we have ensured that the list of recommended reading accompanying each essay includes at least one reference to a different era in German film history. Additional bibliographical references are provided at the end of each of these introductions to aid in the further pursuit of particular periods, themes, or genres.

As our initial discussion of 1932 illustrates, certain years have clearly offered richer yields in terms of important film historical moments — years in which the impact of political-historical events on the cinema was unavoidable (1968 or 1991–92), years in which technological advancements have coincided with formal innovation (1930), and years in which aesthetic and political shifts have converged in a strange moment of confluence (1924–25). In some cases, the essays can easily be read in relation to one another: Tilman Baumgärtel's essay on 1 February 1968 ("*Herstellung eines Molotow-Cocktails* Promotes Film as a Tool for Political Violence") and Richard Langston's essay on 23 June 1968 ("Alexander Kluge Egged in Berlin, Months Later Awarded Gold Lion in Venice") both address the tumultuous state of West German cinema in the late 1960s. Reading these essays together with Katie Trumpener's essay on the fall of 1968 ("Expulsion of Thomas Brasch from GDR Film School Signals Fate of East German '68ers") and Larson Powell's entry on 1 February 1968 ("Konrad Wolf's *Ich war neunzehn* Evokes an East German Nation in Transition"), readers can discern the similarities and differences in how each Germany confronted social and political conflict both onscreen and in the film academies. If, in turn, one considers these essays in the light of Tobias Nagl's entry on the 1920 outcry by Chinese students against *Die Herrin der Welt*, one gains a new appreciation for the longer-term intersections between movie culture and the culture of public protest. Other entries — Mattias Frey's essay on 23 July 1991 ("ZDF Broadcast of *Ostkreuz* Initiates Darker Reckoning with the *Wende*") and Roger F. Cook's essay on 25 August 1992 ("*Ostalgie* Provides Pushback against Western Views on the East German Collapse") offer contrasting interpretations, reinforcing the notion that the meaning of a historical moment cannot be exhausted in a single reading, and indeed demonstrating the fruitful debates that enliven the discipline of German film studies. In other instances, such as is the case with the essays that cover the years 1924–25, it is only through the juxtaposition of entries that one gets a sense of the variety of linkages between a political shift (like that precipitated by the stabilization of German currency and the implementation of the Dawes Plan) and a cultural or aesthetic transformation: the turn away from expressionism (31 January 1924), the exploration of new film technologies (23 December 1924), the onset of a more permissive cultural period (16 March 1925), and even the beginnings of the turn toward a more nationalistic stance (14 February 1924 and 10 May 1924).

In collecting these complementary and contradictory accounts of over one hundred years of German cinema, this volume seeks, in the end, to challenge the very notion of a single film history, bringing together essays that illustrate the numerous vantage points from which German film history can be viewed. By presenting well-known works alongside underexamined aspects of this history, this volume explores German film in dialogues that span generic, temporal, and even territorial distinctions. For the film scholar familiar with these works and well versed in German cinema, we hope our volume will spark renewed interest and reevaluation of particular areas, texts, or genres; for the initiate, we wish that our volume may point toward new avenues of research that will bridge existing work and the as-yet unexplored terrain of German film history.

Notes

[1] Valentina Vitali, "Film Historiography as Theory of the Film Subject: A Case Study," *Cinema Journal* 50, no. 1 (Fall 2010): 141–46; here 142.

[2] Barbara Klinger, "Film History Terminable and Interminable: Recovering the Past in Reception Studies," *Screen* 38, no. 2 (Summer 1997): 107–28.

[3] Andrew Higson, "The Concept of National Cinema," in *Film and Nationalism* (New Brunswick, NJ: Rutgers UP, 2002), 52–67; here 53.

[4] Robert Sklar, "Does Film History Need a Crisis?" *Cinema Journal* 44, no. 1 (Autumn 2004): 134–38; here 134.

Selected Bibliography • Introduction

Allan, Seán, and John Sandford, eds. *DEFA: East German Cinema, 1946–1992*. New York: Berghahn Books, 1999.

Alter, Nora M. *Projecting History: German Nonfiction Cinema, 1967–2000*. Ann Arbor: U of Michigan P, 2002.

Bergfelder, Tim, Erica Carter, and Deniz Göktürk, eds. *The German Cinema Book*. London: BFI, 2002.

Bock, Hans-Michael, and Tim Bergfelder, eds. *The Concise Cinegraph: Encyclopaedia of German Cinema*. New York: Berghahn Books, 2009.

Brockmann, Stephen. *A Critical History of German Film*. Rochester, NY: Camden House, 2010.

Douglas, Thomas B. *The Early History of German Motion Pictures, 1895–1935*. Washington, DC: Thomas International, 1999.

Elsaesser, Thomas, and Michael Wedel, eds. *The BFI Companion to German Cinema*. London: BFI, 1999.

Feinstein, Joshua. *The Triumph of the Ordinary: Depictions of Daily Life in the East German Cinema, 1949–1989*. Chapel Hill: U of North Carolina P, 2002.

Finney, Gail, ed. *Visual Culture in Twentieth-Century Germany: Text as Spectacle*. Bloomington: Indiana UP, 2006.

Frieden, Sandra, Richard W. McCormick, Vibeke R. Petersen, and Laurie Melissa Vogelsang, eds. *Gender and German Cinema: Feminist Interventions*. Providence, RI: Berg, 1993.

Geiss, Axel. *Filmstadt Babelsberg: Zur Geschichte des Studios und seiner Filme*. Berlin: Nicolai, 1994.

Gersch, Wolfgang. *Szenen eines Landes: Die DDR und ihre Filme*. Berlin: Aufbau-Verlag, 2006.

Ginsberg, Terri, and Kirsten Moana Thompson, eds. *Perspectives on German Cinema*. New York: G. K. Hall, 1996.

Hake, Sabine. *German National Cinema*. Revised 2nd edition. London: Routledge, 2007.

Halle, Randall, and Margaret McCarthy. *Light Motives: German Popular Film in Perspective*. Detroit: Wayne State UP, 2003.

Hantke, Steffen, ed. *Caligari's Heirs: The German Cinema of Fear after 1945*. Lanham: Scarecrow, 2007.

Helt, Richard C., and Marie E. Helt. *West German Cinema since 1945: A Reference Handbook*. Metuchen: Scarecrow, 1987.

Jacobsen, Wolfgang. *Babelsberg: Ein Filmstudio 1912–1992*. Berlin: Argon, 1992.

Jacobsen, Wolfgang, Anton Kaes, and Hans Helmut Prinzler. *Geschichte des deutschen Films*. Revised 2nd edition. Stuttgart: Metzler, 2004.

Jordan, Günter, and Ralf Schenk. *Schwarzweiss und Farbe: DEFA-Dokumentarfilme 1946–92*. Berlin: Filmmuseum Potsdam & Jovis, 1996.
Kreimeier, Klaus. *The Ufa Story: A History of Germany's Greatest Film Company, 1918–1945*. Translated by Robert and Rita Kimber. New York: Hill & Wang, 1996.
Kuzniar, Alice A. *The Queer German Cinema*. Stanford: Stanford UP, 2000.
McCormick, Richard W., and Alison Guenther-Pal. *German Essays on Film*. New York: Continuum, 2004.
Murray, Bruce A., and Christopher J. Wickham, eds. *Framing the Past: The Historiography of German Cinema and Television*. Carbondale: Southern Illinois UP, 1992.
Petro, Patrice. *Aftershocks of the New: Feminism and Film History*. New Brunswick, NJ: Rutgers UP, 2002.
Pflaum, Hans Gunther. *Germany on Film: Theme and Content in the Cinema of the Federal Republic of Germany*. Translated by Richard C. Helt and Roland Richter. Detroit: Wayne State UP, 1990.
Pflaum, Hans Günther, and Hans Helmut Prinzler. *Film in der Bundesrepublik Deutschland: Der neue deutsche Film von den Anfängen bis zur Gegenwart*. Munich: Hanser, 1992.
Prinzler, Hans Helmut. *Chronik des deutschen Films, 1895–1994*. Stuttgart: Metzler, 2005.
———. *Träume Bilder, Bilder Träume: Die Geschichte der UFA von 1917 bis heute*. Berlin: Nicolai, 2007.
Reimer, Robert C., and Carol J. Reimer. *Historical Dictionary of German Cinema*. Lanham, MD: Scarecrow, 2008.
Schenk, Ralf, and Christiane Mückenberger. *Das zweite Leben der Filmstadt Babelsberg: DEFA-Spielfilme, 1946–1992*. Berlin: Henschel, 1994.
Schindler, Stephan K., and Lutz Koepnick, eds. *The Cosmopolitan Screen: German Cinema and the Global Imaginary, 1945 to the Present*. Ann Arbor: U of Michigan P, 2007.
Silberman, Marc. *German Cinema: Texts in Context*. Detroit: Wayne State UP, 1995.
Töteberg, Michael, ed. *Metzler Film Lexikon*. Revised 2nd edition. Stuttgart: Metzler, 2005.
Vogt, Guntram. *Die Stadt im Film: Deutsche Spielfilme 1900–2000*. Marburg: Schuren, 2001.

Part I: 1895–1918

The Wilhelmine era represented a turning point in the history of the newly unified Germany. After nearly twenty years of rule under Bismarck, with the Kaiser playing a secondary role to the chancellor, Germany took on a much different character with the succession of Kaiser Wilhelm II. Unlike other European monarchs who saw their roles and influence diminished, Wilhelm II reasserted the power of the emperor. When Bismarck offered his resignation in 1890, the Kaiser gladly accepted and, with the support of the military, plotted a more engaged and aggressive course for Germany. The Wilhelmine period was marked by several characteristics: rapid industrialization, a rise in social tensions, and an increase in nationalism and military aggressiveness.

Together with industrialization came a significant population explosion, the rate of which far exceeded other European countries. In 1890, Germany had approximately 49.4 million residents — by 1914 this had grown to nearly sixty-seven million. Much of this growth took place in German cities, with many doubling, even tripling in size. By 1910, the capital city of Berlin could claim over two million residents. In addition to reflecting a high rate of growth, this shift reflected the migration of significant numbers of Germans from the country to the city, where they hoped to find work in the burgeoning chemical and electrical industries.

The concentration of industrial workers in urban areas fueled the growth of trade unions and the rise of the Sozialdemokratische Partei Deutschlands (Social Democratic Party of Germany, SPD). In 1890, anti-Socialist legislation of the Bismarck period lapsed, allowing the SPD to present electoral lists and play an increasingly oppositional role. Although the SPD favored total revolution and theoretically rejected reformism — i.e., joining the "bourgeois" government in order to overthrow the system from within — in practice, the SPD ran for and won increasing numbers of votes and seats. Despite attempts by the Kaiser to counter the SPD by implementing his own social reforms — the regulation of working hours for women and children, greater pension benefits, and the establishment of courts for industrial arbitration — the SPD continued to gain support and by 1912 was the single largest party in the Reichstag. The changing socio-economic picture predictably led to heightened class tensions, particularly since the government remained strongly pro-industrial throughout the period. While social concessions were made, the Bismarck-era *Bündnis aus Roggen und Eisen* (marriage of iron and rye) — the alliance between agrarian and industrial elites — was revived during the Hohenlohe government, and while elites were not always in agreement, they often saw it in their mutual interests to unite against the growing working class.

One of the most significant — and consequential — breaks with the Bismarck period concerned foreign policy. Bismarck took a decidedly *Realpolitik* (practical politics) approach, both domestically, to ensure that Prussia remained the dominant state, as well as internationally, most notably in his manipulation of victories over Austria and France to assert control over the Germanic states and unify the country despite not demanding territory from a defeated Austria. This *Realpolitik* continued throughout the late nineteenth century, with Bismarck cultivating a complex but calculated system of multiple alliances, with the goal of strengthening Germany's position in Europe without engaging in military conflict. By contrast, Wilhelm II was far more aggressive, and replaced *Realpolitik* with *Weltpolitik* (world policy), the goal of which was most clearly articulated by then Foreign Minister Bernhard von Bülow's statement, "we do not want to place anyone into the shadow, but we also claim our place in the sun." The nationalist sentiment that fueled unification was directed outward in order to turn Germany into a true superpower via the creation of a colonial empire and a naval fleet superior to the British Royal Navy.

The complex set of alliances of the Bismarck period gave way to a more divided Europe. When Wilhelm II allowed the "Reinsurance Treaty" between Germany and Russia to lapse, Russia looked elsewhere for allies, leading to the Franco-Russian alliance, which developed gradually and formalized in 1894, the Anglo-French Entente Cordiale of 1904, and an Anglo-Russian agreement of 1907, all of which culminated in the Triple Entente between Great Britain, France, and Russia. This alliance was seen as a necessary counterweight to Germany's remaining alliance — namely, the Triple Alliance between Germany, Austria, and Italy.

Throughout the early twentieth century, tensions between Germany and the Triple Entente powers increased. Germany's military and colonial aspirations were perceived as a threat to Great Britain, leading to a European arms race, while the formation of the Triple Entente provoked fears that Germany was surrounded by hostile forces. A number of diplomatic incidents heightened these tensions. The First Moroccan Crisis of 1905, when the Kaiser, resentful of France's increasing dominance of Morocco, went to Tangier and spoke in favor of Moroccan independence, found France supported by all major European powers except Germany and its ally Austria. Six years later, Germany provoked the Second Moroccan Crisis when it deployed the gunboat *Panther* to the Moroccan port of Agadir. Both situations led to the hardening of the alliance against Germany and Austria and increased mistrust between the two European power centers. Meanwhile, the decline of the Ottoman Empire during the end of the nineteenth century led to an unstable political situation in the Balkans. The Balkan Wars of 1912–1913 effectively removed the Ottoman Empire from the region and heightened nationalist tensions.

On 28 June 1914, the Austrian Archduke Franz Ferdinand was assassinated while visiting Sarajevo by Gavrilo Princip, a member of the Young Bosnia movement. While such an act would not normally have been enough to provoke a conflict, long simmering tensions between Austria-Hungary, Germany, Russia, France, and Great Britain prompted the so-called July Crisis. With Germany's support, Austria-Hungary delivered the July Ultimatum to Serbia, a series of intentionally unacceptable demands designed to provoke a war. When Serbia agreed to only eight of the ten demands, Austria-Hungary declared war on 28 July 1914. One day later, Russia mobilized to protect its presence in the region. When Germany began to mobilize on 30 July, France began its mobilization on 1 August, with Germany declaring war on Russia on the same day.

The initial response to the war was one of nationalist enthusiasm on both Left and Right, with even members of the SPD voting on 4 August to approve the war bonds requested by the imperial government. This reflected both the SPD's view of Russia as the most reactionary, anti-Socialist government, as well as the political calculation that opposing a popular war could cost them seats in the Reichstag. Even the trade unions agreed to refrain from labor strikes and demands for higher wages during the war. The Kaiser welcomed this *Burgfrieden* (civil peace) declaring, "Ich kenne keine Parteien mehr, ich kenne nur noch Deutsche!" (I know no more parties, I only know Germans). This also led the left and far-left wing of the party to split from the SPD, first under the auspices of the Rosa Luxemburg–founded Gruppe Internationale (Group International) — from which emerged on 1 January 1916 the Spartakusbund (Spartacus League) — and then led to the founding of the Unabhängige sozialistische Partei Deutschlands (Independent Socialist Party of Germany, USPD) under the leadership of Hugo Haase on 9 April 1917.

For some, the war was a chance to pursue grandiose dreams of empire; for others it was a distraction from — and potential solution to — the social tensions of the period. At the onset, many thought that it would end in a matter of months. Not wanting to engage in battles on two fronts simultaneously, Germany adopted the Schlieffen Plan, which involved defeating France first by invading the neutral countries of Belgium and Luxembourg (which led to Great Britain entering the war) and encircling and crushing the French forces along the Franco-German border. Only then would Germany engage Russia. At first the attack was successful, but the French and British armies successfully defended Paris at the First Battle of the Marne, forcing the Germany army to retreat. This defeat ended hopes of a quick victory, and the war became a long, drawn-out conflict with heavy casualties and little in the way of territorial advancement. Germany had no easy way out. Peace without victory was not only financially impossible, but would have brought all of the domestic problems masked by the war back to the forefront. As the war dragged on, high casualties, worsening living conditions, food riots, and major strikes led to low morale at home and civic unrest. While some of the more strident nationalists still believed that Germany could achieve victory and conquer new territories, much of the population was eager for the conflict to end.

Prompted in part by Germany's unrestricted submarine attacks and the sinking of several US merchant ships, the United States ended its policy of isolation and entered the war on 6 April 1917, turning the tide against Germany and Austria. When Germany imposed the humiliating Brest-Litovsk peace treaty on now-Bolshevik Russia on 9 February 1918, marking Russia's exit from the war, it was too late. Facing rising discontent at home and the very real possibility of revolution, the military leadership (by 1916 Germany had essentially become a military dictatorship run by Field Marshal Paul von Hindenburg and Generalquartermeister Erich Ludendorff) handed over government control to civilian hands to negotiate an end to the war.

The class tensions in the period also found expression in tensions within Germany's cultural life. On the one hand, the new Empire sought to legitimize its existence through culture — monuments, paintings, festivals — that glorified empire and foregrounded heroism and sentimentality. Although the nobility was losing political power to a growing upper middle class, the bourgeoisie sought to imitate the aristocracy in an effort to gain the social recognition they felt they deserved. This "feudalization of the bourgeoisie" allowed the militaristic and paternalistic culture of the nineteenth century to continue to flourish into the twentieth century.

However, many artists chafed at these values, and sought to highlight the tensions and contradictions in bourgeois society, critically depicting the economic and psychological stresses brought on by Germany's industrialization and urbanization. Building on sociological analyses of the experience of life in the modern city such as Georg Simmel's "Die Großstadt und das Geistesleben" ("The Metropolis and Mental Life"), artists and thinkers examined the implications of industrialization, Taylorization, and the anonymity of urban life. Across the spectrum of the arts, artists broke with the conventions of the past, developing new, critical ways of understanding the relationship of form to content. The combination of technological development and the concentration of population in urban areas led to the rise of mass commercial culture, geared primarily at the lower-middle and working classes, which proved to be fertile ground for the cinema.

The development of film occurred in many countries simultaneously, but the first public exhibition of moving pictures took place in Germany. Max and Emil Skladanowsky demonstrated their Bioscop (a double-projector system) at the Berlin Wintergarten on 1 November, 1895, over a month before the first public performance by the Lumière brothers in Paris. The Wintergarten program was modeled on the variety format, with a lineup that featured acrobatic acts, animal scenes, and folk dances.

Initially, the emphasis was on the technical novelty of film projection, its ability to create the illusion of the motion picture. As such, there was a great deal of experimentation with projection systems and film effects. Oskar Messter was responsible for many of the innovations in early German film, most notably the Maltese Cross projection system, which offered a flicker-free alternative to the Lumière claw movement. Messter also invented *Ton-Bilder* (sound images) that synchronized gramophone sound with film images. Messter produced fictional shorts that featured some of the first examples of close-ups, animation effects, and speeded-up motion effects and, as early as 1897, newsreels.

In its first decade, films were shown as part of traveling shows, and could be divided into two basic styles: a documentary or realist style, associated primarily with Lumière, that focused on recording the visible world, and a fantastic style associated with Georges Méliès that focused on the use of filmic effects to create images that could not be seen in real life. Shows featured a mix of short films — newsreels, nature scenes, travelogues, humorous sketches, and acrobatic acts. By 1905, movies were popular enough to warrant their own exhibition spaces. Early films were shown in *Kinntopps* — bars, storefronts, and coffee houses — that were usually located downtown in urban areas, to attract a varied clientele: the working class, middle-class women, and teenagers. Movies were shown on a continual basis, with audiences coming and going throughout the day. By 1906, the first permanent theater was established in Germany in Mannheim. Others soon followed: by 1910, over a thousand cinemas could be found throughout Germany.

Over the next decade, a number of factors were responsible for transforming film from a technical curiosity to a recognized — though still critically debated — art form. The first was the consolidation of resources and the development of film distribution systems. Early film exhibitors had to buy all of the films that they showed, but beginning in 1905, distributors began moving toward renting exclusive rights to films, eliminating competition between theaters on a local level. Continued streamlining as well as the acquisition of smaller film companies by larger ones increased the efficiency of the industry and left more resources available for the films themselves. Alfred Duskes GmbH (1905) was the first film producer to double as a distributor, while Paul Davidson, having acquired the ubiquitous Union-Theater chain in 1906, created the first German joint-stock film company, the Projektions AG Union (PAGU), in 1909. Berlin became a center of filmmaking, with most studios located there. The years 1907 and 1908 also marked the founding of the earliest trade papers, *Der Kinematograph* and *Die Lichtbild-Bühne*. In 1913 the first serious reviews appeared in daily newspapers and sustained public debate about the artistic merit of film in mainstream publications.

Although early audiences were fairly heterogeneous, the growing popularity of film with the lower class was met with criticism from the bourgeoisie and the upper class. This was partly due to bourgeois anxieties about their own cultural status and the status of Germany as a cultural nation, and also due to fears that film was a degenerate and possibly revolutionary influence on the working class. Critics argued that the realism of early film — its portrayal of everyday life in its mundane and often seedy aspects — did not offer the same rewards as literary arts that aspired to higher goals. These criticisms led to greater controls, both in terms of censoring supposedly objectionable content, and in terms of regulating audiences, exhibition spaces, and the like. Initially, censorship was left up to individual states, leading to a variety of versions of early films, but when Prussia publicized its censorship decisions as a reference for other states, censorship guidelines became more standardized, and in 1907, films were required to have a censor's certificate. Films also became subject to entertainment taxes similar to those levied on alcohol and tobacco.

But film was not without its supporters among the educated middle class, who recognized its educational as well as artistic potential. Artists and intellectuals began pushing back against the cinema's critics in what became known as the *Kino-Debatte* (cinema debate). Filmmakers themselves sought to build on the popularity of film and legitimate it as an art form. The period from 1910 to 1914 saw a number of changes in the films themselves. The first of these was the emergence of longer narrative films, which required an increased attention to film as a storytelling medium. Production companies began drawing on the traditions of literature and theater, hiring famous writers and actors capable of providing films with consistent and believable character development and psychological motivation. Studios also focused on the development of a star system, thus facilitating audience identification across films. Film stars, who frequently were described as displaying "Germanic" characteristics, provided continuity from film to film. This was furthered by the strong sense of physical presence and intimacy upon which silent film relied, and which was embodied by two of the era's key female actresses: Asta Nielsen and Henny Porten. Many studios also became identified with a particular genre, so that audiences brought educated expectations to their productions. Another change was the introduction of new techniques related to camerawork, editing, and mise-en-scène. The creation of film-specific language allowed film to move beyond a reliance on other media and assert its unique characteristics. The rapid expansion of the industry continued throughout the early teens, as more and more movie theaters were built. These theaters also became progressively more elegant, as movies became recognized as a legitimate form of elite entertainment. By 1919, Germany boasted over 2,800 theaters, with a capacity of nearly one million.

Prior to the First World War, film remained essentially international, both in orientation and distribution. While the output of German cinema increased significantly (more than 350 new films were released in 1913 alone) demand for films was so great that German companies began to import films from England, Italy, America, France, and Denmark, with the latter two supplying the most films. Prewar, domestic productions accounted for only 10–20 percent of all films shown. With the onset of the war, however, French films, which had dominated international cinema up to that point, were banned from Germany, allowing German film producers to grow nearly without competition. The Danish company Nordisk, which had an agreement to be able to distribute films in Germany, gradually lost its presence in favor of domestic productions. The German film industry, seeing the need for further economic consolidation, continued to tilt toward fewer, but larger companies. Kaiser Wilhelm had long been interested in film, recognizing its potential as a form of publicity and propaganda, and the government began to offer support for the centralization of the industry for military and political reasons. Just as film had earlier been seen as a potential danger for its ability to incite the masses, now it was viewed as an essential tool for gaining their support. German companies began producing more newsreels about the war as well as patriotic dramas. With the entry of the United States into the war in 1917, Ludendorff concluded that more drastic measures should be taken to meet the general wave of anti-German propaganda coming from Hollywood and ordered the founding of the army's own propaganda unit. He also strengthened the bond with private producers such as Oskar Messter, leading on 18 December 1917 to the formation of Ufa (Universum Film A.G.), which brought together prominent financiers and industrialists with the largest film companies in Germany.

Selected Bibliography • 1895–1918

Andriopoulos, Stefan. "The Terror of Reproduction: Early Cinema's Ghostly Doubles and the Right to One's Own Image." *New German Critique* 33, no. 3 (2006): 151–70.

Birett, Herbert. *Lichtspiele: Der Kino in Deutschland bis 1914.* Munich: Q-Verlag, 1994.

Castan, Joachim. *Max Skladanowsky oder der Beginn einer deutschen Filmgeschichte.* Stuttgart: Füsslin, 1995.

Cherchi Usai, Paolo, and Lorenzo Codelli, eds. *Before Caligari: German Cinema, 1895–1920.* Madison: U of Wisconsin P, 1991.

Elsaesser, Thomas. *Filmgeschichte und frühes Kino: Archäologie eines Medienwandels.* Munich: Text und Kritik, 2002.

Elsaesser, Thomas, and Michael Wedel, eds. *A Second Life: German Cinema's First Decades.* Amsterdam: Amsterdam UP, 1996.

———. *Kino der Kaiserzeit: Zwischen Tradition und Moderne*, Munich: Text und Kritik, 2002.

Fullerton, John. *Celebrating 1895: The Centenary of Cinema.* Sydney, Australia: John Libbey, 1998.

Fuhrmann, Wolfgang. "Local Entertainment and National Patriotism: The Distribution of Colonial Films in Early German Cinema." In *Networks of Entertainment: Early Film Distribution, 1895–1915*, edited by Frank Kessler and Nanna Verhoeff, 246–49. Eastleigh, UK: John Libbey, 2007.

Garncarz, Joseph. "Early Forms of Film Distribution in Germany, 1896–1905." In *Networks of Entertainment: Early Film Distribution, 1895–1915*, edited by Frank Kessler and Nanna Verhoeff, 255–59. Eastleigh, UK: John Libbey, 2007.

Jelavich, Peter. "'Am I Allowed to Amuse Myself Here?': The German Bourgeoisie Confronts Early Film." In *Germany at the Fin de Siècle: Culture, Politics, and Ideas*, edited by Suzanne Marchand and David Lindenfeld, 227–49. Baton Rouge: Louisiana State UP, 2004.

Jung, Uli, and Martin Loiperdinger, eds. *Geschichte des dokumentarischen Films in Deutschland. Band I: Kaiserreich 1895–1918.* Stuttgart: Reclam, 2005.

Kaes, Anton, ed. *Kino-Debatte: Texte zum Verhältnis von Literatur und Film 1909–1929.* Tübingen, Max Niemeyer, 1978.

Ligensa, Annemone, and Klaus Kreimeier, eds. *Film 1900: Technology, Perception, Culture.* New Barnet, UK: John Libbey, 2009.

Loiperdinger, Martin. *Oskar Messter: Filmpionier der Kaiserzeit.* Basel: Stroemfeld/Roter Stern, 1994.

Mühl-Benninghaus, Wolfgang. *Vom Augusterlebnis zur Ufa-Gründung: Der deutsche Film im 1. Weltkrieg.* Berlin: Avinus, 2004.

Müller, Corinna. *Frühe deutsche Kinematographie: Formale, wirtschaftliche und kulturelle Entwicklungen, 1907–1912*. Stuttgart: Metzler, 1994.
Oksiloff, Assenka. *Picturing the Primitive: Visual Culture, Ethnography and Early German Cinema*. New York: Palgrave, 2001.
Prawer, Siegbert Salomon. *Between Two Worlds: The Jewish Presence in German and Austrian Film, 1910–1933*. New York: Berghahn Books, 2005.
Schlüpmann, Heide. *The Uncanny Gaze: The Drama of Early German Cinema*. Translated by Inga Pollmann. Champaign: U of Illinois P, 2010.
———. "Cinema as Anti-Theater: Actresses and Female Audiences in Wilhelminian Germany." *Iris* 11 (Summer 1990): 77–93.
Thomas, Douglas B. *The Early History of German Motion Pictures, 1895–1935*. Washington, DC: Thomas International, 1999.
von Zglinicki, Friedrich. *Die Wiege der Traumfabrik: Von Guckkästen, Zauberscheiben und bewegten Bildern bis zur UFA in Berlin*. Berlin: Transit, 1986.

Max Skladanowsky posing before his Bioscop projector, labeled a "holy relic" of German cinematography. Credit: Bundesarchiv Koblenz.

1 November 1895: Premiere of Wintergarten Program Highlights Transitional Nature of Early Film Technology

Janelle Blankenship

THE RECENT INTERACTIVE DISPLAY The Boulevard of Stars, a public-private partnership of the city of Berlin and the Boulevard of Stars Association, aims to "reanimate" German film history. The instructive placard flanking the film history Walk of Fame on Potsdamer Platz invites spectators to look through a "magical camera" and see a shadowy image of their favorite film personality floating over their commemorative brass star. Using the proto-cinematic technique of Pepper's Ghost (a nineteenth-century magic lantern illusion), a spectral apparition of a film star is projected onto a red asphalt walkway. Among the forty spectral film personalities selected to grace the red carpet — many of them Berlin-to-Hollywood exiles such as Billy Wilder, Marlene Dietrich, Fritz Lang, and Peter Lorre — is a forgotten figure of the silent screen, early German film pioneer Max Skladanowsky. In a full-body shot, Skladanowsky strikes a classic inventor's pose beside his Bioscop dual projector. Although the inscription on his star commemorates the 1895 Wintergarten film premiere, the black-and-white photograph one glimpses through the Pepper's Ghost camera dates to the 1930s, an uncanny reminder of the inventor's musealization under National Socialism. Indeed, it was not only the name Skladanowsky that was "resurrected" in numerous museum exhibits, tours, anniversary screenings, and national ceremonies of the 1930s, the inventor's eccentric and unwieldy projector was also itself christened a "holy relic" of German cinematography. Thus the modern-day spectator is invited to relive both the premiere of the 1895 Wintergarten films and the 1930s rehabilitation of the inventor and his work. The interactive display not only educates the viewer on the art of obscure nineteenth-century optical technology, it also explicitly invites viewers to read film history through a political palimpsest of signs and erasures. The Boulevard's home page explicitly acknowledges that "Berlin also stands for breaches in the development (of film history) — for exile and flight and the usurpation of cinema and television for propaganda."

The German film pioneers and variety theater showmen Max and Emil Skladanowsky have often been written out of film history. Overshadowed by the Lumière cinematograph, Max Skladanowsky's Bioscop dual projector has been viewed as an experimental apparatus that straddles two worlds — flickering between the perfected "dissolving views" of magic lantern projection and the imperfect stuttering of "silent" cinema in its first decade. And yet, the German showmen were responsible for the event generally regarded as the first projection of moving pictures in Europe to a paying audience: on 1 November 1895, two months prior to the Lumière debut of the cinematograph at the Grand Café in Paris, Max and Emil Skladanowsky premiered celluloid "copies" of variety theater attractions (including the "Gymnastics Family Grunato" and the "Boxing Kangaroo") as a fifteen-minute "side show" act screened with live orchestral accompaniment. The six- to sixteen-second loop films were rear-projected at the Berlin Wintergarten Varieté onto a translucent screen using Max Skladanowsky's self-constructed Bioscop dual projector (an apparatus based on a biunial magic lantern projector) and a magic lantern for intertitles.

Although the initial success of the Wintergarten program is undisputed, film historians have often focused on the failure of the Skladanowskys to found a film industry or invent an apparatus that would prove economically viable for a world market. Film historian Charles Musser famously deemed the Skladanowsky Bioscop "the most eccentric and commercially unimportant of European inventions."[1] The practice of feeding alternating film strips through a double projector was certainly unwieldy, but was conveniently linked to Skladanowsky's experience with dissolving view effects: a magic lantern with a dual projection system featuring two optical lenses allowed the lanternist to superimpose two images on the same screen. The Bioscop, in a manner befitting the spectacular technology of the "cinema of attractions," was advertised as the "most interesting invention of modernity," yet the machine itself was shrouded in secrecy prior to and during the Wintergarten debut, obscured from view behind a translucent screen. The program and apparatus also utilized traditional magic lantern showmanship, technology and tricks, surprising the audience with looped or repeated movements and "life-size copies" of attractions projected onto a large screen. The film program featured burlesque body-movement, one-shot circus-act spectacles, and carefully choreographed moments of direct address. The brothers twice stepped out from behind the curtain to bow to the audience, first on screen in the film's apotheosis and then on the Wintergarten side stage, breaking the boundaries between diegetic space and live variety performance. Just as the brothers considered the Bioscop films to be "copies" of variety theater "scenes" (reminiscent of the copying of historical motifs in their magic lantern slides), the projector itself was dubbed a reproduction machine: "it reproduces the Wintergarten production in bluffingly true, life-size copies." The Bioscop not only reproduced variety attractions, it also copied dissolving-view lantern technology, a biunial projection trick affiliated with the dissolving-view apparatus Max Skladanowsky had earlier employed for the magic lantern programs of Carl Skladanowsky & Sons. The company toured Germany, Austria, and Eastern Europe from 1879 until the late 1890s, advertising the magic lantern program as *edutainment*, a sightseeing spectacle that used magical light reflexes to educate and disseminate the "light of culture."

The Bioscop, albeit eccentric, was not dissimilar to the dissolving view apparatus. Two separate optical systems staggered and projected looped film strips, creating the illusion of continuous movement. Its illuminated *Momentphotographien* (moment photographs) were exhibited at numerous venues in Germany, the Netherlands, and Scandinavia where the Skladanowsky Brothers had previously debuted with "dissolving views." However, the Bioscop's fame as electric novelty was short lived. After the debut of the Lumière Cinematograph, several billings were cancelled, including an engagement at the Folies-Bergère in Paris. A memoir unearthed by film historian Deac Rossell indicates that the Brothers had a short engagement at the Empire Theatre in London in 1896. By that time, however, there was little interest in Skladanowsky's shorts: rather than featuring the Bioscop, the theater displaced the act from the stage to "a structure in the foyer and charged 1S entrance, but it still failed to attract, and the engagement was concluded."[2] In a matter of months, the Skladanowsky apparatus had been demoted from the side stage of the Wintergarten Varieté to a lobby display.

In classic film histories, the Skladanowsky "living photographs" projected at "lightning speed" are often denigrated as "primitives" that pale in comparison to the pioneer work of French directors and studios. Lotte Eisner in a foreword to *The Haunted Screen* describes them as "dull little moving snapshots" that "have nothing in common with the lively topicalities being produced by August Lumière at that time."[3] Certainly, if the Wilhelmine "Welt-Theater" and biunial magic lantern of Skladanowsky & Sons had perfected the dissolving view play of light and darkness, the Bioscop living pictures, due to light-insensitive film stock, overexposure to sunlight and camera angle used, were literally bathed in imperfect shadow, creating a second "copy" or reproduction of the physical movement within the scene. In the Wintergarten program, these shadows even served as an unintended second projection of the variety theater acts, an uncanny repetition of the burlesque bodies on the screen. Although generally well-received, one contemporary reviewer subsumed the Bioscop films under the term "shadow play," rendering the Skladanowsky films an amateur play of precinematic light and shadow.

Yet it is precisely this dual or transitional nature of the Bioscop projector and its relationship to precinematic spectacle and magic lantern culture that is most valuable, from the perspective of a revisionist film historiography. The Skladanowsky archive provides unique evidence for the nuanced role the magic lantern played within fin-de-siècle art of moving picture projection, pointing to how porous the boundaries are between film and slide projection in the early period. It is significant in this context that Skladanowsky commences his archival composite film of the late 1920s and 1930s with a series of magic lantern slides (comic slip slides, dissolving view slides, and chromatrope color wheels), even using intertitles after the transition to sound film to claim that his slides are the first sound and color "living pictures."

Max and Emil Skladanowsky frequently alternated between slides and living photographs — standard practice from 1895–1900, when the cinematograph was often viewed as a "supplement" to magic lantern projection. In 1895 — the year the Bioscop apparatus was unveiled — the inventor also premiered a new, bi-directional lantern with an electric light source at the Circus Renz. The directors Dorn and Baron not only booked the Bioscop for the Wintergarten for the month of November 1895 (for the royal sum of 2,500 reichsmarks), they also booked the Skladanowsky Brothers' protocinematic "Electro-Mechanic-Pyrotechnic Water-Display-Theater" for the month of October. Skladanowsky's 1895 Bioscop patent certificate, which lists his occupation as "dissolving view showman" (*Nebelbilderdarsteller*), situates Skladanowsky in a legacy of inventors and showmen who did not divorce themselves from earlier magic lantern screen practice. In 1896, when the popularity of the Bioscop dual projector itself started to wane, the brothers fell back on their familiar repertoire of lantern slides. In one variety theater program, we see the showmen double billed at the Tivoli Theatre in Sweden.[4] In the first act they appear with their sensational novelty, the Bioscop; in the second act they reappear under their French-Belgian alias "Professor Morieux" to present chromatropes, comic slides, and twenty-four dissolving-view slides narrating "Dr. Nansen's Expedition to the North Pole."

The final screening of the Skladanowsky Bioscop program (enhanced with new actualities similar to the Lumière shorts) took place in Stettin, Germany, on 30 March 1897 with the Bioscop II, an improved single-film band projector. As fate would have it, Max Skladanowsky's trade license as an exhibitor had expired and the Berlin authorities refused to grant him a new one, arguing "too many film licenses were already in circulation."

Overshadowed by more powerful commercial figures like Edison, the French inventors, and more successful German film industry pioneers like Oskar Messter and Guido Seeber, in the teens and early twenties Skladanowsky slipped into obscurity. In 1924, however, as the thirty-year anniversary of the "birth of cinema" neared, the Berlin photographer and family friend Wilhelm Frenz published an article beseeching the German film industry and public to finally give the aged pioneer "the credit" that he had been denied "three decades earlier."[5] In the mid- to late 1920s, numerous commemorative events and exhibits on the history of film gave Skladanowsky an opportunity to showcase his Bioscop projectors and archival films in an increasingly nationalist setting. 1933 marked a decisive turning point in the inventor's career. In 1933 (the year Max Skladanowsky turned seventy), the National Socialists founded the Committee to Honor the Contributions of the German Film Inventor Max Skladanowsky to pay the inventor his due. The committee hosted a gala dinner to honor the inventor and spearheaded a fundraising campaign. The fundraising press release instrumentally asserted that the Weimar government, itself debt ridden and shamed into paying international reparations, had created a further negative legacy by failing to recognize Germany's own inventors. The committee invited individuals and theater owners to contribute to the campaign, to be chaired by Reichsminister Goebbels, as a means to pay off a "national debt." In 1936, the commission, in letters written on behalf of the Reichsfilmkammer, pressed directors and cinema owners to fulfill "their honorable duty" and book Skladanowsky's archival film, *Aus den Archiven des Erfinders Max Skladanowsky* (From the archives of the inventor Max Skladanowsky), for a commemorative engagement. Skladanowsky's composite film was screened as supplemental cultural programming alongside such patriotic fare as *Menschen ohne Vaterland* (People without a fatherland, 1937) and *Im Trommelfeuer der Westfront. Ein Film vom Heldenkampf unbekannter Soldaten* (Drumfire on the western front: The heroic struggle of unknown soldiers, 1936), as well as box-office hits featuring Greta Garbo or Marlene Dietrich. The film even traveled beyond Germany to Prague, Vienna, Copenhagen, and Lithuania, with Skladanowsky's private secretary Richard Ohrtmann serving as a silent "film barker." In special screenings, Skladanowsky himself appeared in a top hat and frock to speak to the public. The outmoded Bioscop was set up as a museum display in theater lobbies. Although the Reichsfilmkammer did not directly fund the endeavor, the regime instrumentally used the film pioneer's history to forward their own agenda: Skladanowsky's film was one of the first reels deposited at the Reichsfilmarchiv, only two weeks after its grand opening on 4 February 1935.

On the fortieth anniversary of the "birth of cinema," Skladanowsky's archival film was screened in Stuttgart on the very night that Riefenstahl's *Triumph des Willens* (*Triumph of the Will*) premiered. Newspapers announced this screening of both films as a special event in the creation of a national film history, linking both films as "the starting point and final culmination of the tremendous development that film has undergone since its first public exhibition in the year 1895."[6] Newspaper articles proclaimed that Skladanowsky's strips seemed made to last for "eternity," arguing that "after the thousand screenings in German theaters the artifacts would wander back into the archive to teach later generations about the first work behind [the invention of] film, . . . an instrument for education and propaganda."[7]

Even before the founding of the Reichsfilmarchiv, Skladanowsky's motion picture relics were strategically linked to a techno-nationalist fantasy. In a 1934 radio interview, Skladanowsky claimed US newspaper magnate William Randolph Hearst had offered to purchase his Bioscop for a Hollywood museum. Numerous interviews and articles quote Skladanowsky as having stated that he "naturally" refused to sell the artifacts to an American museum. In press releases, Skladanowsky further asserted that he had offered to donate his artifacts to the Deutsches Museum, on the condition that his collection would be used to found a new German film archive.

Other German film pioneers were not pleased to see Skladanowsky step into the limelight. To complicate matters, Skladanowsky was not an official member of the Nazi Party and, in a misguided attempt to reinforce his pioneer status, he attempted to backdate his inventions on museum placards and in newspaper articles. An "inventor's argument" ensued, with a vicious debate between Skladanowsky and Oskar Messter regarding who could lay claim to the title "German" inventor of film. The Reichsfilmkammer, although they had initially protected Skladanowsky, finally intervened and subjected all parties to a gag order. Nevertheless, the Reichsfilmkammer and Propaganda Ministry officially sanctioned his commemorative tour.

Although Skladanowsky's "tour of honor" ended abruptly with his death in 1939, his archival film continued to travel posthumously. Shortly after the Reichsfilmarchiv opened, Museum of Modern Art Film Division curators Iris Barry and John E. Abbot acquired a copy of a fragment of his archival composite film. During the 1936 Olympics, they acquired the print that they catalogued as *Skladanowsky Primitives*, along with other classic German silents.[8] The fragment from Skladanowsky's archival film was used in at least three different MoMA film programs in the 1930s and 1940s. On the one hand, the MoMA film division clearly viewed the Skladanowsky primitives as less important than the postwar films of Germany, arguing in a didactic intertitle to the "Film in Germany: Legend and Fantasy" program that only postwar films like *Das Cabinet des Dr. Caligari* (*The Cabinet of Dr. Caligari*) and *Der letzte Mann* (*The Last Laugh*) had a highly individual style" and "were striking innovations at that time."[9] On the other hand, the "Skladanowsky Primitives" were seen as an innovative example of early animation, or even as forerunners to the avant-garde. In 1945, the "Skladanowsky Primitives" appeared in a program at the

San Francisco Museum of Art entitled "Precursors to the Avant-Garde Film" (part of a larger exhibit on "Art in Film").

Despite the film's link to National Socialist interests, the years after the Second World War saw a second German and European tour for the film Skladanowsky deposited with the Reichsfilmarchiv, after a copy surfaced in the newly established GDR State Film Archive. Erich Skladanowsky resurrected his father's archival film to lecture on his father's career at numerous museums and institutions in East and West Germany and in major European cities. In his popular lecture entitled "Vom bunten Nebelbild zum Weltumspannenden Zelluloid" (From vibrant dissolving views to world-encompassing celluloid), Erich Skladanowsky put a socialist spin on the family archive by emphasizing his father's support of trade unions and labor. Even Wintergarten film titles were rewritten to reflect this new political agenda: the "Gymnastic Family Grunato" became "Artists at Work."[10] For a brief moment, in the years preceding the hundred-year anniversary of Max Skladanowsky's birth — in a constantly shifting play of political interests — the film pioneer became an East German legend. Erich Skladanowsky's tour and lecture, like the complicated afterlife of the Bioscop films, provide yet one more example of the manner in which each political state effectively interrupts the archive, inscribing a new layer of meaning onto its celluloid surface.

See also:

- 23 May 1920: *Das Cabinet des Dr. Caligari* Brings Aesthetic Modernism to the Fairground
- 14 September 1922: Schüfftan Process Reconciles Artistic Craftsmanship with Demands of Entertainment Industry
- 28 March 1935: Premiere of *Triumph des Willens* Presents Fascism as Unifier of Communal Will

Notes

[1] Charles Musser, *The Emergence of Cinema: The American Screen to 1907* (New York: Scribner and Macmillan, 1990), 91.

[2] Deac Rossell, *Living Pictures: The Origins of the Movies* (Albany: State U of New York P, 1998), 17.

[3] *The Haunted Screen: Expressionism in the German Cinema and the Influence of Max Reinhardt*, trans. Roger Greaves (Berkeley: U of California P, 1973), 7.

[4] 8 August 1896. Kristall-Salongen, Stockholm Program (BA N 1435/112).

[5] Wilhelm Frenz, "An der Wiege des Films," *Der Kinematograph* 894 (1924):15–16; here 16.

[6] "Die Rache der Frau Schultze: Max Skladanowsky erzählt von der Erfindung des Kinos," *Stuttgarter Neues Tagesblatt* (30 March 1935).

[7] "Der Erfinder des Films in Tilsit. Max Skladanowsky will 115 Jahre alt werden: Ein Plauderstündchen über die ersten Anfänge der Weltmacht Film," *Beiblatt der "Memelwacht"* (13 September 1938).

[8] See Mary Lea Bandy, "New York Friends Look at Documentary Films," in *Filming Robert Flaherty's Louisiana Story: The Helen van Dongen Diary*, ed. Helen Durant and Eva Orbanz (New York: Museum of Modern Art, 1998), 13.

[9] Museum of Modern Art, Reel S-3124.

[10] "Ein Eimer Wasser stand immer dabei: Die 'Flimmerkiste' der Gebrüder Skladanowski," *Neueste Nachrichten* (Potsdam) (29 October 1953).

22 September 1907: Sigmund Freud Is Attracted to the Movies but Feels Lonely in the Crowd

Tan Waelchli

IN THE SECOND HALF of the twentieth century, psychoanalysis and film engaged in a famously fruitful exchange. While directors such as Alfred Hitchcock, Woody Allen, Roman Polanski, and David Lynch explored Freudian subjects, psychoanalytic theorists such as Christian Metz, Michel Chion, and Slavoj Žižek made significant contributions to film studies in the wake of Jacques Lacan. But when film and psychoanalysis first rose to fame in the early twentieth century, the relation was much more distanced, if not to say downright antagonistic. Freud, for his part, remained strangely silent about film: he hardly ever went to the cinema, and in 1925 he declined offers by both Samuel Goldwyn and Hans Neumann to collaborate on feature films.[1] He viewed with dismay the decision by Karl Abraham and Hanns Sachs to work with Neumann and director G. W. Pabst on *Die Geheimnisse einer Seele* (*Secrets of a Soul*, 1926). At the same time, Freud's negative view of film found its counterpart in the negative portrayal of psychoanalysis in such famous German features as *Das Cabinet des Dr. Caligari* (*The Cabinet of Dr. Caligari*, 1920) and *Dr. Mabuse, der Spieler* (*Dr. Mabuse: The Gambler*, 1922), in which evil analysts use their hypnotic power to control helpless subjects and to inflict severe damage to the order of society.

If one were to write the history of this mutual rejection, one might start in late September 1907. The first encounter between psychoanalysis and film seems to have taken place in Rome, where Freud was alone on vacation for two weeks. Staying at a hotel close to Piazza Colonna, he would spend the lovely, late-summer evenings on the open square, among a crowd of Romans promenading, listening to music, chatting, and from time to time viewing lantern slides and short movies, which were projected on a screen on a nearby rooftop. The encounter was a remarkable one for Freud, as can be concluded from a letter he wrote to his children on 22 September:

> On the roof of a house at the other end of the piazza there is a screen on which a *società Italiana* projects lantern slides (*fotoreclami*). They are actually advertisements, but to beguile the public these are interspersed with pictures of landscapes, Negroes of the Congo, glacier ascents, and so on. But since these wouldn't be enough, the boredom is interrupted by short cinematographic performances.... They are stingy with these tidbits, however, so I have had to look at the same thing over and over again. When I turn to go I detect a certain tension in the crowd, which makes me look again, and sure enough a new performance has begun, and so I stay on. Until 9 P.M. I usually remain spellbound; then I begin to feel too lonely in the crowd, so I return to my room to write to you all.[2]

The passage reveals an ambivalent stance for Freud. While he is clearly attracted to the films, it seems that what actually makes him watch — instead of returning to the hotel — is the "tension" he detects "in the crowd." Freud, in other words, seems to be mostly "spellbound" by the effects the films evoke in the audience. And what is most remarkable about this effect is the seemingly endless repetition.[3] While only a few films are played "again and again" (the German text says *wiederholt*), Freud notices that the repetition is part of the spell as it forces the audience — and him — to turn around and "look again."

Twelve years later this description strangely resonates in the one single text of Freud's in which a film is mentioned. When in "Das Unheimliche" ("The Uncanny," 1919), in the context of his discussion of the doppelganger, Freud briefly refers to Paul Wegener's *Der Student von Prag* (*The Student of Prague*, 1913), the old letter from Rome comes to mind for two reasons. For one, part of Freud's definition of the uncanny is that it underlies a compulsion to repetition, which forces a repressed belief from childhood to appear again and again. This means that film — that medium of spell and repetition, which Freud had come to know in 1907 — might now be understood as uncanny *per se*. And the comparison is strengthened when Freud explains that the uncanny figure of the doppelganger, specifically, can be dated back to a "childish" belief in eternal life, which once found expression in images of the dead carved in materials by the ancient Egyptians. As much as these old depictions, the new medium of film seems to provide "living" images and thus to guarantee the depicted a kind of eternal "life," so that it can be said to bring about the uncanny return of the old Egyptian belief.

These parallels indicate that "Das Unheimliche" implicitly contains an outline for a Freudian theory of film. Such a theory would understand film as an uncanny doppelganger, which, fueled by a repressed belief in "living" images and eternal "life," is forced to appear again and again. And this might explain why Freud's view of film was mostly negative: from his standpoint, the new media falls under the same critique as other uncanny phenomena, which Freud generally considers to be psychopathic. In addition to being based on "childish" beliefs, uncanny phenomena gain their specific force in a twofold process of repression and return of the repressed, which makes clear that the old beliefs have not actually been abandoned.

As stunning as such an approach might seem, we should not forget that a similar comparison between film and the doppelganger is already established in *Der Student von Prag*. The moment when the hero's double — created by a devilish villain, a moneylender — steps out of a mirror is frequently read as a depiction of the medium of film itself.[4] And here too this doppelganger/film is cast in a highly critical light. As it turns out in the course of the story, it not only drives the hero into madness and suicide, but it also kills the single heir to the throne and thus destroys the royal dynasty, which for centuries had provided the constitution of society.

While Freud's negative assessment of film as a doppelganger comes close to the view expressed in *Der Student von Prag*, two significant differences emerge if one compares his approach to Wegener's. First, Freud would never claim that the uncanny phenomenon is actually dangerous (much less threatens to destroy society as a whole). Indeed, Freud's analysis of the doppelganger reveals that the perception of danger is a *distortion caused by the repression* of the "childish" belief. In ancient times, he explains, the lasting image of the dead was regarded as much more friendly and entirely unthreatening. Secondly, Freud would also reject the assumption that the uncanny is brought about by an evil agent such as the moneylender in *Der Student*. Incorporating an old belief once repressed and now returned, the doppelganger obviously originates in the psyche of the subject.

These differences allow for "Das Unheimliche" to be read as a text written *against* Wegener's film. It seems as if Freud, by revealing that the uncanny doppelganger/film arises from the repressed belief of the subject, is pointing out that the evil agent — which brings about the doppelganger/film in *Der Student* — is a mere cover up. And this analysis is sustained in a short passage in which Freud discusses uncanny persons that are believed to bring about uncanny phenomena through supernatural powers. While he does not mention the moneylender from *Der Student*, Freud refers to Mephisto in Goethe's *Faust* as well as to the *Gettatore*, a figure of Romantic superstition. His third example is the author himself! "I should not be surprised to hear that psychoanalysis, which is concerned with laying bare these hidden forces [that bring about the uncanny], has itself become uncanny to many people for that very reason."[5] This is a remarkably dialectical point: according to Freud, the evil agent that is being portrayed as the cause of the uncanny is in fact trying to help the subject to get rid of it. If we apply this again to *Der Student*, we can observe that Freud reevaluates the role of the villainous magician, thereby identifying with him.

Freud's identification with the figure of the cinematic villain is particularly striking given that Wegener's evil agent bears little obvious similarity to a psychoanalyst. The choice seem less strange, however, if we consider the possibility that Freud was aware of the increasingly popular perception that had developed in the course of the 1910s according to which psychoanalysis and film were closely related phenomena. The common denominator for both was seen in hypnosis, which Charcot had practiced and which Freud and Breuer had applied in their early treatment of hysteria (prior to Freud's invention of the Oedipus complex in the fall of 1897). Thus when in 1913 Walter Hasenclever stated that movies "hypnotize the audience," and when three years later Hugo Münsterberg explained that cinema was superior to theater because its effect on the audience was comparable to that of the "hypnotizer," their language evoked aspects of psychoanalytic praxis.[6] The comparison was confirmed when in 1918, Ernst Simmel, a prominent psychiatrist close to Freud, described the process of remembrance that Freud and Breuer had tried to initiate by means of hypnosis as a film "made to roll again."[7]

Read against this background, "Das Unheimliche" reveals a sense in Freud that the association of psychoanalysis and film could finally make *him* the object of that critique, which, as in *Der Student von Prag*, was directed against film as an uncanny, harmful doppelganger. As if to prevent that conclusion, Freud agreed on the critique of the medium, while modifying it in three major aspects. First, according to Freud, the doppelganger/film is not harmful, but psychopathic. Second, it is not produced by a villain, but caused by a repressed belief of the subject. And finally, psychoanalysis is far from being responsible for the doppelganger/film; rather it tries to understand the uncanny phenomenon and to help the subject overcome it.

Freud's intervention notwithstanding, shortly after the publication of "Das Unheimliche" in 1919, two major films did indeed depict psychoanalysis as uncanny and harmful. Both Dr. Caligari and Dr. Mabuse are evil analysts whose uncanny hypnotic powers are closely associated with the power of film. Caligari, who in many regards seems to be modeled after Charcot, presents his somnambulist on the fairground (i.e., on the very site where most of the earliest films were shown), and when the somnambulist suddenly comes to "life," one is reminded of the way still images are animated at the moment a movie begins.[8] Mabuse lectures on psychoanalysis — in a scene deleted from the version of the film most widely distributed today — and the connection between hypnosis and film is made explicit in the famous scene in which he tries to hypnotize Wenk while playing cards with him. When, all of a sudden, we as viewers of the film see Mabuse from Wenk's point of view, this indicates that we fall under his spell as well.[9]

In retrospect, the overwhelming success of those two movies makes Freud's attempted self-defense in "Das Unheimliche" appear both prophetic and futile. The battle — if that is an apt term — between psychoanalysis and early film seems to have been won by the movies. However the last footnote to the story stems from an advocate of Freud's. In a review of *Dr. Mabuse*, published in 1922, Freud's niece Margit Freud rightly pointed out that her uncle had long ago abandoned his early method of treatment, and that psychoanalysis was, in fact, "the opposite of hypnosis."[10] If we accept the comparison between film and hypnosis common at that time, we might conclude that psychoanalysis was, in the 1910s and 1920s, the "opposite of film."

See also:

- 23 May 1920: *Das Cabinet des Dr. Caligari* Brings Aesthetic Modernism to the Fairground
- 4 March 1921: With *Das Floss der Toten*, the Dead Come Back to Town
- 31 January 1924: Premiere of *Orlacs Hände* Marks Beginning of the End of Expressionism

Notes

[1] Stephen Heath, "Cinema and Psychoanalysis: Parallel Histories," in *Endless Night: Cinema and Psychoanalysis, Parallel Histories*, ed. Janet Bergstrom (Berkeley: U of California P, 1999), 25–56; here 25, 51.

[2] *Letters of Sigmund Freud*, ed. Ernst L. Freud, trans. Tania and James Stern (New York: Basic Books, 1960), 261–62.

[3] Laura Marcus, "Dreaming and Cinematographic Consciousness," in *The Dreams of Interpretation: A Century Down the Royal Road*, ed. Catherine Liu, John Mowitt, Thomas Pepper and Jakki Spicer (Minneapolis: U of Minnesota P, 2007), 197–214; here 200–201.

[4] Friedrich Kittler, "Romanticism — Psychoanalysis — Film," trans. Stefanie Harris, in *Literature — Media — Information Systems*, ed. John Johnston (Amsterdam: Overseas Publishers Association, 1997), 85–100; here 96–97; Thomas Elsaesser, *Weimar Cinema and After: Germany's Historical Imaginary* (London: Routledge, 2000), 63–65.

[5] Sigmund Freud, "The Uncanny," trans. Alix Strachey, in *Psychological Writings and Letters* (New York: Continuum, 1995), 120–53; here 144.

[6] Stefan Andriopoulos, *Possessed: Hypnotic Crimes, Corporate Fiction and the Invention of Cinema* (Chicago: U of Chicago P 2008), 116–117. As Andriopoulos goes on to explain, later this view was confirmed by Robert Musil and Jean Cocteau.

[7] Anton Kaes, *Shell Shock Cinema: Weimar Culture and the Wounds of War* (Princeton: Princeton UP), 49.

[8] Kaes, *Shell Shock Cinema*, 63–64; 57–58.

[9] Andriopoulos, *Possessed*, 104–6.

[10] Andriopoulos, *Possessed*, 104.

Spring 1911: At Munich's Frankfurter Hof a Comedy Team Is Born

Christian Rogowski

Karl Valentin and his boss's wife, Frau Kuhn (Liesl Karlstadt) enjoy coffee with whipped cream in Der Sonderling *(1929). DVD capture.*

WITHIN A FEW MONTHS of their first meeting in Munich's Frankfurter Hof, Elisabeth Wellano appeared in a small supporting role as a wedding guest in *Karl Valentins Hochzeit* (Karl Valentin's wedding, 1912). Under the name Liesl Karlstadt, she was to become Valentin's partner and sidekick in hundreds of stage and radio skits and dozens of films over a period of more than twenty-five years. Although much of their material was developed jointly, often via improvisation, Karlstadt was hardly, if ever, given credit as a writer, her considerable comedic talent largely eclipsed by his idiosyncratic genius, to which she provided the necessary foil.[1] Valentin's accomplishments would have been unthinkable without Karlstadt's input: together, they formed the greatest, and most popular, German film comedy duo of their time.

Valentin, born Karl Ludwig Fey in Munich, started off (disastrously) as a musical clown with his "living orchestrion," a self-built contraption for a comedy routine that featured him struggling awkwardly with up to twenty-four instruments at the same time. His breakthrough as a comedian came in 1908 with the success of his stage monolog "Das Aquarium" (The aquarium). Delivered in the broad Bavarian accent of his hometown and combining absurdist wordplay with grotesque physical humor, it provided the blueprint for much of Valentin's later work: his persona, incapable of distinguishing the literal from the figurative dimension of discourse, inevitably gets tangled up in the inscrutable and imperfect logic of language; physically awkward, he constantly bumps into things, adrift in a bizarre world of recalcitrant objects that defeat his increasingly frantic efforts to claim or maintain control.

Such emphasis on physical comedy is rare in early German film. While German audiences enjoyed physical humor and slapstick imported from France (Max Linder) and the United States (Charlie Chaplin, Buster Keaton), there were few domestic performers who excelled at emulating or innovating the format. There were notable exceptions: Curt Bois, who at eight became Germany's first child star as "Willy," a clever boy who plays impish pranks on adults; Gerhard Dammann, who in the 1910s developed two comedic characters in a series of shorts, "Luny," who outwits his opponents in dicey situations through his mental and physical agility, and "Bumke," a pompous and physically inept dimwit; Anna Müller-Lincke, always starring as "herself," who crafted the persona of the spinsterish matron ridiculed for her physical rigidity; and Ernst Lubitsch, who as an actor in his early short films created a popular German-Jewish schlemihl, an underdog and social climber who, by shrewdly exploiting other people's weaknesses, usually gets both the job and the boss's daughter. In the late 1920s, there were even efforts to emulate the American comedy formula developed by Stan Laurel and Oliver Hardy, with the pairing of English-named characters "Beef" (Siegfried Arno's spidery zany persona) and "Steak" (Kurt Gerron as the fat straight-man). On the whole, though, slapstick and physical humor were not very widespread in early German film, remaining largely episodic.[2]

For decades, though, comedies did constitute the bulk of Germany's genre film production, culminating, in the wake of the Great Depression, in the era of early sound film, when — astonishingly — up to two thirds of all films produced in Germany were comedies.[3] Much of the output of the silent era has not survived, and the countless sound comedies, many produced in multiple language versions, often simply languish in the archives. Valentin's misanthropic masochistic humor is squarely at odds with the conciliatory humor of tame military farces (with their mild critique of pompous officers and bumbling recruits) and the schmaltziness of romantic comedies (with their clichéd boy-meets-girl scenarios of mistaken identities, amorous entanglements, and happy reunions) that predominated in German movie theaters. Nor does Valentin's filmic humor have anything in common with the immensely popular operetta films of the period (in many senses the precursors of today's Broadway musicals). These were sometimes syrupy and sentimental, revolving around Viennese aristocracy, vacations in romantic Rhine valleys, or Heidelberg student days, but at their best demonstrated a sophisticated charm and tongue-in-cheek satirical wit — a rich tradition all but destroyed when the Nazis came to power and expelled the genre's largely German- and Austrian-Jewish creators.[4]

Though an outsider in the German film industry, Valentin can rightfully be considered a pioneer: his involvement in film began in 1912, two years before Charlie Chaplin first appeared in Mack Sennett's Keystone comedies. While Chaplin's carnivalesque humor revolved around the "tramp" persona, the underdog whose resourcefulness enables him to outwit a hostile environment, Valentin's anarchic persona is that of the neurotic petit bourgeois (*Kleinbürger*), who stubbornly refuses to accept the constraints of an overpowering reality. His early silent short film comedies center on his distinct misfit persona and seek to find visual equivalents for his stage routines, which combined verbal, physical, and (often) musical humor. Like many of his films that were to follow, the title of *Karl Valentins Hochzeit* (the oldest of Valentin's short comedies still extant) conflates character and actor and banks on the tremendous popularity Valentin had achieved prior to turning to film. The short was written and shot shortly after Valentin's real wedding in 1911 to Gisela Royes, his parents' former chambermaid with whom he already had two daughters out of wedlock.

Lasting some five-and-a-half minutes, the surviving version comprises five short scenes: Valentin, excessively gaunt and tall, his skeletal limbs emphasized by tight, ill-fitting clothes, sits at his desk, reading an ad in the newspaper from a woman seeking marriage. He timidly visits the address, only to find himself in the clutches of an oversized matron (played by Georg Rückert in drag); the sofa collapses under her weight as she pounces upon him amorously and forces him to sign a wedding contract. Quick cut to the married couple leaving the registry office, with mayhem ensuing as the bride stumbles trying to climb into a horse carriage. Likewise, the wedding party at the bride's home ends in chaos, as the dancing newlyweds trip and the bride falls on top of the luckless groom. A chase sequence ensues, incongruously provoked by an escaped canary; running across a field, Valentin stumbles and is almost crushed when again his bride lands on him; the film ends with the relatives hoisting his lifeless body into a wheelbarrow, carting him off-screen.

It is difficult not to read this early short in Freudian terms as reflecting profoundly ambivalent feelings about sexuality in general, and women in particular. Valentin is constantly overpowered, and the two partners are grotesquely mismatched. Much of the physical humor comes at the expense of Valentin's character, who is incapable of maintaining control over his environment. The audience is invited to laugh at, rather than with, his inept figure, taking a sadistic form of pleasure at his predicament and the ensuing mishaps while at the same time feeling uneasy about the actor's freakishly grotesque — but all too real — physicality.[5]

The formula developed here is brought to fruition in Valentin's only full-length silent feature film, Walter Jerven's *Karl Valentin, der Sonderling* (Karl Valentin: The odd one, 1929). A sequence of skits is loosely held together by a thin plot revolving around Valentin (again appearing under his real name) as a tailor's apprentice who becomes the reluctant object of affection of his master's wife, Frau Kuhn (played by Karlstadt). Here, too, there is a Freudian dimension to the sadomasochistic humor. Valentin is shown at the outset fussing over his collection of stamps. As he vainly tries to glue stamps in his album, his elbow squashes a tube of adhesive, creating a squirting oozy mess that ruins his precious collectibles. Later, alone with Frau Kuhn, Valentin is shown absentmindedly heaping spoonful after spoonful of whipped cream onto his coffee until the cup overflows. The references to repressed and misplaced sexual desire, with such symbolic quasi ejaculations, are obvious. The very premise that Valentin — excessively tall, thin, and gauche — should be an object of female desire appears ridiculous. Equally incongruous is the notion that Frau Kuhn — short and portly — could be capable of unabashed (and adulterous) sexual passion. A later episode finds Frau Kuhn astride a runaway motorbike she cannot control, culminating in her bringing a group of gentlemen (her husband's choral society) to collapse as she encircles them with a clothesline that is entangled in her bike. The frenetic pace of the sequence is enhanced by repeated cross-cutting between Frau Kuhn's fearful motorized escapade and a side-plot featuring an exuberant roller-coaster ride: Frau Kuhn's niece Anni, a pretty, independent-minded flapper (Dutch actress Truus van Aalten), fends off the precocious advances of the adolescent clockmaker's apprentice Toni (fifteen-year-old actor Gustl Stark-Gstettenbaur) on a visit to a fair. In a rare instance of extended physical slapstick, the sequence serves as a set-up for the conclusion of the film, when Valentin — despondent after several unsuccessful suicide attempts over suspicions that he embezzled money to buy a coveted rare stamp — declines Frau Kuhn's offer to go on a joint motorbike ride, because, as an intertitle tells us, he is wary of putting his life at risk with her at the wheel.

Jerven's film is both typical of and exceptional in Valentin's filmic output. It features many of the trademark characteristics of his distinct physical comedy while also displaying a certain filmic sophistication absent from Valentin's shorts in terms of mise-en-scène, camera work, and editing. Most of Valentin's other short films, both silent and sound, are little more than straightforward records of the stage skits he and Karlstadt had honed in dozens, sometimes hundreds, of performances. The camera usually remains static, primarily recording the interaction between the characters, with little effort to translate the theater experience into film-specific terms. The focus is on the idiosyncratic interactions between Valentin's oddball persona and Karlstadt as exasperated sidekick, with Valentin punning, spewing syllogisms, manhandling Bavarian dialect, and contorting conceptual logic. The skits never culminate in a traditionally happy ending, but rather slip toward the worst possible outcome; intrinsically innocuous situations gradually derail and escalate to their usually bitter end. In the early silent *Der neue Schreibtisch* (The new desk, 1913), Valentin fails in his efforts to level the four legs of his new desk, trimming them to the point that he is forced to sit on the floor. As he drills holes in the floor to accommodate his long legs, he ends up falling through the ceiling into the shop below. In the sound film *Orchesterprobe* (The orchestra rehearsal, 1933), he struggles vainly as a percussionist with the conflicting demands of keeping the beat on various instruments while wrestling with a faulty music stand, wayward sheet music, and fogging glasses. Physical and linguistic humor converge when, during an increasingly frantic performance, Valentin mistakes the conductor's cue of a musical "pause" by attempting to take a break and down a stein of beer. His befuddled incompetence drives the conductor (Karlstadt) insane, and the scene ends in utter chaos.

Valentin and Karlstadt would appear together in nearly four dozen short films ranging in length from one minute to about half an hour, with most of the sound skits of the 1930s averaging around twenty minutes. While Valentin more or less always played the same character — the comically awkward, misanthropic, hypochondriac, neurotic *Kleinbürger* — Karlstadt as his straight sidekick would play a wide variety of roles of both genders, ranging from naïve young boys and incompetent coworkers to irascible authority figures, from shrewish matrons and nosy neighbors to exasperated salesladies.[6] Some of their films were artistically significant, like their collaboration with playwright Bertolt Brecht and director Erich Engel in the experimental, surrealist silent farce *Mysterien eines Frisiersalons* (*The Mysteries of a Hairdresser's Shop*, 1923). Some were highly ephemeral, like advertisements aimed at luring tourists to Munich. On her own, Karlstadt also had a reasonably successful career in minor parts in films from the 1920s through the 1950s. Together, Valentin and Karlstadt appeared in four full-length sound film comedies: as supporting players in Max Ophüls's *Die verkaufte Braut* (The bartered bride, 1932) and Hans Deppe's *Straßenmusik* (*Street Music*, 1936), and in starring roles in two films by Erich Engel, *Kirschen in Nachbars Garten* (The grass is always greener, 1935), and *Donner, Blitz und Sonnenschein* (Thunder, lightning, and sunshine, 1936). Their most ambitious short sound film, Jacob Geis's *Die Erbschaft* (The inheritance, 1936) revolves around a poor married couple that is put under pressure by their landlord and the bailiff. Receiving news that they have inherited some valuable furniture, they celebrate by destroying their old shabby furniture for firewood, only to find out that the new — absurdly small — set was intended for their midget-sized neighbor. Crushed by debt, the couple ends up in an empty apartment. The Nazi censors banned the bleak film for its "defeatist tendencies." Valentin's dream of eventually directing a full-length feature of his own never came to fruition.

Valentin's blend of Bavarian provincialism and anarchic subversion has lived on in emulation, however. Munich-based filmmaker Herbert Achternbusch evokes Valentin in such absurdist low-budget tragicomedies as *Bierkampf* (*Beer Chase*, 1977) and *Das Gespenst* (*The Ghost*, 1982). The Valentin/Karlstadt brand of humor further serves as a model for later comedic pairings in mainstream German film, notably the uptight Prussian Loriot (Vicco von Bülow) and his tight-lipped sidekick Evelyn Hamann, or, closer to home, the bumbling Bavarian Gerhard Polt and unflappable Gisela Schneeberger. In 2008, director Jo Baier brought the couple's tempestuous creative and personal relationship back to the screen and into public awareness with *Liesl Karlstadt und Karl Valentin*, securing the pair's presence as comedic masters for the new century.

See also:

- 21 January 1914: Premiere of *Die Firma heiratet* Inaugurates Fashion Farce
- 31 December 1995: *Der bewegte Mann* Sells 6.5 Million Tickets to Mark Peak of New German Comedy
- 21 October 2001: Television Provides Platform for Record Box-Office Success of *Der Schuh des Manitu*

Notes

[1] Michael Schulten, *Karl Valentin in Selbstzeugnissen und Bilddokumenten* (Reinbek bei Hamburg: Rowohlt, 1968).

[2] Thomas Brandlmeier, "Early German Film Comedy, 1895–1917," in *A Second Life: German Cinema's First Decades* (Amsterdam: Amsterdam UP, 1996), 103–13. Hans-Michael Bock, Wolfgang Jacobsen, eds., *Der komische Kintopp*. Filmmaterialien 10 (Hamburg: CineGraph, 1997).

[3] Ulrich von Thüna, "Die deutsche Filmkomödie der Depressionsjahre 1930–33," in *Photokina-Katalog* (Cologne: Messe- und Ausstellungsgesellschaft, 1980), 317–25.

[4] Jan Distelmeyer, ed., *Spaß beiseite, Film ab: Jüdischer Humor und Verdrängendes Lachen in der Filmkomödie bis 1945* (Munich: edition text + kritik, 2006). Michael Wedel, *Der deutsche Musikfilm: Archäologie eines Genres 1914–1945* (Munich: edition text + kritik, 2007).

[5] Jan-Christopher Horak, "Laughing until It Hurts: German Film Comedy and Karl Valentin," in *Prima di Caligari: Cinema tedesco, 1895–1920/Before Caligari: German Cinema, 1895–1920*, ed. Paolo Cherchi Usai and Lorenzo Cordelli (Pordenone: Edizione de Biblioteca dell' Imagine. 1990), 202–29.

[6] Gunna Wendt, *Liesl Karlstadt: Münchner Kindl und Travestie-Star* (Berlin: Edition Ebersbach, 2007).

27 May 1911: Asta Nielsen Secures Unprecedented Artistic Control

Heide Schlüpmann

IN 1910 THE FILM INDUSTRY found itself in a period of transition. The familiar short films had begun to give way to longer feature films, now running as long as 40–50 minutes. The distribution of film copies, initially occurring in the form of sales, was gradually replaced by the lending system that we know today, and so-called monopoly distributors began to take over. Finally, stars began to emerge, as figureheads who would help viewers navigate among a multitude of new film titles. These stars afforded a means by which the film production company, the distributor, and the movie theater could ensure strong audience attendance. Although these changes resulted from an economic crisis in the film industry, the solution did not derive solely from economic principles or mechanisms. The crisis opened up a space for new aesthetic and social forces. Danish actress Asta Nielsen embodied this kind of dual potential.

Asta Nielsen had burst upon the world scene with *Afgrunden* (The abyss, 1910), as a figure whose novelty simultaneously captivated and offended viewers. The film's physically palpable exposure of the female body and sexual drama elicited strong reactions. It was her first film following many years in the theater. In the immediate aftermath, Nielsen, who had become famous overnight, seemed to be at a standstill with her film career: she received no offers in Denmark and made just two films with Bioscope in Germany. But behind the scenes in the European market, plans were already being drawn up for her. The result, on 27 May 1911, was a contract between Nielsen and cinema company Projektions AG Union (or PAGU) — an already active firm that was bent on innovation. The group that gathered at the company's office in the Kaiserstraße in Frankfurt am Main included the director of PAGU, Paul Davidson, the monopoly distributor Christoph Mülleneisen as well as his son, along with Urban Gad, the Danish director of *Afgrunden*, and their future star, Asta Nielsen. Nielsen was fully aware of what she meant to the industry and negotiated a commensurate part in any profits. With this, she secured not only the economic foundation for her independence as an actress, but also her influence on the films themselves.

The contract, signed in the presence of an attorney, committed Gad and Nielsen to making eight to ten movies a year through the end of 1914; the event was photographed for posterity. Even in retrospect, the moment was significant: it marked the beginning of a *Spielfilmkino*, a cinema marked by playing, in the development of which Nielsen would play a singular role, reshaping public and critical consciousness of the medium's aesthetic and social significance.

The 1914 Nielsen film *Die Filmprimadonna* (*The Film Primadonna*) grants a look at the ways in which this star does not merely play a role, but rather influences the entire creation of a film. She selects the script, she chooses her partner, she controls the shooting and discussions with the camera people, she controls the darkroom to look on while the film is developed. What the film does not explicitly show, because it is already self-evident, is the manner in which Nielsen acts in constant dialogue with the camera. Together with the camera, she organizes the cinematic space into which the other actors are introduced, while she herself steps outside of it and toward the audience. In her bodily movements, her gestures, and facial expressions, she exposes an interior space to the outside world. The camera focuses on this exterior, the moving surface of a female body.

Nielsen, as we read in her autobiography, also picked out the fabrics and patterns of her costumes herself. After all, they were her second skin — they had to convey her bodily expressions. But this was not her sole interest — she also wanted to bring to life the social reality of the women she portrayed. Women's thoughts, wishes, and hopes, *and* the social reality in which they lived, were of equal importance to her. To have brought both of these things to equal reality before the camera is Nielsen's achievement. She developed a new cinematic aesthetic, one that brought the ruptures in modern society, its changes and new beginnings, hopes, and possibilities, into the movies — particularly as it affected women. As a result, cinema earned its place among the other modern social movements of the time: the women's movement, the sexual reform movement, and the workers' movement.

The first full-length feature films juxtaposed documentary shots with narrative scenes. They translated, so to speak, the variety format of early cinema — the rapidly changing "views" from all over the world or the neighborhood, the little staged stories and trick scenes à la Méliès — into a single film. What was lost was the vitality of the cinematic situation in which the "numbers" were embedded. Asta Nielsen gave new life to the more or less varied sequence of the film — the life of acting in the sense of *Spiel* (play). The fascinating presence of her performance functioned like an overtone for the sequence of changing scenes. But it was not music alone that she brought to the cinema as it transitioned from an earlier program format to the full-length feature film; she also accomplished a different and unique translation — namely, the translation of the reality from which the film draws its material into the reality of the audience in the movie theater. This interplay became both the common thread and the medium/mediation of these realities. In a lovely essay titled "Der Dichter und das Phantasieren" ("The Relation of the Poet to Day-Dreaming," 1908), Sigmund Freud describes how children adapt their fantasies to reality and take this means of relating to reality as seriously as grown-ups take "real life." In the name of the latter, we are forced to conceal our daydreams. Spielfilm, the photoplay of cinema, grants those fantasies a public space. Nielsen establishes that space as a form of cinema and cinema-going in which the woman before the camera and the audience play together. The effect is emancipatory — a form of film and cinema that liberates from social taboo.

In her first film, *Afgrunden*, Asta Nielsen plays a young woman from Copenhagen. In her dress and manner she belongs in the modern metropolis. The camera watches her appear among other passers-by, following her as she moves confidently in the public space, enters a streetcar, and drinks coffee with a chance acquaintance in the park before hurrying on to work. She is independent, earning her living giving piano lessons. Thus far, the protagonist mirrors liberal society's notion of an emancipated woman. She attracts the attention of a young gentleman, the son of a Protestant minister who finds her pleasing. But as the brief story approaches its "happy ending" in marriage, Nielsen reveals that behind the figure of this modern woman there resides a deeply hidden desire, a longing for a freedom quite different from the bourgeois one.

The film initially proffers images of this longing in shots of itinerant circus performers and the proud figure of a man on horseback in their midst. Only a little nudge is necessary, we can see, and the man will burst the framework of her present world — he literally climbs through the window frame — to mobilize a passion that makes the protagonist, for her part, break out of her previous life like a prisoner escaping from jail. And yet, true to the realism of the documenting camera, the promise of liberation that emanates from the exotic images is soon shown to be sheer illusion. The melodramatic course of the story seems predictable. But Nielsen unpredictably asserts herself against realism and its disillusionment, clinging to the lasting reality of her most intimate desire, clinging to the wish that is contained in the images, with their longing and the departure that is continually renewed in them.

The center and high point of the film is a boot-stomping gaucho dance that mirrors Nielsen's approach to acting. She shows not only that, but also how she breaks with the conventions of the stage, turning away from the varieté audience portrayed in the film and toward the camera. It is for the camera that she dances: with it she transforms her dance- and film-partner into the object of her performance; toward it she directs her imagination; through it, she reveals a dark, hidden side of human existence. The protagonist of this drama knows very soon after their first meeting that the man she is after represents the wrong addressee for her utopian vision of a liberated life. But Nielsen simply shifts her address — instead of the male partner in the drama, she turns toward the camera, which documents the slightest movements of her body and reveals them to us, her audience.

The subjects and stories that Urban Gad and Nielsen chose were, on the one hand, everyday events; on the other hand, they embodied dreams and fantasies, wishes and hopes. In everyday reality, as a rule, the latter exist only in fragmented form, transformed into art or hidden within individuals. But they do not just originate in reality, they also press for realization. Nielsen drew on her own desire as a means of representing the childlike capacity for play and did away with the separation of exterior and interior. Adapting her fantasies to camera-mediated reality, she acted and played in and with this reality. Today it seems almost unimaginable that actresses once had such freedom, but the 1910s were a period in which the dominance of directors and producers had not yet been established. In Germany there were scattered attempts at developing an *Autorenfilm* (authors' film) based on literature and the theater, but this tendency only became established in the 1920s. In it, the fantasy that has been liberated in film turns back into art and separates itself, once again, from reality. This occurs at the expense of the autonomy of the actress and actor. Before the war, by contrast, under the sign of the Asta Nielsen series, Nielsen worked with a producer and director in a contractually secured constellation in which all the freedom was hers.

In the 1910s, Nielsen played proletarian girls — *Die arme Jenny* (*Poor Jenny*, 1912), *Vordertreppe und Hintertreppe* (Frontstairs and backstairs, 1915) — as well as daughters of the bourgeoisie (*Der fremde Vogel* [The strange bird], 1911). Again and again she portrayed artists, in settings ranging from honky-tonk to more established varieté theaters — *Den sorte drom* (The black dream, 1911), *Der Totentanz* (*The Dance of Death*, 1912), *Die weißen Rosen* (The white roses, 1916) — and even movie actresses, as in *Zapatas Bande* (*Zapata's Gang*, 1914), *Die Filmprimadonna* (*The Film Primadonna*, 1913), or *Die falsche Asta Nielsen* (*The False Asta Nielsen*, 1915). All these roles bear the stamp of her personal experience and observation. Together with Gad, Nielsen fulfilled her contract with an immense production of cinematic dramas and comedies: before the First World War put an end to the collaboration with PAGU, she starred in thirty-four films. Her incomparable ability to express suffering and pain was matched by an equally unique comedic talent (especially captivating in her performance in *Engelein* [Little angel], 1914). In 1916, Nielsen was able to return to Berlin and to make eight more movies with various directors using her own money. Among them was one with obvious contemporary relevance: *Die Börsenkönigin* (The queen of the stock exchange, 1916), in which she plays the part of a mine owner. After a brief interlude in the Danish film industry, she again returned to German cinema in 1919. But despite her continued popularity with audiences, she would not make movies at her previous prolific pace. After the early 1920s, she appeared only occasionally in films, but made more frequent appearances in variety theaters. In 1933, the National Socialists assumed complete control of German film production; Nielsen turned her back on the industry altogether, and in 1937 she returned to Denmark.

The history of Asta Nielsen's feature films is very closely interwoven with the social and political history of Germany. This is already visible in the breaks and interruptions of her career. Nielsen's cinematic work also experienced breaks and resistance of a film-historical nature. The relations of production after 1918 were radically different from those in prewar Germany. Nielsen was now dealing with directors who saw themselves as the authors of their films, and who insisted on their authority over actresses — even one as experienced and successful as she. Nielsen did not accommodate them. Her fierce debates with Ernst Lubitsch during the making of *Rausch* (*Intoxication*, 1919) — based on the play by August Strindberg, by whom Nielsen set great store — were public knowledge. At issue were not just conflicts of authority, but above all differences of aesthetic and even political conception. Montage was being put forward as an increasingly popular means of addressing the audience, both for reasons of artistic merit and as a tool of enlightenment. It came to dominate the interplay of actress and camera — an interplay dedicated to translating filmic space into the space of cinema, thus mobilizing a capacity for play among audiences. Nielsen also found little support from film producers. PAGU's absorption into Ufa (Universum Film A.G.) in 1917 was indicative of the changing historical situation. The ideological overwriting of reality and real-world conflicts led to the suppression of the playful interweaving of the forces of dream with reality.

For a while, Asta Nielsen attempted to continue with her way of working by creating her own movie production company, Art-Film GmbH. With it, she was able to realize, among other films, *Hamlet* (1921) — a film that reprises her predilection for *Hosenrollen* (pants roles) and that at the same time gave her a turn away from comedy. But she was no longer able, as a producer, to create the constellation between director, camera, and actress that she required for her work and her impact dwindled. Yet she continued, even in these reduced circumstances, to attempt to seize possibilities and make the best of them according to her own standards. Thus, for example, she gave a socially and also cinematically critical turn to the role of the prostitute, which had frequently been offered to her. In films such as *Der Absturz* (*Downfall*, 1923), *Dirnentragödie* (Tragedy of the street, 1927), or *Die freudlose Gasse* (*The Joyless Street*, 1925), she managed to convey her objection to the socially degrading presentation of women/actresses as objects. Soon she earned a reputation as "difficult," and in 1925–26 she was virtually boycotted by the film industry. In 1927, she played in another five films, and in 1932 Nielsen made a triumphant return, appearing in front of her audience one last time. The "talkie" *Unmögliche Liebe* (*Crown of Thorns*, 1932) gives the lie, even today, to the rumor that Nielsen failed because of the introduction of sound. Quite the opposite: she treated spoken language in a way that was similar to the way she handled the visual language of her physical gestures and facial expression.

Asta Nielsen's film-historical reception was oriented toward the 1920s. It was, however was the 1910s during which she gained a worldwide following and helped to shape international film production — for example, influencing the Italian divas and the early Russian actresses. But, like early film altogether, this fell prey to oblivion. In the 1920s, Nielsen had lost her stature in film production, even if the public remained faithful to her. Film critics, intellectuals, and artists, too, recognized that there was something special about her, and attempted to make this something public. They constituted a weak opposition to Nielsen's expulsion from film production. This opposition is weak also insofar as it virtually reproduces the kind of isolation she experienced by being reduced to a "mere" actress, having acted as a creative player within a network before. In the appraisal of Nielsen, the form of the films that she had once brought to life was forgotten. Instead, we find hymns to the persona of the actress, declarations of love for the appearance on the silver screen in the early film theory of Béla Balázs, the poems of Richard Behrens and Hans Siemsen, or, a bit later, in the Belgian lyric expressionism and painting of the Dutchman Pyke Koch. Film history has continued this adulation. Asta Nielsen has not been forgotten, unlike so many early actresses and, above all, female directors. But her importance in the history of the emergence of *Spielfilmkino*, a cinema bent on playing, has been lost. In this regard, film history has participated in the repression and distortion of this particular cinema. The material fate of the films of Asta Nielsen reflects this ignorance. For a long time, unless they were made by known Weimar directors, they failed to garner any archival interest. Worldwide, one can often find only poor-quality copies in the archives, and half of her films must be considered lost. And yet through the preserved films, even today — after all the critical attention that has been paid to narrative cinema and fiction films — Asta Nielsen has the power to make us aware of the existence of another, aesthetically and politically emancipatory form of feature film. In this form of *Spielfilmkino*, the woman-as-actress was producer in every sense of the word.

Translated by Susan H. Gillespie

See also:

- 15 October 1920: Ernst Lubitsch Fuels Debate over Tears in the Cinema
- 16 August 1949: Ilse Kubaschewski Founds Gloria-Filmverleih, Sets the Course of Popular West German Film
- 11 February 2008: Ulrike Ottinger's *Prater* Wins German Critics' Award for Best Documentary Yet Highlights the Director's Ties to Both Fiction and Nonfiction Film

18 December 1913: *Atlantis* Triggers Controversy about Sinking of Culture

Deniz Göktürk

THE TITANIC DISASTER was in the air before it actually happened. In Slavoj Žižek's words, "'the time was waiting for it': . . . there was already a place opened, reserved for it in fantasy-space. It had such a terrific impact on 'social imaginary' by virtue of the fact that it was expected. It was foretold in amazing detail."[1] Žižek refers to a novel by Morgan Robertson, published in 1898, about a fabulous Atlantic liner named Titan, which hit an iceberg and sank one cold April night. Newspapers carried reports about disasters at sea, and *Sensationsfilme* (sensational films) about shipwrecks appeared in cinemas well before the Titanic's fateful journey in 1912. The glory and demise of transatlantic transportation technology converged in the popular imaginary with the production and circulation of moving images. The focus here is on one particular shipwreck narrative and its journey through various media: a novel by Nobel Prize-winning author Gerhart Hauptmann, its cinematic adaptation, and the film's reception.[2]

The rise of cinema was accompanied by a variety of reflections in literature. Writers felt threatened, challenged, and at times inspired by the new form of popular entertainment offered by the *Kintopp*, as Berlin audiences lovingly called the new show business of projected moving images. In Germany, probably more than in any other country, long-established ideals of *Bildung* triggered heated debate about the question of film's status as art. Writing, evolving around the rise of the new medium in what was termed the *Kino-Debatte* (cinema debate), constituted the discursive field wherein cinema gained significance as a cultural institution.[3]

The film adaptation of Gerhart Hauptmann's novel *Atlantis* by the Danish Nordisk Films Kompagni in 1913 was an event of broad cultural impact. The marketing of *Atlantis* as a "Gerhart-Hauptman-Film" followed Nordisk's policy of acquiring film rights for famous books and using names of well-known literary authors as trademarks to gentrify the lowbrow entertainment of cinema by promoting quality *Autorenfilme* (author films) — an early predecessor of the French "Tradition of Quality," which likewise attributed authorship to the writer of adapted works.

Nordisk's literary agent, Karl Ludwig Schroeder, who worked mostly in Berlin, signed contracts around the same time with other writers such as Max Halbe, Clara Viebig, Bertha von Suttner, and Arthur Schnitzler. Schroeder also wrote the film script for *Atlantis*. Hauptmann's publisher Samuel Fischer was himself interested in the potential of the new medium for increasing book sales, just as serializations in newspapers and journals had helped to sell books to a literary audience, and a letter from the publisher reveals that Hauptmann was extremely well paid by Nordisk (receiving a 20,000 mark guaranteed payment and 4 percent royalty).[4] Although Hauptmann did not write the screenplay himself, *Atlantis* was generally billed as his film. The director was August Blom, who had previously made film dramas about the abduction of white slave girls — a popular genre and another Nordisk specialty.

Atlantis's Berlin premiere occasioned the grand opening of the picture palace Kammer-Lichtspiele on Tauentzienstraße on 18 December, a week before the first Danish screening at the Copenhagen Paladsteatret on 26 December. Rumors of colossal expenses and ambitious technology had been circulating for months before the film was released. The press emphasized the high gross production costs (ca. 500,000 marks), the army of actors (close to eighty starring actors, one hundred supporting actors, and as many as five hundred extras for the ship scenes), as well as the chartered flotilla (including an ocean liner, three trans-Atlantic steamships, two tugboats, an extravagantly constructed wreck, and many motorboats).[5] Critics generally hailed the ship disaster as the dramatic highpoint of the performance. The opulent sets and the high quality of the cinematography are still impressive today. The film's length was no less spectacular: an unprecedented 2280 meters plus 128 intertitles, or about two hours long, although, in a sign of cinema's prewar internationalism and its tendency to cater to specific tastes, Nordisk representatives in many countries demanded that it be edited down according to the preferences of their audiences. *Atlantis* remained in distribution in Germany throughout the war years, selling out among urban and provincial audiences alike.

The story follows one middle-class intellectual's fascination with trivial, lowbrow entertainment as represented in *Atlantis* by a precocious and wicked child-dancer. Starring in this role at the author's request was Ida Orloff, an established actress at the Vienna Burgtheater, who had bewitched Hauptmann back in 1905 in a stage appearance in Berlin. Casting Orloff to play the variety dancer Ingigerd Hahlström was a controversial choice, as the contemporary critical reception indicates. In stark contrast to the character Hahlström, the actress Orloff was renowned for her performances of modern high literature at leading German theaters. In the novel, Hauptmann identifies the variety stage dancer with the revolting world of the entertainment industry; she is a tightrope-walking girl, a puppet from the panopticon. She lures the bacteriologist Friedrich von Kammacher (played by a brooding Olaf Fønns, who would later play the lead role in the *Homunculus* series), recuperating from a failed marriage, across the ocean to the land of unscrupulous modernity where quantity reigns over quality, distraction over contemplation, business and sensationalism over genuine value. The traveler's fascination with this feminized sphere of dubious entertainment precedes his arrival in America, the land of "dollar-mania" and "the lust for sensation"; temptation sets in back home in Berlin. On this transformative journey to America, the bourgeois intellectual's passion turns into disgust and a general rejection of the city. He recovers from the madding crowd in the purifying solitude of a Walden-like log cabin in the woods and finally, purged of his temptations, returns to Europe.

Fascination with female dancers and artists was in vogue among literati at the turn of the twentieth century. Hauptmann himself had met leading representatives of expressionist dance, including Ruth Saint-Denis, Isadora Duncan, and Saharet (Clarine Campbell). In the tradition of Nietzsche, he saw dance as a Dionysian inebriation, an expression of elemental experience to which the modern city-dweller had no access. The aesthetic fascination with dancing child-women and the demonization of female sexuality emerge as central themes throughout Hauptmann's work. Yet he was not alone among modernist authors in his ambivalent feminization of the primitive and the trivial. Gustave Flaubert, for example, was — despite his claims to the contrary — not identical to his Madame Bovary, the wayward reader of sentimental love romances. As Andreas Huyssen has argued, "the diminutive association of mass culture with the sphere of the feminine was written into the aesthetic program of modernity from the beginning."[6] Keeping with efforts to elevate cinema as art, however, explicit feminine eroticism was downplayed in *Atlantis*. In stark contrast to seduction scenarios in other contemporary films, such as the social dramas of Danish actress Asta Nielsen, acting and body language in *Atlantis* appear rather stiff and subdued.

Hauptmann and other European writers imagined modern mass culture as not only feminized, but also Americanized. Their ambivalence toward modern civilization, technology, and commerce found its target in America. New York, with its hectic swarms of people, chaotic traffic jams, merciless competition, clamoring advertisements, sensationalized press, and compulsion for amusement, served as the ultimate modern metropolis, which offered the appropriate setting for the fate of an individual overwrought with inner turbulences.

In the film, such city views corresponded with audience demands for simulated travel. Moving pictures set locations on the move; in fact, they offered ersatz journeys to the armchair traveler, and in many ways also enticed and promoted tourism.[7] For the Berlin shots, Nordisk sent the actors with a team to Berlin. Olaf Fønns rode a taxi by the Siegessäule, the Stadtschloß, and other sights, enacting an impression of organic movement in the city traffic. In addition, the film production crew acquired documentary footage of New York, which Marguerite Engberg rediscovered during the reconstruction of the film at the Danish Film Museum in Copenhagen. The production company had sent not actors but a cameraman to New York, whose footage of the port, the skyline, the Statue of Liberty, the city traffic, newspaper boys, and the entryway to a music hall were incorporated in the final montage of the film.

The reenactment of life on board an ocean liner delivered similar thrills of virtual travel. The luxurious upper deck was juxtaposed with contrastive cuts to below, showing arranged tableaux of steerage passengers staged for bourgeois eyes. The shots below deck betray the film's reliance on traditional pictorial representations of gypsies and bohemian milieus. Appearing in these scenes are not the poor, mostly Russian Jewish emigrant families that one could expect to see, but rather — as in the novel — the exotic, erotic projections of the men "above." In the film, the middle-class man peered into the cavernous realms of the *lumpenproletariat*, grouped in a painterly tableau around a dark guitar player; von Kammacher offers a cigarette to a dark, mysterious beauty. The sinking of the ship served as an opportunity to enact class hierarchies. Panic among the passengers and the crowds pushing onto the lifeboats were augmented through dramatic editing.

The extensive incorporation of location footage as well as stage acts resulted in the ambitious production of *Atlantis* ultimately failing to hold together, with contemporary critics deriding the film as a patchy collection of individual scenes. The narrative thread based on the protagonist von Kammacher, which the novel had maintained, no longer functioned in the film. *Atlantis* thus embodies a turning point in the transition to the long feature format, while still absorbing elements of variety stage entertainment and the "cinema of attractions."[8] Stopping by a New York variety show, von Kammacher visits a performance by the "Armless Wonder" Carl Unthan. The artist Unthan was a travel acquaintance of Hauptmann during his Atlantis crossing in 1894, becoming Arthur Stoll in the novel. Unthan had appeared in short films before and later on published his memoir titled *Das Pediskript*.[9] In the film version of *Atlantis*, Unthan plays himself. The stage act of this armless artist playing the trumpet, performing card tricks, lighting a cigarette, opening a wine bottle and pouring a glass of wine, blowing his nose, writing on a typewriter — all with his feet — takes up extensive time in the film, also pointing to a prenarrative "cinema of attractions" with its roots in variety theater. These scenes show that the film remained somewhat undecided between narrative integration and display of spectacle and stage attractions.

Atlantis further displays an unresolved tension between literary and visual forms of communication. Literary culture at the beginning of the twentieth century was still grounded in the image of an intact creative individual, who conducted his life as if it were a nineteenth-century *Bildungsroman* and, on the basis of his own experiences, created his works in a solitary chamber. Authorial practice was quite different, however, and inevitably evolved in competition and cooperation with the despised, flashy visual media. *Atlantis* is thus less a symbol of the demise of bourgeois society or a vision of the imminent world crisis and war catastrophe than a vision of the downfall of the literary bourgeoisie. Although he himself consented to the filming of his novel, Hauptmann nonetheless repudiated the American lust for trivial sensations through his hero Friedrich von Kammacher's return to Europe. The cultivated individual was thereby saved. Yet among Hauptmann's works, it was *Atlantis* — with its rejection of the city and metropolitan mass culture — that inaugurated his occasional enterprises in the realm of the entertainment industry.

The release of *Atlantis* generated controversial responses about relations between cinema and literature, the cultural status of adaptations, and more generally accelerated circulation in capitalist modernity, perceived projectively as the "Americanization" of culture. Although the production values and the attempt to create serious art cinema were noted, critics expressed uneasiness about the representation of character psychology and concluded that cinema was not the appropriate medium to convey complex interior turmoil. More generally, these debates around the film adaptation picked up on a critique, already voiced in the novel, of a commercialization of art in modern-day capitalism associated with America. There was no American connection in this Danish adaptation of a German novel (the extra Mihály Kertész had not yet embarked on his American career as Michael Curtiz). Nonetheless the conservative critic Erich Schlaikjer wrote in January 1914, alluding to *Atlantis*: "The destruction of a venerable work of art by the film industry, aiming to draw with a famous author's name, is an American strategy, and the whole cinema as is it today has something American about it."[10] While to many America epitomized the excesses of capitalist exploits, in Europe, too, various media circuits were already networked by 1913, the borders between high art and trivial entertainment were becoming porous, and the commercialization of cultural values was causing concern — as this case study of *Atlantis* indicates. While later mobilizations of "auteur cinema" as a quality label shifted the emphasis to the creative genius of a film's director rather than the writer, the fundamental concern with branding and valorizing individual creativity still permeates these debates. The author is always already a function of the market.

After 1920, the *Atlantis* case was still cited as an emblem of the degradation of the true poetic spirit and individual creativity in the media competition — a lament for the end of literature, which resonates in ever new ways in debates about authorship and "new" media today. The novel denigrated the obsession with the loose variety dancer by blending it with a strong dose of cultural anti-Americanism. The author thus positions himself against the threatening rise of a feminized mass culture by writing an apologetic parable about seduction and redemption, almost apprehensively legitimizing his first contract with the film industry. His novel constitutes a fictionalized contribution to the *Kino-Debatte*. In the *Atlantis* scenario images of virtual travel and female sexuality are conflated with a critique of modern mass culture, cast in oppositions between Europe and America — a constellation that has been equally virulent in the myth of the Titanic and has lived on in debates on modernity, mobility, and the media.

See also:

- 15 October 1920: Ernst Lubitsch Fuels Debate over Tears in the Cinema
- 3 June 1929: Lloyd Bacon's *The Singing Fool* Triggers Debate about Sound Film
- 11 December 1930: Ban of *All Quiet on the Western Front* Highlights Tensions over Sound Technology

Notes

[1] Slavoj Žižek, *The Sublime Object of Ideology* (London/New York: Verso, 1989), 69.

[2] A more detailed account of this case study in intermediality was published in Deniz Göktürk, *Künstler, Cowboys, Ingenieure . . . Kultur- und mediengeschichtliche Studien zu deutschen Amerika-Texten 1912–1920* (Munich: Fink, 1998), 38–79. Thanks to David Gramling for help with translation and condensation, and to Nicholas Baer for corrections and suggestions.

[3] Anton Kaes, ed., *Kino-Debatte: Texte zum Verhältnis von Literatur und Film 1909–1929* (Tübingen: Max Niemeyer, 1978).

[4] Dierk Rodewald and Corinna Fiedler, eds., *Samuel Fischer, Hedwig Fischer: Briefwechsel mit Autoren* (Frankfurt am Main: Fischer, 1989), 303.

[5] *Erste Internationale Film-Zeitung* (20 September 1913): 31.

[6] Andreas Huyssen, "Mass Culture as Woman; Modernism's Other," in *After the Great Divide: Modernism, Mass Culture, Modernism* (Bloomington: Indiana UP 1986), 44–62.

[7] Tom Gunning, "The Whole World Within Reach: Travel Images Without Borders," in *Virtual Voyages: Cinema and Travel*, ed. Jeffrey Ruoff (Durham, NC: Duke UP, 2006), 25–41.

[8] Gunning, "The Cinema of Attraction: Early Film, Its Spectator and the Avant-Garde," *Wide Angle* 8, nos. 3/4 (1986): 63–71.

[9] Carl Hermann Unthan, *Das Pediskript: Aufzeichnung aus dem Leben eines Armlosen* (Stuttgart: Robert Lutz, 1925).

[10] Erich Schlaikjer, "Amerikanismus," *Kunstwart und Kulturwart* 27, no. 8 (January 1914): 104.

21 January 1914: Premiere of *Die Firma heiratet* Inaugurates Fashion Farce

Mila Ganeva

Director Lubitsch, in character, guides a model down the runway in Schuhpalast Pinkus *(1916). DVD capture.*

JANUARY 21, 1914 MARKED the Berlin premiere of *Die Firma heiratet: Drei Kapitel aus dem Leben einer Probiermamsell* (Marriage in the company: Three chapters from the life of a fashion model), directed by Carl Wilhelm. In the next two months it played over five hundred times to audiences that "laughed, neighed, and screamed" with excitement (*Lichtbild-Bühne*, 24 January 1914). The comedy features Ernst Lubitsch in a breakthrough role as a sales apprentice in a clothing store and exposes the intrigues of Berlin's garment district. A few months later, on 30 July 1914, the same director released a sequel, again starring Lubitsch: *Der Stolz der Firma: Die Geschichte eines Lehrlings* (The pride of the company: The story of an apprentice). Lubitsch went on to set the first two films he directed himself — the slapstick situation comedies *Schuhpalast Pinkus* (Shoe palace Pinkus, 1916) and *Der Blusenkönig* (The blouse king, 1917) — in the social and geographical milieu of Berlin's *Konfektion* (fashion) industry, thereby directly addressing the themes of consumerist desires and infatuation with fashion.

In studies of early cinema these films are mentioned, if at all, only in the context of Lubitsch's screen persona: his performance style, his indebtedness to popular forms of entertainment — vaudeville, circus, pantomime — his Jewish humor, and his interest in stories related to the fashion and garment industries. The popularity of these early comedies has been attributed to Lubitsch's convincing performance as a shrewd, scheming, opportunistic, and yet likable apprentice in the rag business, appearing under the names of Moritz Abramowsky, Siegmund Lachmann, Sally Katz, or Sally Pinkus. Critics have emphasized the affinity between Lubitsch's petit-bourgeois characters and his own social background. Growing up among Eastern European Jews in Berlin, he was very familiar with the Jewish *Konfektion* environment.[1] In fact, before joining Max Reinhardt's theater, Lubitsch had worked as an apprentice in a garment store in Berlin. More than any other filmmaker, Lubitsch shows how connected cinema is to commerce, marketing, consumer goods, and fashion, and how the *Konfektion* milieu as a world of make-believe "effectively mirrors or parodies cinema itself."[2]

With fashion constituting an essential part of both mise-en-scène and plot, the films with and by Lubitsch provide a preview of broader emerging cinematic and cultural trends. These works chart the direction in which Lubitsch's comedic style develops during his "German period" (1914–22), and they additionally reveal the complex relationship between film and fashion in early and Weimar cinema. The fashion theme shaped distinct cinematic conventions associated with a new subgenre, known as the *Konfektionskomödie* (fashion farce). This subgenre's rise coincided with the flourishing of Berlin's mostly Jewish-owned garment industry. Lubitsch's films about fashion were also among the first to link early German comedy to Jewish humor and Jewish characters and to the themes of masquerade, cross-dressing, and the transformative effects of clothing.

The rediscovery of these fashion farces of the 1910s and 1920s not only fills a blind spot in German film history, but it also reveals the mechanisms by which popular culture became relevant. The impetus for both critique and theoretical reevaluation of the role of fashion in film can be traced back to Siegfried Kracauer's essentially disparaging film essays in the *Frankfurter Zeitung*. Kracauer saw fashionable images in film primarily as an empty vehicle for entertainment — escapist, conformist, and unrealistic. In "Film 1928" he characterized contemporary films as "the most daring *escape attempts*," in which "social reality is evaporated, petrified, and distorted. . . . [The protagonists] chauffeur themselves, live in Berlin, in Paris, and on the Riviera, dress almost exclusively in sports clothes or in full evening attire, and fall on hard times only once (at most) in order to marry into money immediately afterward."[3] Yet Weimar cinema's enormous appeal for contemporary audiences — an appeal documented in numerous reviews including in Kracauer's own writing — was compelling enough to merit a closer look at how exactly the pleasurable visual experience was constructed through the theme of fashion.

Kracauer believed that despite its strong roots in capitalism and consumer culture, cinema as a mass medium could be instrumental in the process of democratizing culture. In his 1926 essay "Cult of Distraction," as well as in other critical writings around that time, he suggested that the film experience was predicated upon a pervasive form of distracted consumption that replaced the contemplative fascination associated with highbrow, bourgeois art. Although Kracauer focused primarily on the "elegant surface splendor" of Berlin's movie theaters, the representation of glamour and fashion on the screen, too, offered pleasurable distraction and shaped cosmopolitan urban audiences. In his early writings Kracauer still saw this "distraction," this mass experience of visual pleasure, as a redeeming and socially useful phenomenon, because cinema offered the possibility of "self-representation of the masses subject to the process of mechanization."[4] He read the entertaining and popular features of film as subtle signs of resistance to the pressures of a depersonalized capitalist society. By engaging a heterogeneous public on the most immediate level, the level of the senses, as Kracauer scholar Miriam Hansen argues, film introduced its mass audience to new forms of perception, awareness, and attention and, as a result, helped it navigate an increasingly complex modern environment. Thus if cinema presents, as Hansen proposes, an incarnation of a "vernacular modernism," a modernist aesthetic that articulates and mediates a wide array of quotidian cultural practices, then fashion (within film), given its distinct visuality and its obvious connections to everyday usage, can be considered one of the most pronounced forces shaping the experience of modernity for the masses.[5]

Between 1914 and 1933 over two dozen fashion comedies were released. They exhibited alluring locations, events, and products associated with the modern lifestyle of the German metropolis — designer salons, upscale department stores, fashion parades, and stylish clothes. The sites and fashion practices displayed were quite familiar to even lower- and middle-class women, who were drawn to them if not as customers then at least as avid window-shoppers and consumers of visual delights. The protagonists in these films were also appealing to a mass public. On the one hand, there was always the shrewd male shop assistant who knew how to cater to capricious and vain customers. By the mid-1920s, a crop of new comic talent emerged following in the footsteps of Lubitsch: the new stars of *Konfektionskomödie* were now Curt Bois and Siegfried Arno, who played in the nationally and internationally popular comedies *Der*

Fürst von Pappenheim (*Masked Mannequin*, 1927) and *Moritz macht sein Glück* (Moritz makes his fortune, 1931), respectively. On the other hand, there was the ambitious, smart, indispensable female fashion model (*Konfektionsmädel, Probiermamsell, Gelbstern,* or *Konfektioneuse*) who hoped to acquire middle-class status, to become a fashion queen, an actress, a film star, or the owner of a designer salon. Taking cues from her popular predecessor Thea Sandten, who was cast as the fashion model in Otto Rippert's 1912 film *Gelbstern*, Henny Porten played in *Die Dame, der Teufel und die Probiermamsell* (The lady, the devil, and the mannequin, 1919) and created what the press then called "a new type: the German fashion model" (*das deutsche Konfektionsmädel*).[6] Actresses as diverse as Camilla Horn (in *Ich geh' aus und du bleibst da*), Charlotte Ander (in the remake of *Die Firma heiratet*), Lya Mara (in *Yvette, die Modeprinzessin*), Maria Korda (in *Eine Dubarry von heute*), Grit Haid, Helga Molander, and Elisabeth Pinajeff (in *Die drei Mannequins*), Truus van Aalten (in *Jennys Bummel durch die Männer*), Mona Maris and Dina Gralla (in *Der Fürst von Pappenheim*), Lia Eibenschütz and Lee Parry (in *Luxusweibchen*), Uschi Elliot (in *Gelbstern*), Hella Moja (in *Die Warenhausprinzessin*), Evi Eva and Lilly Flohr (in *Die Kleine aus der Konfektion*) all aimed at stardom by playing top models in fashion farces.

As a subgenre, the *Konfektionskomödien* are remarkable for the way in which they combine a focus on gender and class issues with visual pleasure. The central character of the model embodies erotic initiative and social ambition of almost utopian proportions, which helps her resist the intentions of the men around her. Moreover, models — usually young women of lower-class background — could be considered the female doubles of the ambitious Jewish apprentices, recent arrivals from the provinces, since both groups were "social climbers" and "adventurous hedonists" who mastered perfectly the tasks of advancement, assimilation, and achieving maximum success in life.[7]

On-screen, unlike in real life, the girls who modeled the glamorous outfits were allowed to display temperament, opinions, and ambition of their own, thus inviting the audience to identify with them on several levels. As part of her job, the model presented clothes that she possessed only temporarily during the show, and in reality could never buy. Nevertheless, the fashionable attire and the experience of wearing it seemed to embody her dreams of future fame and prosperity. She liked to think that her involvement with fashion was just the first step toward her imagined future realization as a real actress. Similarly, for the female audience, the spectacular display of fashion on the screen could easily serve as a reminder of what it neither owned nor could afford. Nevertheless, the viewers preferred to indulge, at least for the duration of the film, in the visual pleasure of such fashions and in the fantasy of one day becoming such an image. It is in this act of doubling powerful on- and off-screen illusions that the fashion models in the farces also emerged in the peculiar function of role models for an upwardly mobile yet still very constrained female audience. And the fashion farces as a whole offered access — or what Jeanne Allen calls "ownership by viewing" — to an often inaccessible material environment, to a way of dressing and living that consumerism "promised to the viewer ideologically, but awarded only to the eye."[8]

The fashion farce offers a credible milieu study of Berlin's fashion scene in part because it sheds light on the life of a typical model: she parades dresses for upper-class customers yet she is often not allowed to talk to them or to collect any commission from sales. At the same time, these films tend to favor the exhibition at the expense of the story or artistic sophistication. Setting substantial parts of the film in a clothing store serves as an excuse to stage numerous parades of fashionable clothes, shoes, and accessories — pure visual extravaganzas that contribute little to the development of the plot but fulfill other functions. The fashion shows within the film served as effective advertisement for the Berlin designer houses that supplied the costumes and were mentioned by name in the credits, intertitles or programs. At the same time, these parades on the screen directly contributed to the democratization of modern fashions. Since in real life the fashion shows were cast as a form of exclusive entertainment, accessible only to small, elite audiences that paid high entrance fees, movies provided for the masses an occasion to enjoy for free the same visual attractions that only the select few could enjoy in the fashion salons.

By the mid-1920s, there emerged a new generation of screenwriters that demonstrated exceptional familiarity with the Berlin fashion trade and brought its ambience, rituals, and characters into the stories of *Konfektionskomödie*. These writers — the most famous among them, Ruth Goetz and Ola Alsen — had worked as professional fashion journalists for *Die Dame*, *Elegante Welt*, and *Der Modenspiegel*. Ruth Goetz wrote the script for *Die Kleine aus der Konfektion* (The salesgirl from the fashion store, 1925), a comedy of errors and mix-ups, which starts as a melodrama but continues with a spectacular series of fashion shows that constituted the primary draw of this film, especially for the women in the audience. According to the critics, "the female viewers will be thrilled to see much more than they paid for when they watch the long parades of mannequins. . . !" (*Film-Kurier*, 28 February 1925). Ola Alsen scripted the 1925 movie *Luxusweibchen*, another fashion farce with scenes of nightclubs, designer salons, and incessant fashion shows, which earned the label "Baedecker of the world of elegance" (*Film-Kurier*, 21 April 1925).

The pioneer actor and director of the fashion farces, Ernst Lubitsch, did not continue working in this subgenre. His subsequent career, however, in Berlin as well in Hollywood, remains marked by an interest in a filmic narration that is inseparably and often comically entangled with the sensual immediacy of clothes and accessories. In almost all of his later films — from *Sumurun* to *Ninotchka* and from *Bluebeard's Eighth Wife* to *The Shop Around the Corner* — a garment (pajamas, silk stockings, a polka-dot blouse) figures prominently in the economy of vanity and desire and in the spectacles of flattery and attraction. Within the later Lubitsch films and within the Weimar fashion farces more generally, the display of fabulous clothing resulted in significant breaks in the narrative flow, offering spectators a glimpse of an earlier cinema of attraction preserved fragmentarily in the fabric of popular story-based cinema. At the same time, the disruptions provided by the fashion show of Weimar cinema, even in the most straightforward and trivial narratives, spoke to the core experience of modernity — increasing distraction, disjunction, and fragmentation.

See also:

- Spring 1911: At Munich's Frankfurter Hof a Comedy Team Is Born
- 10 January 1927: Brigitte Helm Embodies Ambivalence of the New Woman
- 16 December 1927: Debut of *Familientag im Hause Prellstein* Provokes Debate about Jewish Identity in Popular Cinema

Notes

[1] Michael Hanisch, *Auf den Spuren der Filmgeschichte: Berliner Schauplätze* (Berlin: Henschel, 1991), 284.

[2] Thomas Elsaesser, "Early German Cinema: A Second Life?," in *A Second Life: German Cinema of the First Decades*, ed. Thomas Elsaesser and Michael Wedel (Amsterdam: Amsterdam UP, 1992), 9–37; here 25.

[3] Siegfried Kracauer, "Film 1928," in *The Mass Ornament*, ed. and trans. Thomas Y. Levin (Cambridge, MA: Harvard UP, 1995), 308–10.

[4] Siegfried Kracauer, "Berliner Nebeneinander: Kara-Iki — Scala-Ball im Savoy — Menschen im Hotel," *Frankfurter Zeitung*, 17 February 1933; reprinted in Kracauer, *Kleine Schriften zum Film*, ed. Inka Mülder-Bach, vol. 6, bk. 1 (Frankfurt am Main: Suhrkamp, 2004), 418.

[5] Miriam Bratu Hansen, "The Mass Production of the Senses: Classical Cinema as Vernacular Modernism," in *Reinventing Film Studies*, ed. Christine Gledhill and Linda Williams (London: Arnold, 2000), 332–50.

[6] C.B., "Die Dame, der Teufel und die Probiermamsell," *Der Film*, 25 January 1919, 36.

[7] Jürgen Kasten, "Der Stolz der deutschen Filmkomödie: Die frühen Filme von Ernst Lubitsch 1914–1918," in *Die Modellierung des Kinofilms: Zur Geschichte des Kinoprogramms zwischen Kurzfilm und Langfilm 1905/06–1918*, ed. Corinna Müller and Harro Segeberg (Munich: Wilhelm Fink, 1998), 301–32; here 308.

[8] Jeanne Allen, "The Film Viewer as Consumer," *Quarterly Review of Film Studies* 5 (Fall 1980): 481–99.

Part II: 1918–1932

In October 1918, the military leadership that had run Germany since 1916 handed over power to a civilian government to negotiate an end to the war. Max von Baden was appointed chancellor, and undertook a number of constitutional reforms designed to help quell unrest and fulfill one of the preconditions for an armistice set out by Woodrow Wilson in his "Fourteen Points" speech: ministerial responsibility was to be returned to parliament, the armed forces were to come under the control of a civilian government, and the Prussian three class voting system was to be discarded in favor of universal suffrage.

Military leaders, however, were not ready to end the war — allowing a civilian government to negotiate peace was a ploy to deflect blame and to allow them to claim that defeat was the result of sabotage by domestic enemies, not military failure. This *Dolchstosslegende* (the myth of a stab in the back) would be a source of discontent throughout the Weimar Republic. At the end of October, naval leaders ordered one final, suicidal attack on the British fleet. However, when the Wilhelmshaven fleet was ordered out on 28 October, a majority of sailors mutinied. Demonstrations in Kiel on 3 November led to a more general mutiny, and throughout November Germany found itself in the midst of widespread revolutionary upheavals. Both the Chancellor and Kaiser Wilhelm were forced to resign.

On 9 November, Baden handed over power to Friedrich Ebert, leader of the SPD (Sozialdemokratische Partei Deutschlands, or Social Democratic Party of Germany). The "German Republic" was proclaimed by Philipp Scheidemann at the Reichstag in Berlin; two hours later, a "Free Socialist Republic" was proclaimed nearby at the Berliner Stadtschloss by Karl Liebknecht in the name of the *Spartakusbund*. Meanwhile, on 8 November in Munich, the socialist Kurt Eisner announced the formation of a Bavarian Socialist Republic. At first, Ebert sought to pacify demonstrators and unite the working class parties and was willing to bring the USPD (Unabhängige sozialistische Partei Deutschlands, or Independent Socialist Party of Germany), as well as Liebknecht, into his government. But pressure from more revolutionary elements forced Ebert to agree to a compromise government, consisting of a Council of People's Representatives.

At the same time, Ebert secretly negotiated a pact with General Wilhelm Groener, who offered the support of the army if Ebert pursued a more moderate path and suppressed the radical councils. As Germany continued to experience social unrest and revolutionary upheaval,

Ebert increasingly turned to military force, including use of the *Freikorps* — paramilitary groups made up largely of returning soldiers — to quell revolts. In January 1919, when a general strike in Berlin led to armed battles known as the Spartacist uprising, the police chief Gustav Noske enlisted the army and the *Freikorps* to suppress the revolt. Spartacist leaders Karl Liebknecht and Rosa Luxemburg were arrested, murdered, and their bodies crudely dumped in the Spree River. In Munich, the assassination of Eisner and the arrival of military and Freikorps soldiers led to the end of the *Räterrepublik* there. When the violence finally subsided, thousands of Germans had been killed in the course of these conflicts. The hostility between the left wing, particularly the KPD (Kommunistische Partei Deutschlands, or Communist Party of Germany), and the SPD would linger throughout the Republic.

On 11 November, in a railway car in the forest of Compiègne, the armistice agreement ending the war was signed. In no position to negotiate, Germany had capitulated without any Allied concessions. The territorial terms of the peace would continue to be negotiated until the Treaty of Versailles was signed on 28 June 1919. The terms of the treaty were extraordinarily harsh: Germany lost large areas of land including Alsace-Lorraine, West Prussia, Upper Silesia, Danzig, and Posen. Germany was also forced to relinquish its colonies, and was barred from forming an alliance with Austria. The left bank of the Rhine was demilitarized under Allied supervision, with a gradual phasing out of Allied occupation over the next decade.

On 11 August 1919 the Weimar Constitution officially took effect. For its time, it was a progressive document: the constitution allowed direct popular vote for president, who was vested with considerable powers, including the right to appoint/dismiss the chancellor, dissolve parliament and call new elections, and call national referenda; it outlined a voting system of proportional representation; and it provided universal suffrage for men and women. However, the political system of proportional representation and numerous small parties meant that no party was able to gain an overall majority, while radically divergent views made it difficult for main parties to form sustainable coalitions. As a result, the only choice was to form a minority cabinet, which led to a succession of cabinets and frequent presidential interventions.

Throughout 1919 to 1923, the Republic endured a series of attacks from both right and left. The contrast in how each group was treated was significant: right-wing extremists tended to be treated leniently by the conservative judiciary; left-wing revolutionaries faced harsh sentences, and often the death penalty. Moreover, the army often refused to fight against right-wing revolts, such as the 1920 Kapp Putsch. Only a general strike in Berlin enabled the Ebert government, which had fled to Stuttgart, to regain control. When Communists unsuccessfully revolted in Saxony and the Ruhrgebiet, however, the army was quite eager to engage them.

Reparations further complicated Weimar politics. Since Germany had financed the war through a series of loans and bonds, rather than new taxes, debt was already a problem. The Allied Reparations Committee levied $33 billion in war reparations debt against Germany; it ordered the handing over of 26 percent of all exports for forty-two years and billed the Germans immediately for 12 billion marks, with the total repayment sum set at 132 billion marks. With few options, Germany began printing more paper money, and quickly entered an extended period of hyperinflation. The exchange rate in early 1921 was roughly 60 marks per US dollar; by the end of the year, it stood at nearly 320 marks, and by September 1923, it had ballooned to 60,000,000 marks per dollar, rendering the German currency worthless, and leaving millions penniless. It was only with the introduction of the rentenmark (one rentenmark equaled 1 trillion marks, or $4.2 US) in November 1923 that the currency was stabilized.

Meanwhile, political unrest continued. When Germany fell behind in its coal and wood deliveries, France sent troops to occupy the Ruhrgebiet. Germany's strategy of passive resistance garnered international sympathy, but further exacerbated the financial crisis. The other major revolt was the *Hitlerputsch* (Hitler's "Beer Hall Putsch") on 8–9 November 1923. Hitler sought to overthrow the Bavarian government, but overestimated his political support, and the Putsch was quickly quelled. Arrested, tried and sentenced to prison for five years, Hitler served only eight months in the fortress of Landsberg, where he wrote much of *Mein Kampf*. After his release, he adopted a different strategy for taking power (namely, through the political system).

From 1924 to 1929, Germany enjoyed an extended period of stabilization, thanks in part to the foreign policy of Gustav Stresemann. Stresemann, of the Deutsche Volkspartei (German People's Party, DVP), regularized foreign relations with the West; signed pacts with Poland and Czechoslovakia; and in April 1926 signed the Berlin Treaty with Russia, guaranteeing German neutrality were Russia at war with a third party. On 29 August 1924, the parliament ratified the Dawes Plan, which, though it made Germany more dependent on US loans, facilitated reparations payments and by July 1925 led to the removal of Allied troops from the Ruhrgebiet. In September 1926, Germany became a member of the League of Nations. In August 1929, the Young Plan was adopted, reducing annual compensation to be paid by Germany, removing foreign controls, and ending the Rhineland occupation in June 1930, five years before the Versailles Treaty stipulated.

Still, Germany was not without its problems during this period. The split between the SPD and the far Left continued; the Right continued to propagate the *Dolchstosslegende*, and there was a general nostalgia for imperial Germany and a time when Germany was a dominant power in Europe, as evidenced by Hindenburg's election as president in 1925.

When the worldwide economic crisis occurred in late 1929, Germany was hit hard. The economy was dependent on short-term loans from abroad, which were withdrawn after the crash. Unemployment skyrocketed: in September 1929, 1.3 million workers were unemployed; by the beginning of 1933, this number reached six million. The financial crisis led to a political crisis as well. After Brüning took over as prime minister in 1930, the parliamentary system was essentially ignored and power returned to the hands of the old elite who had never accepted either the peace treaty or the republic. Parliament met less and less frequently, with the government ruling by a series of emergency decrees. Fearing a return of hyperinflation, the government focused its efforts on loan repayment, which only exacerbated the financial crisis. In 1932, the Hoover Moratorium brought an end to reparations, but this did little to help.

The end of the Republic, like the beginning, was characterized by polarized political positions. Both the KPD and the National Socialist party gained a significant number of seats from 1930 to 1932, but it was the Nazis, with the support of industrialists keen to end the democratic experiment, who emerged as the largest party. Tapping into a general discontent with the democratic system, they were able to broaden their base beyond the petit-bourgeois rural voters and gain support in the educated, professional, and upper-middle class. Despite the fact that the Nazis actually lost votes in the November elections, business leaders continued to put pressure on Hindenburg to bring Hitler into the government. On 30 January 1933, Hitler was constitutionally appointed as chancellor of a coalition government, setting the course for the eventual dissolution of Germany's first democracy and twelve years of dictatorial rule.

Amid all of the turmoil, the cultural sphere enjoyed a period of great intellectual and creative activity. Just as the old political system was being overturned, so too were traditional notions of art and science being challenged. Arnold Schoenberg's experiments with atonality, Bertolt Brecht's Epic Theater, the critical theory of the Frankfurt School and Walter Benjamin may all be traced back to this period. Weimar also saw the development and institutionalization of new forms of mass culture, particularly film. During the stabilization period, a modern consumer culture aimed at the new class of white-collar office workers emerged. But these transformations were not universally celebrated, and the political tensions between those who sought to return to the old ways of the monarchy and those who called for radical political change also found expression in judgments about culture. The Right was extremely critical of what it saw as a decadent turn — a laxity in sexual morals, a shift away from traditional values, and, most significantly, a transformation in women's identity, as embodied in the concept of the New Woman. The Left, though it embraced aspects of mass culture, was critical of its costs, and railed against the evils of modern capitalism, the suffering of the working class, and the de-individualization of modern society.

German cinema, too, experienced a period of tremendous creativity and growth during the years from 1918 to 1932. Lacking foreign competition domestically, the film industry boomed. Ufa (Universum Film A.G.) continued to dominate, acquiring smaller studios, building new theaters, and publishing books and journals. It also invested in larger, prestige projects and art films to improve Germany's market share abroad. Hyperinflation actually helped the industry to prosper; not only were filmmakers able to borrow money that would be devalued long before it was repaid, but the worthless German currency made the German market unappealing to international film companies. The quality of many of the films produced during the period reflected a need for cheap, quick products, but Germany was also producing works that were both critically and artistically successful, such as Robert Wiene's expressionist classic, *Das Cabinet des Dr. Caligari* (*The Cabinet of Dr. Caligari*, 1920).

Expressionism first took root in the Wilhelmine period in the visual arts and then in poetry, literature, and the theater. Its main themes — patricide, the New Man, the struggle against authority — reflected the deep divisions of the time. Although expressionism had run its course in other fields by the end of the war, the social upheaval of early Weimar, as well as expressionism's use of dark, moody symbolism and psychological themes, made it particularly appropriate for a cinema that sought to produce films that were both artistic and reflective of the turmoil of the time. Moreover, with sound still years away, film remained a visual medium, making it particularly well-suited to the exaggerated acting styles, nonrealistic sets, and play between light and shadow that characterized films such as *Caligari*, Paul Wegener's *Der Golem: wie er in die Welt kam* (*The Golem*, 1920) and F. W. Murnau's *Nosferatu* (1922). By the mid-1920s, expressionism was supplanted by *Neue Sachlichkeit* (New Objectivity), characterized by a focus on social themes and a return to realism (not coincidentally at the time when Germany was in its stabilizing period), but it continued to influence both German and international cinema well into the 1950s.

A variety of styles and genres followed, some of which, like the *Straßenfilm* (street film) or the *Kammerspielfilm* (chamber play film), drew on expressionism, and some of which, like the *Bergfilm* (mountain film), combined more realist tendencies with a glorification of nature and myth. Although many of the most well-known films of the Weimar period were art films, easily recognizable as the work of particular directors such as Lubitsch, Murnau, Lang, and Pabst, popular genres — big-budget historical dramas, light comedies, and melodramas accounted for most of the commercial successes of the period. Avant-garde film also flourished during the Weimar era, as filmmakers experimented with new technologies and new conceptualizations of what defined film.

The legitimation of film as art was advanced by the growing discipline of film criticism. Industry-sponsored publications such as *Lichtbild-Bühne* and *Kinematograph* were joined in 1919 by the film daily *Film-Kurier*, which self-consciously discussed the nature of film criticism. Other critics such as Rudolf Arnheim, Béla Balázs, Siegfried Kracauer, and Lotte Eisner wrote reviews and articles for a variety of publications. Criticism centered not just on questions of film aesthetics, but on the social and economic implications of and themes in contemporary film. Film was consistently interpreted with an eye toward its historical and cultural context: even essentially escapist films were read in terms of concepts such as distraction, consumerism, and subjectivity.

The end of inflation in the mid-1920s made the German market again appealing to foreign productions, particularly those from the United States. German films no longer monopolized the domestic market, which was split between Germany and the United States. In an effort to bolster the industry both home and abroad, Ufa entered into a reciprocal distribution agreement with Paramount and Metro-Goldwyn-Mayer, though financial troubles led to Ufa being purchased by Alfred Hugenberg in 1927. Germany also developed exchanges with the Russian film industry, exporting films to the Soviet Union and importing films such as Eisenstein's *Battleship Potemkin* (1926) and Pudovkin's *Mother* (1927). European directors and filmmakers began a period of international collaboration, with actors and directors from Russia, Austria, and Scandinavia working on and influencing German productions. In the early 1930s, many German actors and directors also began moving to Hollywood, joining a migration that began with figures such as Murnau, Lubitsch, and Jannings in the 1920s.

While internationalism was a byword for many directors, film was also a means for articulating a particular German national identity. Films such as Fritz Lang's two-part *Nibelungen* epic (1924), and historical epics such as Arzén von Cserépy's four-part *Fridericus Rex* (1922–23) and Hans Behrendt's *Danton* (1931) engaged audiences' desire for nostalgia and nationalistic pride.

The advent of sound dramatically changed the economic and aesthetic landscape of German cinema. Silent film was easily marketable abroad, but sound films had less appeal internationally. Studios began casting French, British, and even American stars and shooting multiple foreign-language versions of films. Critics attacked sound film, fearing that sound would deprive film of its unique focus on visuality and diminish its aesthetic potential. But just as filmmakers had experimented with montage and mise-en-scène, directors made innovative use of sound, both as a means to provide their narratives with greater emotional depth and through new techniques of sound montage. The first German full-sound film, *Melodie des Herzens* (*Melody of the Heart*, 1929), was quickly followed by Josef von Sternberg's *Der blaue Engel* (*The Blue Angel*, 1930, shot simultaneously in German and English), which made an international icon out of Marlene Dietrich, and demonstrated the artistic potential of sound. By 1932, the production of silent films had effectively ceased in Germany.

With Hitler assuming power as chancellor, one of the most productive and diverse periods of German film came to a close. A cinema that produced both nationalist epics and socially engaged films, traditional melodramas and experiments in sound and abstract image, would give way to a tightly controlled industry that sought to eliminate divergence and critique, and instead bring the nation's film production in line with the political, cultural, and propagandistic aims of the regime.

Selected Bibliography • 1918–1932

Calhoon, Kenneth S., ed. *Peripheral Visions: The Hidden Stages of Weimar Cinema*. Detroit: Wayne State UP, 2001.

Coates, Paul. *The Gorgon's Gaze: German Cinema, Expressionism, and the Image of Horror*, 18–73. Cambridge: Cambridge UP, 1991.

Doge, Ulrich, Thomas Elsaesser, and Laurence Kardish. *Weimar Cinema 1919–1933: Daydreams and Nightmares*. New York: MOMA, 2010.

Dyer, Richard. "Less and More than Women and Men: Lesbian and Gay Cinema in Weimar Germany." *New German Critique* 51 (Fall 1990): 5–60.

Eisner, Lotte. *The Haunted Screen: Expressionism in the German Cinema and the Influence of Max Reinhardt*. 2nd Edition. Berkeley: U of California P, 2008.

Elsaesser, Thomas. *Weimar Cinema and After: Germany's Historical Imaginary*. New York: Routledge, 2000.

Gander, Gero, ed. *Der Film der Weimarer Republik: Ein Handbuch der zeitgenössischen Kritik*. Berlin: de Gruyter, 1993.

Guerin, Frances. *A Culture of Light: Cinema and Technology in 1920s Germany*. Minneapolis: U of Minnesota P, 2005.

Gunning, Tom. *The Films of Fritz Lang: Allegories of Vision and Modernity*. London: British Film Institute, 2000.

Hagener, Malte. *Geschlecht in Fesseln: Sexualität zwischen Aufklärung und Ausbeutung im Weimarer Kino 1918–1933*. Munich: edition text + kritik, 2000.

Hall, Sara F. "Moving Images and the Policing of Political Action in the Early Weimar Period." *German Studies Review* 31, no. 2 (2008): 285–302.

Hogan, Patrick Colm. "Narrative Universals, Nationalism, and Sacrificial Terror: From *Nosferatu* to Nazism." *Film Studies* 8 (Summer 2006): 93–105.

Isenberg, Noah, ed. *Weimar Cinema: An Essential Guide to Classic Films of the Era*. New York: Columbia UP, 2009.

Kabatek, Wolfgang. *Imagerie des Anderen im Weimarer Kino*. Bielefeld: Transcript, 2003.

Kaes, Anton, ed. *Kino-Debatte: Texte zum Verhältnis von Literatur und Film 1909–1929*. Tübingen, Max Niemeyer, 1978.

———. *Shell Shock Cinema: Weimar Culture and the Wound of War*. Princeton: Princeton UP, 2009.

Kardish, Laurence, ed. *Weimar Cinema, 1919–1933: Daydreams and Nightmares*. New York: Museum of Modern Art, 2010.

Kelly, Andrew. "From the Defeated: *Westfront 1918*, *Kameradschaft* and *Niemandsland* — the German Cinema and the War." In *Cinema and the Great War*, 82–100. London: Routledge, 1997.

Kester, Bernadette. *Film Front Weimar: Representations of the First World War in German Films of the Weimar Period (1919–1933)*. Translated by Hans Veenkamp. Amsterdam: Amsterdam UP, 2003.

Kosta, Barbara. *Willing Seduction: The Blue Angel, Marlene Dietrich, and Mass Culture.* New York: Berghahn, 2009.

Kracauer, Siegfried. *From Caligari to Hitler: A Psychological History of the German Film.* Princeton: Princeton UP, 1974 [1947].

Kreimeier, Klaus. *The Ufa Story: A History of Germany's Greatest Film Company, 1918–1945.* Translated by Robert and Rita Kimber. New York: Hill & Wang, 1996.

Kühn, Gertraude, Karl Tümmler, and Walter Wimmer. *Film und revolutionäre Arbeiterbewegung in Deutschland, 1918–1932: Dokumente und Materialien zur Entwicklung der Filmpolitik der revolutionären Arbeiterbewegung und zu den Anfängen einer sozialistischen Filmkunst in Deutschland.* Berlin: Henschelverlag Kunst und Gesellschaft, 1978.

McCormick, Richard W. *Gender and Sexuality in Weimar Modernity: Film, Literature, and "New Objectivity."* New York: Palgrave, 2001.

Meskimmon, Marsha, and Shearer West. *Visions of the "Neue Frau": Women and the Visual Arts in Weimar Germany.* Aldershot, UK: Scolar Press, 1995.

Murray, Bruce Arthur. *Film and the German Left in the Weimar Republic: From Caligari to Kuhle Wampe.* Austin: U of Texas P, 1990.

Nagl, Tobias. *Die unheimliche Maschine: Rasse und Repräsentation im Weimarer Kino.* Munich: edition text + kritik, 2009.

Petro, Patrice. *Joyless Streets: Women and Melodramatic Representation in Weimar Germany.* Princeton: Princeton UP, 1989.

Prawer, Siegbert Salomon. *Between Two Worlds: The Jewish Presence in German and Austrian Film, 1910–1933.* New York: Berghahn Books, 2005.

Rickels, Laurence. "The Demonization of the Home Front: War Neurosis and Weimar Cinema." In *Dancing on the Volcano: Essays on the Culture of the Weimar Republic*, edited by Thomas W. Kniesche and Stephen Brockmann, 181–93. Columbia, SC: Camden House, 1994.

Roberts, Ian. *German Expressionist Cinema: The World of Light and Shadow.* London: Wallflower, 2008.

Rogowski, Christian. "The 'Colonial Idea' in Weimar Cinema." In *German Colonialism, Visual Culture, and Modern Memory*, ed. Volker M. Langbehn, 220–38. New York: Routledge, 2010.

———, ed. *The Many Faces of Weimar Cinema: Rediscovering Germany's Filmic Legacy.* Rochester, NY: Camden House, 2010.

Saunders, Thomas J. "Film and Finance in Weimar Germany: The Rise and Fall of David Schratter's Trianon-Film, 1923–25." *Film History* 23, no. 1 (2011): 38–56.

———. *Hollywood in Berlin: American Cinema and Weimar Germany.* Berkeley: U of California P, 1994.

Scheunemann, Dietrich, ed. *Expressionist Film — New Perspectives.* Rochester, NY: Camden House, 2003.

Thompson, Kristin. *Herr Lubitsch Goes to Hollywood: German and American Film after World War I.* Amsterdam: Amsterdam UP, 2005.
Wager, Jans B. *Dangerous Dames: Women and Representation in the Weimar Street Film and Film Noir.* Athens: Ohio UP, 1999.
Ward, Janet. *Weimar Surfaces: Urban Visual Culture in 1920s Germany.* Berkeley: U of California P, 2001.
Weinstein, Valerie. "Dissolving Boundaries: Assimilation and Allosemitism in E. A. Dupont's *Das alte Gesetz* (1923) and Veit Harlan's *Jud Süss* (1940)." *The German Quarterly* 38, no. 4 (Fall 2005): 496–516.
Whitney, Allison. "Etched with the Emulsion: Weimar Dance and Body Culture in German Expressionist Cinema." *Seminar: A Journal of Germanic Studies* 46, no. 3 (2010): 240–54.

6 March 1920: Chinese Students Raise Charges of Racism against *Die Herrin der Welt*

Tobias Nagl

The threat of white slavery in Die Herrin der Welt *(1920).*
Credit: Deutsche Kinemathek.

WITH A TOTAL LENGTH of sixteen kilometers, a budget of 5.9 million marks, twelve hours of screen time, two codirectors (Uwe Jens Krafft and Karl Gerhardt), thirty thousand extras, and a plot that was set in meticulously recreated locales ranging from Denmark to China, Africa to the United States, Joe May's eight-part adventure serial *Die Herrin der Welt* (Mistress of the world, 1919) certainly fulfilled all the requirements for a screen spectacle. When *Die Herrin der Welt* premiered in weekly installments during the winter season 1919/20 in Berlin, it was the most expensive and lavish German production to date. Produced by May-Film and heavily subsidized by distributor Ufa (Universum Film A.G.), it was not the production values alone, however, that helped *Die Herrin der Welt* set new standards for the creation of what Karen Pehla calls a "Kinoerlebnis" (cinema experience): already the shooting of the series on a huge studio lot in Woltersdorf outside of Berlin had been part of a gigantic multimedia publicity and commercial tie-in campaign that kept the public mesmerized for several months before the film's premiere. Journalists were invited to Woltersdorf to attest to the authenticity of the exotic sets and extras; newspaper ads and posters plastered the city months ahead of its bombastically staged premiere in the Tauentzien-Palast, and a commissioned novel of the same name by the popular journalist and adventure romance specialist Karl Figdor, who had also written the extensive program notes and collaborated on the script, appeared in serialized form in several newspapers (reaching a record circulation of 40,000 only four months after the premiere).

Inspired by Henri Pouctal's French serial *Le Comte de Monte Christo* (*The Count of Monte Christo*, 1918) and conceived by Joe May as a customized star vehicle for his wife Mia, an actress and operetta singer already popular in Wilhelmine Germany, *Die Herrin der Welt* focused on the exploits of heroine Maud Gregaards over a span of fifteen years. As a result of her father's involvement in an espionage plot, Maud gives birth to an illegitimate child in prison and after her release accepts a position as a private tutor in Canton, where she is abducted by Chinese white slave traders and taken to a brothel. Rescued by her two platonic admirers, the Westernized Chinese Dr. Kien-Lung (Henry Sze) and Consul Madsen (Michael Bohnen), she heads an expedition that takes her first to an ancient synagogue in China and then to East Africa, where Maud hopes to find the treasure of Queen Sheba, but instead is adorned by the "natives" in the mythical city of "Ophir" as a reincarnation of the White Goddess Astarte. In the second half of the series, her new lover, the engineer Stanley, constructs a pacifist sci-fi ray gun to "smelt all weapons," while May gets involved in a "newspaper war" between two publishing houses in the United States, founds a philanthropic "Academy of Mankind," and is finally reunited with her now-teenaged son.

Attempting to entertain economically depressed audiences with images of unseen material splendor and far-away, non-European places, *Die Herrin der Welt* provided the blueprint for an entire cycle of often multipart Orientalist action-adventure films that peaked in popularity between 1920 and 1922, and included films such as *Die Jagd nach dem Tode* (The hunt after death, 1920), *Das indische Grabmal* (*Mysteries of India*, 1921), *Der Mann ohne Namen* (The man without a name, 1921), and *Lebende Buddhas* (*Living Buddhas*, 1925). Regarding the promise of such films, the trade journal *Der Kinematograph* jokingly quipped: "If you want to see the world today, you have to be an actor."[1] The experience of a cinematic "time-space compression"[2] that these films offered to their audience was extratextually prepared and stabilized by a pseudo-scientific discourse on ethnographic authenticity, linking the "film city" in Woltersdorf with its "exotic" extras (many of them former German colonial subjects), the Chinese and African decoration of Berlin's first-run theaters, and the global narrative space of the film's plot to a larger cultural archive of Orientalism and colonial fantasy that had provided a framework for the ever popular *Völkerschauen* (ethnographic exhibitions) during Germany's imperialist heyday. "When it comes to non-European building," set-designer Martin Jacoby-Boy revealed in the trade-journal *Film-Kurier*, "one should not take into consideration what is real, but how a spectator imagines, for example, Canton and what he rightfully expects to see.... If a Chinese saw the sets in *Die Herrin der Welt*, he would be amazed and would have a sensation of absolute originality, he would find everything remarkably beautiful."[3] It is precisely this authority to seemingly effortlessly unveil and recreate the inner "truth" of the East that, according to Edward Said, contributes to the "flexible positional superiority" of Western knowledge formations.

But despite its innovations in marketing and set-design and its impact on the modernization of the German film industry, *Die Herrin der Welt* was at the same time characterized by residual moments of both form and content that pointed back to the cinema of the Wilhelmine era. Whereas its plot combined the rather worn-out sensationalist and melodramatic formula of the "white slavery" genre of the prewar period (popularized in the 1910s by Danish productions) with tropes and devices derived from imperial romances, penny dreadfuls, and science fiction novels, its monumental form — the *Film in Fortsetzungen* (serial installments) — represented a belated local appropriation, perhaps even a solid misunderstanding of the American silent film serial, of which German critics after the First World War seemed ignorant, just as they were of earlier German experiments with the format by Joe May and others (*Miss Nobody*, 1913; *Stuart Webbs*, 1914–15; *Homunculus*, 1916–17). In fact, the editing patterns of the German epics and "serials" that hit the American market during the German film export "invasion" after 1921 were so slow and their cinematography still so indebted to the tableau-like, frontal staging of theater and early cinema, that it became standard practice among American distributors to establish separate units specialized in editing down German fare. Nevertheless, it was precisely the monumental set-design and the serial form that German critics perceived as Joe May's key innovations and as expressions of a much needed "Americanism." At the same time, May's gigantomania was hailed in nationalistic and revisionist terms as an attempt to rebuild the German film industry after the war; if Germany's army had lost the war on the battlefield, many critics fantasized that the film industry could win back the former German *Weltgeltung* (world relevance) and bloodlessly "conquer" former enemy nations with their film exports. In his seminal *From Caligari to Hitler*, Siegfried Kracauer, departing briefly from his reading of Weimar cinema as a dark harbinger of Nazism, reads the popular "sex" and adventure films of the early 1920s as a condensed and displaced response to the historical trauma of the First World War. "The whole group of films, with its craving for exotic sceneries, resembled a prisoner's daydream," Kracauer writes on these "space-devouring films," arguing that they functioned as cinematic "substitutes" for a "suppressed desire for expansion" and the "involuntary seclusion" of Germany after the war. Films like *Die Herrin der Welt* facilitated an *Ersatz*-colonialism that allowed for the "average German" to virtually "reannex the world, including Ophir."[4]

Kracauer's symptomatic observations not only resonate with more recent studies of Germany's "imperialist imagination," they are also productive when brought into a dialogue with an archive-based film historiography. Until recently, a curious fact about the public reception of *Die Herrin der Welt* remained almost completely unknown: using public and political channels, the small but well-connected Chinese community in Berlin campaigned vehemently against the film, claiming that its two Chinese episodes promoted "racial hate" and stressed "racial difference" in a distorting manner. While the eight-part premiere of *Die Herrin der Welt* was still enjoying great success during the 1919/20 holiday season in Berlin's first-run theaters, Chinese journalists and diplomats had already filed a complaint with the Commissioner for Export Questions at the Foreign Ministry, who immediately put a preliminary ban on the export of two parts of the series.

These protests were initiated by the Chinese Student Club, an organization that was first established in the late 1880s and existed until 1941. Unlike Chinese sailors and peddlers or African colonial migrants, who were often seen as a social problem by the German authorities, Chinese students with their private or state stipends were considered welcome agents of modernization who would take home a positive image of Germany. In light of both the relative weakness of German foreign policy one year after the First World War and the belated recognition of cinema by the national elites in Germany, it seems hardly surprising that the Chinese intervention received support from self-declared East Asia specialists, academics, foreign policy makers, cinema reformers, and even colonial veterans who had served in the former protectorate Tsingtao. The success of the Chinese student protest was also aided by the fact that the abolition of film censorship during the November Revolution of 1918 and the perceived subsequent flood of "sex" and "morality" films had created a situation in which the supposed limits of the new-found representational freedom were hotly debated: cries for a centralized censorship system arose across the entire political spectrum.

The German public was first introduced to the protests in early February 1920 by an article written by Max Linde, a Lübeck doctor, patron of the arts and secretary general of the Association for the Far East, in which he detailed the allegations brought forward by the Chinese students against the racial stereotyping of the film. The extensive plot analysis focused on two main aspects: the nexus of violence and sexuality that the "white slavery" episode *Die Freundin des gelben Mannes* (*The Dragon's Claw*) established, and the presumption of an inherited, traditionally Chinese xenophobia in *Der Rabbi von Kuan-Fu* (*The City of Gold*). In particular the Chinese objected to the torturing of Mia May in an underground water hole, the complicity of a high-ranking Chinese police official with the white slave ring, and the fact that the only positive Chinese character, the Westernized Dr. Kien-Lung, turns out to be a rascal in the end. Linde feared that *Die Herrin der Welt* could harm political and economic relations between Germany and China and thwart national reconstruction: "Germany is depleted of friends in the world. One of the few peoples that bears sympathy for us is the Chinese."[5]

In the following weeks the battle over *Die Herrin der Welt* raged. Ufa, the distributor and financer of the film, publicly rejected and ridiculed the criticism, filing an objection against the export ban. Nonetheless, the Foreign Ministry forced Ufa to organize two special screenings of the incriminating episodes that were attended by several professors, diplomats, politicians, scholars, and Chinese representatives. In response to these screenings, several "scientific" reports were submitted to the Foreign Ministry, all of them supporting the initial critique. These reports also explored ways to alter the film's thrust through the insertion of new intertitles. On 6 March, the Chinese Student Association finally decided to demand the total prohibition of the film in Germany, since they felt that the film's representational politics were based on completely erroneous objectives and could not be changed.[6] In a written statement that might be considered the first antiracist film critique written by people of color in Germany, they repeated and expanded on several of the issues put forward by Max Linde (e.g., the depiction of China as a land of poverty and beggars or the exploitation of interracial sexuality), while, on the other hand, generously forgiving the Orientalist set-designs and costumes as a mere result of "technical impossibilities" and a "lack of knowledge." Interestingly, in their rhetoric the Chinese Student Association strategically aligned themselves with the reformist arguments that resurfaced during the "censorship-free period" of the immediate postwar period. Locating the true essence of cinema in its educational function, they argued that cinema was one of the "most significant achievements of the last decades." However, phenomena such as "inflammatory propaganda" and "so called sexual education films" proved that the cinematograph could easily be exploited and "needed censorship."[7]

After all sides had been heard, the Foreign Ministry ruled that the Ufa company would have to change the film significantly to make it suitable for the international market — an essential venue if the film were to create the revenues the German film industry so badly needed. This, however, was easier said than done and in its attempt to meet the criticism, the studio submitted multiple, frequently ridiculous drafts. One version, for example, simply transposed the action to a fictive Asian island named "Ku-ra-ra." A compromise was finally reached after months of negotiations, when Joe May declared that he was willing to change not only many of the obvious offensive racial markers on the title cards (the "yellow inhabitants" of Canton became "old inhabitants"), but also to alter the plot by shooting new scenes that would challenge notions of Chinese cultural inferiority. These newly shot scenes followed a "positive" images approach: they showed a wise old Chinese father eagerly awaiting the arrival of the Western teacher or a Westernized main Chinese character (Kien-Lung) wearing traditional clothes (for a change) and praying in a temple.

All these changes are contained in the surviving archival prints of *Die Herrin der Welt*. They form an integral part of a cinematic text whose authorship until now has been attributed solely to Joe May. Even more significant are the institutional traces the Chinese intervention left in the history of German cinema. The integration of a passage on the "breach of Germany's foreign relations" into the film censorship law of May 1920 is, at least in part, a response to the very conflicts outlined above. Furthermore, the Chinese protests against *Die Herrin der Welt* established an important precedent and matrix for the discursive and institutional normalization and regulation of racial representations in German cinema during the interwar years. Despite German attempts to counterbalance racial stereotyping and national interests, Chinese voices from Berlin and abroad continued to campaign against German celluloid racism until the outbreak of the Second World War. The Chinese intervention thus marks an important point of departure for a postcolonial and transnational perspective on German cinema, as it attests to the existence of an "oppositional" gaze *within* German film history long before contemporary debates on cinema and migration.

See also:

- 16 December 1927: Debut of *Familientag im Hause Prellstein* Provokes Debate about Jewish Identity in Popular Cinema
- 31 January 1929: Limits on Racial Border-Crossing Exposed in *Piccadilly*
- 10 February 1999: Berlinale Premier of Four Turkish-German Films Signals New Chapter in Cinematic Diversity

Notes

[1] Ludwig Brauner, "Seine Exzellenz von Madagaskar," *Der Kinematograph* (15 January 1922).

[2] The notion of "time-space compression" according to David Harvey refers to historical processes that overcome spatial and temporal distances (including communication technologies, travel, and economics) and require a new mapping of the world system. These processes are inherent to modernity and should not only be understood as ideological or cultural, but also as an integral part of capitalist accumulation cycles and imperialism's drive towards the creation of a world market. See David Harvey, *The Condition of Postmodernity: An Inquiry into the Origins of Social Change* (Oxford: Blackwell, 1990), 260–83.

[3] Martin Jacoby-Boy, "Der künstlerische Beirat," *Film-Kurier* (2 September 1919).

[4] Siegfried Kracauer, *From Caligari to Hitler: A Psychological History of German Film* (Princeton: Princeton UP, 1966), 56–57.

[5] Dr. Max Linde, "Film und auswärtige Politik," *Der Sonntag* (1 February 1920). Also published under the same title in *Ostasiatische Rundschau*, 1, no. 2 (15 February 1920).

[6] Chinese Student Association to Foreign Ministry, 8 March 1920, and appendix "Entschließung" of General Assembly, BAB (Bundesarchiv-Berlin) R 901/72197, 36 f.

[7] "Wie die Chinesen über Karl von Figdor's Film *Die Herrin der Welt* denken," BAB (Bundesarchiv-Berlin) R 901/72197, Bl. 51–52.

23 May 1920: *Das Cabinet des Dr. Caligari* Brings Aesthetic Modernism to the Fairground

Paul Dobryden

The visual melding of old-fashioned amusement and modernism in the fairground set of Das Cabinet des Dr. Caligari *(1920). DVD capture.*

CLOSED DURING THE GREAT WAR, Berlin's Luna-Park, located at the west end of the Kurfürstendamm, reopened for business on 23 May 1920. On that holiday weekend, the city's largest, most modern amusement park offered a concert, fireworks, and a number of new attractions. In addition to roller coasters, a "Foxtrot Machine," and a Wild West show, visitors were treated to latest popular style: expressionism. A number of artists, including Novembergruppe member Rudolf Belling, had been hired to decorate parts of the park in the bold, angular aesthetic that had come to be associated with the expressionist movement in painting and theater. The Luna-Park was not alone in embracing expressionism for commercial purposes; indeed, after the war it had become a fad. For some intellectuals this marked its death as an avant-garde movement. In 1921, the poet Yvan Goll wrote that "expressionism, that cardboard Lunapark . . . is being dismantled. The carousel operator is counting his cash."[1]

Robert Wiene's *The Cabinet of Dr. Caligari* is the most famous example of Germany's brief infatuation with expressionism. The film premiered on 26 February 1920 in Berlin's Marmorhaus, also on the Kurfürstendamm, and was still playing throughout the country when the Luna-Park reopened. The distorted, uncanny sets designed by Hermann Warm, Walter Reimann, and Walter Röhrig caused a sensation, and helped inaugurate what came to be known as German expressionist cinema. The film announced the presence of German cinema to international audiences, and has been a touchstone of cinema history and criticism ever since. The following sketch is resolutely local, meant to situate the film within the landscape of popular amusements on offer in Berlin around 1920. It seeks to place Wiene's film within the context of a broader aesthetic and cultural transition underway at this very juncture, from a tradition of fairground amusement to a new culture of modern, surface entertainment — exploring the film's invocation of both older and newer sites of urban leisure.

Like the famous Luna Park in Coney Island, on which it was partly modeled, Berlin's Luna-Park was a temple to modernity. As the new face of amusement in Germany, its attractions celebrated the triumphs of technology in light shows and high-speed roller coasters. The modernity of such parks did not go uncontested, as they began to replace traditional sites of amusement like the *Jahrmarkt* (annual fair). "More and more, the colorful magic of the old fairgrounds is disappearing," wrote Carl Zuckmayer in 1923, "their odd attractions and oriental Bazaar-like quality making way for a pure extract of intoxicating velocity, an American worship of speed."[2] In the face of what Siegfried Kracauer would later call the "organized happiness" of the Luna-Park, many felt nostalgic for the messier, more illicit pleasures of carnival and fairground.

Caligari returns to the old world of the fairground as described by Zuckmayer. The yearly fair at Holstenwall where Caligari (Werner Krauss) presents his exhibit — the somnambulist clairvoyant Cesare (Conrad Veidt) — is the antithesis of the clean, orderly amusement of the Luna-Park. In the first shot of the fairground in action, an organ grinder with a monkey stands frame right, in the foreground; behind him, the tops of two carousels spin wildly at odd angles, while curious spectators in vaguely nineteenth-century dress wander in and out. In the next shot, a packed crowd walks among a row of tents that trails into the background. The film's fairground is dark, chaotic, and, compared to 1920s Berlin, thoroughly unmodern. We then see Dr. Caligari as a sideshow barker, advertising his exhibition by standing in front of his tent and unfurling a poster with a drawing of Cesare. As Kurt Tucholsky noted in a 1920 review of Berlin amusement parks, this was a dying practice: "In the large amusement parks, the barker is being replaced by façades."[3] The modern designs of park attractions advertised themselves, rendering the barker obsolete.

Dr. Caligari's somnambulist exhibit is a traveling freak show, a fairground and circus amusement that reached the height of its popularity in the late nineteenth century. Traveling exhibitors and humbug illusionists would often call themselves doctors or professors, lending their shows a playful air of scientific legitimacy that visitors easily saw through. As we follow Francis, the film's protagonist, and his friend Alan into Caligari's tent, the camera lingers on the Doctor's showmanship: he stands on stage, gesturing dramatically with his cane before opening a large box that contains the motionless Cesare. Such theatrical presentation was an essential freak show practice, providing suspense and story to the exhibit. Cesare's tricot — a tight one-piece jersey favored by acrobats and contortionists — further emphasizes the exhibit's roots in nineteenth-century carnival entertainment. Before the days of standing movie theaters, film was also a traveling amusement exhibited at fairgrounds, and the scene further resembles an early movie show. These references to late nineteenth-century entertainments display the film's allegiance to the anarchic spirit of the fairground. At a crucial moment, however, film technology takes over for the sideshow barker: a close-up displays Cesare's face as he slowly opens his eyes. Caligari has been blended out; the camera alone lends an unsettling intensity to the tiny movements of Veidt's eyelids.

Caligari's narrative can be understood as an elaborate play on what Neil Harris, writing about P. T. Barnum's traveling circus, has called the "operational aesthetic." Harris argues that an important aspect of spectatorial pleasure at the circus lay not in believing the illusions on display, but in seeing through the trick and figuring out how it worked. This also characterized early film audiences, who were as curious about the technology of cinema as they were about the images on the screen. In Wiene's film, Cesare is not just a somnambulist, but also, Caligari claims, a clairvoyant; during the show, Cesare prophesies that Alan will die before dawn, and he is murdered that night. Francis is skeptical of Cesare's clairvoyance, and believes that Caligari is behind the murder of his friend. In the detective story that follows, Francis takes it upon himself to unmask the humbug — he tracks Caligari back to an insane asylum, where he discovers that Caligari is the director. Caligari's diary reveals the doctor as a madman. Indeed, the prophecies were a trick; Caligari has been using his control over Cesare to commit murders. In the film's sensational epilogue, however, we find out that Francis — who has been narrating the story all along — is himself an inmate of the insane asylum. The bulk of the film's narration is unmasked as the fantasy of a madman. Like the viewer at a fairground illusion, *Caligari*'s spectator takes pleasure in having been tricked for so long, and is invited to reflect upon the workings of its curious narrative.

The story of a doctor who compels his patient to commit murder reflected a deep skepticism after the First World War regarding psychiatrists, who had used their medical authority to declare traumatized soldiers fit to kill on the battlefield. Exhibiting medical anomalies in public settings, however, was a common practice at the turn of the century. Rudolf Virchow's Pathological Museum opened in Berlin in 1899, where on Sundays the public could view any number of human deformities preserved in plaster, jars, and cases; alternatively, some of Virchow's exhibits could also be seen at the popular Passage-Panoptikum. Similarly, Berlin's Ethnological Museum, founded in 1873, drew crowds curious to see exotic artifacts, while anthropologists frequented the Passage-Panoptikum's *Völkerschauen*, live exhibits of colonial peoples. By 1920, however, science and popular amusement had grown further apart, as doctors and scientists sought to dissociate themselves from the gawking and quackery of the fairground.

In postwar Berlin, fairground entertainments were on the decline in the face of more modern amusements like the cinema and the Luna-Park. If the fairground attractions so popular in the nineteenth century still had a home, it was in the city's arcades, located on Friedrichstraße. Beginning in 1901, the Passage-Theater in the Kaisergalerie arcade featured circus-style magic and acrobatic acts. The Passage-Panoptikum, which opened in the Kaisergalerie in 1889, contained dozens of rooms, each with a different kind of visual entertainment, including recreations of exotic architecture, wax figures, and a freak show (the "Hall of Abnormalities"). After the war, however, such exhibits were more rare, the arcades less popular. In 1922, Egon Erwin Kisch described the Passage-Panoptikum's portrait gallery, an archive of the freaks who had passed through. For Kisch, the photographs, "fading from year to year," memorialized a bygone era of amusements.[4]

In many ways, the world of *Caligari* is that of Berlin's arcades. Not, however, as a place of modern consumerism, but as Siegfried Kracauer imagined them in his childhood — a "site of murderous assaults," as he would write in 1930. "What united the objects in the Linden Arcade," Kracauer claims, "was their withdrawal from the bourgeois façade."[5] The arcades were a "protest" against these façades — a dark, secret space, away from the street, that promised danger and a release from bourgeois respectability. Wiene's 1920 film mimics this logic of the arcade, each scene offering a new cabinet, a new thrill, a new look behind the bourgeois façade: Caligari's tent, the prison cell of the falsely accused murderer, Caligari's office at the insane asylum. In one scene, Francis's love interest Jane (Lil Dagover) is alone at the fairground; Caligari invites her into his tent, where he excitedly opens his cabinet, revealing Cesare to the terrified girl. This moment of erotic display is reminiscent of the "Secret Cabinet" of the Passage-Panoptikum's "Anatomical Museum," where curious spectators could view representations of sex organs and venereal diseases. The arcades remained for some a more accurate representation of the postwar world — see George Grosz's grotesque 1918 depiction of Friedrichstraße — than the bright consumerist modernity of the Kurfürstendamm and the Luna-Park.

The canted angles and painted shadows of *Caligari*'s mise-en-scène are usually appreciated for the way they visually convey the uncanny world of the narrative, expressing trauma and madness in the very spaces of the film. At the same time, however, the modernist sets take part in the burgeoning façade culture of the Kurfürstendamm. As much as *Caligari* indulges in nostalgia for the illicit amusements of the fairground, its use of expressionism marks the film as hypermodern. Its expressionist façades appealed to a desire for the absolutely contemporary, as well as a pleasure in surfaces. Although reviewers complained of the visual disjuncture between the film's real human actors and its patently unreal sets, this would have been a common experience at the Luna-Park, where visitors walked among a variety of artificial, painted worlds. Tucholsky remarked that just looking at the Luna-Park's "cubist-expressionist" roller coaster could make one seasick — in other words, its visual aesthetic alone effected bodily disorientation, the primary pleasure of the roller coaster. *Caligari* is cinema as modern amusement park — as roller coaster. Its artificial sets aim for a kinesthetic spectatorship that transcends the visual logic of the curiosity cabinet. Rather than offer the strange and wonderful as ostensibly real, the film's expressionist mise-en-scène discards realism; instead it addresses the spectator's whole body, producing a sense of instability and imbalance.

The Cabinet of Dr. Caligari registers the modernization of popular amusement in the twentieth century. Nostalgically invoking the unseemly world of the arcades, it simultaneously draws inspiration from the surface culture of the Kurfürstendamm and the Luna-Park. The film's ambivalence is captured in its advertising campaign, which in the weeks preceding the premiere had Berliners repeating its enigmatic slogan: "You must become Caligari." While the figure of Caligari stood for the dying world of fairground amusements, the film's expressionism carried the unspoken imperative of virtually all advertising: "You must become modern."

See also:

- 22 September 1907: Sigmund Freud Is Attracted to the Movies but Feels Lonely in the Crowd

- 1 April 1921: Walter Ruttmann's *Lichtspiel: Opus 1* Shapes Culture of Abstract Filmmaking
- 21 June and 30 August 1957: *Jonas* and *Berlin — Ecke Schönhauser* Link Urban Reconstruction to National Cinema in Both West and East

Notes

[1] Ywan Goll, "Das Wort an sich," *Die neue Rundschau* 2 (1921): 1082.

[2] Carl Zuckmayer, "Von Zirkus, Karussell und Jahrmarkt, von Schiffschauklern, Gauklern und Vagabunden," *Die Weltbühne* 19. 13 (1923): 363.

[3] Kurt Tucholsky, "Berliner Rummelplätze," in *Gesamtausgabe: Texte und Briefe*, 22 vols., ed. Antje Bonitz, Dirk Grathoff, Michael Hepp, and Gerhard Kraiker (Reinbek bei Hamburg: Rowohlt, 1996), 4:577–80; here 579.

[4] Egon Erwin Kisch, "Das Geheimkabinett des Anatomischen Museums," *Das Tage-Buch* 3, no. 50 (1922): 1732.

[5] Siegfried Kracauer, "Farewell to the Linden Arcade," in *The Mass Ornament: Weimar Essays*, trans. and ed. Thomas Y. Levin (Cambridge, MA: Harvard UP, 1995), 337–42; here 337, 341.

15 October 1920: Ernst Lubitsch Fuels Debate over Tears in the Cinema

Michael Wedel

Magda (Asta Nielsen) mourns over her fallen lover in Afgrunden *(1910). DVD capture.*

On 15 October 1920, director Ernst Lubitsch addressed an open letter to actress Asta Nielsen. Lubitsch was responding to an interview given by the actress the week before, published only a few days earlier, in which Nielsen had criticized a certain *Hervordrängung des Technischen* (foregrounding of the technical) that would increasingly limit the *Ausbreitung des Künstlerischen* (broadening of the artistic), and thus considerably reduce the artistic quality of the German cinema.[1] Their public dispute would polarize into two axiomatic positions, bringing into the open a fundamental underlying tension between acting and directing, and highlighting larger shifts in cinematic performance styles.

In the interview, Nielsen spoke of her painful experience with this tendency in the course of Lubitsch's adaptation of Strindberg's stage play *Rausch* (*Intoxication*, 1919). Arguing that in Strindberg's play, the "meaning and emotional content [*der seelische Gehalt*] . . . are not to be found outside the narrative" but would reside directly in "the events and sensations" themselves, Nielsen contended that a successful interpretation was only possible if the external dramatic action and the internal emotional content of the drama could be brought together through the performative act of the actress, and these then transmitted to the audience via the immediate experience of sensual perception. But, as Nielsen pointed out, current audience taste demanded nothing more than "pure narrative action, sensation after sensation": "The artist isn't given any time anymore to fully develop her acting skills [in front of the camera]. Or, if the time is granted to her during shooting, the scissors of the director are taking it away again after the fact: as superfluous."[2] In a very concrete sense, Nielsen here alludes to a scene in *Rausch* in which she brought to the fore one of her most succinct expressive gestures as an actress: a close-up shot in which she weeps in order to communicate to her audience an inner emotion authenticated by the physical act of shedding "real" tears.

Lubitsch immediately understood what Nielsen was getting at, not least because it very likely had been Lubitsch himself who (in a characteristic play on words) had called Nielsen's extended crying "überflüssig" (meaning "excessive," but also a pun on "overly fluid"). Responding to Nielsen's only half-disguised protest, his open letter sought to save the situation, in a move only too typical for the director, by turning his abridgement of the scene into a coded compliment: "You still cannot forgive me that I let you cry in close-up for only two meters instead of five. But believe me, your tears were running from your eyes over your cheeks onto your blouse so realistically that the audience was completely captivated and moved by it already after two meters of film."[3] Lubitsch could invoke a critical reaction that had celebrated his film as a "masterpiece" and had been full of praise for his innovative use of close-up framing and fast editing, of the very sort that probably surrounded the contested close-up.

In the ensuing public debate, one position, represented by an anonymous actor supposedly familiar with Nielsen and eager to disclose some inside knowledge, claimed that the tears she shed on the *Rausch* set were nothing other than the artificial products of a standard acting routine, equal in status to all the other techniques at the medium's disposal, like editing, framing, and mise-en-scène. He asserted that Nielsen's tears weren't real at all, but drops of glycerin applied before the filming — and thus far more effective than the genuine article because of the visible trace the chemical substance left on her make-up, shimmering under bright studio floodlights.

This position, neatly subsuming Nielsen's tears under cinema's efficient "power of the false," was countered by a diametrically opposed second opinion, voiced by the celebrated stage and screen actor Paul Wegener. Wegener underlined the genuinely artistic nature of Nielsen's performance, arguing it would always infuse an otherwise technical process of representation with subjectivity and originality of expression. In late 1920, Wegener had been Nielsen's costar in *Steuermann Holk* (Helmsman Holk), and invoking this recent experience, Wegener countered the contention about the synthetic nature of Nielsen's tears by declaring that the tears he kissed from Asta's cheeks had not had the "greasy and sweet" taste of glycerin, but rather were "watery and salty."[4]

It is easy to see how the debate around "false" and "real" tears echoes Nielsen's principal distinction between acting as the art of individual performative expressivity and acting as merely one among many external techniques of cinematic simulation. What emerges from this debate is the fact that exactly this relationship between the actress and her audience had entered into a state of crisis. With changes in filmic standards around 1920, now dominated by fast, analytical, and narrative-driven editing, the very conditions of Nielsen's relationship with the audience underwent a thorough transformation. In the early 1910s, when Nielsen rose to stardom as Germany's first genuine film actress, her broad popularity and artistic reputation were built on the special physical quality of her acting style and the unique affective potential it carried. The public debate around the authenticity of her tears in 1920/21 indicates a more general and far-reaching stylistic climate change in German film history, in the context of which this particular signature — at odds with a new order of cinematic discourse — grew increasingly problematic. Hence, what is so illuminating here is not so much the focus on the real or fabricated quality of the actress's tears, but instead the question it raises as to how, if at all, the particular sensation of immediate emotional intimacy that Nielsen's tears were able to evoke in audiences could be integrated into the emergent discourse of the art film of the Weimar period.

In a different context, philosopher Slavoj Žižek once described the "fright of real tears" in the cinema as the anxiety of entering into a realm of phantasmatic intimacy that one should access only via a "move into fiction" in order to avoid the "pornographic trespass into intimacy."[5] This transition into an intermediate space of de-sublimated perceptual empathy, characterized by Žižek as a fundamental violation of the symbolic order, has been qualified by Heide Schlüpmann as a central feature of the perceptual culture of early cinema where "the movie theatre still constituted a sphere where the individual spectator could let go of his or her habitual defense shields and forget their bourgeois personalities, where the bodies could extend and reach out without being hurt."[6]

This phenomenon of phantasmatic intimacy between star and audience has left numerous traces in the early reception of Nielsen's films. In her study of early cinema audiences, Emilie Altenloh noted that, above all, the films of Asta Nielsen were not only most popular with the audience but also enabled spectators to feel a greater degree of empathy and compassion with what is shown on screen: "Indeed emotional identification really is the crucial factor here, for film representations have a very direct effect, sweeping spectators along with the action and enabling them to experience the hero's predicaments."[7] With the emergence of an institutionalized, professional film criticism in the early 1920s, the very forms of admiration changed, and with them the stylistic parameters to which they were related. Two critical models illustrate this shift in perception. The first is well known: it derives from the early writings of Béla Balázs and continues to be influential in shaping our view of Nielsen. The second critical model, contemporaneous with that of Balázs, was put forward with no less consistency and poetic elegance by the film critic and screenwriter Willy Haas.

For Balázs, the cinema is the agent of a purely sensual, nonalienated language without words, an "image-language" of movements and gestures with a direct expressive impact on the perception of the audience. At the center of what he calls the illusion of lifelike emotional expressivity is the "tacit understanding" that the audience would show toward the presence of a human face in close-up. Nielsen's extremely reduced mimic vocabulary came to stand as the very epitome of this encounter: "The extraordinary artistic standard of Asta Nielsen's eroticism stems from its absolute intellectual quality. It is the eyes, not the flesh, that are of most importance. As a matter of fact, she has no flesh at all. The dressed Asta Nielsen can show obscene nakedness *in her eyes*, and she can smile in a way that is liable to make police feel the film ought to be seized on account of pornography."[8]

Willy Haas, too, called Nielsen's face the "creative center" of her expressive powers, but without insisting on the primacy of the close-up as their ultimate condition of possibility. Rather, Haas saw the specific quality of Nielsen's acting style as directly opposed to — or, at least, in a fundamental tension with — the new formal standards of scene dissection, such as the emotionally intensifying close-up and fast, narrative-driven analytical editing. His reading thus retains a sense of a directly felt, immediate physicality, as had been so characteristic of her early films and as was now, in her films of the 1920s, being redefined to suit a completely different stylistic system and cinematic mode of audience address. Within this new framework, Nielsen's unique talent for transmitting a direct physical effect and emotional impact to her audience was reduced to what Haas called single isolated "moments of genius" in which one could witness the "emotional explosion of the individual."[9]

Haas finds one such rare moment in *Dirnentragödie* (*Tragedy of a Whore*, 1927), preserved like a time capsule between two cuts. Haas takes director Bruno Kastner to task for his editing that — partly for reasons of dramatic pace, partly in order to achieve simple erotic effects — shows no respect for the unique qualities of Asta Nielsen's acting. For the briefest moment, Haas has the pleasure of sensing the distinctive emotional pull of Nielsen's acting, before it is destroyed by the intrusion of an untimely cut. In the shot in question, Nielsen, playing an aging prostitute, "lies crying in front of a locked door, behind which some stupid chap with whom she had fallen in love amuses himself with a much younger prostitute" — in Haas's words, "a well thought-out scene, indeed." And yet, as a result of unfortunate cuts, Haas contends, the whole scene ultimately fails to unleash its complete emotional effect on the audience; here, as throughout the whole film, "it is not the light touch of a finger-tip that commands the editing."[10]

What is so instructive about Haas's ambivalent perception of this climactic scene is that it highlights a trademark element of Nielsen's acting, which was the motion of breaking down onto the floor in an emotional mixture of love and desire, grief and despair. Nielsen concluded any number of her tragic or melodramatic films thusly. These are moments in which she seems to cry with the whole of her body, clearly distinct from those shots that reduce her expressive register to close-ups of her tears. Haas here lights upon a marked difference that characterizes her films of the 1920s, even in those that evidence formal moments reaching back to her films from the 1910s: the later films refrain from cutting into the shot and leave intact the stable performative space of the long, tableau shot.

This shift in Nielsen's style comes to the fore if one compares examples of her early and late films. In the penultimate shot of Nielsen's film debut *Afgrunden* (*The Abyss*, 1910), her character suddenly breaks down in tears over the body of the man that she just killed. Carefully calculated in all its seeming spontaneity and unprompted by any cut to a closer framing, what erupts in the sudden vertical trajectory of her entire body moving across the stable action space of the long tableau shot is a performative, physical energy yet untamed by cinematic discourse. It is a moment of shock, but also of recognition and insight: it is only in the very instant of the body collapsing that the depth of her feeling of love and sexual bondage becomes clear, and the extent to which the killing of her ex-lover constitutes less an act of liberating violence than the climax of their physical passion. The shot thus represents not so much the dramatic endpoint of a narrative conflict, but rather resonates as a performative echo that closes the circuit of an energy flowing between the two since their famous gaucho dance.

A comparable, yet far from equivalent "tragic explosion" comes in the closing shot of *Vanina* (1922). Nielsen, playing the title character, breaks down in front of a heavy wooden door behind which her lover has just gone to the gallows — a lover whom she believed she had saved but who now faces certain death. The motion of her despair — a drawn-out glide down the hard surface of the door, her arms slowly following the trajectory of her body — reiterates the lines of the historically stylized set. Perfectly in tune with the stylistic conventions of the *Kammerspielfilm* (chamber play film) — a genre that was all about the symbolic inscription of hidden emotional energies into the topographical space of the action — Nielsen's performative gesture is here safely contained by the very fact that it does nothing more than redraw the lines of an architectural space to which her movement symbolically assimilates itself. There is no cut to interrupt the execution of the gesture or close-up to highlight its emotional intensity, and what is revealed in this shot could be called the very "emotional content" of the drama, making visible in the performative act itself the source of her downfall. But in a marked contrast to the shot from her earlier film, in *Vanina* the emotional charge that results from the friction between space and movement only contributes to the creation of an image that, in its perfect composition, forestalls any performative explosion; an image that is only brought into its appropriate pictorial form, as it were, by this hopeless expenditure of energy.

Paul Wegener stars once more alongside Nielsen in *Vanina*, in the role of her despotic father, but his style of acting differs sharply from his partner's. Dependent on a pair of crutches and thus almost completely robbed of physical mobility, the execution of the Wegener character's political and patriarchal power assumes a spectral quality that turns the Turin castle into a haunted house and the Governor himself into its cyborg-like prosthetic extension. Wegener's inert interpretation stands as paradigmatic for an alternative acting style gaining dominance in 1920s Weimar art cinema — one that Willy Haas aptly called "Maskenschauspielerei" (mask acting).[11] In Haas's understanding, it constituted a mode of inhibited gestural expression that radically moved away from establishing an intimate emotional contact between actor and spectator, creating a distance necessary to endow film with a higher degree of formal coherence and thus elevate the medium into the ranks of art. If one considers the trajectory of Wegener's own film career from *Der Student von Prag* (*The Student of Prague*, 1913) via his interpretation of the Golem legend in *Der Golem* (*The Golem*, 1915) and *Der Golem, wie er in die Welt kam* (*The Golem: How He Came into the World*, 1920) to the string of historical films he made in 1922 — *Vanina, Lucrezia Borgia, Monna Vanna* — it becomes clear that he exemplified this second historical acting tradition of pictorial stylization into a "character mask," just as much as Nielsen's body language of unforeseen emotional eruption and extended melodramatic gesture seems to exemplify the first one. Wegener's style, carried over from the 1910s into the early 1920s, was bound to the artistic dominance of a "pictorial style" pervading the early fantasy films, expressionist films and *Kammerspielfilme* in the German cinema between 1913 and 1924.

Both modes of acting, however, were soon to be surpassed by a third historical configuration between camera and character, cinematic space and performative gesture, pioneered by Lubitsch already around 1920 but most clearly signaled by Emil Jannings's performances in F. W. Murnau's *Der letzte Mann* (*The Last Laugh*, 1924) and E. A. Dupont's *Varieté* (1925): the turn to cinematographic virtuosity and a more subdued acting mode of psychological "realism."

See also:

- 27 May 1911: Asta Nielsen Secures Unprecedented Artistic Control
- 27 May 1921: *Scherben* Seeks Cinematic Equivalent of Theatrical Intimacy
- 19 September 1958: Douglas Sirk's *A Time to Love and a Time to Die* Tests Limits of Postwar Feeling

Notes

[1] Dr Walter Steinthal, "Bei Asta Nielsen," *Lichtbild-Bühne*, 13, no. 41 (9 October 1920): 42.

[2] Quoted in Steinthal, "Bei Asta Nielsen."

[3] Asta Nielsen und Ernst Lubitsch. "Ein offener Brief an Asta Nielsen," *Lichtbild-Bühne*, 13, no. 43 (16 October 1920): 31–32; here 31.

[4] The first, anonymous accusation appeared in "Die Tränen der Asta Nielsen," *Lichtbild-Bühne* 13, no. 49 (4 December 1920): 49. Wegener's response was published as: "Paul Wegener und Asta Nielsen," *Lichtbild-Bühne* 14, no. 3 (15 January 1921): 48.

[5] Slavoj Žižek, *The Fright of Real Tears: Krzysztof Kieslowski between Theory and Post-Theory* (London: BFI, 2001), 75.

[6] Heide Schlüpmann, *Abendröthe der Subjektphilosophie: Eine Ästhetik des Kinos* (Frankfurt: Stroemfeld/Roter Stern, 1998), 61.

[7] Emilie Altenloh, "A Sociology of the Cinema: The Audience" (1914), *Screen* 42, no. 3 (Autumn 2001): 249–93; here 259.

[8] Béla Balázs, "Die Erotik der Asta Nielsen" (1923), in *Schriften zum Film*, vol. 1, *Der sichtbare Mensch/Kritiken und Aufsätze zum Film 1922–1926*, ed. Helmut H. Diederichs, Wolfgang Gersch, Magda Nagy. (Berlin: Henschel, 1982), 185–86. Emphasis in the original.

[9] Willy Haas, "Genialität in der Filmdarstellung" (1920), in Haas, *Der Kritiker als Mitproduzent: Texte zum Film 1920–1933*, ed. Wolfgang Jacobsen, Karl Prümm, Benno Wenz. (Berlin: Edition Hentrich, 1991), 45.

[10] Haas, "Dirnentragödie" (1927), in Haas, *Der Kritiker als Mitproduzent*, 204.

[11] Haas, "Gibt es eine Schauspielermaske im Film? Filmdramaturgische Notizen" (1924), in Haas, *Der Kritiker als Mitproduzent*, 46–47.

4 March 1921: With *Das Floss der Toten*, the Dead Come Back to Town

Philipp Stiasny

WHAT HAPPENS WHEN a man presumed dead returns home alive and unexpectedly knocks at the door? This very conundrum served as the basis for numerous returnee films that emerged in the years following the First World War. Taken together, the films — which featured literal returning soldiers as well as more allegorical travelers seeking home — formed a cycle that provided a key public forum for exploring a broad constellation of domestic issues confronting postwar German society: the trauma of marital separation and infidelity, the bonds of male friendship and their violation through betrayal, and, obliquely, the death of millions of men who did not survive the mechanized mass death that characterized trench warfare.

One day in Berlin in the summer of 1920 a dead man comes knocking: a soldier swallowed by the war, later held captive in Siberia and reported missing. After waiting six years without word, his wife has had him declared dead and has remarried. Now he is back and there is one husband too many. Legally, the returnee, whose death has been officially established, no longer even exists. A true story, it merited no more than a short paragraph in the tabloid *B.Z. am Mittag*, which reported the story on 29 July 1920. One week later the trade journal *Der Film* announced the production of a new movie whose fictional story closely resembled the real one related in the newspaper.

Das Floss der Toten (The raft of the dead), directed by Carl Boese, opened in theaters on 4 March 1921. It tells the story of two European engineers, Roland Ford (Otto Gebühr) and John Kelley (Carl Clewing), who are working abroad on a railway construction site in colonial Africa. Both are in love with Maria (Aud Egede Nissen), but she chooses Roland. On their journey back to Europe, the two friends are shipwrecked and lose contact with each other. While John succeeds in making his way home, Roland — rescued by fishermen on a remote island — suffers from shock-induced amnesia. He has become a man without a name. A year passes and Roland is declared dead. Maria, already the mother of Roland's child, succumbs to John's courting and marries him. Some time later, however, Roland regains his memory, returns to Europe and finds Maria together with his child and a second from her marriage to John. He retreats into solitude as the keeper of a lighthouse. Meanwhile John admits he had long known that Roland survived the shipwreck. Now Maria persuades him to ask for Roland's forgiveness. When John confronts his former friend with this confession, the latter attacks him in a rage and both men die.

Nowhere in *Das Floss der Toten* does one find a direct reference to the First World War (at least not in the one incomplete version with English subtitles that has survived in the Library of Congress). Yet the film touches a vital nerve in contemporary discourse about the War and its aftermath, principally through its evocation of the era's manifold experiences of loss: political (national defeat and loss of the African colonies); existential (death, memory, identity, manhood); and moral (loss of moral certainty). German audiences in 1921, who shared this frame of reference, certainly would have understood the code.

Concrete analogies between this film narrative and the war also abound. During the First World War, millions shared the experience of ruptured family relations with husbands, fathers, and sons fighting, wounded, or missing in action. Communication between the front and homeland broke down for many reasons, including physical and psychological injuries (among them, amnesia), the gruesome effects of modern weaponry that left thousands of human bodies unidentifiable, and captivity. Fourteen percent of all mobilized soldiers became prisoners of war, including approximately one million Germans. Some of these POWs were unable for years to send letters to their families. Even fifteen years after the war's end, the fate of 100,000 German soldiers remained unknown. Meanwhile the plight of German POWs in France and Russia — where many were held until 1920 — became the subject of heated debate. Doctors and psychiatrists examined the long-term effects of captivity and what was called "barbed wire disease" on their health, psyche, and sex drive. Lawyers established regulations on the status of missing persons as well as procedures for declaring a person's death in the absence of his body, and the formalities of remarriage.

In stories about returnees, ancient myth, literary fiction, and reality merge in a peculiar way. In contemporary accounts, the supposedly dead soldier returning home from war has occasioned comparisons with figures from older tales. There was a rich tradition on which postwar filmmakers might draw. The most famous example is certainly Homer's Odysseus/ Ulysses, who returned to Penelope after many years of wandering in the wake of the Trojan War. But there is also Balzac's Colonel Chabert. A severely wounded officer of the Napoleonic army who is thrown into a mass grave after a battle, Chabert manages to make his way back to the living. Returning home after many years with a horribly disfigured face, he finds his wife remarried and ultimately withdraws from the world. In a similar vein, Tennyson's ballad "Enoch Arden" recounts the story of a shipwrecked sailor who is reported dead and nevertheless returns home ten years later to learn that his wife, after waiting faithfully for a long time, has now married his best friend. Only after his death from a broken heart is the secret of Enoch Arden's identity revealed and his heroic self-denial acknowledged. In the period before and after the war, these three literary figures — Ulysses, Chabert, and Enoch Arden — inspired numerous writers. Around 1920 they became popular heroes on German cinema screens as well, where they also serve as models for *Das Floss der Toten* and other home-comer films.[1]

Most films of this genre were produced shortly after the war and avoid any direct reference to the immediate past or the present.[2] In the realm of fantasy production, however, these returnee films engaged in an oblique, allegorical working through the trauma of painful war experiences. While Freud's work proved crucial in the postwar period for the establishment of a medical and legal understanding of trauma and its workings, Freudian theory has also been particularly useful for exploring the figure of the living dead. Particularly his concept of the "return of the repressed" has served to open up to new readings these figures of the living dead, like the haunting vampire Nosferatu in *Nosferatu, eine Symphonie des Grauens* (1922).[3]

By the mid-1920s, with greater historical distance, allegory was gradually replaced by realism, and a number of films openly identify the mythical figure of the home-comer with the returning soldier from the First World War.[4] The most prominent of these later films is *Heimkehr* (Homecoming, 1928) — an adaptation of Leonhard Frank's story "Karl und Anna" (1926), directed by Joe May and produced by Erich Pommer for Ufa (Universum Film A.G.). Here Richard (Lars Hanson), a German prisoner of war in Russia longing for his beloved young wife Anna (Dita Parlo), attempts to escape captivity together with his friend, Karl (Gustav Fröhlich). While the former is caught by the Russians, the latter returns to Germany where he meets Anna and the two lonely people fall in love. The armistice, however, leads to an inevitable confrontation. Scared and angry, the returnee first considers killing his rival, but then defers to him as the former comrade who once tried to save his life.

Despite their many differences, *Das Floss der Toten* and *Heimkehr* share a common focus on men who begin as comrades and manage to survive together under extreme conditions — in the first case in Africa, which as an environment hostile to white men can be read as code for the First World War, and then in Russian captivity. In both films, the two central male figures become separated and undergo different developments. One remains an outsider because of amnesia or captivity, while the other transitions from a soldier into a civilian who seeks fulfillment in love for the wife of his friend. Comradeship and male friendship are displaced by rivalry over a woman.

The conflict does not ensue simply as a result of female infidelity, however. The female heroine in this love triangle does *not* appear unfaithful. On the contrary, she is a woman who waits for her missing husband for a long time, guards his letters, and cherishes his memory. Only the belief that he is dead makes the new relationship possible. *Das Floss der Toten* emblematically portrays the heroine as a mother of two children by different fathers between whom she ultimately has to choose, knowing that a morally correct answer to her dilemma does not exist.

Other, more conventional films than these tended to provide drastic solutions to the conflict arising from the return of the man once presumed dead. These films depicted the home-comer as a dangerous intruder who — in both appearance and temperament — behaves like a wild animal or even turns out to be a downright villain. *Das Floss der Toten* and *Heimkehr* avoid such polarized characterizations of their returnee figures. Instead, they suggest solutions that rest on forgiveness and reconciliation. The heroine in *Das Floss der Toten* stands by her second husband, his guilt notwithstanding — even if, in the end, her attempt at reconciliation fails, the melodrama develops into a tragedy, and she is left to mourn both men. *Heimkehr* goes still further and refrains altogether from this kind of melodramatic excess. In lieu of catharsis, it offers a nonviolent resolution that depends on breaking with the military ideals of the past.

Compared to German war films produced in the second half of the 1920s and early 1930s, which are primarily concerned with the reconstruction of famous battles and the experience of soldiers in combat on the front, with an emphasis on male bonding, the home-comer films turn their attention away from the enemy outside and toward the inner conflicts engendered by war both within and among men.[5] Confronting contemporary audiences with a troubled past that reaches into the present, they focus on changes in gender relations, anxieties about recovery, and questions of memory and mourning. Although the love triangle at the center of both film narratives addresses such emotionally laden issues as marital fidelity and betrayal, it does so without judgments about right and wrong. Instead there remains a moral dilemma, in response to which outbursts of violence appear as little more than helpless cries. Notably, these films do not subscribe to the sorts of simplistic ideas of loyalty and betrayal promoted after the war by the *Dolchstoß* (stab-in-the-back legend). Engaging urgent problems of their time, these returnee films — in a gesture that parallels the popular Weimar-era literary genre of returnee plays — offer a liberal and nonmilitaristic view of ruptured family relationships, where happy endings are denied and easy solutions yield to ambivalence.

See also:

- 22 September 1907: Sigmund Freud Is Attracted to the Movies but Feels Lonely in the Crowd
- 18 May 1945: *Welt im Film* Newsreels, Rubble Films Model "Cool Conduct"
- 19 September 1958: Douglas Sirk's *A Time to Love and a Time to Die* Tests Limits of Postwar Feeling

Notes

[1] On these literary reworkings, see Walter Neumann, *Grundzüge der Technik des Heimkehrerdramas: Ein Beitrag zur Technik des Dramas der Gegenwart* (Würzburg: Richard Mayr, 1936) and Hedwig Röttger, *Das Motiv: Der heimkehrende Gatte und sein Weib in der deutschen Literatur seit 1890* (Bonn: L. Neuendorff, 1934). Related returnee films included: *Die Heimkehr des Odysseus* (The homecoming of Ulysses, 1918), *Die Toten kehren wieder — Enoch Arden* (The dead return, 1919), *Oberst Chabert* (Colonel Chabert, 1920), *Die Heimkehr des Odysseus* (The homecoming of Ulysses, 1922), and *Graf Chargon* (Count Chargon, 1922).

[2] See *Der Leidensweg der Inge Krafft* (The passion of Inge Krafft, 1921), *Das Medium* (The medium, 1921), *Hintertreppe* (Backstairs, 1921), *Versunkene Welten* (Lost worlds, 1922), *Brüder* (Brothers, 1923), *Der Turm des Schweigens* (The tower of silence, 1925).

[3] Anton Kaes, *Shell Shock Cinema: Weimar Culture and the Wounds of War* (Princeton, NJ: Princeton UP, 2009).

[4] See *Der Mann aus dem Jenseits — Feldgrau* (Malice, 1925), *Ich hatt' einen Kameraden* (I once had a comrade, 1926), *Ein Tag der Rosen im August, da hat die Garde fortgemusst* (One rosy day in August, the guards had to leave, 1927), *Doktor Bessels Verwandlung* (The transformation of Dr. Bessel, 1927), and the adaptation of Balzac's novel, *Colonel Chabert, Mensch ohne Namen* (The man without a name, 1932).

[5] Bernadette Kester, *Film Front Weimar: Representations of the First World War in German Films of the Weimar Period (1919–1933)* (Amsterdam: Amsterdam UP, 2003).

1 April 1921: Walther Ruttmann's *Lichtspiel: Opus 1* Shapes Culture of Abstract Filmmaking

Gregory Zinman

Abstraction of the image in Lichtspiel: Opus 1 *(1921). DVD capture.*

THE CINEMATIC AVANT-GARDE in Germany sprouted from seeds sown by European art movements in the aftermath of the First World War. Painters and sculptors from Hungary, France, and Russia flocked to Weimar and Berlin, spurred by new social and economic ties between Germany and their birth nations, social unrest back home, and the establishment of the Weimar Bauhaus in 1919. As Dada, expressionism, and constructivism waxed and waned, a small cadre of artists sought to overturn the cultural primacy of easel painting via the creation of a new art form that would more comprehensively represent modernity while capturing a burgeoning mass audience. These artists embraced film as the site for this new art, and their efforts more closely resembled the era's abstract painting than its popular filmmaking. The resulting works were at once part of Weimar film and outside of it, part of the avant-garde yet flirting with the mainstream. Spawning new cinematic processes and goals, these artists and films separated from one another and came back together like a double-helix, running parallel at times, at others, diverging from one another.

On one track lay the "absolute" abstract films of Walther Ruttmann, Viking Eggeling, and Hans Richter, who sought to "paint in time." On the other resided the experiments of László Moholy-Nagy, Ludwig Hirschfeld-Mack, and Kurt Schwerdtfeger at the Bauhaus, wherein various apparatuses were constructed in order to "paint with light." At their intersection stood Oskar Fischinger, who brought together film and the light play. His viewing of Ruttmann's *Lichtspiel: Opus 1* in Frankfurt on 1 April 1921 produced the filmic substance that would eventually bind these strands together. Like the structure of DNA, these two strands of experimentation — with Fischinger at their center — can be read as the genetic code for the cinematic avant-garde that would follow.

Following the First World War, Ruttmann, a painter, had moved from expressionism to full-blown abstraction. As early as 1917 — the same year that Ufa (Universum Film A.G.) was established — Ruttmann argued that filmmakers had "become stuck in the wrong direction," due to their misunderstanding of cinema's essence.[1] Shortly thereafter, the pages of the Dutch journal *De Stijl* were filled with discussions of a "machine aesthetic" bringing together technology and abstraction in the pursuit of a universal language. The twinned investigation of the technical and the abstract would indeed provide the very elements giving rise to the cinematic avant-garde. By 1919, Ruttmann had laid out his own plan for using the technologically derived medium of film to produce new art, calling for "a new method of expression, one different from all the other arts, a medium of time. An art meant for our eyes, one differing from painting in that it has a temporal dimension (like music), and in the rendition of a (real or stylized) moment in an event or fact, but rather precisely in the temporal rhythm of visual events. This new art-form will give rise to a totally new kind of artist, one whose existence has only been latent up to now, one who will more or less occupy a middle-ground between painting and music."[2]

Here we see not only the proleptic desire for an art of intermedia *avant le lettre*, one that borrows from multiple arts (music, painting) while positioning the artist as a liminal figure straddling various media. In place of easel painting, Ruttmann proposed a technological art that matched the "speed of our times," one that would mimic the pace set by the "telegraph, express trains, stenography, photography, printing presses, etc," via machine abstraction.[3] Ruttmann's desire to paint "with the medium of time" thus combines constructivist rigor and expressionism's subjectivity with a dash of the anything-is-possible permissiveness that had been unleashed by Dada — which would soon enjoy its high-water mark in Berlin in the summer of 1920 at the First International Dada Fair.

Answering his own challenge, Ruttmann devised and patented a unique process to realize his vision. His *Lichtspiel: Opus I* was an eleven-minute work in three movements, set to music by Max Butting. He composed the film by painting on layers of glass, filming each frame separately, before hand-tinting and toning various sections of his film to produce heretofore-unseen moving images. Ruttmann completed a version of the film in 1920, painstakingly assembling the dozens of hand-colored fragments into a single print before turning the film over to his university friend Butting. Butting composed a score for the film, a meticulously timed piece for string quartet for which Ruttmann played cello during screenings. Viewers saw gliding circles, rippling flag-like forms, and encroaching triangles fill the screen in full color. In April 1921, it became the first abstract film to be screened for the public.

While Ruttmann had warned of the new film's limited commercial appeal, he realized that even a mildly successful movie would be seen by many more people than a painting hanging in a gallery or museum. *Opus I* was nevertheless met with accolades. Critic Bernhard Diebold, who had previously called for artists to take up the mantle of *Bildmusiker* (visual musicians) to create abstractions that would combine and supersede all other arts, wrote in the *Frankfurter Zeitung* that the film had cast aside the photographic "naturalism" of other films in order to produce "a new art. The ocular music of film."[4] What's more, Diebold explicitly contextualized *Opus I* in terms of the relationship between film and painting, noting that Ruttmann took "his speed from the cinematic rush of the futurist canvas."[5]

Diebold's invocation of futurism speaks to the welter of art-world influences operating on German cinema at that time. From the first decade of the twentieth century, expressionism had been the aesthetic approach dominating German painting. This valorization of subjectivity over a realistic representation of the world was expressed in the electric colors of Ernst Ludwig Kirchner, the savagely distorted caricatures of George Grosz, and Wassily Kandinsky's abdication of representation altogether in favor of spiritually informed abstractions. Although it had been more or less exhausted in painting, expressionism reached its filmic apotheosis in the Weimar cinema of 1920, the year of Robert Weine's *Das Cabinet des Dr. Caligari* (*The Cabinet of Dr. Caligari*) and Carl Boese and Paul Wegener's *Der Golem*. Both of these "artistic" films proved major commercial successes for Ufa, thus broadening the movie-going public's palate of comedy, crime, adventure, and historical films that had previously proven to be the most popular film entertainments. Significantly, both films also made use of color tinting processes resembling Ruttmann's, producing sepia, violet, and aqua hues intended to dramatize action or represent emotion.

While Ruttmann's paint-on-glass techniques were much more precise and varied than those of the expressionist dramas, their palettes are similar. And where the dramas still relied on narrative, *Opus I* reflected the art world's shift toward valorizing pure form and movement. Indeed, the influence of Kandinsky — who would join the Bauhaus faculty a year later — on Ruttmann seems particularly pronounced in the neophyte filmmaker's reliance on the nonobjective shapes traversing the screen.

Though the handmade and fragmentary nature of *Opus I* meant that no single master print existed, and consequently that the film was not widely screened, the piece nevertheless attracted the attention of advertisers. Fragments of *Opus I* found their way into two ads: "Der Sieger" (The winner) for Excelsior automobile tires, and "Das Wunder" (The miracle) for Kantorowicz liqueur. That Ruttmann's avant-garde intentions gave little pause to the businessmen bemused by his sprightly animations demonstrates how these works could circulate in myriad ways to different audiences — a pattern that would be repeated by Fischinger and numerous other experimental filmmakers.

While Ruttmann self-produced his first film, Richter and Eggeling began working under the auspices of Ufa. Richter, an original member of Dada, had become increasingly interested in the confluence of simplified forms, machine aesthetics, and utopian spirit espoused by Russian and Dutch constructivists. With Swedish painter Viking Eggeling, he developed a system of scroll painting in Berlin around 1920 before both men turned to traditional animation. Eggeling and Richter cowrote an essentially constructivist manifesto that same year, "Universal Language," arguing that abstraction held the promise of an entirely new art capable of translating "both simple and most complex notions, emotions, and thoughts, objects and ideas" into pictorial form.[6]

A year later, Richter joined Dutch painter Theo van Doesburg and the polymath El Lissitzky — who had arrived in Berlin in 1921 as a cultural ambassador from Russia — as a member of the International Fraction of Constructivism at the First International Congress of Progressive Artists. The group released a statement arguing against subjectivity in favor of "new principles of artistic creation by systematically organizing the media to a generally understandable expression."[7] Ruttmann, too, would push his work further in a constructivist vein, as evinced by his *Opus III* (1924) with its black-and-white compositions of harder-edged squares, rectangles, and trapezoids strongly reminiscent of Richter's *Rhythmus 21* (1921).

Moholy-Nagy, meanwhile, had arrived in Berlin in 1920. By 1923 he was given the charge of heading up the Foundation Course at the Bauhaus, the year the institution adopted the slogan "Art and Technology — A New Unity," further signaling Weimar's constructivist turn away from expressionism. Moholy's own interest in synthesizing media was expressed by his stated desire to create a means of "light composition," in which "light would be controlled as a new plastic medium, just as color in painting and tone in music."[8] In his landmark *De Stijl* essay of 1922, "Production-Reproduction," he exhorted artists to rethink their use of technology to create, rather than capture, new sounds and visions. He praised both Ruttmann and Danish inventor Thomas Wilfred, whose color organ produced shifting miasmatic clouds and shapes of brilliant color and vibrancy, for their foregrounding of motion in their moving images. He heaped even greater approbation on the experiments of Richter and Eggeling, before concluding that kineticism should be the goal of the moving picture.

Moholy further suggested that filmmakers use the medium's resources of "color, plasticity and simultaneous displays, either by means of an increased number of projectors concentrated on a single screen, or in the form of simultaneous image sequences covering all the walls of the room."[9] Bauhaus students Ludwig Hirschfeld-Mack and Kurt Schwerdtfeger constructed hand-manipulated color organs played by up to four people at once to project layered, full-color moving geometric forms onto a transparent screen. After two years of experiments building various apparatus with liquids, mirrors, moving lenses, and colored lights, Hirschfeld-Mack published an explanatory booklet describing this "future art," and gave performances of his *Reflektorischen Farbenlichtspiele* (Reflective colored light plays) in Berlin and Vienna, Weimar and Leipzig. That these pursuits were taken as being in line with those of Ruttmann, Eggeling, and Richter is borne out by the fact that all of them were shown in the "Absoluter Filmabend" show of 1925.

Even before then, abstract cinema's influence had begun spreading rapidly. Twenty-year-old machine engineer and aspiring artist from Munich Oskar Fischinger was taken by Diebold to a private rehearsal screening of *Opus I* at a Frankfurt theater at the beginning of April 1921. Fischinger was so impressed by *Opus I* that he decided to try his hand at abstract filmmaking. He did not wish, however, merely to copy Ruttmann's style. True to his nature as a tinkerer, Fischinger quickly developed a wax-cutting machine that allowed him to animate thin cross-sections of wax on a frame-by-frame basis, a process resulting in shifting abstractions reminiscent of both tidal pools and swirling galaxies. Impressed by this innovation, Ruttmann asked Fischinger if he could license the wax-cutting machine to produce backgrounds for his animations of a flying horse for the opening sequence for Lotte Reiniger's *Die Abenteuer des Prinzen Achmed* (*The Adventures of Prince Ahmed*, 1926).

By that time, Fischinger was working with composer Alexander Lázló on *Farbe-Licht-Musik* (*Color-Light-Music*), a visual music extravaganza that toured throughout Germany in 1925 and 1926. The performance incorporated colored spotlights and multiple slide projectors, as Fischinger projected hand-colored films. Eager to pursue his own project, Fischinger developed *R-I: Ein Formspiel* (*R-1: A Form Play*), which further refined the techniques he had initiated with Lázló. The multi-projector work culled footage from many of Fischinger's film experiments, including the deliquescing wax imagery that had so intrigued Ruttmann, hand-tinted reels of abstract imagery, and animated geometric cut-outs of paper and wood.[10]

Fischinger's *R-1* was in many ways a technical and aesthetic extension of the possibilities first introduced by *Opus I*, and Ruttmann lectured on his younger colleague's work at the Bauhaus, as did Moholy. Fischinger dubbed his work "*Eine neue Kunst: Raumlichtmusik*" (A new art: Spacelightmusic), and argued for its teleological significance: "Of this Art everything is new and yet ancient in its laws and forms. Plastic-Dance-Painting-Music become one. The Master of the new Art forms poetical work in four dimensions . . . Cinema was its beginning . . . Raumlichtmusik will be its completion."[11]

In less than a decade's time, however, the utopian ambition percolating through this avant-garde strain of Weimar Cinema had been smothered by the rise of the Third Reich. Confronted by a regime in which abstract art was considered "degenerate," Ruttmann, Moholy, Richter, and Fischinger took radically different paths. Ruttmann abandoned abstract filmmaking in favor of directing industrial films, before finally collaborating with Leni Riefenstahl on *Triumph des Willens* (*Triumph of the Will*, 1935). Fischinger's ludic animated films caught Hollywood's eye, and allowed him to leave Nazi Germany for Los Angeles in 1936. There he produced some of his greatest films, although he often did not receive proper credit or payment for his work, and had a disastrous stint at Disney working on *Fantasia* (1940). Moholy moved around Europe before taking refuge in Chicago in 1937 as director of the short-lived New Bauhaus, and Richter taught film in New York starting in 1940. Temporarily expunged by fascism, the resilient genetic code of Weimar's abstract cinema would eventually resurface in postwar experimental cinema as an influence on direct animators, kinetic artists, and expanded cinema practitioners.

See also:

- 3 May 1925: French and German Avant-Garde Converge at *Der absolute Film*
- 17 June 1927: Amateur Film League Aids Invention of Film Culture
- 8 June 1986: Farocki's *Wie man sieht* Urges New Ways of Seeing

Notes

[1] Quoted in Walter Schobert, "'Painting in Time' and 'Visual Music': On German Avant-Garde Films of the 1920s," in *Expressionist Film — New Perspectives*, ed. Dietrich Scheunemann (Rochester, NY: Camden House, 2003), 237–50; here 237.

[2] Walther Ruttmann, "Painting with the Medium of Time," in *The German Avant-Garde Film of the 1920s*, Walter Schobert (Munich: Goethe-Institut, 1989), 102–3.

[3] Sara Selwood, "Color Music and Abstract Film," in *Light Art from Artificial Light: Light as a Medium in 20th and 21st Century Art*, ed. Peter Weibel and Gergor Jansen (Ostfildern, Germany: Hatje Cantz, 2006), 418.

[4] William Moritz, *Optical Poetry: The Life and Work of Oskar Fischinger* (Bloomington: Indiana UP, 2004), 3–4.

[5] Peter Weibel, "The Development of Light Art," in *Light Art from Artificial Light*, 168.

[6] Selwood, "Color Music and Abstract Film," 420. Contrary to Richter's claims elsewhere, *Rhythmus 21* from 1921 was not the first abstract film, and was in fact preceded by Ruttmann's *Opus I*.

[7] Justin Hoffman, "Hans Richter: Constructivist Filmmaker," in *Hans Richter: Activism, Modernism, and the Avant-Garde*, ed. Stephen Foster (Cambridge, MA: MIT Press, 1998), 84–85.

[8] László Moholy-Nagy, "Production-Reproduction," in *Moholy-Nagy*, ed. Krisztina Passuth (London: Thames & Hudson, 1985), 289–90.

[9] Ibid.

[10] Cindy Keefer, "Space Light Art": Early Abstract Cinema and Multimedia, 1900–1959," Center for Visual Music, accessed 20 December 2011, http://www.centerforvisualmusic.org/CKSLAexc.htm.

[11] Keefer, "Space Light Art"; ellipses in the original.

27 May 1921: *Scherben* Seeks Cinematic Equivalent of Theatrical Intimacy

Patrick Vonderau

ON 27 MAY 1921, *Scherben* (*Shattered*) opened in two Berlin cinemas frequented by those who considered themselves members of the cultured classes, the Ufa-Theater Kurfürstendamm and the Mozartsaal. *Ein deutsches Filmkammerspiel: Drama in fünf Tagen* (A German cinematic chamber play: drama in five days), as the picture's subtitle read, was meant to stand out from the several hundred feature films premiering in the spring of 1921. At the time, 360 production companies were registered in Berlin alone, with an annual output of about 650 long features that could be screened in more than 400 local cinemas. The market was oversaturated with mystery and adventure films, melodramas, comedies, and historical epics of monumental proportions. In addition to Germany's own diversified production, foreign imports had been readmitted to the German market after a war-related import ban was lifted in January 1921.

New European and US American inroads prompted a heated debate on the condition and competitiveness of German cinema, carried out in trade papers and film magazines that only recently had seen an unparalleled upswing of their own. In this vibrant film culture, indicating the growing social importance of cinema internationally, *Scherben* (directed by Lupu Pick and written by Carl Mayer) was placed as a programmatic demonstration of film's potential as an art form. The term *Kammerspielfilm* (chamber play film, referring to an intimate melodrama) has come to be associated particularly with three films scripted by Carl Mayer — *Scherben*, *Hintertreppe* (The back stairs, 1921), and *Der letzte Mann* (*The Last Laugh*, 1924) — that revived naturalist themes and combined them with a foregrounding of formal qualities, resulting in films that often favored composition and atmosphere over narrative development and presented highly emotional, even existential situations in static cinematic tableaus.[1]

These three films' aesthetic and promotional references to the chamber play were not intended to stir up public debate in the fashion of *Das Cabinet des Dr. Caligari* (1919), also scripted by Carl Mayer, with its widely advertised appropriation of popular contemporary Gothic romanticism and expressionist stylization. As a cinematic chamber play, *Scherben* and the short-lived cycle of films following it instead drew on a tradition of earlier attempts to elevate cinema dating back to the *Autorenfilm* (author films) of the early 1910s. References to Max Reinhardt's prestigious productions, the chamber play tradition, and the modernist approach to stage drama associated with the "Intimate Theatre" had also been invoked by three earlier adaptations of August Strindberg works — *Rausch* (*Intoxication*, 1919), *Fräulein Julie* (*Miss Julie*, 1921), and *Kameraden* (*Comrades*, 1919) — with the last production even featuring Strindberg's widow Harriet Bosse in a main role, although with limited success. Yet if *Scherben* was not perceived as new or revolutionary in its programmatic reference to high art, it certainly was in its omission of intertitles. It was as though through the absence of the written word, the cinema would finally become an art form on par with contemporary theater and literature — an art at the same time meant to be easily identified with "Germanness" and Germany's cultural role in Europe after the First World War. Those at least were the expectations raised by the German press and trade papers, expectations to whose underlying paradoxes this essay will return.

The plot of *Scherben* revolves around four nameless persons entangled in a tragedy that unfolds in a period of just five days in an unspecified, wintry locale. An old railway worker (Werner Krauss) in charge of patrolling the tracks lives with his wife (Hermine Straßmann-Witt) and grown-up daughter (Edith Posca) in a petit-bourgeois home close to the railway line. Into this secluded space of nature, marked by the slow routines of work and a pietistic family life, an arrogant young railway inspector (Paul Otto) intrudes, arriving by train from a far-away city. Without much hesitation the inspector seduces the girl, to the utter chagrin of the observing mother, who dies almost immediately thereafter because of spending the night out in the cold praying at a wayside cross. The daughter desperately tries to convince her seducer to take her with him, and when he refuses she takes revenge by informing her father about the root cause of her mother's sudden death. The father, numbed by incidents whose meaning he fails to grasp, strangles the inspector. Afterwards, he stops an approaching train and confesses to its more or less unconcerned passengers, in what becomes the picture's one and only intertitle, "I am a murderer." His daughter, in a state of growing madness, watches the train depart from the roof of her shattered homestead.

Contemporary reviews criticized *Scherben*'s plot as overly linear and kitschy. One critic sarcastically summed up the film's storyline as "What the Girl and That Inspector Did," and compared it to *Hintertreppe*, the second installment in a short *Kammerspielfilm* cycle, with its consequential treatment of the question, "Why the Other Girl Fell from the Roof."[2] Both pictures and also two subsequent ones scripted by Carl Mayer, *Sylvester* (1924) and *Der letzte Mann*, nevertheless bore some formal resemblances to the program of intimate art as first laid out by Strindberg in his preface to *Miss Julie* (1888). The chamber play on stage had been defined by a perceived "inwardness," resulting from, among other things, the detailed and often psychologically refined performances of only a few actors, a limited number of sets, and a dramaturgy driven by unresolved familial conflicts lurking behind the façade of bourgeois well-being. Similarly, and in a marked contrast both to expressionist and popular genre cinema, *Scherben* and Mayer's other works from that era focused on the emotional pain and on the life's lies of the protagonists. Mayer's highly evocative scriptwriting for *Scherben* and Lupu Pick's mise-en-scène not only worked out the psychological aspects of an otherwise rather stereotypical narrative, but the picture also reminded its audience of the *Kammerspiel* in its use of the Aristotelian unities of time, place, and action, in its interest in the drama of the everyday, and in Werner Krauss's detailed performance. Similar to Maurice Maeterlinck's "static dramas" in its depiction of the human subject as a defenseless object of death, but unlike Gerhart Hauptmann's plays in its apolitical treatment of the human condition, *Scherben* also seemed to comment on the fragmented identity of the subject in modernity. Apart from these outward resemblances, however, the allusion to the chamber play fall short of explaining *Scherben*'s novelty, as it by no means constituted an end unto itself. Indeed, Mayer's script for *Scherben* and consequently also Lupu Pick's mise-en-scène did not so much attempt to replicate the chamber play as spelled out by Strindberg, Ibsen, or Wedekind, as it strove for a cinematic equivalent of theatrical intimacy.

The program of the Intimate Theater had developed in historical conjunction with psychoanalysis, most notably Breuer's and Freud's research on hysteria. By 1921, familial problems had become the stuff of both therapy and theater; art, therapy, and even journalism shared an interest in psychological causation and the most intimate confessions of the soul. Cinema, however, had largely abstained from investing narrative situations and characters with emotional depth, at least in Germany, where expressionism had been particularly dismissive of contemporary psychology's explanations of mental life. When foreign films reentered the German film market in 1921 after having been absent for more than a year, reviewers and practitioners alike bemoaned the backward techniques and outmoded themes of German storytelling. Despite its quantitatively insignificant production output, it was especially Swedish cinema that set a new benchmark for psychological realism. The films of Mauritz Stiller and Victor Sjöström were heralded as points of reference for a future German cinema, and *Scherben* was even considered a first step toward the goal of achieving comparable psychological plausibility. Yet in opposition both to the chamber play and Swedish cinema, Pick's and Mayer's *Kammerspielfilm* limited itself to illustrating the psychology of internalized social norms. Instead of full-fledged characters, *Scherben* presented "allegorical characters."[3] While the Intimate Theater attempted to explain human individuality in its social environment and used the interior spaces of its stage settings to convey that explanation, *Scherben* relied on social typologies and a reduced set design marked by a symbolically accentuated realism. Its psychology and "inwardness," then, was founded on features uncommon on either stage or screen.

Most remarkable about *Scherben*'s composition in this context was its almost complete lack of intertitles, a technique later perfected by and subsequently associated with the personal style of Friedrich Wilhelm Murnau and *Der letzte Mann*. Critics and early theorists of German cinema repeatedly described this strategy as a means of inducing a feeling of intimacy in the audience. Reviewers found novelty in the "abandonment of text" and also in the "uninterrupted progression of action" resulting from that technique.[4] Since most cinemas in Berlin allowed patrons to enter the auditorium at any point during a screening, watching films from beginning to end was by no means an established practice. Hence the often lamented dramaturgic predilection for pure spectacle, endless subplots, and logically unconnected scenes; German cinema lacked the narrative integration common to American motion pictures as early as 1915.[5] However stereotyped *Scherben*'s motifs were, then, their treatment in a fully visualized, stringent narrative underlined the film's opposition to the outward sensationalism of monumental epics or detective thrillers of its day. *Scherben*'s programmatic break with Germany's "cinema of attractions" consequently also had an intended disciplining effect on its audience. The lack of any textual explanation made it advisable to follow the story from beginning to end and it demanded close observation, especially of the actors' individual performances. Further, the lack of intertitles bore an intimate connection to the critical appreciation of *Scherben* as a work of art. For only the absence of words allowed the film to "visually express everything related to the soul."[6] Indeed, the very definition of film art as it circulated in early Weimar film culture rested precisely on its relation to the soul. According to the contemporary understanding, film would only qualify as an art when it succeeded in stirring the soul — an idea that was not grounded in recent psychology or stage theory, but in Goethe's idealist philosophy of the arts.

Scherben was produced by Rex-Film, a small, independent production company headed by the film's director, Lupu Pick. The majority of the shooting took place in January–February 1921 in Rex-Film's Berlin studios, with a few exteriors shot on location in the province of Silesia. Since Pick was involved in both producing and directing, he has sometimes been credited with having had the initiative to make the film, while explicit authorship has been credited to Mayer. In fact, the production also resonated well with the overall aesthetic program of Ufa (Universum

Film A.G.), to which *Scherben* had more than incidental ties. Rex-Film produced the picture on commission for Ufa, with Ufa bearing 90 percent of the production costs. Ufa was also involved in the distribution (via the affiliated Hansa-Verleih) and exhibition of *Scherben* (by way of its theater chain), and its widely circulating promotional leaflets such as *Die Ufa-Blätter* informed both reviews and later historical accounts of the film to a striking degree.[7] Despite its affinity to the themes and motifs of Mayer's scriptwriting, then, *Scherben* should also be seen as part of a larger production portfolio whose main concerns in 1921 were rising inflation and competition in the European film market. In the trade papers, a debate raged about German films suited for export, and experts recommended investing in "inexpensive pictures that address contemporary society and that endow human fate with some psychological depth." Others in turn advised strictly against any form of individualized character psychology, as it was perceived to trouble foreign audiences.[8] *Scherben*'s "transient aesthetic," mediating between vague categories of "expressionist" and "realist" style, looks in retrospect like an attempt to find a way out of this discursive binary.[9] Its narrative investigation into the relationship of the individual to society deliberately blurred the line between psychological and idealist notions of the soul, taking up the motifs of sensational newspaper reportage as well as modernist literature — a practice in keeping with Ufa's trademark popularization of common cultural knowledge. Yet the *Kammerspielfilm* was never meant to become a genre akin to Hollywood's strategic genre development, as later historians have suggested; indeed, genres were dismissed per se as antithetical to film as an art. In the then-abundant critical discourse on film, the making and experience of art was still seen to be irreproducible; an "aura" could only be attributed to the uniqueness of the artwork.

Caught in their contradictory ambition of redefining film art by relating industrial production to the German soul, *Scherben*'s creators soon found themselves confronted with reports that both domestic and foreign audiences had difficulties understanding the picture without intertitles. "German character," it seems, did not translate directly into a poetics of German cinema. Regardless of how we judge the film's audience success from the vantage of today, however, it remains a key work for its effort to develop a cinematic intimacy, translating the proximity of contemporary theater into visual form.

See also:

- 22 September 1907: Sigmund Freud Is Attracted to the Movies but Feels Lonely in the Crowd
- 23 December 1924: *Der letzte Mann* Explores Limits of Modern Community

- 7 April 1968: Straub, Huillet, and Fassbinder Share the Stage at Munich's Action-Theater

Notes

[1] Marc Silberman, *German Cinema: Texts in Context* (Detroit: Wayne State UP, 1995), 21; see Patrice Petro, *Joyless Streets: Women and Melodramatic Representation in Weimar Germany* (Princeton: Princeton UP, 1989), 175.

[2] Cinemax, "Von Menschen und Dingen," *Film-Kurier* (13 April 1922).

[3] Siegfried Kracauer, *Von Caligari zu Hitler: Eine psychologische Geschichte des deutschen Films* (1947; repr. Frankfurt am Main: Suhrkamp, 1995), 111.

[4] Kurt Pinthus, "Sylvester," *Das Tage-Buch* (19 January 1924).

[5] Patrick Vonderau, *Bilder vom Norden. Schwedisch-deutsche Filmbeziehungen, 1914–1939* (Marburg: Schüren, 2005), 140–85.

[6] Heinz Riedel, "Der Gebildete und der Film," *Film-Kurier* (13 March 1922).

[7] Kracauer, for example, based his account on the *Ufa-Blätter*.

[8] Paul Ickes, "Wie erhalten wir den deutschen Film exportfähig?" *Film-Kurier* (11 August 1921). Joe May, "Der Stil des Exportfilms," *Film-Kurier* (4 August 1922).

[9] Jürgen Kasten, *Carl Mayer: Filmpoet. Ein Drehbuchautor schreibt Filmgeschichte* (Berlin: Vistas, 1994), 124.

14 September 1922: Schüfftan Process Reconciles Artistic Craftsmanship with Demands of Entertainment Industry

Katharina Loew

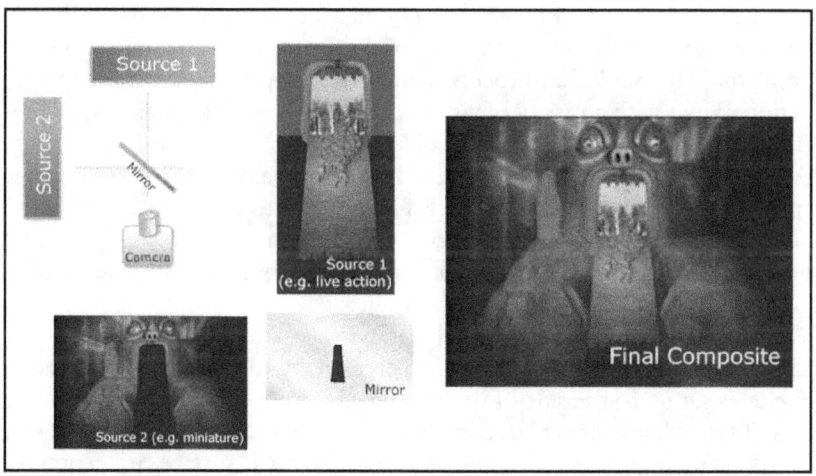

The principle of the Schüfftan process. Credit: K. Loew.

WITHOUT WHAT HAS BECOME known as the "Schüfftan process," many of Weimar cinema's spectacular effects would have been inconceivable. The Schüfftan process permitted German film technicians to create illusions in films like *Varieté* (*Variety*, 1925) and *Metropolis* (1926) that staggered film professionals and audiences worldwide. On 14 September 1922, the young painter Eugen Schüfftan initiated the first patent application for this mirror-based trick technological invention, which became Germany's only internationally marketed special effect and the most widely used compositing technique in European filmmaking until the 1950s.[1]

In the history of special effects, the 1920s represent a key transitional period. Before that time, special effects were used sparingly, typically for representations of supernatural events or superhuman physical feats. Film technicians usually devised tailor-made trick technological solutions for specific aesthetic problems. Around the latter half of the 1920s, however, an industrialized approach gained popularity and special effects became increasingly prevalent. Cinematic illusions were now primarily employed to simulate physical reality, usually for financial reasons. Ever since the final years of the silent era, the vast majority of illusions used in professional filmmaking have belonged in this category.

Carrying features of both of these tendencies, the Schüfftan process epitomizes this crucial transition phase. More generally, the technique highlights a constitutive feature of Weimar cinema — namely, the effort to reconcile the demands of an emerging capitalist entertainment industry with aspirations to an almost preindustrial artistic craftsmanship. In contrast to previous practices employed in Europe. The Schüfftan process was not conceived to solve only one specific problem, but rather to serve as an all-purpose technique, implementable in a large number of contexts. The Schüfftan process made possible the combination of live-action scenes with a variety of visual components of different sizes, including photographs, models, and projected images, both still and moving. Although its inventor had originally devised it as a means to "visualize the imagination,"[2] the Schüfftan process turned out to be an excellent tool to subtly reduce costs on large, expensive sets. Because the technique could account for all purely scenic décor, only the parts of the set where actors actually performed had to be built in full size.

The basic principles of the Schüfftan process are simple. Consider the famous Moloch scene in *Metropolis*, created by means of this process: a model is set up to the side of the camera while a live-action scene is staged straight on. A mirror is placed at a forty-five degree angle directly in front of the camera and parts of the mirror's reflective surface are removed. The visual elements located next to the camera (e.g., the model) thereby are reflected in the mirror's remaining silvered portions and replace parts of the view directly in front the camera. Optically the two scenes merge and may then be recorded simultaneously.

The Schüfftan process opened up tremendous new possibilities for filmmakers. It was the first trick technique that allowed moving models to be integrated smoothly with live-action footage. In addition, "Gulliver" effects — the rendering of extreme size differences — became convincing and flexible enough to sustain a feature film. The Schüfftan process was also capable of rendering astonishing transformations, which is apparent from its first application in a commercial motion picture. In Fritz Lang's first Nibelungen film, *Siegfried* (1924), the eponymous hero slays Alberich, king of the Nibelungen, whereupon the dwarfs who are chained to the king's treasure basin turn into stone. The masterful execution of the dwarfs' petrifaction remains impressive today. To achieve this shot, two treasure basins were constructed, one in front of the camera for the live actors to carry, and another replica with petrified dwarfs beside the camera. As it would have been exceedingly complicated to create mirror-inverted molds of the actors, two mirrors were used, one fixed and fully reflective and one that was partially transparent and could slide up and down. Initially, the live-action scene was shot through the transparent part of the sliding mirror. At the moment of transformation, the mirror would slowly move up, allowing the reflective part to replace the live actors with their plaster copies. The effect is spectacular: the dwarfs gradually transform into stone, and they helplessly follow the process in horror, contorting their faces with excruciating pain. Set decorator Erich Kettelhut recalled the reactions of on-set observers and subsequent audiences: "One could not help but share the astonishment, the fear, and despair expressed in the dwarfs' faces as their bodies slowly turned into stone from their feet upward."[3]

Conventionally, this scene would have been realized as a dissolve, gradually transitioning from a shot of the live actors to another one of their stone surrogates. However, it would have been impossible to represent a gradual transformation from the bottom up and it is precisely this aspect that gives the shot such an eerily "realistic" quality. Indeed, the transformation of the dwarfs is staged in such a way as we might imagine a petrifaction to look in real life. The Schüfftan process's technical ability to render scenes "as if" they existed in physical reality heralded a critical shift in the role of cinematic illusions in European filmmaking. In contrast to previous practices, this technique privileged efficiency over creative experimentation. The prospect of consistently achieving "flawless" illusions made the Schüfftan process attractive as an economizing measure on expensive sets. The reasons for this can be traced back to Schüfftan's ambition to invent a truly "magic" device — the least obtrusive and the most flexible of all trick techniques.

Although the Schüfftan process appeared quite industrialized compared to the work of earlier trick technicians, it was still very much rooted in traditions of craftsmanship and echoed a nineteenth-century fascination with optical illusions and stage magic. The ardor of German pioneer inventors resonates in the dedication with which Schüfftan refined his process over a ten-year period, developing a substantial number of rather complex modifications that involved a variety of mirrors, lenses, prisms, and projectors. The Schüfftan process requires the meticulous precision of a craftsman-technician, which might explain why it never gained a foothold in American professional filmmaking. An assessment by William Stull, editor of the trade journal *American Cinematographer*, reveals that by contemporary Hollywood's standards, the process was still far too inefficient: "It is one of the most intricate of all special effects processes, as it requires microscopically perfect alignment of camera, prisms, miniature, and people."[4] In Europe, by contrast, the Schüfftan process was considered one of the most evident symptoms of the modernization of the national film industries.

German film production during the 1920s grew progressively rationalized, standardized, and globalized as the demands of an international and profit-oriented entertainment industry prevailed. In the field of special effects, the Schüfftan process surged ahead in terms of streamlining and commercialization. Between 1922 and 1930, Schüfftan was granted over forty patents in at least eight countries for variations of his process and he subsequently embarked on an unprecedented global business strategy. In August 1925, Schüfftan sold a two-year license to Universal Pictures for commercializing his patents in North America and in January 1927, he sold the world rights (except for Germany and North America) to British National Pictures, allowing Hitchcock to employ the technique in several of his British films including *Blackmail* (1929) and *The Man Who Knew Too Much* (1934).[5]

In April 1925, Schüfftan began cooperating with Ufa (Universum Film A.G.), which generated considerable publicity and established the process in the German film industry. Ufa set up an in-house mirror-trick department that was subsequently merged into the Spiegeltechnik GmbH & Co., a specialized company that produced made-to-order Schüfftan shots for the entire German film industry.[6] As a consequence, the Schüfftan process first became available to German studios other than Ufa in October 1926. By 1927, one out of every ten German films contained Schüfftan shots. Such encouraging numbers notwithstanding, the profitability of Spiegeltechnik GmbH & Co. fell short of expectations. This was largely due to the company's inflated operating expenses, combined with infighting and miscalculations on the part of Ufa. Despite substantial investments in Spiegeltechnik GmbH & Co., Ufa itself only rarely employed the Schüfftan process.

To be sure, commentators were enthusiastic about the technique's allegedly unlimited possibilities and even associated it with utopian visions of artistic renewal. The Schüfftan process's international promotion as the hallmark of German technological excellence also triggered considerable national pride. Accordingly, the Schüfftan process was featured prominently in Ufa's prestigious flagship productions such as *Varieté*, *Metropolis*, and *Die Liebe der Jeanne Ney* (*The Love of Jeanne Ney*, 1927). In the case of smaller-scale productions, however, where first-level management had greater control, widespread apprehension about the ongoing transformations in the film industry led to the Schüfftan process rarely being used. According to a 1927 report, "certain circles within [Ufa's] production departments sabotage the Schüfftan process. Despite the sympathetic support from the head of production . . . it has not been possible to obtain orders from directors or set designers, even though there have been plenty of opportunities to shoot scenes using the Schüfftan process."[7] Indeed, many filmmakers saw this all-purpose trick system as a threat to their artistic freedom. Cinematographers, for instance, felt limited in their creativity: "The cameraman has to content himself with turning his handle in the usual way. His personal skills come less into their own, because the process ... already prefabricates everything before the take."[8] Fearful for their livelihood, set designers and set decorators in particular viewed the Schüfftan process with trepidation, as it was supposedly "a cinch to predict that the future belongs to this invention [the Schüfftan process] and that the set designer and the huge set will be ousted with its help."[9]

By the end of the silent period, the dominant function of special effects had irrevocably become the imitation of physical reality. Large sets were rarely built to full-size but were now conveniently faked by means of special effects. Although the requirements of sound recording equipment certainly played a major role in this, the trend toward increased efficiency and realism in the field of special effects had already begun years earlier. By the 1930s, Hollywood and subsequently also European studios began investing heavily in high-tech composite systems like rear-projection and traveling matte techniques. In comparison with these, Schüfftan's mirrors began to seem painstaking and antiquated. Nonetheless, the Schüfftan process continued to play a major role in European filmmaking into the 1950s. Cheap, low-tech, unobtrusive, and capable of providing the highest image quality, it proved particularly advantageous for tight-budgeted studios such as East Germany's state-owned film company DEFA (Deutsche Film-Aktiengesellschaft), where filmmakers employed the Schüfftan process routinely into the 1980s.

Like no other technique, the Schüfftan process epitomizes the ingenuity and extraordinary aesthetic accomplishments of German film technicians during the 1920s. It stands for an attempt to reconcile ideals of artisan filmmaking with the demands of an international entertainment industry that also characterizes Weimar cinema as a whole. That this idealist experiment was not crowned with lasting success does not diminish its importance.

See also:

- 1 November 1895: Premiere of Wintergarten Program Highlights Transitional Nature of Early Film Technology
- 16 March 1925: *Wege zu Kraft und Schönheit* Educates Audiences in the Art of Nudity
- 3 September 1942: With Venice Premiere of *Die goldene Stadt*, Veit Harlan Enters Debate on Color Cinema

Notes

[1] The first patent application specifying the Schüfftan process was filed under the name of Schüfftan's sponsor Willy Köhler in Germany on 14 September 1922 but rewritten and reissued in 1926: Willy Köhler, 1926, *Verfahren und Einrichtung für kinematographische Aufnahmen*, Deutsches Reichspatent 428,589, issued 10 May 1926.

[2] Gertrud Isolani, "Gespräch mit Eugen Shüfftan," *Basler Nachrichten* (19 October 1965), 9.

[3] Erich Kettelhut, *Der Schatten des Architekten*, ed. Werner Sudendorf (Munich: Belleville, 2009), 93.

[4] William Stull, "Process Cinematography," *The Complete Photographer* 8 (1943): 2994–3005; here 3000.

[5] See "Vereinbarung Universal Pictures Corp. New York und Akt. Ges. für Spiegeltechnik vom 11.8.1925," in the Bundesarchiv Berlin (R109/I2070) and "British National Strengthened," "Britain's Hollywood: Facts about the Elstree Equipment," and "Camera Magic: British National's Big Scoop," *Kinematograph Weekly*, London (13 January 1927), 56; 105. See also François Truffaut, *Hitchcock*, transl. Helen G. Scott (New York: Simon and Schuster, 1985), 65.

[6] See the files of the Deutsche Spiegeltechnik GmbH & Co. K.-G. Berlin in the Bundesarchiv Berlin, particularly "Angebot der Universum-Film AG an die Deutsche Spiegeltechnik GmbH &Co, Berlin W9, Köthenerstrasee 1/4 vom 15. September 1926" (R109/I2070); "Bericht über Zwischenrevision der Geschäftsbücher und der Bilanz per 28. Februar 1927" (R109/I2455); and "Bericht über Revision der Geschäftsbücher und der Bilanz für das am 30. September 1927 abgelaufene Geschäftsjahr" (R109/I2456).

[7] "Bericht über Zwischenrevision der Geschäftsbücher und der Bilanz per 28. Februar 1927," Bundesarchiv Berlin (R109/I2455).

[8] Guido Seeber, *Der praktische Kameramann*, vol. 2, *Der Trickfilm in seinen grundsätzlichen Möglichkeiten* (1927) (Frankfurt am Main: Deutsches Filmmuseum, 1979), 141–42.

[9] "Das Ende der Dekoration," *Kinematograph* 950 (3 May 1925).

13 October 1922: Alexander Kolowrat-Krakowsky Sets Course of Austrian (Inter)National Film

Robert von Dassanowsky

THE NEW YORK-BORN, Bohemian aristocrat Count Alexander "Sascha" Kolowrat-Krakowsky is traditionally labeled the father of the Austrian film industry, but the first Germanophone Austrians to produce feature films were the team of female film pioneer Louise (or Luise) Veltée, her husband, Anton Kolm, and their cameraman Jakob Julius Fleck. In 1910, the trio founded the first official Vienna-based film company; its production of *Der Müller und sein Kind* (The miller and his child, 1911) is today considered the first true Austrian feature film. Prior to the First World War, the only true rival to the Kolm/Fleck team was Sascha Kolowrat, as he was known professionally. Socially and financially secure after having inherited his parents' wealth and impressive estates, by 1916 he held a monopoly in Vienna's newsreel creation. Often manipulating war documentaries with studio effects and fictional scenes, Kolowrat not only learned from the emotional power of sensationalized images about the medium's attraction, but also gleaned a formula for its exploitation: "Nothing appears as real as an illusion."[1] The successes of Kolowrat's Austrian war films inspired German imitation, and in 1917 the German Universum-Film firm, better known as Ufa, was founded in Berlin for the specific purpose of creating cinematic war propaganda.

The collapse of the Austro-Hungarian monarchy in 1918 radically transformed the Austrian film industry. Germany had become a republic, but despite loss of some territory, remained intact. Austria-Hungary, however, splintered into several Central European republics. The remnant core, a German-speaking territory carved imprecisely from the tatters of the Empire, became a small, impoverished republic wrestling with its identity. Kolowrat succeeded in manipulating the tragedy into a beneficial situation for his company. Due to the location of his land holdings, he was now a Czechoslovakian citizen and unlike his vanquished Austrian colleagues, he could therefore maintain healthy contacts with film and government sources in Paris and London. He assumed the Austrian representation of Hollywood's Paramount Pictures and replaced the studio network he had built throughout the Empire with a commonwealth of production branches that bore different names designed to appear homegrown, but that were actually run by his Sascha-Film.[2]

Kolowrat admired American films and their easy exportability, and his goal — devised during the war years — was to create an Austrian national cinema both universal in theme and groundbreaking in presentation. In 1919, he put two notable Hungarian filmmakers under contract: Michael (Mihály) Kertész (known to world audiences as Michael Curtiz through his successful career in Hollywood) and Alexander (Sándor) Korda. Both had fled to Vienna following involvement with the cultural committee of the short-lived Marxist commune in Budapest. Kolowrat's concept for Austrian cinematic triumph was to make films less specifically Austrian. Yet while the romances, dramas, and comedies of Kolowrat's early postwar productions between 1919 and 1921 may have been international in subject matter and locale, their diluted "intellectuality filtered through baroque theater, the representation of the Habsburgs, literary-Romantic scripts, art nouveau and expressionist stage writing, [was] a mixture that could only have come about in Vienna."[3] Korda's adaptation of Mark Twain for *Prinz und Bettelknabe* (*The Prince and the Pauper*, 1920) became the director and producer's first Austrian global commercial success.

Kolowrat visited the United States in 1919 and in 1920 in order to study American film production methods and set up a Hollywood-based releasing company. He returned to Vienna with the desire to utilize the concepts of D. W. Griffith's monumental epics to fulfill his international commercial aspirations for Austrian cinema. Both Kertész and Korda enthusiastically agreed with Kolowrat's plan and his Hollywood rivalry, but their own developed, and Korda also found it difficult to work with an intrusive producer. The first monumental film of the Kertész-Kolowrat partnership is considered a highpoint in the history of Austrian silent film. *Sodom und Gomorrha: Die Legende von Sünde und Strafe* (*Queen of Sin and the Spectacle of Sodom and Gomorrah*, 1922) was easily understood by critics of the era as a condemnation of the forces of capitalism in the impoverished fledgling republic. Kertész had indeed succeeded in advancing the style of Griffith's *Birth of a Nation* (1915) and *Intolerance* (1916). Following through on the erotic promise of its subtitle, it was the longest, most spectacular film created in Austria to that date. The film was shown in two parts and, at a length of 3,900 meters, it ran three hours at its Vienna premiere on 13 October 1922. Like its American counterpart, the Austrian biblical epic consisted of a dream sequence framed by a contemporary story: Mary Conway, the young daughter of a banker's mistress, is forced to marry a wealthy widower who has ruined many lives. Developing into a femme fatale, she nearly causes her husband's suicide and seduces his innocent son. Her biblical dream, which underscores her sins, ultimately transforms her and she returns to an equally penitent husband. Kertész's wife, Lucy Doraine, portrays both the central contemporary (Mary) and biblical (Lot's Wife) female roles in the film. The banker's offspring was the first film role for Austrian and later Hollywood star Walter Slezak, son of opera singer Leo Slezak. Head cameraman was future film director Gustav Ucicky, son of Austrian Secessionist artist Gustav Klimt. Although there remains no actual record, the number of extras is believed to have ranged anywhere from 3,000–14,000. Among them were several significant names from Austrian and German cinema to come: director/actor Willi Forst, actors Paula Wessely and Hans Thimig, and film writer/theoretician Béla Balázs.

The production gave thousands of unemployed craftspeople work as set builders, technicians, carpenters, metalworkers, prop creators, and pyrotechnicians. Kolowrat managed to utilize much of Vienna's available film crew talent as cameramen, hair stylists, make-up artists, costume designers, tailors, wardrobe personnel, and their assistants. The film's architectural façades, including the mammoth temple of Sodom, were created by three set designers under the direction of Julius von Borsody (of the future Austrian filmmaking dynasty) and betray strong influence from Viennese *Jugendstil* and the Secessionist architecture of Josef Hoffmann. Alexander Korda's costly epic *Samson und Delila* (1922) for rival Vita-Film found similar success the same year, and made his wife Maria Corda a star. Unlike Kertész's epic, which locates its thematic duality by defining aspects of morality and immorality, Korda's concentrates on the opposition between innocence and decadence, and on class conflict in its contemporary story frame. Set in a doomed ocean liner on the high seas, the special effects suggest the *Titanic* myth and matched the film's immense biblical scenes.

Kolowrat and Kertész answered the inflation crisis of 1923 with another monumental epic, *Die Sklavenkönigin* (The slave queen, 1924). The film was conceived as a direct challenge to Hollywood, where Cecil B. DeMille was in production with his own biblical epic, *The Ten Commandments* (1923). Kertész turned to H. Rider Haggard's novel *The Moon of Israel* as the basis for his new spectacle, a sprawling costume drama climaxing with a scene in which Moses (Hans Marr) leads the Israelites through the parting of the Red Sea. Competing with DeMille for new effects, Kertész created a miniature set for the manipulation of the Red Sea sequence and in an astoundingly successful early matte-process, placed the actors between the parted and closing waves of the Red Sea. The film was a critical and popular success internationally, but Paramount Studios bought the American rights to the film in order to block distribution in the United States and allow DeMille's film to gain advantage over Kertész's version.[4]

The success of *Der junge Medardus* (*Young Medardus*, 1923), Kertész's monumental film of Arthur Schnitzler's play, which recreated war-torn Vienna during Napoleon's occupation, implied that popular epic films need not be biblical. It led to a unique but problematic collaboration between film and a name synonymous with Viennese literary and dramatic prestige, Hugo von Hofmannsthal. The author hailed cinema art and published "Der Ersatz für Träume" (The replacement for dreams) in 1921, one of the earliest essays dealing with mass reception of the medium.[5] His libretto for Richard Strauss's 1911 opera, *Der Rosenkavalier* (The cavalier of the rose) became the final grand-scale Austrian film of the silent era. Directed by *Das Cabinet des Dr. Caligari*'s Robert Wiene in 1925, the French coproduction boasted location shooting at Belvedere Palace and lavish sets recreating rococo Vienna crafted by the director of set design for the Vienna Opera, artist Alfred Roller. Approximately 10,000 extras were used in the film, which featured an international cast. Although Hofmannsthal soon disassociated himself from the project because his script adaptation was not used, the opulent visuals make for a landmark film.

Despite the global popularity of Wiene's German *Caligari* film, true cinematic expressionism never took root in Austrian cinema, and only three works stand out as an attempt to bring "Caligarism"[6] to Vienna: an obvious reworking of the original in Friedrich Feher's *Das Haus des Dr. Gaudeamus* (The house of Dr. Gaudeamus, 1921), which also utilized other stylistic elements such as *Jugendstil* and Italian futurism in its heady mixture; screenwriter Ida Jenbach's shock ending to H. K. Breslauer's satire on antisemitism, based on Hugo Bettauer's controversial novel *Die Stadt ohne Juden* (*The City Without Jews*, 1924); and Robert Wiene's *Orlacs Hände* (*The Hands of Orlac*, 1925). Directors of German monumental films of the era (some of them originating in the former Austria-Hungary, such as Fritz Lang and G. W. Pabst) were uninterested in biblical themes or finding a Hollywood-like internationalist formula. Given their access to larger production venues and markets than those available in Vienna, Berlin-based filmmakers concentrated on displaying the cutting-edge quality of film technology and art at Ufa. Lang's two-part saga based on myth and Richard Wagner, *Die Nibelungen* (*The Nibelungen*, 1924), and his blend of expressionism and New Objectivity in Thea von Harbou's futuristic fable on class and technology, *Metropolis* (1927), provided metaphors for modern society that were not as reductively moralistic as the biblical and historical epics of Vienna or Hollywood. The German counterparts instead attracted debate on power structures and social construction, on fate and mythology. Hungarian-born director Arzén von Cserépy's grandiose four-part series, *Fridericus Rex* (1922–23), enraged the Left and began a genre that celebrated Prussian history and authoritarian benevolence (into the Third Reich) in a way that would not have been possible in an Austrian Republic traumatized by its immediate Habsburg past, territorial collapse, and rejection by the states created from its imperial dissolution. Austrian silent film generally avoided imperial settings (and the 1914–18 war) except as a backdrop to comedy/satire, the opera/operetta film, musical biographies, and folk stories.

With *Das Spielzeug von Paris* (also know as *Célimène, la poupée de Montmartre*; *Red Heels*, 1925) Kolowrat and Kertész moved from monumentalism to lavish decadence in an attempt to match the flamboyant look and extravagant costumes of mid- to late 1920s Hollywood. Most importantly, however, the film's overriding theme of choice between love and art would become vital to Austrian film following the onset of sound. In 1927, Kolowrat produced *Die Pratermizzi* (Mizzi of the Prater), a nostalgic period piece with folk music set in Vienna's artist milieu, directed by Gustav Ucicky from a script by Walter Reisch. It was Kolowrat's final production but it set in motion the development of a new concept and style that would be associated with Austrian cinema into the 1960s.

Rather than the progressive social melodramas and proletarian films that briefly intersected with cinema genres of the Weimar Republic, or the biblical epics that gave nascent Austrian film its image, it was artist biographies and operetta themes enforcing the identity of Vienna as a city of music that, with the onset of sound, ultimately came to define the new Austrian national film style. In mild contradiction to Kolowrat's silent era theory, those films that emphasized their *romanticized* Austrian origins now attracted international attention. These various elements were best synthesized by actor and director Willi Forst (who claimed influence from French director René Clair, but detectably utilized aspects of the bourgeois tragedy and the theme of love versus art), and Kolowrat's *Pratermizzi* writer, Walter Reisch, into the Viennese Film, which gave Austrian cinema its most identifiable genre throughout the 1930s and 40s. Launched by the pair's Schubert romance film, *Leise flehen meine Lieder* (*Unfinished Symphony*, 1933), and followed by the Forst-Reisch *Maskerade* (*Masquerade in Vienna*, 1934), Reisch's *Episode* (1935), Forst's *Burgtheater* (Court theater, 1936), Reisch's *Silhouetten* (Silhouettes, 1936), and Austrian/transnational coproductions like Max Neufeld's *Hoheit tanzt Walzer* (*Highness Prefers a Waltz*, 1935), the core Viennese Film blended the traditions of the Austrian period film, the literary and cultural myth of the self-sacrificing Viennese artist, and the aural pleasures of opera/operetta film.[7]

So indelible was the genre's identification with Austria, that along with operetta and what can be called the melocomedy (a forerunner of the screwball style of Hollywood and specialty of the Austrian *Emigrantenfilm*, or emigrant cinema), it became part of the official cinematic mission for Forst and his emulators at the centralized Viennese studio, Wien-Film, during the Third Reich.[8] After figuring ambiguously in pan-German cultural propaganda, it carried over into the postwar era, eventually providing the stylistic basis for a series of sumptuous Agfacolor royal fantasies by Ernst Marischka and Franz Antel known as the *Kaiserfilme* (emperor films). Along with the reborn *Heimatfilm,* these imperial pictures gave Austria its 1950s commercial film boom (at the cost of developing a critical neorealism that critics had encouraged) and myths for nation building, and competed against Hollywood's Technicolor musicals and cold war biblical epics, as well as with later West German variants and coproductions.

The best known of the *Kaiserfilme* are Marischka's *Sissi* trilogy (1955–57) with Romy Schneider as the young Empress Elisabeth of Austria, but others like Antel's *Kaisermanöver* (Emperor's maneuver, 1954) and *Kaiserball* (Emperor's ball, 1956) are also classics of the form. Into the 1960s, cinematic Austria was thus to be found in re-adaption of the genre that held its forbidden identity in trust during the Reich — the Viennese Film. But unlike the late-silent/early-sound period, Habsburg and imperial Vienna fantasy now represented a "better" past that articulated high-art historical grandeur (along with the evergreen operetta film and composer biopics), a benevolent history framed in the context of visual pleasure. This durable genre, and its eventual deconstruction into sprawling musical-comedy and even sex farce before its demise in the 1960s, was in fact a successor to the Kolowrat epic formula of the 1920s. Ironically, the producer's insistence that the national cinema's success lay in being "less specifically Austrian" was now true once more: the *Kaiserfilme* were indeed less *accurately* Austrian in a world in which the neorealistic orientation of Italian, French, Scandinavian, and British film had changed the cinematic landscape. Also according to Kolowrat's concepts, these were highly accomplished entertainments that created employment in the film sector, exploited international fascination for a trend (in this case postwar royalty) in a grand Hollywood manner, and insured lasting national box-office success.

Critics continue to be conflicted about the value of these nostalgic/escapist films and their attempt to delineate Austria's past and culture away from Germany, and to solidify a positive national identity for tourism, while ultimately fighting a losing battle against television and Hollywood imports. The small critical Austrian film that began in an impoverished independent fashion in the wake of the collapse of Vienna's commercial film industry in the late 1960s had no other choice but to depict a real Austria to the Austrians and abandon market-driven concepts of entertaining on an international scale. It was greeted with a different kind of national and then international attention as it matured into the late 1990s and early 2000s. In this broadly defined new wave, Austrian auteurs looked back to the socially critical and proletarian melodramas of the silent and early sound era that had been suppressed by the internationalist studio entertainment style of Kolowrat and his legacy.

See also:

- 14 February 1924: *Die Nibelungen* Premieres, Foregrounds "Germanness"
- 29 February 1935: *Der alte und der junge König* Instrumentalizes Myth of Prussian Nationalism
- 22 December 1955: *Sissi* Trilogy Bridges Hapsburg to Hollywood through Hybrid Blend of Film Genres

Notes

[1] Günter Krenn points out that these reportages were masterpieces of narrative cinema in their own right. Günter Krenn, "Der bewegte Mensch — Sascha Kolowrat," in *Elektrische Schatten: Beiträge zur österreichischen Stummfilmgeschichte*, ed. Francesco Bono, Paolo Caneppele, Günter Krenn (Vienna: Filmarchiv Austria, 1999), 37–46; here 41–42.

[2] Krenn, "Der bewegte Mensch," 42.

[3] Gyöngyi Balogh, "Die Anfänge zweier internationaler Filmkarrieren: Mihály Kertész und Sandor Korda," in *Elektrische Schatten: Beiträge zur österreichischen Stummfilmgeschichte*, 83.

[4] Elisabeth Büttner and Christian Dewald, "Michael Kertész. Filmarbeit in Österreich bzw. bei der Sascha Filmindustrie A.-G., Wien, 1919–1926," in *Elektrische Schatten: Beiträge zur österreichischen Stummfilmgeschichte*, 101–37; here 106.

[5] See Assenka Oksiloff, "Archaic Modernism: Hofmannsthal's Cinematic Aesthetics," *The Germanic Review* 73:1 (1998): 70–85.

[6] Fritz, *Im Kino*, 106.

[7] Rather than the generally understood concept of the Viennese Film as one merely emphasizing the clichés of the city and its myth as a nexus of music and charm, I refer to the stricter definition used to categorize the Forst/Reisch creations and its development into the late 1940s. These had specific formalistic and narrative elements — most importantly the theme of sacrificing personal life and love for artistic creation.

[8] The term refers to Austria's secondary film industry between 1933–38, which included émigré talent from Germany and Austrian talent deemed racially "unacceptable" for films exported to Germany. These films were mostly coproduced with studios and talent in Hungary and Czechoslovakia (but also Netherlands and Sweden). It featured such stars as Hans Jaray, Franziska Gaal, and S. Z. Sakall in mostly Hollywood-style comedies and musical films, and was both popularly and critically successful at home and in international (including US) distribution.

29 November 1923: Karl Grune's *Die Straße* Inaugurates "Street Film," Foreshadows Film Noir

Anton Kaes

IF THE STREET IS the quintessential site of urban modernity, Karl Grune's underappreciated feature film *Die Straße* (*The Street*, 1923) epitomizes German modernity in all its ambivalence. The film investigates the experience of a nameless protagonist who suddenly decides to flee his domestic sphere to seek adventure in the nocturnal city streets. Driven by desire, he pursues a prostitute, gets entangled in a card game, and barely escapes being framed for murder. After a night in the city, which has seen him alternately exhilarated, frenzied, and forlorn, he returns home. His wife silently serves him the warmed-up soup from the night before. The quest is over, the allure of the street now proven dangerous.

The film begins with the protagonist watching moving shadows thrown from the street window to the ceiling. Passing vehicles refract the light into myriad luminous rays and produce a flicker effect reminiscent of film projection. As if in a movie, he sees a flaneur address a woman and follow her. Transfixed and aroused by the spectacle, the man sits up, visibly yearning for the bustling life behind the shadows. He looks out the window, down onto the street. Another space — urban and kinetic — opens up. A close-up of his face registers his captivated gaze. In a film-within-the-film insert, demarcated as a daydream, the film shows us what he imagines seeing: cars and trains in wild motion, thrill-seekers enjoying themselves on fairground rides, a circus clown making faces, an organ-grinder. The final image, held longer than all other shots, is of a smiling young woman who beckons him with her eyes. Compressed within a frame, these overlapping vignettes of the city produce, like a cubist painting, multiple perspectives, temporal simultaneity, and dizzying dynamics. The window itself has become the screen (doubling the actual screen) as we see the man watch the spectacle in his own home. Gripped by sudden impulse, the man grabs his hat and umbrella, runs out the door, down the stairs, and into the street. The camera cuts away from him to an endless procession of vehicles and pedestrians streaming by; he has become no more than a particle swept along in the maelstrom of a busy metropolitan street at nightfall.

It may have been this scene that caught Siegfried Kracauer's interest as he engaged with *Die Straße* in several reviews, calling it the first film in which urban modernity is expressed in ways only available through film.[1] The urban flaneur (also an object of fascination for Walter Benjamin) loses himself for the moment and merges with the urban environment in a delirious state of *Straßenrausch* (street frenzy).[2] Because silent film puts people and things on the same representational plane, they become interchangeable. For Kracauer, the big city commodified life to the extent that human subjects became mere objects. In a review of Grune's *Die Straße*, Kracauer wrote:

> The individuals of the big city streets have no sense of transcendence, they are only outer appearance, like the street itself, where so much is going on without anything really happening. The swirl of the characters resembles the whirl of atoms: they do not meet, but rather bump up against each other, they drift apart without separating. Instead of living connected with things, they sink down to the level of inanimate objects: of automobiles, walls, neon lights, irrespective of time, flashing on and off. . . . Love is copulation, murder is accident, and tragedy never occurs. A wordless and soulless coexistence of directed automobiles and undirected desires.[3]

Kracauer's analysis of the reification and instrumental rationality pervading modern city life suggests the extent to which the urban landscape had radically reshaped the status and role of the subject in the city. This revolutionary shift may explain the fascination that the metropolitan street held in the 1920s for philosophers and filmmakers alike. It was in the medium of film that the modern subject could be made visible as fragmented (in close-ups), minimized (in high-angle shots of masses), and observed by the surveilling gaze of the camera.

Such contradictory reactions to urban experience encapsulate the range of emotions associated with the big city throughout modern history, running the gamut from intoxication and elation to condemnation and feelings of anxiety and apocalypse. *Die Straße* resonates with these attitudes, ultimately emphasizing the negative view that responded to the historical moment in which the film appeared. Only three weeks before the film opened, on 9 November 1923, Hitler and his followers had marched through the streets of Munich, intending to overthrow the government (the putsch and the "national revolution" were stopped within hours); on 16 November, the wildly galloping inflation had finally come to a halt (the rentenmark was introduced after the exchange rate to the dollar exceeded 4000 billion marks); unrest and separatist activities continued in the occupied Rhineland; and Communist-inspired revolts in Saxony and Hamburg at the end of October had cost several lives. Assassinations in broad daylight, violent mass demonstrations, and street fights offered an apocalyptic scenario of a civil war raging within Germany that left its citizens confused, fearful, agitated. *Die Straße* makes no explicit reference to these political events, but implicitly takes part in the denigration of the public sphere. It depicts the street as a perilous site, rife with vice and crime, doubly harmful because of its seductive lure. The film is about the politics (and the price) of desire: blinded by his hunger for life, the protagonist enters the street as a phantasmagorical space in which appearances deceive and imagination runs wild. Women are prostitutes, men gamblers, cheats, and murderers, the street itself a cesspool of cruelty and decadence.

Die Straße inaugurated a filmic subgenre, the *Straßenfilm* (street film), that at the time was seen in opposition to the *Kammerspielfilm* (chamber play film), named after the intimate *Kammerspiel*, which Max Reinhardt had developed at the turn of the century for the staging of intimate, psychologically complex melodramas. Examples like Lupu Pick and Carl Mayer's *Scherben* (*Shattered*, 1921) and *Sylvester* (*New Year's Eve*, 1924); and Leopold Jessner's *Hintertreppe* (*Backstairs*, 1921) explore psychic spaces, emphasizing subtle gestures and silences that speak volumes. These films unfold their melodramatic plots (keeping to the Aristotelian unity of space and time) in a domestic narrative with claustrophobic sets consisting of bedroom, kitchen, and stairs. An occasional glimpse of the dark and gray outside provides no relief from the unremitting gloom of the private sphere, with all its repressed and pent-up emotions that inexorably lead to murder or suicide. These films present the criminal act as an escape from the unbearably monotonous lives in which the protagonists find themselves. As with Naturalist theater, the working-class or lower middle-class characters are shown to be essentially instinct-driven creatures without a language, and whose lack of speech and rational thought finds refuge in compulsive gestures and physical violence. Silent film, with its emphasis upon gesture and facial expression, as well as close-ups and extreme light/dark contrasts, was the perfect medium for communicating unspoken and inexpressible pathos. F. W. Murnau's *Der letzte Mann* (*The Last Laugh*, 1924), not unlike *Die Straße*, juxtaposes two settings: the static, narrow, and repressive one of the home (the realm of old haggard housewives) and the mobile, cosmopolitan, and adventurous site of the street with its elegant hotel, glistening streets, and flirtatious young women. Again, as in *Die Straße*, the glorious life of the big city is shown as deceptive: on account of his age, the man loses his job as a hotel porter and is stripped of his uniform. The experience of the street as an alluring but ultimately ruinous site is replayed in many other films of the period: G. W. Pabst's *Die freudlose Gasse* (*Joyless Street*, 1925), *Tagebuch einer Verlorenen* (*Diary of a Lost Girl*, 1929), and *Die Büchse der Pandora* (*Pandora's Box*, 1929), as well as Bruno Rahn's *Dirnentragödie* (The tragedy of a prostitute, 1927) and Josef von Sternberg's *Der blaue Engel*

(*The Blue Angel*, 1930). Even Murnau's *Sunrise*, made for Fox Studios in Hollywood in 1927, follows the basic grammar of the Weimar street film: a simple farmer is drawn to the city by a woman who conjures up a montage of luminous city attractions similar to the one in *Die Straße*. At the very end, after the woman dares him to murder his wife, he wakes up to reality and, with his wife saved, returns home. As moral tales of urban living, these films work through escapist fantasies only to reject them, a structure that is similar to the movie experience itself: after exposing oneself to transgression and the dark side of human nature, we return from the alternative dream space into the reality of daily life.

One of the last silent films, Joe May's crime film *Asphalt* (1929), again exhibits the characteristic nexus of the street film: forbidden sexuality and transgression of the law in the milieu of a hectic and sensually animated metropolis. A young policeman falls in love with a young jewel thief and, because of her, falls under suspicion of having murdered her former lover. Out of a sense of duty, his own father, a senior constable, is forced to arrest him. But the woman, who herself has fallen in love with the policeman, testifies that he acted in self-defense. The pulp fiction material, signaled by the subtitle "The Policeman and Diamond Else," was elevated through high production values that spared no expense. As with other street films, even the outdoor shots were highly stylized, their interior and exterior sets all studio-built, resulting in a completely controlled "realism." "This film was created from the visual possibilities of the milieu and its effects upon the life of individuals," wrote the producer Erich Pommer. "This street is no longer merely environment, no longer background. Fate appears, and the path of an individual is altered, naturally, simply, and nevertheless incomprehensibly. A scene springs to life, its emissions alter a person's life. The street becomes, then, a symbol of human life — an unending conjoining of fates."[4]

In this way, the street became the existential site of modernity, in which the individual is both the object of, and unwitting participant in, a series of incomprehensible and uncontrollable processes. The dynamization of the setting in the street film is only a symptom of how the urban landscape had radically reshaped the relationship of the subject to his surroundings. In this genre, the street stands emblematic for the metropolis, a central theme of literary modernism from Rainer Maria Rilke's *Die Aufzeichnungen des Malte Laurids Brigge* (*The Notebooks of Malte Laurids Brigge*, 1910) to Alfred Döblin's *Berlin Alexanderplatz* (1929), from Georg Heym's poem "Gott der Stadt" ("God of the City," 1911) to Bertolt Brecht's poetry collection entitled *Aus dem Lesebuch für Stadtbewohner* (A primer for those who live in cities, 1926–27). Like the rich literature about the big city, the street film bears witness to Germany's tormented experience of modernity.

The street film also developed a visual grammar for the crime stories that take place in public spaces: streets, stations, squares, towers and derelict buildings that loom over or close in on the protagonist who tries — in vain — to escape his fate. Classic urban crime film such as Fritz Lang's *M* (1931) and the entire genre of American film noir partakes of this tradition. It is not surprising that in the 1940s and 1950s, many of the exile filmmakers in Hollywood reinvented the traditional American gangster film in the image of the Weimar street film. Enamored of those films for their angst-ridden look and their existential message, French film critics after the Second World War dubbed the American street film "film noir." Titles like *The Naked Street*, *Asphalt Jungle*, *The Street with No Name*, *Scarlet Street*, and *Sunset Boulevard* suggest film noir's affinity to the street film genre and its emphasis on sex, crime, and the social order. Fritz Lang, Billy Wilder, Robert Siodmak, among many others, used techniques that derived from what critics called the German School: low-key lighting, heavy shadows, sharply angled architecture, and subjective camera angles that suggested dislocation and disorientation, fear and paranoia — the dark side of urban modernity. Film noir's emphasis on milieu, mood and atmosphere (in combination with Hollywood's usual emphasis on action and editing) produced a distinct visual style that dates back to the German street film and it is still evident in today's neo-noir films and television crime serials.

See also:

- 23 December 1924: *Der Letzte Mann* Explores Limits of Modern Community
- 4 February 1930: *Menschen Am Sonntag* Provides New Model of Cinematic Realism
- 21 June and 30 August 1957: *Jonas* and *Berlin — Ecke Schönhauser* Link Urban Reconstruction to National Cinema in Both West and East

Notes

[1] Siegfried Kracauer, "Ein Film," *Frankfurter Zeitung* (4 February 1924). See also his reviews of the film in *Frankfurter Zeitung* (3 February 1924 and 5 May 1925).

[2] See Eckhardt Köhn, *Straßenrausch: Flanerie und kleine Form* (Berlin: Das Arsenal, 1989).

[3] Siegfried Kracauer, "Filmbild und Prophetenrede," *Frankfurter Zeitung* (5 May 1925).

[4] Erich Pommer, "Kritische Filmschau," *Deutsche Filmzeitung* (12 April 1929).

31 January 1924: Premiere of *Orlacs Hände* Marks Beginning of the End of Expressionism

Paul Coates

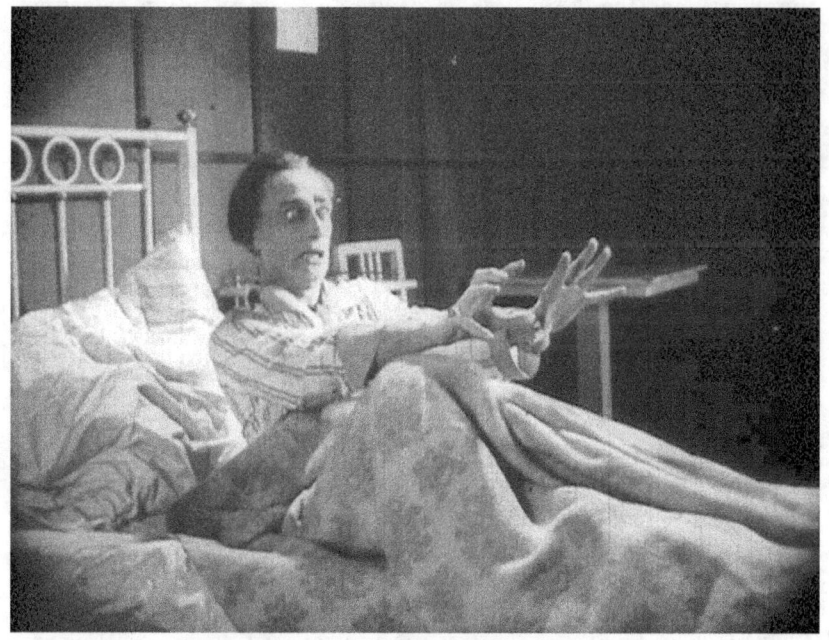

Orlac recoils from his wayward hands in
Die Hände Orlacs *(1924). DVD capture.*

ROBERT WIENE'S ORLACS HÄNDE (*The Hands of Orlac*, 1924), one of the few surviving works from his 1924 to 1926 period as the star director of Vienna's Pan Film, serves as an appropriately ambiguous marker of the moment of "the beginning of the end" of expressionism, as an expressionist sense of horrific fantasy that envelops reality was replaced by a New Objectivity that cast fantasy in terms of individual derangement, and even outright deception. Wiene's earlier *Das Cabinet des Dr. Caligari* (*The Cabinet of Dr. Caligari*, 1920), which has been characterized as the expressionist film par excellence, has at times threatened to engulf Wiene's later work within its expressionist shadow. The terms in which Uli Jung and Walter Schatzberg criticize John D. Barlow for highlighting only the expressionist motifs in *Orlacs Hände*, however, suggest its positioning at a transitional moment: "The film's motifs seem to fit his thesis, whereas the representation of these motifs does not. Consequently, he exaggerates the significance of the expressionist motifs and neglects the many nonexpressionist elements of the film."[1] This double status reflects the film's own transformation from a work of horror and possible delirium to a criminal investigation with a robustly material villain located firmly outside the mind of Paul Orlac, the protagonist. An expressionist preoccupation with uncanny doubling, phantoms, trauma, substitution, imminent apocalypse, and the death-dealing qualities of modernity's machines and exact time-keeping (think, for instance, of Freder's agony when seeking to synchronize himself with the Moloch machine clock in Lang's *Metropolis*, 1927) gives way to a rationalist disclosure that the supernatural is only apparent, the specters are physical, and science brings healing knowledge. This "beginning of the end" of expressionism in *Orlacs Hände* also inaugurates its director's movement away from the school with which he most completely identified. Wiene's best-known films — *Dr. Caligari*, *Genuine* (1920), *Raskolnikow* (1923) — had matched visual stylization to the disturbed consciousness of a male protagonist, a style that Lotte Eisner later faulted in her assessment of *Genuine*: "The set was muddled and overloaded" and "the naturalistic actors just vanished into it."[2]

The ramifying central event of *Orlacs Hände* sees a railway accident rob Paul Orlac of his hands, his piano-playing gift, and his reason for living. Shortly after an operation sought by his wife Yvonne has given him new hands, he lies in bed as she visits. As she prepares to kiss his bandaged hands, a mysterious face appears in the upper right of the screen. Orlac perceives it as staring at his hands and laughing, but when Yvonne turns her head in its direction it has vanished, prompting spectators to grant it an uncanny provenance as either the real ghost of Vasseur, the executed criminal whose hands have replaced Orlac's, or an hallucination by Orlac himself, whose trauma may threaten his sanity. Shortly thereafter, as he sleeps, his bed appears as a matchbox-sized image in the screen's bottom left-hand corner. A cloud that resolves into a larger version of the watching head appears right of screen, after which the clenched fist of an enormous arm pushes straight into the bed from the upper right-hand corner. This may seem simply dreamlike, but since Paul, awaking in terror, subsequently discovers a note stating that his new hands belonged to a murderer, the oneiric intersects enigmatically with reality's material transactions. As Paul comes to fear that evil is inherent in the hands, flowing from them into his soul and rendering him his father's murderer, it is little wonder that he declares himself unable to distinguish truth from dream. Distraught, he exudes the terror of those hands, either extending them before him, in a never-ending sleepwalk, as if metaphorically holding them "at arm's length," like Vasseur's deadly dagger, or clamping them rigidly to his side. Splayed, they are either held up for inspection, or bristlingly electrified by some unseen force. Reminiscent as they are of the hands of Nosferatu in *Nosferatu: Eine Sinfonie des Grauens* (*Nosferatu*, 1922), they reinforce Orlac's terrified self-image as a creature given over to night, as if he were wondering whether his own true name might be the "Count Orlok" of the earlier film.

Within Weimar cinema a small set of films transforms the doubling motif by placing the double *within* the body, at its extremity, knotting together hand, glove, and "hand-as-shadow." In doing so they appear to begin declining the phantom world of expressionism into a greater corporeality, anticipating the New Objectivity best represented by that masterchronicler of human physicality, G. W. Pabst. In this regard, *Orlacs Hände* can be grouped with *Schatten — eine nächtliche Halluzination* (*Warning Shadows*, 1923) and *Metropolis* (1927). Whereas the first two films focus intensively on one character's hands, a more varied use of real and metaphorical prosthetic hands shapes *Metropolis*, whose industrialist Fredersen places a Napoleonic hand inside his jacket, whose mad inventor Rotwang has lost a hand, and whose militant workers are described as hands directed by a head doubly, and therefore schizophrenically, embodied in Fredersen and Rotwang. A similar metaphor of head-hand subordination is employed by the figure of Dr. Serral, who has operated on Orlac's hands, and whose response to Orlac's worry whether his hands will play again is that hands obey head, spirit, and will. Inasmuch as any penalty for Serral's possibly overweening experiment appears to recoil upon Orlac, the "sorcerer's apprentice" scenario of several key Weimar films gives way to a concern with otherness as a fifth column within the patient's body: at its borders, perhaps, but working its way up into it insidiously.

Allegorically minded readers might ponder the scenario's implications for the self-understanding of an Austria stripped of empire by the war, which is strongly suggested by the devastation of the train wreck. (Indeed, war trauma imagery recurs when Orlac returns home and stands immobile within the door, unable to step forward to greet Yvonne.) At the same time, the Professor's secure anchoring in a realm of unproblematic medical expertise permits the final neat operation that separates madness from science, and fantasy (Nera's claim that he is Vasseur, whose head has been reattached after guillotining, was deemed ludicrous by Béla Balázs) from the feasible (hands can indeed be reconnected to arms).[3] The doctor's mention of the importance of the will ascribes to it a role in mastering internal chaos inevitably reminiscent of Prussian disciplinary rhetoric and anticipatory of that of the National Socialists. Moreover, the frequency with which characters stand behind one another translates into a recurrent image of a situation in which, like the German army of 1918, one might be "stabbed in the back": in which even the doctor's social position does not bestow security. The frequency with which characters either adopt this position, or fail to face one another (in the hospital, Orlac's wife lays her head *beside* his) validates Orlac's fearfulness by suggesting an inherent danger in standing before a person, within hand's reach. (It also, of course, allows audiences to observe both faces simultaneously within a mise-en-scène with a theatrical predilection for long and extreme long shots — criticized by some viewers — and no shot-counter-shot mechanism.)[4] On learning that Vasseur was innocent, Orlac voices no regrets over his death but simply rejoices that his own hands have remained clean. The real villain, Nera, the assistant of Dr. Serral, fashioned wax impressions of Vasseur's fingerprints and stamped them upon rubber gloves he used to murder with impunity, killing Orlac's father before blackmailing Orlac himself as the presumptively guilty inheritor. This revelation sets up an ending that rhymes with the beginning, as Orlac's hands close around Yvonne's head to stroke her hair, as envisaged in his opening note to her. Not surprisingly, they occupy the middle of the screen. The satisfaction in the film's rounding off probably differentiates this ending from that of *Caligari*, whose eponymous hero's donning of his glasses lends a sinister air to his mention of a cure for his patient. Or does this ending retrospectively drain the earlier one of some of its ambiguity?

Among other things, *Orlacs Hände* dramatizes artists' fears of becoming disposable, sacrificeable parts in a smoothly running modernity: fears that are structurally, and possibly significantly, homologous with contemporary ones of the contamination of the body politic by engrafted "alien parts," such as a Lombroso-like congenitally criminal class, or another race. Orlac may disclaim criminality, but the doubling endemic to expressionism, to which this film is more than half-indebted, raises the possibility of classifying much of its narrative as an artist's denial of responsibility for deeds whose symbolic, dreamlike enactment is nevertheless in a sense psychically all-too-real. The scenario's undertones recall Thomas Mann's contemporary assertions of a kinship between criminal and artist, a theme well known to Wiene himself from *Caligari*, whose eponymous protagonist is both. If Orlac's opening letter to Yvonne envisages how her body trembles under his caress, can he claim complete innocence of intentions of sowing fear?

Orlacs Hände is preoccupied also with precise temporal measurements: the thirty minutes before Paul's scheduled homecoming, the exact time of his train's arrival, the brief respite the four Kafkaesque, synchronized creditors allow Yvonne. In expressionist fashion, this preoccupation with time-keeping correlates with a view of modernity as an instrument of amputation: events can be cut off before they have run their course, merely because of a mechanical measure of time, a stopwatch held by Procrustes. Other forms of mechanism and technique also suggest danger.

The doctor says he will give Paul back to Yvonne piece by piece (as if he has disintegrated), starting with the face. The cutting mechanism of film itself separates the pianist's hands from his body even before he loses them, while modern media seem to target him for loss with a newspaper headline announcing "Paul Orlac's last concert." Does this announcement draw one possible conclusion from the fact that his piano playing occurs in Benjamin's "age of technical reproducibility" and has been recorded (after the accident, he disconsolately stares at a record bearing his name), as if rendering artists themselves superfluous? Such suspicions concerning modernity represent equivalent surface-structure transformations of a deep-seated expressionist fear of the machine: thus the train wreck becomes a metaphor for the "machine" of the First World War, which at least one contemporary reviewer felt it recalled.[5] Meanwhile, Paul's victimization appears to be intensified by a newspaper language whose apparently rational pursuit of economy translates paradoxically into an economy of desire that pegs Vasseur's hands as "Mörderhänden" (murderer-hands), shedding adjectives and fusing nouns to imbue the part that is the hand with the entire identity of the person who has committed one particular act with them: exactly what Paul himself fears. Like the shadows characterizing expressionist mise-en-scène, the overspill of that action swells to blot out all the other deeds the hands might perform. The degree to which parts metonymize (absorb) wholes is underlined when Nera instructs the maid Regine not to seduce Orlac, as one might expect, but his hands.

Orlacs Hände mediates complex interactions within expressionism itself — in particular, that between visions underwriting a supernaturalism and the hallucinations of madness. (For instance: is that fist punching down into the bed otherworldly, or an exteriorization of a dream-enlarged image of a material reality? Is Balázs correct to link the darkness lapping many images to "the mystical"?)[6] The copresence within expressionism of supernaturalist or visionary explanations of fantastic events and their materialist ascription to madness can be seen as potentially deflating the visions from the outset, rendering more comprehensible the speed with which the antisupernaturalist New Objectivity supplanted it. Since this internal tension resembles that of *Caligari*, with its opening that mentions spirits abroad in the world, but an end that identifies its starting point as the site of delusive visions, an asylum, one may wonder whether expressionism in film in general was in a sense "ending" even as it "began."

This internal duality is reflected in that of the film's legacy, its transitional status rendering it partly compatible with, and hence equally partially assimilable by, both the "primary process" movement par excellence, surrealism, and a Hollywood rooted in realism. If the secondary processes of reason and realism finally prevail, as they do in New Objectivity, this closing parti pris is surely the main reason why this narrative alone among expressionist ones should have passed almost directly into an American cinema that habitually dismantled expressionism into a set of shock effects to be deployed strategically. Thus *Orlacs Hände* is the exact source of *Mad Love* (1935) — which reworks the Maurice Renard novel underlying Wiene's film — and is strongly echoed in *The Beast with Five Fingers* (1946), their continuity underscored by Peter Lorre's appearance in both Hollywood films. The revolt of self against self parabolically embodied in that of a hand, being partial, is more manageable than that of the double who appropriates all the body; the scenario, less dark in its upshot than *Caligari*'s, is more friendly to Hollywood than that film's. Moreover, the debunking of visionary magic as trickery (or happily fading dream) would be a frequent closing gambit of American film, its most-beloved instance crowning *The Wizard of Oz* (1939), with the unmasking of the eponymous Wizard. Nevertheless, because *Orlacs Hände* is a genuinely transitional work, expressionism persists intensely in some of its parts. An expressionist aura of derangement surrounds Conrad Veidt's haunted, traumatized tottering, planting a question mark in the margins of realism's eventual triumph. Meanwhile, of course, the film's fixation on the fetish of the disembodied, living hand was shared by the surrealists, prompting Luis Buñuel to set one crawling on the ground, like a human version of one of his beloved insects, both early in his career (*Un Chien Andalou*, 1929) and, much later, in *El ángel exterminador* (*The Exterminating Angel*, 1962). He and his fellow surrealists would also have discerned tell-tale meaning in Orlac's hiding of his dagger in his piano — as would have Freud.[7]

See also:

- 23 May 1920: *Das Cabinet des Dr. Caligari* Brings Aesthetic Modernism to the Fairground
- 13 October 1922: Alexander Kolowrat-Krakowsky Sets Course of Austrian (Inter)National Film
- 4 September 1959: *Der Frosch mit der Maske* Moves Popular Cinema from Idyllic Pastures to Crime-Infested City Streets

Notes

[1] Uli Jung and Walter Schatzberg, *Beyond Caligari: The films of Robert Wiene* (Oxford: Berghahn, 1999), 116–17.

[2] Lotte Eisner, *The Haunted Screen: Expressionism in German Cinema and the Influence of Max Reinhardt* (London: Secker and Warburg, 1973), 27.

[3] Béla Balázs, *Schriften zum Film. Erster Band "Der sichtbare Mensch." Kritiken und Aufsätze 1922–1926* (Munich, DDR-Berlin: Carl Hanser, 1982), 305.

[4] Ibid.

[5] See Andrew J. Webber, "The Manipulation of Fantasy and Trauma in *Orlacs Hände*," in *Words, Texts, Images*, ed. Katrin Kohl and Ritchie Robertson (Bern: Peter Lang, 2002), 157n5.

[6] Balázs, *Schriften zum Film*, 305.

[7] A list of some other films featuring disembodied living hands may be found at www.eatmybrains.com/showtopten.php?id=29. Their low-grade horror status would, of course, have been no impediment to surrealist enthusiasm for them.

14 February 1924: *Die Nibelungen* Premieres, Foregrounds "Germanness"

Adeline Mueller

In full costume, the cast of Die Nibelungen *poses with the director and crew, ca. 1924. Credit: Deutsche Kinamathek, Berlin.*

LIKE ALL FILMS, Fritz Lang and Thea von Harbou's *Die Nibelungen* (*The Nibelungen*, 1924) invites multiple readings, but its polysemy bears unique scars. The epic two-part film was adapted from a medieval poem whose composite character had already left it amenable to centuries of reinscription; from the outset, it was the locus of competing cultural and political interests, a token of Germany's self-image following the First World War. Ever since that time, the film has been read as either a balm to a wounded nation, or a subtle critique of the decadent and ultimately self-destructive pursuit of fatalist glory. The first reading is often associated with screenwriter Harbou, the second with director Lang, in an interpretive clash that establishes *Die Nibelungen* as an exemplar of increasingly specialized, competitive models of film authorship. Yet the way these opposing subtexts have been reinforced by later interpreters shows how difficult it is to avoid the pull of the national in the reception of an interwar-period German film, especially one based on a national myth.

The circumstances of *Die Nibelungen*'s premiere did much to distinguish it from other blockbusters of the early 1920s. Part 1, *Siegfried*, opened at the largest picture palace in Germany, Berlin's 1,740-seat Ufa-Palast am Zoo, with the usual contingent of celebrities, press, and cinephiles now augmented by a host of local and national political figures that included the president of the Reichstag, members of Parliament, the chief of Berlin police, the director of the Reichsbank, and the defense minister. The Ufa-Palast's atmosphere of sacralized excess — which extended from the Gothic-scripted premiere invitation to the lobby decorations reproducing the obsessive symmetries of the film's mise-en-scène to the grandly somber original musical score performed by the seventy-member Ufa-Palast orchestra — suggested that attendance was akin to participation in a holy rite, approximate to one of the ceremonies shown in the film at Worms Cathedral.[1] In her contribution to the lavish souvenir program distributed at the premiere, Harbou added to the transcendental atmospherics, declaring that the legend of the Nibelungen had "chosen" her (not the other way around) in order to remind Germany of a glory that it had almost forgotten.[2] The film's opening titles included the stirring dedication, "Dem deutschen Volke zu eigen" (for the German people), while the colossal scale of the picture — with its extravagant set design, elaborate special effects, and hundreds of extras — appeared at one stroke to efface the previous two years of devastating hyperinflation. The grandest and most expensive to date of producer Erich Pommer's films, *Die Nibelungen* was certainly a "watershed in the history of filmmaking," as one trade paper put it. But as the same article argued, it was also intended, at least on the part of Ufa (Universum Film A.G.), to serve as an olive branch to the Entente Forces, an alternate peace treaty that would for once benefit Germany, both financially and politically. Pommer engineered a massive banquet following the premiere at which some 170 government and business leaders gathered to hear Foreign Minister Gustav Stresemann declare *Die Nibelungen* a masterpiece of education and edification for the German people and for the world, a means of bringing all nations closer together in mutual sympathy and understanding.[3]

Many of the elements that characterized *Die Nibelungen*'s initial presentation were later marshaled as evidence for what is still the most influential critical account of the film, Siegfried Kracauer's *From Caligari to Hitler*. In it, Kracauer read the film's static blocking, claustrophobic visual patterning, and towering physical and natural landscapes as adumbrations of the fascist triumph of the ornamental that would soon characterize Nazi ideology. The fact that *Die Nibelungen* was beloved by the Nazi leadership appears at first glance to bear out Kracauer's proleptic reading. Four months after the 1933 seizure of power — and two months after Goebbels identified *Die Nibelungen* as one of four model German films, in a speech to an association of German filmmakers — the Ufa-Palast am Zoo hosted the premiere of a reedited, soundtracked version of *Siegfried*, now titled *Siegfrieds Tod*, which was heralded in the press as "a truly German film."[4] And the Third Reich's appropriation of the film did not end there: in 1935, Goebbels was planning a completely new, all-talking film adaptation of the legend, with Harbou herself on board as screenwriter. According to an entry in Goebbels's diary, the script was complete by April and casting was about to begin. The project never came to fruition, but as late as 1941 Hitler was still hoping for yet another remake of this "genuine classic of German film art."[5]

Kracauer's take on *Die Nibelungen* has prompted a range of counter-arguments and elaborations, nearly all of which sanction his backshadowing even when taking issue with it. Some historians emphasize that those same visual elements that appeared protofascist to Kracauer may be just as plausibly attributed to the influence of the *Wiener Werkstätte*, German Romantic painting, or even the medieval epic itself and contemporaneous decorative and architectural aesthetics. Others have pointed to the collapse in the second film, *Kriemhilds Rache* (*Kriemhild's Revenge*, 1924), of the social order established in *Siegfried*, arguing that the sequel does not end up privileging the moral compass of the Burgundians over those of Brunhild or Etzel. Tom Gunning, for instance, asserts that the film is at least as much an elegy on the death of heroism as a rousing etiological myth or paean to German blood purity.[6] Gunning's perspective echoes comments Lang himself made in response to postwar critiques of the film by Kracauer and Lotte Eisner. In a 1968 letter taking issue with Eisner's observations on *Die Nibelungen*, Lang urged his fellow expatriate to revisit its source epic, the *Nibelungenlied*:

> You will see it is not at all a heroic poem of the *German people*; that's what the Rightist imbeciles before and under Hitler made it. . . .
>
> Even Harbou, who is a thorn in your side as much as mine, realized this. . . .
>
> It is a "heroic" poem of the ruling upper class! Where is there any reference to the people?!
>
> I saw the Burgundian kings with their magnificent robes as a decadent social class that was already on the decline.[7]

Lang insists here that his film was meant not as a rallying cry, but as a cautionary tale. And yet only a significant stretch of the imagination could square these remarks with Lang's own original subtitle to the film — *Ein deutsches Heldenlied* (A German heroic poem) — or with his hyperbolic rhetoric in the original souvenir program, in which he claimed the film would help bring about a "revival of the world of myth for the twentieth century."[8] It is even more difficult to substantiate Lang's assertion, eighteen years after her death, that Harbou's intentions had been concurrent with his own. The retroactive assignment of a critical subtext to the film, in other words, might in the end tell us more about California in 1968 than about Berlin in 1924.

No matter which historical moment we privilege, *Die Nibelungen*'s meaning proves elusive. If we look to the film itself, we find a set of inscrutable characters marching with severe grandeur and little in the way of relatable psychology toward a tragic end that is presented as virtually preordained. *Die Nibelungen*'s flawed heroes and sympathetic villains belie any simplistic good-evil dichotomy, and the intertitles that introduce each of its "Gesänge" (cantos) retain an archaizing distance from the events they report, eschewing moral commentary. Even the film's original score, which composer Gottfried Huppertz developed in close consultation with Lang and Harbou, undermines narrative authority at virtually every turn. For instance, the "voice" of the bardic character Volker — understood by many as a self-reflexive proxy for the film's implied author — constitutes an often problematic presence in the score, whether split among several instruments (as in Volker's introductory scene in *Siegfried*) or slipping between the realms of diegetic and nondiegetic music (as in the night-watch episode in *Kriemhilds Rache*). All told, *Die Nibelungen*'s skillful preservation of its sources' opacities, silences, and lacunae leaves the film as open to contradictory reappropriations as the materials on which it was based.

Some reviews, particularly those that followed the premiere of *Kriemhilds Rache*, resisted the triumphalist national rhetoric that surrounded *Siegfried*'s opening. In contrast to the studio-driven panegyric of the trade papers (which, if nothing else, demonstrates how much was at stake for the industry if this precedent-setting blockbuster failed), these oppositional reviews tended to appear more frequently in newspapers and general-interest periodicals. Journalist and author Kurt Pinthus observed that "the material of the Nibelungen is a crude tale of adventure, murder, loyalty and vengeance that is remote and alien to our hearts. With a sense of relief, we may safely conclude that this material will never again be put on the screen."[9] Even more revealing is screenwriter and critic Roland Schacht's somewhat rueful complaint about *Die Nibelungen*'s "fuss with Germanness . . . in a time when there is no such thing as Germanness."[10] At least some viewers, then, remained unconvinced that the film spoke to the concerns of interwar Germany. And yet the issue of "Germanness" persists, even in the midst of its very negation. It even vexes the author of the essay accompanying the 2008 DVD of the restored print, who leaves his own summary question — "Left or Right, black or white?" — unanswered.[11] It seems necessary, then, to continue to historicize and particularize the dichotomous, politically charged reception of *Die Nibelungen*. Only when we have more thoroughly succeeded in belaboring the issue can film historians hope to suggest other things to "fuss with."

See also:

- 11 December 1930: Ban of *All Quiet on the Western Front* Highlights Tensions over Sound Technology
- 11 May 1931: With Premiere of *M*, a Gala Hit Becomes a Cultural Controversy
- 22 January 2007: Film Establishment Attacks "Berlin School" as Wrong Kind of National Cinema

Notes

[1] Klaus Kreimeier, *The Ufa Story: A History of Germany's Greatest Film Company, 1918–1945*, trans. Robert and Rita Kimber (New York: Hill and Wang, 1996), 114.

[2] Thea von Harbou, "Vom Nibelungen-Film und seinem Entstehen," in *Die Nibelungen: Ein deutsches Heldenlied* [premiere souvenir program] (Berlin: Ufa, 1924), 7.

[3] "Der Wendepunkt," *Lichtbild-Bühne* 17, no 17 (16 February 1924): 9, 12.

[4] "'Siegfrieds Tod' begeistert in tönender Fassung: Zur Neuaufführung des Nibelungen-Films im Ufa-Palast am Zoo," *Kinematograph* 27, no. 102 (30 May 1933): 1. There appears to be no public evidence directly linking either Lang or Harbou to *Siegfrieds Tod*, although they were presumably at least aware of it; they and their biographers are pointedly silent on the 1933 version, whose credits list a "Franz Biermann" as responsible for the adaptation.

[5] Diary entry dated 22 November 1941. Joseph Goebbels, *Die Tagebücher von Joseph Goebbels: Teil II, Diktate, 1941–1945*, vol. 2, *Oktober-Dezember 1941*, ed. Elke Fröhlich (Munich: K. G. Saur, 1996), 344.

[6] Tom Gunning, *The Films of Fritz Lang: Allegories of Vision and Modernity* (London: British Film Institute, 2000), 43.

[7] Fritz Lang, Letter to Lotte Eisner, 3 October 1968, quoted in *Fritz Lang: Leben und Werk, Bilder und Dokumente*, ed. Rolf Aurich, Wolfgang Jacobsen, and Cornelius Schauber, English trans. Robin Benson et al. (Berlin: Jovis, 2001), 97–98. Emphasis Lang's.

[8] Fritz Lang, "Worauf es beim Nibelungen-Film ankam," in *Die Nibelungen: Ein deutsches Heldenlied*, 12–13.

[9] Kurt Pinthus, "Der Nibelungenfilm," *Das Tage-Buch* 18 (3 May 1924): 603, quoted in *Fritz Lang: Leben und Werk*, 96.

[10] Roland Schacht, *Das Blaue Heft: Freie Deutsche Bühnen Berlin*, quoted in Rainer Fabich, *Musik für den Stummfilm: Analysierende Beschreibung originaler Filmkompositionen*, European University Studies Series 36, Musicology 94 (Frankfurt: Lang, 1993), 196.

[11] Jan-Christopher Horak, [untitled essay], *Die Nibelungen* (dir. Fritz Lang), Kino Video, 2002, DVD.

10 May 1924: *Der Berg des Schicksals* Inaugurates the Genre of the "Mountain Film"

Kamaal Haque

The drama of ascent in Der Berg des Schicksals *(1924). DVD capture.*

MOVIEGOERS ATTENDING THE Theater am Nollendorfplatz in Berlin on 10 May 1924 were astounded. On the screen they beheld a dramatic story, filmed on-location and at great risk to cast and crew, about a mountain climber who loses his life trying to climb a new route. As a reviewer for the *Lichtbild-Bühne* exclaimed three days later, "A crowning achievement! A crowning achievement not only in the athletic arena, but also in photographic technique. Technique? No, no longer technique, but the highest art! Words are not powerful enough to describe what this film offers our eyes and our minds."[1] The reviewer and others who saw *Der*

Berg des Schicksals (The mountain of destiny) during its four-month run were witnessing the first fully formed example of the *Bergfilm* (mountain film). The earliest Alpine film dates back to at least 1901, when an unknown cameraman made a short film of the Matterhorn. In 1909, renowned mountain photographer Vittorio Stella filmed part of an Italian expedition to K2.[2] Yet it was Arnold Fanck, director and screenwriter of *Der Berg des Schicksals*, who merged on-location mountain filming with melodramatic plots to form a new cinematic genre, one that would flourish in the 1920s and 1930s but remained largely limited to the German-speaking world.

Traditional interpretations of the *Bergfilm* have followed several trajectories. Numerous critics have followed the lead of Siegfried Kracauer in declaring the *Bergfilm* a product of a protofascist aesthetic.[3] More recently, Eric Rentschler has drawn attention to the technological innovation required to shoot these works on-location, and Nancy Nenno has placed the contemporary interest in these films within the larger context of burgeoning Alpine tourism in the first part of the twentieth century.[4] Along these lines, it is important to recognize that *Bergfilme* reflected the ongoing technological and ideological developments of European mountaineering, responding to and shaping a growing cultural fascination with German heights.

Fanck's first forays into directing were a ski film, *Das Wunder des Schneeschuhs* (The miracle of skis, 1920), and the filming of an ascent of Monte Rosa, the second-highest mountain in the Alps, entitled *Im Kampf mit dem Berge* (In battle with the mountain, 1921). Both featured innovative on-location photography. Indeed, the cameramen's athletic abilities had to match those of the actors in order to film the sequences as Fanck wanted. The director coupled the mountain-climbing and artistic skills of his cameramen with the latest technology. Fanck bought and used a very expensive (and heavy!) Ernemann camera to shoot the slow-motion sequences in *Das Wunder des Schneeschuhs* (Fanck, 117–18). The weight of the camera equipment, the necessity of transporting it to often almost inaccessible shot locations, and the fragility of early film in the Alpine cold all posed substantial problems to filming, all of which Fanck overcame.

Fanck soon determined that combining the latest in film technology with daring Alpine athleticism would not secure the longevity of his film career or the genre. According to his autobiography, Fanck was approached by one viewer after the premiere of *Das Wunder des Schneeschuhs* and warned: "Your film is wonderful, Herr Fanck, and I congratulate you. Believe me, however, that you will not be able to have long-term success with films without dramatic plots. Man and his psychological experiences belong in [film], even in the mountains" (Fanck, 125). Fanck himself came to the same conclusion after noticing the reactions to his second film. Determined to make a film with a plot, he returned to the topic of skiing in the sequel to *Das Wunder des Schneeschuhs*, entitled *Eine Fuchsjagd auf Skiern durchs Engadin* (A fox hunt on skis through Engadin, 1922). This film, with a prolonged chase-sequence performed on skis, did not play the seminal role in the development of the *Bergfilm*, however. This success came with the release of *Der Berg des Schicksals*, which established Fanck as both the founder and master practitioner of the *Bergfilm*.

Der Berg des Schicksals dramatizes the true story of Carlo Garbari (Carbarie, in Fanck's version), who in 1897 attempted to climb the Campanile Basso in the Italian Dolomites. Upon failing to ascend a particularly difficult section for the fifth time, Garbari placed a sign at this point that read, "To this point and no further — no one will ever set foot on the peak of the Campanile Basso" (Fanck, 142). Garbari then changed his mind, removed the plaque, and attempted the climb once more, only to suffer a fatal fall. In *Berg des Schicksals*, Fanck embellishes upon the original by adding the story of the mountain climber's son, who later climbs the Campanile Basso as part of a rescue operation to save other climbers.

This pattern — in which a difficult, usually never-before-completed climb is attempted, the climbers encounter difficulties and need to be rescued — repeats itself in such Fanck films as *Der heilige Berg* (*The Holy Mountain*, 1926) and *Die weiße Hölle vom Piz Palü* (*The White Hell of Piz Palu*, codirected with G. W. Pabst, 1929), both of which, unlike *Der Berg des Schicksals*, are wholly fictional accounts. In these two later films, climbers attempt the dangerous north face of Alpine peaks, and in both cases one climber sacrifices himself for his climbing partners (successfully in *Die weiße Hölle vom Piz Palü*, in that the partners are rescued, and in vain in *Der heilige Berg*). In many ways, this progression of Arnold Fanck from *Der Berg des Schicksals* to *Der heilige Berg* and *Die weiße Hölle vom Piz Palü* reflects the changes in mountaineering in the early twentieth-century. Indeed, though it is often said that Fanck's ski films helped popularize skiing within the German-speaking world, his high-altitude mountain climbing films may also be seen as indices of his era's broader emergent interest in mountain climbing in the Alps and beyond.

The plot in *Berg des Schicksals* corresponds to the phase of classic alpinism, which was the middle of the nineteenth century, when most of the classic Alpine peaks were first climbed. By the early twentieth century, the focus of many mountaineers in the Alps had shifted toward attempting the more difficult routes on those peaks that had already been climbed. Chief among these "problems," as they were called, were the north faces of the Matterhorn, Grandes Jorasses, and Eiger. Although these routes were first climbed successfully in the 1930s, there were many attempts to scale them in the 1920s — the precise period in which Fanck was directing many of his most famous *Bergfilme* about such unsuccessful ventures. Films such as *Der Berg des Schicksals*, *Der heilige Berg*, and *Die weiße Hölle vom Piz Palü* prepared the German viewing public for the reports and newsreels from the Eiger, both of the unsuccessful attempts of 1935 and 1936 and the successful 1938 ascent.

The *Bergfilme* did not simply reflect developments in Alpine mountaineering; the genre was also instrumental in making the mountains known to a broader public. As Stefan König points out, Fanck introduced mountain scenery "to a majority of people for whom it was something distant and foreign. . . . Pleasure travel and tourism were limited to the upper-class. Those who did not live in or near the mountains were entirely unfamiliar with them."[5] Fanck's films contributed to the popularization of the mountains, particularly the Alps, as a real destination and as a virtual space of projection and identification. It is little coincidence that membership in the *Deutscher und Österreichischer Alpenverein* (German and Austrian Alpine Club, D.u.Ö.A.V.) grew exponentially in the early 1920s; the club tripled its size between 1919 and 1923, and by 1924 it boasted 250,000 members.[6]

Most famously, Fanck's films kindled the interest of a young Leni Riefenstahl. As she recounts it, Riefenstahl was waiting for a train when she saw a poster advertising *Der Berg des Schicksals*. So taken with the image of a mountain climber ascending a dangerous rock chimney, Riefenstahl not only missed her train, but also went immediately to a movie theater to see the film. The beauty of the mountains surprised her: "That mountains are so beautiful — who would have thought that! I was familiar with them through postcards — they look lifeless and frozen there and now they rushed in front of my eyes in unexpected grandeur. . . . I decided before the film was over to get to know the mountains" (quoted in Fanck, 151). Only a few weeks later, Riefenstahl herself traveled to the mountains, intent on acting in Fanck's next film. Her campaign was successful, and Riefenstahl would go on to star in several Fanck films before embarking on a directorial career of her own.

Today, of course, Riefenstahl is better remembered for her Nazi-era propaganda films, *Triumph des Willens* (*Triumph of the Will*, 1935) and *Olympia* (1938). Her presence in several *Bergfilme* inevitably raises questions concerning the genre's connections to National Socialism. Several critics have written on this issue, with the consensus being that although Nazis never appear in Fanck's *Bergfilme*, the films are, as Kracauer phrases it, "rooted in a mentality kindred to Nazi spirit."[7] This mentality consists of the exultation of feats of strength and will, coupled with a martial understanding of mountain climbing (besieging the mountain, then conquering it). A look to the history of German mountaineering in this time supports such a reading. Most sections of the D.u.Ö.A.V. had adopted the Aryan paragraphs by 1921. These clauses in the organization's bylaws allowed membership only to those of "Aryan" descent. The D.u.Ö.A.V. officially excluded all Jewish members in 1924. The preponderance of

Nazi thought among mountaineers led Adam Wandruszka to declare: "The Third Reich begins one thousand meters above sea level."[8] We should be cautious, however, about overstating the connection between alpinism and antisemitism with regard to Fanck's films — as Christian Rapp points out, the director made all of his most successful films prior to the Nazi takeover in 1933.[9] Yet there can be little doubt that Fanck's early mountain films participated in a popular culture of Alpinism with deep ties to the development of German fascism.

Beyond its most successful days in the late 1920s and early 1930s, the path of the *Bergfilm* has been winding. Fanck's most obvious influence was upon his actors Leni Riefenstahl and Luis Trenker, both of whom became successful directors, including as *Bergfilm* creators. Riefenstahl directed *Das blaue Licht* (*The Blue Light*, 1932), while Trenker is best known for *Der Berg ruft* (*The Mountain Calls*, 1937/1938). Fanck's films also exerted influence on the next generation of mountain documentarians. When mountaineering shifted its focus from the Alps to the Himalayas in the late 1930s, German-speaking filmmakers followed. The films that resulted from these expeditions, *Nanga Parbat* (1936) and *Kampf um den Himalaja* (Struggle for the Himalayas, 1938, released in 1951 as *Deutsche Himalaja-Expeditionen* [German Himalaya expeditions]), would be unthinkable without the pioneering on-location high-altitude camerawork by Fanck and his cameramen.

More recently, the *Bergfilm* has seen a rebirth in German cinema. The film *Nordwand* (*North Face*, 2008), directed by Philipp Stölzl, adopts many of the conventions of the genre in telling the story of the ill-fated attempt of the first ascent of the Eiger North Face, adding, however, explicit connections between Nazism and the conquest of the Alps missing in the classical mountain film. *Nanga Parbat* (Vilsmaier, 2010) tells the story of the 1970 ascent of this Himalayan peak from the point of view of Reinhold Messner, whose brother Günther perished in the attempt. Echoes of the *Bergfilm* genre further continue to surface in contemporary cinema in films set far away from the high mountains. Quentin Tarantino repeatedly references *Die weiße Hölle von Piz Palü* in *Inglorious Basterds* (2009), although he credits Pabst as the director (and not codirector with Fanck). And as Robert von Dassanowsky has argued, elements of *Titanic* (1997) can be traced back to the genre.[10]

Within the German tradition, it is Werner Herzog whose work perhaps most prominently embodies the lasting impact of the *Bergfilm*. Herzog's conscious reworking of the genre goes beyond iconography and encompasses his absolute commitment to remote on-location filming, coupled with his preoccupation with main characters who are driven by quests that routinely take them through and over the mountains. In Herzog's films (among them, not only *Cerro Torre: Schrei aus Stein* [Cerro Torre: Scream of stone], 1991, but also *Aguirre, der Zorn Gottes* [*Aguirre, Wrath of God*],

1972, and *Fitzcarraldo*, 1982) the *Bergfilm* lives on, not only in the mountains, but also in the jungles of the Amazon.

See also:

- 17 June 1927: Amateur Film League Aids Invention of Film Culture
- 30 August 1936: Luis Trenker Tries but Fails to Sidestep Nazi *Filmpolitik*
- 30 April 1999: Werner Herzog's "Minnesota Declaration" Performs Critique of Documentary Cinema

Notes

[1] Quoted in Arnold Fanck, *Er führte Regie mit Gletschern, Stürmen und Lawinen: Ein Filmpionier erzählt* (Munich: Nymphenburger Verlagshandlung, 1973), 146. Hereafter cited in text.

[2] Stefan König, "Der Mythos vom heiligen Berg: Kleine genealogische Abhandlung in Sachen deutscher Bergfilmtradition," in *Berge, Licht und Traum: Dr. Arnold Fanck und der deutsche Bergfilm*, ed. Jan-Christopher Horak and Gisela Pichler (Munich: Bruckmann, 1997), 105–23; here 105.

[3] Siegfried Kracauer, *From Caligari to Hitler: A Psychological History of the German Film*, revised and expanded. ed. Ed. Leonardo Quaresima (Princeton: Princeton UP, 2004); here 110–12, 257–59.

[4] Eric Rentschler, "Mountains and Modernity: Relocating the *Bergfilm*," *New German Critique* 51 (1990): 137–61; Nancy Nenno, "Postcards from the Edge: Education to Tourism in the German Mountain Film," in *Light Motives: German Popular Film in Perspective*, ed. Randall Halle and Margaret McCarthy (Detroit: Wayne State UP, 2003), 61–84.

[5] König, "Der Mythos," 106.

[6] Christian Rapp, *Höhenrausch: Der deutscher Bergfilm* (Vienna: Sonderzahl, 1997), 35.

[7] Krakauer, *From Caligari to Hitler*, 112.

[8] Quoted in Rainer Amstädter, *Der Alpinismus: Kultur — Organisation — Politik* (Vienna: WUV-Universitätsverlag, 1996), 371.

[9] Christian Rapp, "Im Banne der Politik: Der deutsche Bergfilm um 1930," in *Bergfilm: Dramen, Trick und Abenteuer*, ed. Stefan König, Hans-Jürgen Panitz and Michael Wachtler (Munich: F. A. Herbig, 2001), 85–87; here 85.

[10] Robert von Dassanowsky, "A Mountain of a Ship: Locating the *Bergfilm* in James Cameron's *Titanic*," *Cinema Journal* 40, no. 4 (2001): 18–35.

23 December 1924: *Der letzte Mann* Explores Limits of Modern Community

Robert Schechtman

LONG CONSIDERED A MAJOR WORK of the silent film era, Friedrich Wilhelm Murnau's *Der letzte Mann* (*The Last Laugh*, 1924) poses several paradoxes. Widely acclaimed by contemporary critics as a creative masterpiece, this story of a simple man's downfall was nevertheless a failure with the general viewing public. Though the narrative offers a critique of the fast-paced, impersonal conditions of life in urban modernity, the pace of the film itself is often plodding, while a subtext suggests a simultaneous critique of what was popularly considered in Germany to be modern society's superior counterpart — local community. Moreover, although the film's widely noted lack of intertitles helped to foreground the new medium's visuality and its supposedly international appeal, the work was described abroad as too German in both form and content. Indeed, the inability of several of the country's top film talents to translate artistic innovation into commercial success is emblematic of the struggles of the entire German film industry at the time.

In its day, the film was hailed as groundbreaking. Apart from a brief introduction to the epilogue, almost no text intrudes on the visual flow of a work that essentially presents a silent cinematic monologue by the main character. Lead actor Emil Jannings artfully depicts the struggles of an aging hotel doorman who is demoted from his prestigious post and sent to work as a lowly washroom attendant; his gestures emphasize the disparity between a proud man walking tall and a disgraced figure cowering before his fellows. Berlin's *Film-Kurier* cited the work as exemplary: "*Der letzte Mann* shows that film without words is no Utopia. Its universal achievement remains one of the greatest challenges to film art" (24 January 1925). Additionally, cameraman Karl Freund put the recently *entfesselte Kamera* (unchained camera) in motion as never before, adding new dimensions to the subjective camera shot. In the opening sequence, for example, the camera descends in an elevator and passes through the hotel lobby to the revolving front door, where Jannings stands at his post, framed in the rapidly turning panes of glass — an image that both gestures toward the mechanisms of filmic apparatus and also symbolizes the rapid pace of modernity. Later, the old man's drunken hallucinations during his daughter's wedding party are portrayed through double-exposures and a wildly tilting camera. Reviewers were astounded. *Kinematograph* praised Freund's innovative techniques as "towering above everything created up to this point" (4 January 1925), while an American writer suggested the camera was the film's star.

Formally, *Der letzte Mann* plays a transitional role in German film history, bridging the emerging New Objectivity movement with the expressionism of earlier film classics. Although reviews stressed the work's realism, the unnamed character types ("The Porter," "The Aunt") are an overtly expressionist device, and moments of visual excess — buildings appearing to descend upon Jannings as he walks home after his demotion, faces of laughing neighbors spinning at him derisively in multiple exposure, the whirling camera in the drunken dream sequence — draw upon earlier visual tropes. With a focus on common people, minimal intertitles, and strongly contrasting visuals, *Der letzte Mann* echoes elements of screenwriter Carl Mayer's earlier *Kammerspiel* (chamber play) films.

Even before its lavish premiere at the Ufa-Palast in Berlin on 23 December 1924, *Der letzte Mann* received critical praise. Two weeks earlier, producer Erich Pommer had hosted a prescreening in New York, and an eager German press spread the news of the film's subsequent booking in major New York theaters. In early reviews, Vienna's *Kino-Journal* lauded the work as "the highest expressive possibility of film art" (6 December 1924), and Berlin's *Film-Kurier* declared it "an historic turning point in the development of film" (20 December 1924). After its debut, the enthusiastic reception continued. London's *Bioscope* termed the work "perhaps the greatest film ever made" (26 March 1925), and the *Ciné-Journal* of Paris wrote, "one is faced with the impossibility of comparing this film with any other that we know" (10 April 1925). Many reviewers considered the film to be the pinnacle of contemporary cinematic art.

Still, despite extensive positive press, the film was not a financial success. Even Berlin bookings were only average, and *Variety* later dismissed the work as "a critics' picture" (22 April 1925). Given that few of its celebrated techniques were truly novel, its critical reception must be read in the context of a German film industry struggling for cultural legitimacy at home and battling against a flood of imports — mostly American — from abroad. *Der letzte Mann* was part of the Ufa (Universum Film A.G.) studio's creative response to a highly competitive international film market. The strategy did not pay off, however; before long, a wave of transatlantic partnerships would lead much of Germany's top talent to emigrate to Hollywood. Nevertheless, the work influenced countless contemporary filmmakers, among them Alfred Hitchcock, who was working for Ufa in Berlin while Murnau was filming.

Der letzte Mann focuses on the tribulations of a working man, depicting the disgrace that befalls Jannings's character after he is relieved of his post for struggling with heavy luggage one rainy night. Too ashamed to return home in the plain garb of a washroom attendant, he steals back his former grand uniform to wear to his daughter's wedding, but he is humiliated by his neighbors' reaction when his farce is discovered. Rejected even by his own family, he returns to the hotel, where a sympathetic night watchman comforts him. An ironic epilogue then follows: the old man miraculously inherits the fortune of an American millionaire who dies in his arms. The film's closing shot shows Jannings and his watchman friend riding off in a carriage, laughing heartily.

Since its release, *Der letzte Mann* has sustained numerous readings. The decline-and-fall narrative offers an allegory of Germany's geopolitical situation following the country's defeat in the First World War and the subsequent inflationary chaos. Similarly, the doorman's struggles illuminate the perilous position of the lower middle class in Germany at a time of rapid economic decline, a predicament later detailed by Siegfried Kracauer's *Die Angestellten* (*The Salaried Masses*, 1930). The hotel's name, "Atlantic," and the film's deus ex machina epilogue — imposed by Pommer upon a reluctant production team — suggest both a parody of American happy endings and a commentary on the Dawes Plan, which had recently revived the German economy. In addition, traces of the period's idolization of youth culture are apparent in a narrative that the *Süddeutsche Film Zeitung* described as "the tragedy of becoming old" (20 February 1925), while the film's misogynist and homosocial undertones have prompted recent gender-based critiques. The emphasis placed on the doorman's uniform not only recalls Gottfried Keller's novella *Kleider machen Leute* (*Clothes Make the Man*, 1874) but also the various adaptations of *Der Hauptmann von Köpenick* (*The Captain of Koepenick*, 1926, 1931, and 1956), though the focus on uniformed authority led some international reviewers to label the film as too German.[1] Still, the work was so illuminating of its time that film historian Thomas Elsaesser has termed Jannings's doorman "an icon of the Weimar Republic."[2]

Der letzte Mann must be read within a broad discourse in the Weimar Republic that was highly critical of modernity. The film's German title (The last man) and its pessimistic main ending call to mind Oswald Spengler's widely read polemic against a supposedly over-rationalized, urbanized, Anglo-French *Zivilisation*: "The last man [*Mensch*] of the world-city," Spengler wrote in 1922, "no longer *wants* to live." Moreover, the impersonal setting of the metropolitan hotel in which Jannings finds his end recalls sociologist Ferdinand Tönnies's oft-cited critiques of "cold" capitalist society, which he described as "the realm of business [or] travel" in which "everybody is by himself and isolated." According to Tönnies, the "real and organic life" of human community (*Gemeinschaft*) was increasingly being eroded by modern society (*Gesellschaft*). By 1924, when *Der letzte Mann* premiered, popular calls to revive community as a remedy for the perceived ills of modernity were so pervasive that German philosopher Helmuth Plessner dubbed community "the idol of this age." In this context, the film has long been considered a critique of anonymous, globalized urban space.[3]

Yet to read the film simply as depicting a crisis of community is to overlook crucial details. Certainly, the hotel is a realm where rational commerce prevails and relationships are superficial at best, while the apartment block where the old man lives exemplifies what Tönnies termed "urban community," a place of familiarity and intimacy where friends greet each other, children play, and a young couple celebrate their wedding. Nonetheless, although the doorman is quite literally defrocked in the hotel, his fellow workers do not reject him. On the contrary, a brief insert shows the manager's note to him: "In consideration of your long service with us, we have found another position for you by arranging for our oldest employee to be admitted to a Home, so from to-day you will take over his duties." Here, the hotel's management displays a certain degree of compassion — at least toward Jannings's character. In the following scene, the former doorman is led down a hallway toward his new workplace in the hotel basement. In a shot paralleling Jannings's later homecoming, several people lean out of windows to watch him pass. In stark contrast to his reception in the tenement, however, nobody is laughing. The mood is somber, but not degrading.

The ridicule and rejection he does receive comes only after he returns home — foregrounded by the multiple-exposure shot of neighbors' laughter — and after he faces his family, who scowl at him mercilessly while he trembles before them. As if to emphasize the point, the aunt who discovers his demotion starts to laugh when he turns to flee. Conversely, in the next and final scene, set in the hotel, the kind watchman drapes his own jacket over Jannings's shoulders as the cast-out man slumps in a chair. A close-up shows the watchman's hand gently stroking the protagonist's head, while a cross cut shows the darkened tenement courtyard. The contrast is clear: the film's ultimate tragedy occurs within the man's own community. Seen in this light, even the strange epilogue may be read as a recuperative gesture for the public sphere, depicting the hotel as a space of opportunity and mobility, if only through the (albeit fantastical) kindness of strangers.

While emphasizing the limits of uniformed prestige, *Der letzte Mann* also explores the atomizing effects of urban existence and free-market capital on human relations — resonant themes in 1920s Germany. But contrary to a popular discourse that proposed a neoromantic vision of community as the antidote to society, the film points to the communal space of the urban courtyard apartment as equally problematic. Filmed at the peak of Germany's popular craze for *Gemeinschaft*, *Der letzte Mann* suggests that local community may hold no refuge for the effects of "cold" society in the modern age. In the same year, Helmuth Plessner's book *Grenzen der Gemeinschaft* (*The Limits of Community*, 1924) cautioned against idealizing communal intimacy. Because we are all imperfect creatures, Plessner argued, every life is threatened by irony, "disintegrating a world to nothing through its laughter."[4] Such laughter destroys the film's hero when he is seen for what he is — a vulnerable human being trying to cover his imperfections in a temporary cloak of glory. The film ultimately leaves the question of human relations in the modern era unresolved, just as its own paradoxes — in its reception, its form, and its interpretation — remain irresolvable.

See also:

- 29 November 1923: Karl Grune's *Die Straße* Inaugurates "Street Film," Foreshadows Film Noir
- 29 May 1929: Oscar for Emil Jannings Highlights Exchange between German and American Film Industries
- 6 December 2007: Indie Film *Für den unbekannten Hund* Seeks Space for Marginalized Male Heroism

Notes

[1] "Isn't it . . . eminently German," asked France's *Cinémagazine* (10 April 1925), "the directorial idea of this work, based solely on the prestige of the uniform?" Later, Lotte Eisner termed it "pre-eminently a German tragedy, [that] can only be understood in a country where uniform is King." Lotte Eisner, *The Haunted Screen: Expressionism in the German Cinema and the Influence of Max Reinhardt*, trans. Roger Greaves (Berkeley: U of California P, 1969), 207.

[2] Thomas Elsaesser, *Weimar Cinema and After: Germany's Historical Imaginary* (London: Routledge, 2000), 232.

[3] Oswald Spengler, *The Decline of the West*, 2 vols. 1920–22, trans. Charles Atkinson (New York: Alfred Knopf, 1945), 2:103 (original italics); Ferdinand Tönnies, *Community and Society*, trans. Charles Loomis (East Lansing, MI: Michigan State UP, 1957), 34, 65; Helmuth Plessner, *The Limits of Community: A Critique of Social Radicalism*, trans. Andrew Wallace (Amherst, NY: Prometheus, 1999), 65.

[4] Plessner, *Limits of Community*, 117.

16 March 1925: *Wege zu Kraft und Schönheit* Educates Audiences in the Art of Nudity

Britta Herdegen

Embracing the beauty and vigor of the nude body.
Wege zu Kraft und Schönheit *(1925). DVD capture.*

WILHELM PRAGER AND NICHOLAS KAUFMANN'S 1925 educational film *Wege zu Kraft und Schönheit: Ein Film über moderne Körperkultur* (*Ways to Strength and Beauty*) represents a distinctively German variation on the documentary film — the *Kulturfilm* (cultural film). Despite Weimar audiences' general lack of interest in these types of films and preference for fiction films, *Wege zu Kraft und Schönheit* achieved commercial success not only in Germany but also internationally. The film's success can be attributed, at least in part, to its radical departure from the normative, conservative cultural films generally approved for public viewing — a departure that allowed for a redefinition of the *Kulturfilm*. Unlike its conservative contemporaries, Prager and Kaufmann's film openly depicts public nudity, strong and active women, and multicultural tolerance, while also invoking elements of popular entertainment. It achieves this break from the norms of the *Kulturfilm* (and avoids the era's censorship strictures) through deliberately artistic representations of the nude body that link ancient traditions of physical culture with modern preoccupations with health and fitness.

During the early Wilhelmine era, film imitated more established forms of entertainment of the time, including vaudeville and burlesque performances devoted principally to entertainment. Advocates of *Kinoreform* (cinema reform) attacked both these so-called *Schundfilme* (a term referencing films deemed shoddy and without educational value) and Hollywood imports for their appeal to mass audiences, which the critics believed would lead to the degeneration of German society and threaten the stability of the republic.[1] The *Kulturfilm* was seen as a positive, edifying, as well as more conservative alternative. Early popular subjects included travel accounts, wildlife expositions, historical reports, and footage of the imperial family and Prussian military. After 1918, educational films emerged as a key subgenre of the *Kulturfilm*, and Germany's leading film studio, Ufa (Universum Film A.G.), created a separate division dedicated solely to their production, particularly medical films treating matters of public health and hygiene. These films were considered invaluable pedagogical tools for a society in flux.

The development of the *Kulturfilm* genre was closely bound up with the emergence of film censorship. Despite numerous reforms, the Weimar Republic did not provide an unconditional climate of artistic experimentation and innovation. The oft-cited *zensurlose Zeit* (time without censorship) — a result of the newly formed republican constitution, the end of the war, and the removal of the *Kaiser* — supposedly ushered in an era without film censorship, but as Malte Hagener and Jans Hans have argued, this concept has been overgeneralized and simplified consistently by (film) historians.[2] Indeed, although the new constitution allowed for freedom of speech and initially aided the removal of stringent censorship laws, the *Reichslichtspielgesetz* (Reich Film Law) went into effect in 1920 as a result of continued pressure from propagators of cinema reform. These critics, aside from asserting that film could corrupt the moral values of the masses, argued that film needed to be elevated to the level of other artistic media following the tradition of German theater and literature. Unlike these arts, which under the new constitution were allotted complete artistic freedom, cinema had to face the scrutiny of newly formed censorship boards based in Berlin and Munich — the *Filmoberprüfstellen* — which assessed a film's appropriateness for a mass audience. The boards not only strictly monitored fiction films, but also those works intended to educate the public, and only a small portion of the era's educational films were released for public viewing.

Wege zu Kraft und Schönheit managed to bypass many of these censorship obstacles and offer a radical alternative to the prevailing practices of the Weimar *Kulturfilm* by incorporating elements of high-art forms that enjoyed the stamp of legitimacy. The film thus made public nudity acceptable by tying it to Greco-Roman tradition. Throughout, the film features Greco-Roman statues and recreations of daily Roman life, representing them as instantiations of a lost ideal. The film then links this ancient past to contemporary high culture, depicting author and playwright Gerhart Hauptmann scantily clad and sunbathing. Hauptmann not only provided visible evidence of the benefits of exercise and fresh air, but conferred a certain gravitas on the film as one who had played a key role in the 1910s as a legitimator of the cinema. As Max Osborne, a contemporary critic wrote:

> The presence of nude bodies in the film . . . has nothing to do with tawdriness. Far from being treated as something secondary, the problem is taken up with great seriousness. . . . Eroticism in its ancient sense rises up out the murky waters of the darker urges that have pulled down this godly element of our lives, sullied it and made it unrecognizable. Eros emerges as a thing apart from sex, and hence becomes the foundation for a more highly evolved free morality.[3]

Most educational films of the time focused exclusively on the dangers and consequences of neglecting the care of one's body, particularly the corporeal effects of a modern, industrialized society, including war and modern diseases. Educational films such as *Die Wirkung der Hungerblockade auf die Volksgesundheit* (The effects of the hunger blockade on national health, 1921) or *Feind im Blut* (Enemy in the blood, 1931), directed by Walter Ruttmann and intended to school audiences in the dangers of syphilis, used jarring imagery to scare viewers.[4] The body was not depicted as an organic whole but rather soberly and clinically as a series of disparate parts. These films paraded patients before the camera, inscribed their bodies with topographical illustrations, and frequently employed modern microscopic filming techniques. Women appeared predominately as a threat to the nation's health and stability, for example, as the main source for transmitting sexual diseases. These works consistently reinforced an idealized role of woman as child bearer through juxtapositions of the figure of the happy mother versus the desolate, barren prostitute.[5]

Wege zu Kraft und Schönheit, by contrast, takes a holistic view of the body and emphasizes the importance of synergy between mind, body, and spirit. It restricts its use of negative imagery to the opening scenes of the film and even then oscillates between visual illustrations and the intercutting of text. References to Goethe lauding the culture of Greek antiquity and its tradition of cultivating body and mind are juxtaposed with a scene that aligns the lifestyle and values and the German petite-bourgeoisie with shallow materialism and a blatant disregard for the body's well-being. The opening scene depicts a chaotic contemporary family episode that dissolves into a contrasting, idyllic Greco-Roman spectacle of athletic outdoor activity. This historic flashback is followed by a scene of present-day museumgoers gawking at a statue of Venus, their expressions ranging from lustful to apathetic. In contrast to the idealized Greco-Roman figure, the onlookers represent physically imperfect individuals with neglected bodies. An intertext reminds the viewer that it is not enough to simply study antiquity; individuals should incorporate classical ideals into everyday life. While the onlookers appear prudish and old-fashioned, the nude Venus appears as the epitome of physical beauty, health, and harmony, providing a role model for spectators to emulate and thereby reform their destructive lifestyles.

The Venus episode in *Wege zu Kraft und Schönheit* stands out in particular because, to the astonishment of the spectators within the narrative as well as the original audience, the inanimate marble statue morphs into a living human being. The scene exemplifies the film's appeal to both modern cinematic standards and the traditions of high art. On the one hand, it replicates a popular visual trope of trick cinematography commonly employed in contemporary expressionist feature films, for example in *Der Golem* (*The Golem*, 1920) and *Das Wachsfigurenkabinett* (*Waxworks*, 1924). On other hand, the Venus scene is reminiscent of the literary preoccupations of German romanticism, like the Venus statue that comes to life in Joseph von Eichendorff's *Das Marmorbild* (*The Marble Statue*).

As one of the first films to depict the naked body as integral to better personal and collective health, *Wege zu Kraft und Schönheit* participated in the contemporary life-reform movement, which encompassed *Freikörperkultur* (nudist culture) and "sought to change the Germans and Germany . . . by reforming the individual," and "freeing the body of the moral chains that shamed and bound" it.[6] Residents of Weimar Germany displayed a significant shift in attitudes toward nudity. Nudity came to be seen as having therapeutic value, since it allowed for the healing power of nature and sunlight to reach the unbridled body. New laws in 1918 allowed for public nude bathing, and by the beginning of the 1920s, public nudity had become relatively common. Nude bathing even became a popular weekend family activity — viewed as an outlet for stress caused by hectic workdays and fast-paced city life.

Although *Wege zu Kraft und Schönheit* emphasizes a critique of degenerative petite-bourgeois lifestyle practices, the call for lifestyle reform that the film propagates was not limited to one particular social class or political ideology. As Michael Hau has emphasized, this movement was not "apolitical."[7] Educational efforts spread across both left and right-wing ideological groups, albeit each with separate distinctive agendas.[8]

In addition to stressing the importance of outdoor activity and the benefits of exposure to natural sunlight, the film's focus on the benefits of physical fitness also suggests a certain progressivism, particularly in its privileging of dance. It highlights dance as a universally instinctual form of activity and holds up non-Western cultures as exemplary, celebrating their unique contributions to dance and emphasizing global unity through this shared activity. The film also devotes significant attention to modern dance. Notably, it praises the work of Mary Wigman, whose choreography famously challenged the "traditional eroticization of the female dancer."[9] Modern dance, characteristic for its rejection of suppressed and restricted forms of movement, not only offered alternative avenues of bodily expression that were both free and more natural, but also allowed for a reversal in traditional gender roles. In modern dance generally, and Wigman's work specifically, women were not just confined to the role of the performer, but could also be responsible for the choreography.

Although *Wege zu Kraft und Schönheit* was a domestic and international success, and, as film historians note, one of the few cultural films included in the German film canon, it has drifted into relative obscurity within contemporary film studies. The few references that are made are often brief and somewhat superficial. Within these rare discussions, the film is generally positioned as a forerunner to the "cult of the body" created by National Socialist propaganda films, such as Leni Riefenstahl's *Triumph des Willens* (*Triumph of the Will*, 1934) and *Olympia* (1938). Photographic stills of *Wege zu Kraft und Schönheit* in film history books are often limited to images depicting Greco-Roman scenes that recall the subsequent racist and antisemitic practices of the Nazi period. These visual excerpts, according to scholars, establish a connection between the film and National Socialist ideology because of their similarity to the opening scenes Riefenstahl uses in *Olympia*. In reading *Wege zu Kraft und Schönheit* through such a limited sample as emblematic of the prehistory of Nazi ideology, this line of argument risks negating the film's larger autonomy.

Without doubt, there were those among the propagators of popular hygiene and the life-reform movement during the Weimar era who supported an aesthetic ideology that fostered racism and antisemitism, as well as beauty ideals that discriminated against women and the disabled. Under National Socialism, racial hygiene provided the "scientific" justification for mass murder of those who did not conform to prescribed ideals of physical or genetic purity. Because of the film's retroactive association with the Third Reich, however, *Kulturfilm* scholarship has neglected the significance of the film's images and didactic content — overlooking its radical departure from normative contemporary filmic representations of the human body.

See also:

- 14 September 1922: Schüfftan Process Reconciles Artistic Craftsmanship with Demands of Entertainment Industry
- 10 May 1924: *Der Berg des Schicksals* Inaugurates the Genre of the "Mountain Film"
- 13 January 1954: Preminger's Dual-Language *The Moon Is Blue* (1953) and *Die Jungfrau auf dem Dach* (1954) Seek Glocal Success

Notes

[1] Sabine Hake, *German National Cinema* (New York: Routledge, 2002): 31. Hereafter cited in text.

[2] Malte Hagener and Jans Hans, "Von Wilhelm zu Weimar," in *Geschlecht in Fesseln: Sexualität zwischen Aufklärung und Ausbeutung im Weimarer Kino 1918 — 1933*, ed. Malte Hagener (Munich: edition text + kritik, 2000), 7.

[3] Max Osborne, "Der Nackte Mensch im Film," *Wege zu Kraft und Schönheit: Programmheft zum Film*, Berlin 1925, 28, cited in Ingo Starz, "Kunstort oder Sportplatz? Aesthetische Aufrüstung zwischen Dekadenz und Faschismus," in *Fitness: Schönheit kommt von aussen*, ed. Andreas Schwab and Ronny Trachsel (Bern: Palma3, 2003).

[4] Ulf Schmidt, "Der Blick auf den Koerper," in *Geschlecht in Fesseln: Sexualität zwischen Aufklärung und Ausbeutung im Weimarer Kino 1918 — 1933*, ed. Malte Hagener (Munich: edition text + kritik, 2000): 25.

[5] Hake, *German National Cinema*, 40–41.

[6] Chad Ross, *Naked Germany: Health, Race and the Nation* (New York: Berg, 2005): 35.

[7] Michael Hau, review of *Naked Germany: Health, Race and the Nation*, by Chad Ross, *Medical History* 52, no. 4 (October 2008): 557–58.

[8] For more on the left-wing lifestyle reform movement during the Weimar period, see Nick Hopwood, "Producing a Socialist Popular Science in the Weimar Republic," *History Workshop* 41 (1996), 117–53.

[9] Susan A. Manning, *Ecstasy and the Demon: Feminism and Nationalism in the Dances of Mary Wigman* (Berkeley: U of California P, 1993): 15.

3 May 1925: French and German Avant-Garde Converge at *Der absolute Film*

Joel Westerdale

IN LATE APRIL 1925, popular film culture in Weimar-era Berlin was still reeling from the recent visit of Tom Mix; *Wege zu Kraft und Schönheit* (*Ways to Strength and Beauty*, 1925) continued to fill theaters, and the public awaited the next comic farce with Ossi Oswalda. In this setting there appeared a rather modest announcement for a "one-time" matinee, *Der absolute Film* (Absolute film), to be held on 3 May at the small Ufa-Theater on Kurfürstendamm. The event promised to make "works of absolute film-art" available for the first time to "a broader audience." As ever, funding and spectators for experimental film were scarce, but this show found both: its organizers, the *Novembergruppe* (November Group),[1] had the support of the *Kulturfilm* (documentary culture film) division of Ufa (Universum Film A.G.), and the nine-hundred–seat theater sold out easily. So great was the show's success that this "one-time" event was repeated the following Sunday. In bringing together for the first time Germany's pioneer avant-garde filmmakers — Hans Richter, Viking Eggeling, and Walter Ruttmann — the matinee has since become "legendary."[2] But perhaps of greater consequence for the further development of German avant-garde film was the program's inclusion of works by French directors Fernand Léger and René Clair. For even as the event celebrated the achievements of the German avant-garde, it also fundamentally changed it, ushering in a new phase that merged the diverse aesthetic impulses and technological methods of both the German and French contingents represented that day.

According to the program, *Der absolute Film* was to begin with Ludwig Hirschfeld-Mack's *Dreiteilige Farbensonatine* (Three-part color-sonatina), followed by Hans Richter's *Film ist Rhythmus* (Film is rhythm), Viking Eggeling's *Symphonie Diagonale* (Diagonal symphony), and Walter Ruttmann's *Opus 2, 3,* and *4*; the performance would then present *Images mobiles* (Mobile images, 1924) by Fernand Léger and Dudley Murphy, and conclude, somewhat playfully, with René Clair's *Entr'acte* (Intermission, 1924). Though unstated, the program fell into two distinct halves, first featuring shorter abstract works of animation produced in Germany,

DER ABSOLUTE FILM

EINMALIGE FILMMATINEE
veranstaltet von der
NOVEMBERGRUPPE
in Gemeinschaft mit der
KULTURABTEILUNG DER UFA

PROGRAMM

Dreiteilige Farbensonatine — Hirschfeld - Mack
Reflektorische Farbenspiele — Bauhaus Dessau

Film ist Rhythmus — Hans Richter Berlin

Symphonie Diagonale — Viking Eggeling Berlin

Opus 2, 3 und 4 — Walther Ruttmann Berlin

Images mobiles — Fernand Leger
und Dudley Murphy, Paris

Entr' Acte — Scénario de Francis Picabia
adapté et réalisé par René Clair

Hoboken - Presse, Charlottenburg, Fasanenstraße 13

3. 5. 25

*The original program for the "Absolute Film" matinee.
Credit: Deutsche Kinemathek.*

then showing lengthier French films composed largely of live-action footage. The lack of musical accompaniment for the French films reinforced the distinction between the two groups.[3] Even if both sets of films were united in their rejection of narrative development — earning them the label "absolute" — their aesthetic and technological differences were as conspicuous as their division along national lines.

The German contributions share a preoccupation with the promise of "optical music."[4] The opening piece by the Bauhaus artist Ludwig Hirschfeld-Mack, like the films to follow, emphasized form, color, and motion over figurative representation, developing in a manner more akin to music than narrative. Unlike the works to follow, however, and despite the matinee's title, Hirschfeld-Mack's *Dreiteilige Farbensonatine* wasn't actually a film, but rather moving color projections of abstract forms produced by an altogether different apparatus designed by the artist and operated by a small crew. The first actual film of the day was to be Richter's *Film ist Rhythmus*. This film is difficult to identify decisively. Censorship records make no mention of it, though on 21 April 1925, the same day censors approved the films by Eggeling and Ruttmann, a forty-five-meter work by Hans Richter appears: *Ohne Haupttitel* (Without a title). This work-in-progress likely combined elements from his *Rhythmus 21* (Rhythm 21, which, despite its 1921 imprint, probably premiered in 1923) and *Rhythmus 23* (Rhythm 23, 1923). Regardless of the exact composition of *Film ist Rhythmus*, the film was still not ready for the initial matinee, and was only included the following Sunday. Thus despite what the program says, the first *film* to reach the screen on 3 May was not by Hirschfeld-Mack or Richter, but Viking Eggeling.

Symphonie Diagonale (1924), made by the Swedish-born but German-based Eggeling with the assistance of animator Erna Niemeyer, introduced a form of filmic optical music distinct from Richter's (though he and Richter had been painters together in Zurich, where they both developed an interest in adding movement to their abstract paintings). In *Symphonie*, Eggeling realizes his dream of "cinemorphism," a painting style he conceived of before turning to film. His earlier cinemorphic works depict long sequences of distinct but similar shapes of increasing and decreasing intricacy; likewise, his *Symphonie* portrays the emergence of largely static figures that vary in complexity as portions are revealed and masked. Whereas the figures in his paintings develop sequentially in space over the length of a long roll of paper, the figures in his film unfold in time, exploiting film's illusion of movement. The result is a 149-meter film with figures far more complex than Richter's, though they fail to create the three-dimensional sense of depth featured in the *Rhythmus* films.

The three contributions by Walter Ruttmann, his *Opus 2*, *Opus 3*, and *Opus 4*, continued the event's exploration of musical abstraction. Ruttmann also began as a painter; his goal was to create "painting in time" by adding motion to his canvases. For him, too, the metaphor of music is operative. Like Eggeling's *Symphonie*, these works forego the illusion of depth, but exhibit a dynamism alien to both the preceding works. His forms do not simply unveil themselves or advance and retreat; they transform and interact. By Richter's own admission, Ruttmann's films were technically superior. Ruttmann, however, spent less effort theorizing his work than Richter, who responded to the former's greater skill by insisting that his own initial forays into abstract film came first.[5] Contemporary critical reception magnifies their distinct profiles: whereas avant-garde publications such as *De Stijl* and *Ma* discuss the works of Richter and Eggeling, they all but ignore Ruttmann, while the more popular press like *Kunstwart* and *Lichtbild-Bühne* reference Ruttmann while largely overlooking the other two.[6]

The popular appeal of Ruttmann's works derives not only from their technical virtuosity, but also from their capacity to generate an emotional response by bringing abstract shapes to life. In his review of *Der absolute Film*, a young Rudolf Arnheim praised Ruttmann's forms for behaving "in a very human way."[7] This talent for true "animation" enlivens Ruttmann's renowned work on dream sequences for Fritz Lang (*Nibelungen*, 1924) and Paul Wegener (*Lebende Buddhas* [Living buddhas], 1925), though it also drew criticism for its potentially erotic qualities, leading Munich censors to ban at least one of his *Opera*.[8] Theorists and artists like László Moholy-Nagy may have preferred the lack of representation in the works of Richter and Eggeling, but the popularity of Ruttmann's early abstract work is bound precisely to its anthropomorphic quality. And this quality aligns his work with that of the matinee's French contingent.

Like Ruttmann's *Opera*, Fernand Léger's *Images mobiles* (better known under the title *Ballet mécanique* [Mechanical ballet]) and René Clair's *Entr'acte* were a hit with the German audience, even more so than in France. Reviews frequently mention the applause and whistles provoked by Léger's repeated shots of a woman climbing the stairs without reaching the top, or Clair's fast-motion funeral march. As "absolute" films, these works emphasize form over story, but they do not actually forego representation. Even if the triangles and circles Léger intersperses through his film encourage spectators to attend to formal aspects, and Clair's inverted oblique shots of rooftops recall Eggeling's diagonal symphony, the woman on the stairs is effective because she is a person perpetually failing to reach the top; the oddly paced funeral is funny precisely because it is a funeral. Even as the filmmakers defamiliarize the image, its affective success is bound to its representationality.

The German critics largely dismissed the abstract works of Richter and Eggeling and accused Ruttmann of failing to break new ground (they were already familiar with his first two *Opera*). The press was more responsive to Léger and Clair — "They have ideas!" exclaimed *Der Film*

(10 May 1925) — and judging from the subsequent works of Richter and Ruttmann, they, too, were convinced. Though Eggeling died a few weeks after the matinee, Richter and Ruttmann continued to produce films for many years; neither returned to purely abstract animation. As Walter Schobert notes, the release of Eisenstein's *Potemkin* in 1925 may also have contributed to Richter and Ruttmann's turn to live-action footage, but their frequent use of imagery suggestive of *Images mobiles* and *Entr'acte* points to the legacy of *Der absolute Film*. Richter's *Filmstudie* (Film study, 1927) and *Rennsymphonie* (Race symphony, 1928) feature the kaleidoscopic effects of *Images mobiles*, while his *Inflation* (1928) borrows its zero-motif and his *Vormittags-Spuk* (Ghosts before breakfast, 1928) its oblique angles, inversions, and leaping of the axis.[9] Many shots from Ruttmann's *Berlin. Die Sinfonie der Großstadt* (*Berlin: Symphony of a Great City*, 1927) likewise recall Clair and Léger, from the vertiginous rollercoaster sequence familiar from *Entr'acte* to the natural rhythm of machinery reminiscent of *Images mobiles*. Both Richter and Ruttmann would also establish personal relationships with their French counterparts, helping to promote a transnational film avant-garde.

Neither Richter nor Ruttmann entirely abandoned their earlier aesthetic program — rather, their work developed into a hybrid of these two aesthetic impulses. Ruttmann's magnum opus even begins by plotting a trajectory from his early abstract work to the present montage: *Berlin* opens with a close shot of slowly rippling water that dissolves into the ripples of abstract lines that clearly cite his *Opus 4*; these abstract images then transform through a match-cut into a falling rail barrier. This not only draws attention to the film's formal priorities, but it also identifies its lineage in early abstract film, suggesting that although Ruttmann's technique may have changed, his aesthetic program had not. While this may have led to Carl Mayer's criticism of *Berlin*'s "surface approach," it attests to the film's continuity with early German avant-garde's first phase, a phase of abstract experimentation and visual musicality that would reach its pinnacle at — and ultimately be transformed by — the matinee *Der absolute Film*.

See also:

- 1 April 1921: Walter Ruttmann's *Lichtspiel: Opus 1* Shapes Culture of Abstract Filmmaking
- 13 June 1930: *Weekend* Broadcast Tests Centrality of Image in Cinema
- 28 May 1942: Bertolt Brecht and Fritz Lang Write a Hollywood Screenplay

Notes

[1] With a name evoking the 1918/19 revolution that toppled the German monarchy, the *Novembergruppe* drew from diverse avant-garde movements and included such figures as Max Pechstein, Lyonel Feininger, Walter Gropius, Ludwig Mies van der Rohe, and Alban Berg.

[2] Christine Noll Brinckmann, "Experimentalfilm, 1920–1990: Einzelgänge und Schübe," in *Geschichte des deutschen Films*, ed. Wolfgang Jacobsen, Anton Kaes, and Hans Helmut Prinzler (Stuttgart, Weimar: Metzler, 1993), 417–50; here 422.

[3] George Antheil's *Ballet mécanique* did not premier until June of 1926, and Erik Satie's composition for *Entr'acte* — "Cinéma. Entr'acte symphonique de 'Relâche'" — was not performed at the matinee, likely due to restrictions on time and funds. Contemporary reviews of the matinee frequently criticize the failure of the organizers to provide these last two films with musical accompaniment, though Eggeling's short film was likewise, though intentionally, free of music. When shown, Richter's film was accompanied by atonal music by the twenty-three-year-old Stefan Wolpe, but it is difficult to determine what exactly accompanied Ruttmann's films; when shown in London later that year, they were accompanied by drums, and at the Dutch Filmliga in 1927, by the amplified sound of the projector. See Jeanpaul Goergen, ed. *Walter Ruttmann: Eine Dokumentation*. Berlin: Freunde der Deutschen Kinemathek, 1989, 109; Hanns Eisler's music for *Opus 3* would premiere in 1927.

[4] See Joel Westerdale, "The Musical Promise of Abstract Film," in *The Many Faces of Weimar Cinema*, ed. Christian Rogowski (Rochester, NY: Camden House, 2010), 153–66.

[5] William Moritz, "Restoring the Aesthetics of Early Abstract Films," in *A Reader in Animation Studies*, ed. Jayne Pilling (Sydney: John Libbey, 1997), 221–7.

[6] Holger Wilmesmeier, *Deutsche Avantgarde und Film: Die Filmmatinee "Der absolute Film" (3. und 10. Mai 1925)* (Münster, Hamburg: Lit, 1994), 109.

[7] Quoted in Walter Schobert, "'Painting in Time' and 'Visual Music': On German Avant-Garde Films in the 1920s," in *Expressionist Film — New Perspectives*, ed. Dietrich Scheunemann (Rochester, NY: Camden House, 2003), 237–49; here 241.

[8] Wilmesmeier, *Deutsche Avantgarde*, 52–53. According to Goergen, Ruttmann's *Opera* were censored not due to their erotic qualities, but as part of a government education campaign against hypnosis (*Walter Ruttmann: Eine Dokumentation*, 23).

[9] Schobert, "'Painting in Time'" 242. Richter freely acknowledges the kinship of his later films with these French works in *Der Kampf um den Film* (Munich/Vienna: Hanser, 1976), 42–43.

Brigitte Helm strikes an arch pose in a publicity still for Die Gräfin von Monte Christo *(1932). Credit: Friedrich-Wilhelm-Murnau-Stiftung.*

10 January 1927: Brigitte Helm Embodies Ambivalence of the New Woman

Valerie Weinstein

BRIGITTE HELM'S DOUBLE ROLE in Fritz Lang's now canonical *Metropolis*, as whorish robot and saintly leader of an underground movement, catapulted the unknown nineteen-year-old, a slim, angular blonde, to fame as one of the German film industry's leading ladies. Helm's brief career, which ended in 1935 when she did not renew her Ufa (Universum Film A.G.) contract, reflects the vexed, contradictory, and ambivalent figure of the "New Woman" in Weimar cinema. Perceived as public, independent, androgynous, sexually liberated, and cosmopolitan, the New Woman was assigned conflicting images and values, a tension that Helm enacted in her various roles. Helm employed her own statuesque beauty, awkward yet compelling movements, and seductive but cold emotional range so effectively that in her day she was seen as the authoritative "Vamp" — hypersexualized, dangerous, domineering, and associated with technology and foreignness.[1] Uncomfortable having been typecast as a Vamp, however, Helm fought to secure roles in which she could represent herself as the modern urban "Girl," the more mundane, pragmatic, and less fatal permutation of the New Woman: trim, athletic, cosmopolitan, and self-reliant. As a result, Helm's persona and her films often conflated and confused the images of the Vamp and the Girl and, in doing so, offer a particularly useful illustration of Weimar's ambivalent fascination with the New Woman.

The construct of the New Woman in Weimar Germany signified women's real and imagined postwar social, economic, and sexual liberation. Modern women's work outside the home, particularly white-collar work in offices, shops, and the professions, along with young urban women's perceived independence vis-à-vis previous eras, were construed as androgynous, even mannish. This image was underscored by the fashion and the preferred body-types of the era, which accentuated lines, angles, broad shoulders, flat chests, and narrow hips, and favored short skirts, menswear looks such as that of the girl-boy (*garçonne*), and short hairstyles like the pageboy bob (*Bubikopf*).

Representations of New Women in the media took a variety of forms — from the fashion-forward consumer to the legible lesbian, from athletic, American-style "Girls" to elegant society women — whose images melded easily with those of the Vamp or femme fatale. These New Women were associated with new technologies such as the typewriter, the telephone, the automobile, and motion pictures; with transgressive behaviors such as cigarette smoking and extramarital sex; and with their counterparts abroad, especially, but not exclusively, in the United States.

Attitudes toward the perceived modernization and masculinization of women were as varied as their representations, occupying every position on the spectrum between enthusiasm and condemnation. Many young women in urban centers embraced the economic and sexual freedom promised by images of New Women, even as the social realities of the Weimar Republic limited their opportunities. Hyperinflation and unemployment created conditions in which many men treated working women as a threat to their status as breadwinners. The dislocation caused by economic and political turmoil and the concomitant urbanization and modernization was met in many corners with fierce resistance, which frequently construed women's sexual and social independence as a challenge to German cultural traditions.

As a site where these tensions over modernization were played out, the New Woman figured prominently in the Weimar cultural imagination and, correspondingly, in Weimar cinema as heroine, antagonist, and set-dressing. From the earliest days of the feature film and throughout the Weimar Republic, the popular Asta Nielsen dramatized modern female sexuality, androgyny, and their perils, in a range of genres from melodramas to literary adaptations. In G. W. Pabst's *Die freudlose Gasse* (*Joyless Street*, 1925), Nielsen played opposite Greta Garbo, illustrating, respectively, working-class and white-collar women's responses to the economic and sexual pressures faced by the New Women of the 1920s. Comic darling Ossi Oswalda showcased the New Woman's pluck and challenge to traditional gender roles in many popular films. Like Helm, the American Louise Brooks, with her signature black bob, as well as Betty Amann and Marlene Dietrich, embodied the New Woman's dangerous sexual allure. Dina Gralla, Renate Müller, and Hertha Thiele represented the fresh, athletic, somewhat boyish, and down-to-earth Girl with androgynous sexual appeal, akin to that of Nielsen, Dietrich, or the stage and screen actress Elisabeth Bergner.

Brigitte Helm, a brilliant national and international star, reflected notions about the New Woman in a multifaceted way. Labeled as *the* Vamp of German film, her star sign is in fact more complex.[2] Helm has been read as an onscreen mannequin, representing contemporary fashion and its exhibition practices, and serving as a site of identification, spectacle, and marketing.[3] She has been described as having fit neither the flapper paradigms of the 1920s nor the "homely and healthy" paradigms of the nationalist 1930s and as having had more affinities with Art Deco aesthetics and the Hollywood star system than other Weimar-era German stars.[4] Moreover, it has been suggested that Helm's vampish performance and her role as saint in *Metropolis* both served as templates for her future career.[5] Taken together, these readings point to Helm's cultural significance: more than any other Weimar star, Helm, as a site of both identification and aversion, awkwardly performed tensions between visions of saints and whores, Vamps and Girls.

Helm invests her star persona with these tensions and ambivalences toward the New Woman in her first and defining double role as Maria in the futuristic *Metropolis*. In this film, Helm plays two very disparate women who, despite the obvious differences in their behavior, are mistaken easily for one another. The human Maria leads the oppressed workers and eventually unites them with management into an organic body of hands, heart, and brain, in part because of her physical and spiritual beauty, and in part because of the machinations of her robot double. The robot, the embodiment of technology, cinema, and their dangers and attractions, uses blatant sexuality to unite the same workers and masters into a frenzied, destructive mass, which Maria domesticates after she saves their children. Lang's use of a sexualized female to outline the homogenizing effects of mass culture is consistent with historical discourses linking the New Woman and her sexuality to technology, modernity, and mass culture.[6] The human Maria, however, also represents a variation of the New Woman, one who works, takes a public role, and extends her presumed maternal instincts to politics and society, as did women leaders of the socialist, social democratic, and social work movements in the early twentieth century. Maria's youth, natural beauty, slender frame, and athleticism (she can outrun a mad scientist and save children from floods) combine with those elements of the Girl image. This good Maria is the authentic one, the bad one a product of fantasy, technology, and capital. Yet, central to the plot and mise-en-scène is the notion that these figures are interchangeable, and that both can seduce the masses. Such ambivalent and simultaneous embodiment of both positive and negative visions of the New Woman would remain typical for Helm.

Helm's further career was marked by just such a tension between nightmare visions of the New Woman and more positive forms. Soon after *Metropolis*, Helm performed in two films directed by G. W. Pabst that built on both her roles in *Metropolis*, as a gentle blind girl in *Die Liebe der Jeanne Ney* (*The Love of Jeanne Ney*, 1927) and as an elegant society wife who indulges in Weimar's decadence (dancing, alcohol, drugs, and affairs with an artist and a boxer) in *Abwege* (*The Devious Path*, 1928). Another of Helm's signature roles, *Alraune*, merges Vamp and Girl in a single figure, and renders them both seductive and monstrous.[7]

With the coming of sound, Helm struggled to shift her image away still further from the Vamp and gradually toward that of the Girl.[8] This shift was well received and produced influential films such as *Eine von Uns* (*One of Us*, 1932), Johannes Meyer's film version of Irmgard Keun's best-selling novel *Gilgi*. But Helm's performances continued to evoke the danger of the Vamp and staged ambivalence toward the New Woman. We see this in *Die Gräfin von Monte Christo* (*The Countess of Monte Christo*, 1932). In this depression-era fantasy, a film extra named Jeanette becomes famous by pretending to be a countess, checking into a luxury hotel, becoming involved with con men (Rudolf Forster and Gustaf Gründgens), and eventually turning herself in. Helm begins easily as the Girl — a modern, attractive young woman with relationship and money troubles, working at the lowest rung of a glamorous industry. Her daring, luck, beauty, and confidence, as well as plausible acting and spectacular costumes — not to mention criminal fraud — make possible her transition to a flashier and more successful type. The New Woman is an attractive figure of identification in *Gräfin* — beautiful and upwardly mobile, the onscreen incarnation of little shop girls' dreams.[9] Yet despite Jeanette's underlying goodness and honesty, which surface repeatedly at key moments, she still is dangerous. She steals a car from the film studio, obtains lavish products and services from the hotel management, and seduces a hardened con man, albeit seemingly unintentionally, into sacrificing his own well-being and freedom for her. Jeanette is more personally attractive than Helm's Vamps of the 1920s, and domesticated through marriage and capitalist fantasies, but she remains a risky figure for those around her.

By the end of the Weimar years, attitudes toward and images of the New Woman remained ambivalent, and Helm's roles still danced between them. As the Nazi regime took increasing control of the film industry, representations and characterizations of the New Woman shifted further; its most dangerous variations such as Helm and Dietrich left, and narratives domesticated or replaced the modern women that remained.

Helm's role in *Gold* (1934), one of the Third Reich's few science fiction films, illustrates the problems in adapting Helm's ambivalent versions of the New Woman to a Nazi ideal of femininity. The film is about turning lead to gold, pitting idealized German science against capitalist corrupted, foreign technology. Helm plays Florence Wills, a millionaire's daughter who in dress and gesture resembles Helm's earlier Vamp roles. She finds her foil in the figure of Margit Möller (Lien Deyers), fiancée to protagonist Werner Holk (Hans Albers). Margit — whom Holk will choose in the end — represents the ideal type of modern woman that would replace ambivalent Weimar portrayals in the 1930s, and might be described, cautiously, as a domesticated version of the Girl. Competent, physically attractive, and up-to-date, Margit balances strength and good health (even donating blood to save Holk's life) and subservience: instead of challenging or rivaling him, she dotes on, supports, and obeys her man, who is so superior to her that he affectionately calls her "child."

By contrast, while Florence behaves — and those around her treat her — as if she were independent and imperious, her actions always end up serving the needs of powerful men, first her father and then Holk. Helm continues to look seductive and dangerous, but other than her desire for Holk, her character's motivations are opaque and seemingly inconsistent. Florence Wills reveals the strain inherent in the effort to adapt the Weimar-style Vamp to National Socialist ideals. Her dangerous appearance of sexual and narrative agency simply does not work, cinematically, within ideological constraints of feminine subordination and obedience. While glamorous, the character of Florence Willis is awkward, illogical, and superfluous. Unthreatening and marginal to the plot, Helm's defanged Vamp in *Gold* enters the narrative late and exits noticeably early.

Wishing to retire to private life and to abandon fully her career as Vamp, Helm refused to renew her Ufa contract in 1935, married, and moved to Switzerland. Her years as an onscreen model of dominant, seductive, and dangerous femininity had come to an end, and with her disappeared an influential image of the New Woman's power that was both compelling and threatening. Nazi-era temptresses, such as those played by Zarah Leander, would have softer edges, and ultimately suffer for their transgressions in ways that Helm's heroines rarely did.

See also:

- 27 May 1911: Asta Nielsen Secures Unprecedented Artistic Control
- 21 January 1914: Premiere of *Die Firma heiratet* Inaugurates Fashion Farce
- 24 June 1974: Launching of *Frauen und Film* Creates Lasting Forum for Feminist Film Writing and Practice

Notes

[1] Oskar Kalbus, *Vom Werden Deutscher Filmkunst: Der Stumme Film* (Altona-Bahrenfeld: Cigaretten Bilderdienst, 1935), 129–30. Robert Müller, "Die Frau aus Marmor: Brigitte Helm — ein deutscher Vamp," in *Schauspielen und Montage: Schauspielkunst im Film*, ed. Knut Hickethier (St. Augustin: Gardez!, 1999), 15–30.

[2] Daniel Semler, *Brigitte Helm: Der Vamp des deutschen Films* (Munich: Belleville, 2008).

[3] Mila Ganeva, *Women in Weimar Fashion: Discourses and Displays in German Culture, 1918–1933* (Rochester: Camden House, 2008), 130–41.

[4] Tim Bergfelder, Sue Harris, and Sarah Street, *Film Architecture and the Transnational Imagination: Set Design in 1930s European Cinema* (Amsterdam: Amsterdam UP, 2007), 148.

[5] Andrea Böhm, "Brigitte Helm — Heilige und Vamp," in *Grenzgänger zwischen Theater und Kino: Schauspielerporträts aus dem Berlin der Zwanziger Jahre*, ed. Knut Hickethier (Berlin: Ästhetik und Kommunikation, 1986), 194–212; here 202–11.

[6] See, among others, Andreas Huyssen, *After the Great Divide: Modernism, Mass Culture, Postmodernism* (Bloomington: Indiana UP, 1986), 43–62; Janet Lungstrum, "*Metropolis* and the Technosexual Woman of German Modernity," in *Women in the Metropolis*, ed. Katharina von Ankum (Berkeley: U of California P, 1997), 128–44; Peter Wollen, "Cinema/Americanism/the Robot," in *Modernity and Mass Culture*, ed. James Naremore and Patrick Brantlinger (Bloomington: Indiana UP, 1991), 42–69; here 50–53.

[7] Valerie Weinstein, "Henrik Galeen's *Alraune* (1927): The Vamp and the Root of Horror," in *The Many Faces of Weimar Cinema: Rediscovering Germany's Filmic Legacy*, ed. Christian Rogowski (Rochester, NY: Camden House, 2010), 198–210.

[8] See Böhm, "Brigitte Helm," 198–99.

[9] See Siegfried Kracauer, *From Caligari to Hitler: A Psychological History of the German Film*, revised and expanded edition, ed. and introd. Leonardo Quaresima (Princeton: Princeton UP, 2004), 213–14.

17 June 1927: Amateur Film League Aids Invention of Film Culture

Martina Roepke

The BUND DER FILM-AMATEURE (Amateur Film League, BDFA) was founded in Berlin on 17 June 1927, in order to "propagate film sport and stimulate its culturally uplifting development."[1] Among the founding members of the BDFA were representatives of the film industry and the association of movie theaters, journalists, and individual film amateurs. Only a few years earlier, in 1923, Kodak's 16-millimeter safety stock had reached Germany, prompting manufacturers and industry to create a market for the new technology and free it from censorship and safety regulations.

Compared to the United States and Great Britain, the German Amateur Film League was quite small in terms of its membership, having only two hundred members in 1928, six hundred in 1932, and about four thousand in 1944. The cities of Berlin, Halle, and Dresden clearly spearheaded the movement and occupied its center, along with active local film clubs in various other cities, including Munich, Hamburg, Dresden, and Halle. At the outset, the League instituted a monthly competition to stimulate exchange and ambition among its members. The official National Amateur Film Competition was first held in 1935. As in all amateur cultures, these competitions played an important role in shaping the League's cultural identity by defining its relation to both film professionals and hobby filmmakers. Like other leagues that spread worldwide, the German Amateur Film League had a constituency comprised of anything but mere hobbyists. Born mainly out of economic interests, the BDFA evolved into a group of ambitious film practitioners, authors, screenwriters, critics, and cinephiles who made significant contributions to the "invention of film culture"[2] during the Weimar years.

Film für Alle (Film for all), published in Halle from 1927 through 1944, was Germany's first amateur film journal. It was joined by *Der Filmamateur* (The Film amateur), which was published in Berlin from 1927 through 1943 and became the first official organ of the BDFA (later replaced in 1937 by competitor *Film für Alle*). Both journals not only provided information about technological developments and club activities, but also engaged in lively debates about the cultural space of amateur filmmaking within Weimar film culture. A crucial question for amateur cultures in general and for film amateurs in particular was the relationship between amateur filmmaking and professional or semiprofessional filming. Should one allow amateurs to earn money with their "work"? A certain permeability between the professional, semiprofessional, and amateur realms of filmmaking was characteristic for the Weimar amateur film culture — resulting in a productive grey zone that changed profoundly after 1933 with the introduction of the new *Reichslichtspielgesetz* (Reich Film Law), which hindered such crossovers and sought to restrict amateur engagement to the private sphere.

During the 1920s numerous innovations profoundly changed the field of amateur film technology. Pathe's "Baby," a complete home movie system for 9.5-millimeter film (1923), and Ica's "Ica-Kinamo" (1927), the first camera with automatic release, were the most famous examples. Ambitious film amateurs were challenged by these technological developments and joined professionals in exploring the field. In Berlin, BDFA-members joined regular meetings at the Osram Lichthaus or the Ufa-Kulturfilmabteilung (Universum Film A.G.'s cultural film division) to test new equipment and to evaluate the new 16-millimeter stock, which, due to its high optical qualities, reached beyond amateur circles, influencing science, education, and the arts.[3]

Eager and ambitious as they were, club filmmakers were careful to keep their distance from family and hobby filming. For these amateurs, filming was understood as something more than a leisure activity for fathers: rather, it represented the proper occupation for the urban, modern, and mobile citizen. In this regard, the discourse on amateur film articulated broader attitudes toward technology and debates on modernism so central to Weimar culture. Film amateurs embraced technological innovations, and with their light, mobile cameras, they saw themselves as flaneurs of the big cities, capturing images on their way.

In their search for a genuine amateur-film aesthetics, these serious amateurs clearly preferred nonfiction to fictional filmmaking, primarily for budgetary reasons. The small 16-millimeter cameras could be carried along on trains and boats, and their light weight and small size allowed filming from extraordinary or even hidden positions. With respect to the documentary qualities of filmmaking, these filmmakers were fully aware that careful staging would eventually aid in the unfolding of reality before the camera (following Winfried Basse's definition of documentary film as an "artistic and concentrated performance [Darstellung] of reality; and the use of reality as performer [Darsteller]").[4] Béla Balázs's *Der sichtbare Mensch* (*The Visible Man*, 1924) and Rudolf Arnheim's *Film als Kunst* (*Film as Art*, 1932) further influenced the somewhat fragmentary poetics of amateur filmmaking, propagating new ways of looking at the most familiar things. Alongside the emphasis on documentary, however, members of the BDFA also successfully experimented with other genres. Richard Groschopp's animated film of a battle on a chessboard, *Eine kleine Königstragödie* (A little king's tragedy, 1934), even gained international recognition. Fictional films — from detective stories to comedies — were realized on a local level as forms of group activity and collaborative filmmaking.

Amateurs learned filming by doing but also by watching films and even copying the work of professionals. Walter Ruttmann's *Berlin. Die Symphonie einer Großstadt* (*Berlin — Symphony of a City*, 1927) was very popular within amateur film circles and by the mid-1930s instructions on how to make a cross-section film (*Querschnittsfilm*) had made it into books on amateur filmmaking.[5] Some professionals like Guido Seeber and Willy Zischler shared their insights with amateur colleagues, introducing them to the technique of double-exposure and the "unchained camera" and teaching them how to mount a camera on a bicycle. A key role in transferring knowledge from professional filmmaking to amateur circles was surely played by Alex Strasser, a father and author of numerous books on amateur film who was also closely associated with the Internationale Liga des unabhängigen Films (International League of Independent Film).[6]

In 1932 Kodak introduced the first 8-millimeter film, cameras, and projector, which led to a further reduction of costs, but in this case at the expense of cinematographic quality. For many amateurs, subscribing to this format represented a barrier to public or even semipublic distribution venues, even as the format conquered the domestic market for home movies. Marketing strategies for amateur equipment adapted to this situation, redefining film as a home entertainment for the whole family rather than a hobby for the technically versed. Filming is easy, the slogan was, and life should be, too. The literature directed at this new generation of film amateurs clearly aimed at bringing film as *Heimkino* into living rooms and instructed the whole family on how to act in a varied film program. For the purposes of home entertainment, self-made films could be programmed alongside reduction prints of popular fiction films, uplifting cultural films, or even propaganda films, all of which were available from the early 1930s via 16- and 8-millimeter film libraries.[7]

Hitler's rise to power and the National Socialist Party takeover prompted a further retreat by many amateurs into the private sphere. In 1934, the Amateur Film League was subsumed by the Reichsfilmkammer (Film Chamber of the Reich) and from then on, all members were required to provide proof of so-called Aryan descent. Any public screening of small-gauge films, whether amateur productions or not, became subject to censorship. Within a year, the boards of the BDFA and *Der Film-Amateur* were replaced by official representatives of the Nazi regime. Karl Melzer, at that point secretary of the Reichsfilmkammer, became president of the BDFA in 1935 and announced closer cooperation between the BDFA and the Reichsstelle für Unterrichtsfilm (Reich Office for Educational Film), granting the amateur filmmaker a role in producing films about German customs and traditions.

At this point, not surprisingly, the genre of the family film, disdained by ambitious amateurs in the 1920s and early 1930s for its lack of aesthetic quality, celebrated its renaissance in the form of the *Familienkulturfilm* (family cultural film). In 1935, the *Film-Amateur* defined this genre as the proper remit of the amateur, one of high cultural importance, instilling cultural values such as home, family, and tradition in line with the National Socialist ideology. This shift was confirmed at the 1936 National Amateur Film Competition, which awarded prizes to two such films. Second prize went to Herbert Plessow's *Der Napfkuchen* (The bundt cake), an instructional film on cake baking and a family comedy at the same time. First prize was taken by Richard Groschopp for his *Bommerli*, a short family film with the director's daughter as main actor and character. Groschopp's talent was widely recognized within and even beyond the German amateur film community. His animated film *Eine kleine Königstragödie* (A minor kingly tragedy) had been the distinguished winner of the same competition the previous year, prompting Dresden's Boehner-Film to finance a high quality remake of the film for theatrical release that later screened publicly together with Veit Harlan's feature film *Der Herrscher* (The ruler, 1937).

The success of *Bommerli* symbolizes both the peak of German amateur filmmaking and its most problematic turning point. With the rise of the *Familienkulturfilm* to the national stage, the German amateur film officially proved itself "worthy" of the new regime. While close analysis of this genre reveals a certain ambiguity and even potential moments of resistance — for example, in moments of mockery with respect to gender roles — the elevation of the family film into the realm of *Kulturfilm* coincided with a period of extensive cooperation and complicity. In the following years, leading BDFA members more or less openly aligned themselves with NS ideology, in the hopes that amateur film would be assigned a crucial role in Nazi politics.[8] Richard Groschopp entered the professional world of filming with Leni Riefenstahl before he joined Boehner-Film in Dresden and later the DEFA-Studios (Deutsche Film-Aktiengesellschaft, East Germany's state-owned film company), eventually becoming president of the National Center of Amateur Film in the GDR in 1960. For the majority of even the most serious German amateurs, however, filmmaking now meant a retreat into the private sphere. In 1943 the headquarters of the BDFA were bombed; the league stopped all activities the same year, and would not reemerge until its postwar rebirth in Braunschweig in 1949.

See also:

- 10 May 1924: *Der Berg des Schicksals* Inaugurates the Genre of the "Mountain Film"
- 3 May 1925: French and German Avant-Garde Converge at *Der absolute Film*
- 30 April 1999: Werner Herzog's "Minnesota Declaration" Performs Critique of Documentary Cinema

Notes

[1] Quoted from the statute in Barbara Zimmermann, "Hundert Jahre Film — 75 Jahre BDFA," in *Das BDFA-Handbuch: Nachschlagwerk für alle Film und Video-Freunde*, ed. Bund Deutscher Film und Video-Amateure (Gütersloh: Flöttmann, 1997), 12–35; here 13.

[2] Malte Hagener, *Moving Forward, Looking Back: The European Avant-garde and the Invention of Filmculture 1919–1939* (Amsterdam: Amsterdam UP, 2007).

[3] Niels-Christian Bollbrinker, "Von Emulsionen, Objekten und Tonlampen: Anmerkungen zur Entwicklung der Filmtechnik," in *Geschichte des dokumentarischen Films in Deutschland*, vol. 2, ed. Klaus Kreimeier, Antje Ehmann, Jeanpaul Goergen (Stuttgart: Reclam, 2005), 301–21.

[4] Winfried Basse's definition of documentary film was published in *Film für Alle 1932*. See Jeanpaul Goergen, "Die Avantgarde und das Dokumentarische," in *Geschichte des dokumentarischen Films in Deutschland*, vol. 2, 493–526, here 518.

[5] Alexander Stüler, *So wollen wir filmen: Anregungen für die inhaltliche Gestaltung des Amateurfilmens* (Stuttgart: Frankh'sche Verlagshandlung, 1932), 9.

[6] Goergen, *"Die Avantgarde und das Dokumentarische,"* 511.

[7] Ralf Forster, Jeanpaul Goergen, "Ozaphan. Home Cinema on Cellophane," *Film History* 19, no. 4 (2007): 372–83.

[8] Schenke, Eckhard. *Der Amateurfilm: Gebrauchsweisen privater Filme* (PhD diss., Georg-August-Universität Göttingen, 1998), 160.

16 December 1927: Debut of *Familientag im Hause Prellstein* Provokes Debate about Jewish Identity in Popular Cinema

Daniel H. Magilow

UNTIL IT APPEARED on the program of the 2004 Cinefest program *Spaß beiseite: Jüdischer Humor, 'Arisierung' und verdrängendes Lachen* (Kidding aside: Jewish humor, aryanization, and repressive laughter), the film comedy *Familientag im Hause Prellstein* (Family day at the Prellsteins, 1927) had almost disappeared from German cinematic history. An adaptation of a cruder and raunchier eponymous play produced for the *Jargon* theaters in 1905 (*Jargon* being a synonym for Yiddish), *Familientag im Hause Prellstein* draws many of its laughs from stereotypes derived from the intimate setting of bourgeois Jewish family life. The film's mobilization of these stereotypes made it a flashpoint in its day for debates about German-Jewish cinematic representation.

In Wilhelmine and Weimar Berlin, *Jargon* theaters, like the one owned by brothers David Donat Herrnfeld and Anton Herrnfeld, uniquely combined and caricatured traditional modes of Jewish drama (such as the *purimshpil* or Purim play) with non-Jewish burlesque and variety shows. With its mixture of German and Yiddish and bawdy sketches about family disputes, adultery, and unrequited love, this form of popular entertainment attracted urban middle-class audiences consisting primarily (but not exclusively) of Jews.[1] In so doing, the *Jargon* theater became an important venue for the "presentation and negotiation of Jewish identities 'in and through the presence of Gentiles.'"[2] Its audiences were multiple: the theatrical viewership consisted largely of self-identified Jewish viewers who could laugh at a satirical spectacle of cultural self-effacement. Meanwhile, the *Jargon* theater provided non-Jewish Germans an image of private Jewish life that, while caricatured and vulgar, still humanized Jews.

Like the original play, the film version of *Familientag im Hause Prellstein* tells the story of a debt-ridden patriarch. It is a tale of domestic anarchy, rife with sexual innuendo, puns, and ridiculous nomenclature, which produces a chaotic and mocking image of the money-hungry bourgeoisie, Jewish or otherwise.[3] Sami Bambus ("Bamboo" — silly names were a staple of the *Jargon* theater) fakes his own death in order to punish his jealous ex-wife Flora, now remarried as Flora Prellstein. Sami and Flora's marriage had fallen apart when Flora discovered payment references in Sami's notebooks, which she mistook for remittances to a prostitute but which in fact were made to a moneylender who had financed Sami's secret gambling. In faking his demise, Sami seeks to punish Flora by burdening her with these debts, of which both she and his other relatives remain entirely unaware. Falsely believing Sami to be a wealthy man, Sami's brothers call for a "family day at the Prellsteins'" where they jockey for control over Sami's estate through a variety of tricks and schemes.

If the transformation of the *Jargon* play aimed principally at urban Jewish audiences into a mass-market film for a broader viewership of mainly non-Jewish Germans resulted in a somewhat forgettable cinematic adaptation, it nevertheless raised important questions about minority self-representation in popular media. In terms of its intended viewers, the film *Familientag im Hause Prellstein* was clearly aimed at mixed audiences. It premiered at the Ufa-Palast Königstadt, in today's Prenzlauer Berg, in close proximity to Berlin's Jewish neighborhoods. With a seating capacity of 1,500, this centrally located venue, one of the city's largest, could and did accommodate large audiences of diverse backgrounds. At the same time, the fact that the 16 December 1927 issue of the Zionist *Jüdische Rundschau* included an advertisement for *Familientag im Hause Prellstein* alongside ads for a "Chanukah Concert Ball" and an announcement for a "Gathering of the Central Group of the Jüdischen Volkspartei" suggest that the film was also specifically marketed to Jewish viewers.[4]

When critics of the film in 1927 praised it for its entertainment value or criticized its Jewish stereotypes, they rehearsed a long-standing debate. This debate focused on questions that remain topical to this day, concerning the meaning of humor about a historically disenfranchised group: when an audience consists primarily of non-Jews — as did the viewership of mass market films adapted from *Jargon* theater — do the tropes of Jewish humor reinforce prejudices? Or do hyperbolic stereotypes provide a critical, ironic mode that unmasks antisemitism's absurdity? And are the two possibilities necessarily mutually exclusive? If an entertainment commodity's producers and consumers are themselves Jewish, are they somehow "inoculated" against accusations of bigotry? Does the understandable scholarly focus on prewar antisemitic actions obscure the need to understand Jewish-gentile interactions within specific, localized contexts?

Familientag im Hause Prellstein's reliance on Jewish stereotypes concurrently evoked voices of praise and criticism. In this silent film, these stereotypes manifested themselves specifically in the casting of actors and actresses such as Sig Arno, Erika Glässner, and Paul Morgen (born Morgenstern) who, Jewish or not, could physiognomically "pass" as such.

Promotional stills from the film suggest that the stereotype of the nervously gesturing Jew also found a ready space for expression in this comic melodrama because, like many silent films, it had to rely disproportionately on bodily gestures to convey meanings along with intertitles. As such, the film offers an opportunity to examine how culturally diverse audiences perceived ethnic humor. The issue of differentiated audience perception has received only little attention in canonical histories of Weimar cinema, because the history of Jews in Weimar cinema history is understandably overdetermined by the subsequent horrors of Nazism and the Holocaust. Today, the stakes of this debate appear far more significant than in their own time. In a 17 December 1927 review, critic Georg Herzberg alludes to several aspects of *Familientag im Hause Prellstein* that situate the film firmly within the pre-1933 debates about the representation of Jewish identity to German-Jewish and non-Jewish German audiences and, at the same time, further explain its lapse into cinematic obscurity:

> Hans Steinhoff has created a tidy film out of available and no doubt meager resources, a film you can have a few hearty chuckles over and whose viewers, apart from the hopeless anti-Semites, will find a diversion from Heidelberg, the Rhine, and operettas.... As a second film, the work will be quite serviceable in the programs of cinema-owners.

Contemporary readers would understand this review as basically dismissing *Familientag im Hause Prellstein* as a mediocre comedy. Some of that mediocrity undoubtedly arises from film's attempt to appeal to a broad viewership. Where the theatrical versions had played to largely Jewish audiences and hence could rely on their understanding a humor that demanded familiarity with certain linguistic and cultural codes, the filmic *Familientag im Hause Prellstein* was "toned down" — that is, made more comprehensible and consumable to the non-Jewish Germans who lacked such knowledge.

To readers today, however, Herzberg's review reads far more ominously. The most startling detail must be the name of the film's director: Hans Steinhoff. Six years after *Familientag im Hause Prellstein*, the conservative-nationalist Steinhoff became one of Nazi Germany's leading film propagandists with the tremendous success of his fascist coming-of-age film *Hitlerjunge Quex* (1933). Steinhoff's cozy relationship with Nazi Propaganda Minister Joseph Goebbels and the use of scenes from *Familientag im Hause Prellstein* in antisemitic "documentaries" such as *Juden ohne Maske* (Jews without masks, 1937) and *Der ewige Jude* (*The Eternal Jew*, 1940) retroactively colored perceptions of this film and his pre-1933 work in general. In addition to *Familientag im Hause Prellstein*, Steinhoff's pre–Third

Reich films included internationally distributed comedies, melodramas, and literary adaptations, many reviewed positively by Siegfried Kracauer in the *Frankfurter Zeitung* but that have faded into obscurity in the light of Steinhoff's later work.

Yet as is clear from a 1937 review (itself racist) of the propagandistic compilation film *Juden ohne Maske*, which used footage from *Familientag im Hause Prellstein* to reveal the supposedly "true face" of the Jew, the antisemitic content of Steinhoff's work, which to later critics has seemed self-evident, was by no means obvious during the film's own period. Indeed, critics during the Nazi years referenced the excerpt of the Prellstein film *as* Jewish and accused it of mocking Aryan ideals. "We see," the *Münchner neueste Nachrichten* reported in its review of *Juden ohne Maske*, "how in Jewish hands, the harmless material of a droll story is so transformed such that a strong, powerful movement . . . is damned into ridiculousness." This bizarre critique is only possible, of course, because it omits the central role that one of the regime's premiere propagandists played in the making of the film. The review is sympathetic to the compilation film's project, and hence it must ignore the historical specificity of its component scenes. When it uses vague Nazi clichés like "in Jewish hands," the review falsely implies that only Jews would make or consume films with Jewish themes and/or Jewish actors, and that a Jewish take on something as sacred as family life would invariably present it in a demeaning way.

While we may be rightly wary of ascribing too much value to a review that espouses such obviously hateful views, the piece is instructive insofar as it highlights the mutable nature of caricature and stereotype in the cinema. Moreover, it points toward the risks of reading Steinhoff's film solely through a retroactive lens. For if readers buy into the later notion that *Familientag im Hause Prellstein* was just antisemitic pabulum made for antisemitic viewers, they unwittingly fall prey to a logic alarmingly similar to that advanced by the reviewer of *Juden ohne Maske* — that is, they assume that only Jews would be interested in positive representations of Jewish themes or that only antisemites would ever make fun of Jews, when neither is true. They assume that, because of Steinhoff's compromised politics, *Familientag im Hause Prellstein* must have been conceived as an antisemitic film. Yet in its day, low aesthetic quality and theater jokes that simply "did not translate" to the screen provided equally convincing reasons to dismiss it.

In a strange historical irony, this vein of Nazi-backed anti-Jewish criticism in the 1930s echoed a trend of earlier "anti-antisemitic" objections to caricatured representations of Judaism in popular entertainment, especially in the German-language Jewish press. Although they disdained "Jewish" films for different reasons, Nazis found themselves in line with those Jews who, during the *Jargon* theater's heyday in the early twentieth century, had also attacked popular forms of Jewish entertainment that relied on stereotypes. Writing in *Die jüdische Rundschau* in 1908 about the Herrnfeld brothers' theatrical version of *Familientag im Hause Prellstein*, the critic "N. N." argued that the Herrnfeld brothers had for years "been at pains to defame Judaism and the Jewish character in the crudest manner imaginable, and to present the entirety of German Jews as rubes or vagabonds."[5] In 1921, Alfred Döblin similarly denounced the Herrnfelds' theater as "self-prostituting."[6] Because of this history of critiques of anti-Jewish caricatures, one can easily dismiss the filmic *Familientag im Hause Prellstein* as an expression of Jewish self-hatred or an ugly predecessor to more explicitly anti-Jewish Nazi-era films.

But as Georg Herzberg aptly noted, the odds of *Familientag im Hause Prellstein* ever achieving cinematic notoriety were slim from the outset, regardless of how it negotiated Jewish ethnic identity. A key factor for the film's slide into obscurity was simply that it was a comedy, and an adaptation rather than an original screenplay, at that. Ernst Lubitsch, one of the few comic filmmakers whose work has stood the test of time, presciently remarked in 1919 that German film studios "are beholden to the frankly barbaric idea that comedy is a lower art form than the drama."[7] This status as a "low" form or disposable mass cultural commodity also bears upon the issue of the Jewish film's stereotypes. On the one hand, mass culture could attract a larger audience of (in this case, non-Jewish) consumers who, in turn, would be exposed to its stereotypical images and themes. If audiences were to consume these images uncritically, this argument runs, the film could ultimately corrode German-Jewish relations. On the other hand, this same status as mass cultural artifact would surely have dissuaded many viewers from accepting it as the legitimate vehicle for any kind of political message — antisemitic or otherwise.

And yet, as Lubitsch once wrote, the perceived problem that "stereotypically Jewish" films generate prejudice does not rest exclusively on the shoulders of filmmakers or audiences, but on a combination of poor filmmaking and misinterpretation:

> It has often been said that films set in Jewish milieus are offensive. This position is simply unbelievable. Should such a film prove displeasing, then that is due entirely to a mode of presentation that simply does not "get" the essence of Jewish humor, in which case the filmmaker should simply leave the matter be; or else it is due to inappropriate exaggeration, which would be detrimental to any artistic effort and its desired effects. Jewish humor, regardless of where it turns up, is appealing and artistic, and it plays such an all-around important role that it would be ridiculous for filmmakers to ignore it.[8]

While not explicitly pinpointing the "essence" of Jewish humor, Lubitsch offers a compromise position between those who would accuse the makers of films that incorporate Jewish stereotypes of self-hatred and those who would blame bigotry on an audience's inadequate interpretive abilities, its failure to "get the joke." He suggests that production aesthetics and audience reception work in tandem. As the debate around *Familientag im Hause Prellstein* further indicates, the diegetic construction of ethnic identity is not solely a product of the text itself, but of an ongoing interaction and negotiation between the film and its viewers. Georg Herzberg said as much in his review of the film. He believed that most moviegoers would welcome the shift away from stereotypically "German" subject matter to focus instead on a Jewish family comedy. These film viewers, "apart from hopeless anti-Semites," would recognize the film's exaggerated Jewish stereotypes for their comic intent. In that way, they would resemble the "more Jewish" theatrical audiences who also "got the jokes."

Herein lies the major reason that *Familientag im Hause Prellstein* has been nearly forgotten: in 1927, a play first lost its viewership when the film was marketed to non-Jewish Germans. After 1927, it lost its audiences for commercial reasons: newer films supplanted it in movie theaters. After 1933, it lost its audience when potential viewers were, in the case of Jewish Germans, exiled, persecuted, and murdered, and, in the case of non-Jewish Germans, discouraged from consuming Jewish themes in favor of *völkisch* ones. By 1945, long fallen into obscurity, the film was, to the extent it was remembered at all, lumped together with the later oeuvre of a Nazi propagandist. Only in the twenty-first century has Steinhoff's film remerged to present itself for different readings. More than anything else, it clearly shows that to interpret Jewish cinema in Weimar Germany as merely a precursor to the Third Reich or the Holocaust, or to judge the film as "antisemitic," are approaches lacking in nuance. Rather, the matter of ethnic representation in Weimar film demands close attention to questions of audience.

See also:

- 21 January 1914: Premiere of *Die Firma heiratet* Inaugurates Fashion Farce
- 6 March 1920: Chinese Students Raise Charges of Racism against *Die Herrin der Welt*
- 18 January 1943: Bateson Analysis of *Hitlerjunge Quex* Stresses Value of Film as Key to National Culture

Notes

[1] Marline Otte, *Jewish Identities in German Popular Entertainment, 1890–1933* (Cambridge: Cambridge UP, 2006), 126.

² Anselm Heinrich, "Circus not Einstein." Review of *Jewish Identities in German Popular Entertainment, 1890–1933.* http://www.jewish-theatre.com/visitor/article_display.aspx?articleID=2802.

³ Horst Claus, "Komische Juden oder Komische Typen? Hans Steinhoffs *Familientag im Hause Prellstein*" in *Spaß beiseite, Film ab: Jüdischer Humor und verdrängtes Lachen in der Filmkomödie bis 1945*, ed. Jan Distelmeyer (Hamburg: edition text + kritik, 2006), 22–25.

⁴ *Jüdische Rundschau* 100–101 (16 December 1927): 723.

⁵ N. N. "The Anti-Semitic Brothers Herrnfeld, N. N., *Jüdische Rundschau* 13, no. 35 (28 August 1908): 346.

⁶ Alfred Döblin. "Deutsches und Jüdisches Theater" *Prager Tagblatt*, 46, no. 303 (28 December 1921).

⁷ Quoted in Artur Vieregg, *Lichtbild-Bühne* 28 (12 July 1919).

⁸ Julius Urgiss, "Künstlerprofile: Ernst Lubitsch," *Der Kinematograph* (30 August 1916).

31 January 1929: Limits on Racial Border-Crossing Exposed in *Piccadilly*

Cynthia Walk

Censoring interracial desire: the forbidden kiss, implied but not shown. Picadilly *(1929). Credit: Deutsche Kinemathek.*

THE INVESTMENT OF Weimar German cinema in the cooperative venture known as Film Europe involved extensive exchange with other film industries of continental Europe and Great Britain from the mid-1920s through the early 1930s.[1] During this period E. A. Dupont became the most prominent émigré film director in London. A veteran of popular as well as prestige art filmmaking in Germany, with success abroad (*Varieté* [*Variety*], 1925) and first-hand experience in Hollywood (*Love Me and the World Is Mine*, 1927), Dupont was recruited to help rebuild the national film industry of Great Britain and position it to compete effectively in the international market.[2] His tenure as General Manager of Production for British International Pictures (BIP) in the new Elstree studios between 1927 and 1930 spanned the transition from silent to sound film technology. Dupont met this challenge with several multilinguals produced in English, French, and German versions, in a pioneering effort to make sound films with a broad reach on the global market — notably *Atlantic* (1929), the first fully synchronized sound film released in Europe, and *Piccadilly*, long considered a masterpiece of late British silent cinema and more recently celebrated as a cult classic and star vehicle for the Chinese-American actress Anna May Wong.

Wong's acting career had begun in Hollywood with bit parts as a generic Asian woman cast in stereotypically orientalized roles, such as the Mongol slave girl in *The Thief of Baghdad* (1924). Because of legal constraints against miscegenation at the time, the American film industry avoided government censorship through self-regulation and — long before the Production Code was enforced in 1934 — tacitly restricted onscreen interracial romance. Realizing that her options in Hollywood were limited, Wong went abroad in search of a culture more open to nonwhite actors in leading roles, joining an emigration of performers of color to Europe in the 1920s that included the African-American celebrities Josephine Baker and Paul Robeson. Indeed Wong's hybrid Chinese-American identity served to her advantage abroad. She not only succeeded in securing seven leading film roles in Germany and Britain between 1928 and 1934, but Karen J. Leong argues that Wong also "increasingly sought to employ racial and gender politics . . . to enhance her celebrity status in Europe . . . that had eluded her in Hollywood."[3] The actress achieved her own breakthrough to celebrity with *Piccadilly*, a film that thematizes the rise of an Asian performer to stardom. Wong's performance in the film has been read by Yiman Wang as an ironic ethnic masquerade and an "allegory of how Wong negotiated her status as a Chinese in the Euro-American cinema of the 1920s and early 1930s."[4]

A typical Film Europe initiative, *Piccadilly* was financed as an Anglo-German coproduction under the BIP umbrella. Dupont and his German team (art director Alfred Junge, and cinematographer Werner Brandes) offered the UK film industry an entrée to the modern urban culture of distraction promoted so successfully in *Varieté*. Here again (as in Dupont's first British silent film, *Moulin Rouge*, 1927), the show-business milieu of a major European city is represented with a self-reflexive display of flamboyant design, lighting effects, and camerawork. The narrative formula in these backstage melodramas is a romantic intrigue launched by an outsider who disrupts established professional and personal relationships. In *Piccadilly*, the outsider figure is a working-class Asian woman, who spikes the familiar mix of culture clash and class conflict with racial difference. The film's depiction of interracial desire was a controversial issue throughout its international market. Miscegenation represented a social taboo in Britain and the colonies of the Empire as well as Europe, while it was widely regarded as illegal in the United States, where in 1929 thirty out of forty-eight states had antimiscegenation laws banning racial intermarriage and often also criminalizing sex between white and nonwhite groups (including Blacks as well as Native Americans and Asians).

"Just imagine — the whole place being upset by one little Chinese girl in the scullery!" Shosho (Anna May Wong) explicitly enters the film as a disturbance, a threat to the status quo. Her sultry backstage dance disrupts business-as-usual in the Piccadilly Club and launches the plot by interrupting the narrative with the spectacle of her racial otherness. Valentine Wilmot (Jameson Thomas), the white nightclub owner, is captivated. Focused on the commercial appeal of Oriental exoticism, he hires Shosho as a novelty for his faltering entertainment business, underestimating the social and personal complications that will ensue. When the Chinese dishwasher becomes the dancing sensation of Piccadilly, she displaces Mabel Greenfield (Gilda Gray), a white English woman who becomes her rival on and offstage. The mixed-race melodrama leads to jealousy and murder in a resolution that demonizes the Asian intruder as a scheming femme fatale and underscores a conservative cautionary message against interracial romance. Yet while accepting this version of Yellow Peril racism, promoted in Britain at the time by the popular Fu-Manchu novels and film serials, Dupont's film also challenges it through a frank critique of Black racism in the East End pub scene. In a night on the town, Valentine and Shosho visit a public bar where they witness a disturbance on the dance floor: a white woman is expelled for dancing with a Black man, exposing the taboo of their own mixed relationship. In effect this scene juxtaposes two interracial couples to highlight the position of Asians and Blacks as outsiders in a white-dominated society, subject to exclusion when they cross the color barrier. On the issue of race *Piccadilly* proves an intriguingly contradictory text.

Film Europe offered Wong substantial leading roles, but she never completely escaped the strictures against interracial romance. The editing of the seduction scene with Shosho and Valentine in *Piccadilly* is emblematic: a hard cut interrupts the lovers' embrace just before their lips meet. This represents a departure from the story by novelist Arnold Bennett ("'Kiss me. I like you.' He kissed her lips."),[5] and even more so from the shooting script, which calls for passionate lovemaking:

> CLOSE UP With an infinitely charming, sensual smile Shosho points lightly to her lips. A moment later Valentine has thrown himself at her and chokes her with his kisses; both disappear in the flood of the soft cushions that bury them.

CLOSE UP With a last exertion Shosho's naked arm stretches up to the light switch on the wall — and then everything is dark.[6]

Reports differ on whether the censors intervened here or the studio acted preemptively to accommodate the requirements of the international market. In any case, what was planned and shot as a sexual encounter between a white man and an Asian woman is only implied in the actual film, which ends the scene abruptly via an editing change that reinstates the American taboo against onscreen interracial kissing.[7] Even so, the gesture in the penultimate shot anticipates what has been suppressed. This intervention at the climax of the film exposes the paradox between the film's international aspirations and the limits imposed on the representation of racial border-crossing.

Critics at its London premiere on 31 January 1929 saw *Piccadilly* as a vindication of their hopes for the future of the British film industry. Calling it Dupont's most important film since *Varieté*, the best film ever produced in the UK, and indeed the first to meet international standards, they portrayed it as a response to skeptics who doubted Britain's ability to produce world-class films for the global market. *Piccadilly* toured Germany the following month, where a poster for the Berlin premiere previewed a strikingly different investment in the film. Retitling the film *Nachtwelt* (Night world), the German marketing conjured a provocative vision of modern urban nightlife in a collage of publicity photographs confronting whiteness with the ascendancy of racial difference. It was Wong's performance of Oriental exoticism, onscreen and off, that fascinated German critics — even Walter Benjamin[8] — and dominated their reviews of *Piccadilly* as well as the other films she made before and after for producer-director Richard Eichberg in Berlin and London.[9] Despite this reception, *Piccadilly* went unnoticed in the annals of film history — a casualty of changes in film technology, as a silent work premiering at the very moment when cinema was transitioning to sound. It was not rediscovered until the 1990s, when the international aspirations of Film Europe's early projects began to resonate anew with contemporary debates around multiculturalism and media globalization.

See also:

- 6 March 1920: Chinese Students Raise Charges of Racism against *Die Herrin der Welt*
- 14 September 1922: Schüfftan Process Reconciles Artistic Craftsmanship with Demands of Entertainment Industry
- 13 January 1954: Preminger's Dual-Language *The Moon Is Blue* (1953) and *Die Jungfrau auf dem Dach* (1954) Seek Glocal Success

Notes

[1] The pioneering work on Film Europe as a strategy for pan-European cooperation in the cinema is Andrew Higson and Richard Maltby, eds., *"Film Europe" and "Film America": Cinema, Commerce and Cultural Exchange 1920–1939* (Exeter: U of Exeter P, 1999). Two essays in the anthology are important sources for the argument and factual information in this article: Andrew Higson, "Polyglot Films for an International Market: E. A. Dupont, the British Film Industry, and the Idea of a European Cinema, 1926–1930," 274–301; and Tim Bergfelder, "Negotiating Exoticism: Hollywood, Film Europe and the Cultural Reception of Anna May Wong," 302–24. On the political implications of Wong's films in Germany in the context of postwar colonial loss, see Cynthia Walk, "Anna May Wong and Weimar Cinema: Orientalism in Postcolonial Germany," in *Alterity and Affinity: German Encounters with East Asia*, ed. Qinna Shen and Martin Rosenstock (Oxford: Berghahn, forthcoming).

[2] Tim Bergfelder, "Life is a Variety Theatre — E. A. Dupont's Career in German and British Cinema," in *Destination London: German-Speaking Émigrés and British Cinema, 1925–1950*, ed. Tim Bergfelder and Christian Cargnelli (Oxford: Berghahn, 2008), 24–35.

[3] Karen J. Leong, "Anna May Wong and the British Film Industry," *Quarterly Review of Film and Video* 23 (2006): 13–22; here 16.

[4] Yiman Wang, "The Art of Screen Passing: Anna May Wong's Yellow Yellowface Performance in the Art Deco Era," *Camera Obscura* 20, no. 3 (60): 159–91; here 174.

[5] Arnold Bennett, *"Piccadilly": Story of the Film Illustrated with Scenes from the Photo-Play* (London: Readers Library Publishing Company Ltd., 1929), 161. Compare the scene in Bennett's novel with a frame enlargement from the film that is captioned with this line of dialogue, at the very point in the seduction scene where the kiss is preempted by a cut (Ibid., 128–29).

[6] Unpublished typescript at the British Film Institute, shots 511–12.

[7] Among conflicting reports one attributes this cut to a decision negotiated with the actors: "In *Piccadilly*, her most famous British film, they shot a scene where the London idol, Jameson Thomas, kissed her, but both players agreed it was better to cut this scene out. 'In England,' Mr. Thomas (now in Hollywood) explains, 'we have less prejudice against scenes of interracial romance than in America. . . . But we are very careful to handle such scenes tactfully.'" Quotation from an interview with Audrey Rivers, "Racial Barrier Prevents Star's Finding Happiness: Anna May Wong Sorry She Cannot Be Kissed," *Movie Classic* 1, 3 (1931): 39.

[8] Walter Benjamin, "Gespräch mit Anna May Wong: Eine Chinoiserie aus dem alten Westen," *Gesammelte Schriften* vol. 4, bk. 1 (Frankfurt: Suhrkamp, 1972), 523–27. Compare Benjamin's interview with Bergfelder's analysis of Wong's reception in Germany in terms of projective exoticism. In Bergfelder, "Negotiating Exoticism," 318–19.

[9] *Song* (Show Life, 1928), *Großstadtschmetterling* (*Pavement Butterfly*, 1929), and *Hai-Tang: Der Weg zur Schande* (German version of the multilingual, *Hai Tang: The Flame of Love*, 1930).

Emil Jannings poses with his Oscar statuette. Credit: Deutsche Kinemathek.

29 May 1929: Oscar for Emil Jannings Highlights Exchange between German and American Film Industries

Gerd Gemünden

IN THE SPRING OF 1929, Emil Jannings became the first actor ever to win an Academy Award. The now-famous photo showing him proudly holding the statuette, however, was not taken at the 29 May inaugural awards ceremony, but several months earlier in the Paramount publicity department. That first year the winners were announced about three months ahead. By the time the awards were officially celebrated, Jannings was already back home in Germany, his highly successful two-and-a-half year run at Paramount having come to an abrupt end when the studio converted to sound. By the time Hollywood professionals wanted to crown the best male actor among them, he was no longer in their midst. Today, Jannings's time in Hollywood identifies him as the German film professional who was most successful in straddling the cultural divide of the mid- to late 1920s, building his American star persona on his European success and enlarging his popularity in Germany by virtue of his American experience. But the conversion to sound ended his stint in Hollywood — and the industry's use of stage-trained actors. Ironically, his biggest success, *Der blaue Engel* (*The Blue Angel*, 1930), was also a clear indicator that his style of acting had run its course, as newcomer Marlene Dietrich stole the movie, and subsequently Jannings's position as the most successful German star in Hollywood.

Jannings had come to Hollywood in October 1926, the last and most celebrated star in a long line of German and European film professionals to sign a contract with an American studio. A character actor who had gained an international reputation with Ernst Lubitsch's two features *Madame DuBarry* (*Passion*, 1919) and *Anna Boleyn* (*Deception*, 1920), he was invited on the strength of two films in particular: F. W. Murnau's *Der letzte Mann* (*The Last Laugh*, 1924), and E. A. Dupont's *Varieté* (*Variety*, 1925). During his time in Hollywood, Jannings acted in six feature films, including Victor Fleming's *The Way of All Flesh* (1927) and Josef von Sternberg's *The Last Command* (1928) — the two films that won him the Oscar — as well as Ludwig Berger's *Sins of the Fathers* (1928), Lubitsch's

The Patriot (1928), Mauritz Stiller's *Street of Sin* (1928), and Lewis Milestone's *Betrayal* (1929). A number of other projects were cut short by Jannings's sudden departure, including a bio-picture of Paul Kruger, the leader of the South African resistance against the British, a production that would eventually be realized as the Nazi propaganda film *Ohm Krüger* (1941). When Jannings left, Edwin Schallert wrote in the *LA Times* that his "leaving culminates [an] exodus of foreign stars. The king of them all has gone. The king of the European film stars. . . . [Jannings's] preeminence as a pantomist actor is unquestioned, and in a sense his going marks the close of a picturesque phase of Hollywood's history" (28 April 1929).

When Emil Jannings first stormed onto American cinema screens as Louis XV in *Passion*, he did so incognito: neither his name, nor that of director Ernst Lubitsch, was included in the credits. Because anti-German sentiment was still strong so shortly after the First World War, the film's origins were intentionally obscured, and in some places it was advertised as a Polish film. By the time Jannings arrived in person in the fall of 1926, matters could not have been more different. The success of *Passion* and *Deception*, together with the critical acclaim for 1920 works, *Das Cabinet des Dr. Caligari* (*The Cabinet of Dr. Caligari*) and *Der Golem* (*The Golem*), had overcome hostility toward German film, and Jannings, now a major international star, received a royal welcome. New York journalists reported the simultaneous docking of ships carrying Jannings and the Queen of Romania with the headline, "Welcome the Queen Maria of Romania! Welcome the King of Dramatic Actors!" while Hollywood film professionals greeted Jannings and his wife Gussy Holl with a banner that read, "American Screen Guild Welcomes Emil Jannings/Screen's Foremost Dramatic Actor."[1] Jannings's meteoric rise to international fame must certainly be attributed to his individual talent, but first and foremost it must be understood as part of the German film industry's stunning postwar recovery, which made it Hollywood's fiercest rival but also its frequent collaborator. Indeed, the competitiveness between German and American film studios was also the guarantee for the German film professionals' compatibility within the US studio system and a reason for their success there.

Emil Jannings is a pivotal figure in the exchanges between the American and German film industries of the mid- to late twenties. Incredibly successful on both sides of the Atlantic, Jannings easily straddled the professional dimension of cultural divide, and became the face of a new form of internationalism. It is important to recall that Weimar cinema, like Weimar culture in general, was truly international, and its film industry was the only European cinema at the time that presented both a commercial and artistic alternative to Hollywood. Hollywood, in turn, was well aware of this competition, both because of the German film industry's artistic and technological advances, and due to its own failure to make the same inroads in Germany that it had made in other European markets after the war. Hollywood's continued efforts to reach German audiences were closely observed by German cultural critics as well as the public at large, and *Amerikanismus* (Americanism) became a buzzword for the contested reception of American culture, be it cinema, music, fashion, sports, or lifestyle in general. While some Germans claimed that American mass culture foreshadowed a homogenization of the world, others considered it to be a force that could subvert the pretentiousness of traditional elite culture. The pros and cons of American popular culture were of central importance, particularly in the discourse surrounding the film industry, and German filmmakers kept a very close eye on Hollywood, using it as a yardstick for their domestic achievements. Yet rather than a unidirectional flow of influence from one national culture to another, there existed considerable two-way traffic between the nations' film industries. While German studios imitated the American standardization of production, the emphasis on publicity, and its star system, American producers were interested not only in conquering a German market (often by setting up subsidiaries in Germany) but also in importing know-how and personnel. While the latter practice led to a genuine enrichment of the American film industry, it also often seemed aimed at weakening its competitors by depriving them of their strongest talent.

The long list of professionals who left Berlin for Los Angeles reveals just a few whose forays met with real success. The only true long-term success story is that of Ernst Lubitsch and his entourage, which included scriptwriter Hanns Kräly (who would win an Academy Award for his script of *The Patriot*), his personal assistant Henry Blanke (who later became an important producer at Warner Brothers), and his main female star, Pola Negri, who rose to be one of the best-paid stars of her time. Lubitsch himself emerged as one of the most consistently acclaimed directors of that decade, successfully straddling the conversion to sound, and for a short while even heading up production at Paramount Studio. Most others who followed in their wake were far less successful: the star producer Erich Pommer was brought in to repeat the feats that had made Ufa (Universum Film A.G.) famous but returned to Germany in the late 1920s; director Dimitri Buchowetzki, who had cast Jannings in *Danton* (1921), *Othello* (1922), and *Peter der Große* (*Peter the Great*, 1922), failed to gain recognition with his American films; F. W. Murnau, whose films with Jannings (*Tartuffe*, *Faust*, and *Der letzte Mann*) made him Weimar's premier director of art film, struggled to preserve his artistic integrity in Hollywood and ultimately grew disenchanted with the studio system. This is not to mention E. A. Dupont and Ludwig Berger, who, for various reasons, did not deliver on the high expectations that their German works had created. Paul Leni's promising beginnings were cut short by his untimely death. Among the actors and actresses besides

Pola Negri, who arrived soon after Lubitsch, only Jannings and his friend Conrad Veidt acquired major star status while Lya de Putti (Jannings's costar in *Varieté*), Lil Dagover (of *Caligari*-fame), and Camilla Horn (the Gretchen in *Faust*) had short-lived careers. Germany, too, had tried from the 1910s onward to make stars out of imported American actors like Fern Andra, Betty Amann, and Louise Brooks, with similarly disparate results. While both industries desired a certain transatlantic traffic, their mutual competition, the emergence of the talkie, and the longer history of international political disputes rendered this flow uncertain.

Both the American and the German trade press followed the import and export of talent closely, and tended to characterize the import of their competitor's cinema in dire terms. From the beginning of the decade, American voices, deeply mistrustful of Germans after the war, warned of "the German invasion," "the deluge," and "tidal waves," while by mid decade, when the numbers of Europeans increased significantly, the rhetoric shifted toward protectionism, and in June 1927, *Variety* issued the headline: "400 Aliens in U.S. Films. Majority Leads of Foreign Birth." German observers, on the other hand, were wary of the perceived drain on the film industry and frequently commented on the "talent raids" by Carl Laemmle, William Fox, Adolph Zukor, and other moguls. In March 1927, the renowned theater critic Herbert Ihering took stock of the German film industry and came up with a dire pronouncement: "Jannings, Conrad Veidt, Murnau, in the near future Ludwig Berger — the last year has cost Germany its most significant film artists. At the same time, the German cinemas have been swamped by an uncontrollable flood of mediocre American films, while German products have not been able to make inroads over there. The German film is destroyed."[2] Yet despite the rhetoric of tidal waves, the actual number of German film professionals in Hollywood was small in proportion; what was big was the interest they created. It was this buzz that greeted Jannings when he arrived in October 1926, and that explains the extraordinarily warm welcome that he received both in New York and Los Angeles.

Having arrived at the height of his fame, Jannings negotiated a very favorable contract that not only paid him the handsome salary of $10,000 per week, but more importantly assured him the right to choose his directors and have a say in the script. He chose to work predominantly with European directors (Lubitsch, Stiller, Berger, the Austrian-born von Sternberg) and writers (von Sternberg, Lajos Biró, and Hanns Kräly). The fact that art director Hans Dreier, another important German import, worked on three of Jannings's six American films assured them the unifying "European" look for which Paramount was striving.

Jannings's two most successful German films in America had been *Der letzte Mann* and *Varieté* — both of which were films in which Jannings played everyday men and their everyday plights, shifting away from his earlier embodiments of kings and other dignitaries — and Paramount's roles for him were meant to be an American extension on the fallen man type he had portrayed in these later films.[3] With the exception of *The Patriot*, *The Street of Sin*, and *Betrayal*, all of his American films are set in present-day America and, as mentioned above, often cast him as American with a German-language background. In *The Way of All Flesh*, he plays the German-American cashier August Schiller who, an ideal father and loyal husband, loses everything through one fateful misstep; similarly, in *Sins of the Fathers*, he plays a German-American restaurateur who inadvertently blinds his son through his bootleg gin, serves a prison sentence, and is redeemed through an unlikely happy ending; and in *Betrayal*, Jannings is the mayor of a small Swiss town involved in a jealousy drama. In these roles, and others such as the crime boss Basher Bill in the London-set gangster drama *Street of Sin*, or Sergius Alexander, a former Russian general now toiling as an extra in Hollywood in *The Last Command*, Jannings plays individuals who strive high and plunge deep — often through the smallest fault — eliciting our compassion for their all-too-human shortcomings. These stories of degradation and humiliation allowed Jannings to employ full range of his melodramatic repertoire, making them of one piece not only with the German films that preceded them, but also *Der blaue Engel*, the film that would enable his German comeback.

There is good reason to consider *Der blaue Engel* an extension of Jannings's American oeuvre. Initiated by Erich Pommer, also just returned from Hollywood, it was meant to be a synthesis of Hollywood and Babelsberg — a multiple-language film made for an international audience by a producer intimately familiar with the tastes of both the American and the German public. It featured an American star director, von Sternberg, able to draw on his Austrian roots; a major international star, Jannings, capable of playing both the German and English language versions; and a new star in the making, Marlene Dietrich. It would be Jannings's biggest success ever — and his last one until he starred as another teacher figure in Carl Froelich's *Traumulus* (1936), a film meant to recast the internationalism of *Der blaue Engel* in decidedly German fashion. But if *Der blaue Engel* marked Jannings return to the German screen, it would launch Marlene Dietrich's career in Hollywood — a success story of unparalleled dimensions that would quickly outshine Jannings's three years with Paramount.

See also:

- 11 December 1930: Ban of *All Quiet on the Western Front* Highlights Tensions over Sound Technology
- 13 January 1954: Preminger's Dual-Language *The Moon Is Blue* (1953) and *Die Jungfrau auf dem Dach* (1954) Seek Glocal Success

- 25 February 2007: *Das Leben der Anderen* Follows Blueprint for Foreign-Language Oscar Success

Notes

[1] Munkepunke [Alfred Richard Meyer], *1000% Jannings* (Hamburg: Prismen, 1930), 101.

[2] Herbert Ihering, *Von Reinhardt bis Brecht: Eine Auswahl der Theaterkritiken von 1909–1932*, 3 vols, ed. Rolf Badenhausen (Reinbek: Rowohlt, 1967), 388.

[3] In Nazi Germany Jannings would return to playing kings (*Der alte und der junge König* [*The Old and the Young King*], 1935) and other leading figures: in politics (*Ohm Krüger*, 1941, and *Die Entlassung* [*The Dismissal*], 1942), in industry (*Der Herrscher* [*The Ruler*], 1937), and in science (*Robert Koch, der Bekämpfer des Todes* [*Robert Koch, Victor over Death*], 1939).

3 June 1929: Lloyd Bacon's *The Singing Fool* Triggers Debate about Sound Film

Lutz Koepnick

On 3 June 1929, almost a year after its American premiere, Lloyd Bacon's *The Singing Fool* opened at Berlin's Gloria-Palast. The distributor's expectations ran high while the critics' diagnostic radar was on extreme alert. As the first fully synchronized sound film shown in Germany, *The Singing Fool* would inaugurate a new era of film production, exhibition, and consumption, one that promised to open new avenues of investment and revenue collection. Though film, of course, had never been entirely silent before — thanks to piano accompanists, film commentators, and unruly viewers who provided their own soundtracks — synchronized sound had the potential to standardize the relationship of image and sound, streamline the often erratic relationships between the production and exhibition sector, and allow for a more effective management of resources and profit margins. Just as importantly, however, synchronized sound also asked filmmakers and viewers alike to revise established codes of realism, illusion, identification, and pleasure, thus threatening what had often been hailed as the distinguishing mark of German cinema during the Weimar era: its self-confident exploration of film as a visual medium, be it through the use of canted camera angles and extravagant set-designs in expressionist cinema, the unchaining of the camera in the work of F. W. Murnau, or the widespread attempt to tell compelling stories without relying on intertitles at all and hence make images speak for themselves. Primarily driven by the commercial interests of the industry, yet clearly aiming at popular appeal, the introduction of synchronized sound film entailed all the elements necessary to add yet another chapter to the protracted story of how German film culture struggled to position cinema somewhere in between the poles of authentic art and the popular, in between auteurist self-expression and industrial mechanization, in between meaning and money.

Starring Al Jolson in the title role, *The Singing Fool* tells the sentimental story of a café waiter whose voice will earn him Broadway fame as he tries to follow the demands of his ill-directed, and ultimately doomed, romantic desire. The film, including Jolson's numerous song interludes, relied on Vitaphone processes, an early sound technology used primarily between 1926 and 1930 in which a film's soundtrack was not yet printed on the actual film strip, but recorded onto a separate record and then played in synch with the projection. Because dubbing techniques had not yet been developed, *The Singing Fool* premiered to German audiences with its original soundtrack, and one might therefore wonder about the extent to which viewers were able to follow the film's narrative, dialogue, and songs. But given the contentious nature of the advent of sound film, neither the critics' nor the general audience's eyes (or ears) were really trained on the film's narrative shapes and melodramatic energies. Instead, what took center stage in the public's attention was the power of the apparatus to unify image and sound in the first place and thus manifest what critics at the time often envisioned as the matrimonial drama of the visual and acoustical. Some reviewers clearly sought to stay calm and distant in face of the new attraction, considering the addition of synchronized sound as merely a short-lived fad or, much worse, a serious threat to the medium's cultural standing. In this, these reviewers echoed the polemical arguments against sound cinema articulated throughout the 1920s by Germany's leading film critics and theorists such as Béla Balázs and Rudolf Arnheim.

Repeated and modified for years to come, Arnheim's position was symptomatic of how many German intellectuals hoped to endow the medium of film with aesthetic and cultural legitimacy. According to Arnheim, synchronized sound threatened what qualified film as art because it undermined the ways in which cinematographic technique explored, structured, and shaped the visual field. Insisting that film was meant to be a visual medium alone, Arnheim feared that the mobility and multidirectionality of the acoustical would pierce the frame of the image, blur the boundary between on- and off-screen space, and thus define cinema as both a heterogeneous medium and as a mere subordinate rather than a strong alternative to theatrical stage art. "Suddenly," Arnheim had written about the role of sound in cinema already a year prior the release of *The Singing Fool*, "the edge of the image no longer is a frame but a mere boundary of a hole, of a theatrical space — sound transforms the screen into a spatial stage!"[1] Synchronized sound, in Arnheim's perspective, had the potential to guide the viewer's attention away from the integrity of the frame; it punctuated what constituted film's formative principle as it invited the viewers' senses to touch upon the unseen and unrepresented. In other words, sound inscribed noise at the very heart of the cinematic image; it unframed the image and destabilized the self-contained character of the filmic work, producing viewers whose inattention could not but deflate any filmmaker's serious aesthetic ambitions.

Arnheim's elitist plea against the use of sound in cinema was echoed by various critics anticipating 3 June 1929 as a mere detour in the history of German film: a vain play with technological ornamentation that added nothing substantial to the art of filmmaking yet nonetheless threatened the integrity of the cinematic image. As if trying to appease some of these critics' discontent, on the night of its German opening, *The Singing Fool* was shown with two short films on the supporting bill: the first presented a performance by an American jazz band; the second featured tenor Beniaminio Gigli intoning Italian opera. The choice was clearly programmatic. It situated sound cinema as a medium able to disseminate a wide range of audiovisual pleasures to diverse audiences — a medium having something to offer for everyone, including high art for culturally demanding audience members. Such gestures of cultural pluralism certainly did very little to encourage highbrow critics to give up their initial misgivings. It succeeded, however, in energizing those eager to join the moment and embrace the addition of sound as cinema's inevitable future. For some, 3 June 1929 marked the beginning of a new task for cinema — namely, to satisfy Germany's long-standing hunger for music and transport this most German of all arts to even the remotest corners of the land. "It is only a matter of time," rejoiced one ecstatic reviewer of *The Singing Fool*, "and La Scala will play for only one *Deutschmark* in small provincial towns."[2] For others, synchronized sound offered mnemonic possibilities far superior to how either photography or simple sound recording had hitherto been able to embalm the present for the future: "Voices have always been there since the beginning of the universe," concluded Fred Hildenbrandt in his review, "but now we have an apparatus that makes a voice and a singer or an actor immortal."[3] Though early sound films were not always as synchronized as they claimed to be and often tended to frustrate their audiences with annoying (although at times quite comical) rifts between sound and image, many critics applauded the new era, not simply because it promised new kinds of cinematic pleasures, but also because it redefined the public role of the movie theater as a site for transmitting vernacular meanings, memories, and visions. The coming of sound fueled the hopes of those trying to reconnect cinematic pleasures to national traditions and local idioms of expression as much as it inspired those envisioning the language of film as at once popular and modernist.

As the principal force driving the transition from silent to sound cinema, the German film industry had little patience with how German critics contemplated the aesthetic pros and cons of synchronized sound. It in fact moved swiftly and rigorously into the new era, augmenting given production facilities, retraining actors and staff, and retooling existing exhibition venues. Six months after the premiere of *The Singing Fool*, the first German 100-percent sound production, *Melodie des Herzens* (*Melody of the Heart*, directed by Hanns Schwarz), hit the theaters, launching a whole series of domestic musicals or music-centered films that, in an effort to make the best use of the new technology, flooded German screens in the months and years to come. "What a relief," wrote critic Ernst Jäger about *Melodie des Herzens* for *Film-Kurier*, "sound film without a saxophone."[4] Though Schwarz's film had all kinds of dramatic flaws, it effectively proved that German studios not only could enter, but also could significantly profit from the race to sound. If *The Singing Fool* had catered to the Weimar fascination with foreign rhythms and different sounds, jazz music in particular, *Melodie des Herzens* helped producers and critics anticipate a future in which native voices and domestic musical idioms would recenter German spectatorship and contain the increasing internationalization of leisure activities and profit margins. In face of the darkening clouds over the economy in the late 1920s, the industry hailed the arrival of the talkie as an opportunity to reduce American market shares in Germany and German-speaking Europe. In 1929, German studios still produced 175 silent and only 8 sound films; in 1930, the ratio diminished to roughly 2:1. In 1931, the total number of silent film productions decreased to 2, and in 1932, German studios shot no silent pictures at all.[5]

Arnheim's initial worries about the coming of synchronized sound were surely not entirely off the mark for at least three reasons: first, unwieldy recording equipment caused early sound films until the early 1930s to lack much of the visual virtuosity of Weimar art film; second, due to the radical increase in production and distribution costs of sound films, the late 1920s and early 1930s witnessed a significant waning of modernist sensibilities and avant-garde experimentation; and third, the industry's initial focus on the production of multilanguage versions and hence on working with multiple casts led to a certain decrease of thespian excellence in front of the camera. But it would be wrong to think that the transition to sound resulted in a profound crisis of German filmmaking, as initially feared by some of the leading critics of the 1920s. On the contrary: acclaimed directors such as G. W. Pabst, Fritz Lang, and Robert Siodmak were quick not only to develop imaginative strategies to integrate sound and image effectively, but also to shoot films in which the presence and materiality of the acoustical took center stage. One prime example is Lang's masterpiece *M* (1931), a film as much dedicated to the possibilities of (cinematic) sound as to the precarious dynamic of modern city life. German audiences, too, embraced the new rhythms, noises, and voices on screen swiftly and without much hesitation. The speed of this conversion in fact remains quite astonishing. It is indicative of the fact that much more was at stake than merely a makeover of aesthetic preferences and modes of narrative identification. What is important to remember here is the fact that the breakthrough of sound film coincided with the fundamental rupturing of the social, economic, and political fabrics around 1930. Whereas the economic crash of 1929 and the ensuing turmoil of late Weimar Germany resulted in an unprecedented contraction of spatial and temporal coordinates, the streamlined temporality of sound cinema offered viable channels to articulate or even counteract feelings of displacement, to restructure memory, and readjust fantasy. In contrast to the often-unpredictable temporality of silent film projection, talkies enabled structures of experience that differed from the chaotic flexing of time outside the movie theater. Far from merely serving as an anesthetic, sound film thus offered nothing less but new means of sounding out — in however distorted a form — fundamental anxieties about a bleak present and an unsettling future.

See also:

- 14 September 1922: Schüfftan Process Reconciles Artistic Craftsmanship with Demands of Entertainment Industry
- 11 December 1930: Ban of *All Quiet on the Western Front* Highlights Tensions over Sound Technology
- 13 June 1930: *Weekend* Broadcast Tests Centrality of Image in Cinema

Notes

[1] Rudolf Arnheim, "Der tönende Film," in *Die Seele in der Silberschicht: Medientheoretische Texte. Photographie — Film — Rundfunk*, ed. Helmut H. Diederichs (Frankfurt am Main: Suhrkamp, 2004), 68.

[2] R. K., "Filmbesprechung: Der singende Narr," *Licht-Bild-Bühne* (4 June 1929).

[3] Fred Hildenbrandt, "Der Singende Narr" (4 June 1929), Archive of Stiftung Deutsche Kinemathek, Berlin.

[4] *Film-Kurier* (17 December 1929).

[5] Anton Kaes, "Film in der Weimarer Republik: Motor der Moderne," in *Geschichte des deutschen Films*, ed. Wolfgang Jacobsen, Anton Kaes, and Hans Helmut Prinzler (Stuttgart: Metzler, 1993), 86.

4 February 1930: *Menschen am Sonntag* Provides New Model of Cinematic Realism

Noah Isenberg

A moment of bucolic relaxation offers distraction from urban life.
Menschen am Sonntag *(1930). Credit: Deutsche Kinemathek.*

SHOT ON THE EVE of the Great Depression, with almost no budget to speak of, an equally modest cast of amateur actors, a relatively untested, unknown crew, and no major studio backing, the late silent film *Menschen am Sonntag* (*People on Sunday*, 1930) has a production history like no other of its era.[1] After seasoned director Rochus Gliese abruptly abandoned the project due to the lack of proper support, the picture was codirected by two aspiring filmmakers, Robert Siodmak and Edgar G. Ulmer, neither of whom had ever directed a feature film. It was more or less scripted, though not in any formal sense, by Billy (then "Billie") Wilder, with input from Curt (then "Kurt") Siodmak. Veteran special effects technician Eugen Schüfftan operated the camera with assistance from Fred Zinnemann, and the project was produced by "Filmstudio 1929," a one-off production company cobbled together by crewmembers and theater impresario Moriz Seeler and nominally backed by Nero-Film producer Heinrich Nebenzahl. Almost every person originally associated with the film — most notably, Ulmer, the Siodmak brothers, and Wilder — would later, after migration to Hollywood and after the film's cultural cachet had accrued over time, take considerably more credit for the film than the historical record allows them. The question of who deserves the lion's share of acclaim, or even a legitimate director's credit, will likely never be definitively resolved. In fact, given the highly collaborative nature of the film, *Menschen am Sonntag* does not fit terribly neatly into the framework of *Autorenkino* or auteur cinema.

In terms of its formal innovation, *Menschen* takes the "city film," commonly associated with Walter Ruttmann's *Berlin. Die Sinfonie der Großstadt* (*Berlin: Symphony of a Great City*, 1927), in a new direction. Unconcerned with merely capturing a cross-section of the German metropolis, the film cannily blends avant-garde documentary and narrative cinema into something that is less abstract, more improvised and natural, and more unabashedly romantic than its predecessors. While it continues to draw on the once dominant trend of *Neue Sachlichkeit* (New Objectivity), with a strong focus on popular advertising, photography, design and technology — and, more generally, on the wider contemporaneous trend in Europe and America in capturing the pulsating city life on celluloid — its main conceit is its utter defiance of prevailing modes and industry norms. The film turns its back on studio production, instead allowing the city and its many inviting locations — its boulevards, cafes, lakes, boardwalks, beaches, and other places of leisure and recreation — to substitute for the standard reliance on sets, while at the same time allowing amateurs to play the roles otherwise reserved for bona fide film stars.

That the film was initially greeted by critics with such enthusiasm (pronounced "a grand success" in most of the city's leading newspapers), and in the meantime has been repeatedly hailed by film historians on both sides of the Atlantic, many of whom have championed its presaging of Italian neorealism and the French New Wave, has cast upon it a certain afterglow. Similarly, the film's vague origins — it was ostensibly conceived during a series of conversations among the crew, then scribbled on napkins at Berlin's Romanisches Café — only adds to the mystique. Now that the film has found a firm place in the canon of Weimar cinema, however, *Menschen am Sonntag* deserves to be reappraised on its own very basic terms, to be seen in the history of German cinema as an essential and unusually influential film (a favorite among the Oberhausen signatories and beyond), and to be recognized for the small gem that it is.

The premise of the film could not be any simpler: in the heart of the city, near the Bahnhof-Zoo subway station, amid the intense bustle of commerce and traffic, a modern boy-meets-girl story transpires before our eyes. A chance encounter between two young, slightly aimless urban strollers results in a serendipitous scheme for a Sunday outing, which, after each one shows up with a best friend in tow, becomes a frolicsome double date at one of Berlin's nearby lakes. In a witty twist, the fifth member of the cast manages to oversleep the entire outing. What ultimately unfolds over the mere hour or so of remaining screen time is a remarkably straightforward depiction, by turns affectionate and comical, of courting rituals, leisure activity, and mass entertainment circa 1930. We see the four protagonists listening to music, swimming, enjoying a picnic, riding a pedal boat, alternating their love interests, and trying in general to squeeze the most out of the day. The style of the film is natural, the setting universal, and the atmosphere, perhaps the core of the entire film, shamelessly flirtatious. More than anything else, the filmmakers strove for a new kind of directness, an unmediated, unvarnished representation of everyday life as experienced by members of a young, urban consumer class; quite fittingly, one of the film's working titles was *So ist es und nicht anders!* (This is how it is, and no different!).[2]

By using amateur actors (who retained their real names and day jobs) extracted from the same sector of society as the protagonists — the minor professions of a burgeoning young, urban, white-collar work force — the film crew was able to offer an unusually honest, verité rendering of the values, mores, dreams and anxieties of this social class. In the opening credits, following the initial intertitle announcing that the film's five lead characters appear here before the camera for the first time and that they are today back at their real jobs, we are immediately introduced to the characters in their true settings. These are the jovial taxi driver Erwin Splettstößer, seated behind the wheel of a cab bearing the Berlin license plate "IA 10088"; the charming record salesgirl Brigitte Borchert in front of the Electrola shop, who last month, so the title reads, sold 150 copies of the hit song "In einer kleinen Konditorei" (In a little pastry shop); the tall, dark, and slender Wolfgang von Waltershausen, a former officer, farmer, antique dealer and gigolo, currently working as a traveling wine merchant; the very chic, urbane Christl Ehlers, who enters what appears to be a casting studio, and who we are told, "wears down her heels as a film extra"; and, finally, Annie Schreyer, a model, here reclining, filing her nails, and waiting for the next job. Much like their predecessors in Russian films (such as those by Sergei Eisenstein, Abram Room, and others), each of these characters serves as a kind of social type, easily recognizable to the audience. Moreover, they participate actively in forming the very mass culture that they represent on the screen, the culture with which the audience so readily identified. "The five people in this film," implored Billy Wilder at the time of the production, "that's you and that's me" (Vogt, 226). Admittedly, the film's primary viewpoint — with its occasional flourishes of voyeurism, its unabashed prankster sensibility, and boyish bravado — is quite masculine. The audience serves, in part, as witness to Wolfgang and Erwin's youthful exploits, and their fraternal bonds, from their chummy card game near the start of the film to their final splitting of a last cigarette, are unmistakably deep. Yet the leading women, whose roles shift and evolve throughout the picture, are not without their share of complexity and individual development; they challenge their male counterparts, seeing through their schemes and standing their own ground.

Though the film was made at an especially fragile moment in history, between the recent stock market collapse and the rise of National Socialism, it evokes a strange sense of calm, purity, and innocence. As Lutz Koepnick has observed, "it can be understood as having allowed audiences to take a final breath before being caught in the vortex of violence and mass mobilization."[3] The chief concerns of the film, or of the film's characters, are indeed trivial — fighting over matinee idols, burning one's tongue on a hot dog, scrounging together enough money to pay for a boat ride — compared to the grand historical events taking place off screen. This does not, however, render the film distant from the spirit of the times. Its sustained focus on such comparatively banal matters is perfectly in keeping with the Weimar preoccupation with leisure and the still rather new idea of "Weekend." Thus, *Menschen am Sonntag* is to a notable degree a visual commentary on such hit songs as "Wochenende und Sonnenschein" (Weekend and sunshine) and on the vivid photo portraiture of August Sander, and is also very much an exploration of the new cultural habits of the petite bourgeoisie, similar to Siegfried Kracauer's more scholarly and critical 1929 study of white-collar workers.[4]

Still, despite the seemingly apolitical, even escapist nature of the film, there are overt strains of political satire. For example, relatively late in the story, just after a quick cut to the *Siegessäule* (Victory Column), the central monument devoted to the glorious Prussian battles of the 1860s and 1870s, we observe an elderly fellow walking along the Tiergarten's monumental promenade, the Siegesallee, with hat and cane. Perhaps a war veteran or merely someone who outlived Imperial Germany, he represents an era that was brought to a halt with the advent of Weimar, as he stands in front of the monuments, first watching a small procession of soldiers march by and then taking in the statues of Prussian leaders and heroes. As Schüfftan's camera assumes the old man's perspective, we zoom in on the imposing figures, thereby gaining a privileged view; he finally sits down in front of former Duke of Prussia and Elector of Brandenburg Georg Wilhelm (1595–1640), and removes his hat, as if to show respect and offer a salute to the Prussian past. Many members of the contemporary audience would no doubt recognize these towering historical figures, and might even recognize in the seemingly innocuous, marginal character of the old man a satirical allusion to Paul von Hindenburg, Reichspräsident since 1925 and a notorious monarchist, who embodied a Weimar-era nostalgia for a political past that was no more. As one critic put it, referring to the famed Weimar political satirist Kurt Tucholsky, the film has "a bit of Tucholsky-Germany."[5]

Even if the film's meandering plot — more akin to an episode from a late twentieth-century American television sitcom like *Seinfeld* than a Weimar-era feature film — eschews a more sophisticated, politically minded critique, *Menschen* certainly tested the limits of filmmaking at the time. It broke new ground in the final phase of silent film production, introducing a fresh model of independent cinema and a bare-bones realism that would have a deeper impact both at the time of and many years after its release. In the *Berliner Tageblatt*, the critic Eugen Szatmari took special joy in noting the ways in which a film like *Menschen* undermined studio production:

> Young people got together and with laughably little means — without sets or ballrooms or opera galas, without stars, with a few human beings that they drew from their professions — they shot a film and achieved a total success for which one has to congratulate them and which hopefully will finally open up the eyes of the film industry. (Vogt, 230)

Regardless of whether these young cineastes effected the change hoped for by Szatmari, the model espoused by *Menschen* is one that filmmakers would continue to emulate internationally, from *nouvelle vague* and New German Cinema up to the more systematic efforts in the name of *Dogme 95*, and whose legacy endures to this day.

See also:

- 17 October 1930: Bertolt Brecht's *Threepenny Opera* Lawsuit Identifies Contradiction between Individual Creativity and Collective Production in Cinema
- 30 April 1999: Werner Herzog's "Minnesota Declaration" Performs Critique of Documentary Cinema
- 11 February 2008: Ulrike Ottinger's *Prater* Wins German Critics' Award for Best Documentary Yet Highlights the Director's Ties to Both Fiction and Nonfiction Film

Notes

[1] An earlier, slightly condensed version of this essay appeared as the booklet essay to accompany the 2011 Criterion Collection DVD release of *People on Sunday*.

[2] According to Wilder's contemporary account of the production, "Wir vom Filmstudio 1929," published in *Tempo* 2, no. 169 (23 July 1929), other titles included *Sommer 29* and *Junge Leute wie alle* (Young people like us). Cited in Guntram Vogt, *Die Stadt im Film: Deutsche Spielfilme 1900–2000* (Marburg: Schüren, 2001), 226. Hereafter cited in text.

[3] Lutz Koepnick, "The Bearable Lightness of Being: *People on Sunday* (1930)," in *Weimar Cinema: An Essential Guide to Classic Films of the Era*, ed. Noah Isenberg (New York: Columbia UP, 2008), 239.

[4] See Petra Löffler, "The Ordinary Life of Ordinary People: *Menschen am Sonntag*," in *Edgar G. Ulmer: Essays on the King of the Bs*, ed. Bernd Herzogenrath (Jefferson, NC: McFarland, 2009), 54–55.

[5] On this line of inquiry, see Ludwig Bauer, "Zeichen und kulturelles Wissen: Die Rekonstruktion des Bedeutungspotentials visueller Zeichen am Beispiel von *Menschen am Sonntag* (1930)," in *Der Stummfilm: Konstruktion und Rekonstruktion*, ed. Elfriede Ledig (Munich: diskurs film, 1988), 60–62.

13 June 1930: *Weekend* Broadcast Tests Centrality of Image in Cinema

Brian Hanrahan

WEEKEND, WALTER RUTTMANN'S 1930 *Hörfilm* (radio film), is a hybrid work, made on film, but produced for a radio broadcast. A "film without images," consisting only of a soundtrack, it represents, as one critic put it, "a limit case of film," a work that questions the centrality of the image in film, and marks the porous boundary between film and other media.[1] In formal-aesthetic terms, Ruttmann's piece incorporates new kinds of acoustic verisimilitude and indexicality into interwar montage aesthetics. In its production history, it was a direct result of institutional collaboration and technology transfer between film and radio, an example, albeit a formally atypical one, of the particularly close relation between the two media in the late Weimar period.

A coproduction of the Reichsrundfunkgesellschaft (RRG), the *Berliner Funkstunde* station, and the Tri-Ergon sound-film company, *Weekend* was first broadcast on 13 June 1930, in a simultaneous transmission in Berlin and Breslau. However, Ruttmann's eleven-minute sound montage was made on film: to gather the sounds for his "blind film," he toured Berlin, using a Tri-Ergon film camera, its lens cap left on, to record fragments of noise, voices, and music. From this material, he constructed an acoustic portrait of a weekend in the metropolis, deploying the techniques of rhythmic and associative montage he had developed to considerable popular and critical success in earlier, visual films like *Berlin. Die Sinfonie einer Großstadt* (*Berlin: Symphony of a Great City*, 1927) and *Melodie der Welt* (Melody of the world, 1929).

Although it is more modest in its scope, *Weekend* is more difficult and ambitious than either *Berlin* or *Melodie der Welt*. Eschewing explanatory frame, identificatory voices, and dramatic dialogue, it functions largely by sonic evocation and association. Ruttmann uses a variety of formal techniques in his dense assemblage of 240 sound samples, combining futurist-inspired noise collage with word association and fleeting hints of narrative. Dense, noisy passages are interspersed with slower, unedited samples that highlight the spatial properties of recorded sound and silence. An overture, entitled "Jazz of Work," thrusts the listener without warning into the noise of industrial machines, department store elevators, bells, and sirens, as the piece strives to convey the tense dissatisfaction and expectation of the end of the working week. In a subsequent excursion into the spaces around the city, traffic and trains give way to pastoral sounds and the noise of brass bands and beer garden revelers. Finally, with the weekend's close, "free time" segues back into the working week. Monday morning's eternal return is heard in alarm clocks and traffic, the grind of machine tools, the "ching!" of cash registers and the hubbub of work conversation.

Weekend was not only an innovative work of sonic modernism, but also a piece of demonstration software, commissioned to test and promote the compatibility of two separate technologies. Ruttmann's piece is the only work of lasting aesthetic interest to emerge from an experiment to develop and sell Tri-Ergon optical sound film as a recording medium for radio. This moment of shared technology, lasting from 1927 to 1930, formed part of the first phase of the intermedial relations of German radio and film, a period that sharply differs from later stages.[2] In its earliest years, radio had been hampered by the lack of electric recording technology, forcing the medium to depend almost entirely on live broadcasting and performance. Recording would allow precise preediting of programs, the capture of live events and their integration into news and sports reports, the establishment of sound and program archives, as well as improved sound effects and training. In 1928, Tri-Ergon film, which recorded sound as a graphic trace on celluloid, running alongside the images, offered a plausible solution to radio's recording problem, although the technology was initially developed for the synchronous recording of image and sound.

The technology offered more than sound storage. Easy to cut and rearrange, it overcame the recalcitrant materiality of grooves cut into disk, enabling straightforward sound editing. Moreover, the relative portability of the Tri-Ergon camera, used with long-cable radio microphones, allowed the sound recording of "real world" events, including the compelling reality-effects of local spatial timbre and ambient sound. For Tri-Ergon, selling sound film to the radio market promised a lucrative sideline to its main businesses in sound cinema and music publishing, a chance to outflank its disk- and magnetic-recording competitors. Experimental broadcasts began in 1928, with test transmissions of film-recorded excerpts from sports events, public speeches, operas, and concert performances.

If film-recording for radio primarily promised advantages in day-to-day programming, it also held out possibilities for more ambitious uses of radio. In radio-aesthetic discourse, film had long been held up as a possible countermodel to the theatricality and vococentricity of the early radio play, offering more fluid acoustic dramaturgies and the integration of material and location-recorded sound.[3] Experiments with Tri-Ergon seemed to offer a technical realization of these ideas. Hans Flesch, director of the *Berliner Funkstunde* station and the most prominent institutional supporter of experimental radio, turned to Ruttmann — fresh from *Berlin*'s success with populist modernism — to produce a sound work that would go beyond the "mere reproduction" of events and performances, and that would use the new technical constellation to create innovative form in radiophonic art.[4]

For Ruttmann, *Weekend* formed part of wider experiments with sound montage, which he began in his first RRG/Tri-Ergon commission, the sound film documentary *Tönende Welle* (Sounding wave, 1928; originally titled *Deutscher Rundfunk* [German radio]). In this forty-five-minute cinema advertisement for the medium of radio, and in 1929's *Melodie der Welt*, he had made limited experiments with the use of asynchronous sound montage. This reflected Ruttmann's belief, shared with many of his avant-garde contemporaries, that the aesthetic value of sound film lay not in simple synchronization, but in the interplay of two semiautonomous montages, one in image, one in sound. The *Weekend* project offered his first opportunity for concentrated work in sound montage: it was, in part, a training exercise for the director, with which to develop techniques of sound recording and editing.

Unlike some experimental filmmakers, who used Tri-Ergon's visible, alterable sound trace to create synthetic sounds without a natural referent,[5] Ruttmann emphasized the "photographic" properties of filmed sound. In keeping with his mid-1920s turn away from cinematic abstraction, his acoustic practice centered on the recording of "unstylized, worldly" sounds. With new technologies of sound recording and montage, he wrote, "everything audible in the whole world has become material," available for selection and associative juxtaposition. Tri-Ergon allowed the "forming and compositional arrangement of the natural materials [i.e., unstaged, location-recorded sound] which radio . . . has at its disposal."[6] In particular, Ruttmann was fascinated by what he termed the "photography of acoustic space," the recording of spatial timbre and ambient sound, whose powerful effects of verisimilitude and presence had been previously audible on radio, but, unrecorded, were impossible to incorporate into complex aesthetic form.

The emphasis on sonic photomontage underlies Ruttmann's avoidance of distortion and mixing on *Weekend*. Even fading is used sparingly in the piece. Where it appears, it is immanent to the sound event, internal to the sample, as when a passing brass band moves out of earshot, or the murmur of a conversation dies away. As in his visual montage, Ruttmann's main device is the cut, which audibly divides one sound sample from the next. Sharp cuts accentuate the internal rhythms of the piece and their miniature ruptures emphasize its assembled nature, but they also serve to frame the sounds, even at a fraction of a second, preserving their discreteness and cognizability and helping maintain an audible indexical link to an original sonic event. Thus, while Ruttmann's sounds participate in melody, rhythm, and discordance, his audio assemblage never fully becomes music, even of a sonically expanded kind. It remains, to use his favored generic term, "photographic sound art."

The combination of palpability and signification in Ruttmann's assemblage of "photographed" sound enables complex formal effects. *Weekend* is structured by a set of oppositions that blur the divide between the semantic and somatic. Male/female, city/nature, work/leisure, pleasure/displeasure are signified by recognizable sonic elements, but also experienced acoustically in the interplay of sound and silence, acceleration and deceleration, loud and quiet, low-reverb and high-reverb sound. To this, Ruttmann adds layers of different temporalities: narrative time compresses forty-eight hours into eleven minutes, while the piece's own time is marked out in irregular and fleeting rhythms. Repeated motifs form their own patterns, while also creating semantic associations, and complicating the piece's narrative time by embedding tiny flashbacks and flashforwards into its linear progress.

Much of this formal complexity went unperceived. Commenting after the film's broadcast, Ruttmann reflected on the work's relative failure. "The experiment," he observed "was not quite a success. The film was difficult and incomprehensible, listeners got lost in a sea of sounds, grasped a few associations and connections, but essential aspects slid past unnoticed."[7] More than anything, the director's auto-critique highlights the passive role assigned to the early radio listener: today, a digital media player (which, like a Tri-Ergon editing suite, makes listening a matter of the coordination of hand, ear, and eye) allows a better appreciation of *Weekend* as an intricately wrought modernist work.

In another sense, too, *Weekend* enjoys a medial afterlife beyond its original conditions of production. Contrary to its commissioners' hopes, Ruttmann's *Hörfilm* did not launch a new era of hybrid radio-films. It marked the experiment's end. Sound film, it turned out, was overpriced and overspecced for day-to-day radio use, and was soon superseded by a new generation of portable disk recorders. The celluloid copy of *Weekend* was lost in the 1930s, though the work survived as a privately made recording on shellac disk and was later digitized and made available online for more listeners than ever heard it on the airwaves.[8] If Ruttmann's work questioned the relation of sound to (absent) image, and asked which works on film can be considered *films*, it now poses an additional set of questions, centering on the historical migration of forms across different media. *Weekend* was produced by one historical constellation of radio and film; it was a creation — technically, institutionally, and aesthetically — of *both* film and radio. Today, the same work, the same sound, survives as something else again.

See also:

- 1 April 1921: Walter Ruttmann's *Lichtspiel: Opus 1* Shapes Culture of Abstract Filmmaking
- 3 May 1925: French and German Avant-Garde Converge at *Der absolute Film*
- 8 June 1986: Farocki's *Wie man sieht* Urges New Ways of Seeing

Notes

[1] Michel Chion, *Audio-Vision: Sound on Screen* (New York: Columbia UP, 1994), 143.

[2] After 1930, the central phenomenon linking the two media was a highly effective synergy based on the marketing of popular songs. For an account of the interrelationship of film and radio, see Wolfgang Mühl-Benninghaus, *Das Ringen um den Tonfilm: Strategien der Elektro- und der Filmindustrie in den 20er und 30er Jahren* (Düsseldorf: Droste, 1999), especially 53–81, 251–87.

[3] Media-aesthetic ideas linking film and radio are perhaps best summed up in Rudolf Arnheim's text "Hörfilm tut not!" See Rudolf Arnheim, *Rundfunk als Hörkunst* (1936; repr. Frankfurt am Main: Suhrkamp, 2001), 82–85.

[4] On Flesch and *Weekend*'s commissioning, see Hermann Naber, "Ruttmann & Konsorten: Über die frühen Beziehungen zwischen Hörspiel und Film," *Rundfunk und Geschichte: Mitteilungen des Studienkreises Rundfunk und Geschichte* 32, no. 3/4 (2006): 5–20.

[5] See Thomas Y. Levin, "'Tones from out of Nowhere': Rudolph Pfenninger and the Archeology of Synthetic Sound," *Grey Room* 12 (Summer 2003): 32–79.

[6] Walter Ruttmann, "Neue Gestaltung von Tonfilm und Funk: Programm einer photographischen Hörkunst" (1929), reprinted in Jeanpaul Goergen, *Walter Ruttmanns Tonmontagen als Ars Acustica* (Siegen: Medien und Kommunikation, 1994), 25–26; here 25.

[7] "Jerzy Toeplitz im Gespräch mit Walter Ruttmann" (1933). In *Walter Ruttmann: Eine Dokumentation*, ed. Jeanpaul Goergen (Berlin: Freunde der deutschen Kinemathek, 1989), 89–90; here 90.

[8] *Weekend* is available on numerous Web sites. A remastered version is available on the recent DVD edition of Ruttmann's 1920s films: Walter Ruttmann, *Berlin, die Sinfonie der Großstadt & Melodie der Welt*: 2 DVD set (Vienna: Edition Filmmuseum, 2008).

17 October 1930: Bertolt Brecht's *Threepenny Opera* Lawsuit Identifies Contradiction between Individual Creativity and Collective Production in Cinema

Marc Silberman

BERTOLT BRECHT WAS unusual among German artists and intellectuals of the Weimar Republic in that he did not fear the entertainment industry as a threat to artistic practices. On the contrary, he sought out opportunities to use it as a platform to launch polemics against conservative and progressive intellectuals alike who clung to traditional art forms as if they were not affected by the new media. Nothing illustrates this practice better than the fate of *Die Dreigroschenoper* (*The Threepenny Opera*) in its metamorphosis from the most successful stage production of the Weimar Republic, to the film scenario commissioned for a commercial film adaptation, to the actual film directed by G. W. Pabst, to the *Dreigroschenroman* (The threepenny novel) that Brecht wrote during his first year of exile in Denmark. Accompanying these creative stages were the court injunction initiated by Brecht and composer Kurt Weill against the film production company for copyright infringement and the book-length essay about the trial called *Der Dreigroschenprozeß* (*The Threepenny Lawsuit*). Here Brecht formulated his only extended theoretical reflection on the cinema as well as his most incisive contribution to a new kind of media history that explored, on the one hand, the competition unleashed by capitalist production practices between the theater and the cinema, and, on the other hand, artists' rights to control their ideas when they encounter new mass media.

The legendary success of *Die Dreigroschenoper* launched Brecht's international theater career when it opened in Berlin in August 1928. Based on the popularity of Weill's music and the provocative decadence of the play's characters, Nero-Film bought the adaptation rights in May 1930, which included a proviso that Brecht and a team of collaborators would write the film scenario. Though the contract gave Brecht the right to demand changes if the final cut did not follow their scenario, it also obliged the collaborators to follow the original play's content and style. Yet by 1930 Brecht's views had changed, and when it became clear in the course of the summer that his film scenario would differ in essential ways from the stage play, Nero-Film, under pressure to begin the shoot on deadline in September, sought some kind of accommodation with Brecht. When that failed, the production began with a new but not altogether different script under the direction of G. W. Pabst — and Brecht went to court.

The bone of contention was the text of "Die Beule" (The Bruise), Brecht's *Dreigroschen* film scenario, the thrust of which was substantially different than that of the play. Not only had Brecht's own views about capitalist society shifted through his study of Marxism, but his turn to a more didactic style in his *Lehrstücke* (learning plays) was at odds with the mix of politics and entertainment that characterized the original work. Moreover, the market crash in October 1929 had created a politically more polarized context than was the case in 1928, and Brecht took the adaptation as an occasion to change the play's characters and setting to construct a more radical image of class struggle.[1] Since Nero-Film was interested in cashing in on the stage hit, Brecht's revision did not serve their ends of reproducing the original.

Cinephiles have celebrated the film as one of Pabst's masterpieces, while Brecht fans and scholars have largely regarded it as a betrayal of the anti-illusionistic thrust that characterized his Epic Theater experiments of the time.[2] In fact, the film version of *Die Dreigroschenoper*, which opened to enthusiastic reviews in Berlin in February 1931, undoubtedly contributed to the play's international fame as well as to Brecht's. Meanwhile, Brecht and Weill filed suit on the grounds that Nero-Film had not fulfilled its contractual obligation of "protecting" the integrity of the original work, thereby threatening the company's entire investment with a court injunction to stop the shoot. The trial lasted four days, from 17–20 October 1930, and generated an unusually large press response owing to Brecht's notoriety and to the fact that the case had a signal function in articulating the contradictory positions of literary intellectuals and the stakeholders in the entertainment industry.

Brecht must have been pleased with the fact that he lost in the court's judgment of 4 November 1930, for if he had won he would have had to recognize that the capitalist system was *not* following its own rules.[3] The lawsuit essay, which appeared slightly more than a year later, represents Brecht's analysis of how this system functions, exposing the intersection of power, false ideas, and art. Although the lawsuit against the film production company was the point of departure, the text neither documents the trial nor raises the issues of cinematic adaptation surrounding his scenario or, for that matter, Pabst's film (there is no evidence that Brecht actually saw it, although he was an avid moviegoer). Rather, Brecht presents himself in the role of the naïve artist who goes to court to defend the inviolability of intellectual property guaranteed by the liberal, democratic constitution. There he discovers that the validity of individual ownership is measured against economic consequences; in the case of new media, such as cinema, the economic risk is so great that the profit motive in producing the commodity (the film) is deemed more important than the right of the author to his immaterial property (the ideas). In short, Brecht shows that, contrary to what many artists would like to believe, the work of art, like other commodities, is subject to market forces. *Der Dreigroschenprozeß*, subtitled "A Sociological Experiment," is a brilliant demonstration of the implications of this insight and, from today's perspective, a document of a significant media shift taking place during the interwar period.[4]

Divided into five unequal sections, the essay comprises a montage of press reports about the 1930 court case, excerpts from contracts and lawyers' arguments, reports on discussions, as well as Brecht's own commentaries, witticisms, and polemical theses. In a brief introduction he spells out the purpose of this formal construction as the means of "staging" his own experience with the movie industry so that the difference between the actual practices and the ideas of how culture, law, and public opinion function become visible. In one section he investigates the consequences of the lawsuit's possible resolutions, only to conclude, as the court did, that the artist's "ideal" — that is, the belief that contractual law protects ideas — is false. Like all property rights, they can be purchased by capital. This was, in effect, the actual outcome of the court case, and the press excerpts Brecht liberally cites indicate that the court judgment corroborated traditional and even leftwing attitudes about the incompatibility of art and commerce. If he had stopped there, he argues, he would have achieved at least one important concession from the court: the public demonstration that legal precedent, oriented exclusively toward notions of individual creativity, was incompatible with a capitalist mode of production based on the sort of collective production found in the movie industry.

Brecht goes a step further by developing a critical theory of the media. He argues that art can neither reject nor simply avoid the new mass media as "bad" since the technologically most progressive media define the standard for all other arts, including traditional forms of poetry and drama. This is an issue not merely of collective forms of production but also of reception. The fact that traditional forms of art still dominate the cinema, for example, in the adaptation of a stage play, results from an obsolete ideology of individualism — "the" author — in a historically specific phase of capitalism. Yet the audiences for the work of art perceive reality differently — they read novels and they go to the theater knowing how the new mass media represent reality. Brecht not only takes aim here at the still widespread adherence to Romantic aesthetics with its cult of the genius and insistence on the aura of originality, he also criticizes an understanding of reality based on introspective psychology and anthropomorphism. His growing interest in behaviorist psychology and materialist philosophy in the late 1920s drew his attention to the process of "looking from the outside" as a means to capture the social, intersubjective nature of human behavior.

A note included in "Die Beule" indicates that Brecht was exploring cinematic representation in response to the technological advances of the new media: "The camera searches for motives, it is a sociologist."[5] The camera becomes here the ideal instrument for "looking from the outside"; the camera as sociologist allows the filmmaker to construct each sequence with distinct cinematographic techniques and a visual rhythm dictated by external action rather than by the subjective perspective of the main character(s). Brecht's critique of mimesis and illusionism in the theater transfers here to the cinematic medium, where the goal cannot be the documentary replication of external reality, as if it simply exists "out there," waiting to be reproduced. In a frequently cited passage of *Der Dreigroschenprozeß* he uses still photography to critique this notion of realism as verisimilitude:

> The situation has become so complicated because the simple "reproduction of reality" says less than ever about that reality. A photograph of the Krupp works or the AEG reveals almost nothing about these institutions. Reality as such has slipped into the domain of the functional. The reification of human relations, the factory, for example, no longer discloses those relations. So there is indeed "something to construct," something "artificial," "invented." Hence, there is in fact a need for art. But the old concept of art, derived from experience, is obsolete.[6]

Visible surfaces and the content of visual images, such as a Krupp munitions factory or the electrical company Allgemeine Elektrizitäts-Gesellschaft, no longer communicate the structural conditions of capitalism. For that the dramatist, the photographer, and the filmmaker must find a new approach to reality.

In *Der Dreigroschenprozeß* Brecht staged an original and fundamental critique of an outmoded, idealist understanding of art. He recognized the revolutionary nature of the capitalist process of commodity circulation that was changing the entire system of artistic production and reception, and at the same time he greeted capitalism's self-destructive power, which promised to release transformative cultural energies like those that fed his own lawsuit. Contrary to the actual trial, the publication of the lawsuit essay over a year later had little resonance and — like much late Weimar intellectual ferment — sank into oblivion when Hitler came to power. In the broader context of postwar Brecht and media studies, the *Dreigroschenprozeß* was rediscovered only after the publication of Brecht's collected works in sixteen volumes in 1967, which ignited more generally a renaissance in serious Brecht reception. Today the text is seen as a forerunner or crucial influence on Walter Benjamin's more familiar essay "The Work of Art in the Age of Mechanical Reproduction" (1935) or is compared to Max Horkheimer and Theodor Adorno's critique of the culture industry in *Dialectic of Enlightenment* (1947) and Marshall McLuhan's reflections on media technology in *The Gutenberg Galaxy* (1962). Unlike these, however, Brecht's *Dreigroschenprozeß* is a striking collage that stages contradiction both as form and as method. The conviction in the practical power of contradiction explains not only its unique argument but also the epigram that introduces it: "Unsere Hoffnung sind die Widersprüche!" (148, "Contradictions are our hope!").

See also:

- 4 February 1930: *Menschen am Sonntag* Provides New Model of Cinematic Realism
- 28 May 1942: Bertolt Brecht and Fritz Lang Write a Hollywood Screenplay
- 30 April 1999: Werner Herzog's "Minnesota Declaration" Performs Critique of Documentary Cinema

Notes

[1] Bertolt Brecht, "The Bruise," in *Brecht on Film and Radio*, trans. and ed. Marc Silberman (London: Methuen, 2000), 131–43.

[2] On the reception of Pabst's film *The Threepenny Opera*, see Thomas Elsaesser, "Transparent Duplicities: *The Threepenny Opera* (1931)," in *The Films of G. W. Pabst: An Extraterritorial Cinema*, ed. Eric Rentschler (New Brunswick, NJ: Rutgers UP, 1990), 103–15. The film was produced in German and French language versions, with separate lead actors; they are available in a double DVD edition from the British Film Institute.

[3] The court actually separated the cases of Weill and Brecht and found composer Weill's rights to have been abridged, while Brecht's were not. Brecht could have appealed his judgment, but he settled out of court with Nero-Film. For a detailed discussion of the actual court case, judgment, and settlement, see chapter 1 in Steve Giles, *Bertolt Brecht and Critical Theory: Marxism, Modernity and the Threepenny Lawsuit* (Bern: Peter Lang, 1997), 13–37.

[4] Bertolt Brecht, *The Threepenny Lawsuit*, in *Brecht on Film and Radio*, 147–99. Brecht wrote the essay in Spring/Summer 1931 and then revised it while working on the galleys in the Fall. It was published as "Versuch 10" (Experiment 10)

together with *Die Dreigroschenoper*, "Anmerkungen zur *Dreigroschenoper*," and the unfinished scenario "Die Beule," in volume 3 of Brecht's series *Versuche* (Berlin: Gustav Kiepenheuer Verlag, [December] 1931).

[5] Brecht, "The Bruise," 135n12.

[6] Brecht, *The Threepenny Lawsuit*, 164.

11 December 1930: Ban of *All Quiet on the Western Front* Highlights Tensions over Sound Technology

Dayton Henderson

Paul joins the ranks of the fallen at the end of
All Quiet on the Western Front *(1930). DVD capture.*

On 11 December 1930, the German Ministry of the Interior released an official communiqué detailing the decision to ban the American sound film *All Quiet on the Western Front*. The verdict came exactly one week after the film's debut in Berlin's Mozartsaal, and although the censorship board vehemently denied it, many observers felt it was a concession to the National Socialists. American and German newspapers reported with consternation that approximately 30,000 Nazi activists protested throughout Berlin due to the film's alleged anti-German subtext.

Agitators inside cinemas released snakes and white mice among the spectators, while Joseph Goebbels interrupted viewings by leading antisemitic chants and waving his parliamentary identification card in order to demonstrate his immunity from prosecution. Critics argued that this hysterical public response influenced the film's prohibition, which was uniquely based on both the version submitted to the German censors and the original, English-language copy screened in America.

Right-wing rabblerousing unquestionably affected the popular perception of *All Quiet on the Western Front*. But the film also received a curious reception within the German film press that resonated not with the lingering pall of the "Great War," but rather with the sound film "patent war," which lasted from 1928 to 1930. This dispute, in which German and American multinational corporations were often depicted as national combatants, took the form of a protracted race to equip the world for the "coming of sound." Although it was resolved shortly before the debut of *All Quiet on the Western Front*, the "war" created a climate of animosity toward American sound technology that is echoed both in the reviews of the film and in the critical justification for its censure. Retracing the international sound film dispute enables a more complete understanding of the fraught atmosphere into which *All Quiet on the Western Front* was released, providing new insight into this notorious occasion in German film history.

Hollywood's early foray into sound film threatened film markets throughout the world because of the potential for monopolistic control over the means to produce and screen the new media. Unlike German innovators, who constituted the vanguard of sound film development but were haphazard in its implementation, Hollywood benefited from an early, sustained, and coordinated investment into sound film through close alliances with the electronics industry. Western Electric, a subsidiary of AT&T, not only dominated the advancement of sound technology in America, it did so with over $188 million in assets and $263 million in sales.[1] This financial clout enabled exclusive contracts with the major Hollywood studios, which in turn allowed the corporation to control both sound recording and sound reproduction. Specifically, Western Electric secured agreements stipulating that films recorded with their equipment would only be exhibited on apparatus that were "not inferior to their own."[2] This qualification provided the company with leverage in foreign markets. Unless theater owners bought Western Electric's projectors and speakers, they would not have access to talkies such as *The Jazz Singer* (1927), or the popular and lucrative *The Singing Fool* (1928). Hollywood used this tactic to penetrate and control the European sound market quickly. By September 1928, Western Electric had already employed over 500 men to wire cinemas in Great Britain at the rate of three per day.

German industrialists only coordinated their investment into sound film once confronted with Hollywood's aggressive development. Heinrich Brückmann, the majority stockholder in Deutscher Ton-Film-AG, formed Tobis AG on 30 August 1928 as a response to American expansion. Tobis AG facilitated the collaboration of European patent holders in electrical industries in order to standardize German research into sound-producing equipment and accelerate development of competitive technology.[3] As one commentator writing in *Film-Kurier* noted on 20 July 1928, the stakes were high: "Without unity, only ruin will await the German sound film . . . only a focus on standardization can save us from foreign competition."

In order to ensure that standardization, Tobis pooled numerous European patents. On 13 March 1929, the firm signed a contract to share technological rights with Klangfilm (formed through a collaboration between Siemens & Halske and the Allgemeine Elektrizitäts Gesellschaft). The agreement between the two corporations allowed Tobis AG to outfit studios with the machinery necessary for making sound films, while Klangfilm manufactured and equipped cinemas with speakers and amplifiers — a merger that suddenly offered the German film industry a viable alternative to Western Electric. An article in the paper *Kinematograph*, titled "Tonfilmeinigung in Deutschland" (Sound film agreement in Germany, 14 March 1929), heralded the moment as a decisive opportunity for Germany to assume a "rightful" position at the forefront of the new medium: "It is to be expected that the new technology resulting from this merger will shortly dominate not only European markets, but overseas markets as well. Years ago we missed the opportunity to lead in this new field — a field first discovered through the Germanic spirit of invention. A new opportunity now presents itself." In less than two years the German sound film apparatus, born out of a reaction to Hollywood's expansion, was seamlessly incorporated into the symbolic vernacular of national pride.

Tobis's collection of patents enabled it to litigate against Western Electric's European expansion. On 20 July 1929, shortly after the Berlin debut of *The Singing Fool*, which one columnist for the *New York Times* claimed "fell like a bombshell"[4] on the Kurfürstendamm, Tobis-Klangfilm received an injunction that required Western Electric to dismantle its equipment unless it paid a licensing fee of 3 percent of the total box office gross for every film it screened in Germany.[5] American filmmakers answered this demand by boycotting the market. Hollywood ceased exports to Germany in order to place pressure on German theater owners, who they felt would lose business without the attraction of American films. Hollywood simultaneously stopped importing German films to America. The objective was to place Germany's film industry under an economic siege.

Between 19 June and 12 July 1930, William Hays brokered a peace between RCA, Western Electric, and Tobis-Klangfilm that reopened the German market for the Americans and provided Tobis the assurances that their apparatus would be relevant for future developments in sound film. The "Paris Peace Accords" followed seventeen lawsuits between Tobis-Klangfilm and Western Electric, which were estimated to total $1 billion. The ubiquity of the term "patent war" in the press led Hays to stress the peaceful potential of sound film as he opened the negotiations. One columnist for *Film-Kurier* noted that, "Will Hays used his opening speech, in which he noted that sound film could be the 'greatest peace instrument of mankind,' as the platform for a political address that was embellished with the friendliest sort of flattery for Germany."[6] Given the proximity of Paris to Versailles, it also seems likely that Hayes wanted to tread lightly to avoid invoking further unpleasant associations with the earlier treaty.

Hays later remarked that the German representatives were defensive, continually insisting that they must "protect" their markets. Conversely, the Americans employed a laissez-faire attitude toward maintaining a free market economy. The accord attempted to compensate both parties' wishes through three primary agreements. First, it designated that Western Electric, Tobis-Klangfilm, and RCA pool their patents and terminate all lawsuits against each other. Second, it guaranteed interchangeability between the sound reproducing apparatus in all countries, ensuring that there would be no mechanical incompatibility between films of different countries. Finally, the agreement opened the global market for both European and American sound film technology. The participants divided the world into three "patent zones" and charged film companies licensing fees for the right to show sound films in each respective zone. Tobis received the patent rights for all German-speaking countries and many central European states. Western Electric received the rights to the United States, North America, and Australia. The United Kingdom, Italy, and France were shared between the American and German systems.

In spite of the conciliatory tone of the compromise, the German press reported discord between the American and German participants. Immediately after the Paris talks concluded, one article in *Film-Kurier* noted that the Germans received too few concessions and too many territories in which America had already established control through previously wired cinemas. Another article, titled "Miesmacher in Amerika" (Troublemakers in America, 1930), reported that the American studios and electric companies felt Germany had received *too many* concessions, and were contemplating a second removal of American films from the German market.

Perhaps because of this renewed tension, the producers of *All Quiet on the Western Front* incorporated reminders of the sound film reconciliation into its advertising campaign in Germany. One full-page advertisement in *Kinematograph*, published on 29 November 1930, prominently notes that the American film not only is a "German-language sound film," but also that its soundtrack is a product of both Western Electric *and* Tobis. In order to mitigate the impression that Western Electric should get first billing, a second mention of both corporations' apparatus appears directly under director Lewis Milestone's name. The brief text notes that the film was recorded with both "Licht- und Nadelton" technology. *Lichtton* references Tobis's method of using light to record sound on film, while *Nadelton* describes Western Electric's usage of the "Vitaphone" process, in which sound is recorded onto a record that is played in synchronous conjunction with the camera. Posters placed throughout the Mozartsaal for the premiere of *All Quiet on the Western Front* similarly emphasized the German and American imprint on the film, listing both Western Electric and Tobis underneath the director's name and directly above the list of actors. The repeated references to not only Tobis, but also Tobis's recording methods in German advertisements for *All Quiet on the Western Front*, point to an attempt to placate the German market. In reality, Tobis's technology was not used to make the film. Universal relied exclusively on Western Electric's apparatus while filming.

Nonetheless, the advertising campaign for *All Quiet on the Western Front* failed to alleviate German film critics' and the German censorship board's reservations about *how* American talkies employed their sound apparatus within German borders. One central issue for the censors was the fact that Germans were watching a version of the film that differed fundamentally from that being screened elsewhere: "The producers cannot deny that a different version of the film is being shown abroad than here. If Carl Laemmle is upset that the film has not been well received in Germany, perhaps he should ask himself why he produced a film that can't be shown in Germany as it is in the rest of the world?"[7] Film critics noted that the film's producers changed the dialogue while recording the German soundtrack, and the press argued that the synchronization from English to German might be used to cover up disparaging messages that were being openly voiced in other countries:

> Hollywood apparently does not know, or does not want to know, that the dialogue is not translated literally. Rather, it has been consciously edited according to conditions in Germany. Hollywood ... therefore does not understand the deeper issue. This version of the film is only a secondary problem. The main issue is that Germans will no longer tolerate it when propaganda is translated for the sake of political expediency or economic demands.[8]

A 9 December 1930 piece in *Kinematograph* cited the film's German soundtrack as an alleged attempt to camouflage American malice, and felt that was enough justification to ban the film: "It is our position that this film should not be shown, in order to convince the Americans once and for all that we will not tolerate our nation being denigrated beyond our borders by a film that later attempts to profit from us simply through a different translation." Ironically, the German press's anger about the film's synchronization was a consequence of Hollywood's attempt to remove anything that might prove incendiary within Germany's sensitive political climate.

Five months after the conclusion of the Paris negotiations, *All Quiet on the Western Front*'s premiere elicited a far graver response from German trade press than when *The Singing Fool* "dropped like a bombshell" on the Gloria Palast. Many film critics felt it represented a continuation of Hollywood's hegemonic disregard for European cinema, and their indignation often paralleled popular rejections of the film for its depiction of "German defeat." Moreover, the critics' nationalist sensitivity was often bound up with a critique of the patent war's recent conclusion and the American employment of the sound apparatus itself—signifying a worry that the talkie's presence in Germany might portend another sort of defeat altogether. Tobis-Klangfilm may have won the courtroom battle, but Western Electric could still help Americans win the larger war. In a review titled "Zirkus Nollendorfplatz" (Circus Nollendorfplatz, 1930), one critic argued that the film's mere presence typified Hollywood's attitude that Americans "must appear . . . harsh in order to ultimately belittle both the German film industry and the German cinema owner." The same author implies Hollywood returned to Germany in bad faith following the Paris agreement: "Perhaps observers will now realize that American 'Filmpolitik' in Germany is currently not in the best hands. [The Americans] must have thought it was an empty threat when certain German politicians explained, months ago, that the period of negotiations was over. Now we must call their bluff." Another critic of the film took aim at William Hays, who had no role in producing the film whatsoever but who was central to the Paris negotiations, by calling him a hypocrite for his July assertion that film should foster a "peaceful" relationship between nations: "Mr. Hays decreed recently on behalf of his organization that film producers are obligated to reconcile the people of different nations. Unfortunately these are just words, while actual deeds continue to be alarming."[9]

Ultimately, the critics' anger about the two soundtracks coalesced with that of the general public. Parliament quickly allowed the censor to consider the film's suitability for public viewing based not only on the German dubbed version, but also on the original copy shown outside of Germany. Its verdict, that the film fomented civil disorder domestically, was thus complimented by a new accusation that the English version tarnished Germany's reputation abroad. This latter charge contributed greatly to the film's censure, and evidences the unfortunate legacy of mistrust between two of the world's great film industries during a key juncture in German cinema history.

See also:

- 3 June 1929: Lloyd Bacon's *The Singing Fool* Triggers Debate about Sound Film
- 13 June 1930: *Weekend* Broadcast Tests Centrality of Image in Cinema
- 13 January 1954: Preminger's Dual-Language *The Moon Is Blue* (1953) and *Die Jungfrau auf dem Dach* (1954) Seek Glocal Success

Notes

[1] Douglas Gomery, *The Coming of Sound* (New York: Routledge, 2005), 33.

[2] Wythe Williams, "German Movie Men Turn to Silent Film," *New York Times* (21 April 1929), 54.

[3] Karel Dibbets, "Tobis, Made in Holland," in *Tonfilmfrieden/Tonfilmkrieg: Die Geschichte der Tobis vom Technik-Syndikat zum Staatskonzern*, ed. Jan Distelmeyer (Frankfurt: edition text + kritik, 2003), 25–33; here 25.

[4] "German Films Face a Crisis," *New York Times* (2 March 1930), 123.

[5] "Die Debatte: Tobis — 'Der Deutsche': Die Patent-Anerkennungsgebühren," *Film-Kurier* (19 May 1930).

[6] "Paris verhandelt streng geheim über das Schicksal der Weltfabrikation," *Film-Kurier* (21 June 1930).

[7] Ministerialrat Dr. Seeger (Vorsitzender), *Zur Verhandlung über die Anträge der Regierungen von Sachsen, Thüringen, Braunschweig, Bayern und Württemberg auf Widerruf der Zulassung des Bildstreifens "Im Westen nichts Neues,"* 11 December 1930, 12.

[8] "Zirkus-Nollendorfplatz," *Kinematograph* (11 December 1930), 2.

[9] "Zensurverschärfung für ausländische Filme," *Kinematograph* (6 December 1930).

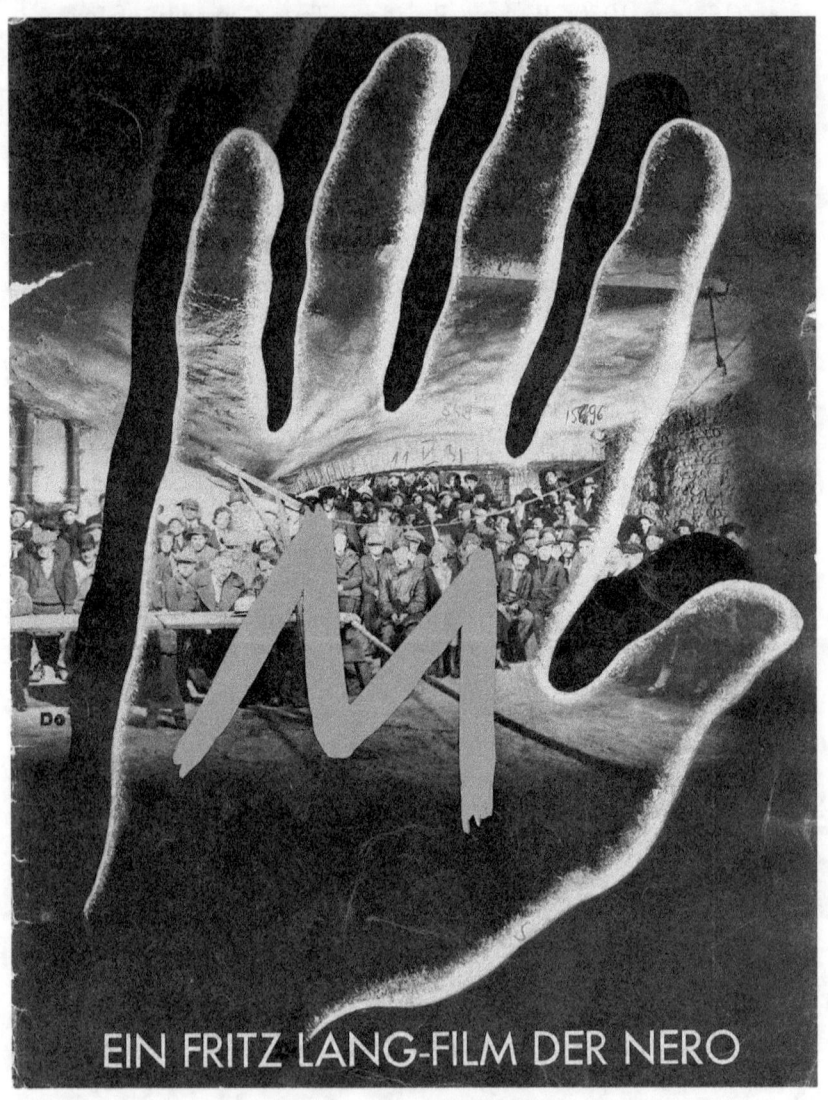

The premiere program for M. Source: Deutsche Kinemathek.

11 May 1931: With Premiere of *M*, a Gala Hit Becomes a Cultural Controversy

Sara F. Hall

THE SPECTATORS ATTENDING the sold-out premiere of *M* at Berlin's grand Ufa-Palast sat captivated, their attention broken only occasionally by spontaneous bursts of applause.[1] When the action stopped and the house lights went up, director Fritz Lang, screenwriter Thea von Harbou and prominent members of the cast and crew were summoned forward for multiple curtain calls.[2] Anticipation for the gala event had been high, and the film appeared to deliver the timeliness, suspense, and virtuosity promised. As a writer for the promotional magazine *Filmwelt* had pronounced in a late May photo spread featuring *M*, it had seemed only a matter of time before the notorious deeds of the serial killers Fritz Haarmann in Hannover, Karl Grossmann in Berlin, and Peter Kürten in Düsseldorf became fodder for the big screen. With Lang and von Harbou's reputation as Germany's most ambitious, uncompromising, and provocative writer-director team firmly established and themes and plot points drawn directly from the day's most sensational true crime news, the duo's newest production seemed guaranteed to stand out from anything that had come before. As early as September 1930, gripping ads for the film (then billed with the ominous title *Mörder unter uns* [Murderer among us]) ran in publications targeted at theater owners and exhibitors such as *Lichtbild-Bühne* and *Der Kinematograph*. Regular reports updated insiders each step of the way as the project went from a reality-based draft in May 1930 to a complex final script in November 1930, and again as shooting ran from December through April. Readers continued to follow along closely as *M* underwent censors' scrutiny on 27 April and emerged in the final cut in May.[3]

A steady stream of increasingly controversial reviews and filmmaker interviews began appearing for the general readership of the daily papers during the days before and after the premiere. While Weimar-era audiences had come to admire Lang and von Harbou for their ability to match an emotionally gripping and suspenseful narrative with technically precise yet expressive imagery unique to each film's particular setting and subject matter, film journalists in 1930–31 were not letting readers forget the financial failure of the grand spectacle *Metropolis* (1927) and the ambivalent reception of Lang's adamant hold-out against the transition to sound, *Die Frau im Mond* (*The Woman in the Moon*, 1929). How, they asked, would this duo's latest collaboration, a film made not with the commercial powerhouse Ufa (Universum Film A.G.), but instead with Seymour Nebenzahl's smaller and more independently minded company, Nero, look — and sound?[4] Could the filmmakers and their new producer make such controversial subject matter successful, either formally or commercially?

Certainly cinema historians of the later twentieth and early twenty-first centuries have concurred that the results were and remain unparalleled. *M* is a masterpiece of suspense cinema, stands as the first internationally successful police procedural film, and is often named as the single most powerful cinematic exploration of criminal pathology, the social ills of urban modernity, and the moral dilemmas involved in balancing individual rights, personal safety, and the collective good. For those qualities, along with its evocative cinematography, pitch-perfect acting, and unprecedented use of sound as an integral plot element (a quality shared, albeit to a lesser degree, by other Nero productions of the transition period), *M* was selected in a 1995 survey as the single most important German film of all time and is listed in various international critics' top-100 lists. Lang considered *M* his most enduring work; Joseph Losey took it as the inspiration for a 1951 film noir remake; and Lang's acolytes and admirers have quoted and cited it in numerous films and video works. Each rerelease, either in the form of a restoration or reconstruction on the basis of newly discovered footage or archival materials, or in a new exhibition format such as Blu-Ray, refreshes audience interest and inspires another burst of critical celebration, scholarly evaluation, revival screenings, and DVD sales.

At the time of *M*'s unveiling, German movie producers and distributors often collaborated with the fan magazine *Der Film Kurier* on the production of a series of illustrated program brochures. The installment in that series featuring the latest Lang release fueled the excitement of audiences. On its eye-popping cover, a negative image of an enormous hand marked by the unmistakable chalk letter "M" overlay a still photo of the famous kangaroo court scene, with the fiery eyes of criminals and parents glaring out at the viewer; together these elements evoked the parallel plotlines of crime, criminal identification, the organized criminal underworld, and public outrage. The brochure contents included a collection of photos and short texts compiled by the *Illustrierter Film Kurier*'s movie program editor, Alexander Alexander, which not only teased readers with the usual images of actors and hints at compelling plot details, but also offered exceptionally socially engaged position statements by the filmmakers and contributions from criminal justice experts to place the film squarely in its real-world context. Renowned public defender Dr. Frey used the figure of Hans Beckert as the basis for a fictionalized criminal profile. Berlin Criminal Court Lead Prosecutor Dr. Steinbeck endorsed the movie as a deterrent to crime, praising its vivid description of the dangers of modern delinquency and its impressive evocation of possible preventive measures. Criminal Investigator Geissel, the director of Berlin's Crime Museum and Public Information Center, described a series of recent murder cases and included facsimiles of letters exchanged over the course of the Peter Kürten case as documentation. Leo Heller, a popular writer of true tales from the criminal underworld, offered an account of the organized syndicates he knew so well.

This blend of factual objectivity, emotional arousal, critical acumen, and the enthusiasm of marketing was complimented by the reflective tone of the essays by the filmmakers, Lang's "Tatsachenberichte — ein Film" (A factual report — a film),[5] and von Harbou's answer to the question, "Warum gerade ein solcher film?!" (Why a film like this?!). The director expounded on his desire to draw on the details of present realities for storylines more fantastic than the most elaborate fantasies of storytellers of yore. Especially intriguing to him was the repetitive horror of recent murder cases and the borderline psychotic responses of those who, again and again, came forth to falsely denounce others and even themselves. He embraced what he saw as a moral responsibility to draw on these events in order to sound a warning to contemporary audiences. Von Harbou's piece spoke to readers who responded to the idea behind *M* with shock and dismay, especially those amazed that a woman could inure herself to the emotional effects of such gruesome material. Describing her working environment as a veritable murderer's den or chamber of horrors, piled high with newspaper clippings, wanted posters, and photos of both perpetrators and victims, the screenwriter confessed to being haunted by the image of the child murderer, and expressed the wish to speak out for the thousands of working men and women who could not spend their days standing protectively beside their children. The screenwriter closed by exhorting readers to cease being apathetic and self-centered and to see and appreciate this film for its educative and warning message. A journalist covering marketing news for the *Lichtbild-Bühne* insisted that this movie program, with its copious ancillary documentation and commentary, belonged in the hands of anyone who wanted to engage in a discussion about the film and the events it portrayed. According to the marketing scheme it represented, discussion and debate were as much a part of the work as were the images, sounds, and storyline.

Rousing curtain calls may have been the response at the front of the house at the premiere screening, but according to Leo Hirsch, reporting for the *Berliner Tageblatt*, the assessment coming from critics and other audience members on the floor and in the lobby was not entirely positive. They began to reconsider: could this film, with its potentially tasteless exploitation of themes so blatantly drawn from the recent Kürten trial and its perhaps cheap attempt to capitalize on Germany's death penalty debates, really be considered a "great film?"[6] The longer *M* played in Germany's cinemas, the more ambivalent, and sometimes outraged, public reactions became. Critics pondered whether the film's strength lay in its reflection of social reality and its weakness in its lofty attempts at mixing moralizing with cinematic poetry, or the other way around. Numerous commentators expressed astonishment that this harrowing work, with its derisive portrayal of an ineffectual police force paralleling a comparatively heroic depiction of the organized criminal underworld, made it past the censors, whereas so many other crime dramas were subjected to radical cuts and revisions. Increasingly, the filmmakers were called to task for capitalizing for profit and renown on the nation's crisis of physical and emotional security and for exploiting the audience's emotional vulnerability. In the meantime, Lang and von Harbou's program brochure essays were reproduced in publications ranging from the fan papers *Mein Film* and *Die Filmwoche*, to the urban daily the *Berliner Volks-Zeitung*, which simultaneously doused and fanned the flames of controversy.

The debates surrounding *M* reached the upper echelons of German cultural criticism in early June when Gabriele Tergit, a respected nonfiction writer, court reporter, and emergent novelist, declared in the left-leaning literary journal *Die Weltbühne* that the film represented an unmistakable attempt to cash in on the events of the Kürten case. She raged at the inconsistency of the censors who had not halted the release or demanded changes and cuts.[7] Art and film critic Rudolf Arnheim responded in the same issue, asking if Lang's film really warranted such a vehement response and warning Tergit and others against calling for the kinds of interventions so resented when imposed on the work of progressive artists.[8] He suggested that squabbling over this film (especially among those on the Left) would serve parties like the National Socialists, who remained unified regardless of the debate waged. Interestingly, Arnheim left unaddressed Tergit's charges of crass commercialism and her related response to the eager applause she witnessed at the premiere during the kangaroo court, wherein she noted that individual viewers who did see the film would probably experience enthusiasm not just (or necessarily) for the artistry of the film, but also (or instead) for its ability to resonate with certain political viewpoints and social anxieties. Tergit railed that film played to the conditioned instincts of people who wanted the immediate satisfaction of a prompt and forceful meting out of justice, choosing to ignore the nuance and additional insight that the latest advances in the science of criminal psychiatry might bring to a case. Arnheim may have sensed that her suspicions here were correct. Indeed the reviewer for the NS paper *Der Angriff* praised the film as presenting a convincing argument against death penalty opponents.[9] Despite the fact that Seymour Nebenzahl and Nero were responsible for some of the most powerful cinematic messages of antifascism and pacifism of the late 1920s and early 1930s, including G. W. Pabst's *Westfront* (1930), Josef Goebbels wrote in his diary that *M* was fantastic, antihumanitarian, well made, and supportive of the death penalty.[10] Just the same, it may have been members of the extreme Right whom Lang intended to implicate in his "factual report" essay when he described his film as pointing an admonishing finger at the threat lurking among criminally inclined individuals who threatened the lives and livelihoods of society's most vulnerable members.

Even with all the controversy it engendered, Lang and von Harbou's film did not rank among Germany's top ten features that year, and its box-office returns were modest.[11] In other words, it did not turn out to be the hit that the amount of applause at the debut screening on 11 May 1931 might have presaged. Perhaps certain members of the public consumed the film through the surrounding discourses alone, never feeling compelled to spend the additional time or money to see the film itself. Perhaps some were turned off by the idea of the movie industry making a profit off of real victims' misfortunes. There is no complete record of who applauded that evening, and in response to what, or of why individual viewers chose to attend or avoid subsequent screenings. The breadth of the range of reactions in the press does show that the film's cultural life extended well beyond the walls of movie houses. Its reception was a cultural event in its own right, perhaps one as significant as the work itself. And as decades of scholarly and critical reception have proven, *M* is a film whose historical afterlife has far exceeded its initial commercial value.

See also:

- 14 February 1924: *Die Nibelungen* Premieres, Foregrounds "Germanness"
- 28 March 1935: Premiere of *Triumph des Willens* Presents Fascism as Unifier of Communal Will
- 16 February 1952: Peter Lorre Leaves Germany Again

Notes

[1] "S. Nebenzahls Lang-Film," *Lichtbild-Bühne* 113 (12 May 1931); B. E. Werner, "Fritz Lang: 'M.' Nero-Film — Ufa-Palast am Zoo," *Deutsche Allgemeine Zeitung* (12 May 1931).

[2] Dr. Hans Wolkenberg, "Filmbesprechung: 'M.' Fritz Lang-Film der Nero, Verleih: Star/Ufa-Palast," *Lichtbild-Bühne* 113 (12 May 1931); K. Gl. "'M' — Fritz Langs erster Tonfilm. Uraufführung im Ufa-Palast am Zoo," *Berliner Morgenpost* 113 (13 May 1931); U. H. "Filmschau: *M*," *Neue Preussische Kreuz Zeitung* (16 May 1931).

[3] Todd Herzog, "Fritz Lang's *M* (1931). An Open Case," in *Weimar Cinema: An Essential Guide to Classic Films of the Era*, ed. Noah Isenberg (New York: Columbia UP, 2008), 291–310; here 294.

[4] Erika Wottrich, ed., *M wie Nebenzahl. Nero — Filmproduktion zwischen Europa und Hollywood* (Munich: edition text + kritik, 2002).

[5] Republished nine days later as "Mein Film M: ein Tatsachenbericht," *Filmwoche* 9 (20 May 1931).

[6] Leo Hirsch, "Fritz Lang: 'M.' Ufa-Palast am Zoo," *Berliner Tageblatt* 221 (12 May 1931). See also Heinz Pol., "Fritz Langs Film vom Kindermörder: Ufa-Palast am Zoo," *Vossische Zeitung* (13 May 1931).

[7] Gabriele Tergit, "Der Film des Sadismus," *Die Weltbühne* 23 (9 June 1931). Reprinted in *Fritz Lang: Leben und Werk, Bilder und Dokumente*, ed. Rolf Aurich, Wolfgang Jacobsen and Cornelius Schnauber (Berlin: Film Museum Berlin — Deutsche Kinemathek, 2001), 148–50.

[8] Rudolf Arnheim, "Eine Minute Pause!" *Die Weltbühne* 23 (6 June, 1931). Reprinted in *Fritz Lang: Leben und Werk*, 151–53.

[9] Anon. "M," *Der Angriff* (30 May 1921). Cited in Herzog, 308.

[10] Cited in Tom Gunning, *The Films of Fritz Lang: Allegories of Vision and Modernity* (London: BFI Publishing, 2000), 192.

[11] Anton Kaes, *M* (London: BFI Publishing, 2000), 7.

Part III: 1933–1945

When Hitler assumed the chancellorship in 1933, Germany was still a parliamentary democracy. Von Papen and Hindenburg had calculated that bringing Hitler into the government would enable them to control him, particularly since support for the Nazis in the November 1932 elections had actually dropped. New elections were called for March, but before they took place, the Reichstag was engulfed in a fire on 27 February 1933. While there remains some dispute about the precise role the Nazis played in the fire, there is no doubt that they used the event as a pretext to consolidate political support. Hitler persuaded Hindenburg to issue the Reichstag Fire Decree declaring a state of emergency and suspending most civil liberties, and used these emergency powers to ban Communist publications, institute mass arrests of Communist political leaders (include all their parliamentary delegates), and suppress their participation in the next election.

Together with their partners the Deutschnationale Volkspartei (German National People's Party, DNVP), the Nazis now held a parliamentary majority. Once Hitler was able to gain the support of the Center Party and several smaller, right-wing parties — and after harassing and detaining members of the SPD (Sozialdemokratische Partei Deutschlands, or Social Democratic Party), he had the two-thirds majority needed to pass the *Ermächtigungsgesetz* (Enabling Act) on 23 March, which legally established Germany as a dictatorship, giving Hitler the authority to pass laws without parliamentary approval. While the position of president was retained, Hindenburg was effectively rendered powerless, and he retreated from the public eye. When he died in August 1934, Hitler combined the offices of president and chancellor in his position as *Führer*, and took command of the armed forces, which now were compelled to swear their allegiance to him.

In the following months, the Nazis moved quickly to eliminate opposition and institute their policy of *Gleichschaltung* (coordination). All parties other than the Nazi Party were either outlawed or disbanded themselves, and the creation of new parties was made illegal. The Nazis also purged the civil service of political opponents and Jews, and took control of regional and state governments. On 30 January 1934, the upper chamber of parliament was abolished and the federal system was terminated.

Hitler also consolidated power within his own party by purging the Nazis of the SA (*Sturmabteilung*, or Storm Division) on what became known as The Night of the Long Knives. Under the leadership of Ernst Röhm, the SA had been instrumental in the rise of the Nazi Party, inciting violence and intimidating opponents. But as an organization of nearly one million members loyal to Röhm, the SA was also a rival for both the SS and the regular army. On the evening of 30 June 1934, leaders of the SA, leaders of the more "leftist" Nazi faction such as Gregor Strasser and Kurt von Schleicher, as well as anyone else deemed unreliable by Hitler were arrested and executed. The remaining SA was absorbed into the army and the SS, under the command of Heinrich Himmler.

Hitler also sought to build wider public support for his regime by implementing a series of social welfare policies aimed at revitalizing the economy. A number of large-scale work-creation projects, such as building the Autobahn, coupled with the upswing that had already begun before 1933, put the economy on a more solid footing. The concept of a new *Volksgemeinschaft* (people's community) was designed to give people a greater sense of participation and a stake in the country's affairs. Through programs such as *Schönheit der Arbeit* (Beauty of Labor) and *Kraft durch Freude* (Strength through Joy), as well as a variety of social organizations such as the *Hitler Jugend* (Hitler Youth) and the *Bund Deutscher Mädel* (League of German Girls), the Nazis organized leisure activities and holiday excursions, and promoted *Winterhilfswerk* (winter relief) campaigns where people could donate money to help the less fortunate. These initiatives were advertised to the population through government propaganda that presented Germany as strong, vital, and, above all, "Aryan." Together with the increased availability of consumer goods, these measures in the prewar years lead to a greater sense of national pride and support for Nazi policies.

But this national community did not include everyone. The first concentration camp in Germany was opened at Dachau in March 1933 with others soon to follow. Criminals, political opponents, homosexuals — anyone deemed "antisocial" — were arrested and sent to these forced labor camps, where they were subject to torture, malnutrition, overwork, and murder. German Jews were increasingly deprived of their civil rights. In 1935 the Nuremberg Laws were enacted, forbidding marriage and even sexual relations between Jews and Aryans, depriving German Jews of their citizenship, and forbidding them from displaying the national colors. In 1936 German Jews were prohibited from participating in elections, and in 1938 a series of laws restricted their economic activity and ability to work, including a law requiring them to carry cards identifying them as Jews. All of these measures were accompanied by a barrage of antisemitic propaganda that denigrated Jews as racial inferiors and characterized them as threatening to the German state.

On 28 October 1938, seventeen thousand Jews of Polish citizenship, including those who had lived in Germany for decades, were arrested and relocated across the Polish border where they were interned in "relocation camps" on the frontier. Herschel Grynszpan, the son of one of these deportees, upon hearing the news in Paris, went to the German embassy intending to assassinate the German ambassador. Unable to find him, Grynszpan instead shot Third Secretary Ernst vom Rath, who died two days later on 9 November. The Nazis used this as a pretext for launching a pogrom against German Jews. SA storm troopers systematically attacked Jewish property, burning or demolishing destroying over 175 synagogues and 7,500 shops, killing nearly one hundred people, and arresting thirty thousand Jews. German Jews themselves were held responsible for these events, and were fined 1 billion marks for the assassination of vom Rath and 6 billion marks for property damages. *Kristallnacht* (The Night of Broken Glass), as it became known, began a major acceleration in the deportation of remaining German Jews. While thousands of Jews and political opponents of the regime emigrated, many could not, and German Jews who remained found their property confiscated and lives subject to ever-greater restrictions. With the commencement of war, the Nazis implemented a new phase in their persecution of German Jews with deportations to Polish ghettos.

At first, Hitler took a more diplomatic stance in his relations with other nations, stressing his peaceful intentions but all the while pursuing an aggressive rearmament policy. He cultivated relationships with Italy, forming a military alliance on 1 November 1936, and with Japan, with whom he signed an anti-Comintern pact on 25 November 1936. He even attempted to pursue an alliance with Great Britain, though beyond the signing of the Anglo-German Naval Agreement on 18 June 1935, this did not bear any fruit. In a meeting with Army leaders in 1937, Hitler made it clear that the military was to prepare for war within the next five years. By 1938, he had purged the Army leadership of critics of his plans and began maneuvering Germany to expand its borders.

The first country to be absorbed by the Nazi empire was Austria. While Austria would describe itself after the war as Hitler's first victim, the 12 March 1938 *Anschluss* (annexation) of Austria was a relatively peaceful affair. Pressure to make Austria part of a "Greater Germany" had been building for years, when the Austrian Chancellor Kurt Schuschnigg called for a referendum on the issue. But a coup d'état by the Austrian Nazi Party rendered the vote moot. Austrian troops were ordered to give no resistance to the incoming German troops, who were welcomed by cheering Austrian crowds. On 12 March 1938, Austria officially became part of the German empire.

In the summer of 1938, tensions flared between Germany and Czechoslovakia, which had a sizeable ethnic German population, prompting the intervention of British Prime Minister Chamberlain. But after the Munich conference of September 1938, Chamberlain's "appeasement policy" — under which Germany was given large border areas of Czechoslovakia in exchange for a promise not to wage war — only delayed the inevitable invasion in March 1939, an act that drew no help from other Western European powers.

It was Germany's invasion of Poland that finally triggered the Second World War. Poland refused to cede Danzig back to Germany, receiving assurances from Britain that they would come to Poland's aid should Germany use military force. Germany, which had just entered into a pact with Soviet Russia on 23 August 1939 (the Hitler-Stalin pact), believed that Britain would not make good on its promises. To garner public support for the invasion, the SS staged a phony raid on the German radio station in Gleiwitz, Upper Silesia on the night of 31 August. A number of prisoners from Dachau, including a German known for having Polish sympathies, were killed or wounded and left at the scene. But the international community was skeptical of Germany's account, and when Germany invaded Poland on 1 September, Great Britain and France declared war on Germany.

After Poland fell in a matter of weeks, there followed a long period of inactivity, as France and Britain did not directly engage Germany. In mid-1940, Germany began its campaign to conquer Northern Europe. Between mid-1940 and mid-1941, Germany took control of Denmark, Norway, France, Holland, Belgium, and Luxembourg. Germany also began fighting Britain directly, attacking the Royal Air Force and conducting bombing raids of London. Bolstered by his domestic popularity (a result of the military's rapid victories), and confident that Britain, too, would soon be defeated, Hitler decided to invade Russia and begin a two-front war on 22 June 1941.

At first, the German army was able to conquer vast stretches of territory, encircling Leningrad and advancing to within twenty miles of Moscow. However, a combination of tactical mistakes, Stalin's scorched-earth policy that left few resources behind as the Soviet army retreated, and the German army's unpreparedness for a long winter campaign, meant that Germany would remained bogged down in Russia, suffering significant casualties throughout the rest of the war as well a demoralizing defeat in its failure to capture Stalingrad. When Germany also declared war on the United States following the Japanese attack on Pearl Harbor, Germany became engaged in a protracted conflict that it was unable to sustain. Over the next three years, Germany would suffer a series of military defeats and territorial losses, as its army was driven back on all fronts. This, coupled with the devastating air raids on German cities conducted by Allied forces, lead to material deprivations and significant loss of life and morale at home.

By the spring of 1945, it was clear that the war was lost. Hitler retreated to his bunker in Berlin. On 29 April 1945 he married Eva

Braun, and the pair committed suicide the next day, their remains incinerated by his remaining soldiers. Over a dozen other officers and high ranking Nazi leaders also committed suicide, including Joseph Goebbels and his wife Magda, who poisoned their six children before having themselves shot. Berlin fell to the Russians on 2 May and in the night of 7–8 May, 1945, the unconditional surrender of Germany was signed.

After the German invasion of the Soviet Union, the Nazis began rounding up Jews from the Soviet territories as well and deporting them to the Jewish ghettos in Poland. These were, in effect, overcrowded prisons where hundreds of thousands died of starvation and disease from 1940 to 1942. The Nazis also began mass killings of Jews, first through large-scale executions committed by SS formations known as *Einsatzgruppen*, then through the use of vans equipped with sealed compartments into which engine exhaust was pumped. On 20 January 1942, Nazi leaders held a conference at Wannsee to plot what was called the Final Solution, a plan to accelerate the genocide of European Jewry. Six camps located in Poland were designated as extermination camps. The ghettos in Warsaw, Lodz, and other Polish cities were evacuated, with all of the inhabitants sent to one of the extermination camps. Many were killed in gas chambers on arrival; others were forced into slave labor. When they could no longer work, they too were executed. By the end of the war, six million Jews had perished in the Holocaust, nearly 75 percent of the prewar European Jewish population. An estimated five million non-Jewish victims also died at the hands of the Nazis between 1933 and 1945.

Even before Hitler took power, the Nazis recognized the importance of mass media for the dissemination of propaganda and for generating support for Nazi ideology. As part of its policy of *Gleichschaltung*, the Nazi regime, under the administration of Joseph Goebbels's Reichsministerium für Volksaufklärung und Propaganda (Ministry of Public Enlightenment and Propaganda) established the Reichsfilmkammer (Chamber of Film) to control the system of film production and distribution. Anyone involved in the film industry was required to be a member of the Reichsfilmkammer; this led to the exclusion of Jews and anyone considered politically undesirable from the industry, and also allowed Goebbels to control those who were involved.

With non-Aryan film professionals banned from employment, and many others simply refusing to live in Nazi Germany, close to a thousand members of the Weimar film industry, including actors, directors, producers, technicians, and film journalists fled the country. What was a significant blow to the creative pool of the German film industry was a boon to Hollywood. Directors such as Fritz Lang, Billy Wilder, and Douglas Sirk, actors such as Marlene Dietrich, Peter Lorre, and Conrad Veidt, and film professionals such as the cameraman Rudolf Maté and the composer Friedrich Hollaender, were all able to continue their film careers with great success. Many others, however, found themselves relegated to one-dimensional bit parts or felt stifled by the constraints of this new system. Even those who were successful often felt that they remained foreigners. Yet they were able to use this outsider status, making films that straddled Europe and Hollywood and that productively engaged with German and American film traditions.

Less than two months after the Nazis took power, Goebbels delivered a speech at the Kaiserhof on 28 March 1933, in which he outlined the new principles for German film. Not only would German cinema need to be more committed to National Socialism — and free of the "degenerate" influence of Jewish artists — but it needed to provide audiences with films that were both well-made and entertaining, able to compete with Hollywood both domestically and internationally. This latter point was a key part of Nazi film policy, albeit one that is often overlooked. Certainly, the Nazi government exercised nearly complete artistic and eventually financial control over the German film industry, passing a law in 1934 that instituted a policy of film censorship both before and after films were released, banning film criticism entirely in 1936, and gradually assuming control of the industry so that, by 1942, all German film companies were part of one large holding company called Ufa-Film GmbH.

The Nazis pursued a complex approach toward using film as propaganda. In cinemas, it was mandatory for a feature film to be proceeded by a *Wochenschau* (newsreel) and a short *Kulturfilm*, both of which would contain overt propaganda and nationalistic messages. Two of the best-known propaganda films from the period — Leni Riefenstahl's ostensible documentary of the 1934 Nazi Party Congress in Nuremberg, *Triumph des Willens* (*Triumph of the Will*, 1935) and Veit Harlan's antisemitic account of the life and death of Joseph Süss Oppenheimer *Jud Süß* (1940) — skillfully blended Nazi ideology and artistic vision to provide two of the most lasting and iconic visual depictions of the Third Reich. But crude and transparent propagandistic films such as Fritz Hippler's *Der ewige Jude* (*The Eternal Jew*, 1940) were met with unease by the general public. Indeed, very few feature films dealt directly with the Nazi Party or organizations such as the Hitler Youth or SA. Since one of the main goals of Nazi film policy was to provide audiences with light, escapist entertainment, blatantly political or propagandist films accounted for less than 15 percent of the some 1,100 feature films made during the period. Most fell into traditional genre categories — adventure films, historical dramas, musicals, and comedies. To be sure, the ideological subtext of these films reinforced Nazi values — the importance of *Heimat*, traditional gender roles, and national community — but overt political messages were usually absent.

The modernist techniques that defined much of Weimar cinema were rarely to be found in Nazi cinema. Instead, films focused on illusion and fantasy, avoiding any subjects that were unwelcome or that might challenge the values that the government sought to reinforce. Relying on the conventions and styles of traditional Hollywood features, Nazi filmmakers sought to create worlds free of strife and danger, providing audiences with a respite from reality, something that became increasingly important as the war dragged on. At the point when the tide of the war began to turn against Germany, the popularity of the cinema was at its all-time peak: total admissions in 1943 were close to 1.1 billion, for an average of fourteen visits per person per year.

The star system remained an important part of the film industry in the Nazi period, albeit with a new set of stars — actors such as Zarah Leander, Lil Dagover, and Heinz Rühmann. Even this system was highly controlled, with careful attention paid to the frequency and variety of films in which actors appeared, and strong pressure put on stars to participate in official events that supported the war efforts. Female stars tended to conform to certain gender stereotypes (Kristina Söderbaum as the ideal Aryan woman, Ilse Werner as the girl next door), while male stars, who were not to compete with the heroic image of Hitler, instead often stood in for larger issues of national identity (Otto Gebühr embodying Prussian values as Friedrich the Great, Willy Fritsch as a symbol of the new generation).

Nazi cinema was also attentive to new technological developments, in particular the development of color film. Goebbels saw color film as a powerful tool for eliciting emotional reactions from domestic audiences and as a means to overcome American film internationally. After 1940, several major productions, including Josef von Báky's *Münchhausen* (1943) and Veit Harlan's *Kolberg* (1945) were shot in Agfacolor. *Kolberg* exemplified cinema's status as a vital tool to maintain morale at home. Begun in 1943 when the war had already turned against Germany, the film was the most expensive of the period, costing more than 8 million marks. Thousands of soldiers and a hundred railway cars were diverted from the front to depict the siege of a city and the stubborn resistance of its occupants. The film premiered in a Berlin already devastated by Allied bombing. Film could only do so much — no matter how grand the spectacle, it could not win the war or shield the German public from the destruction and devastation that it faced on a daily basis.

Selected Bibliography • 1933–1945

Ascheid, Antje. *Hitler's Heroines: Stardom and Womanhood in Nazi Cinema.* Philadelphia: Temple UP, 2003.

Bahr, Ehrhard. *Weimar on the Pacific: German Exile Culture in Los Angeles and the Crisis of Modernism.* Berkeley: U of California P, 2007.

Bergfelder, Tim, and Christian Cargnelli, eds. *Destination London: German-speaking Emigrés and British Cinema, 1925–1950.* New York: Berghahn Books, 2008.

Beyer, Friedemann, Gert Koshofer, and Michael Krüger. *UFA in Farbe: Technik, Politik und Starkult zwischen 1936 und 1945.* Munich: Heyne, 2010.

Brook, Vincent. *Driven to Darkness: Jewish Emigre Directors and the Rise of Film Noir.* New Brunswick, NJ: Rutgers UP, 2009.

Bruns, Jana F. *Nazi Cinema's New Women.* Cambridge: Cambridge UP, 2009.

Carter, Erica. *Dietrich's Ghosts: The Sublime and the Beautiful in Third Reich Film.* London: British Film Institute, 2004.

Dimendberg, Edward. "Down These Seen Streets a Man Must Go: Siegfried Kracauer, 'Hollywood's Terror Films,' and the Spatiality of Film Noir." *New German Critique* 89 (Spring/Summer 2003): 113–43.

Fox, Jo. *Film Propaganda in Britain and Nazi Germany: World War II Cinema.* Oxford: Berg, 2007.

———. *Filming Women in the Third Reich.* Oxford: Berg, 2000.

Giesen, Rolf. *Nazi Propaganda Films: A History and Filmography.* Jefferson, NC: McFarland, 2003.

Hake, Sabine. *Popular Cinema of the Third Reich.* Austin: U of Texas P, 2001.

———. "Mapping the Native Body: On Africa and the Colonial Film in the Third Reich." In *The Imperialist Imagination: German Colonialism and Its Legacy*, edited by Sara Friedrichsmeyer, Sara Lennox, and Susanne Zantop, 163–88. Ann Arbor: U of Michigan P, 1998.

Hansen, Jennifer. "The Art and Science of Reading Faces: Strategies of Racist Cinema in the Third Reich." *Shofar: An Interdisciplinary Journal of Jewish Studies* 28, no. 1 (Fall 2009): 80–103.

Hoffmann, Hilmar. *The Triumph of Propaganda: Film and National Socialism, 1933–1945.* Providence, RI: Berghahn Books, 1996.

Hoffmann, Kay. "Propagandistic Problems of German Newsreels in World War II." *Historical Journal of Film, Radio and Television* 24, no. 1 (2004): 133–42.

Jacobsen, Wolfgang, and Hans H. Prinzler. *Siodmak Bros.: Berlin — Paris — London — Hollywood.* Berlin: Argon, 1998.

Koepnick, Lutz P. "Doubling the Double: Robert Siodmak in Hollywood." *New German Critique* 89 (Spring/Summer 2003): 81–104.

———. *The Dark Mirror: German Cinema between Hitler and Hollywood.* Berkeley: U of California P, 2002.

Köppen, Manuel, and Erhard Schütz, eds. *Kunst der Propaganda: Der Film im Dritten Reich.* Bern: Peter Lang, 2007.

Kreimeier, Klaus. *The Ufa Story: A History of Germany's Greatest Film Company, 1918–1945.* Translated by Robert and Rita Kimber. New York: Hill & Wang, 1996.

Kuzniar, Alice A. "'Now I Have a Different Desire': Transgender Specularity in Zarah Leander and R. W. Fassbinder." In *Queer German Cinema,* 57–87. Stanford: Stanford UP, 2000.

Moeller, Felix. *Der Filmminister: Goebbels und der Film im Dritten Reich.* Berlin: Henschel, 1998.

Morgan, Ben. "Music in Nazi Film: How Different is *Triumph of the Will?*" *Studies in European Cinema* 3, no. 1 (2007): 37–53.

O'Brien, Mary-Elizabeth. *Nazi Cinema as Enchantment: The Politics of Entertainment in the Third Reich.* Rochester, NY: Camden House, 2004.

Offermanns, Ernst. *Die deutschen Juden und der Spielfilm der NS-Zeit.* Frankfurt am Main: Peter Lang, 2005.

Petro, Patrice. "Nazi Cinema at the Intersection of the Classical and the Popular." *New German Critique* 74 (Spring/Summer 1998): 41–55.

Peucker, Brigitte. "The Fascist Choreography: Riefenstahl's Tableaux." In *The Material Image: Art and the Real in Film,* 49–67. Stanford: Stanford UP, 2007.

Prager, Brad. "Interpreting the Visible Traces of Theresienstadt." *Journal of Modern Jewish Studies* 7, no. 2 (2008): 175–94.

Rentschler, Eric. *The Ministry of Illusion: Nazi Cinema and Its Afterlife.* Cambridge: Harvard UP, 1996.

Rothberg, Michael. "In the Nazi Cinema: Race, Visuality and Identification in Fanon and Klüger." *Wasafiri* 24, no. 1 (2009): 13–20.

Rother, Rainer. *Leni Riefenstahl: Die Verführung des Talents.* Berlin: Henschel, 2000.

Sakmyster, Thomas. "Nazi Documentaries of Intimidation: *Feldzug in Polen* (1940), *Feuertaufe* (1940), and *Sieg im Westen* (1941)." *Historical Journal of Film, Radio and Television* 16, no. 4 (1996): 485–515.

Schulte-Sasse, Linda. *Entertaining the Third Reich: Illusions of Wholeness in Nazi Cinema.* Durham: Duke UP, 1996.

Smedley, Nicholas. *A Divided World: Hollywood Cinema and Emigré Directors in the Era of Roosevelt and Hitler, 1933–1948.* Bristol, UK: Intellect, 2011.

Spector, Scott. "Was the Third Reich Movie-Made? Interdisciplinarity and the Reframing of 'Ideology.'" *The American Historical Review* 106, no. 2 (2001): 460–84.

Spicer, Andrew, ed. *European Film Noir.* Manchester: Manchester UP, 2007.

Tegel, Susan. *Nazis and the Cinema.* London: Hambledon Continuum, 2007.

Thomas, Sarah. "A 'Star' of the Airwaves: Peter Lorre — 'Master of the Macabre' and American Radio Programming." *Radio Journal: International Studies in Broadcast & Audio Media* 5, nos. 2/3) (2007): 143–55.

Trautwein, Wolfgang. *Werner Richard Heymann: Berlin, Hollywood und kein Zurück*. Berlin: Hentrich & Hentrich, 2011.

Welch, David. *Propaganda and the German Cinema 1933–1945*. London: I. B. Tauris, 2001.

Winkel, Roel Vande, and David Welch, eds. *Cinema and the Swastika: The International Expansion of Third Reich Cinema*. Basingstoke: Palgrave Macmillan, 2007.

Winkel, Roel Vande. "Nazi Newsreels in Europe, 1939–1945: The Many Faces of Ufa's Foreign Weekly Newsreel (*Auslandstonwoche*) versus German's Weekly Newsreel (*Deutsche Wochenschau*)." *Historical Journal of Film, Radio and Television* 24, no. 1 (2004): 5–34.

Witte, Karsten. "The Indivisible Legacy of Nazi Cinema." *New German Critique* 74 (Spring/Summer 1998): 23–30.

28 March 1933: Goebbels's Kaiserhof Speech Reveals Tension between National and International Aims of Nazi Cinema

Laura Heins

A model for Nazi melodrama: Greta Garbo in Love *(Anna Karenina).*
Credit: BPK/Deutsche Kinemathek/Art Resource.

LITTLE MORE THAN two weeks after taking his post as the head of the new Ministry for Propaganda and Popular Enlightenment, Joseph Goebbels appeared before a group of film producers and journalists at the Hotel Kaiserhof in Berlin. The speech he delivered there gave the first major indication of the regime's plans for the film industry, and alluded to the exclusion of Jews that was to follow in June 1933. From the remaining filmmakers, Goebbels demanded an ideological and aesthetic revolution, the development of a uniquely German film art that would be National Socialist and broadly popular. Nazi filmmakers, he said, were to create a national cinema that would simultaneously dominate the world market. The Kaiserhof speech thus introduced a tension between Goebbels's demands for a culturally specific and propagandistically effective film style, on the one hand, and his desire for global box office success, on the other — a success that would depend on non-German and even anti-Nazi models.

Goebbels's speech contained few specific directives to filmmakers, and demonstrated that his concept of Nazi aesthetics was still undefined. In the most concrete indication of what would be expected of Third Reich filmmakers, Goebbels cited four films of the past decade that had deeply impressed him and that should serve as prototypes for Nazi filmmaking: Sergei Eisenstein's *Battleship Potemkin* (1925), Greta Garbo and Edmund Goulding's version of *Anna Karenina* (*Love*, 1927), Fritz Lang's *Nibelungen* (1924), and Luis Trenker's *Der Rebell* (*The Rebel*, 1931). These were surprising choices, given the foreign or Jewish origins of all the filmmakers listed, yet each of these examples is paradigmatic of Nazi cinema's conflicted position in regard to other national cinemas. While its aesthetic exchanges with other hypernationalist cinemas were limited, National Socialist cinema ultimately modeled itself after the most globalized of film forms, Hollywood classicism.

The first of the films cited in the Kaiserhof speech, Goebbels claimed, is "film art without parallel," even if it supported an opposing political system.[1] *Potemkin* stood for Goebbels as an admirable example of aesthetic innovation and a singularly effective piece of propaganda. His enthusiasm for the masterwork of Soviet montage is consistent with his initial openness to other forms of modernism, as with his Weimar-era embrace of expressionism — an inclination that Goebbels subsequently repudiated in order to conform to Hitler's taste for neoclassicist kitsch. Although it was presented as a model for Nazi films, *Potemkin* was banned a few days before the Kaiserhof speech and German filmmakers were not given access to Soviet films for study purposes, since Goebbels considered them too dangerously convincing.[2] A few traces of Soviet influence remained, however. The Boer massacre sequence in *Ohm Krüger* (1941) imitated Eisenstein's Odessa Steps sequence, and echoes of Vertov and Pudovkin remain in the dynamic (though not dialectical) editing of Riefenstahl's *Tag der Freiheit* (*Day of Freedom*, 1935) and *Olympia* (1938), as well as in some of Walter Ruttmann's fascist-era Italian work (particularly *Acciaio/Steel*, 1933).

Although resembling each other in moments of patriotic pathos, the Soviet cinema distinguished itself markedly from Nazi cinema through its focus on labor and production. Nazi features attempted to disguise the material nature of the cinematic and wartime apparatus, hiding the presence of the camera and avoiding scenes of factory work. Those Nazi films that did take place in industrial settings, such as *Der Herrscher* (*The Ruler*, 1937) and *Diesel* (1942), most often concerned an inventor or corporate executive, and tended to naturalize technology by describing it as the result of the virile generative processes of exceptional men.[3] The Nazi resistance toward revealing the actual mechanics behind industrial and cultural production was demonstrated characteristically in 1940, when Goebbels sharply chastened a magazine editor for publishing a photo of a record, because it revealed that a musical fanfare commonly transmitted over the radio was prerecorded rather than live. Goebbels then issued a directive threatening all journalists with internment in a concentration camp if they dared to publish any similarly "disillusioning" information about Nazi radio or film in the future.[4]

Third Reich feature film thus conformed to the illusionary nature of classical film aesthetics, most often emulating American rather than Soviet cinema. Goebbels's second example in the Kaiserhof speech ultimately proved indicative of the stylistic tendencies of the Nazi cinema as a whole. A large number of Third Reich films imitated Hollywood melodrama, offering uninspired versions of international literary classics and Garbo substitutes. The Tolstoy adaptation *Love*, Goebbels claimed, proved that film was no "surrogate for the theater," but a wholly independent medium (*Tagebücher*, 154). Goebbels's notion of cinematic specificity lay as much in its mass effects as in its formal properties. As Horkheimer and Adorno presumed when they described Nazi cinema as merely another version of the capitalist culture industry, what Goebbels particularly admired about Hollywood was its superior ability to repackage old high culture and sell it as world popular culture.[5] Hollywood has long been successful on the global market precisely because it does not promote itself as a national cinema and does not rely heavily on notions of national-cultural specificity, addressing its spectators instead with a set of cultural values it most often posits as universal. Goebbels admired Hollywood's ability to harness the utopian desires of the international masses, and attempted to copy Hollywood's hegemonic policies toward the film industries of other nations, as well as its stylistic formulas.[6]

Goebbels's third Kaiserhof model was perhaps the most curious, and points to the ambiguous Nazi position in regard to Weimar cinema. Fritz Lang's expressionist version of the medieval *Nibelungenlied* epic, Goebbels effused, was "so modern, so close to the times," and proved that filmic modernity was not a matter of subject, but of style (*Tagebücher*, 154–55). Yet Lang's most recent film, *Das Testament des Dr. Mabuse* (*The Testament of Dr. Mabuse*, 1933) was banned the day after the Kaiserhof speech, in keeping with the Nazi paranoia about baring the cinematic device — Goebbels apparently recognized too many parallels between the fictional Mabuse's reliance on hidden recordings and illusionism to extend his power and the Nazis' own media ambitions. After the half-Jewish Lang escaped Germany in late 1933, most attempts at developing an innovative visual style akin to Lang's were banished as well. One such attempt was Frank Wysbar's *Fährmann Maria* (Ferryman Maria, 1936), an allegorical film that features a personification of death in the manner of Lang's *Der müde Tod* (*Destiny*, 1921). Goebbels rejected the film as an unwelcome aesthetic experiment, and Wysbar soon followed Lang into Hollywood exile. Hitler despised anything resembling Gothic style, and so those fascinations of the early Weimar cinema to which Lang had contributed so much — modernist expressions of fatalism and horror, the fantastic and the uncanny — rarely found entry into Third Reich cinemas. This elimination of expressionism from National Socialist film was, ironically, also an expulsion of the only major cinematic style that had been hitherto recognized as a specifically German film aesthetic.

Goebbels's other Weimar model, Luis Trenker's *Der Rebell*, followed a more classical pattern, but does reveal some continuities in German cinema of the pre- and post-1933 eras. Although the Nazi press most often referred to Weimar cinema as a degenerate product of the "Systemzeit" (system era), many of the stars, directors, and genres of Third Reich cinema had been inherited directly from the Weimar industry. Trenker was one of these, and although a South Tyrolean with Italian citizenship, he delivered pan-German propaganda through the *Bergfilm*, a genre marked by protofascist sensibilities.[7] *Der Rebell*, in which Trenker himself played the leader of an early nineteenth-century insurgency against Napoleonic occupation, belonged to a string of Weimar nationalist productions (*Fridericus Rex*, 1922 to *Morgenrot* [*Dawn*], 1933). Goebbels saw the film as an exceptionally skillful delivery of contemporary ideological content in the guise of an historical film, since it actually served to militate against the Treaty of Versailles. Such a treatment of twentieth-century conflicts through the lens of eighteenth- and nineteenth-century wars was characteristic for the later Nazi cinema. Goebbels final filmic mega project of the Third Reich, *Kolberg* (1945), was just one of the many Nazi films that followed Trenker's model in its attempt to validate imperialist aggression by means of a spurious siege rhetoric, according to which a foreign power supposedly aimed to colonize and exterminate the Germans.

The example of Luis (Luigi) Trenker further highlights the Nazi cinema's conflicted relations with Italian Fascist cinema, since Trenker also contributed to Italian national cinema with his 1937 German-Italian coproduction *Condottieri*. German-Italian film collaborations predated the Nazi takeover, but under the banner of a transnational European fascism, the Nazis cultivated these relationships even further, sponsoring coproductions and cultural exchanges with the Italians and inviting several Italian directors (Carmine Gallone, Augusto Genina, and Mario Camerini) to come work in the German studios. Less than two months after the Kaiserhof speech, Goebbels visited Italy to speak about his plans for the new Reich Film Chamber. Following the Nazi model, an Italian Press and Propaganda bureau was set up in 1934, and Goebbels's counterpart Luigi Freddi similarly called for state intervention and the creation of a specifically Italian film style. In 1938, Mussolini's son Vittorio visited the Ufa (Universum Film A.G.) studios in Berlin-Babelsberg for insight into Nazi production methods. Although influenced by Nazi practices in institutional and industrial organization, on a stylistic level the Italians, too, ultimately oriented themselves toward America.

Despite some pan-European rhetoric, Goebbels was never genuinely interested in establishing an equal exchange with Italian Fascism. Goebbels insisted that Italy, like the rest of world, should be dominated by German national cinema. Jealous of the competition that Italian Fascist cinema presented on the European market, he viewed such films as inferior to both German and American productions. Although the more fascist of Italian films, such as *Scipione l'africano* (*The Defeat of Hannibal*), clearly shared the Riefenstahlian aesthetics of ornamental masses, Goebbels did not view the two cinemas as sharing a common aesthetic. On several occasions he considered banning Italian imports on artistic grounds alone, because they displayed a melodramatic style too reminiscent of silent cinema. Problematically also, the two cinemas diverged ideologically in regard to the church. Italian Fascist cinema, like Spanish film under Franco, made common use of religious iconography in an attempt to blend the authority of Catholic tradition with the revolutionary rhetoric of fascism, while the Nazis tried to develop racial politics and the cinema itself into substitute cultic realms. Trenker, Goebbels's favorite nationalist filmmaker at the time of the Kaiserhof speech, fell out of favor soon after the premiere of *Condottieri*, which struck the propaganda minister as being too Catholic and politically too close to Rome.

Goebbels ended his first speech as propaganda minister with the slogan: "May Germany lead the world!"[8] The path to global German domination was, he claimed, a resolutely national cinema: "The more sharply a film reveals *völkisch* contours, the greater are the possibilities of conquering the world" (*Tagebücher*, 155). The tension between these two competing demands left many of his listeners uncertain about how to proceed, and Goebbels soon began lamenting the disappointing performance of Third Reich filmmakers such as Trenker. Goebbels's efforts to promote a racialized film aesthetic based upon theories of German genius through the short-lived German Film Academy[9] did not mitigate his recurrent sense of failure. In 1940, at a special screening of *Gone With the Wind*, the Minister admitted partial defeat. The Nazis had been unable to produce a comparable film, he explained, because they did not have the same recourse to the talent of foreign technicians as Hollywood.[10] Nazi films did score some export successes, particularly during the war and in countries where Hollywood's access was restricted.[11] However, they never realized Goebbels's initial ambition of a worldwide Nazi cinematic empire that would simultaneously support nationalistic objectives, display ethnic and aesthetic specificity, and conquer global audiences.

See also:

- 14 February 1924: *Die Nibelungen* Premieres, Foregrounds "Germanness"
- 28 March 1935: Premiere of *Triumph des Willens* Presents Fascism as Unifier of Communal Will
- 13 January 1954: Preminger's Dual-Language *The Moon Is Blue* (1953) and *Die Jungfrau auf dem Dach* (1954) Seek Glocal Success

Notes

[1] Joseph Goebbels, *Tagebücher*, ed. Ralf Georg Reuth (Munich: Piper, 1992), 154. Hereafter cited in text.

[2] Felix Moeller, *Der Filmminister: Goebbels und der Film im Dritten Reich* (Berlin: Henschel, 1998), 79.

[3] Linda Schulte-Sasse, *Entertaining the Third Reich: Illusions of Wholeness in Nazi Cinema* (Durham: Duke UP, 1996), 274–87.

[4] Bundesarchiv File BArch R55/20001c, 87.

[5] Max Horkheimer and Theodor Adorno, *Dialectic of Enlightenment* (Stanford: Stanford UP, 2002), 94–136.

[6] Eric Rentschler, *The Ministry of Illusion: Nazi Cinema and its Afterlife* (Cambridge, MA: Harvard UP, 1996), 216.

[7] Ibid., 34–37.

[8] Joseph Goebbels, "Dr. Goebbels's Speech at the Kaiserhof on March 28, 1933," trans. Lance W. Garmer, in *German Essays on Film*, ed. Richard W. McCormick and Alison Guenther-Pal (New York: Continuum, 2004), 153–58; here 158.

[9] Erica Carter, *Dietrich's Ghosts: the Sublime and the Beautiful in Third Reich Film* (London: BFI, 2004), 41–48.

[10] Bundesarchiv File BArch R 55/20001e, 41–42.

[11] Ernst Offermanns, *Internationalität und europäischer Hegemonialanspruch des Spielfilms der NS-Zeit* (Hamburg: Dr. Kovacs, 2001), 89–93.

29 February 1935: *Der alte und der junge König* Instrumentalizes Myth of Prussian Nationalism

Martina G. Lüke

ADOLF HITLER'S PLAN to centralize political power was aided in 1932 with the *Preußenschlag* (Prussian coup), when, under a pretext, Reichspräsident Paul von Hindenburg issued an emergency decree dismissing the cabinet of Prussia. Until that time, the government of Germany's largest state had been a powerful republican force against antidemocratic powers in the Weimar Republic. This notwithstanding, the National Socialists were eager to claim the legacy of Prussian history. As Reich Propaganda Minister Joseph Goebbels commented in his diary in March 1942: "Film becomes a first-class political means of education. It is just what we need nowadays. We are living in a time that needs the Frederickian spirit."[1] With this in mind, the Reich Ministry for Propaganda, which from March 1933 on oversaw the entire cultural production of Nazi Germany, undertook a program of filmmaking that sought, among other things, to instrumentalize Prussian history for political ends. Under Goebbels, the Nazi film industry produced a series of historical films that blurred the boundaries of history, propaganda, and entertainment, and transformed existing cultural narratives and traditions into aesthetic mystifications of Prussian militarism and nationalism.

Der alte und der junge König (The old and the young king, 1935) inaugurated this series of Nazi-era films concerned with Prussian history and the so-called Prussian virtues of discipline, loyalty, and obedience. These Prussia films represented one important strand in the regime's larger cinematic project to justify its present policies through a strategic recreation of the German past in historical dramas.[2] In keeping with the regime's propaganda aims, *Der alte und der junge König* emphasizes self-sacrifice, the need to obey orders, and the neglect of personal fulfillment in favor of following the demands of duty and *Staatsraison*. Based on a script by Thea von Harbou and directed by Hans Steinhoff (also behind such infamous propaganda films as *Hitlerjunge Quex*, 1933, and *Ohm Krüger*, 1941), *Der alte und der junge König* takes popular anecdotes on the difficult relationship of Frederick the Great (Werner Hinz) and his father, Frederick William I (Emil Jannings), as case studies for the necessity of submission to paternal authority. This conflict of personal feelings and political reasoning escalates when Frederick, the free-spirited heir to the throne, who, as a Francophile philosopher and musician is not the least interested in Prussian military politics, attempts to escape. After being caught and imprisoned, his best friend and collaborator Hans Hermann von Katte (Claus Clausen) is sentenced to death for high treason, while Frederick, who is forced to watch the execution, remains in custody until he submits to his father. Father and son remain estranged, until, persuaded by the celebrated General-Field Marshal Leopold I von Anhalt-Dessau (Rudolf Klein-Rogge), they reconcile at the deathbed of Frederick William. Frederick, like his father, becomes an authoritarian monarch and patriarchal head of the Prussian state. Throughout, the film legitimizes authoritarian modes of education and discipline, whether in the scene portraying the burning of Frederick's books — possibly an echo of the Nazi book burnings of May 1933 — or in those moments that, evoking the methods of the Hitler Youth, highlight the need to "harden" male youth through military instruction, physical fitness, deliberated brutality, and political instruction. *Der alte und der junge König* thereby transforms eighteenth-century sentimentality and moralizing humanity from phenomena that seem antithetical to the Nazi war machine into principles that undergird idealized views of warfare and soldierly nationalism. Featuring important military figures and absolute monarchs of German national and cultural identity such as the legendary *Soldatenkönig* Frederick William, Frederick the Great, or the "Alte Dessauer," the film incorporates characters that also implicitly justify totalitarian control by a powerful leader.

The mobilization and exploitation of Prussian history did not commence with Steinhoff's film, however. As early as September 1926, during a visit at Sanssouci, Goebbels had become aware of the legacy's propaganda potential, and the future propaganda minister appeared in 1929 as a speaker at a presentation of the four-part epic *Fridericus Rex* (1922–23). In adopting and adapting the myth of Prussia, the National Socialists built on older historiographic, literary, and cinematic traditions from the Weimar Republic and Imperial Germany. Early movies included *Der alte Fritz* (Old Fritz, 1896), *Theodor Körner* (1912), and *Der Film von der Königin Luise* (The Film of Queen Luise, 1913), which were released in coincidence with the centennial of the Wars of Liberation (1813–15). While popular works by historiographers Heinrich von Sybel or Heinrich von Treitschke had already established a national and authoritarian perception of Prussia in Imperial Germany, the cultural mass production and new mass media in the Weimar Republic popularized these existing perceptions, as can be seen in Walter von Molo's 1918 biography on Frederick the Great, or Arzén von Cserépy's already mentioned, highly successful series *Fridericus Rex*, which also initiated actor Otto Gebühr as the impersonator of the Prussian king. These postwar depictions also epitomize the era's genuine longing for restoration and an overall glamorized vision of Prussian legends and myths. *Der Choral von Leuthen* (The Leuthen chorale, 1933) and Gerhard Lamprecht's two-part movie *Der alte Fritz* (1928), for example, portray an exhausted but strong-minded Frederick the Great during the Seven Years War and the troublesome but successful reconstruction of Prussia; *Flötenkonzert von Sanssouci* (The flute concert of Sanssouci, 1930) evokes the search for national identity and an intact world after Germany's defeat and the demoralizing Treaty of Versailles. There are also cult-of-personality films like *Die elf Schillschen Offiziere* (Schill's eleven officers, 1926), *Die letzte Kompanie* (The last company, 1930), and *Marschall Vorwärts* (Marshal Forward, 1932), as well as the remakes *Königin Luise* (1927/1928), *Luise, Königin von Preußen* (*Luise, Queen of Prussia*, 1931), and *Theodor Körner* (1932). Lighter invocations of the Prussian past, such as *Die Tänzerin von Sanssouci* (The dancer of Sanssouci, 1932) and *Der schwarze Husar* (*The Black Hussar*, 1932), focus on romantic situations and can be seen as the culmination of an imaginary escape from the modernity and socioeconomic crises of the Weimar Republic.

The National Socialist film industry drew upon these existing traditions, transforming historically oriented escapism and the longing for a reactionary restoration into potent material for contemporary political propaganda and utopian fantasies. Immediately after Hitler's rise to power, performative acts like the "Day of Potsdam" (21 March 1933), on which Adolf Hitler and Paul von Hindenburg met at the gravesides of Frederick the Great and Frederick William I, offered images of a synthesis of "old" and "new" elites. Furthermore, Hitler himself considered the political and military struggles of Frederick the Great as the historical model for himself and the National Socialist movement. A fictionalized Prussia thus served as a fantasy object for both the initiator as well as the receivers of the modern totalitarian mass movement. Through a selective representation of fictionalized Prussian historical figures and events, the National Socialists cultivated nostalgic national myths as a means to foster support for both the regime and the war. Leaving out unwanted political, ethical, and cultural developments (e.g., the emancipation of the Prussian Jews or the Prussian Enlightenment linked to philosophers such as Immanuel Kant and Moses Mendelssohn), the National Socialists stylized Prussia as a totalitarian state that made unscrupulous use of its military powers. With their antimodern projection, mystification of the Prussian past, and emphasis on figures of (military) genius, Nazi-era Prussia films provided narratives tailor-made to fuel irrational mass desires.[3]

Nazi-era Prussia films focused on three main aspects of the state's history: Frederick the Great and the rise of Prussia as a leading European power; the defeat of Prussia in 1806 and her political resurrection in the Wars of Liberation; and Otto von Bismarck and German unification (1870/71). *Der alte und der junge König* was thus followed by films such as Johannes Meyer's *Fridericus* (1937) and Veit Harlan's *Der große König* (The great king, 1942), which portrayed Frederick the Great as a determined leader who, despite facing a string of personal and military defeats, overcomes internal and external tensions and finally succeeds. Released in the year when the German offensive came to a halt on both the Eastern and Western fronts, *Der große König* in particular sought to portray the monarch simultaneously as a model of identification in times of personal hardship and as an enduring supreme strategist — a carefully refashioned projection of the *Führer* myth.

The theme of the misunderstood rebellious genius and Nietzschean *Übermensch* in tragic solitude was linked to Otto von Bismarck in *Bismarck* (1940) and *Die Entlassung* (The dismissal, 1942). In both films the chancellor faces intrigues at the domestic and foreign level. In *Die Entlassung*, Bismarck is defeated by opponents in parliament, the royal court, and an overly ambitious William I — a propagandistic reflection of both the 1934 outlawing of all monarchist organizations in Nazi Germany and the regime's contempt for all democratic institutions. By omitting the fact that Bismarck negotiated to avoid war and that his foreign policy after unification succeeded for decades without entering another armed conflict, *Bismarck* manages to portray the statesman as a dominant *Führer*-figure and a "blood and iron" ruler. With these aestheticized transformations of well-known historical narratives, Hitler appeared as the implicit successor of Prussian icons.

As in *Der alte und der junge König*, films concerning the Wars of Liberation and the end of Napoleonic occupation like *Der höhere Befehl* (On higher order, 1935) or *Der Katzensteg* (1937) emphasized the value of duty and self-sacrifice for a higher cause, and presented military and war experience as opportunities for personal development and comradeship. Films made after the beginning of the Second World War increasingly linked personal sacrifice to death on the battlefield. *Kadetten* (Cadets), for example, was finished in 1939, but in keeping with the nation's larger military aims, it was not released until December 1941, months after the attack on the Soviet Union.[4] In an uncanny resemblance to the military mobilization of German youth by the National Socialists, it takes as its focus the defense of the fortress Spandau by child cadets against invading Cossacks. Indeed, pupils of the Nationalpolitische Lehranstalt (NAPOLA) boarding school in Potsdam participated as actors.

The final Prussia film of the National Socialist era was *Kolberg* (1945), directed by Veit Harlan, who also made *Der große König* and other commissioned works, including Nazi cinema's most contested film, the anti-semitic *Jud Süß* (Jew Süss, 1940). *Kolberg* represents the apotheosis of Nazi Prussian historical propaganda and the cinematic celebration of total war. Much like *Der Choral von Leuthen* or *Fridericus*, the film transforms a hopeless military situation, the siege of the Pomeranian fortress, into a moral triumph. This *Durchhaltefilm* (perseverance film) stylizes the myth of Prussian/German invincibility grounded in national unity and male military and civic collaboration — a narrative in which women are generally consigned to passive supporting roles. Harlan's film concluded a tradition of cinematic instrumentalization of history begun with *Der alte und der junge König*. The two films serve as the end markers of a cinematic narrative that mobilized constructions of Prussia as a militaristic, nationalistic, and antimodern state in which royal authorities ruled as absolute leaders and National Socialist aggression as appeared as the fulfillment of a long tradition. Offering fragments of the monarchical past of Brandenburg-Prussia and systematically assembling historical legends to meet the aims of mass manipulation, the National Socialists sought to establish a continuity of German history from 1640 to 1933. Despite the tradition of republican resistance destroyed by the *Preußenschlag* and the fact that two-thirds of the participants in the last attempt on Hitler's life on 20 July 1944 were members of the old Prussian nobility, in the end "it was the Nazi view of Prussia that prevailed":[5] the equation of "Prussianism" and National Socialism became the foundation for Law Number 46 of the Allied Control Council, passed on 25 February 1947, which formally dissolved Prussia.

See also:

- 14 February 1924: *Die Nibelungen* Premieres, Foregrounds "Germanness"
- 18 January 1943: Bateson Analysis of *Hitlerjunge Quex* Stresses Value of Film as Key to National Culture
- 9 March 1954: *Ernst Thälmann — Sohn seiner Klasse* Marks High Point of Socialist Realism

Notes

[1] Cited in Jo Fox, *Film Propaganda in Britain and Nazi Germany* (Oxford: Berg, 2007), 215–16.

[2] On the Nazi fascination with period dramas, see Linda Schulte-Sasse, *Entertaining the Third Reich: Illusions of Wholeness in Nazi Cinema* (Durham: Duke UP, 1996).

[3] On the subject of "genius films," see Eric Rentschler's discussion of *Paracelsus* (Pabst, 1943) in his standard work on Nazi cinema, *The Ministry of Illusion: Nazi Cinema and Its Afterlife* (Cambridge, MA: Harvard UP, 1996), 171–91.

[4] Udo W. Wolff, *Preußens Gloria im Film* (Munich: Heyne, 1981), 31 and 34. On this topic see also the still excellent essential discussions in Axel Marquart and

Heinz Rathsack, *Preussen im Film: Eine Retrospektive der Stiftung Deutsche Kinemathek* (Hamburg: Rowohlt, 1981).

[5] Christopher Clark, *The Iron Kingdom: The Rise and Downfall of Prussia, 1600–1947* (Cambridge, MA: Harvard UP, 2006), 670.

28 March 1935: Premiere of *Triumph des Willens* Presents Fascism as Unifier of Communal Will

Michael Cowan & Kai Sicks

The pomp-filled opening of Triumph des Willens.
Credit: Licht Bild Bühne 75/1935: 1.

DURING THE SECOND HALF of March 1935, in the weeks leading up to the premiere of Leni Riefenstahl's *Triumph des Willens* (*Triumph of the Will*), Berlin's premiere movie palace, the Ufa-Palast am Zoo, received a major makeover. Among other things, the building's façade was expanded and equipped with a massive pedestal in order to accommodate a golden German eagle measuring some twenty-five by twenty-eight feet (seven and a half by eight and a half meters), flanked by nineteen swastika flags.[1] The redesigning of the Ufa theater was only the latest installment in a monumental and costly film project. While recording the Nuremberg party rally of 1934, Riefenstahl used the nearly unlimited financial support of Hitler to employ a crew of some 170 artists, technicians, and workers — including eighteen camera teams and various contraptions for setting the cameras into motion — in her effort to make a new and improved "document" (as she dubbed the film) of a Nazi Party rally after the less impressive results of her 1933 documentary *Sieg des Glaubens* (*Victory of Faith*).[2] After some seven months of editing 130,000 meters of material down to 3000,[3] *Triumph des Willens* premiered on 28 March to an audience of party elites that included Josef Goebbels and — arriving in a motorcade and accompanied by a massive array of bodyguards as well as his own orchestra — Hitler himself.

Redesigning movie theaters for film premieres was in itself nothing new: Germany's larger picture palaces had long been decorated to match the film being shown. But the preparations for *Triumph des Willens* were the most expensive and most monumental ever undertaken. The team of architects in charge of retrofitting the theater was led by Hitler's chief architect Albert Speer, who had also designed the gigantic sets for the 1934 Nuremberg rally and planned to transform all of Berlin into the monumental "World Capital Germania." Nor was the Berlin Ufa-Palast the only movie theater to participate in the event: during the 1934 rally, the Nuremberg cinemas themselves, as reported in trade journals, were at the "front ranks" of the activities — decorating their façades with flags, national emblems, festoons, and images of the *Führer*, and programming films to fit the occasion.[4] The Nuremberg Ufa theater, for example, featured a rotating series of propaganda films including *SA Mann Brand* (1933), *Hitlerjunge Quex* (1933), and *Ein Mann will nach Deutschland* (*A Man Wants to Get to Germany*, 1934).

This mobilization of movie theaters both during and after the 1934 Nuremberg rally formed part of a much broader "media event," understood in the sense outlined by Daniel Dayan and Elihu Katz, as the mediation of political rites that "integrate societies in a collective heartbeat and evoke a renewal of loyalty to the society and its legitimate [or in the case of the Nazi regime, illegitimate] authority."[5] Staged just after Hitler's assassination of the rebellious SA leader Ernst Röhm, the 1934 Nuremberg rally aimed precisely to command loyalty to the new regime — "Treue" is a recurrent keyword in the speeches featured in the film — not only from the masses present at the rally, but also the general population, to whom the events were broadcast via a complex interplay of mixed media including *Wochenschauen* (newsreels), radio shows, and the daily press. Seen within this context, Riefenstahl's film can be understood less as an individual or unique work than as one element of a complex set of mediations.

Film-historical debates about Riefenstahl have tended either to condemn *Triumph des Willens* as the ultimate example of the cinema's instrumentalization in the service of evil, or (echoing Riefenstahl's own revisionist accounts) to defend the film as an aesthetic masterpiece and a milestone of documentary, whose director, emerging from the Weimar mountain-film genre, happened to break through in the wrong place and the wrong time. But the film also represented a rearrangement of mass mediations already familiar to Germany's media consumers at the time. Not by chance did one reviewer write that Riefenstahl was able to shorten Hitler's speeches for the film because "one could assume that the public already knew their entire content from the press, from radio broadcasts and from newsreels."[6] To these formats, Riefenstahl added strategies of aestheticizing the political by means of filmic techniques such as montage (through Riefenstahl's editing, even a cat appears to join the excitement surrounding Hitler's arrival, turning its head to follow his motorcade), camera angles (particularly the low-angled shots used to establish Hitler's authority), and camera movement (e.g., the famous tracking shots used to depict the masses of followers as endless geometrical formations). Such techniques have been analyzed repeatedly in research on *Triumph des Willens*, but understanding what happened *around* the film, as well as the film's role within the broader mediations of the 1934 rally, is no less important than understanding its aesthetics. Like the Nuremberg rally itself, the premiere of *Triumph des Willens* was covered in newspapers, movie magazines, radio shows, and newsreels. In this way, the events surrounding the film's release constituted a collective act of remembering the party rally and sought to reinforce the integrative function of the rally itself.

Indeed, it is no exaggeration to say that the course of events at the film's Berlin premiere was organized largely to repeat, at least in part, the rally as shown in the film. The premiere included many of the same "stars" and even the same marching tunes featured in the film. Most importantly, perhaps, the premiere party reenacted the film's famous opening sequence in staging the wait for Hitler's arrival and the masses' joy at his messianic appearance. As a writer for *Lichtbild-Bühne* described the scene for publication the following day: "For hours, countless masses of people have been waiting all around the Ufa-Palast for the spectacle [*Schauspiel*] of the ministers' arrival.... Shortly before 9:30, the car of the *Führer* drives up. A storm of enthusiasm moves through the masses. Jubilatory calls of 'Heil!' greet the *Führer*" ("Ein epochales Filmdokument," 1). In this scene, as in the film, Hitler's role as political leader merges with his role as star actor. Thus *Triumph des Willens* not only serves as propaganda in a strict political sense (e.g., by showing disciplined masses or speeches of leading Nazi politicians), it also tries to establish Hitler as a star of popular media — a reading that is supported by cover images of Hitler in film journals like *Kinematograph* the day after his appearance at the Berlin premiere. In this sense, Hitler's arrival at the premiere not only reenacted his broadcasted arrival in Nuremberg, but also evoked traditional appearances by famous movie stars at the premiere of their latest blockbuster.

The coordination of media around the Nuremberg rally and Hitler in which Riefenstahl's film participated was in keeping with the theme of the film itself. *Triumph des Willens* is nothing if not the "document" of a *totale Mobilmachung*: a complete mobilization of bodies, resources, and media in the service of the new movement. Famous above all for its panorama shots of mass ornaments, in which individual bodies meld into a unified *Volkskörper* (national body), the film sought to render in visual terms the absolute unification of national energy around a single goal and the single figure of Hitler. Thus, Riefenstahl's montage constantly associates Hitler's face with visions of unified masses arranged statically and representing elemental groups in fascist German society — workers, youth, military, SA, and SS — interspersed with close-ups of enthusiastic individual faces within the crowd. Indeed, the theme of unification runs throughout Hitler's many speeches in the film, which constantly emphasize the transition from political and economic conflict toward unity. "We want to be one people," he tells the Hitler Youth, "and through you to become this people; we want a society without classes or rank." The same theme also formed the central trope in the film's reception; trade journals repeatedly described *Triumph des Willens* as a vision of "the new Germany become one," or "the document of the unification of the people."[7]

Such a staging of national unification takes up a broader narrative, central to Nazism's self-understanding, about the transition from Weimar parliamentary democracy to National Socialism. As is well known, the film was originally intended to begin with a prologue about the Weimar years shot and edited by Walter Ruttmann, who had already constructed condemnations of Weimar decadence in films such as *Blut und Boden* (*Blood and Soil*, 1934), where he used recycled footage from his own *Berlin. Die Sinfonie der Großstadt* (*Berlin: Symphony of a Great City*, 1927) to oppose the unhealthy conditions of Weimar urban life to the beauty and strength of the blood-and-soil lifestyle propagated by Nazism. According to reports, Ruttmann's prologue for *Triumph des Willens*, consisting of found footage and scenes shot at the Ufa (Universum Film A.G.) Studios, relied primarily on what Vsevelod Pudovkin had dubbed the montage of "contrast" to picture Weimar culture as a period of stark political and economic dichotomies: the orgiastic extravagancies of the upper classes contrasted with visions of starving mothers and laid-off workers, prostitutes and reveling jazz musicians juxtaposed with wounded and traumatized soldiers, etc. Although the prologue was ultimately removed — primarily in order to avoid celebrating Röhm and the SA — it was clearly intended to figure Weimar as a period of conflict, as one writer put it, "before the new Germany-become-one showed its manifestation of faith and will in the Nuremberg rallies."[8] In the final version of the film, echoes of the prologue are still evident in the opening titles, which describe the Nuremberg rallies as the manifestation of a national "rebirth" after the humiliations of the Great War and the Weimar Republic ("sixteen years after the start of German suffering") and in the lengthy sequences honoring the war dead.

This desire to stage the unification of national energy also informed the film's title. According to various reports, the title *Triumph des Willens* came not from Riefenstahl but from Hitler himself ("Ein epochales Filmdokument," 1).[9] The preoccupation with the will and willpower had, in fact, a longstanding tradition in Germany and Europe stretching back to the nineteenth century, in which the will was seen as a cure for the ills of mass modernity — understood as a state of chaotic and conflicting influences, tendencies, styles, or drives — whether in the individual body or on a collective level. National Socialism largely adopted this rhetoric of the will to describe their political and economic endeavors, and above all to narrate the transition from the chaos of Weimar democracy to the coordinated (*gleichgeschaltet*) society of fascism. The psychologist Erich Grassl, for example, explained in a 1937 book entitled *Die Willensschwäche* (Weakness of will) how Hitler's ascent had ushered in a new era of willpower after the weakness of Weimar: "The German people had entered an advanced stage of will decay, which manifested itself in all domains of life in the form of indolence and lack of energy.... But *Adolf Hitler*, the leader of our people, whose life path was and is itself a triumph of the will, put an end to all of this."[10] That Riefenstahl's film and title were understood in a similar sense can be seen, once again, in the film's reception in trade journals. As one writer for *Lichtbild-Bühne* described it, "For anyone who had any doubt, this film shows that the *Führer* and his followers in Germany have become one, ruled by one will, which has triumphed over everything that previously impeded it — and which will also triumph over all obstacles in the future" ("Ein epochales Filmdokument," 1).

If Riefenstahl's film sought to stage the unification of national energies around this new fascist "will," it should also be seen as part of a broader effort to coordinate and unify audio-visual media — including the cinema — in the service of a state-controlled media event. After the Ufa-Palast screening, the festivities surrounding the Berlin premiere would be repeated in miniature around the country in screenings tightly regulated by the newly formed Reichsfilmkammer (Film Chamber of the Reich). Among other orders, the film was to be screened alone, unaccompanied by the usual array of short films. In addition, theaters were obliged to charge a nonprofit ticket price for members of NS organizations and children. A writer for *Deutsche Filmzeitung* might have sensed some of the significance of this regulation of movie theaters when he described *Triumph des Willens* as a mixture of *Wochenschau* and *Vereinsfilm* (club or association film), the latter a genre long used by sports clubs and other associations to forge collective identifications through commemoration of significant events in private screenings. *Triumph des Willens*, the writer continues, carries such private acts of commemoration to the public and the national level: "But since the 'association' has developed into a first-rate political party and finally into the sole bearer of power, indeed into the state itself, the commemorative film has developed into an act of national and state memory."[11] *Triumph des Willens*, seen as part of a broader media event, can be understood precisely as an effort to transform the public cinema into the space of an all-encompassing national "association": a forum for commanding loyalty to the will of the new state.

See also:

- 1 November 1895: Premiere of Wintergarten Program Highlights Transitional Nature of Early Film Technology
- 18 December 1913: *Atlantis* Triggers Controversy about Sinking of Culture
- 28 March 1933: Goebbels's Kaiserhof Speech Reveals Tension between National and International Aims of Nazi Cinema

Notes

[1] "Triumph des Willens: Der Ufa-Palast am Zoo als Festspielhaus," *Kinematograph* 29, no. 62 (28 March 1935): 1.

[2] "Was der Reichsparteitagfilm zeigen soll," *Lichtbild-Bühne* 27, no. 196 (24 August 1934): 2; "*Triumph des Willens*. Festaufführung im Ufa-Palast am Zoo," *Der Film* 20, no. 13 (30 March 1935), erste Beilage; Peter Zimmermann, "Der Parteitagsfilm der NSDAP und Leni Riefenstahl," *Geschichte des dokumentarischen Films in Deutschland. Band 3: "Drittes Reich,"* ed. Peter Zimmermann and Kay Hoffmann (Stuttgart: Reclam, 2005): 511–30; here 517.

[3] "Ein epochales Filmdokument: 'Triumph des Willens,' Fest-Premiere im Ufa-Palast," *Lichtbild-Bühne* 28, no. 76 (29 March 1935): 1–2, hereafter cited in text; "'Triumph des Willens': Festaufführung im Ufa-Palast am Zoo in Anwesenheit des Führers," *Kinematograph* 29, no. 64 (30 March 1935): 1–2.

[4] See "Nürnberger Kinos während der Festtage," *Lichtbild-Bühne* 27, no. 210 (10 September 1934): 2.

[5] Daniel Dayan/Elihu Katz, *Media Events: The Live Broadcasting of History* (Cambridge, MA: Harvard UP, 1992), 9.

[6] "Der Triumph des Willens," review, *Deutsche Filmzeitung* 14 (28 March 1935), 3.

[7] "Aufnahmen zu 'Triumph des Willens,'" *Kinematograph* 28, no. 196 (10 October 1934): 3; "'Triumph des Willens': Festaufführung im Ufa-Palast am Zoo in Anwesenheit des Führers," 2.

[8] "Aufnahmen zu 'Triumph des Willens,'" 3.

[9] See also Jürgen Trimborn, *Leni Riefenstahl: A Life*, trans. Edna McCown (New York: Faber & Faber, 2008), 114.

[10] Erich Grassl, *Die Willensschwäche: Gleichzeitig ein Beitrag zur Theorie des Willens, der Willensentwicklung und Willenserziehung* (Leipzig: Verlag von Johann Ambrosius Barth, 1937), 2.

[11] "Triumph des Willens," film review, *Deutsche Filmzeitung* 14 (28 March 1935): 3.

19 June 1935: Celebration of Lilian Harvey's Return Belies Ideological Incongruence in Nazi Entertainment Films

Antje Ascheid

Filmwelt *featured Lilian Harvey's high-publicity welcome upon her return to Germany in 1935. Credit: ns-archiv.national-socialism.org.*

IN JUNE 1935, LILIAN HARVEY'S return to German cinema was celebrated with great pomp at Berlin's Tempelhof Airport. Ufa (Universum Film A.G.) star Willy Fritsch, her long-term *Traumpartner* (dream partner) going back to the Weimar era, film director Paul Martin, and Ufa board representative C. M. Köhn were in attendance, as were the international press and plenty of photographers. News articles and postcards documenting the event soon circulated and the National Socialist media began to spin its earlier condemnation of Harvey's relocation to Hollywood and secure a successful reintegration of the actress into Ufa's star firmament. "The emancipation of the day," so Ernst Bloch wrote in 1937, "was the return of the prodigal daughter."[1] Accordingly, Harvey was represented as reformed, indeed tired of Hollywood superficiality, having discovered "that Hollywood wasn't the perfect film paradise."[2]

Behind the scenes, things were not running quite as smoothly. Following her arrival in Germany, she was privately presented with a significant fine as a penalty for her previous *Reichsflucht* (escape from the Reich), which was only lifted after she successfully complained to Reichspropagandaminister Joseph Goebbels about it. And while the next few years saw the production of some of the most popular pictures of the Nazi era, many of which starred Harvey, the actress upset the administration with her private behavior, particularly through her continued friendship with former Jewish colleagues. Her second "defection" from Nazi Germany in 1939, following her break-up with Martin, confirmed their suspicions. Indeed, biographies of the actress stress that it was solely for romantic reasons (Martin couldn't find his feet in Hollywood) that she returned to Germany at all. When Martin left her for a younger actress, the estranged couple struggled to finish *Frau am Steuer* (Woman at the wheel, 1939), a film Harvey resented for its regressive antifeminist politics; then Harvey left Germany once again.

As this biographical information suggests, even though Harvey's initial Weimar star image as the "sweetest girl in the world" suggests innocence and political ignorance, her private persona, well hidden from the public, contradicts this perception. Indeed, one may wonder why NS officials were so keen on her repatriation at all. What did she have to offer Nazi cinema? As I have argued elsewhere, I believe that the discourses surrounding Lilian Harvey's 1933 departure for Hollywood, her subsequent return to Ufa, as well as her second and final emigration in 1939, illustrate the NS film ministry's oxymoronic desire for German popular cinema and its star culture to be both competitive with and distinct from Hollywood models. Harvey's phenomenal success with films like *Glückskinder* (Lucky kids, 1936) exemplifies the delicate attempt to produce what Karsten Witte has referred to as "Germanized" American pictures.[3]

While NS film culture was, as Joseph Goebbels's many comments on the question of politics and propaganda suggest, deeply committed to the party's political causes, it was also fundamentally inscribed in antecedent cultural traditions as well as influences from abroad. In terms of the cinema, not only were entertainment films to avoid propagandistic content on the surface in favor of "working invisibly so to speak," many film historians have shown that there are also a good number of NS films that function predominantly along cultural frameworks deeply steeped in Weimar and Hollywood culture. Both Lilian Harvey as a star figure and Harvey's NS films are significant examples of that trend.

Harvey's Weimar star image suggested an adorable ingénue whose petite figure and lithe frame seemed almost prepubescent, a body type fundamentally connected to 1920s flapper culture. Once paired with Willy Fritsch, the duo dominated the media as Ufa's premier dream couple. Her subsequent appearances in Hollywood in turn foregrounded Harvey as a glamour star, the "prize package of Europe," who arrives in Hollywood with the finest automobile ("a snow-white Mercedes coupé... longer and more spectacular than any other motor seen in Hollywood"), soon to be pictured in the company of Gary Cooper and other established Hollywood celebrities.[4] Her return to Ufa in 1935 thus strongly emphasizes continuity over reinvention. The Nazi press addressed this implicit contradiction by stressing that despite Harvey's association with celebrity excess her life nonetheless consisted of "a lot of effort and work."[5] By the time the NS journal *Filmwelt* asserted in 1941 that "the film heroine of today is one of us . . . there is nothing left of the man-eating villainy of the vamp, of the playful moodiness of the capricious or worldly lady,"[6] Harvey had emigrated once again. Yet a closer look at her most popular films made during this time undercuts the notion that the erasure of former models of womanhood had been successfully attempted at all.

The Harvey/Fritsch vehicle *Glückskinder*, directed by Paul Martin, was so closely based on Frank Capra's 1934 screwball comedy *It Happened One Night* with Clark Gable and Claudette Colbert that many critics even speak of a remake. Set in New York City, the film centers on the comedic battle between the sexes as Gil Taylor (Fritsch) and Ann Garden (Harvey) find themselves married without knowing each other. The continuing complications driving the screwball plot are further enlivened by witty banter and musical numbers, including enduring favorites like the song "Ich wollt' ich wär ein Huhn" (I wish I were a chicken). The narrative conclusion restores traditional gender hierarchies through the couple's romantic union.

The film was an instant success. Indeed, the leading journal *Film-Kurier* jubilated: "Bravo! Bravo! What the Americans can do, we can do too! Maybe no one wanted to believe that the German language can compete with the American slang in terms of its dry humor, *Glückskinder* proves the opposite."[7] In a number of ways, the film was Ufa's answer to Goebbels's 1935 warning against making too many ideological (*weltanschauliche*) pictures, and took up the suggestion that the majority of German films should play like *It Happened One Night*. *Glückskinder* not only quoted (or, if you will, appropriated) the narrative elements of the earlier American screwball comedy, it was also set in New York, directed by a *Spielleiter* with Hollywood experience, and featured an international star — namely, Harvey.

However, while audiences responded positively and even Hitler liked the film, the SS journal *Das schwarze Korps* complained:

No one can convince us that a *Schlager* [popular song], which expresses the stirring sentiment: "I wish I was a chicken, I wouldn't have much to do," is even just a tiny bit better or smarter than the often invoked garbage [of earlier times: jazz]. No, this type of art production bears a distinct resemblance to the behavior of certain companies that while announcing loudly to the world that they are now Aryan still maintain their Jewish methods.[8]

The film's humor primarily derived from its deviation from dominant NS codes, and, according to Witte, any deviation from any code is funny (106). Having fun in the cinema, however, is a far cry from engaging critically with contemporary politics. That said, the film stays far away from giving lessons in Nationalist Socialist thinking. Without suggesting that the film's avoidance of political complicity — achieved primarily through its "Germanized Americanism" and its reliance on surviving traditions of the popular — worked as a destabilizing cultural force, we can nevertheless assert that it also didn't help to popularize the ideological messages of National Socialism.

Karl Ritter's 1938 production *Capriccio*, in which Harvey's character spends most of her time being mistaken for a man, is an even stronger example of ideological incongruence in Nazi entertainment films. If *Glückskinder* had delighted audiences that included the Nazi leadership and negative responses limited themselves to a condemnation of the film's musical styles, *Capriccio* angered both Hitler and Goebbels. *Promi* issued devastating criticism and reprimanded its director, Karl Ritter, several times. Ritter's unrestrained approach to the material was certainly a surprise for a director whom Witte sees as more instrumental to the establishment of militant Nazi pictures than Hans Steinhoff or Veit Harlan (18). Nonetheless, the film constituted an astonishing aberration from what was otherwise acceptable in Nazi cinema. The narrative, set in nineteenth-century France, follows Madelone (Harvey), who was raised as a boy by her uncle, as she escapes an arranged marriage to an undesirable local prefect and disguises herself as a young man. A tumultuous plot unfolds as she joins two other young nobles and falls in love with one of them. The film's utter lack of respect toward many traditional values and its technique of deriving comic energy from ridiculing virtually every public institution not only thoroughly overstepped the limits of the traditional burlesque, it also exhibited a radical farcical anarchy that was fundamentally antiauthoritarian. *Capriccio* was a provocation, proposes Witte, not only in its distance from the everyday production standards of 1938, but also in its "flagrant violation of what was considered in good taste, in its overstepping the norm, and ... in its falling short of it unpunished" (153). In addition, Lilian Harvey's job in the narrative is to negotiate masculine and feminine impulses and concerns within herself, while escaping the externally oppressive forces of male domination at the same time. This newly discovered Lilian Harvey, reads an undated *Ufa Filmblatt* pamphlet available in the Deutsches Filminstitut,

> casts off the shackles of holy traditions and as a knight and a gentleman with a shining sword in her hand fights her way through adventures of love and amusement. . . . Next to her natural femininity stands adventurous dare-devilishness, next to the sweet charms of a noble lady stands the superior humor of a swaggering ladies' man . . . next to elegance, grace and female charm stands aggressiveness, temerity, and the enjoyment of male actions, such as carousing, horseback-riding, fencing, gambling . . . Lilian Harvey, more enchanting than ever!

Only *Frau am Steuer* (Woman at the wheel, 1939), Harvey's last film made in Nazi Germany, deliberately stresses the importance of taming the independence in Harvey's characters. And while Harvey's private relationship with Paul Martin was not known to the public during this period, their final film together not only marks the dissolution of their romance, but also strikingly illustrates the ideological attempt to redress questions of female emancipation in public discourse. The German men of NS cinema, argues Ula Stöckl, had "the task to 'clean-up' women, . . . off the stairways into apartments, off the streets into houses, out of the professions into the nursery."[9] Nowhere is this move from the office to the nursery more directly literalized than in this German version of the comedy of remarriage. The film's overt goal may be easily described in Paul's (Fritsch) repeated suggestion that he has to humble Annie (Harvey) to eventually assume complete power over her at the end. The filmic narrative — set in Budapest — centers on Annie, an ambitious career woman who is unwilling to give up her job for marriage. When her husband Paul loses his job, she hires him as her assistant, which in turn provokes a marriage crisis. Once the big boss finds out about this situation, he promotes Paul to Annie's position and the enraged Annie quits, only to admit to Paul that very evening that she has since discovered that she is pregnant and thus happy to stay at home anyway. *Frau am Steuer* further met with fierce resistance by Harvey. Having been forced into production, Harvey wrote,

> [by now] it is pointless to attest that thousands of married couples pursue a professional life in perfect harmony, . . . that [the film] treats every problem from a male perspective, offering the completely wrong approach regarding women's psychological viewpoints, and that there is the danger that the female audience will not be won by the film.[10]

Three years later Lilian Harvey, now back in exile, was officially expatriated. Yet National Socialist newspapers were told not to take notice.[11] The narrative return of the prodigal star daughter had collapsed; perhaps an embarrassment too bitter to be publicly acknowledged or effectively absorbed into Nazi wartime rhetoric.

See also:

- 10 January 1927: Brigitte Helm Embodies Ambivalence of the New Woman
- 30 December 1940: Von Borsody's *Wunschkonzert* Mobilizes Melodrama for Total War
- 20 June 1977: DEFA's Biggest Star, Manfred Krug, Leaves the GDR

Notes

[1] Ernst Bloch, "Die Frau im Dritten Reich," *Die Neue Weltbühne* (2 April 1937).

[2] Edith Hamann, *Lilian Harvey: Ein Leben für den Film* (Berlin: Herman Wendt, n.d.), 32–33.

[3] Karsten Witte, *Lachende Erben, Toller Tag: Filmkomödie im Dritten Reich* (Berlin: Vorwerk 8, 1995), 133 (hereafter cited in text). For my own, longer study, see Antje Ascheid, *Hitler's Heroines: Stardom and Womanhood in Nazi Cinema* (Philadelphia: Temple UP, 2003).

[4] Virginia Sinclair, "Lilian Drives 'Em Wild!" *Screen Play* (May 1933): 33, 58.

[5] Hamann, *Lilian Harvey*, 8–9.

[6] Ellie Tschauner, "Tapfere, kleine Frau," *Filmwelt* 4 (14 January 1941): 85.

[7] "S-k" in *Film-Kurier* 220 (19 September 1936), reprinted in Ulrich Kurowski, ed., *Deutsche Spielfilme 1933–1945: Materialien III*, 2nd rev. ed. (Munich: Stadtmuseum Munich and Münchner Filmzentrum, 1980), 167.

[8] "Ich wollt', ich wär ein Huhn . . .," *Das Schwarze Korps* (26 November 1936), reprinted in Ulrich Kurowski, ed., *Deutsche Spielfilme 1933–1945*, 172–77.

[9] Ula Stöckl, "Appell and Wünsche und Traumbilder" in *Wir tanzen um die Welt*, ed. Helga Belach (Munich: Carl Hanser, 1979), 101.

[10] Lilian Harvey, statement regarding script submission of *Frau am Steuer*, unpublished typescript, cited in Christiane Habich, ed., *Lilian Harvey: Ein Leben für den Film* (Berlin: Haude & Spencer, 1990), 148.

[11] Press orders dated 9 October 1942, documented in Joseph Wulf, *Theater und Film im Dritten Reich: Eine Dokumentation* (Frankfurt am Main: Ullstein, 1983), 346.

30 August 1936: Luis Trenker Tries but Fails to Sidestep Nazi *Filmpolitik*

Carola Daffner

Director Luis Trenker receives the Mussolini Cup. Credit: BPK/ArtResource.

IN AUGUST 1936, LUIS TRENKER's film *Der Kaiser von Kalifornien* (*The Emperor of California*) won the Mussolini Cup for Best Foreign Film at the Venice Biennale. The event inspires a new reading of Trenker's work as a Southern Tyrolean actor, director, and film producer, and accentuates the ambivalence of working as an artist in the Third Reich. It also shows — and here the *Kaiser von Kalifornien* reveals its role as a true register of the inherent contradictions and power struggles in Nazi cinema — the treacherous illusion of subversive action within the film industry in Nazi Germany. Trenker's cinematic deviations from Nazi *Filmpolitik* (meaning both the politics and policies of film) paradoxically allowed the director to suppress his own doubts about the regime while continuing to finance his work through the propaganda ministry. Although Trenker claimed that both movie and award served his efforts to undermine Goebbels's vision of mass manipulation, he remained entangled in a film industry in the service of propaganda.

A photograph dated 1 May 1937 illustrates the challenge when approaching Trenker's work during the Third Reich. It shows a smiling Trenker, as he — according to a description on the back of the photograph dating to the 1950s — receives the Mussolini award in Berlin, surrounded by key Nazi leaders. The authenticity of the photo, however, remains unclear: looking closely, Baldur von Schirach and Heinrich Himmler seem to be edited into the image, complicating the meaning of the constellation. The photograph raises larger questions about Trenker's true motives and those of the fascist regime: were Trenker's sympathies genuine, or were they a fabrication, imposed when the photograph was produced during the Nazi period, or perhaps even by postwar critics?

As a former filmmaker in the Third Reich, Trenker and his oeuvre have been the subject of considerable controversy since 1945. Whereas Trenker insisted on his innocence, his participation as an actor in the leading *Bergfilme* (mountain films) of the 1920s, coupled with his own directorial work after 1933, have led critics to consider his work an integral part of Goebbels's *Filmpolitik*. Trenker's early film *Der Rebell (The Rebel*, 1932) particularly complicates the discussion of his artistic integrity under National Socialism. Set in a Tyrolean village during the Napoleonic wars, the film bears the dubious honor of having been cited as a model for the future of film by Joseph Goebbels in his first speech as minister of propaganda on 28 March 1933.

According to Goebbels, effective propaganda could only be transmitted successfully through entertainment films, and Trenker's *Rebell* had achieved this. Goebbels declared that future films should, like Trenker's *Rebell*, show patriotic conduct (*Haltung*) and the strong attitude (*Gesinnung*) of a charismatic leader, and should capture the spirit of the united German nation, elevating German cinema to the status of a world power. *Völkisch* (folk) themes, German dialects, as well as stories rooted in the "German soil" would transform the movie of the future into an explosive weapon, the dangerous but mighty power of which could only be regulated by the government.[1]

Goebbels believed Trenker's film "could even overwhelm the non–National Socialist."[2] Trenker's crowd scenes and his portrayal of nationalistic uprisings particularly impressed both Goebbels and Hitler when they viewed *Der Rebell* in January 1933, just days before the latter took power. Underscoring Trenker's importance for the conceptualization of Nazi *Filmpolitik* even more, Goebbels wrote in his diary: "Here you really see what can be done with the film as an artistic medium."[3] The Reichsminister's glowing appraisal gave way to Trenker's continued (if not rising) stardom in the Third Reich, a career in which Goebbels and Hitler invested much hope. In the early years of the regime, Trenker would become one of the main forces behind Nazi cinema's media dictatorship, which focused on the production of light entertainment films infused with Nazi ideology. By 1935 Trenker was well established in the ranks of Nazi cinema's elite and was a "welcome guest of Goebbels" at various receptions held by the regime.[4]

Trenker's *Der Kaiser von Kalifornien*, which premiered on 21 July 1936 at the Reich Ministry in Berlin, represented a pioneering work in the history of the European Western and a paragon of propagandistic fiction film. Shot in 1935 in locations throughout the American Southwest and Europe and based on the historical account of Swiss pioneer Johann August Sutter, Trenker's film tells the story of a revolutionary refugee, who, persecuted by local German authorities for his political agitation, flees to America. Inspired by the spirit of poet, publisher, and vocal Napoleon critic Ernst Moritz Arndt, Sutter (played by Trenker himself) determines to conquer the world.

On both aesthetic and narrative levels, Trenker's *Kaiser* follows Goebbels's vision of how film could be deployed as a mode of public persuasion and propaganda. In a gesture sure to capture the attention of the German audience, Trenker's film combines a well-known story with popular images from the Wild West, employing them to offer a clear critique of American capitalism. In California, Sutter leads his fellow immigrants as they transform his region into "paradise," irrigating and cultivating the land "just like the Lord when he created the world." This oasis is destroyed soon thereafter, however, when gold is discovered on Sutter's estate and anarchy takes hold. The film jumps ahead ten years, when Sutter's appearance at the California Supreme Court causes a riot that leads to the burning of San Francisco. The film concludes with a scene of an aged Sutter dying on the Capitol steps after the spirit of Ernst Moritz Arndt has conjured images of America's future in the age of industrialization and capitalism.

Embedded in this escapist fantasy is a focus on National Socialist themes: the film couples agricultural mystification, *Blut und Boden* motifs, and *Lebensraum* fantasies ("I need land," Sutter remarks several times) with a charismatic German *Führer* who repeatedly battles (and triumphantly conquers) nature's power in a foreign terrain, all while never losing his Southern Tyrolian inflection. This dynamic leader further employs his charisma to unite his fellow immigrants: "He plowed the land. He built streets. He gave work and bread to thousands. He gave a new homeland to several thousands." As such, *Der Kaiser von Kalifornien* hews closely to quintessential National Socialist iconography and motifs, and it is hardly surprising that recent critics have classified Trenker's film as a "Nazi Western."[5]

It cannot be denied, however, that Trenker's ambivalent relationship to the National Socialist regime, which, like the photograph of the Mussolini award, fluctuated between blatant opportunism and suppressed rebellion, also permeates *Der Kaiser von Kalifornien*. After all, the film includes moments independent of Goebbels's *Filmpolitik*: the topos of the rebel who battles higher authorities, a heavy reliance on Catholic iconography, and landscape portrayals reminiscent of those of *Bergfilm* director Arnold Fanck, who had been a mentor for Trenker since the 1920s. More importantly, Trenker's movie also shows direct divergences from Goebbels's concept of film as narrative playground for National Socialist ideas.

Above all, the portrayal of Sutter's battle against his former workers defies Goebbels's insistence on a charismatic leader. For Goebbels, leaders were only useful when they had prestige.[6] In Trenker's film, uncontrolled tirades undermine the alleged absolute authority of his protagonist. As Sutter rises to deliver his fiery speech in the Supreme Court Building, imitations of Hitler's mannerisms turn into a grotesque farce. The audience watches the transformation of Sutter's charismatic leadership into a screaming and stomping frenzy, further supported by a shift to low-key lighting and an increased audio-volume. The rage of the main character, which could be read as lampooning Hitler, interrupts the flow of the plot and becomes pure spectacle — a characteristic central to the effectiveness of propaganda films, but that here appears seemingly at odds with a purely positive reading of this *Führer* figure.

The ghostly character of Arndt poses another intriguing addition to the movie and embodies the ideological ambiguity that characterizes both the film's and Trenker's motives. As the instigator for Sutter's travels, Arndt provokes Sutter into a colonial fantasy of conquering the world. And when Arndt advises Sutter at the film's conclusion that he should be content with his life achievements in the knowledge that he has "served the world" purposefully, the film seems again to play to National Socialist ideas of self-sacrifice for one's country. Simultaneously, however, Arndt advises Sutter that "the world has enough room for everyone," a statement that contradicts the National Socialist regime's emphasis on the need for *Lebensraum* and its murderous policies of racial "cleansing" of non-Aryan populations. Moreover, Arndt urges Sutter to let go of futile attempts to stem the tide of things to come, such as the eternal power of machines and the beauty of the city. The moment thereby complicates possible *Blut und Boden* interpretations of the film, seeming to condone the very sorts of progress that Nazi leadership denigrated as the "Jewification" of the world. Arndt leaves a satisfied Sutter with a profound if vague musing that is characteristic of the movie's effort to find balance between extremes: "Right or wrong: Who can know?" The very end of Trenker's movie, then, fails to deliver a return on the propagandistic premise prevalent for most of the film. Unsurprisingly, Hitler himself was particularly disappointed by the ending of *Der Kaiser von Kalifornien*, writing that it was "without any ethics or morals."[7]

How, then, should one assess the *Kaiser von Kalifornien* and its receipt of the Mussolini prize in the larger context of Trenker's involvement in the Third Reich? According to the director's eldest son Florian, Trenker intended *Der Kaiser von Kalifornien* to be an apolitical piece of art that would remain free of any ideology or possible misuse as a pawn of political interests.[8] Scholarship on the film, meanwhile, has rejected as illusion any assertion of a public sphere free of politics during the Third Reich.[9] Trenker's own comments on the film have further fueled debate: while refusing to admit any sympathies with the regime, the director quoted the award, of all things, as proof of *resistance* against the Nazi media dictatorship — placing the bestowal of the Mussolini Cup at the center of discussions about artistic responsibility and integrity.

According to an anecdote from Trenker's memoir, Goebbels wrote of his esteem for Trenker's film in diary entries from mid-June 1936, but also indicated some concerns with the ending as well as his focus on the United States. Trenker avers that he was pressed by Goebbels to modify the film but refused, defending his recalcitrance by citing the Mussolini Cup. This anecdote, while certainly not intended to be an apology for Trenker's affiliation with the National Socialist regime, complicates *Der Kaiser von Kalifornien*'s ideological message. According to Trenker, the film's success in Venice forced Goebbels to release the film against his wishes, and the prestigious award thus provided the director an opportunity to assert some independence, however limited, against the all-powerful Minister of Propaganda.

Despite later claims of subversion, however, Trenker's *Kaiser von Kalifornien* fails as a piece of resistance: for contemporary audiences, any discrepancies from Nazi film politics or subversive elements in the film were probably inadequately transparent. Trenker's film was and is still a product of Nazi Germany and remains rightfully marked by the moment of its aesthetic creation as well as its reception — just as the Mussolini Cup was and still must remain connected to the Fascist regime of Benito Mussolini. After all, the Mussolini Cup was not the first recognition Trenker received for his cinematic style; his work was first validated by Joseph Goebbels himself. More importantly, the support from Mussolini only connected Trenker to the constraints of another repressive regime — Fascist Italy.

Whatever possibilities the award promised, it came with an equal number of limitations, and Trenker never succeeded in his attempts both to please the National Socialist leadership and maintain a modicum of artistic independence. To some extent the award may have helped Trenker to save his movie from Goebbels's censorship, and thereby created a (temporary) buffer for his continuing work. But Trenker did not anticipate the influence that receipt of the Mussolini Cup would have: far from strengthening the director's position, the award enhanced Goebbels's mistrust, brought the Reichsminister's attention to more dissonant elements in Trenker's films and led him to disfavor Trenker, his chosen prodigy and once an integral part of his *Filmpolitik*. Trenker's movie *Condottieri* (1937), which showed Hitler's SS men and Mussolini's Blackshirts as actors kneeling in front of the Pope, resulted in further disfavor with the regime.

The situation only worsened with Trenker's ambivalence over the South Tyrol Option Agreement between Hitler and Mussolini in 1939. Hesitation over whether to opt for Mussolini's Italy or Hitler's Germany, as well as rumors that Trenker had advised people in South Tyrol against siding with Germany, quickly made Trenker a persona non grata in the eyes of the Nazi leadership. Trenker's later work, *Der Feuerteufel* (*The Fire-Devil*, 1940), about a revolt of the people of Kärnten against Napoleonic oppression, made thinly disguised parallels between Napoleon and Hitler and guaranteed the director's break with the regime. Although Trenker continued, Janus-faced, to insist upon his support for the regime — acting in the colonial film *Germanin* (1943) and drafting sycophantic letters to Hitler — the Film Ministry rejected of all his new projects, and Trenker moved to Italy in 1943.

Luis Trenker's German career flourished again after the war, and he made dozens of Alpine films that earned him cult status in Austria and Southern Germany. This popular success aside, however, he has remained dogged by accusations of fascist opportunism. In the end, it would seem, Trenker succumbed to his own desires — whether witting or naïve — simultaneously to succeed in and rebel against the parameters of National Socialist cinema.

See also:

- 10 May 1924: *Der Berg des Schicksals* Inaugurates the Genre of the "Mountain Film"
- 28 March 1933: Goebbels's Kaiserhof Speech Reveals Tension Between National and International Aims of Nazi Cinema
- 28 May 1942: Bertolt Brecht and Fritz Lang Write a Hollywood Screenplay

Notes

[1] See Joseph Goebbels, "Dr. Goebbels' Rede im Kaiserhof am 28.3.1933," in *Der Film im Dritten Reich: Eine Dokumentation*, ed. Gerd Albrecht (Karlsruhe: Schauburg and Doku, 1979), 26–31; here 26–29.

[2] Ibid., 27.

³ Diary entry on 18 January 1933 in Goebbels, *My Part in Germany's Fight*, trans. Dr. Kurt Fiedler (New York: Howard Fertig, 1979), 201.

⁴ See Felix Moeller, *The Film Minister: Goebbels and the Cinema in the "Third Reich,"* trans. Michael Robinson (Stuttgart: Axel Menges, 2000), 167.

⁵ See Lutz Koepnick, *The Dark Mirror: German Cinema between Hitler and Hollywood* (Berkeley: U of California P, 2002), 99–134.

⁶ See Leonard W. Doob, "Goebbels' Principles of Propaganda," *The Public Opinion Quarterly* 14, no. 3 (Autumn 1950): 419–52; here 434.

⁷ Adolf Hitler, *Adolf Hitler: Monologe im Führerhauptquartier 1941–1944; Die Aufzeichnungen Heinrich Heims*, ed. Werner Jochmann (Munich: Heyne, 1982), 355.

⁸ See Stefan König and Florian Trenker, *Bera Luis: Das Phänomen Luis Trenker; Eine Biographie* (Munich: Berg & Tal, 2006), 173.

⁹ See Sabine Hake, *Popular Cinema of the Third Reich* (Austin: U of Texas P, 2001), 22.

30 December 1940: Von Borsody's *Wunschkonzert* Mobilizes Melodrama for Total War

Jaimey Fisher

A radio broadcast collapses the distance between the front line and home front. Wunschkonzert *(1940). DVD capture.*

PREMIERING ON 30 DECEMBER 1940, *Wunschkonzert (Request Concert)* was the first war film made during the Nazi regime that became the top grossing film of its year; it was also the first successful film of the wave of releases between 1940 and 1942 that were timed to coordinate with the start of the Second World War. Joseph Goebbels declared the film "one of the most important films of recent times," and, indeed, that it was "no mere feature film" and was to be "carefully dealt with and presented" because it was to bridge from the celebratory era of the Olympics to the sobrieties of war.[1] Beyond its breakthrough popular appeal and its bridging a watershed moment, *Wunschkonzert* also represents a significant moment in German film history particularly because, as much as any work from the Nazi years, it demonstrates what Eric Rentschler has called the "polyphonic" principle of the Nazi regime's approach to film — that is, its coordinated effort to utilize multiple modalities and various channels to reach, and coordinate, the *Volk*.[2] Like many films between 1940 and 1942, the film aimed to make palatable the Nazis' war effort, but did so via a deliberately diverse deployment, including the pageantry of the 1936 Berlin Olympics, the personal and catalyzing presence of the *Führer* (who would thereafter increasingly disappear from the screen), and a well-loved radio program suddenly more useful than ever to the Nazis, given the country's division between war and home fronts.

Wunschkonzert focuses on the budding romance between Inge Werner and Herbert Koch, a pilot/lieutenant in the air force, and underscores how successful Nazi cinema could be in exploiting popular genres for its propagandistic projects. Inge and Herbert meet at the 1936 Berlin Olympics, from which the film shows stock footage, and within a few days of Blitzkrieg courtship they decide to marry, only to be separated abruptly by Koch's mobilization as part of the Condor unit in the Spanish Civil War. A few years later, with Germany mired in the Second World War, they are reunited when (now Captain) Koch requests the Olympic Fanfare on the eponymous *Wunschkonzert*, a radio program that plays requested music for charitable donations. When faraway Inge hears the fanfare and the source of its request, she commits herself to finding Herbert and rekindling their romance. A number of subplots complicate the romantic trajectory of the narrative. First, Inge's other suitor, her childhood friend Helmut, happens to serve in Herbert's unit and, by exaggerating his relationship to her, discourages Herbert's intentions to resume their relationship. Then a series of peripheral characters, including other couples and a mother and her musician son, serve as parallel stories of the sacrifice, suffering, but also deeper meaning of mobilization for the Nazis' total war.

Analyses of *Wunschkonzert* have tended to emphasize the film's function as propaganda.[3] While not diminishing the film's polyphonic propagandistic operations, it might, in fact, be more important to analyze, in concert with the film's propagandistic aspects, the film's myriad visual pleasures and its subsequent popularity, especially since, as Sabine Hake has emphasized, one of the most remarkable aspects of this era was the astounding growth in film viewership.[4] It is for this reason that the date of the film's premiere, and not that of Goebbels's first interventions in its production, represents the breakthrough moment for this film — as that date on which the carefully crafted work was released to German audiences, who rapidly rendered it a case study for successful audience effects. Such pleasures and popularity come into sharper focus when one compares *Wunschkonzert* to one of the few Nazi films that was even more successful — notably, likewise a "home-front" war film — Rolf Hansen's *Die große Liebe* (*The Great Love*, 1942). In both films, a central aspect of what Rentschler terms their polyphonic efficacy are their genre operations as a particular kind of wartime melodrama, as retooled genre works that would extend their appeal beyond the female audiences conventionally drawn to such films.

Die große Liebe features one of the biggest stars of the Nazi years, Zarah Leander, as a singer, Hanna Holberg, who falls in love with an air force pilot, Paul Wendlandt (Viktor Staal). As in *Wunschkonzert*, the two rapidly establish their love in Berlin, and the film then follows the couple's struggles to be together despite her singing and his bombing schedules. Both *Wunschkonzert* and *Die große Liebe* manifest many of the markers of the conventional melodrama or woman's film: external circumstances force a deferral of love for Inge and Herbert as well as for Hanna and Paul; the disruptive intervention of fate prompts the suffering of all four characters, often musically scored; an emphasis on quotidian but charged objects siphons off the pathos associated with that love and subsequent suffering (Helmut's picture of Inge, which Herbert misunderstands; Paul's unsent letters to Hanna; the ubiquity and importance of telephones); and generational, familial, and social impediments hinder the fulfillment of desire (Inge's aunt and then grandmother against her romance with Herbert; even Herbert's conflict with Helmut).

The films manifest a particular kind of melodrama, however, since both deliberately transcend the domestic sphere, usually coded as female, on which the melodrama traditionally focuses. Both films were frequently characterized at the time of their release as home-front films that negotiated between the "war front" versus the "home front," a distinction that scholars have generally observed and repeated ever since. But it is precisely this distinction that must be examined and reconsidered in these two melodramas. The recent turn in cinema studies to space, spatial relations, and their imbrication in the wider political, social, and cultural relations of a specific historical moment, allow the binary of "war front" and "home front" to be elucidated anew. Reexamining *Wunschkonzert* and *Die große Liebe* in light of such theories of space suggests that these films are not merely or simply homefront melodramas, but rather mobilization films. The films function as mobilization films because of the very deliberate and very modern way in which they manipulate melodrama via mobility, geography, and space in order to achieve their narrative goals, including, perhaps above all, the extension of their audience from the conventionally female-oriented melodrama to male viewers as well. In both films the temporal and agnition functions of melodramas recurring "too late" are emphatically spatial as well: too-lateness and its emotional vicissitudes are deliberately remapped spatially by the films' representations of the war versus home fronts.

In *The Geopolitical Aesthetic,* Fredric Jameson argues that the cinematic operations of cognitive mapping become intensified — at least representationally — when it is revealed that there is a secret or secondary map behind the presumed spatial order of things: a second, initially unknown layer permits a shift to a different landscape (literally) of agency.[5] These mobilization films begin, quite quickly, with the early stages of a courtship and accordingly visit the familiar venues of the romantic picture: the couples meet in public places (the Olympic Stadium in *Wunschkonzert,* the theater in *Die große Liebe*); proceed to semipublic places to develop their acquaintanceships (restaurants and/or nightclubs and/or parties); and eventually head toward the privacy of the bedroom. But in both cases, this early topography of romance, overlapping with the conventional terrain of the melodrama and women's film, is rapidly undercut and displaced by a secondary mapping coded as male: that of the military and, in particular, the *Wehrmacht*'s wartime mapping of Europe. The melodramatic tensions in both pictures are precisely the tensions between these two topographies — ostensibly, at least, at odds spatially — and the films cut between them as two different contemporaneous spaces. In both cases, the secondary, military mapping is very deliberately kept secret from the female leads and their romantic dreams, but then erupts into the narrative to interrupt the expected trajectory of courtship.

With this secrecy of the secondary map, the films activate another of the basic operations of many melodramas, which tend to foreground the secret (and/or misunderstood) virtue of their (usually female) protagonists.[6] These melodramas tend to derive their strong affective charge from the suffering caused by this virtuous secret and secret virtue. Narratively speaking, such melodramas frequently unfold this pathos through a series of scenarios in which viewers know of the reason for the (usually female) suffering while other characters do not, a mechanism of viewer knowledge that cements empathy with the suffering women. What is unusual in these mobilization melodramas is that this secret is based on a second, military map that threatens to overcome the usual domestic focus of the melodrama and that the secret is held by the male protagonist: the male leads sport their own secret virtue on the clandestine map of war.

In *Wunschkonzert,* Herbert is called up suddenly and has very little time to inform Inge, to whom he has already proposed marriage. Moreover, he is even forbidden to tell her why he is going so abruptly or to write her subsequently about it, although viewers know the military secret that subverts their marital plans. At this point, the film introduces the secondary map into their urban courtship, as the film cuts to a map of Spain to explain Herbert's whereabouts and bombing mission. The film then spends most of its narrative after the initial twenty-minute setup crosscutting between their parallel plots. Viewers know the whole time of his secret, dutiful departure, even as they watch the suffering Inge try to comprehend how the man she was going to marry could disappear so quickly. The crosscutting between protagonists and their maps serves, in this fashion, to heighten the melodrama at the same time it extends the domestic spaces of the melodrama and its subsequently gendered — now both female and male — appeal.

In *Die große Liebe*, Paul is called up from leave repeatedly when he thinks he might have a few romantic days with Hanna. Cinematically speaking, the spaces of German romance are similarly thrown over for the aerial shots mentioned above, the topography of Berlin in each case replaced by literal maps of European conquest — exactly the spatial ensemble at which the Reich was aiming. This narrative navigation and tension between the amorous (civilian, private, intimate) and the military (official, public, coldly impersonal), supported by the spatial tension between the romantic metropolis and war-torn continent, is paradigmatic for these mobilization melodramas. In both cases, the term "war film" seems a misnomer, since the front's homosocial camaraderie is not at the center of the plots. These genre mechanisms foreground instead, to paraphrase the title of Christine Gledhill's watershed collection on melodrama, that home might indeed be where the heart is, but the films arrive at this melodramatic insight belatedly and via a second, very male map that has to be reconciled with the repeatedly deferred domestic sphere of the conventionally female-oriented melodrama.

If these spatially emphatic narratives interrupt their initial urban spaces with secondary maps of the military, they offer a parallel shift in the location of the narrative's (agentized) power and desire, as if these two key facets of any narrative are run through a refracting prism between the films' double maps. In this manner, these war films manipulate and manage not only desire and fantasy, as Linda Schulte-Sasse has argued, but also place and space.[7] Jameson argues that the double mapping within such a cartographic narrative undergoes a triangulation effect, among the two different layers and the observer, who comes to see the surface as well as deeper map over which the surface is stretched.[8] These mobilization films similarly remap agency via the double layer sketched above: where agency seemed to reside and reign — for example, with the romantic leads, as it might in conventional romance or melodrama — is abruptly transformed by the secondary map, and in spatially emphatic ways. Suddenly, the center of the film's agency, via military time and space, shifts to a third space that does not so much reconcile the home and war fronts, but rather includes (and thereby sublates) them both, and, indeed, for both genders, in the greater space of the nation.

In *Wunschkonzert*, after Herbert Koch's secret mobilization undercuts the trajectory of his courtship of Inge Wagner, the eponymous radio program (*Wunschkonzert*) emerges to mediate between them. Given the spatial shift from Berlin to the wartime front — between which, as noted above, crosscutting emphasizes the subsequent distance between Inge and Herbert — the radio program is able to unite the two lovers when Herbert requests, for all to hear, the march that was playing at the Olympics where they met. The same is true for many of the film's minor characters: the radio program serves to reunite separated couples, dispersed families, and even dead soldiers with their living relations. The implication is that the war would require a remapping: first, that of the mobilization that threatens to undercut intimate life, but then that of the publicly mediated community that the Reich's technology can create with the radio. The publicity pamphlet for the film emphasizes this emphatically spatial force of the (auditory) radio: "A magical ribbon embraces front and homeland. In the dugout in France, in the submarine on an enemy mission, in the airbase on the coast, in the quiet room of a mother, in thousands and hundreds of thousands of homes, everywhere the flood of word and song and music resounds and vibrates . . ."[9] This radio program ultimately brings the couple back together, bridging the gap between the primary and secondary maps of the film. The radio program serves as the solution to the two maps, their resolution in a deliberately produced, ersatz-space of a pure (radio) representation tending to community. In *Die große Liebe*, Paul is called up repeatedly, but Hanna attempts to schedule her musical shows in European metropolises where a military man might be able to meet her: first Paris and then Rome, both cities that had, in the intervening years, been incorporated into the expanding sphere of the Reich.

In her important contribution to melodrama scholarship, Linda Williams has argued that melodrama is not so much a genre as a mode that frequently and tellingly alternates extreme sentiment with moments of sudden and surprising action.[10] In *Wunschkonzert* and *Die große Liebe*, the narrative obstacles in these films' romantic melodramas — those fateful events that constitute the deferral and denial of desire — are consistently those of action-packed mobilization, such that the oscillations of melodrama and action of which Williams writes are emphatically spatial. After the melodramatic and spatial vagaries outlined above, both films conclude in hospitals, with dutiful women tending their wounded pilots, endings that underscore their overarching melodramatic frameworks. But their protagonists land in the hospital not due to some internal (read: domestic) disease, as in many of the celebrated melodramas and/or woman's films, but rather due to spatial and aerial daring that offer the films their (masculine) visual pleasures. Whether it be, as in *Wunschkonzert*, the new technology of radio that negates and absorbs spatial distances, or, as in *Die große Liebe*, the remapping of Europe by Nazi conquest, the films have transformed their melodramatic plots spatially and in the direction of war and of the male viewers about to fight it. This was a generic mixture that proved among the most popular of cinema under the Nazis.

See also:

- 15 October 1920: Ernst Lubitsch Fuels Debate over Tears in the Cinema
- 18 May 1945: *Welt im Film* Newsreels, Rubble Films Model "Cool Conduct"
- 19 September 1958: Douglas Sirk's *A Time to Love and a Time to Die* Tests Limits of Postwar Feeling

Notes

[1] David Welch, *Propaganda and the German Cinema 1933–1945* (London: I. B. Tauris, 1983), 98.

[2] Eric Rentschler, *Ministry of Illusion* (Cambridge, MA: Harvard UP, 1997), 21.

[3] David Bathrick "Making a National Family with the Radio: The Nazi Wunschkonzert," *Modernism/Modernity* 4, no. 1 (1997): 115.

[4] Sabine Hake, *Popular Cinema of the Third Reich* (Austin: U of Texas P, 2001), 72–75.

[5] Fredric Jameson, *The Geopolitical Aesthetic: Cinema and Space in World Cinema* (Bloomington: Indiana UP, 1995), 15, 33.

[6] Linda Williams, "Melodrama Revisited," *Refiguring American Film Genres: History and Theory*, ed. Nick Browne (Berkeley: U of California P, 1998), 48.

[7] Linda Schulte-Sasse, *Entertaining the Third Reich: Illusions of Wholeness in Nazi Cinema* (Durham, Duke UP, 1996), 6–8.

[8] Fredric Jameson, "Spatial Systems in *North by Northwest*," in *Everything You Always Wanted to Know about Lacan but were Afraid to Ask Hitchcock*, ed. Slavoj Žižek (New York: Verso, 1992), 47–72.

[9] The program for the film — a standard marketing for films at this point — is quoted at length in Mary-Elizabeth O'Brien, *Nazi Cinema as Enchantment: The Politics of Entertainment in the Third Reich* (Rochester: Camden House, 2004), 123.

[10] As her fourth attribute of melodrama, Williams writes: "4. Melodrama involves a dialectic of pathos and action," Williams, "Melodrama Revisited," in *Refiguring American Film Genres*, ed. Browne, 69.

18 February 1941: *The Devil and Daniel Webster* Puts American Politics on Trial

Simon Richter

ON 18 FEBRUARY 1941, a few months after dissolving his contract with Warner, William Dieterle sent the script of his first film on a more independent footing to three addressees: Stephen Vincent Benét, author of the 1936 award-winning story; Joseph Breen, head of the studio relations department at the PCA, whose moral vision of America had a shaping influence on all Hollywood films at the time; and Max Horkheimer at the Institute for Social Research, relocated from Frankfurt to Columbia University in New York. If the first two are unexceptional, the third is surprising. Is *The Devil and Daniel Webster* a point where Hollywood and the Frankfurt School converge in a productive relationship, even as Max Horkheimer and Theodor Adorno were criticizing the culture industry? Might the practice of critical theory yet be a possibility in Hollywood?

In 1940, Dieterle was at the peak of his prestige.[1] Between 1937 and 1940, he had directed three successful biopics: *The Life of Emile Zola* (1937), *Juarez* (1939) and *Dr. Ehrlich's Magic Bullet* (1940), all starring Paul Muni. Film scholarship has regarded the biopic as inherently less ambitious than the sort of film that would overshadow Dieterle's efforts — that is, the film noir and other films enabled by events related to the Second World War. But of all the émigré directors (Curtiz, Lubitsch, Wilder, etc.) few could engage critically and directly with American political issues or address National Socialism before the United States declared war in December 1941. Fritz Lang's *Fury* (1936) and Anatole Litvak's *Confessions of a Nazi Spy* (1940) were exceptions to the rule. *Casablanca* was produced in 1942 and the first noir films date to 1944. Throughout the 1930s, emigration and exile for moviemakers accustomed to the cinematic avant-garde of Berlin was a matter of finding a way to survive (often thanks to the efforts of the European Film Fund that Dieterle's wife Charlotte helped set up) and compromising with a capitalist film industry reviled by the Frankfurt School. As Saverio Giovacchini puts it, initially the Hollywood exiles were largely "confined to the Hollywood 'operetta milieu.'"[2] Dieterle's biopics were among the foremost politically engaged films of the 1930s, and his exile contemporaries knew it. With *The Devil and Daniel Webster* and plans for two other films (one on the history of jazz and another on the life of Samuel Gompers, the Jewish-American founder of the American Federation of Labor), Dieterle seemed poised to exploit the critical potential of Hollywood.

Classified on the PCA's Analysis Chart of 2 July 1941 as a "(Social Problem-Drama) (1840–47) FANTASY," *The Devil and Daniel Webster*'s closest predecessor in genre and visual style are two films by F. W. Murnau: his adaptation of Goethe's *Faust* (1926), in which Dieterle played the role of Valentin, and *Sunrise* (1927), Murnau's first Hollywood film, a contrast of rural and urban archetypes. While Murnau, renowned for his innovative camera work and editing, supplied an aesthetic model, Dieterle also recurred to the sort of social engagement evident in his preemigration film *Geschlecht in Fesseln* (*Sex in Chains*, 1927), in which he grappled with manifestations of sexual desire in the German prison system. With its folksy tall-tale tone, Benét's story, which establishes the legend of the senator from Massachusetts, Daniel Webster, while scarcely developing the Faustian partner to the bargain, Jabez Stone, was the perfect American counterpart to Murnau's (and Goethe's) *Faust*. Dieterle maintains the focus on Webster, but scraps the hyperbole in order to counter legend with history as a mode of critical theory and social intervention. As a historical figure Webster is famous for upholding the Missouri Compromise and ensuring passage of the Compromise of 1850 and the Fugitive Slave Act. Although he found slavery repulsive, Webster's first priority was the integrity of the Union. What Dieterle accomplishes in his superbly crafted film, marshaling the diverse talents of Benét, First World War vet and playwright Dan Totheroh, and composer Bernhard Herrmann, who had just completed *The Magnificent Ambersons* and would go on to score *Citizen Kane* and many Hitchcock films, is nothing short of a confrontation with the legacy of historical injustice and reflection on the possibility of political legitimacy. Dieterle puts America on trial.[3]

Horkheimer writes back to Dieterle on 20 March 1941.[4] He hails Dieterle as the creator of significant biopics. Horkheimer categorically states that, in contrast to most other Hollywood films, the script of "'The Devil and Daniel Webster' takes a step in the direction of philosophy, i.e., the question of meaning" (20). In Horkheimer's view, William Dieterle Productions and the Institute for Social Theory pursue the same goal: "We approach whatever you produce with unconditional seriousness, for you are concerned with truth, as are we" (23).

It is not unusual that Dieterle was acquainted with Horkheimer. Dieterle left Berlin to join Warner in 1930 and helped Max Reinhardt find his footing in Hollywood in 1935. Horkheimer's American exile began in New York in 1934. Horkheimer's letter implies that he and Dieterle had discussed cinema previously. In a 1941 issue of the Institute's *Studies in*

Philosophy and Social Science, Dieterle contributed an essay about Hollywood's response to Hitler, alongside articles by Horkheimer and Adorno. Dieterle was a respected intellectual partner prized for his insider knowledge about the film industry. A month after posting the letter to Dieterle, Horkheimer moved to Los Angeles for health reasons, right around the time shooting for *The Devil and Daniel Webster* began. Given the close contacts within the progressive German and European exile community, it is safe to assume that Horkheimer and Dieterle met during shooting. Even if they did not discuss his film again (and this is unlikely), Horkheimer's letter prompted Dieterle to rethink his conception of the film.

The story of *The Devil and Daniel Webster* plays in the mid-nineteenth century. By poignantly evoking the oppressive poverty of rural America, Dieterle achieves a timelessness that allowed audience members to recognize their own recent experience in the Great Depression. On the point of eviction and bankruptcy, Jabez Stone sells his soul to Scratch (Walter Huston), the American incarnation of the devil, in exchange for seven years of prosperity. When the time is up and Scratch is on the point of claiming his property, Stone's wife Mary begs the famed Daniel Webster to intervene. Having directed a trial scene in *Zola*, and with the trial scene of Lang's *Fury* also in mind, Dieterle seizes the opportunity to explore the ambiguities of American history in a cinematic court of law. The iconicity of this scene is confirmed by its later adaptations in popular culture, most memorably in a fourth-season episode of the American animated television series *The Simpsons*, titled "The Devil and Homer Simpson."

Horkheimer's letter to Dieterle provides a summary of the discussion of the film by members of the Institute. A prominent issue involves the political valence of collective action by small farmers oppressed by historical circumstances (i.e., technological progress). Dieterle's script included statements that to Horkheimer's ear allow for reactionary interpretation, "rebellion in the wrong direction" (Horkheimer, 22). He pleads for scrupulous philosophical accuracy in the treatment of these issues. As a result of Horkheimer's interventions, Dieterle refines his filmic representation of "farm politics." He has three New England farmers suggest the formation of a grange as a communitarian organization to represent farm interests in Washington. While this is historically inaccurate since the Grange was founded in 1869 and reached its peak in the 1890s, for Dieterle, the idea of the Grange is progressive, essentially communitarian, and consistent with the politics of the New Deal. Dieterle believes communitarian action can ameliorate the capitalist excesses of individuals with selfish motives. Even though Horkheimer did not immerse himself in small-town American culture in the manner of Fritz Lang, he and Lang shared a justified suspicion vis-à-vis the propensities of the mob explored by Lang in *Fury*.

Horkheimer's second major concern has to do with nationalistic ambiguities in the powerful rhetoric of Daniel Webster's speech to the Jury of the Damned. Both Dieterle and Horkheimer were of course painfully aware of the current political situation in 1941, a point at which the United States had not yet declared war on Nazi Germany or Japan. Horkheimer is worried that viewers might respond uncritically to a nationalistic tone in Webster's speech. In other words, like Lang, Horkheimer is extremely sensitive to fascist potential on American soil, but felt that such ambiguity "could be avoided by including a clear anti-fascist message" (23). In this instance, however, Dieterle proves subtler than his fellow exile in his analysis of the situation and in his cinematic intervention. Although both Dieterle and Benét opposed American isolationism, it is a mistake to read the film as a transparent allegory and plea for military action on a nationalistic basis. The film's complexities and ambiguities do not allow it. *The Devil and Daniel Webster* is about putting Daniel Webster and the political history of the United States on trial, neither in order to condemn them out of hand nor to relieve them of moral responsibility in a gush of patriotic excess, but rather to place them under the greatest possible critical pressure and to discern what Horkheimer would call their truth.

When Breen read the script of 18 February, he must have wondered what Dieterle was thinking.[5] Scenes of excessive drinking abound. Not only did the script call for Webster to be shown drunk, but also the town squire and other public officials. The Code clearly stated: "The use of liquor in American life, when not required by the plot or for proper characterization, will not be shown."[6] We can assume that Dieterle larded his script with extraneous drinking so that, even after Breen's numerous cuts, the necessary scenes would remain — and they do, with the censor's stamp of approval: "The several scenes of drinking and drunkenness are necessary for plot motivation and characterization."[7] In one of those scenes, Webster holds a mug indirectly provided by the devil and praises Medford rum as "a breath of the promised land." On the campaign trail, his imbibing prevents him from speaking, and Jabez speaks in his stead. This situation will be reversed when Webster speaks for Stone during the trial, but not before Webster and Scratch have engaged in a drinking contest. But what meaning did Dieterle attribute to Medford rum?

The point of the rum is to achieve an exceptionally nuanced and critical characterization of Webster and the nation he represents. Medford rum is named for its origin in the town of Medford, Massachusetts. Medford's first distillery opened in 1735 and the profitable industry flourished until 1905. The main ingredient for rum is molasses derived from sugar cane. Medford-built ships imported molasses from the West Indies where slaves labored in brutal conditions. The slaves came from Africa, where they were purchased in exchange for rum. These three geographical points make up what was known as "triangle trade." When Webster receives the cup from the hands of Scratch and breaks into reverential praise of Medford rum, only to fall into an unexpected languor that prompts Jabez to speak on his behalf, Dieterle achieves a remarkable level of critical symbolic compression. Dieterle subtly links the idea of America as Promised Land with slavery, one of the nation's two founding acts of injustice, and with the devil, who proffered the cup.[8] It is not Webster's individual moral weakness that is on display, but a tragic flaw in the history of the nation.

Dieterle knew that a lot was riding on the Jury of the Damned scene. In an letter to Benét on 8 January 1941, he writes: "This speech . . . must be the ultimate thing. The picture stands and falls with the power of words and thoughts conveyed to a jury which sits in the theatre as well as in our scene."[9] Horkheimer concurred and offered advice: the effect of the film could be increased through a "more drastic shaping . . . and a more fundamental conceptualization of Webster's speeches" (23). He refers to the closing speech in *The Great Dictator* (1940), in which Chaplin directly addresses the cinema audience in praise of liberty, surmounting national boundaries, and achieving peaceful democracy, and wonders whether Webster's speech might not accomplish something similar. Dieterle takes Horkheimer's advice seriously, construing solidarity to mean New Deal communitarian politics and offering a redemptive vision of liberty based on faith in the people, more in line with American progressive thought than with Horkheimer's European skepticism.

But — and this is the ultimate achievement of Dieterle's cinematic practice of critical theory — the speech and the entire film pivot on the image of Medford rum. As Webster decides whether or not to address the jury, a vision of the jug of rum shimmers like a perverse grail, challenging and condemning him and the nation he represents. Mustering all his determination, Webster addresses the Jury of the Damned, an array of American traitors and criminals, and constructs a redemptive vision of liberty that acknowledges and points beyond historical wrong and bloodshed. While the jury is swept up in the rhetorical embrace of his speech, Scratch is identified and rejected as the "oppressor." Webster prevails and the jury releases Jabez from his contract. The film concludes in a flurry of images that emphasize communitarian politics and a fresh start. But the final image, a close-up of Scratch surveying the film's audience for his next victim, fixing on the viewer and pointing his finger, uncannily mimics the 1917 military recruitment poster of Uncle Sam. Visually the film ends with a renewed call to bargain with the devil and engage in necessary political violence in a new theater of war. The ambiguous politics of the American nation continue. Dieterle's film captures this with critical precision.

See also:

- 29 May 1929: Oscar for Emil Jannings Highlights Exchange between German and American Film Industries

- 28 May 1942: Bertolt Brecht and Fritz Lang Write a Hollywood Screenplay
- 30 June 1970: A Faltering Berlinale Founders on *o.k.* Controversy

Notes

[1] The best available account of Dieterle's career is Marta Mierendorff, *William Dieterle: Der Plutarch von Hollywood* (Berlin: Verlag, 1993).

[2] Saverio Giovacchini, *Hollywood Modernism: Film and Politics in the Age of the New Deal* (Philadelphia: Temple UP, 2001), 61.

[3] Fritz Lang also puts "America on trial" in the trial scene of *Fury*. See Anton Kaes, "A Stranger in the House: Fritz Lang's *Fury* and the Cinema of Exile," *New German Critique* 89 (2003): 33–58, especially 41–45. Of course, mob justice and a trial scene are crucial for Lang's *M* (1931).

[4] Horkheimer's letter is in Max Horkheimer, *Gesammelte Schriften*, 19 volumes, ed. Alfred Schmidt and Gunzelin Schmid Noerr (Frankfurt am Main: S. Fischer, 1995–96), 17:20–24. Hereafter cited in text.

[5] Breen's correspondence with RKO is available at the Margaret Herrick Library of the Academy of Motion Pictures and Sciences.

[6] The full text of the 1930 Code is available at http://www.artsreformation.com/a001/hays-code.html.

[7] PCA analysis chart 7/2/41 at the Margaret Herrick Library.

[8] The cinematic subtlety and power of this gesture is similar to the way Dieterle finessed the prohibition against explicitly representing Dreyfus as a Jew in *Zola*, as well as to Lang's circumvention through visual means of the proscription against dealing squarely with lynching as a racial issue. See Kaes, "A Stranger," 48–52.

[9] Dieterle's letter to Benét can be found in the Beinecke Rare Book Library of Yale University.

28 May 1942: Bertolt Brecht and Fritz Lang Write a Hollywood Screenplay

Jonathan Skolnik

The defiant conclusion of Brecht and Lang's exile collaboration Hangmen also Die! *(1942). DVD capture.*

THE STUDY OF GERMAN EXILE CULTURE in the United States in the 1930s and 1940s will always be marked by the paradox that it gave rise to some of the most damning critiques of the "culture industry" as well as to some of Hollywood's most memorable films. Horkheimer and Adorno's *Dialectic of Enlightenment* and Brecht's poetic résumé of Hollywood as "the marketplace where lies are bought" were both composed just a short drive away from where Fritz Lang, Ernst Lubitsch, and Billy Wilder (to name only the most prominent among scores of others) worked. *Hangmen Also Die!*, produced by Arnold Pressburger Films and released by United Artists on 15 April 1943, is a film situated at the fault line of this paradox. Not only does it represent one of the most important documents of cultural-political resistance to National Socialism, but it is also a film that engages creatively with many of the central tensions within German exile culture: the contradictions evident when combining political engagement, modernist aesthetics, and mass cultural forms in the context of antifascist praxis.

Shortly after American newspapers reported the assassination attempt on the notorious Reichsprotektor Reinhard Heydrich in Prague in late May 1942 (he died on 4 June), Fritz Lang approached fellow-exile Bertolt Brecht with the offer to collaborate on a film that would dramatize this act of anti-Nazi resistance. The story of their collaboration is controversial (compounded by Brecht's legal contestation of the screen credits), and for many years Lang's revisions were widely thought to have severely compromised Brecht's role. Recent discoveries of the original story (entitled *437!! Ein Geiselfilm* [437!! A Hostage Film], registered on 30 June 1942), an expanded English-language version with the title *Never Surrender!* (registered 16 July 1942), an early version of the script labeled "Final Draft" (dated 16 October 1942), and other documents prove that the ultimate film script evolved from intense, complex, sustained collaboration and compromise between Brecht and Lang. They were joined by John Wexley (an experienced Hollywood screenwriter brought in by Lang, Wexley wrote *Angels with Dirty Faces* and the anti-Nazi film *Confessions of a Nazi Spy*, knew German, and had leftist political views), Sam Coslow (a well-known Broadway and Hollywood songwriter), and Hans Viertel as a translator.[1] Yet although Brecht's coauthorship of the film is now indisputable and his imprint on the final version is clearly legible, the question of the struggle within the film over the imperatives of modernist art and left-wing politics versus those of commercial filmmaking remains.

This question cannot be reduced simply to a struggle between "European" and "Hollywood" styles, nor to a personal struggle between Brecht as an uncompromising radical literary idealist versus Lang as an industry-savvy, market-oriented film director.[2] For Brecht's part, *Hangmen Also Die!* represented his one successfully realized film out of some fifty Hollywood screenplay ideas on which he worked. Brecht's enthusiasm for American gangster films like *Scarface* and his 1932 production *Kuhle Wampe* evidence his deep interest in the subversive narrative potential of film as a mass art form within a capitalist market system. Fritz Lang, on the other hand, came to *Hangmen Also Die!* with his own experience of the sacrifices and accommodations necessary for socially critical filmmaking in code-era Hollywood. Lang's first American exile production — *Fury* (1936) — about a lynch-mob, implicitly took on both German fascism and American racism, yet had to cut specific references to African Americans in deference to Hayes Office pressures.[3]

Hangmen Also Die! is the story of the Heydrich assassination and the German reprisals, told as the tale of the Gestapo's hunt for a lone gunman from a local resistance group (historically not factual) and the personal/political conflict that arises when the assassin and Masha, a young woman who has sheltered him, weigh a terrible choice: whether or not to surrender the one man the Gestapo wants in order to save the lives of hundreds of hostages whom the Nazis will murder in his place, including the woman's own father. The hostages are coldly murdered but the resistance scores a victory by framing a collaborator, Czaka, as the assassin. The heroes of the film are the anti-Nazi resistance and the Czechoslovakian people who nobly bear the sacrifice. Brecht and Lang struggled over how to cast the film, deciding to have the Nazis played by German exiles with accents, including Hans Heinrich von Twardowski and Alexander Granach, while the Czechs are all played by native English speakers, including Brian Donlevy, Walter Brennan, and Anna Lee (Lang instructed her to speak with a Midwestern accent, so she hired a language coach). Further, the German characters often speak in untranslated German, to simulate the estrangement of occupation for an American audience and to foster identification with the resistance. Some critics have pointed to the casting choices as an element of weakness and imbalance[4] (with the use of well-known popular US actors from light genres distracting from the film's gravitas and Granach's charisma undermining the Gestapo villain role he portrays). The way in which exiled actors negotiate the transition in their performance conditions represents an important theme for scholars of the era, however, and *Hangmen Also Die!* remains central to that discussion.

Ian Wallace is one critic who sees the Brechtian theme of the individual opposed to the collective in a revolutionary context (so central to his *Lehrstücke*) insufficiently developed in *Hangmen Also Die!*, whereas James K. Lyon sees the film's final script as thematically related to other Brecht works of the mid-1940s.[5] Signature features of Fritz Lang's directing are some of the film's strongest elements: bank vaults used as the scene of Gestapo dungeons (the film successfully raises questions about the relation of fascism to capitalism and militarism); socially and politically complex crowd scenes (when a mob of ordinary Czechs intimidates Masha, who had considered going to the Gestapo, the implicit praise of street-level solidarity is tempered by the terrible specter of mob justice); and most of all the disciplined, suspenseful integration of converging narrative lines. A Brechtian critique of prefabricated romance plots (*der fühlst-Du-mein-Herz-schlagen-Text*) is successfully joined to a Langian play with sound technology and a concern with surveillance (with echoes of *M*) in a masterful scene where Masha and the assassin fool the Gestapo, who listen in as they read from a script that implies their secrecy is driven by adultery rather than political conspiracy.

Much of the recent discussion of the successes and failures of *Hangmen Also Die!* revolves around Hanns Eisler's film music. It is often noted that Eisler received an Academy Award nomination for *Hangmen Also Die!*. The role of avant-garde art music, agit-prop popular song, and critical theory in this wartime Hollywood feature is certainly worthy of further investigation. Eisler worked together with Theodor Adorno on *Composing for the Films* (published in 1947), and the book draws significantly upon Eisler's experience with *Hangmen Also Die!* Most of the film is unscored, yet Eisler's use of jarring twelve-tone music (a first in Hollywood) as the film transitions from the opening credits and panoramic views of Prague's castle (used as headquarters by the Nazi occupiers) to an oversize portrait of Hitler dominating Heydrich's office is a thoughtful musical contribution to the estrangement effects (*Verfremdungseffekt*) for which both Brecht and Lang aimed.

As Eisler and Adorno explain in *Composing for the Films*, the final scene in *Hangmen Also Die!* is crucial. Onscreen, Nazi officials read a secret report revealing that although the Gestapo knows that the collaborator Czaka could not have been the assassin, the Nazi failure to crush the resistance mandates that the case be closed. Meanwhile, counter to the visual story, the song "No Surrender" (now in an orchestrated mixed choral arrangement) begins and builds to an enthusiastic crescendo as the end titles then exclaim that this is "NOT the end" (i.e., of the fight against fascism). "No Surrender" is an attempt by Eisler and Brecht (and Lang, and others) to create a popular song that would embody antifascist aesthetic-political resistance. Composed in the prison barracks as an act of resistance by the hostages, its offscreen use in the final scenes symbolizes the anonymous resistance of the people as a collective. For Eisler's biographer Jürgen Schebera, the song is "in the best tradition of the Eisler-Brecht *Kampflieder* of the 1930s," and he cites positive mentions of the song in contemporary reviews.[6] James K. Lyon notes that Eisler quotes passages from his own "Kominternlied" (1929) in "No Surrender" and, in the view of the musicologist Sally Bick, this gesture is evidence that "what Brecht could not do with the script, Eisler surreptitiously achieved with the music" — to "outsmart producer, director and censor" and slip in a leftist political agenda.[7] But an additional, alternative reading also becomes available if we consider more fully the film's historical context. 1943 was, after all, the year Warner Brothers produced Michael Curtiz's *Mission to Moscow*; from today's perspective that film is an embarrassing apology for Stalinism in the service of America's ally "Uncle Joe." Did the broad coalition against Hitlerism really need to be disguised in *Hangmen Also Die!*? More important is to consider how the song "No Surrender" functions within the narrative of *Hangmen Also Die!*, which is as a work of art deliberately portrayed as unpolished, raw, and even artistically inferior. This is shown is the scene where the song is composed. As the hostages are held together in the barracks, a simple worker presents his poem "No Surrender" to a fellow-prisoner, a prominent Czechoslovakian poet, apologizing that it isn't much and asking him to "improve" it. "This *is* a scribble," says the great poet, who advises him to leave it as it is.

The barracks scenes in *Hangmen Also Die!* and the theme of the prison-camp song as resistance invite comparison with another antifascist production, the 1938 Soviet film *Bolotnye Soldaty*, directed by Alexander Macheret. The film's title refers to "Die Moorsoldaten," the authentic concentration camp song that Eisler had arranged and made into a popular antifascist anthem in the mid-1930s. *Bolotnye Soldaty* was shown in the United States in 1939 under the title *Concentration Camp* and may possibly have influenced Brecht, Eisler, and Lang (although there is no direct evidence of this). In the Soviet film, the song "Die Moorsoldaten" is not part of the plot (a wordless version accompanies the opening credits). A barracks debate is central to the narrative of this Popular Front-era ideological film: Communists, Jews, and Social Democrats realize their need to unite in the struggle against fascism. In Macheret's film, the wordless song "Die Moorsoldaten" hangs in the background serving as shorthand for this unity. The function of "No Surrender" in *Hangmen Also Die!* is more complex. It shows awareness of the aesthetic negotiations and contradictions in the construction of political art.

Brecht was very dissatisfied with Coslow's English lyrics to "No Surrender," denouncing Coslow in his journal as a "hitparademan" and calling the final product "a piece of incredible crap."[8] Brecht felt it was important to keep a written record of his original song, which allows us to see how words like "comrade" and "slave" were excised from Coslow's version. But Brecht never disowned the song or the film and the discussion of the poem in the barracks scene preserves for the film audience the tensions inherent in the film's production. While it is doubtful that Eisler would intentionally compose a "bad" song, "No Surrender" is arguably one of his weaker tunes. Eisler was a master composer of moving popular songs: in contrast to "No Surrender," "Roter Wedding," "Das Lied vom Wasserrad," and the above-mentioned arrangement of "Die Moorsoldaten" all became genuinely popular.

Never Surrender may have been an early title for this collaborative film project, but it was hardly the film's guiding artistic principle — to make a Hollywood film, Brecht and Lang had to surrender plenty. Figured as a simple but stirring product of the moment, the aesthetically inferior ideological poem stands for the price of combining art and politics in wartime. Brecht, Eisler, and Lang have exposed the machinery of art production for a critical audience. *Hangmen Also Die!* thus becomes a document of the uneasy mixture of avant-garde aesthetics, antifascist politics, and the commercial context of the wartime Hollywood dream factory.

See also:

- 17 October 1930: Bertolt Brecht's *Threepenny Opera* Lawsuit Identifies Contradiction between Individual Creativity and Collective Production in Cinema
- 18 February 1941: *The Devil and Daniel Webster* Puts American Politics on Trial
- 16 February 1952: Peter Lorre Leaves Germany Again

Notes

[1] See James K. Lyon, "*Hangmen Also Die* Once Again: Dispelling the Last Doubts about Brecht's Role as Author," *The Brecht Yearbook* 30 (2005): 1–7; and Sally Bick, "A Double Life in Hollywood: Hanns Eisler's Score for the Film *Hangmen Also Die* and the Covert Expressions of a Marxist Composer," *The Musical Quarterly* 93, no. 1 (Spring 2010): 90–143; here 136n12, 142n87, 142n88.

[2] See the discussion in Gerd Gemünden, "Brecht in Hollywood: *Hangmen Also Die* and the Anti-Nazi Film," *The Drama Review* 43, no. 4 (1999): 65–76, and the general call for a new, nonbiographical approach to German exile cinema in Gerd Gemünden and Anton Kaes, "Introduction," *New German Critique* 89 (2003) Special Issue on Exile Film: 3–8.

[3] On *Fury*, see Anton Kaes, "A Stranger in the House: Fritz Lang's *Fury* and the Cinema of Exile," *New German Critique* 89 (2003): 33–58; and Barbara Mennel, "White Law and the Missing Black Body in Fritz Lang's *Fury* (1936), *Quarterly Review of Film and Video* 20, no. 3 (2003): 203–23.

[4] Jerzy Toeplitz, for example, quoted in Jürgen Schebera, "*Hangmen Also Die* (1943): Hollywood's Brecht-Eisler Collaboration," *Historical Journal of Film, Radio and Television* 18, no. 4 (1998): 567–73; here 570.

[5] Ian Wallace, "*Hangmen Also Die*: Varieties of Collaboration" in *Refuge and Reality: Feuchtwanger and the European Émigrés in California*, ed. Pól Ó Dochartaigh and Alexander Stephan (Amsterdam: Rodopi, 2005), 43–56; and Lyon, "*Hangmen Also Die* Once Again."

[6] Schebera, "*Hangmen Also Die* (1943)," 572.

[7] Lyon, *Bertolt Brecht in America* (Princeton: Princeton UP, 1983), 64 and Bick, "A Double Life," 90–91.

[8] Quoted in Bick, "A Double Life in Hollywood," 131.

3 September 1942: With Venice Premiere of *Die goldene Stadt*, Veit Harlan Enters Debate on Color Cinema

Russell A. Alt

ON 3 SEPTEMBER 1942, German director Veit Harlan's film *Die goldene Stadt* (*The Golden City*) premiered at the Venice Film Festival to an enthusiastic reception. The critical attention that this film garnered and that made it one of the festival's darlings was due in large part to Harlan's novel use of color, an accomplishment for which the film received a special award in cinematography. At base, the excitement surrounding *Die goldene Stadt* stemmed from the newness of color technology in European cinema. Until this point, Hollywood possessed the only reliable (and viable) means for creating full-length feature films in color. However, with the development of Agfacolor in Germany in the 1930s, Europe found a way to challenge Technicolor's hegemony. From an aesthetic standpoint, Agfacolor's soft hues and restrained color palette were often touted as an antidote to the brash Americanism of Technicolor. After several years of refinement to the film stock, Harlan's *Die goldene Stadt* proudly showcased the new technology to an international audience.

Naturally there was more at stake in the release of *Die goldene Stadt* than the mere emergence of a color film process capable of competing with Technicolor. This event represents far more the confluence of a Nazi political agenda, new cinematic conventions, and aesthetics in the service of a deadly ideology at a moment when the world was embroiled in a war not only of bodies, but of images and messages as well. Reich Propaganda Minister Joseph Goebbels was fully aware of film's potential to captivate audiences and he exploited this medium time and again to propound the agenda of the National Socialists and craft the look of the young state. As Eric Rentschler puts it, "if the Nazis were movie mad, then the Third Reich was movie made."[1] Indeed, if the Third Reich was "movie made," then Agfacolor, caught in the crosshairs of the swastika, provided a new look for National Socialism and Veit Harlan was its preeminent colorist.

Scholars have dedicated a lot of ink to Harlan's biography and his cinematic work in Nazi Germany, focusing largely on his agit-prop films *Jud Süß* (*Jew Süss*, 1940) and *Kolberg* (1945). But little attention has been paid specifically to how the rise and contested role of color film fits into the otherwise well-documented period of Harlan's career from 1942 to 1945. During these years, Goebbels consistently privileged Harlan above all other directors with the amplest access to the expensive Agfacolor film stock. Harlan in turn directed and released four color features — a significant accomplishment since only nine color feature films were produced and released in Nazi Germany. Given that Harlan directed nearly half of these, he consequently became an important player in shaping the debate on *why* and *how* color should be used in film.

Although Harlan's de facto entrée into the debate on color in cinema occurred in 1942 with the release of *Die goldene Stadt*, Harlan first articulated his stance the following year in an article titled "Farbfilm" (Color film) that he contributed to the Nazi magazine *Der deutsche Film*. In it, Harlan contends that, "The film artist should adhere [to the notion] that he is not a painter, but rather a photographer," and warns that "it is very dangerous when the color film director directs color itself."[2] Working from the conviction that there are two general uses for color in film — one that faithfully enhances the naturalness of the images, and the other that enhances elements of the unreal, the symbolic, the fantastic, and the imaginary — Harlan clearly argues in favor of the former.[3] Harlan's contemporaries both in Germany and abroad, however, overwhelmingly did not share his preference for a mimetic use of color.

In Germany, the color question arose concurrent to the Nazis' ascent to power. Agfa, a concern of IG Farben, had by 1931 already produced a two-color cinematographic process.[4] The color produced from this process was regarded as inferior, however, and by 1936 a three-color process had been developed that promised a more faithful and natural look. By this time Hitler had taken power and "coordinated" all of the political and cultural enterprises in Germany so that they fell under the aegis of and conformed to Nazi Party lines. For German cinema this meant that the Ministry of Propaganda became its custodian (responsible for approving all scripts, releases, and so on) and Joseph Goebbels the nearly omnipotent overseer.

Some of the first color films to be shot in Germany with Agfa's enhanced cinematographic process came in 1941–42 and took the guise of ideologically inflected short "cultural films," which were always shown in conjunction with a weekly newsreel before the main feature and, unlike most feature films, were often overt in propounding Nazi ideology. Among them were landscape and scientific pictures that concentrated heavily on replicating and revealing nature through color. For critics, the frequent coupling of color film with projects on the natural world indicated that color was being primed as a mimetic instrument. This development fostered genuine apprehension, indeed fear, in the film community. Director Walter Ruttmann, for instance, lamented that, "scarcely was there a time more helpless against color than ours."[5] Expressing a similar sentiment in his boldly titled article "Dämonie der Farbe" (The demonic nature of color, 1943), critic Werner Fiedler described color film as "plagiarism," as an "imperfect imitation [of nature]," and argued that "a primary danger for color film is color."[6] Even Harlan himself, who posited that "the primary essence of film, which stems from photography after all, is to photograph reality faithfully,"[7] took up this language and drew a distinction between the "realistic color film" and the "colorful film" (*Buntfilm*).[8] It was believed that too much color in the cinema — that is to say, color for color's sake — could have only one possible outcome: kitsch. Even worse, according to Harlan, such "colorful kitsch" might have the unintended consequence that audiences would begin to yearn for black and white.

But color did not remain confined to the short cultural films in Nazi Germany. It found its way into full-length features whose often trivial topics, fanciful sets, and special effects called cinematic realism into question, with respect to both the verisimilitude of the events and characters and the faithfully reproduced look of what was captured on film. And as far as the preponderance of light fare in Nazi cinema goes (nearly half of the films made in Nazi Germany were comedies and musicals), Goebbels was one of the biggest proponents of this development. He already recognized its usefulness in early 1942 when he noted that "entertainment films are most important at the moment. 'Good moods' are a war commodity."[9] If cheery dispositions were a war commodity, then even unserious cinema, of a piece with Nazi machinations, could not and did not grant reprieve from the "coordinated" and hyperpoliticized world of the Third Reich.[10]

So how then against this backdrop did Veit Harlan and others perceive his color feature films? To begin, Harlan tried to frame the debate on color cinema and his own particular approach in apolitical terms, even though Goebbels's largesse regarding Harlan and Agfa film stock was without doubt politically motivated. In interviews and articles, Harlan maintained that his films *Die goldene Stadt*, *Immensee* (1943), and *Opfergang* (*The Great Sacrifice*, 1944) were consistent with the principles of naturalism and that color did not play a role in lending nuance, symbolic or otherwise, to the narrative. In writing about his first color film, *Die goldene Stadt*, Harlan mentions, for example, the landscape of the moor in which the protagonist, Anna, commits suicide. Harlan describes the choice he had to make when filming the moor scenes — namely, whether to record and present the terrain as it was, a bucolic still life with trees and sunshine, or to tint the landscape in editing with various hues to effect a more menacing atmosphere. Harlan notes that he opted for the former, acting on his conviction that color should not be manipulated just as one does not "direct" or distort the physical form of objects in film.

In spite of his arguments to the contrary, many critics interpreted Harlan's use of color differently. One reviewer praised *Die goldene Stadt* because "the [film's] color is not, for instance, an arbitrary addition based on the intention of a 'lifelike' reproduction of reality, but rather a dramaturgical component of the film as artwork itself."[11] It would seem that Harlan's defense of filmic realism vis-à-vis color in German cinema was destined to give way to the opposing sentiments of his peers. Indeed, Josef von Báky's opulent fantasy *Münchhausen* (*The Adventures of Baron Munchausen*, 1943) was released amid great fanfare and hailed by the *Deutsche Allgemeine Zeitung* (DAZ). The DAZ's review described how "Ufa's [Universum Film A.G.] anniversary film courageously punctures the façade of reality, a breakthrough for fantasy. And the film-goers follow Ufa curiously and happily on a journey into the colorful, magical world of the unreal."[12] The blow that Báky's film dealt to Harlan's case for color realism was seemingly decisive. Fostered by a war-weary public's demand for distraction and the regime's own political investment in providing entertainment, color film in Germany, much as in Hollywood, became synonymous with lighthearted amusement.

This does not mean that Harlan gave up his preference for a true-to-life look. After *Die goldene Stadt*, Harlan produced three more color films under the Nazis and described each as adhering to the principles of color realism, a claim he felt justified in making by showcasing untouched landscape scenes. But given that these films were produced during the Second World War, one might question whether Harlan was actually re-presenting reality or using color to create one, not unlike von Báky in *Münchhausen*. Much of the action in *Immensee* and *Opfergang* unfolds outside on sunny fields, in verdant forests and on lakeside beaches. While Harlan filmed the outdoor scenes of both pictures in a quiet pocket of Schleswig-Holstein, the image of Germany that he presented to audiences could hardly have conflicted more with the reality of many viewers. By 1944, the beleaguered and increasingly bombed-out cities across Germany were incommensurable with the cheery colors of Harlan's "real" (and intact) idylls. This fact did not escape even Harlan himself. In a rare and candid instance in which he tipped his hand perhaps more than he intended, we find that for all his talk of an objective, even documentary-like approach to filming in color, Harlan uncharacteristically acknowledged the symbolic power of his images. In his 1943 article "The Miracle of Colors," Harlan concludes with an appeal to the German people:

> More than ever we must recognize how beautiful the green of the German forest is [and] the limpid blue in which German lakes gleam. The miracle of colors should reveal the beauty of our German home [*Heimat*] to us, and then we will realize that there is no cost too high to protect this beauty.[13]

Not only does Harlan's maudlin nationalism undercut his own attempt at a color aesthetic free both from symbolic overtones and from a narrative role in visual representations of *Heimat* and Germany, but it also anchors his realism directly in the muck of Nazi propaganda. The importance of choosing to film *Kolberg*, Harlan's rhapsodic paean to sacrifice and the indomitable German spirit, in color is evidence enough of that.

Veit Harlan's view on the union of realism and color cinema attempted, however disingenuously, to circumvent the political animus guiding film production in Nazi Germany. But reading behind Harlan's four color features tells a very different story. The development of the new Agfacolor process during the 1930s along with the "coordinated" use of film to turn the Third Reich into a visual spectacle obviated the possibility of an apolitical cinema. An inspection of Harlan's color films, then, helps to shed more light not only on his role as an artist in Nazi Germany, but also on new cinematic conventions vis-à-vis the larger concern of the intersection of politics, ideology, and aesthetics. A final postscript to this period of Harlan's career helps to give some historical perspective on this ongoing discussion: the Allied military censor deemed none of Harlan's four color films fit for screening in postwar Germany.

See also:

- 18 December 1913: *Atlantis* Triggers Controversy about Sinking of Culture
- 3 June 1929: Lloyd Bacon's *The Singing Fool* Triggers Debate about Sound Film
- 28 March 1933: Goebbels's Kaiserhof Speech Reveals Tension between National and International Aims of Nazi Cinema

Notes

[1] Eric Rentschler, "Germany: Nazism and After," *The Oxford History of World Cinema*, ed. Geoffrey Nowell-Smith (Oxford: Oxford UP, 1996): 374–82; here 374.

[2] Veit Harlan, "Farbfilm," *Der deutsche Film* 7, no. 9 (1943): 7–8; here 8.

[3] Ibid., 7.

[4] Susan Tegel, *Nazis and the Cinema* (London: Hambledon Continuum, 2007): 183.

[5] Walter Ruttmann, "Farbfilm," *Der deutsche Film* 6, no. 8/9 (1942): 16.

[6] Werner Fiedler, "Dämonie der Farbe," *Der deutsche Film* 7, no. 7 (1943): 7, 9; here 7.

[7] Quoted in Leonhard Fürst, "Horoskop des Farbfilms," *Der deutsche Film* 7, no. 8 (1943): 2, 4–5; here 4.

[8] Harlan, "Farbfilm," 7.

[9] Joseph Goebbels, *Die Tagebücher von Joseph Goebbels*, part 2, vol. 3, ed. Elke Fröhlich (Munich: K. G. Saur, 1994), 382–83.

[10] Rentschler, "Germany: Nazism and After," 379.

[11] Helmut Fischbach, "Venedig 1942," *Der deutsche Film* 7, no. 4 (1942/43): 2–5; here 4.

[12] Quoted in Jo Fox, *Film Propaganda in Britain and Nazi Germany: World War II Cinema* (Oxford: Berg, 2007), 257.

[13] Veit Harlan, "Das Wunder der Farben," *Filmwelt: Das Film-Magazin* 9/12 (March 1943): 74.

18 January 1943: Bateson Analysis of *Hitlerjunge Quex* Stresses Value of Film as Key to National Culture

Gary L. Baker

WHEN *HITLERJUNGE QUEX* (1933) became part of New York's Museum of Modern Art's film collection in September 1936, millions had already seen it. Its first showing occurred in Munich on 12 September 1933 before Nazi elite, including Hitler, where it proved to be Ufa's (Universum Film A.G.) first but immediately successful attempt to impress the relatively new National Socialist rulers of Germany. In characterizing Ufa's accomplishment, film historian Klaus Kreimeier writes "once again, Germany's most important film company was indisputably avant-garde."[1] This film presents an example of a privately produced propaganda film that tethers Nazi political goals to audience expectations in a well-made film. Consequently, nine years after its Munich debut, and six years after its acquisition, MoMA commissioned English-born anthropologist Gregory Bateson to analyze *Hitlerjunge Quex* to identify a German "national character" and the Nazi ideals to which it ascended.[2] Bateson began his work in the summer of 1942. His interest in the film was ". . . to establish the basic symbolic equations" of fascism, which he felt could only be done:

> by analyzing a film which showed the Nazis and their enemies explicitly labeled on the screen. Such a film makes it possible to dissect out the relationship between these two fixed points and the whole range of phenomena — parenthood, adolescence, maturity, cleanliness, sex, aggression, passivity and death — which are embraced by the Nazi view of life.[3]

With these ideas in mind Bateson embarked on the study of *Hitlerjunge Quex*, which served as key evidence for his psychosocial interrogation of German national culture.

National character at the time of Bateson's work was a freshly redefined concept. It did not connote the racially deterministic or biologically bound, essentialist conception of character of the nineteenth century, nor the impressionistic, relativistic, narrated experiences of an interlocutor of a given culture, but rather the unique integration of a nation's cultural tradition, individual personality development within its society, and the evolution of its social system. Geoffrey Gorer sets "the birth year of the scientific study of national character" at 1934 with the publication of Ruth Benedict's *Patterns of Culture,* to which he also couples the publication of Freud's essays on hysteria.[4] The synchronicity with which the scholar investigates the group (national) and the individual (character) lay at the center of this approach, one that attempted to determine patterns of behavior in the individual that could also be identified on a national scale. Henry Murray and Clyde Kluckhohn explain, for example, that the "governing ego system" is to the personality what the "leader or government (system of legislators and administrators)" is to the group.[5] Upon the assumption of this interaction between personality and world rests the idea that the group consists in many personalities while the identity of a given group can be thought of as having a collective personality structure: "By extending the concept of role (social role) to include personal role, a personality action system and a social system can be represented as roughly homologous, at least in certain respects."[6]

According to Margaret Mead, the Second World War necessitated the study of national character because the uniqueness of the war experience called for new interdisciplinary collaborations and inquiries into the areas of culture, personality, and the social system.[7] In other words, "the science of man" was to become interdisciplinary and focus the power of its insights on enemy peoples living in societies organized around the institutions and cultures of industrialized nation-states. With the dual individual-and-group focus, scholars whose concentration was primarily the individual (psychology and psychiatry) collaborated with scholars whose focus was primarily the group (sociology and anthropology) to create studies that would lead to understanding Germans, their culture, their patterns of behavior, and ultimately their vulnerabilities in terms of psychological warfare and reeducation. Bateson's work is exemplary for this trend, taking *Hitlerjunge Quex* to create a useable image of the enemy with consequential implications for the distant enemy's society. This is a moment in film history in which a feature film functions as the chief informant in the examination of an enemy culture that was otherwise physically inaccessible.

One of Bateson's observations was the stark opposition that the film establishes between the Communist youth and the Hitler Youth behaviors, which made the film such an instructive specimen for an anthropologist working from a psychologically informed perspective. This led to his conclusion that the Hitler Youth's patterns of discipline and orderliness were more appealing to the film's target audience than the Communist display of disorder and deceit ("An Analysis," 311). It is clear that in the film's representational schema the Communists represent an insalubrious lifestyle marked by sexual promiscuity, disrespect for authority, and dishonesty (not to mention an adherence to internationalism and class-oriented thinking), against the nationalism and primordial orientation of the Nazis. These oppositions between political groups are not played out in political debate, but rather in physical appearance and social values manifest in behavior patterns.

Against the liberties of the Communist way of life, the film projects as desirable personal maturation (in suppressing the fear of death) and conformity (in the ability to submit to an authoritative hierarchy). Bateson points out that in order to accentuate the different camps the director operates with geographic oppositions placing the amusement park against the forest ("An Analysis," 305, 311). The former space represents a self-indulgent, scurrilous illustration of life, replete with organ-grinder ballad, shooting booths, and lotteries, and the Communists' association with the carnival provides a negative political expedient that contrasts starkly with the disciplined and well-groomed presentation of the Hitler Youth. Bateson places special significance on the ominous, dizzying spinning circles of the amusement park as symbols of misguidance ("An Analysis," 314). In acknowledging that life in the Nazi camp seems dull by comparison, Bateson asserts that the appeal of Nazism in the film largely lies in the rejection of the parents and the fundamental substitution of the family by "a system based on what anthropologists call 'age grades'" ("An Analysis," 308), which the viewer sees amply demonstrated in the Hitler Youth structure.

The director Hans Steinhoff would have agreed with the broad strokes of Bateson's findings. Steinhoff was an early Nazi sympathizer, and his portrayal of the national ideals that served the Nazi movement was tied to his personal commitment to them. Such an emphasis on collective ideals infused the film's subtitle: *Ein Film vom Opfergeist der deutschen Jugend* (A film about German youth's spirit of sacrifice). In the figure of the central character, Heini Völker — who rejects his parents' Communist ideology, finds his path to Nazism, and ultimately becomes a Nazi martyr — Steinhoff presents an exemplary life story and an ideal type for audience emulation. In this anthropologically rich material Bateson obliges the director, ascertaining in his analysis several German cultural values, including the absolute dominance of national/patriarchal authority, the indispensability of discipline, the compulsion of social orderliness, the value of loyalty, the subordinate place of the individual in relation to the collective, and the imperative of national allegiance. Bateson then investigates these elements of the film in order to construct "a series of hypotheses about Nazi character structure and dynamics" ("An Analysis," 303). Within the national-character framework of the time, Bateson elevates the individual fate depicted in the film to a collective national fate as a device to shed light on Germany's foreign policy and the appeal of National Socialism to the broader German population.

Interrogating national cultures using psychosocial methods of inquiry was a convention of national-character study. In the rich cross-disciplinary efforts of psychology and anthropology, Bateson found himself in the company of scholars such as Richard Brickner, David Levy, Erik Erikson, and Erich Fromm in his goal to elucidate German behavior; in the field of film studies, he prefigured Siegfried Kracauer's approach in *From Caligari to Hitler*. Kracauer, too, used MoMA's stock of German films for his book and was familiar with Bateson's presentation on *Hitlerjunge Quex*.[8] To be sure, Bateson's (and Kracauer's) assertions would make little sense without the presumption of national boundedness, coherence, and cultural cohesion. Indeed, Bateson's task was to analyze the manner in which Germans defined themselves as a group using this propaganda film's transparency and goal-oriented messaging as an investigative venue. Although the national-character approach lost currency in the early 1950s, numerous analogous assumptions about nations and national culture endure in our conception of national cinema. Andrew Higson adroitly outlines many of these where he reminds us that national cinema is inconceivable without specifying "a coherence and a unity," proclaiming "a unique identity," finding a "stable set of meanings," or seeking out an established "generic narrative image" to fulfill "a particular horizon of expectation."[9] These are achievable because we invent "dominant narrative discourses and dramatic themes," as well as draw on established "narrative traditions."[10] These considerations guide Bateson's approach in analyzing German culture and society via a film such as *Hitlerjunge Quex*. For film history, Bateson and his contemporary Kracauer bring us to the discovery that considering film as an expression of national culture can be conspicuously limiting. Working within a conception of national cinema does not easily accommodate films characterized by liminality, deterritorialization, or marginality. It is also difficult to categorize transnational or postnational filmic interpretations of a world picture largely organized around nation-states.

On 18 January 1943, Bateson presented preliminary findings before the New York Academy of Sciences and showed the first three reels of the film. MoMA showed the film in its entirety on 2 June 1973 in an anthropological cinema series, with Bateson's analysis embedded. For years the film was available only with Bateson's intertitles; in fact the difference between the VHS version of 1996 (with intertitles) and the DVD version of 2007 (without intertitles) is thirteen minutes. Given that the film is contraband in Germany, the reels processed by Bateson served as the source for postwar investigations of the film and ultimately for video copies. The fate of Bateson's version offers a particularly poignant example of how processes of distribution have shaped film history: the exclusive availability of the film with his intertitles has played no small part in shaping the secondary literature that has appeared on it. The enduring interpretations of family substitution and oppositional Communist/Nazi behavior patterns, as tools of the film's power to influence the audiences of its time, make up the basis from which many subsequent analyses of *Hitlerjunge Quex* develop. The key element of Bateson's study, from a contemporary point of view, is the extent to which his method of analysis, derived from a discarded notion of national character, continues to play a central role in taxonomies of cinematic traditions.

See also:

- 14 February 1924: *Die Nibelungen* Premieres, Foregrounds "Germanness"
- 16 December 1927: Debut of *Familientag im Hause Prellstein* Provokes Debate about Jewish Identity in Popular Cinema
- 11 December 1930: Ban of *All Quiet on the Western Front* Highlights Tensions over Sound Technology

Notes

[1] Klaus Kreimeier, *The Ufa Story: A History of Germany's Greatest Film Company 1918–1945*, trans. Robert and Rita Kimber (New York: Hill and Wang, 1996), 207.

[2] David Lipset, *Gregory Bateson: The Legacy of a Scientist* (Englewood Cliffs: Prentice Hall, 1980), 170.

[3] Gregory Bateson, "An Analysis of the Nazi Film *Hitlerjunge Quex*," in *The Study of Culture at a Distance*, ed. Margaret Mead and Rhoda Métraux (Chicago: U of Chicago P, 1949), 302–14; here 302. Hereafter cited in text.

[4] Geoffrey Gorer, "The Concept of National Character," in *Personality in Nature, Society, and Culture*, ed. Clyde Kluckhohn and Henry Murray, 2nd ed. (New York: Alfred A. Knopf, 1953), 246–59; here 247.

[5] Henry A. Murray and Clyde Kluckhohn, "Outline of a Conception of Personality" *Personality in Nature, Society, and Culture*, 3–49; here 18.

[6] Ibid., 18–19.

[7] Margaret Mead, "The Study of National Character," in *The Policy Sciences: Recent Developments in Scope and Method*, ed. Daniel Lerner and Harold Lasswell (Stanford: Stanford UP, 1951), 70–85; here 70 and 75.

[8] Gregory Bateson, "Cultural and Thematic Analysis of Fictional Films," *Transactions of the New York Academy of Sciences*, Series 2: 5, no. 4 (February 1943): 72–78.

[9] Andrew Higson, "The Concept of National Cinema," *Screen* 30, no. 4 (1989): 36–46; here 37.

[10] Ibid., 43.

Part IV: 1945–1961

When, in the early days of August 1945, the Second World War ended in Europe, Germany found itself in a state of political, physical, and moral collapse. With the National Socialist regime thoroughly discredited following the loss of the war and widely publicized revelations of mass murder in the concentration camps, German cities devastated by bombing, and millions in the East displaced whether because of flight before the approaching Red Army or expulsion, the nation's citizens found themselves not only struggling for survival, but also wrestling with knotty problems of guilt, responsibility, and the possibility of recovery after total defeat. As philosopher Karl Jaspers admonished the first entering class at the newly reestablished University of Heidelberg, this question of guilt was "vital . . . for the German soul," for only through a process of self-examination could the nation achieve "inner regeneration."[1] Although famously Jaspers's call went largely unanswered by his contemporaries, his insistence on reckoning with the past would eventually come to shape West German official discourse regarding the proper national relationship to the Nazi past.

The immediate postwar period was a time of judgment, both within and beyond the German border. In November 1945, the Allied occupation forces collaborated to create the first of the Nuremberg Proceedings, which not only brought to trial major figures in the Nazi regime (thereby setting a precedent for future international tribunals), but also raised the ire of many Germans who felt the trials were nothing more than "victors' justice." While the Allies were quick to abandon accusations of "collective guilt," the concept took firm root in the German public imagination, as a rallying point for resisting outside efforts to adjudicate Nazi crimes and dictate the terms of national recuperation from twelve years of Hitler's rule.

It was also the era of the *Stunde Null* — the "Zero Hour" — a term that expressed the longing to start over with a clean slate and to make a break with the past (if not always reckon with its consequences). Despite the physical privation and ethical quandaries of the period, it was also an age of enormous optimism, as political and cultural arbiters sought to locate sources for a German renewal. Newspapers, theater productions, cabaret acts, and art shows flourished in the ruins, and once-banned politicians began the process of reforming alliances, reaching back to the traditions of the Weimar period to refound political parties and begin to construct a new state. Divided under the terms of the Potsdam Declaration into four occupation zones ruled by the Western forces of the United States, France, and Great Britain, and the Eastern force of the Soviet Union, however, postwar Germany began almost immediately to split along political lines. By 1948, the Western occupation zones had instituted a currency reform designed to foster outside investment in Germany and stem the influence of the black market, but that cemented the separation of Germany into two distinct zones. Seeking to hinder the establishment of a western state, the Soviets responded by blockading Berlin. American forces then orchestrated the Berlin Airlift, dropping food and supplies to the city's citizens. It marked the first high point in what would become a long history of cold war conflicts. That same year, commissions in both occupation zones gathered separately to draft constitutions for two new German states, and by 1949 the founding of the German Democratic Republic and the Federal Republic of Germany had completed the national division. In the West, the elections of 1949 saw Christian Democratic Union (CDU) leader Konrad Adenauer best Social Democratic Party (SPD) candidate Kurt Schumacher, setting the course for a conservative restoration period that would extend into the late 1960s. In the East, two former Moscow-exile and "Free Germany" committee members would take the helm: Wilhelm Pieck became the country's first president, while Walter Ulbricht assumed leadership of the central committee of the newly formed Sozialistische Einheitspartei Deutschland (Socialist Unity Party, SED) in 1950, becoming de facto head of state and establishing the emerging state's close ties to Soviet policy.

The first decade in both states was dominated by an ethic of *Aufbau* (building up), but each had a starkly different understanding of the ideal state under construction. In the East, the emphasis was on political and economic reform, as GDR leaders, under the influence of Stalin and later Khrushchev, sought to develop a postwar state in line with Communist ideals. The new government implemented a central planning system, including state-controlled agriculture and industry, and in 1956 — just six months after West Germany created the Bundeswehr, the GDR established its own military, the Nationale Volksarmee (National People's Army). At the same time, the GDR sought to forge a new, classless society, affording new political opportunities for women and the working class, while striving to remove former Nazis from positions of power. In practice, the GDR's early purges were deeply problematic, driving not only former fascists but also mere dissenters from the ruling elite with a rhetoric strongly tinged with antisemitism. The result was a state that early on established political conformism as a key principle. The Workers' Uprising of 1953 offers just one poignant example of the growing rift between the country's stated ideals and its practices. Discontented construction workers went on strike and protests spread throughout the country, prompting violent repression by Soviet occupation forces and the East German police, in an action that effectively turned the state against the very workers it claimed to represent.

In the West, Adenauer and economic advisor Ludwig Erhard implemented a staunchly anti-Communist program of "Westernization" designed to strengthen the fledgling democracy through strong ties to Western Europe and the United States. This effort received substantial monetary support through the American Marshall Plan, ushering in the era of unprecedented economic growth known as the *Wirtschaftswunder* (economic miracle). Integral to Adenauer's quest to stabilize the new democracy through strengthened Western alliances were trade agreements with the country's European neighbors. In 1950, a remarkably short time after the end of a war that had consumed the continent, West Germany, along with France, Belgium, Italy, the Netherlands, and Luxemburg, signed on to the Europäische Gemeinschaft für Kohle und Stahl (European Coal and Steel Community, EKGS). A tariffs agreement, the EKGS became the foundation for the eventual political unification of Europe through the European Union (EU). In political terms, Adenauer sought integration rather than elimination of former Nazis — the CDU-led coalition favored amnesty for convicted war criminals and generally sought to bring even the country's most conservative voters into the political fold, fearing their political force if they remained marginalized. But the era of economic growth also came to be associated with political and cultural stultification, summed up perhaps most famously by Adenauer's campaign slogan of 1957: "Keine Experimente!" (No Experiments!).

Although a rhetoric of eventual unification persisted in the early decades of the postwar period and even beyond, in practical terms the two Germanys grew ever more divided in the years 1945–1961. This division was not only ideological, but also geopolitical: in 1952, the inner German border was closed, soon making Berlin the prime destination for East Germans seeking to flee to the West. Despite increasing GDR restrictions on travel to the West, the numbers of *Mauerspringer* (wall jumpers) were considerable: as many as 3.5 million left the GDR before the Berlin Wall was erected in 1961, a disproportionate number of them members of the educated elite. In late summer of 1961, following urging by Khrushchev to "protect" the GDR from the West and just weeks after US President Kennedy's highly publicized visit to West Berlin, SED Secretary Ulbricht ordered the closure of the Berlin border, only two months after declaring publicly "no intention" of building a wall. The move eliminated the last loophole in the system and put in place the final physical barrier to unification until 1989.

In many respects, the film industries of both Germanys followed these divisions. In the immediate postwar period, under the careful watch of Allied occupiers keen to denazify one of Germany's most powerful wartime propaganda outlets and to themselves use the cinema as a space for reeducation, studios soon began to re-form. In the East, the Soviet administration was quick to recognize the value of cinema as a forum to sway public opinion. Within weeks of entering Berlin, the occupiers began screening banned Soviet films to German audiences. In May 1946, the Soviet authorities granted a license to the studio that would become the exclusive producer of films in the GDR: DEFA (Deutsche Film-Aktiengesellschaft). Housed in the former Ufa (Universum Film A.G.) studios in Potsdam-Babelsberg, it was DEFA that managed to produce the very first postwar production, Wolfgang Staudte's *Die Mörder sind unter uns* (*The Murderers Are among Us*, 1946). It was a prototypical example of early postwar filmmaking and established the course for the emergence of a new genre — the *Trümmerfilm* (rubble film), set in the nation's ruined cities and preoccupied with the central problems of guilt, recovery, and the plight of the returning veteran. It was a short-lived genre, however, as audiences lost their taste for these dark and often tendentious films, and as the divisions between the industries of the East and West grew increasingly pronounced.

In the Western zones of occupation, the reestablishment of film culture took a more decentralized course, with new firms opening by 1946 in cities like Berlin, Göttingen, Baden-Baden, and Hamburg. Under the supervision of the US, British, and French occupation authorities, German filmmakers in the Western zones began to produce films that responded to conditions in the war-torn country — whether adopting the conventions of melodrama, as in *In jenen Tagen* (*Seven Journeys*, 1947) — or even the occasional satire, such as *Der Apfel ist ab* (*The Original Sin*, 1948). Simultaneously, the Western occupiers attempted to sell democracy to the defeated through the importation of their own cinematic productions — a phenomenon that remigrant Billy Wilder famously dubbed a strategy of "propaganda through entertainment," since particularly the Americans endorsed the use of light Hollywood fare to support their denazification pedagogy.

By the early 1950s, the West German box office was ruled by domestically produced entertainment fare, beginning with the revival of the bucolic *Heimat* genre with Hans Deppe's runaway hit *Schwarzwaldmädel* (*The Black Forest Girl*, 1950). These films brought color back to the screen in sensational fashion, and although they would gradually be overtaken by other genres — war films, crime dramas, and Westerns — these early *Heimat* films set the tone for two decades of popular cinematic dominance. While the era had its art-film outliers, such as Ottomar Domnick's *Jonas* (1957), and while with the 1957 establishment of *Filmkritik* a culture of serious film criticism began to emerge, the structure of the industry generally favored directors who were able to achieve conventional box-office success and who frequently had honed their skills in the Nazi film industry. The industry remained difficult terrain for returning exiles as well — although a number of directors attempted to reenter the world of postwar production, the industry and audiences proved highly resistant. The case of Siegfried Kracauer's now landmark study *From Caligari to Hitler* is emblematic in this regard: first published in the United States in 1947, it would not appear in German translation until 1958.

West German cinema of the 1950s was not without its controversies, however: parallel to the rise of popular film clubs, a new ratings system emerged that effectively censored the era's most controversial films, most infamously the Hildegard Knef vehicle *Die Sünderin* (*The Story of a Sinner*, 1950). Central to the discussions of film ratings were questions about the influence of cinema on West Germany's youth, perceived to be at risk for corruption at the hands of a popular, and largely US-dominated, industry. By the end of the decade, the industry was struggling to compete with another threat — television — and although the industry embraced ever-splashier widescreen formats and ever-more-risqué subject matter, audience numbers continued their downward trend. Marking the artistic decline of the FRG's domestic production, in 1961 the German Film Awards granted no prize either for best film or best director. The seeds of change were sown: that same year, the Oberhausen Film Festival recognized two directors who would go on to become leading figures in the Young German Cinema movement, Alexander Kluge and Peter Schamoni.

In the East, DEFA concentrated its efforts during the first decade of the GDR on the production of antifascist films. These films — among them, Maetzig's *Rat der Götter* (*Council of the Gods*, 1950), as well as his epic two-part biopic *Thälmann — Sohn seiner Klasse* (Thälmann — Son of his class, 1954) and *Thälmann — Führer seiner Klasse* (Thälmann — Leader of his class, 1955) — commonly featured critiques of National Socialism as an outgrowth of capitalism alongside depictions of the political conversions of working-class characters intended to inspire audience emulation. The studio's output was not restricted to examinations of the recent past, however: by the 1950s, DEFA was creating cold war youth dramas that thematized East Germany as the healthy alternative to a corrupt West (e.g., Klein's 1957 *Berlin Ecke Schönhauser* [*Berlin Corner Schönhauser*]), as well as a line of children's films that proved successful across Eastern Europe. Despite relatively good access to facilities, however, cinematic output remained relatively low in the first decades of the studio's existence. Although the East now controlled the former Agfacolor film stock factory as well as the studio spaces of Ufa and Tobis, Soviet occupiers had seized much of the equipment in the name of reparations. Ideological battles over the content of films posed another challenge: DEFA's governing board included hard-line members of the ruling SED, and the studio struggled to find scripts that matched the list of desired subjects, and even more to gain approval for those films eventually produced. The case of director Falk Harnack is indicative: the DEFA studio artistic head and former resistance fighter choose to leave the GDR for West Berlin after his 1952 drama *Das Beil von Wandsbek* (*The Axe of Wandsbek*) was accused of depicting its Nazi main character in too sympathetic a light and pulled just weeks after its release. It would become an all-too-familiar pattern in the history of DEFA, as artistic possibilities changed with the political winds and filmmakers faced the challenge of negotiating a fluctuating culture of crackdown and liberalization.

Even before the border between the two Germanys closed in 1952, filmmakers increasingly found themselves forced to choose sides. In 1947, the inaugural Congress of Film Authors held in East Berlin had invited directors from across the zones of occupation to contribute to the task of reshaping German film culture, but just a few years later, the increasing politicization of DEFA and the generally worsening climate of the Cold War rendered such collaboration untenable, and filmmakers who sought to work across the divide faced distrust from both sides. Wolfgang Staudte, for one, eventually opted to retreat into television production after struggling to finance film projects deemed insufficiently in line with the interests of either Germany. Instead of collaboration, a spirit of competition and suspicion developed between the Germanys, with each state closely monitoring its representation in the theaters across the border. In the case of the GDR, this also meant watching the steady traffic of moviegoers as well, who crossed into West Germany in search of the more popular and often more salacious fare on offer. When the Berlin Wall was erected in 1961, it marked a turning point in the national division; in cinematic terms, however, it cemented an aesthetic and political rift that was already well in place.

Notes

[1] Karl Jaspers, *The Question of German Guilt*, trans. E. B. Ashton (Westport: Greenwood, 1948), 28.

Selected Bibliography • 1945–1961

Allan, Seán, and John Sandford, eds. *DEFA: East German Cinema, 1946–1992.* New York: Berghahn Books, 1999.

Baer, Hester. *Dismantling the Dream Factory: Gender, German Cinema, and the Postwar Quest for a New Film Language.* New York: Berghahn Books, 2009.

Baker, Mark. "'Trümmerfilme': Postwar German Cinema, 1946–1948." *Film Criticism* 20 (Fall/Winter 1995/1996): 88–101.

Bathrick, David. "Billy Wilder's Cold War Berlin." *New German Critique* 2010; 37, no. 2 (2010): 31–47.

Becker, Wolfgang, and Norbert Schöll. *In jenen Tagen . . . Wie der deutsche Nachkriegsfilm die Vergangenheit bewältigte.* Opladen: Leske + Budrich, 1995.

Bliersbach, Gerhard. *So grün war die Heide: Der deutsche Nachkriegsfilm in neuer Sicht.* Weinheim: Beltz, 1985.

Boa, Elizabeth, and Rachel Palfreyman. "(Un)Happy Families: Heimat and Anti-Heimat in West German Film and Theatre." In *Heimat: A German Dream: Regional Loyalties and National Identity in German Culture, 1890–1990,* 86–129. Oxford: Oxford UP, 2000.

———. "At Home in the GDR? Heimat in East German Film." In *Heimat: A German Dream: Regional Loyalties and National Identity in German Culture, 1890–1990,* 130–43. Oxford: Oxford UP, 2000.

Bongartz, Barbara. *Von Caligari zu Hitler, von Hitler zu Dr. Mabuse? Eine psychologische Geschichte des deutschen Films von 1946–1960.* Munich: MAKS, 1992.

Brauerhoch, Annette. *"Frauleins" und GIs: Geschichte und Filmgeschichte.* Frankfurt am Main: Stroemfeld/Nexus, 2006.

Cooke, Paul, and Marc Silberman, eds. *Screening War: Perspectives on German Suffering.* Rochester, NY: Camden House, 2010.

Davidson, John, and Sabine Hake. *Framing the Fifties: Cinema in a Divided Germany.* New York: Berghahn Books, 2007.

Fay, Jennifer. *Theaters of Occupation: Hollywood and the Re-education of Postwar Germany.* Minneapolis: U of Minnesota P, 2008.

Fehrenbach, Heide. "Narrating 'Race' in 1950s' West Germany: The Phenomenon of the Toxi Films." In *Not So Plain as Black and White: Afro-German Culture and History, 1890–2000,* edited by Patricia Mazón and Reinhild Steingröver, 136–60. Rochester: U of Rochester P, 2005.

———. *Cinema in Democratizing Germany: Reconstructing National Identity after Hitler.* Chapel Hill: U of North Carolina P, 1995.

Fisher, Jaimey. *Disciplining Germany: Youth, Reeducation, and Reconstruction after the Second World War.* Detroit: Wayne State UP, 2007.

Hackbarth, Doris. *DEFA 1946–1964: Studio für Populärwissenschaftliche Film (und Vorläufer); Filmografie*. Berlin: Henschel, 1997.
Hickethier, Knut. "Heimat-, Kriegs- und Kriminalfilme in der bundesdeutschen Rezeption der 1950er Jahre." In *Film — Kino — Zuschauer: Filmrezeption*, edited by Irmbert Schenk, Margrit Tröhler, and Yvonne Zimmermann, 245–60. Marburg: Schüren, 2010.
Kapczynski, Jennifer. "Postwar Ghosts: Heimatfilm and the Specter of Male Violence." *German Studies Review* 33, no. 2 (2010): 305–30.
———. *The German Patient: Crisis and Recovery in Postwar Culture*. Ann Arbor: U of Michigan P, 2008.
Koepnick, Lutz, and Stephan Schindler, eds. *The Cosmopolitan Screen: German Cinema and the Global Imaginary, 1945 to the Present*. Ann Arbor: U of Michigan P, 2007.
Kracauer, Siegfried. *From Caligari to Hitler: A Psychological History of the German Film*, 15–42. Princeton: Princeton UP, 1974 (1947).
Lindenberger, Thomas. "Home Sweet Home: Desperately Seeking Heimat in Early DEFA Films." *Film History* 18, no. 1 (2006): 46–58.
Ludewig, Alexandra. "Screening the East, Probing the Past." *German Politics and Society* 22, no. 2 (Summer 2004): 27–48.
Moeller, Robert G. *War Stories: The Search for a Usable Past in the Federal Republic of Germany*. Berkeley: U of California P, 2003.
Moitra, Stefan. "'Reality Is There, but It's Manipulated': West German Trade Unions and Film after 1945." In *Films That Work: Industrial Film and the Productivity of Media*, edited by Vinzenz Hediger and Patrick Vonderau, 329–48. Amsterdam: Amsterdam UP, 2009.
Müller, Christoph Hendrik. *West Germans against the West: Anti-Americanism in Media and Public Opinion in the Federal Republic of Germany 1949–1968*. Basingstoke: Palgrave Macmillan, 2010.
Rentschler, Eric. "The Place of Rubble in the *Trümmerfilm*." *New German Critique* 110 (Summer 2010): 9–30.
Schenk, Irmbert. "Populäres Kino und Lebensgefühl in der BRD um 1960 am Beispiel des Krimigenres." In *Film — Kino — Zuschauer: Filmrezeption*, edited by Irmbert Schenk, Margrit Tröhler, and Yvonne Zimmermann, 261–80. Marburg: Schüren, 2010.
Scholz, Anne-Marie. "*The Bridge on the River Kwai* (1957) Revisited: Combat Cinema, American Culture, and the German Past." *German History* 26, no. 2 (2008): 219–50.
Shandley, Robert R. *Rubble Films: German Cinema in the Shadow of the Third Reich*. Philadelphia: Temple UP, 2001.
Schissler, Hanna, ed. *The Miracle Years: A Cultural History of West Germany, 1949–1968*. Princeton: Princeton UP, 2001.
Silberman, Marc. "Learning from the Enemy: DEFA-French Co-Productions of the 1950s." *Film History* 18, no. 1 (2006): 21–45.
Spicer, Andrew, ed. *European Film Noir*. Manchester: Manchester UP, 2007.

Soldovieri, Stefan. "Finding Navigable Waters: Inter-German Film Relations and Modernisation in Two DEFA Barge Films of the 1950s." *Film History* 18, no. 1 (2006): 59–72.

Theuerkauf, Holger. *Goebbels' Filmerbe: Das Geschäft mit unveröffentlichten Ufa-Filmen*. Berlin: Ullstein, 1998.

Urang, John Griffith. "Realism and Romance in the East German Cinema, 1952–1962." *Film History* 18, no. 1 (2006): 88–103.

von Moltke, Johannes. *No Place Like Home: Locations of Heimat in German Cinema*. Berkeley: U of California P, 2005.

Weckel, Ulrike. "The Power of Images: Real and Fictional Roles of Atrocity Film Footage at Nuremberg." In *Reassessing the Nuremberh Military Tribunals: Transitional Justice, Trial Narratives, and Historiography*, edited by Kim C. Priemel and Alexa Stiller. New York: Berghahn, 2012.

Wende, Waltraud "Wara," and Lars Koch, eds. *Krisenkino: Filmanalyse als Kulturanalyse; Zur Konstruktion von Normalität und Abweichung im Spielfilm*. Bielefeld: transcript, 2010.

Wilms, Wilfried, and William Rasch, eds. *German Postwar Films: Life and Love in the Ruins*. New York: Palgrave Macmillan, 2008.

18 May 1945: *Welt im Film* Newsreels, Rubble Films Model "Cool Conduct"

Wilfried Wilms

Surveying a youth ready to rebuild from the rubble.
Irgendwo in Berlin *(1946). DVD capture.*

IN LATE SPRING OF 1945 Germans began to return to their cinemas. The country was on the brink of collapse and in dire need of a strong hand that could provide order and, ultimately, a future for its struggling population. The population itself, of course, was perceived by the victor nations to be in need of more than order: what these Germans required was a thorough lesson. What the attentive pupils might attain in the distant future were a reeducated self and a capacity for sustained democratic and humane conduct that would enable the nation's reincorporation in the ranks of civilized societies.

In the early months of occupation, it was the collaborative British-American newsreel *Welt im Film* (which premiered on 18 May 1945 and ran through 1952) that ensured that the occupied population appreciated the rules and rulers of the new Germany in which it now lived. Initially, the newsreel exhibited a philosophy of carrot and stick. Good will (the distribution of foods and repair of infrastructure) was demonstrated alongside displays of authority and power (executions of plundering Germans). In particular, the German viewing audience could distill from these newsreels certain Allied expectations they were obliged to consider — namely, what the Allies deemed as proper conduct. The Latin *conducere* describes the act, manner, or process of carrying on. And of course nothing was more uncertain in defeated and occupied Germany than *whether* and *how* one ought to carry on now that the Nazi regime was removed from power and the country defeated. Proper conduct in mid-1945 therefore meant deciphering the rules of social engagement that would enable initial survival and a possibly successful future. Besides the Allied-made newsreels and documentaries, Germans had numerous sources at their disposal to determine what was expected of them. There was, of course, the daily contact with the forces on the ground. Hollywood films also flooded the country, dispersing entertainment and putatively teaching democratic behavior along with the fabled British and American "way of life" the conquered were encouraged to emulate[1] (a point that Billy Wilder lampoons wonderfully in his 1948 film *A Foreign Affair*). Placards announced the laws and measures of the military government, and radio, newspapers, and magazines, all supervised by Allied cultural officers, began to reappear.[2]

Beginning with its very first example, Wolfgang Staudte's *Die Mörder sind unter uns* (*The Murderers Are among Us*, 1946), the German *Trümmerfilm* (rubble film) followed the norms and expectations of the occupation and reiterated them within a semifictitious context. This should not surprise us, insofar as these films themselves were shaped by Allied censorship during all phases of production and, consequently, could hardly reject the terms set for their realization. One of the most obvious indications of this pressure may be that the very death and destruction to which the genre owed its existence was by no means at its center. While most rubble films feature as their backdrop the ruins of destroyed cities, civilian death, and hopelessness, zooming in for brief moments on disease and hunger as the inevitable consequences of urban annihilation, the films mostly depict a new humanism emerging from the shared experiences of life in the rubble. One is hard-pressed to find even the beginnings of an extensive reflection on German atrocities in the Nazi concentration camp system, or of German guilt and contrition in general. Critics of German rubble film have focused for decades on this deficiency.[3] At the same time, there is a reflective void in these films concerning the cause of the rubble — namely, the bombing of German cities and their noncombatant inhabitants. The films give little account of how Germans processed, perhaps even debated, their experiences, whether publicly or privately, and how they sought to "come to terms with" such radical devastation. But, of course, the punitive wisdom at the time, born out of postwar emotions, was that Germany's population had reaped what it had sown. The demand for an all-encompassing self-purification was thus the only German response considered appropriate.[4]

It has long been commonplace to evaluate these German products of the years 1946–50 as examples of early (and singular) moral failing. As a recent observer put it so succinctly: "The rubble films' treatment of the past is far from morally satisfying to today's viewers."[5] The general consensus is that these films lack an honest reckoning with the past or ample display of German guilt and remorse.[6] Often seen merely as symptoms of a particular German "malady" — a supposed inability to confront the sins of its immediate past, framed in terms of psychosocial deficiency vis-à-vis a violent past that, until today, is considered a specifically *German* phenomenon — these films have too rarely been examined for their aesthetic qualities and for what they actually *do* depict about postwar German life, attitudes, and fears.

In order to complicate the origins of the assumed *cold persona* of post-Nazi Germany, it seems worthwhile to broaden our limited horizon. If we accept that the political, ideological, and cultural situation after 1945 was, for the individual on the ground, in some essential ways comparable (albeit certainly not identical) with that of the 1920s, it may be fruitful to reconsider the aforementioned "German malady" in the context of what Helmut Lethen has termed "Verhaltenslehren der Kälte" (The rules of cool conduct). With regard to the Weimar years, Lethen writes: "Having lost the mooring of an external metaphysics, people begin scavenging the ruins of historical systems for an orienting codex of conduct, which is to say, the tools of self-stabilization."[7] These codes of conduct developed in reaction to the loss of undisputed legitimacy on the part of social institutions, and were directed ultimately at "strategic self-enactment; the aim is the training of a functional ego."[8] Building on Helmuth Plessner's harsh polemic against the cult of community, *Grenzen der Gemeinschaft* (*The Limits of Community*, 1924), Lethen observes that for the Weimar era's New Objectivity "cool behavior" was the desired response within a culture of shame that ranked personal dignity and the garnering of respect higher than a clear conscience. Following Lethen, we might ask: What was the desired conduct after 1945? What tools were employed by the Allies and Germans alike to achieve self-stabilization, to produce a functional ego in the wake of defeat?[9]

After the loss of the desired or promised "authentic" *Volksgemeinschaft* and every ideal of the Nazi community, it was primarily the Allies who provided codes of conduct for a defeated and disoriented people. An analysis of *Welt im Film* of the years 1945–48 reveals that the Allies encouraged the German audience in nearly every episode to work jointly at the physical rebuilding of their homeland. The visual and narrative codes they provided did not promote contemplation, but rather a willingness to work overtime on Germany's reconstruction. One is hard-pressed to find a single installment that encouraged Germans to reflect on their recent past. Of course there were numerous episodes that reminded the audience of their guilt, such as those addressing the concentration camps or trials of perpetrators. Yet these segments rarely amounted to more than an allocation of proper subject positions — that of the perpetrator with regard to Germans, or that of the liberator and beacon of humanity with regard to the Americans. Furthermore, these scenes and commentaries occupied only a very small percentage of the newsreel's screen time. They were effectively overwhelmed by the vast number of other newsreel pieces focusing on reconstruction and the future. The influence of Allied supervision showed itself most strongly, of course, in what the newsreels, and then later rubble films, did *not* show: for instance, a near complete absence of Allied personnel in these films, or the nonexistence of any discussion regarding Allied war conduct.

The rubble film's dual tendencies toward emphasizing labor and reconstruction and excising introspection and pain are well-illustrated by the example of Harald Braun's rubble film *Zwischen Gestern und Morgen* (*Between Yesterday and Tomorrow*, 1947). Licensed and released by the American military government, the film premiered at Munich's Luitpold Theater on 11 December 1947. In *Zwischen Gestern und Morgen*, Kat (Hildegard Knef) revisits her traumatic past only involuntarily. In a key scene, she remembers her losses: her family members are presumed killed during an air raid and are still buried under the ruins of what used to be Munich; the father of her son is missing. Kat responds to these recollections by applying what appears to be a well-functioning mechanism of repression. Realizing that she has lost herself in her painful past, she jerks herself to her feet, throws some more briquettes onto the fire, and exclaims with a firm voice: "Since then we've set up shop here by ourselves. But it does no good. You've gotta keep living, right? There's no other way!"

Numerous rubble films present precisely such a pairing of apathy or suppression of emotion, on the one hand, and the cherished value of productivity, on the other hand. The films repeatedly depict an objectionable inability to act or work toward the future as the consequence of a crippling preoccupation with a traumatic past. Consider the many examples on celluloid: the drunk Dr. Hans Mertens in *Die Mörder sind unter uns*; the depressive former soldier Walter in *. . . und über uns der Himmel* (*. . . and the Sky above Us*, 1947); Beckmann's and Anna's suicidal tendencies in *Liebe '47* (*Love '47*, 1948); or the two prominent veteran figures in *Irgendwo in Berlin* (*Somewhere in Berlin*, 1946), returnee Paul Iller and the shell-shocked Steidel. The films contrast these failures with a weighty emphasis on productivity and usefulness. What most of these characters and films have in common is their desired and eventual return to the sanity and sanctity of production. The protagonists manage to overcome despair and reinsert themselves into the future of a country whose redemption lies not in introspection or remorse, but rather in an active devotion to labor. In Staudte's *Die Mörder sind unter uns*, Hans and Susanne are able to block out the ruins (figuratively and visually) once they acknowledge their love for one another and join hands in work.

Of course, we could look at these scenes and interpret them precisely the way they have been analyzed in the past: as proof of the Germans' disinterest in or inability of coming to terms with the past. Or, as Shandley views it: as "training films for the attitude of dismissal regarding the Holocaust."[10] But such an interpretation not only lacks nuance, it also disregards the significance of Allied cultural politics and expectations as forces that actively influenced all cultural manifestations of the immediate postwar period. The directors of rubble film did not work in a vacuum. Rather, they inevitably responded, perhaps even adhered, to an external frame of expectations that, whether perceived or real, funneled their aesthetic and thematic decisions. Only then could they dream of having careers in a postwar Germany in which the Allies were the source not only of power, but also of codes of conduct for a defeated German population.

Did Germans like Kat in *Zwischen Gestern und Morgen*, especially when they lost family and friends in the bombings, not discuss the air war? Did they not feel any resentment? One could venture to guess that they did. Yet rubble films like Staudte's or Braun's, at least, did not engage the issue in any way worth mentioning. If the fall of 1946 jumpstarted the visual expression of postwar "German" pain and suffering, it certainly did not in any way identify the victorious Allies as the agents thereof. What dominated Allied news, in turn, was the inherent or explicit expectation that the German people get to work and labor on behalf of their future. At least in these early months and years of reeducation, the process of *Vergangenheitsbewältigung* (coming to terms with the past) can be discussed in terms of what Lethen calls "Affektstabilisierung" (internal affective stabilization), which became part and parcel of Allied cultural politics. The rubble films made under occupation similarly denied space for grief and discouraged introspection. Indeed, we find numerous examples in which introspection and grief are represented as paralyzing and must be abandoned for the sake of embracing a better tomorrow — one only achievable through the formation of a "functional ego" (Lethen), an ego ready to go to work. Kat jettisons her mourning and emphasizes the need to labor on. The question that beckons to be explored is whether the prescribed (or merely perceived) transformation into an expected "armored subject" (Lethen's "gepanzertes Ich"), modeled in Allied newsreels and then the rubble films of the immediate postwar years, aided or even jumpstarted a German withdrawal into a state of affectlessness for which the nation would later be criticized. It is not enough to look at Germany's self-pity and obsession with its own dead in the 1950s when discussing the two major tropes of postwar German history (whether the war generation's failure "to come to terms" with the past, or their "inability to mourn"). The traditional argument has been that the Germans remained silent out of shame or guilt, out of some sense of complicity that, in turn, they were unable to confront. As true as that may be, it also seems that the unwillingness or inability to mourn the victims of their time and place may have had as much to do with a set of projected expectations to which Germans responded as with any psychological or moral disposition.

See also:

- 4 March 1921: With *Das Floss der Toten*, the Dead Come Back to Town
- 22 March 1946: Screenings of *Die Todesmühlen* Spark Controversy over German Readiness to Confront Nazi Crimes
- 19 September 1958: Douglas Sirk's *A Time to Love and a Time to Die* Tests Limits of Postwar Feeling

Notes

[1] See Jennifer Fay's analysis of US attempts to use the soft power of cinema to have Germans "look, act, and think" like Americans. Fay, *Theaters of Occupation: Hollywood and the Reeducation of Postwar Germany* (Minneapolis: U of Minnesota P, 2008), 37.

[2] A recent study by Alexander Badenoch, *Voices in Ruins*, explores how radio helped to shape visions of what would become the Federal Republic of Germany, as well as memories of Germany's recent past. Badenoch, *Voices in Ruins: German Radio and National Reconstruction in the Wake of Total War* (New York: Palgrave, 2008).

[3] More innovative readings of rubble films can be found in a recent collection entitled *German Postwar Films: Life and Love in the Ruins*, ed. Wilfried Wilms and William Rasch (New York: Palgrave, 2008). A traditional but informative reading is provided by Jürgen Berger, Hans-Peter Reichmann, and Rudolf Worschech, eds., *Zwischen Gestern und Morgen: Westdeutscher Nachkriegsfilm 1945–1962* (Frankfurt am Main: Deutsches Filmmuseum, 1989). On ruins and the 1950s, see Ursula Bessen, *Trümmer und Träume: Nachkriegszeit und fünfziger Jahre auf Zelluloid* (Bochum: Brockmeyer, 1989).

⁴ On cinema's role in the construction of postwar German national identity, see Heide Fehrenbach, *Cinema in Democratizing Germany: Reconstructing National Identity after Hitler* (Chapel Hill: U of North Carolina P, 1995).

⁵ Robert Shandley, *Rubble Films: German Cinema in the Shadow of the Third Reich* (Philadelphia: Temple UP, 2001), 4.

⁶ See, for example, Shandley's discussion of *The Murderers Are among Us* in *Rubble Films*, 25–46. For informative yet traditional discussions of postwar film, see Anton Kaes, *From Hitler to Heimat: The Return of History as Film* (Cambridge, MA: Harvard UP, 1989), 2–35; and Sabine Hake, *German National Cinema* (London, New York: Routledge, 2002), 86–118.

⁷ Helmut Lethen, *Cool Conduct: The Culture of Distance in Weimar Germany*, trans. Don Reneau (Berkeley: U of California P, 2002), 50.

⁸ Ibid., 18.

⁹ Becker and Schöll write: "What all these films share is their intention to affect the conscience and morals of the audience, to change, stabilize, and alter them." Wolfgang Becker, Norbert Schöll, eds., *In jenen Tagen . . . Wie der deutsche Nachkriegsfilm die Vergangenheit bewältigte* (Opladen: Leske + Budrich, 1995), 24n3.

¹⁰ Shandley, *Rubble Films*, 5.

22 March 1946: Screenings of *Die Todesmühlen* Spark Controversy over German Readiness to Confront Nazi Crimes

Ulrike Weckel

ON 22 MARCH 1946 it was Berlin's turn. After the US military government (officially, the Office of Military Government for Germany, U.S. or OMGUS) had screened its short documentary about liberated Nazi concentration camps *Die Todesmühlen* (*Death Mills*) first in Bavaria and then simultaneously in Greater Hesse, Württemberg-Baden, and Bremen, the film started a one-week run in the fifty-two movie theaters of the city's American sector. Some members of the intelligence service warned that these would be far too many screenings, but officials declined to alter their plan to show this shocking lesson in reeducation in all of the military district's reopened theaters so that moviegoers that week would have no alternative to seeing it. After a first day of lively attendance, the figures dropped. In early April, a harshly critical article appeared in Berlin's *Tagesspiegel* charging that 75 percent of the sector's inhabitants had been "afraid of the truth" and had refused to feel shame at the sight of the dreadful results of Nazi crimes against humanity.[1] The article triggered numerous letters to the editor, most of them arguing that nonattendance did not necessarily indicate indifference or shamelessness. This contribution summarizes what can be established about German responses to *Todesmühlen* and, on these grounds, discuss the status of the so-called Allied atrocity films in (film) history.

The common belief that the Allies compelled German civilians to watch atrocity films is mostly legend. Numerous Germans remember it this way, and in the literature, too, one often finds the claim that food ration cards were stamped at box offices. One of the few things Billy Wilder ever said regarding his brief involvement in the making of *Todesmühlen* was that this method to ensure attendance had been his idea.[2] In truth, compulsory viewing remained a rare exception. Immediately after the end of the war, British commanders in at least two towns in Northern Germany ordered the local populations to watch a newsreel on the Allies' discoveries in the camps, but the British occupying power soon prioritized reconstruction and the reduction of German apathy over reeducation, and the official British atrocity film went unfinished. For the Soviets and the French, the pedagogy of shock via confrontation with Nazi crimes was never a central part of their occupation policy. It was the Americans who most consistently worked on a documentary for German audiences about the liberation of the camps and who devised a plan for screening it in their zone of occupation. Mandatory attendance was discussed but rejected. When it became known that local authorities in some scattered places had indeed compelled attendance, OMGUS immediately banned the practice and had the ban publicly announced. Nevertheless, the expectation, or suggestion, of compulsion seems to have been widespread. Some moviegoers brought their ration cards to theaters and insisted on getting stamps, while in interviews and polls several Germans recommended obligatory viewing, at least for Nazi Party members. However, it was only because OMGUS had renounced compulsion that attendance figures later could be interpreted as an indicator of Germans' readiness to face the criminal character of Nazi rule, and as such become a subject of controversy.

A second common misunderstanding takes *Todesmühlen* to be part of a first, "punitive" phase of American occupation policy and claims that the film articulated an accusation of collective guilt.[3] The pictures from the various sites of Nazi crimes were indeed shameful, and there is good reason to think that some British and American occupiers saw atrocity film screenings as opportunities to shame Germans. In the case of *Todesmühlen*, however, the filmmakers appear to have made efforts to avoid the impression of a self-righteous Allied accusation. Rather than point his finger at the German people, the film's narrator takes on the role of an ordinary German *Mitläufer* (fellow traveler) who finally, after seeing the horrors, recognizes his personal responsibility and invites the film's viewers to participate in similar self-critical reflection. For the first seventeen minutes of the twenty-minute film, the German-speaking narrator confines himself to presenting relatively matter-of-fact, background information, accompanied by shots of wretched survivors, piled corpses, various camp facilities (including a gas chamber, crematoria, and barracks of loot), Allied delegations, arrested SS personnel, and some Nazi officials being forced to visit a camp. At minute seventeen, however, as viewers learn that "the commanding general" also ordered Weimar's citizens to walk to nearby Buchenwald in order to witness the site, the film takes a more personal turn. Accompanying shots of Weimar residents whose facial expressions change visibly once they have passed through the camp's gate, the narrator switches to the first person singular: "Yes, that was then. When the SA held its victory parade through the Brandenburg Gate I marched with them. Yes, I remember now. At the Nuremberg party rally I yelled 'Heil.' And then, another day, when the Gestapo came for my neighbor, I turned away and asked myself: 'Why should I care?'"

Until this point, the images stand in stark contrast to the words: instead of triumphant SA men in 1933, viewers watch Germans at the end of the war walking among corpses, their heads lowered. But then, Nazi footage of cheering crowds and thousands of arms raised in Hitler salutes indeed do appear on the screen. "Do you remember?" the narrator asks his audience. "1933, 1936, 1939. I was there. What did I do against what was happening?" At this moment, images of enthusiastic Nazi crowds and of the ashamed forced visitors of concentration camps are superimposed. "Millions of Germans who cheered the evil, millions of Germans who were intoxicated by songs of hatred and revenge, millions of Germans who pledged themselves to the death and destruction of free speech and the free spirit, millions of Germans who lent their hands to the attack on defenseless peoples and the murder of innocent human beings."[4] In this way, the film's lesson that broad German approval of the regime made Nazi crimes possible is expressed visually and formulated as the insight of a German *Mitläufer* who does not exclude himself from blame. More than an Allied accusation, *Todesmühlen* presented to its German audiences an example of how to come to terms with their Nazi past.

When *Todesmühlen* was completed and 114 copies produced in January 1946, movie theaters in the American zone had been open for several months and, after a short period of screening only documentaries, their usual programs had come to include feature films. *Todesmühlen*, however, was to be shown solely in combination with the British-American newsreel *Welt im Film* and one or two serious documentaries selected by OMGUS. For the one-hour long program, reduced ticket prices of 60 pfennig were to be charged. It appears as if the concept of screening *Todesmühlen* area-wide without alternative did not aim primarily at taking moviegoers by surprise; rather, it represented a middle course between mandatory attendance and offering the film as one among a variety of choices. At any rate, posters were printed and the local press announced the film, regularly urging the population not to avoid the confrontation with Nazi atrocities.

Evaluating whether attendance was high or low depends on one's expectations. After *Todesmühlen*'s run in Bavaria in late January 1946, most commentators were relieved. Nearly 584,000 people saw the film — several screenings were sold out (especially during the first days), and at some cinemas, visitors even waited in line to get in. Fears turned out to be unfounded: no public protests or mass walk-outs were reported, observers found that most audiences watched in depressed silence, and a broad majority, when asked, answered that they believed everything shown was true.[5] Perhaps the Bavarian results raised expectations about the supposedly more open-minded Berliners. However, American film officer Peter van Eyck disclosed two months later that his section was "for the first time bitterly disappointed in the Berliner."[6]

Only 157,120 people or 16.6 percent of the US sector's total population viewed *Todesmühlen* while the average weekly attendance at programs with feature films had been 247,258 people or 26.2 percent. Subtracting children, the sick, and the elderly, the *Tagesspiegel* article concluded that 75 percent of the sector's nondisabled adult inhabitants had been unwilling to let themselves feel ashamed, and the other 25 percent were ashamed of this fact. The unknown author presumed that the nonviewers still hailed "Herrn Hitler."

If the article was meant to instigate a public debate, the provocation worked. Twenty letters to the editor can still be found in the archives, excerpts from four of which were published by the *Tagesspiegel*. Five authors agreed with the article's interpretation; fifteen repudiated it. Most of the latter argued that the truth was already well known. Some referred to news coverage and the revelations of the Nuremberg trial, others claimed to have family and friends among the victims, and several pointed to their own suffering. The nature of this suffering usually remained obscure, but two authors spoke explicitly of the Western Allies' air raids and the Soviets' conquest of Berlin with the clear intention of indicating that the crimes of both sides were equal or even greater on the side of the Allies. Three authors insisted that attending *Todesmühlen* was no proof of conversion, and one complimented all of the Berliners who had stayed away from this "swindle."[7]

The widespread consensus among scholars that Allied atrocity film screenings failed to impress German audiences, though, is not based on attendance figures or the reasons Germans gave for not attending. Instead, it is repeatedly mentioned that a high percentage of viewers who were polled right after screenings answered questions about whether they felt either personally or collectively guilty of Nazi crimes in the negative.[8] But this was only one answer among several. Questionnaires differed, and the sum of all the answers reveals a broad spectrum of attitudes with many nuances. The consistently low acceptance of national or personal guilt should, therefore, give analysts second thoughts about what the answer to such a question asked in the given situation really indicates about the atrocity film's effects on viewers. Obviously, the large number that denied feelings of guilt includes people with otherwise quite different views. Berlin is once again a telling example. Compared to poll results in Bavaria, Berliners' responses were more favorable: more people returned the questionnaires, 87.2 percent believed the film to be entirely accurate, and 91.4 percent thought that all Germans should see *Todesmühlen*; references to Allied war crimes, one's own misery, and suspicions that the film was Allied "propaganda" were far less frequent. However, even in this group 70.5 percent rejected the claim that — as the Berlin questionnaire phrased it — "the whole German people" shared the guilt for Nazi crimes. Apart from the fact that an unusually high percentage

(26.5) answered this question in the positive, the negative answers in no way indicated that *Todesmühlen* had not impressed those viewers. If one insists on a generalizing conclusion about the many — in part contradictory — detectable effects, the evidence suggests that the atrocity film helped to further discredit the Nazi regime and thereby fostered Germans' postwar dissociation from it.

Beyond a doubt, *Todesmühlen* did not generate a spontaneous, general, political "conversion" in Germany's US zone of occupation in early 1946. Such a conversion, however, seems to have been a widespread hope derived from the power of those images. Several postwar American films play out the chances for such a sudden "change of heart" by including a short sequence of atrocity footage as a film being screened to stubborn characters. While it takes additional dramatic developments in *The Stranger* (1946) and *Judgment at Nuremberg* (1961) to convince a young American woman that she has married a Nazi criminal in hiding or to make an indicted German judge break his silence before the American military tribunal and confess his guilt,[9] the atrocity film triggers an immediate transformation in Franz, a fanatic member of the Hitler Youth in Samuel Fuller's *Verboten!* (1959). When his sister finds out that Franz is part of the local Werewolf gang, which fights against the US military government and denies the Nazi crimes, she takes him to a session of the Trial of the Major War Criminals at Nuremberg. *Verboten!* cuts between a mixture of the various films screened in the real courtroom and close-ups of Franz, whom we see biting his lips, sweating, and finally breaking down in tears. His conversion is completed when he betrays a meeting of the Werewolves to the American authorities.

In German cinema, an atrocity film sequence was first worked into a narrative plot in *Die bleierne Zeit* (*Marianne and Juliane*, 1980). Here, the shock that the two teenage sisters in the late 1950s receive from the film eventually motivates their critical attitude toward the FRG, which in turn leads Marianne to finally join the Red Army Faction. In a telling commentary on this scene, *Die innere Sicherheit* (*The State I am In*, 2000) — a film dealing with the adolescence of a girl whose parents, as former terrorists, live underground — shows a high-school class of the 1990s that remains unimpressed when shown an atrocity film.

Given that the Nazis did not document on film how they treated their prisoners, it is the Allied footage of what they found in the camps after the SS had fled them that comes closest to a historical visual representation of Nazi crimes against humanity. These images have become the most prominent signifier of those crimes; various films and television features have quoted from the footage, and most people in the Western world today have a general idea of what they show. In the post-war period, they were publicized not only by Allied newsreels and the atrocity films of 1945–46 (like *Todesmühlen*), but also by Stuart Schulberg's and Pare Lorentz's documentary of the Nuremberg trial of 1948 and, in 1955, Alain Resnais's famous and sophisticated presentation in *Nuit et Brouillard* (*Night and Fog*). The atrocity images were well-known among postwar Germans but hardly talked about in public. Nevertheless, when the West-German government protested against *Nuit et Brouillard* being shown at the Cannes Film Festival in 1956, many Germans protested their government's protest. In response, a German narration written by the Jewish poet Paul Celan was recorded and the film was screened, not only in theaters, but in schools as well.[10]

Such moments aside, the widespread false recollection among postwar Germans that they were forced to watch an Allied atrocity film remains significant. Rather than priding themselves at having confronted the visual evidence of Nazi crimes voluntarily, and perhaps having experienced a transformation like that of Franz in *Verboten!*, the majority of commentators chose to turn attention away from the images and toward the alleged conditions of the Allied screenings, making them appear as an unreasonable imposition. This invention seems to have succeeded somehow in discrediting the early Allied atrocity films so that scholars can imagine only that they "failed," without asking much about the kinds of effects that realistically could have been expected. It took the next generation — like the sisters in *Die bleierne Zeit* — to publicly discuss the visual evidence of Nazi crimes, not least in order to instrumentalize the images as an accusation against the generation of their parents. The provocative question *Die innere Sicherheit* poses ought to be considered: What happens when there is no longer a direct connection to the generation of the perpetrators, and following generations believe they already know the images of the Holocaust without actually knowing much about them?

See also:

- 19 September 1958: Douglas Sirk's *A Time to Love and a Time to Die* Tests Limits of Postwar Feeling
- 22 January 1979: West German Broadcast of *Holocaust* Draws Critical Fire and Record Audiences
- 8 September 2004: *Der Untergang* Offers Palatable Authenticity

Notes

[1] "Angst vor der Wahrheit," *Tagesspiegel* (9 April 1946).

[2] Heinz-Gerd and Reinhard Wolf, "'Ich nehm' das alles nicht so ernst...': Gespräch mit Billy Wilder," in *Billy Wilders Filme*, ed. Neil Sinyard and Adrian Turner (West Berlin: Spiess, 1980), 9–51; here 48.

³ Dagmar Barnouw, *Germany 1945: Views of War and Violence* (Bloomington/Indianapolis: Indiana UP, 1996); Brigitte Hahn, *Umerziehung durch Dokumentarfilm? Ein Instrument amerikanischer Kulturpolitik im Nachkriegsdeutschland, 1945–1953* (Münster: LIT, 1997), 113–28; and Cora Sol Goldstein, *Capturing the German Eye: American Visual Propaganda in Occupied Germany* (Chicago: U of Chicago P, 2009), 51–57.

⁴ Some misjudgments about the film are based on the false assumption that the sharp denunciations of Germans in the English-language version *Death Mills* were literal translations from the original German narration. However, this passage was altered in *Death Mills* in order to warn occupation soldiers sent to Germany after the end of the war about "fraternization."

⁵ "The Atrocity Film in Bavaria," *Information Control Intelligence Summary* 30 (9 February 1946): 4–5, National Archives, College Park (NARA): RG 260/OMGUS, ICD, MPB, Box 281, Folder Film, Intelligence Reports.

⁶ FTM Sub-Section Report 27 (28 March 1946) NARA: RG 260/OMGBS, Records of Information Services BR, General Records 1945–49, Box 82, Folder Monthly Reports 1945–46.

⁷ Public Opinion Surveys Unit, "The Atrocity Film in Berlin" (8 April 1946), NARA: RG 260/OMGUS, ICD, MPB, Box 281, Folder Film, Intelligence Reports.

⁸ Most borrow the argument from Brewster S. Chamberlin, "*Todesmühlen*. Ein früher Versuch zur Massen-'Umerziehung' im besetzten Deutschland 1945–1946," *Vierteljahrshefte für Zeitgeschichte* 29, no. 3 (1981): 420–36.

⁹ Ulrike Weckel, "Amerikanischer Traum von einem deutschen Schuldbekenntnis. Der Spielfilm *Judgment at Nuremberg* (1961) und seine Rezeption in der deutschen Presse," in *Das Gericht als Tribunal oder: Wie der NS-Vergangenheit der Prozess gemacht wurde*, ed. Georg Wamhof (Göttingen: Wallstein, 2009), 163–85.

¹⁰ Ewout van der Knaap, "Enlightening Procedures: *Nacht und Nebel* in Germany," in *Uncovering the Holocaust: The International Reception of Night and Fog*, ed. Ewout van der Knaap (London: Wallflower, 2006), 46–85.

16 August 1949: Ilse Kubaschewski Founds Gloria-Filmverleih, Sets the Course of Popular West German Film

Hester Baer

With the founding of Gloria-Filmverleih in 1949, Ilse Kubaschewski not only set up the most successful West German film distributor of the 1950s, but she also laid the groundwork for what would become one of the top production companies of the postwar period. Under the auspices of Gloria and its production arm Divina-Film, Kubaschewski distributed and produced over 500 films between 1949 and 1973, including many of the most popular movies of the era. While Gloria was responsible for approximately one in ten films made in the Federal Republic in the 1950s, the company earned a full one-third of film revenue with beloved hits like *Grün ist die Heide* (*The Heath is Green*, 1951), *Ferien vom Ich* (*Vacation from myself*, 1952), the *08/15* trilogy (1954–55), *Liebe, Tanz, und 1000 Schlager* (*Love, Dance, and 1000 Songs*, 1955), the *Trapp-Familie* series (1956–58), and *Der Arzt von Stalingrad* (*The Doctor of Stalingrad*, 1958).[1]

One of the most influential yet overlooked figures in the history of German cinema, "Kuba the Great" played a major role in determining the direction filmmaking would take in the early postwar period, both commercially and artistically. Not only did she rule a film empire (including a chain of prominent cinemas) that dictated production and exhibition practices, but she also left her mark on the aesthetic and stylistic qualities of postwar cinema, not least in the realm of genre, helping to pioneer the postwar waves of *Heimatfilme*, *Schlagerfilme*, war films, and sex films.

Like other auteur producers in the German tradition, including Erich Pommer, Artur Brauner, and Bernd Eichinger, Kubaschewski's remarkable career not only underscores the significance of production and distribution for understanding German film history, but also sheds light on the longstanding transnational dimensions of German cinema. At the same time, Kubaschewski's success and influence as a female tycoon in the male-dominated film industry during the Adenauer Era presents an exemplary case study for examining the ambivalent gender politics of postwar German cinema.

Kubaschewski's often-quoted motto "my reviews are written at the box office" demonstrates both her noted instinct for popular taste and her disregard for the opinions of critics. Yet as her nickname *die*

Schnulzenkönigin (queen of schlock) suggests, Kubaschewski's acumen as a producer has often been underestimated, reduced merely to the innate feel for sentimental stories she was said to possess as a woman from a working-class Berlin background.

Born Ilse Kramp in 1907 to a postal worker father and a pianist mother who accompanied silent films, Kubaschewski grew up in cinemas.[2] After finishing trade school, she entered the film business as an intern at Ufa (Universum Film A.G.). In 1931, she was hired at Siegel-Monopol, a small distribution company specializing in entertainment cinema, in particular *Heimatfilme*, where she began as a stenotypist and moved up through the ranks, working as a secretary, a booker, and finally as assistant to the head of the company. In the early 1940s, Kubaschewski acquired shares in a suburban Berlin cinema, where she learned the trade firsthand, studying audience preferences, completing a required course for cinema owners, and even passing a test that certified her as a film projectionist. When she fled Berlin shortly before the Soviet invasion of her native city in 1945, Kubaschewski's expertise as a cinema operator and her training as a projectionist — together with her relatively clean political background — qualified her to take over a cinema in Bavaria, which she ran throughout the period of occupation. The intimate knowledge of booking practices that she gained in her early career was crucial to Kubaschewski's later success as a distributor and producer.

As a woman with years of experience in the film industry who had never held a position of power during the Third Reich, Kubaschewski was in a unique position to receive one of the first postwar film distribution licenses. In addition to a 30,000 reichsmark bank loan, Kubaschewski's capital included an agreement with the Allies that granted her the rights to eleven box-office hits from the Nazi period, which she had convinced the Allied Film Office to derequisition through the mediation of her husband Hans Kubaschewski, a film advisor to the Allies. Focusing on star vehicles for popular actresses such as Zarah Leander and Marika Rökk, Kubaschewski revived evergreens that still appealed to the predominantly female audiences of the postwar period.

At the same time, she expanded her offerings by signing a distribution contract with Republic Films, a purveyor of Hollywood B-movies. Working with Republic's back catalogue of old serials that had never been seen in Germany, Gloria edited together episodes to create feature-length films. The *Zorro* and *Dr. Fu Man Chu* series became huge hits with West German audiences, and Kubaschewski's flexible repayment plan with Republic meant that she had a steady source of available cash, money she poured back into West German production deals.

Much has been made of Kubaschewski's reliance on powerful men, in particular her husband Hans, whom she married in 1938. A salesman for Ufa in the Third Reich, Hans went to work for the Allied military authorities as an adviser on film issues, including licensing, during occupation. He later managed the West German subsidiary of Warner Brothers, and went on to serve as the trustee of the production company Bavaria, helping to facilitate a merger between Bavaria and Columbia Pictures, which took place in 1963, two years after his death. As Tim Bergfelder has pointed out, "the Kubaschewskis strongly supported each other's business interests. Hans Kubaschewski's international connections and advice served to complement his wife's more parochial outlook and helped to diversify Gloria's profile."[3]

If her husband Hans played a significant role in Gloria's internationalization, Ilse Kubaschewski's connection with Luggi Waldleitner also contributed strongly to the company's success. In 1941, when she met him on a skiing vacation, Kubaschewski began a personal and professional relationship with Waldleitner that lasted for over a decade. Waldleitner, who began his film career as assistant to cameraman Guzzi Lantschner during the filming of Leni Riefenstahl's *Olympia* (1936–38), went on to work for Kurt Ulrich as an artistic consultant at Berolina Film in the early 1940s. After the collapse of the German film industry, Waldleitner joined Kubaschewski, helping her to run a Bavarian cinema and to build up Gloria before splitting off to found his own production company, Roxy-Film, in 1952. While Kubaschewski used Hans's business connections to help diversify her distribution company, she exploited Waldleitner's knowledge of the artistic side of filmmaking in developing her skills as a producer. Remarkably, Kubaschewski was able to conceal her years-long affair with Waldleitner from media exposure, which would have tarnished her carefully constructed reputation as a representative of mainstream, conservative values and tastes.[4] However useful Kubaschewski's relationships with these men were to her business, though, she was the indisputable boss of a company that she steered to dominance in the 1950s.

In the fragmented landscape of postwar filmmaking, characterized by Allied efforts at decartelization and the dismantling of Ufa, Gloria became profitable quickly by adopting the risk-free strategy of flooding cinemas with never before seen Hollywood hits and beloved classics from the Nazi era. In this way, Gloria had the necessary capital to finance its own productions and therefore to influence both style and content. Like other distributors in the 1950s, Gloria maximized profits with blind selling and block booking, which forced cinema owners to rent an entire season's program of as yet unmade and unseen films, including inevitable flops along with star-studded hits. This financial scheme strengthened distribution companies immensely; according to Michael Töteberg, "the distribution bosses were the true film producers in the 1950s and 1960s: film subvention did not yet exist and the films were financed from 70 to 100 percent by the distributor."[5] In this context, the personal tastes and preferences of individual distributors had a remarkable influence on the course of postwar West German film production. Claudia Dillmann-Kühn suggests that eight individuals — four distributors and four producers — "essentially determined what was seen in [West] German movie theaters in the 1950s."[6]

At the top of the list was Kubaschewski, "a powerful woman whose definition of the entertainment film producers scrambled to fulfill."[7] Indeed, as one of the most powerful distributors of the 1950s, Kubaschewski routinely initiated projects, chose the producer, participated in the selection of director and cast, edited the script, oversaw advertising campaigns, and secured all financial arrangements and contracts. Well known for running a very tight ship, Kubaschewski insisted on signing off on all important decisions personally. A tough negotiator, she exploited her well-known instinct for the public taste along with her exclusive star contracts with popular actors like Rudolf Prack in order to secure more profitable booking deals with cinemas. On the other end of her business, she drove the distributor's fee ever higher, collecting the first 30 percent of box office profit, ostensibly in order to cover the costs of distribution, though Gloria's actual costs were typically much lower.[8] Moreover, unlike most other distributors of the era, Kubaschewski was able to avoid entering into West German film guarantee schemes, allowing her to steer clear of high interest loans and government censorship.

A successful female distributor in a profession that has always been a male domain, Kubaschewski represents a cohort of women whose professional mobilization was sped up by the events of the Second World War and the gender imbalance in the German population that ensued. Between 1950 and 1961, the number of female entrepreneurs increased by 77 percent in West Germany.[9] For much of this period women also comprised 70 percent of German cinema audiences, a factor that clearly underpinned Kubaschewski's success. As Bergfelder observes, "Gloria's target audience was assumed to be primarily female.... Kubaschewski's trust in and reliance on her female constituency also explains why Gloria only reluctantly moved into producing more 'male' genres."[10]

Bergfelder compares Kubaschewski to the Fassbinder character Maria Braun because she epitomized both the social mobility and the conservative *Zeitgeist* of the economic miracle. Gloria's success was predicated on Kuba's notorious "nose" for the popular, her ability both to shape and cater to audience tastes. As the film historian Walther Schmieding notes, "The rise of Ilse Kubaschewski has often been ridiculed. She is seen as the trademark of innate German cinematic sentimentality, the embodiment of 'Lieschen Müller' taste, the prototype of the petit-bourgeois longing for kitsch and complete cluelessness about art. Her demeanor and affectations, particularly in the early years of her business, did nothing to dispel this image."[11] As a female player in a male industry, Kubaschewski worked hard to soften her image. Emphasizing her own domesticity, she invited reporters to visit her well-appointed homes, and she became famous as a hostess with the lavish Gloria Film Ball, a celebrity gala that she underwrote each year. In interviews, which she granted very rarely, she emphasized her "feminine instinct" and downplayed her business acumen.

Many stories circulated about Kubaschewski's notorious instinct: she was said to base her decisions on her own lowbrow taste; on consultations with her cook, chauffeur, and cleaning lady; and on the formula "*Heimat* + Song Title = Box Office Hit." Kuba's rules for success were often summarized in the press: "1. No unsympathetic lead characters 2. No flashbacks ('the audience doesn't get it') 3. Even with tragic or touching movies, always a happy ending ('people want to see something nice') 4. Many images of *Heimat*, many shots of animals ('it touches the heart') 5. Lots of music 6. 'Always something to laugh about.'"[12] Many of Gloria's top hits, from *The Heath is Green* to *The Trapp Family*, certainly followed these rules.

However, the longstanding stereotype of Kubaschewski as a peddler of sentimental stories masks not only her business expertise, but also the fact that Gloria's offerings were remarkably diverse: not only did the company serve up *Heimatfilme* and *Schlagerfilme*, but it achieved great success by introducing a new genre to postwar cinema with the war films *08/15* and *The Doctor of Stalingrad*. Kubaschewski also produced a number of critically acclaimed films, including the thriller *Nachts, wenn der Teufel kam* (*The Devil Came at Night*, 1957) and a film adaptation of Gustaf Gründgens's classic stage production *Faust* (1960), both of which won major film prizes.

Typecasting her as the "queen of schlock" also foregrounds Kubaschewski's success in the provincial film landscape of postwar Germany at the price of obscuring the transnational nature of her business practices. Just as she built up Gloria on the basis of transnational distribution deals, Kubaschewski's continued success derived from owning the lucrative West German rights to numerous classics of international cinema, including Tati's *Mon oncle* (1958), Fellini's *La dolce vita* (1960), and Visconti's *Ludwig* (1972). Moreover, Kubaschewski ensured the ongoing profitability of Gloria well into the 1970s, when it remained the last independent distributor in West Germany, by recognizing early on that "national cinema . . . is passé; a 'German film' is no longer attractive — not in Germany and certainly not abroad."[13] Thus she focused on developing international coproductions such as the popular *Angelique* series (1964–67), costume dramas that maintained a veneer of romantic respectability for Gloria's female audiences, while participating in the wave of soft-core sex films that helped revive the flagging West German film industry. Ultimately, the demise of the popular West German cinema caught up with Gloria, and the company began to fail when Kubaschewski continued her patented strategies of producing remakes, series, and star vehicles rather than investing in new technical innovations like widescreen that might have drawn audiences back to the cinemas. Nonetheless, Kubaschewski was able to sell Gloria in 1973 to an American television company for a profit, concluding a remarkable career as one of the most influential women in German film history.

See also:

- 27 May 1911: Asta Nielsen Secures Unprecedented Artistic Control
- 19 September 1958: Douglas Sirk's *A Time to Love and a Time to Die* Tests Limits of Postwar Feeling
- 4 September 1959: *Der Frosch mit der Maske* Moves Popular Cinema from Idyllic Pastures to Crime-Infested City Streets

Notes

[1] "Ilse Kubaschewski: Det greift ans Herz," *Der Spiegel* (23 January 1957): 38–44; here 38.

[2] On Kubaschewski's biography, see "Ilse Kubaschewski"; Annemarie Hassenkamp, "Der Filmboß — eine Frau: Ilse Kubaschewski," in Hassenkamp, *Frauen stehen ihren Mann: Porträts deutscher Unternehmerinnen* (Düsseldorf: Eugen Diederichs, 1966), 198–209; and Tim Bergfelder, *International Adventures: German Popular Cinema and European Co-Productions in the 1960s* (New York: Berghahn, 2005), 74–81.

[3] Bergfelder, *International Adventures*, 79.

[4] The affair between Kubaschewski and Waltleitner is mentioned briefly by Franz Marischka in his *"Immer nur lächeln": Geschichten und Anekdoten von Theater und Film* (Vienna: Amalthea, 2001), 161. My thanks to Waldleitner's biographer Ursula Kähler for clarifying in a personal e-mail the nature of his affair with Kubaschewski. See also her *Der Filmproduzent Ludwig Waldleitner: Leben und Werk im Kontext bundesrepublikanischer Zeit-, Film- und Produktionsgeschichte* (Frankfurt am Main: Peter Lang, 2007).

[5] Michael Töteberg, "Gloria, Die Schnulzenkönigin," in *Der rote Korsar: Traumwelt Kino der fünfziger und sechziger Jahre*, ed. Thomas Bertram (Essen: Klartext, 1998), 149–53; here 150.

[6] Claudia Dillmann-Kühn, *Artur Brauner und die CCC: Filmgeschäft, Produktionsalltag, Studiogeschichte 1946–1990* (Frankfurt am Main: Deutsches Filmmuseum, 1990), 58. In addition to Kubaschewski, these were the distributors Theo Osterwind, Herbert Tischendorf, and Kurt Schorcht, and the producers Walter Koppel, Arno Hauke, Kurt Ulrich, and Artur Brauner.

[7] Ibid., 51.

[8] "Ilse Kubaschewski," 44.

[9] Hassenkamp, "Vorwort," in Hassenkamp, *Frauen stehen ihren Mann*, 10–11.

[10] Bergfelder, *International Adventures*, 75–76.

[11] Walther Schmieding, *Kunst oder Kasse: Der Ärger mit dem deutschen Film* (Hamburg: Rütten & Loening, 1961), 138–39. Fabricated by the film industry to assist in development and marketing, "Lieschen Müller" embodied the prototypical (and notably female) film spectator and soon took on derogatory associations as the emblematic passive consumer of commercial entertainment culture in the postwar Federal Republic.

[12] "Ilse Kubaschewski," 39.

[13] Hassenkamp, "Der Filmboß," 202.

Peter Lorre stands at the crossroads of exile and homecoming. Publicity still for Der Verlorene. *Credit: Deutsche Kinemathek.*

16 February 1952: Peter Lorre Leaves Germany Again

Gerd Gemünden

ON 16 FEBRUARY 1952, Peter Lorre boarded a plane in Frankfurt am Main to return to the United States, carrying with him only a few personal items and a print of his most recent film, *Der Verlorene* (*The Lost One*, 1951).[1] In order to write, direct, and star in this film, Lorre had come to Germany in the fall of 1950, escaping financial troubles in Hollywood while hoping to revitalize a stalling American career in the country that had first made him an international star. Yet the mixed critical reviews of the film and its dismal box office cut short his aspirations, and a disillusioned Lorre bade a hasty farewell. Lorre's first departure from Germany nearly twenty years earlier had been a forced exit, one he shared with so many German-speaking Jewish film professionals; back then Lorre had famously quipped, "Germany is too small for two murderers like Hitler and me." His second departure was free of such dramatic symbols of defiance, but nevertheless traumatic in its own right.

Even among the artistically more ambitious films of the postwar years, *Der Verlorene* stands out for its stark realism (something the press kit labeled "Lor-realismus"), uncompromising pessimism, sudden plot twists, and many haunting close-ups of its protagonist, played by Lorre. The film is staged as a late-night dialogue in the canteen of a displaced persons camp near Hamburg, a reckoning of sorts, as we come to realize, between two men who call themselves Neumeister (Lorre) and Novak. They have assumed these names to extinguish their former identities (when they were called Dr. Rothe and Hoesch, respectively), but their chance meeting in the camp makes the past catch up with them. During the Third Reich, Rothe had become a sexual murderer, while Hoesch, a high-ranking Gestapo man, had covered up Rothe's crime because the organization deemed his medical research significant for the war effort. Now, four years later, Hoesch offers Rothe a pact of mutual silence. In voice-over flashback narration, Rothe and Hoesch reconstruct the past as complementing and competing voices. The frequent cuts between events in Hamburg 1943–44 and the camp in 1947 show how the past encroaches on the present: "The past cannot be neatly cordoned off but repeatedly reasserts itself as it perforates the present moment."[2] In the end Rothe shoots Hoesch. While his murder of his fiancé looked as if another soul had taken possession of him, this is a fully rational execution and followed up by Rothe stepping in front of an oncoming train: he is finally allowed the atonement for his deeds earlier denied him by the Nazis.

Revisiting the crimes of the Third Reich in a postwar setting places Lorre's film in the debates about a coming-to-terms with the past that inform so many post-1945 films. Yet in contrast to, say, *Die Mörder sind unter uns* (*The Murderers Are among Us*, 1946), . . . *und über uns der Himmel* (. . . *and the Sky above Us*, 1947), or *Zwischen Gestern und Morgen* (*Between Yesterday and Tomorrow*, 1947), *Der Verlorene* comes across as far less conciliatory and forward-looking, squarely refusing then-common gestures of *vergeben, vergessen, verdrängen* (forgiving, forgetting, repressing). Whereas the majority of the *Trümmerfilme* (rubble films) highlight timeless humanist values that were meant to facilitate, in time, the moving beyond the horrors of the Nazi past — which they usually portrayed as a period of aberration rather than one with concrete historical origins — Lorre's pessimistic and fatalistic portrait of postwar Germany draws uncanny continuities between the present and a past that refuses to go away, forcefully undermining the rhetoric of a clean break or *Stunde Null* (Zero Hour) that so many films then espoused.

As the only film he ever wrote and directed, *Der Verlorene* is also a journey through the personal film history of Peter Lorre, which in turn is itself emblematic of the experience of so many exile filmmakers. Thus the film revisits Lorre's role as serial killer from Fritz Lang's *M* (1931), which first established his international fame. Both films portray a city in a state of exception: while Lang depicts the mobilization of a paranoid populace that recalls a mobilization for war, Lorre shows the tear in the social fabric in a city suffering from constant air raids, hunger, and economic hardship. Yet it remains unclear why Lorre, who often complained how Hollywood's typecasting of him was influenced by *M*, would write such a similar role for himself in the one film where he was in command.[3]

Apart from its inflection with the rubble film, *Der Verlorene* shares many traits with the two genres with which Lorre (and many exile filmmakers) were most closely associated: film noir and the horror film. The chiaroscuro lighting of Lorre's many close-ups, the angled photography, the convoluted narrative, the flashback voiceover narration, and the overall feeling of doom and fatalism are hallmarks of 1940s films noir, many of which starred Lorre in important supporting roles. Equally strong are the traces of US horror film — a genre that, like noir, has strong antecedents in Weimar cinema. Lorre's uncanny, malicious, and deeply disturbing nature was first on full display in *Mad Love* (1935), where he plays a mad scientist, and followed up in his performances in *Arsenic and Old Lace* (1944) and *The Beast with Five Fingers* (1946), to name only the most well-known examples. As Lorre explained, the story of *Der Verlorene* was strongly influenced by Guy de Maupassant's story "La Horla" (1887), and the script's working title, *Das Untier* (The beast) was kept almost until the film was released. (In the script, the music that flares up each time Rothe is about to commit a murder is called the Horla motif.)

Beyond these generic influences from the many crossroads of German-American film history, the film remains highly self-reflexive about the historical reasons that made these cross-fertilizations of two national cinemas possible — the forced exile (and now potential remigration) of so many German-language film professionals. Its main setting is the displaced persons camp Elbe-Düwenstadt, which harbors refugees from the East, thus illustrating Dr. Rothe's/Lorre's own volatile status in West Germany; yet the location's somber past as a prisoner camp during the Third Reich, signaled by its still extant watchtowers and barbed wire, also suggests the fate that enemies of the state would have faced a few years earlier — people who now find shelter in the camp, including Jews like Lorre.

Lorre's syncretic style of filmmaking, his *Lor-realismus*, impressed a number of critics. Lotte Eisner called it the best German film since 1933. But the film fared poorly when it was first shown. The mixing of conventions derived from different genres (established in films Germans had had few opportunities to see) certainly contributed to its failure. But more importantly, the commercial flop of *Der Verlorene* proved for contemporary observers how out of touch Lorre was with what German audiences at that time sought in the movie theater. With the coming of the Berlin Blockade, films concerned with the past, which were never all that popular with German audiences to begin with, had run their course and been replaced by more upbeat or escapist fare — films like Hans Deppe's *Heimatfilm, Grün ist die Heide* (*The Heath is Green*), and Curt Goetz's comedy *Das Haus in Montevideo* (*The House in Montevideo*, both 1951). Indeed, Lorre was perceived as out of sync not only with German audiences, but with Germany at large. The 1951 failure of *Der Verlorene* marked the distance between the "emigrant" and those who had stayed inside the borders of the Third Reich. Whereas Lorre had meant to probe the wounds caused by the Hitler regime and to confront the murderers still in our midst, most Germans were eager to look forward rather than backward; they certainly did not want to heed the advice of someone who in their view had no right to speak, since he had not experienced the trauma of war on the home front. On a deeper but never fully articulated level, the presence of the emigrants must have caused feelings of shame for those who had followed the wrong leader;

after all, they provided unwanted proof that there had been alternatives. Lastly, the failure of Lorre and other remigrants may have also been caused by the discomfort they must have felt working side by side with film professionals who a few years prior had been in the service of Joseph Goebbels, for in no artistic sector were the continuities between the 1940s and 1950s more pronounced than in the film industry.

The reasons for a return to Germany varied among the remigrants. In Lorre's case it was primarily financial pressure as well as the desire to dodge police supervision of his drug habit, while Lang and William Dieterle hoped to escape black- or gray-listing by the House Un-American Activities Committee, and Robert Siodmak blamed his own return on the demise of the studio system. But Lorre's failed attempt at remigration was not an isolated case. On the contrary, most German-speaking exiles and émigrés who tried to get a foothold in the postwar West German film industry faced similar challenges. (This development stands in stark contrast to the successful remigration of Soviet exiles such as Konrad Wolf, Slatan Dudow, and Gustav von Wangenheim, who would find success at DEFA, Deutsche Film-Aktiengesellschaft, East Germany's state-owned film company.) While some came to similar conclusions as Lorre and left again, others acquiesced to popular tastes. Robert Siodmak won critical acclaim and the 1958 Federal Film Prize for *Nachts, wenn der Teufel kam* (*The Devil Strikes at Night*, 1958) — like Lorre's film also a drama about a serial killer during the Third Reich, but far less daring in its implication of German responsibility and personal guilt. His subsequent films included grossly commercial projects such as the Karl May adaptation, *Der Schut* (*Yellow Devil*, 1964) and a grandiose sandal epic, *Kampf um Rom* (*The Last Roman*, 1968). As Siodmak himself commented on his postwar German films, "I only want to entertain . . . and at any rate, the older generation has given up on itself."[4] Another somewhat successful, though less compromising returnee was Frank Wysbar, who had made a mark in the United States as television producer and scored a number of hits with German war films such as *Hunde, wollt ihr ewig leben* (*Stalingrad: Dogs, Do You Want to Live Forever?*, 1959) and *Nacht fiel über Gotenhafen* (*Darkness fell on Gotenhafen*, 1960), marking a modest success that had eluded him in the Hollywood film industry. Somewhat unique in the group of returning émigrés were Billy Wilder and Douglas Sirk; both made movies set in Germany for American studios, but used these experiences as mere dry-runs for a possible resettling before deciding to continue their careers in the United States (with Sirk ultimately retiring in Switzerland). The majority of directors, however, shared Lorre's fate. Fritz Lang, then still the most famous living German director, made three films in Germany in the late 1950s before returning to Hollywood for good. Two of them were produced by Artur Brauner, himself an exile (a native of Lodz, Poland, he survived the Holocaust by fleeing to the Soviet

Union), who would become a key figure for many returning émigrés and for German popular cinema in general. The young Alexander Kluge, a witness on the set of Lang's *Der Tiger von Eschnapur* (*The Tiger of Eschnapur*, 1959), was dismayed by Brauner's treatment of Lang and began developing his ideas of alternate models of filmmaking. *Die goldene Pest* (*The Golden Plague*, 1954) by John Brahm — who, like Siodmak, was known in the United States mostly for his contributions to film noir — specifically addresses the return to Germany from the United States; so too did Josef von Báky's *Der Ruf* (*The Last Illusion*, 1949), starring Fritz Kortner. While Kortner would find success again on the German stage, Brahm quickly returned to America, where he had a second career in television. Gerd Oswald, the son of Richard Oswald, also enjoyed an only short-lived German intermezzo, during which he made one film each for Artur Brauner and Luggi Waldleitner, before he returned to the United States. Suffering from Hollywood blacklisting for his "premature anti-fascism," William Dieterle returned to Germany in 1958. Like Wilder and Lang, Dieterle was a longtime Hollywood A-list filmmaker, with directing credits for almost seventy American films, yet in Germany he was forced to mostly work in television before returning to the theater where his career had begun in the 1920s. Reinhold Schünzel returned in 1949 and had some success as a stage and screen actor before he died in 1954 at age sixty-five. Wilhelm Thiele, creator of hit musical comedies such as *Die Drei von der Tankstelle* (*Three Good Friends*, 1930), also returned only for a two-year stint with limited success. If beyond these examples we also consider the many émigrés and exiles who never really wanted to return to Germany or Austria — including the likes of Otto Preminger, Fred Zinnemann, and Marlene Dietrich — we come to understand that exile was a ticket of no return.

See also:

- 11 May 1931: With Premiere of *M*, a Gala Hit Becomes a Cultural Controversy
- 18 February 1941: *The Devil and Daniel Webster* Puts American Politics on Trial
- 20 June 1977: DEFA's Biggest Star, Manfred Krug, Leaves the GDR

Notes

[1] The date is based on Stephen D. Youngkin's meticulously researched biography, *The Lost One: A Life of Peter Lorre* (Lexington: U of Kentucky P, 2005).

[2] Jennifer M. Kapczynski, *The German Patient: Crisis and Recovery in Postwar Culture* (Ann Arbor: U of Michigan P, 2008), 177.

³ On Lorre's typecasting in Hollywood, see Gerd Gemünden, "From 'Mr. M' to 'Mr. Murder': Peter Lorre and the Actor in Exile," in *Light Motives: German Popular Film In Perspective*, ed. Randall Halle and Margaret McCarthy (Detroit: Wayne State UP, 2003), 85–107.

⁴ Robert Siodmak, quoted in Joe Hembus, *Der deutsche Film kann gar nicht besser sein: Ein Pamphlet von gestern, eine Abrechnung von heute* (Munich: Rogner & Bernhard, 1981), 137. Ellipsis in the original.

13 January 1954: Preminger's Dual-Language *The Moon Is Blue* (1953) and *Die Jungfrau auf dem Dach* (1954) Seek Glocal Success

Christine Haase

ALTHOUGH THE 1950s were a decade of social, economic, and cultural reemergence and reconfiguration in many parts of the world, this was particularly true for Germany following the devastations of the Second World War. Progressive and conservative forces competed with each other to shape postwar society. By the late 1940s, the critical introspective phase of the *Trümmerfilm* (rubble film) genre had ended, and by the early fifties, the West German film industry had largely settled comfortably into making uncritical and escapist movies for light entertainment, such as the *Schlagerfilm* (contemporary musical comedies — literally, a hit-song movie), historical films, period romances like the *Sissi* series, and, most popular of all, the burgeoning *Heimatfilm* genre. These productions offered distractions with displays of beautiful landscapes and nature scenes, frequently a nostalgic emphasis on premodernist folkloristic culture, and a focus on love and family values. They reaffirmed the existence of a positive "Germanness," distinct and independent from the disastrous version that had been proffered by the National Socialists. These films also arguably helped the nation's healing process by reflecting and mediating, in however veiled a fashion, a variety of new realities in postwar Germany: urban-rural tensions over discrepancies in the food supply; the influx of millions of German refugees from the East; generational conflicts; crises of masculinity and the changing roles of women in general (in a country particularly deprived of men). Yet if these popular films made some acknowledgement of the growing number of working women and the fate of single mothers (often war widows), their heroines, after enjoying initial displays of independence and glimpses of gender equality, habitually returned to the traditional roles of wife and mother at the narratives' end. Candid and enlightened considerations of sexuality and gender politics were near nonexistent in 1950s cinema.

Despite these offerings, German audiences longed for films that looked forward as well: films that explored the resumption of modernity and urbanity, representations of international and contemporary lifestyles — in short, works that offered an escape from national provincialism, isolation, and solipsism. Concurrent with the period's increasing conservatism in the arena of sexual politics (which for a large swath of the German population, as Dagmar Herzog has shown, was actually *more*, not less, restrictive than Nazi Germany),[1] many (especially younger) Germans had a particular interest in the investigation of gender roles and relations. One such investigation was offered in an entertaining and lighthearted yet uncommonly frank and provocative manner by émigré Hollywood director Otto Preminger.

Born in 1905 to Jewish parents in what was then Austro-Hungary, Preminger had left Vienna for America in 1935. In 1952, he embarked on the production of a film set in New York and made in two language versions, *The Moon Is Blue* and *Die Jungfrau auf dem Dach* (The virgin on the roof). This work succeeded in combining the modern and international with a reassuring form of gender interaction that was on the one hand excitingly progressive and sexually open, while on the other — in spite of first appearances — soothingly conservative, traditional, and "family friendly." With this double focus, the films partook in a Janus-faced discourse of preserving the established and welcoming the new that characterized much of the fifties, while also succeeding in negotiating and partially reconciling these opposing tendencies in the course of the narrative. While German society would not come to terms with these contradictions until the political and cultural turmoil of the sixties and seventies, *The Moon Is Blue/Die Jungfrau auf dem Dach* arguably foreshadowed seminal shifts in the sexual and gender politics of their respective cultures and directly impacted the portrayal of and discourse about sexuality in the cinema, not least through their resolute challenge to the Hays Code.[2] Although this proved popular with many audiences on both sides of the Atlantic, it also caused a lot of trouble for the production in the United States. A consideration of the sociopolitical contexts and public reception of the films offers insight into the changing sexual-cultural climates of Germany and America during the fifties and beyond.

The plot of both films is a sexual comedy of manners about a young woman who, pursued by two suitors (a womanizing young architect and a grey-templed charmer), sets the men against each other by declaring that she wants to marry a rich older divorcee who "appreciates" her rather than "drools" over her, and that she plans to remain a virgin until then. Both versions were produced simultaneously in the United States, with the lead actors — William Holden, David Niven, and Maggie McNamarra in the English version, and Hardy Krüger, Johannes Heesters, and Johanna Matz in the German one — taking turns performing on the same sets throughout the filming. The practice of such double shooting had become popular in Europe after the introduction of sound in the late twenties and remained common until about the midthirties. During its heyday, over thirty percent of European sound films were shot in multiple language versions, primarily for English-, German-, and French-speaking markets. The main goal of the practice here was to bolster against the American domination of European film markets. In the United States, double shooting was also popular and remained common well into the fifties. However, stateside it usually meant altering the content and visuals of an American film in preparation for export and was generally undertaken to loosen some of the restrictions placed on a production by the Hays Code — that is, the films were commonly made more sexually explicit in terms of language, content, and visuals for comparatively less prudish foreign markets. As film historian Kerry Segrave states: "Those films were shot vividly for export, and vapidly for domestic consumption."[3] Even though popular, widespread, and well-documented today, the practice, as it did not reflect favorably on Hollywood and the sincerity of the Production Code's moral impetus, was firmly denied in its day by the industry.[4]

Otto Preminger's own double production of *The Moon Is Blue* represented a significant twin act of defiance for the director, who remained at the forefront of challenges to the Production Code throughout the 1950s: firstly, the project marked the beginning of his career as an independent producer-director; secondly, he categorically refused to alter his English-language version to make it comply with the Hays Code (which the MPAA had made stricter in 1951, spelling out even more banned words and subjects). Preminger released his film without the official stamp of approval by the censors, thus directly attacking the authority of the Production Code and, since the movie was highly successful, substantially accelerating its demise. All of this also meant that, in an interesting reversal of the conventions of the Hollywood double production, the director adapted the American version's moral and linguistic standards to those of the commonly more liberal export version. That is, rather than making the American film more constrained and prudish as had been demanded of him, Preminger decided to make the US production just as risqué as the German-language one (however nonrisqué it may seem today).

As a consequence, *The Moon Is Blue* provoked a storm of controversy in America as the first mainstream post-1934 Hollywood film to use "obscene" words such as "sex," "virgin," "pregnant," "seduce," and "mistress," as well as for allegedly ridiculing parental rules for safeguarding the female protagonist's virtue. The Catholic Legion of Decency, an influential American lobbying power, stamped the film "C" for Condemned and it was banned from cinemas in Maryland, Boston, and various other municipal and state areas. Yet rather than hurt the production at the box office, the scandal resulted in a financial success for Preminger and his film was nominated for three Academy Awards, revealing a considerable gap between the standards and prudishness of the public guardians of morals and the views of mainstream American audiences. That version, scripted by playwright F. Hugh Herbert based on his successful Broadway play of the same title, premiered on 3 June 1953. *Die Jungfrau auf dem Dach*, adapted by Carl Zuckmayer, who twenty-five years earlier had written the script for another sexually provocative film, *Der blaue Engel* (*The Blue Angel*, 1930), premiered in Germany on 13 January 1954. In this case, the production met with popular success while inciting none of the public outrage that characterized the American run. This may have indicated greater agreement between official and private assessments of what was considered decent and moral.[5] It seems more likely, though, that the film entered into West German culture at an opportune right moment — coming a few years after a film scandal that had already put public and personal views to the test.

That earlier film was *Die Sünderin* (*The Sinner*, 1951), which caused an outcry reminiscent of the American struggle over *The Moon Is Blue* (albeit involving a more readily discernible offense). Upon its release, official censorship bodies, the Catholic Church, the film industry, and audiences had notoriously clashed over the Hildegard Knef vehicle, which featured the first (however chaste) nude scene in a mainstream German movie, and raised the controversial subjects of suicide and euthanasia (which, given National Socialist practices, caused more outrage than almost any other issue). During the early postwar years, church circles in Germany had already crusaded against the "degenerative moral effect" of feature films in general and then against *Die Sünderin* in particular, without any effect on the film's success. On the contrary: the production became a box office hit partly because it had caused such a scandal. By comparison, Preminger's film — which deployed some sexually charged vocabulary — simply lacked the power to shock.

Clearly, in spite of the fifties' common reputation as a period of conservatism and restoration of traditional Christian morals, progressive and liberalizing developments had their share in shaping German society during that decade, and cast long shadows on those that followed. In fact, it may have been precisely the mixture of preservation of the established *and* a search for the new — as in Preminger's comedy — that defined both the political and cultural life of West Germany and America during the time. Such a contradictory pull between conservatism, on the one hand, and liberalization, on the other, characterized the cultures of both countries, often manifesting itself in the cultural sphere and frequently coming into focus in the realm of sexuality and gender relations, topics that were prevalent in society but largely taboo in the media.

The American objections Preminger's film received were remarkable for their attention to semantics rather than deeds: the public objected principally to what the actors *said* on screen, and not what they *did*. In spite of its "hot" topic, the film remained visually chaste. On the level of speech, the actors frankly bandied about such terms as sex, seduction, virginity, mistress, and pregnancy, but none of this liberal talk was reflected in any way on the level of action. A demure kiss on the lips remains the most sexual thing that happens, and the female lead is ultimately validated as virtuous when she earns respect and a wedding proposal from the seemingly debauched yet good-hearted older playboy (David Niven/ Johannes Heesters), and then the hand of the attractive young bachelor (William Holden/Hardy Krüger) at the film's conclusion. The production thus engages in a clever double-voiced discourse — namely, that of the plot's dialogue versus that of the plot's actions, a split that many viewers clearly appreciated while protesters did not. At the level of action, the production reaffirms the "family values" and Christian morals of West German and American society of the fifties, offering the message that virtue will be rewarded and true love will triumph over rationalism and modern materialism — a preoccupation of many cinematic works from the fifties, including, for example, *How to Marry a Millionaire*. At the level of speech, the film allows for a modern, provocative, sexually open, and experimental exchange between the sexes, without risk or real-life consequences. As a result, audiences could enjoy liberal sexual banter and nonprudish dialogue about a highly relevant contemporary topic without having to commit to the accompanying lifestyles of such talk and without having to abandon conventional and publicly validated life models. In short, the film's success rests at least partially on its ability to offer audiences the best of two opposing yet conjoined worlds. Both film versions partake in this double-voiced discourse of preserving the established and celebrating the new that marked the decade — thereby at least partially reconciling and transcending the two worlds on a fictional level. In real life, these contradictions remained largely irreconcilable and continued to fester, manifesting themselves on political and cultural levels in relatively contained ways until they ultimately coalesced and erupted in the social upheavals of the sixties and seventies. *The Moon Is Blue* and *Die Jungfrau auf dem Dach* are intriguing as cultural products because they represent proverbial canaries in the coalmine, alternately outraging and enticing, frightening and exciting viewers, precisely because they offered a foretaste of the future and the social and cultural sea changes that lay ahead.

See also:

- 31 January 1929: Limits on Racial Border-Crossing Exposed in *Piccadilly*
- 29 May 1929: Oscar for Emil Jannings Highlights Exchange between German and American Film Industries

- 25 February 2007: *Das Leben der Anderen* Follows Blueprint for Foreign-Language Oscar Success

Notes

[1] Dagmar Herzog, *Sex After Fascism: Memory and Morality in Twentieth Century Germany* (Princeton: Princeton UP, 2005).

[2] Officially called "Production Code," but often referred to as Hays Code after Will Hays, head of the MPPDA (Motion Picture Producers and Distributors of America, today known as the MPAA, or Motion Picture Association of America) and the Code's creator. The Production Code governed what was and was not morally acceptable in cinematic productions. It restricted screen language, behavior, and visuals primarily in regard to sexuality, crime, and death. The Production Code was a voluntary code of conduct that all major Hollywood studios — the members of the MPPDA — adhered to until about the late 1950s. After that, there was a constant increase in the number of films that violated the Code (domestic ones as well as foreign ones that were not bound by it to begin with), until it became impossible and meaningless to uphold it. The Code, in effect from 1930 but enforced only as of 1934, was finally abandoned in 1967 and subsequently replaced by the MPAA's age-related ratings system in 1968, which is still in place today.

[3] Kerry Segrave, *American Films Abroad: Hollywood's Domination of the World's Movie Screens* (Jefferson, NC: McFarland, 1997), 197.

[4] See Segrave, *American Films*, esp. 197–98.

[5] Preminger's success was not representative for the German reception of returning expatriates, who were often given a decidedly cold shoulder.

9 March 1954: *Ernst Thälmann — Sohn seiner Klasse* Marks High Point of Socialist Realism

Hunter Bivens

Striding forward to his death, Ernst Thälmann sets the course for the future of the GDR. Ernst Thälmann – Führer seiner Klasse *(1955). DVD capture.*

Director Kurt Maetzig's two-part biopic of Ernst Thälmann, the Hamburg dockworker who led the Communist Party of Germany (KPD) from 1925 until his arrest by the Nazis in 1933, closes with a scene that uncannily stages both the triumphant and the symptomatic registers of East German socialist realism. On the eve of Soviet victory, Thälmann is marched from his cell by two SS guards to be shot. "Well," says one, "you know what's coming, right?" With a steely gaze, directed into an undefined space between the camera and the SS man he is addressing,

Thälmann replies, "Yes, a better Germany, a Germany without you." As Thälmann is escorted down the corridor of the Berlin prison where he has been interred for eleven years, a voice-over intones a quote from Nikolai Ostrovsky's classic Soviet novel *How the Steel Was Tempered*, reminding us that, in the final instance, a human life can be measured against its dedication to the liberation of mankind. Now the SS guards behind Thälmann and the corridor itself are replaced by a fluttering red flag, in front of which Thälmann continues to march, his stern visage and piercing gaze directed into the future: the film's present, where the building of socialism on German soil redeems his ultimate sacrifice.

Consider for a moment what is actually shown in this closing sequence: with the effacement of the backdrop as a point of orientation for the spectatorial gaze, the forward movement of Günther Simon, playing Thälmann, likewise loses its directionality. He approaches the camera as far as a medium close-up and remains at this distance, where his gaze seems blank rather than determined. In this image, the historical telos has been reduced to its zero degree, and the only signifiers of motion are Simon's zombie-like marching in place and the graceful undulations of the red flag. Thälmann seems more undead than immortal, an intuition that is supported by the score, a Wagnerian rendering of the propaganda song "Thälmann Never Died," as though only the filmmaker's own discovery of an ideologically adequate account of Thälmann's life would allow him to come to rest. These two readings of the scene reveal the fault line of Maetzig's *Ernst Thälmann — Sohn seiner Klasse* (Ernst Thälmann — Son of his class, 1954) and *Ernst Thälmann — Führer seiner Klasse* (Ernst Thälmann — Leader of his class, 1955): the heroic depiction of socialist martyrdom, on the one hand, and the uncanny rendering of a historical and political impasse on the other, overdetermined by the uncertain status of the film as fiction *and* history.

The GDR struggled to assert its political legitimacy throughout the Cold War. As the West surged ahead economically in the 1950s, the ruling Socialist Unity Party (SED) increasingly turned to recent history as the justification for a second German state. Following in the footsteps of "Teddy," who had presciently warned against the dangers of fascism during the Weimar Republic and remained unbroken during his long imprisonment at the hands of the Nazis, the SED represented this better Germany even as the Federal Republic was argued to embody Germany's fascist past. In this context, Thälmann was commemorated in speeches, schoolbooks, and public memorials, becoming a sort of public myth standing for the legacy of German resistance to National Socialism. Essentially, the Thälmann cult did two things for the SED. First, it supported the party's claim to embody the legacy of German resistance and persecution under the Nazi regime, as Thälmann's story was increasingly used to crowd out the antifascist claims of other groups, especially those of Europe's Jews, after the late

1940s. Secondly, even as Thälmann (who had played a leading role in the "Stalinization" of the KPD) stood for unquestioning loyalty to the USSR, at the largely unspoken level of the social imaginary, he paradoxically sustained the fantasy of a German socialism different from the coercive model that took hold in the 1950s.[1] If, as Patrick Hall has argued, the nation itself is essentially "a social relation of knowledge and power" masquerading as a "historical subject," Thälmann's image, with his leather jacket and workingman's cap, was the public face of the SED's claim to leadership of the better, antifascist German nation.[2]

The Thälmann film can be read as a test case for the development of the film industry in the GDR's first decade. Plans for the film began in 1949, and from the beginning the Thälmann project was a top priority of the party, with General Secretary Walter Ulbricht personally making corrections to the screenplay.[3] In these years the relative openness that had marked the East German film scene since the founding of the DEFA (Deutsche Film-Aktiengesellschaft, East Germany's state-owned film company) in 1946 was coming to a close. Between 1947 and 1953, the SED sought to impose its views on culture through a variety of campaigns, party and state conferences and commissions, and direct censorship. These methods provoked a crisis for DEFA.[4] While the studio did produce of number of more or less successful films tackling contemporary themes from a socialist perspective, for example Slatan Dudow's *Frauenschicksale* (*The Destinies of Women*, 1952), such films remained the exception, and DEFA's output sunk to a mere six feature films that year. Bureaucratic and ideological roadblocks effectively strangled the studio. In this context, Maetzig, who had intended a film "about a worker who despite great difficulties finds his personal path in political life,"[5] ended up directing a two-part epic that used Thälmann as a symbolic figure to "recreate the entire history of the twentieth-century German workers' movement."[6] While the premier of the first Thälmann film in 1954 was celebrated in the East German public sphere as the highpoint of German socialist realist cinema, the death of Stalin the year before had already led to a de facto relaxation of cultural life in the GDR and a turn to a more quotidian aesthetics in the cinema. The Thälmann films are therefore simultaneously exemplary and exceptional in the annals of GDR film.

Socialist realism was formulated as an aesthetic method at the First All-Union Congress of Soviet Writers in 1934. In his opening speech, Andrei Zhdanov outlined two thematic criteria for socialist realist aesthetics. First, "in our country, the main heroes of works of literature are the active builders of a new life," and second, art should depict life "in its revolutionary development."[7] These two criteria were codified in socialist realist aesthetics as that of popularity and partisanship: on the one hand, a commitment to art's accessibility to the broad masses, and a Marxist-Leninist perspective, on the other. At the same time, the categories of socialist realism always remained vaguely defined. Leonid Heller has argued that the history of socialist realism is a story of unending debates on a limited number of fundamental formal and thematic antinomies. The system and practice of socialist realism was thus "always at once static and constantly changing."[8] This fundamental formlessness of aesthetic categories and endless debate became as much a feature of cultural discourse in the GDR during the 1950s as it was in the USSR. Soviet socialist realism in the 1930s was still capable of drawing on the energies of the October Revolution and the suppressed Soviet avant-garde to produce works that communicated the enthusiasm of "building a new life." By the late 1940s and early 1950s, however, this method had already ossified into an aesthetics of Stalinist monumentalism, and its introduction into the cultural life of the GDR as the socialist realism of the 1950s functioned as an aesthetics of containment.

On a formal level, this can be seen in the numerous crowd scenes in the Thälmann films in contrast to similar moments in Eisenstein or Vertov, or for that matter Slatan Dudow's 1932 *Kuhle Wampe* (with a screenplay by Bertolt Brecht), which Maetzig cites in *Führer seiner Klasse*, scoring a demonstration of striking miners in the Ruhr with the Brecht-Eisler "Solidarity Song." Whereas the crowd scenes of *Kuhle Wampe* had emphasized the collective and mobile character of the masses, those in both Thälmann films serve to emphasize the hierarchical relationship of the working class to the party: we see Thälmann leading the march, or we see Thälmann addressing the masses, in a shot/reverse-shot pattern that juxtaposes Simon's direct yet avuncular oratory stylings with the receptively nodding faces of the crowd. Thälmann is front or center; sometimes he is both at once. Furthermore, the critical realist proletarian films of the 1920s and 1930s had relied on montage, juxtaposing imagery not only to produce specific ideological associations in the spectator, but also to mimetically suggest the acceleration of time itself in a revolutionary situation. Socialist realist cinema tends to the opposite, to long takes, but not in the sense that André Bazin, for example, advocated as the sine qua non of cinematic realism. Rather than attuning the spectator to the ambiguity of the world, its "cruelty and ugliness," and above all contingency of events, socialist realist films tend to portray political speeches, historical battles, and even everyday labor processes, "staged like living paintings."[9] The painterly quality of the film also comes across in its use of color, which is more symbolic than realistic, depending on a pallet where a brilliant red repeatedly erupts like the revolution itself from the drab brown-grays of factories and tenements while the forces of counterrevolution and fascism appear in range of uncanny tones of green.

Freezing the montage-driven velocity of the socially-critical realist aesthetic of Weimar-era avant-garde and proletarian films into the carefully arranged cinematic tableaux of later socialist realism, works like the Thälmann films evoke the historical certainty of Marxist-Leninist doctrine against the messiness of the historical record. Here too, socialist realism is an aesthetic of containment, since most of what is related in the Thälmann films is heavily fictionalized. The striking sequence of the KPD's 1923 uprising in Hamburg, for example, is almost completely fabricated. Far from planning and leading the uprising, Thälmann was at most a marginal figure.[10] Furthermore, one of the film's central protagonists, Fiete Jansen, played by a game Hans-Peter Minetti, is also fictive. While there is nothing specifically socialist realist about fictionalizing aspects of history in the cinema, there is something curious about the work that Fiete does in these films. Jansen provides a point of identification for the viewer, since Simon's portrayal of Thälmann remains largely closed to spectatorial empathy. Fiete, on the other hand, enables the film to introduce elements of character development and romance.[11] The Thälmann films can thus also be read as socialist realist action movies.[12] This tension between mobility, agency, and action, on the one hand, and stasis, inertia, and confinement, on the other, shapes the second film, *Führer seiner Klasse*, where Thälmann is arrested in the first hour. While Thälmann languishes in prison, Fiete fights in the Spanish civil war, accepts the German surrender in Stalingrad, and, while liberating a forced labor camp on the Eastern Front, heals the historic division between German Communists and Social Democrats. In other words, Fiete is Thälmann's fictional supplement, allowing the films to symbolically undo the very real political and historical immobilization of the KPD. The images of Thälmann's confinement allow the film to recognize, while discursively disavowing, both the truth that it was not German Communists but the Red Army who defeated National Socialism, and that the Soviet liberators themselves arrived with their hands bloodied by the Great Purges, the victims of which included many German Communists who had fled to the USSR to escape Hitler.[13] The KPD's impasse in the thirties and forties had taken a different form in the 1950s, and the fundamental contradiction of this decade is that between the unprecedented social transformation and mobility unleashed by the building of socialism in the GDR and the rigid and coercive political form in which that emancipation took place. If the Jansen character is a narrative attempt to sidestep these diachronic and synchronic contradictions, this reading of the Thälmann films' closing scene shows their return at the formal level. Properly read, the artworks of the 1950s, the GDR's most ideologically orthodox cultural period, are powerful hermeneutic tools for revealing the lacunae of the East German social imaginary.

See also:

- 17 October 1930: Bertolt Brecht's *Threepenny Opera* Lawsuit Identifies Contradiction between Individual Creativity and Collective Production in Cinema

- 1 February 1968: Konrad Wolf's *Ich war neunzehn* Evokes an East German Nation in Transition
- 20 June 1977: DEFA's Biggest Star, Manfred Krug, Leaves the GDR

Notes

[1] Annette Leo, "Liturgie statt Erinnerung: Die Schaffung eines Heldenbildes am Beispiel Ernst Thälmanns," in *Ernst Thälmann: Mensch und Mythos* (German Monitor No. 52), ed. Peter Monheath (Amsterdam: Rodopi, 2000): 22, 18.

[2] Patrick Hall, "Nationalisms and History," *Nations and Nationalism* 3, no. 1 (1997): 3–24; here 3. Cited in Susan Hayward. "Framing National Cinemas," in *Cinema and Nation,* ed. Mette Hjort and Scott MacKenzie (New York: Routledge, 2000), 91.

[3] Russell Lemmons, "'Great Truths and Minor Truths': Kurt Maetzig's *Ernst Thälmann* Films, the Antifascist Myth, and the Politics of Biography in the German Democratic Republic," in *Framing the Fifties: Cinema in a Divided Germany* (Film Europa: German Cinema in an International Context, volume 4), ed. John Davidson and Sabine Hake (New York: Berghahn, 2007), 96–97.

[4] Ralf Schenk, "Mitten im Kalten Krieg, 1950 bis 1960," in *Das zweite Leben der Filmstadt Babelsberg: DEFA-Spielfilme 1946–1992*, ed. Ralf Schenk (Berlin: Henschel, 1994), 64.

[5] Martin Brady, "Discussion with Kurt Maetzig," in *DEFA: East German Cinema, 1946–1992*, ed. Seán Allan and John Sandford (New York: Berghahn, 1999), 84.

[6] Lemmons, "'Great Truths and Minor Truths,'" 96.

[7] A. A. Zhdanov, "Soviet Literature — the Richest in Ideas, the Most Advanced Literature," in *Problems in Soviet Literature: Reports and Speeches at the First Soviet Writers' Congress*, ed. H. G. Scott (Westport, CT: Hyperion 1981), 20–21.

[8] Leonid Heller, "A World of Prettiness: Socialist Realism and its Aesthetic Categories," trans. John Hendriksen, in *Socialist Realism Without Shores*, ed. Thomas Lahusen and Evgeny Dobrenko (Durham: Duke UP), 56–57.

[9] André Bazin, "The Evolution of the Language of Cinema," trans. Hugh Gray, in *What Is Cinema?*, vol. 1, ed. Hugh Gray (Berkeley: U of California P, 2005), 27; Schenk, "Mitten im Kalten Krieg," 108.

[10] Erich Wollenberg, "Thälmann — Film und Wirklichkeit," in *Ernst Thälmann: Mensch und Mythos*, 115–16.

[11] Schenk, "Mitten im Kalten Krieg," 78.

[12] Joshua Feinstein, *Triumph of the Ordinary: Depictions of Daily Life in the East German Cinema, 1949–1989* (Chapel Hill: U of North Carolina P, 2002), 39.

[13] Leo, "Liturgie statt Erinnerung," 28.

22 December 1955: *Sissi* Trilogy Bridges Hapsburg to Hollywood through Hybrid Blend of Film Genres

David Bathrick

Ingenue Romy Schneider strikes a regal pose in Sissi: Die junge Kaiserin *(1956). DVD capture.*

THE PRODUCTION OF the *Sissi* trilogy about the Austrian Empress Elizabeth (1837–98) gave birth to a plethora of legends. As the three most commercially successful Austrian films of the 1950s with nineteen million tickets sold in 1956 alone, the three films — *Sissi* (1955), *Sissi, die junge Kaiserin* (*Sissi, The Young Empress*, 1956), and *Sissi — Schicksalsjahre einer Kaiserin* (*Sissi, The Fateful Years of the Empress*, 1957) — came to achieve what would be called blockbuster status today. For director and scriptwriter Ernst Marischka, the *Sissi* trilogy proved to be a crowning achievement cinematically, solidifying his iconic status as the creator of *Marischka* films — almost a genre in itself — while making him a millionaire. The sixteen-year-old Romy Schneider, who played the lead in all three films, achieved with *Sissi I* international stardom — a legacy that was famously to haunt her right up to her early death at the age of forty-three. Finally, Schneider's captivating embodiment of the historical "Sisi" (one "s") succeeded in remythologizing a figure whose assassination at the hands of an anarchist in 1898 had already helped fashion a cult image interestingly at odds with Romy's homage to her some sixty years later. The happy end to *Sissi III* gives closure to a trilogy that does not include diegetically the final, troubled thirty-one years of Sisi's life. Nor does this passionate fairytale of love and the wonders of magisterial power even start to grapple with Austrian or German realities ten years after the Second World War.[1]

The *Sissi* trilogy's production schedule of one film a year for three consecutive years enabled rapid organizational rollover that in turn contributed to a high level of cohesion within the trilogy as a whole. In contrast to the often considerably longer lapses within such classical film trilogies as *The Godfather* (1972, 1974, 1990), *Star Wars* (1977, 1980, 1983), and *Jurassic Park* (1993, 1997, 2001) — not to mention Fritz Lang's *Dr. Mabuse* (1922, 1933, 1960) — the internal continuity informing *Sissi*'s narrative patterns, casting configuration (the main characters in all three parts remain the same, as do the actors who play them), and mise-en-scène, together with its focus on the family as the nexus of ethnic, geographical, and national articulations of *Heimat*, lend to this trilogy the feel of a television miniseries, if not a soap opera. A brief plot summary makes these connections clear:

The *Sissi* story is set in motion by the desire of Duchess Sophie to find a suitable wife for her son Franz Joseph, the Emperor of Austria. Her choice of Princess Nene, the oldest daughter of her Sister Ludovika, the Duchess of Bavaria, finds favor with both families and a meeting is arranged at the Hapsburg Court in Vienna in order to facilitate an engagement. On the first day of their visit in Vienna, Nene's younger sister Sissi sneaks off to do some fishing in a nearby stream and ends up running into the Emperor, who invites her to take a stroll through the woodlands. Neither are aware of who the other is. Both fall deeply in love and on the following day Franz Joseph announces to an astonished court, and to the absolute consternation of his mother, his intention to marry the somewhat untamed Sissi rather than the more docile Nene. Part I ends with the glorious wedding.

Parts II and III consist of reenactments and resolutions of the underlying conflicts introduced in part I. Duchess Sophie finds fault with the new Empress due to the latter's unwillingness to follow a Court protocol that she considers arbitrary. When Sissi gives birth to a daughter,

Sophie insists on removing her from the mother's care due to Sissi's lack of experience in child rearing. Sissi rebels and returns to her home in Bavaria without the child. Franz Joseph finally confronts his mother by abandoning the Court to fetch back his Empress. Sissi and Franz Joseph return to Vienna via a brief "second honeymoon" sojourn in the Austrian Alps. Once back in the Court, Sissi finds political cause in supporting the Hungarian struggle for freedom, whereupon Franz makes her Empress of Hungary, which in turn provides another place of refuge from the wicked mother-in-law. Sissi's final flight in part III is caused by her contracting a potentially fatal lung disease, the cure for which turns out to be months of convalescence on the island of Corfu under the loving care of her mother Ludovico and, finally, the arrival of her ever beloved Franz Joseph. The Emperor will once again bring his Empress back to her "second homeland" — this time by way of a brief stopover and triumphant public appearance on the Piazzo de Marco in Venice, which serves as the grand performative finale to the trilogy.

In placing *Sissi* within the cultural and political landscape of Austrian and German cinema of the postwar period, it is helpful to consider this trilogy in relation to a number of the film genres prevailing at the time. The most compelling superficially is the biopic or what the Germans call the *Historienfilm*.[2] Here two characteristics were definitive that would apply to all three *Sissi* films as well: on the thematic level, the treatment of historically significant and, one must also add, mythically coded figures such as found in films like *Erzherzog Johanns große Liebe* (*Arch Duke Johann's Great Love*, 1950), *Maria Therese* (1951), *Mozart* (1955), and *Ludwig II* (1955).

Even more vital for understanding the box office appeal of Ernst Marischka's versions of the *Historienfilm*, however, was their visual and aural grandeur at the level of mise-en-scène and staging. In the *Sissi* trilogy we are offered lavish sets, extravagant costumes (Sissi's wig was said to have weighed thirteen pounds), excessive pomp and circumstance, magisterial musical accompaniment, and long takes of ceremonial celebration, in which any pretense of a linear narrative gets folded into raw spectacle. This last point was particularly important for all three parts of *Sissi*. While Marischka's script scrupulously adhered to individual "facts" in the historical Sisi's life (her engagement with Hungary, her love for horses, her tendency to flee the court and her mother-in-law, the struggle with the Duchess about raising her child),[3] what he ended up doing diegetically was to rewind these "working points" (*Eckpunkte*), as he called them, into repeated operatic patterns of conflict and withdrawal, followed by ever-more-dramatically redemptive returns by the Empress to her "second" familial and national *Heimat*, the Hapsburg Court.

The *Sissi* trilogy's links to the operetta may be explained in part by the fact that Marischka's engagement with the *Sissi* material began when he and his brother Hubert were conscripted in 1932 to write the libretto for Fritz Kreisler's composition of the immensely popular operetta *Sissi*, which has been described as "a romantic retelling of the courtship of Princess Elizabeth of Bavaria by the young Emperor Franz Joseph."[4] Marischka's borrowings from this operetta for his *Sissi* film, however, go well beyond the plot. The frequent resorting to slapstick and comic relief work to defuse the occasional melodramatic leanings within the story itself, just as the famous "opera scene" in *Sissi II* — where Sissi, Franz Joseph, and mother Sophia appear in public at an opera in order to offset rumors of dissension within the royal family — offers a momentary mise-en-abyme (opera within an operetta) in which the film audience gets to watch the action on the stage from the Emperor's box.

While *Sissi* draws heavily from the topoi of the biopic, the operetta, and even the *Wienerfilm* (Vienna film) in its look back at grander traditions in search of cultural and political legitimation for an Austria and a Germany still reeling from total defeat, it is above all the *Heimatfilm* that leaves the deepest generic imprint. *Sissi I* opens in Possenhofen — a castle (and town) located on the western shore of Lake Starnberg in Southern Bavaria — with a pan across the breathtaking mountain skyline, forest, and lake, accompanied by the diegetic sound and subsequently sight of four male yodeling singers in traditional Bavarian dress paddling a raft. Possenhofen is Sissi's bucolic home and the center of her family's rural identity. It is she and her thoroughly rustic father, Duke Max, who at two portentous moments at the beginning of the trilogy will give voice to the credo defining their notion of *Heimat* that is so basic to the competing binaries of the trilogy as a whole:

> Whenever sorrow and trouble enter your life, open your eyes and take a walk like this through the woods. And every tree and every bush, every animal and every flower will remind you of the almighty power of God and, you will find solace and strength to go on.

Daddy (*Päperle*) Max says these words to Sissi shortly before she departs for the Viennese Court. Sissi emphatically repeats them verbatim to the Emperor on their very first walk through the woods, foreshadowing narratively that in moments of greatest crisis, the couple-to-be always have to go back to nature (and ultimately *Heimat*) to restore their undying commitment to each other.

And how do the repeated crises in the *Sissi* trilogy relate to its status as a *Heimatfilm*? The plot summary above identifies the major narrative turning points revolving around the reoccurring conflicts between Princess Sophie and her truculent daughter-in-law. While such figural confrontations further the action at a dramaturgical level, they also give voice to more basic opposing values vis-à-vis work and everyday life that are central to the postwar *Heimat* ethos.

What the Hapsburg Court intermittently comes to represent for Sissi, in marked contrast to her cherished Possenhofen, is an oppressive world of *Staatsraison* (reasons of state), a denial of genuine spontaneity, and, *most* problematically, a rigid separation of the public and private sphere. In her discussion of the *Heimatfilm* of the 1950s, Heide Fehrenbach stresses the "integrative" qualities of the notion of *Heimat* since the turn of the nineteenth Century: "Encompassing both communal and personal identity, it denotes homeland, home and hearth — with all of their myriad meanings and emotional associations."[5]

In exploring the various strands of thematic and generic patterns that have been woven into this profoundly hybrid *Marischka* film, the goal has been to emphasize the extent to which it cannot be reduced to monolithic meaning. As historical biopic and *Heimatfilm*, it is linked to traditions in German culture extending from the middle of the nineteenth century through the Third Reich. That these same genre types flourished in Austrian and German filmmaking of the 1950s[6] has, not surprisingly, generated competing "readings" as to how they are to be understood in this postwar context. On the one hand, there are those who would see them addressing a need on the part of audiences for notions of nation and community seemingly uncontaminated by the crimes and devastation of the immediate past. And in *Sissi* we do indeed find a "glamorization" of the "Hapsburg monarchy of the nineteenth Century,"[7] as well as a glorification of Possenhofen or the Austrian Alps as respites from everyday social and political conflict; as a *heile Welt* struggling to come to terms with a larger history of postimperial territorial loss.

Countering that interpretation, but not exclusively, would be a reading with less weight on the *Sissi* trilogy as simply a genre film and more on its status as a "Romy Schneider film." It was clear from the response of both critics and audiences that the sixteen-year-old acting novice (she received no prior training) had, in a definitive way, taken over the film. Her extraordinary ability to project emotional excess and melancholia beyond the script and even the role she was playing reinscribed the historical personage of Princess Elizabeth in accordance with the habitus of a "modern" romance of the postwar 1950s[8] — or, in a very different reception of late, in "a queer reading that suggests that the *Sissi* films [and Sissi as gay icon] offer a complex cinematic text, that calls forth highly complicated forms of affect on the part of diverse film audiences."[9] Thus it has been argued that despite *Sissi*'s explicit narrative and architectural tribute to the grandeur of nineteenth-century monarchism, its state-of-the-art production values (Agfacolor film stock, anamorphic lenses, Bruno Mondi camera work, and so on), together with the extraordinary star power of the lead actress, ultimately elicited more Hollywood than Hapsburg.[10]

See also:

- 27 May 1921: *Scherben* Seeks Cinematic Equivalent of Theatrical Intimacy
- 19 September 1958: Douglas Sirk's *A Time to Love and a Time to Die* Tests Limits of Postwar Feeling
- 6 August 1984: *Heimat* Celebrated as "European Requiem for the Little People"

Notes

[1] See in this regard Erica Carter, "Sissi the Terrible: Melodrama, Victimhood, and Imperial Nostalgia in the *Sissi* Trilogy," in *Screening War: Perspectives on German Suffering*, ed. Paul Cooke and Marc Silberman (Rochester, NY: Camden House, 2010), 81–101. Carter discusses the *Sissi* trilogy, focusing on "the relation between the films' melodramatic aesthetic and a victim sensibility that circulated in the films' reception in West Germany around the shock of a dual spatial loss: the loss of a common Germanic, film-aesthetic space and the political loss of Eastern Europe as imperial territory" (82).

[2] *Meyers Taschenlexikon*, vol. 9 (Mannheim: Bibliographisches Institut, 1995), 297.

[3] See Katrin Unterreiner, *Sisi: Mythos und Wahrheit* (Vienna: Christian Brandstätter, 2005), 6–60.

[4] Richard Traubner, *Operetta: A Theatrical History* (London: Routledge, 2003), 299.

[5] Heide Fehrenbach, *Cinema in Democratizing Germany: Reconstructing National Identity after Hitler* (Chapel Hill: U of North Carolina P, 1995), 150.

[6] It has been estimated that between 1947 and 1960, one in five German-speaking films made were *Heimatfilme*, and that in 1956 alone 36 percent of the films made were in that genre. See Willi Höfig, *Der deutsche Heimatfilm: 1947–1960* (Stuttgart: Ferdinand Enke, 1973).

[7] Johannes von Moltke, *No Place Like Home: Locations of Heimat in German Cinema* (Berkeley: U of California P, 2005), 204.

[8] Günter Krenn, *Romy Schneider: Die Biographie* (Berlin: Aufbau, 2008), 68.

[9] Heidi Schlipphacke, "Melancholy Empress: Queering Empire in Ernst Marischka's *Sissi* Films," *Screen* 51, no. 3 (2010): 233. See also Andrea B. Braidt, "'What a Sissy!' Romy Schneider als Schwulenikone," in *Romy Schneider: Film, Rolle, Leben*, ed. Karin Moser (Wien: Filmarchiv Austria, 2008), 259–76.

[10] Georg Seeßlen, "Eine Geschichte vom Mädchen, das Frau werden wollte," *epd Film* 5 (1992): 10–14.

2 February 1956: In Letter to Enno Patalas, Siegfried Kracauer Advocates a Socio-Aesthetic Approach to Film

Johannes von Moltke

GERMAN FILM CULTURE of the 1950s is not remembered for its transAtlantic exchanges. While Hollywood continued to export films for exhibition in West Germany, the parochial nature of the latter's domestic production reached its peak in the decade's *Heimatfilm* wave. Sporadic two-way traffic across the Atlantic — for instance, the temporary remigration of exiles such as Fritz Lang, Robert Siodmak, or Frank Wysbar, or the failed attempts of stars such as Hildegard Knef to find fame and success in Hollywood — merely seems to prove the rule that West German cinema had turned inward, to say nothing of the East German DEFA (Deutsche Film-Aktiengesellschaft) studios. In this context, the budding, if short-lived, correspondence between Siegfried Kracauer and Enno Patalas in the mid-1950s takes on a particular significance for the history of film theory, film criticism, and the future of film culture in Germany.

Kracauer, who had been an eminent cultural critic during the Weimar Republic and had fled to France upon the Nazi seizure of power in 1933, had managed to escape to New York in 1941. He had become a US citizen in 1946 and was in his midsixties when, upon reading a brief article on German cinema in the New York journal *Film Culture*, he struck up an exchange with its author, a young student active in Germany's burgeoning film club movement. In the following year, that student, the twenty-six-year-old Enno Patalas, cofounded the journal *film 56* with Theodor Kotulla. While *film 56* would be extremely short lived, folding after only three issues for lack of funds, in retrospect it can be considered the founding moment of serious film criticism in postwar West Germany: only one year after this first, failed attempt, Patalas founded *Filmkritik*, the flagship journal of West German film criticism that would go on to have a run of 334 issues over almost thirty years (only ceasing publication in 1984). Undoubtedly the most important publication venue for writing on film during the 1960s, *Filmkritik* was Germany's answer to the influential *Cahiers du cinéma* in France, and it was closely identified with both the French and the German New Waves of the decade. To the degree that the journal also had a film-historical agenda, Patalas and his collaborators — Kotulla, Winfried Berghahn, and Ulrich Gregor — mounted a sustained attack not only on the Nazi era but also on the restorative tendencies that followed during the 1950s. Only a few directors (e.g., Wolfgang Staudte) and fewer critics still were exempt from the young students' scathing critique. Among the latter, Kracauer held pride of place as an acknowledged father figure alongside his fellow exile Lotte Eisner.[1] Little wonder, then, that the editors took pride at printing the following passage from a letter that Patalas had received from Kracauer in February in response to the inaugural issue of *film 56*:

> This is a fresh start and *it sets the right tune*. I consider this sociological take on film production absolutely necessary; I would only wish that in the future you would try more systematically to discern what is socio-politically wrong or right in the aesthetic domain as well. At first glance, it appears that you have placed too much emphasis on *the manifest content*. But the manner of photography, the camera take and the editing contribute much that should be considered in the overall evaluation. In other words, I am advocating a melding of the sociological and the aesthetic approach.[2]

This critical endorsement is doubly significant for what it says about Kracauer's film theory and about film criticism in Germany from the midfifties on.

As early as 1932, Kracauer had insisted, in an address at the convention of cinema owners, that "the film critic of note is conceivable only as a social critic. His mission is to unveil the social images and ideologies hidden in mainstream films and through this unveiling to undermine the influence of the films themselves wherever necessary."[3] This critical stance derived from Kracauer's own work as film critic for the influential liberal newspaper *Frankfurter Zeitung* between 1921 and 1933, during which time he reviewed some 740 domestic and foreign productions, wrote articles on film culture and theory, and discussed books in the field. This work prepared the ground for Kracauer's two most influential monographs, which he would publish during his years in the United States: *From Caligari to Hitler: A Psychological History of the German Film* (1947) and *Theory of Film: The Redemption of Physical Reality* (1960).

From Caligari to Hitler, undoubtedly Kracauer's best-known book, was written with the help of American grants at the Museum of Modern Art, which had established a significant film library in 1938. In the book, Kracauer advances a sustained argument about the relationship between film and the collective "psychological dispositions" of a nation. Not only do the films produced in Germany between 1918 and 1933 provide insights into German mentalities during the Weimar Republic, Kracauer claims, they also clearly "presage" the rise of Hitler at its close.

The book has been faulted for crafting an overly teleological narrative with the exile's benefit of hindsight; for basing its historical argument on a narrow selection of prestigious films at the expense of the popular fare that constituted the bulk of Weimar cinema; and for positing an essential German character, to be psychoanalyzed by reviewing the films of the era. The latter argument overlooks Kracauer's explicit claims to the contrary in the introduction to *Caligari*, the consistent historicization of all "psychological" findings throughout the book, and the class-specific focus on the petite bourgeoisie, which had already been the object of Kracauer's important study of white-collar workers, *Die Angestellten (The Salaried Masses)*, from 1930. The former two critiques of *Caligari* carry more weight, but they need to be reevaluated in view of Kracauer's earlier work as film critic, now readily available in toto as part of Kracauer's collected works. As the original articles in the *Frankfurter Zeitung* make clear, Kracauer harbored the same mistrust of the direction German film was taking during the 1920s as he would in retrospect, while the breadth of his reviewing activities in Germany clearly attests to his familiarity with a far broader cross-section of Weimar-era film culture than what ultimately found its way into *From Caligari to Hitler*.

None of this background would have been available to readers in Germany, however, when *Caligari* appeared two years after the exchange between Patalas and Kracauer — thirteen years after its original publication in the United States — in a translation that had been abridged to the point of complete distortion.[4] Not only had the "psychological history" become a mere "contribution to the history" of German film; not only had approximately half the text been cut, including passages devoted to the development of Kracauer's method and his conclusions; but, as critics in East Germany in particular were quick to note, a significant number of political references had been toned down, and references to putatively Marxist categories such as "class" expunged to accommodate the restorative tendencies of a postwar, cold war German readership — as if to prove ex post facto some of Kracauer's most damning points about German audiences from the pre-Hitler years. It would take until 1979 for the first complete German edition of the book to appear at the hands of Karsten Witte.

By the time *Caligari* first appeared in Germany, Kracauer had almost completed his second book and major treatise on the medium, *Theory of Film: The Redemption of Physical Reality*. Projected since the end of his period in France, this study had a prolonged gestation period in which the initial conception shifted often and dramatically.[5] The final result was a book whose emphasis on the recording and revealing function of film quickly earned it a place alongside the roughly contemporaneous work of André Bazin in France as one of the seminal realist theories of the medium. Deriving the specificity of film from the properties of photography, Kracauer develops what he calls "a *material* aesthetics." As a medium, he argues, film has a number of "inherent affinities" for the visible world, which it is uniquely equipped to "record and reveal." Due to these affinities, film gravitates toward the unstaged, the fortuitous, the indeterminate, the flow of life, and the endless. Kracauer argues this theory both systematically and through a plethora of examples that also allow him to explore specific aspects of the medium such as the role of sound and music, different types of films (experimental, documentary, narrative), and the relation between film and its spectator. He resumes the latter concern, in particular, in an important epilogue that locates the "redemptive" aspect of cinema in its promise to break through reification and alienation, reconnect spectators with the materiality of experience, and even work through the traumas of modern history.

Like *Caligari* before it, *Theory of Film* has received its share of criticism. Kracauer's realism has been challenged as "naïve," his aesthetic premises regarding medium-specificity called into doubt, and even the writing and organization of the book have been dismissed as heavy-handed and Teutonic. Moreover, as cinema passes into the digital, *Theory of Film* has shared with all other "ontological" theorizations of film the fate of being discarded as unsuited to the changed technological realities of the postphotographic, digital era. And yet, as work by Miriam Hansen and Lutz Koepnick, among others, emphasizes, *Theory of Film* richly rewards a new look — both for the historical ramifications of the arguments it contains and for how it might speak to basic theoretical concerns across the digital divide.[6]

Whatever their shortcomings, both books still stand as touchstones for some of the central concerns in film studies. *Theory of Film* is a central text for discussions of realism, and *From Caligari to Hitler* has been vastly influential for the study of national cinemas, as well as for sociological approaches to film more broadly. Indeed, as his long-time friend Theodor Adorno would claim, it was Kracauer "who really discovered film as a social fact."[7] This discovery is undoubtedly what attracted the young Patalas to Kracauer, even if the latter would respond by advocating a far more dialectical view of the relationship between film and the social than either Adorno or Patalas's young journal would have ascribed to him: film is a "social fact," Kracauer argues in his letter to Patalas, only to the extent that it is fully understood as a formal, aesthetically constituted text — there can be no social judgment of film's "manifest content" that is not sustained by formal analysis.

It is only fitting, then, that the work at *Filmkritik* would oscillate precisely between these two dialectical poles over the following years. On the one hand, Kracauer's "sociological method" served as a template for the young critics setting out in the 1950s, helping them to define "our relation to film and to society — to *our* film, to *our* society."[8] On the other hand, from the early 1960s onwards, a new aestheticism obtained among some of the editorial staff, including Patalas, who sided with the Munich-based "sensibilists" against the politicization of the journal in the throes of the student movement. Curiously, Patalas would defend this move, in an influential "plea for an aesthetic left," by distancing himself from Kracauer's early influence — not recognizing that the latter's own vindication of a more dialectical approach in the letter from 1956 might have shown the way out of the false dichotomy between the political and the aesthetic: "No other book influenced us all so much in our youth" as *From Caligari to Hitler*, Patalas avers, but "nowadays the exclusively sociological critics no longer grasp the meaning of the important films.... The need for an aesthetic approach to film criticism has become imperative."[9] Until Karsten Witte began restoring Kracauer's thinking to public consciousness through a partial edition of his collected works in 1971,[10] the young critics temporarily abandoned Kracauer's legacies; had they read his letter more carefully for the dialectical approach it advocated, the conversation across the Atlantic might have been more sustained.

See also:

- 22 September 1907: Sigmund Freud Is Attracted to the Movies but Feels Lonely in the Crowd
- 28 February 1962: Oberhausen Manifesto Creates Founding Myth for New German Cinema
- 24 June 1974: Launching of *Frauen und Film* Creates Lasting Forum for Feminist Film Writing and Practice

Notes

[1] Enno Patalas, "Siegfried Kracauer" (obituary), *Filmkritik* 11, no. 1 (January 1967): 5.

[2] Siegfried Kracauer, *film 56* no. 2 (March 1956), reprinted in Siegfried Kracauer, *Werke*, vol. 6, bk. 3, *Kleine Schriften zum Film 1932–1961*, 470–71. Translation mine. Italicized passages are English in the original. The complete letter is in the Kracauer Nachlass, Deutsches Literaturarchiv, Marbach.

[3] Siegfried Kracauer, "The Task of the Film Critic," in *The Weimar Republic Sourcebook*, ed. Anton Kaes, Edward Dimendberg, Martin Jay (Berkeley: U of California P, 1995), 634–35.

[4] See Momme Brodersen, *Siegfried Kracauer* (Reinbek: Rowohlt, 2001), 126–29.

[5] See Miriam Hansen, "Introduction," in Kracauer, *Theory of Film: The Redemption of Physical Reality* (Princeton: Princeton UP, 1997), vii–liv.

[6] See Hansen, "Introduction"; Lutz Koepnick, "In Kracauer's Shadow: Physical Reality and the Digital Afterlife of the Photographic Image," in *Culture in the Anteroom: The Legacies of Siegfried Kracauer*, ed. Gerd Gemünden and Johannes v. Moltke (Ann Arbor: U of Michigan P, 2012).

[7] Theodor Adorno, "The Curious Realist: On Siegfried Kracauer," trans. Shierry Weber Nicholson, *New German Critique* 54 (Fall 1991): 159–77; here 167.

[8] Patalas, "Siegfried Kracauer."

[9] Enno Patalas, "Plädoyer für eine ästhetische Linke," *Filmkritik* 10, no. 7 (1966), 404–6.

[10] See Siegfried Kracauer, *Schriften*, 8 vols. (Frankfurt am Main: Suhrkamp: 1971).

21 June and 30 August 1957: *Jonas* and *Berlin — Ecke Schönhauser* Link Urban Reconstruction to National Cinema in Both West and East

Bastian Heinsohn

Jonas and Nanni survey the lifeless landscape of reconstruction-era West Germany in Jonas *(1957). DVD capture.*

WHEN THE SEVENTH ANNUAL Berlinale film festival opened on 21 June 1957, its venue was emblematic of a wave of reconstruction projects in Germany. The new Zoo-Palast replaced the war-torn Ufa-Palast am Zoo, Berlin hosted the International Builder's exhibition *Interbau 57*, and the city saw a wave of massive urban reconstruction projects. In keeping with this, the festival slogan was *Filmfestspiele in einem neuen Berlin*

(Film festival in a new Berlin). The slogan reflects what may have been the organizers' hope for a link between urban reconstruction and a stagnant national film production heavily dominated by the popular but reactionary *Heimatfilm* genre. One film in competition stood out and promised a novel look at the changing environment: Ottomar Domnick's *Jonas. Eine Filmstudie unserer Zeit* (*Jonas*, 1957). In a move atypical of most West German film of the time, *Jonas* comments critically on the 1950s culture of *Wiederaufbau* (reconstruction), depicting urban space as abstract, menacing, and lifeless, while never suggesting, as the *Heimatfilme* of the period did, that bucolic rural spaces could provide refuge.

The DEFA (Deutsche Film-Aktiengesellschaft, East Germany's state-owned film company) production *Berlin — Ecke Schönhauser* (*Berlin — Schönhauser Corner*, 1957), directed by Gerhard Klein, premiered in East Germany only two months later, on 30 August, and like *Jonas* highlighted the centrality of the city for national rebuilding. *Berlin — Ecke Schönhauser* exploits reconstructed urban space and the trope of the New Berlin to advertise the city as a renewed and prosperous destination. Berlin, at the heart of a clash over issues of identity, culture, and politics, served GDR officials as an ideal setting to promote their own *Aufbau* project through a comparison between the "New Germany" and the West.[1] Taken together, the films reveal significant differences in how both Germanys approached the issues of reconstruction and modernization.[2] The very terminology employed by each state evidences the contrast in approaches: *Wiederaufbau* (reconstruction) implies the reestablishment of something that existed before, while *Aufbau* (construction) suggests to the creation of something new.

Six weeks after the release of *Jonas*, critic Gunter Groll declared that *Jonas* would enter film history.[3] Indeed, Domnick's independently produced work is an exceptional filmic achievement, produced before the elaborate film subsidy system of the 1960s and 1970s would facilitate the production of innovative and nonmainstream films. *Jonas* offers a unique exploration of the 1950s German city at a time when the *Heimatfilm* was establishing a markedly different "map to postwar national space," one that privileged rural over urban settings.[4]

Domnick's black-and-white film tells the story of Jonas, a factory worker living in an anonymous city. When his newly bought hat is stolen in a restaurant, he steals one belonging to another patron, but after discovering a monogram inside it, he is overcome by guilt. The initials remind him of an earlier friend whom he left behind in an unspecified escape from a POW camp. These memories resurface repeatedly, and Jonas develops a severe case of paranoia. He tries to leave the hat behind several times, but it always comes back to him. The faceless city develops into a hostile, labyrinth-like space. For most of the film, Jonas rushes through the city aimlessly, driven by fear and inner voices. His angst steadily increases until the city eventually swallows him up: Jonas attempts to escape, but only vanishes into the darkness of the city.

The depiction of the city in *Jonas* offers a vivid critique of the *Wiederaufbau* wave of the 1950s. While *Jonas* was shot in Stuttgart, Domnick deliberately defamiliarized the look of the city. It appears anonymous, fragmented, and without any identifiable landmarks. This is best illustrated in an early montage sequence: into the seventy-two-second sequence, Domnick inserts forty-seven still images of construction cranes, new and reconstructed buildings, honeycomb-like windows and balconies in strict arrangement, modern glass façades, street signs, abstract architectural contours, and concrete structures of intimidating size. Images of façades are juxtaposed with stills of bricks, printing presses, and numerous cremation urns displayed in walls. Domnick's sequence uses the Eisensteinian technique of "intellectual montage": while the images in themselves appear abstract and meaningless, their linking through editing aims to illustrate and support a particular position.

The tension between text, sound, and image gives *Jonas* an avant-garde character, while Domnick's use of textual commentary, written by Hans-Magnus Enzensberger, adds to the film's sense of alienation and depersonalization. The distanced and at times robotic voices Jonas hears evoke what has been repressed in contemporary German society by reminding him relentlessly of past deeds. The film's use of commentary and abstract sound further mirrors the tension between the urban space and Jonas's life and mental state, marked by fragmentation and alienation.

Jonas's critique culminates in the linkage between the superficiality of the *Kaufwelle* (wave of consumerism) and the *Wiederaufbau* wave of 1950s West Germany, both of which Domnick's film characterizes as moves in the wrong direction. *Jonas* depicts the reconstruction as both bland and menacing, characterized by abstract, hypermodern, and oppressive concrete structures that evoke not only lifeless urban spaces, but also memories of the trenches. Despite the new façades, the city calls forth recollections burdened by questions of guilt. The reconstructed façades cannot repress the past, and in classic Freudian fashion (Domnick was a psychiatrist by training), the repressed resurfaces with a vengeance. At a time when the dominant, largely escapist commercial cinema of the time tended to play to contemporary tendencies to repress and forget, *Jonas* represented a striking and important counterpoint — openly addressing matters like the nation's recent history and the question of guilt.

In the Russian sector, the premiere of *Berlin — Ecke Schönhauser* only a few weeks after *Jonas*'s premiere marked a milestone in DEFA cinema. Klein's Berlin film was highly successful at the box office and was also acclaimed for its artistic, realistic style, and its critical stance in depicting youth in East German society. Party functionaries, however, saw too few positive elements in *Berlin — Ecke Schönhauser* that could promote the socialist state and deemed the film "revisionist." They oversaw and changed early script versions to eliminate excessively negative plot elements. The film's neorealist style was of additional concern to party officials. The film's neorealist depiction of the harsh realities of daily life contradicted the tenets of socialist realism, with its emphasis on exemplary heroic figures and previous Communist achievements as the foundation for a new socialist society. Moreover, neorealist aesthetics were generally deemed inappropriate for portraying the crucial contemporary political and social issues of GDR society.

Despite the qualms of the party, and despite the film's controversial depiction of life in the GDR, *Berlin — Ecke Schönhauser* was released. This can be ascribed to its coincidence with a moment of relative openness in GDR cultural policy. Khrushchev's February 1956 denunciation of Stalin at the Twentieth Party Congress of the Communist Party of the Soviet Union had resulted in an uncertain cultural trajectory in the GDR that permitted greater autonomy in the film industry, and subsequently more critical films. In fact, the film's depiction of contradictions within the GDR struck a chord with audiences, and *Berlin — Ecke Schönhauser* became one of the most successful DEFA productions.

Klein and scriptwriter Wolfgang Kohlhaase locate their film within a clearly defined East Berlin urban setting. In practice, the transitory borders of the city, which allowed the regular infiltration of American culture, significantly complicated the GDR *Aufbau*. Adolescents were especially susceptible to the attractions of Western commodities, fashion, music, and movies. The GDR established the groundwork for its *Aufbau* project as early as March 1951, when the SED announced a search for an authentic German national culture.[5] The filmic medium was to play a crucial role in defining a new sense of "Germanness" that supposedly broke free from the imperialist and fascist past. A key element in the East German cultural productions associated with the *Aufbau* project was the creation of a binary distinction between a "good" socialist East and a dangerous and "uncanny Heimat" in the West.[6]

Berlin — Ecke Schönhauser tells the story of four rebellious adolescents in East Berlin's working class Prenzlauer Berg district, with particular emphasis on the figure of Dieter, a construction worker orphaned in the war. The teenagers each flee family problems to search for the warmth lacking at home among their friends in the street. They adore American film stars like Marlon Brando and demolish street lanterns for a west mark, the currency that grants them access to a fantasy world of dance clubs and Western goods. Whereas Dieter's friend Kohle is drawn to the border cinemas, Karl-Heinz gets involved in petty crime in West Berlin and eventually commits manslaughter. After Kohle and Dieter fear they have killed, knocking Karl-Heinz down in a scuffle, the two flee to a refugee camp in West Berlin. While Kohle accidentally kills himself by drinking a toxic mix of tobacco and coffee, Dieter flees once more, returning to the Eastern sector to be reunited with a pregnant Angela and, as a policeman tells him, to start his life anew. Karl-Heinz, in the meantime, has been sentenced to ten years in prison.

Two scenes in *Berlin — Ecke Schönhauser* illustrate the film's *Aufbau* theme. The opening shot introducing East Berlin extends nearly two minutes with no cuts. An almost complete 360-degree horizontal pan depicts a morning street scene at a busy intersection in working-class East Berlin. The sequence locates the story by framing the sign "Neues Deutschland" (New Germany). Slowly the camera follows a mother with a stroller walking in a circle. There is a newsreel quality to the shot, which captures everyday people in the crowded, random arrangement of an urban street: couples, individuals carrying briefcases, a mother and child, and a schoolboy. Their faces are recognizable and some look toward the camera. The scene evokes the impression that employment and family values are decisive aspects of life in East Berlin, while its morning setting stresses the atmosphere of rejuvenation: it is the start another successful day in the new socialist country. The circular wide-angle shot suggests a whole and complete GDR society well on its way to establishing a cohesive identity, while a calm tune underscores the idyllic atmosphere of the scene.

The sequence introducing West Berlin, by contrast, lacks the order and familiarity of the East Berlin scenes and instead bears a certain resemblance to Domnick's representation of the city space. It is subdivided into three brief sections. The sequence consists of an establishing shot of the Bahnhof Zoo area, a scene inside the station with Karl-Heinz, and a scene at a newsstand. The first scene of these is shot from a static camera position that ends with a sudden pan toward the right. It shows the stop-and-go traffic at the train station as people rush by quickly, their faces blurred. The half-destroyed Kaiser Wilhelm Memorial Church dominates West Berlin, a link to Imperial and Nazi Germany. A newspaper-seller announces headlines that underline the West's presumably imperialist and aggressive nature. The headlines provide a menacing diegetic score that mixes with the hectic street sounds. Karl-Heinz's frantic body movements suggest a constant danger and are highly reminiscent of Jonas's rushed walks through the city, a detail that the film emphasizes throughout via frequent remarks referencing time and the need to hurry.

Within *Berlin — Ecke Schönhauser*, Dieter, despite his rebellious nature, clearly emerges as a role model for young GDR citizens of the *Aufbau* years. Dieter has an overall good and balanced character and, as construction worker, is taking part in the creation of a new Germany. A central scene in the film shows Dieter at work on a building site: he is a diligent, helpful worker among his coworkers. Dieter learns about the degenerative effects of American culture, which makes him an even more loyal believer in the socialist cause. Dieter prefers to maintain his independence: he refuses to join the FDJ (Free German Youth) movement (a detail that may have disquieted party censors), but he is also strong enough to resist the temptations of the West. When the film ends with Dieter starting a new life with Angela, it clearly suggests that participation in the project of *Aufbau* offers the true path to happiness in a socialist society.

The debate surrounding the production and the release of *Berlin — Ecke Schönhauser* exemplifies the GDR deployment of the filmic medium for the project of *Aufbau* — a complex undertaking that aimed to present a new Germany in spatial as well as in ideological and political terms. In Klein's film, *Aufbau* does not, as in *Jonas*, take the form of modernist architecture; rather, the film emphasizes the establishment of social values and convictions. Community, security, and regionalism (reinforced by dialect) mark the film's urban space — ironically, something of a socialist, urban counterpart to the West German *Heimatfilm*, which, too, displayed and promoted a sense of community and security, albeit through a generally conservative, nostalgic orientation that emphasized rural roots and downplayed the *Wiederaufbau*. In the West, it was *Jonas* that inaugurated the cinematic exploration of the links between the *Wiederaufbau* and urban space, through a depiction of contemporary architecture that rendered concrete West German society's dual tendencies toward repression of the past and consumerist escape. Through this emphasis on the need to come to terms with the nation's history, *Jonas* helped pave the way for the critical films of New German Cinema. Emerging in this crucial hour of reconstruction, both *Jonas* and *Berlin — Ecke Schönhauser* provided crucial contributions to the effort by both nations to map and remap themselves, carving out a new future through the space of the city.

See also:

- 29 November 1923: Karl Grune's *Die Straße* Inaugurates "Street Film," Foreshadows Film Noir
- 23 December 1924: *Der letzte Mann* Explores Limits of Modern Community
- 10 August 1994: One Month after Founding of X-Filme, Filmboard Berlin-Brandenburg Paves Way for New Productions in the Capital

Notes

[1] Barton Byg, "DEFA and the Traditions of International Cinema," in *The European Cinema Reader*, ed. Catherine Fowler (London: Routledge, 2002), 153–62; here 154.

² It is important to note that *Jonas* was produced outside the mainstream West German film industry on a low budget by a directorial newcomer. Among the awards *Jonas* garnered were two Deutsche Filmpreise (best direction and best score), the Preis der Filmkritik, and the Bambi award for "Künstlerisch wertvollster deutscher Film" (most artistically worthy German film). Stage actor Robert Graf won a silver Deutscher Filmpreis for supporting actor for his film debut in *Jonas*.

³ Gunter Groll, "Die Avantgarde lebt noch: 'Jonas,'" in *Süddeutsche Zeitung* (25 November 1957). In *Ottomar Domnicks Jonas: Entstehung eines Avantgardefilms*, ed. Guntram Vogt (Stuttgart: ibidem-Verlag, 2007), 175–76.

⁴ Johannes von Moltke, *No Place Like Home: Locations of Heimat in German Cinema* (Berkeley: U of California P, 2005), 23.

⁵ Uta Poiger, "Searching for Proper New Music: Jazz in Cold War Germany," in *German Pop Culture: How "American" Is It?*, ed. Agnes C. Mueller (Michigan: U of Michigan P, 2004), 83–95; here 84.

⁶ Karen Ruoff Kramer, "Representations of Work in the Forbidden DEFA Films," in *DEFA: East German Cinema, 1946–1992*, ed. Seán Allan and John Sandford (New York: Berghahn, 1999), 131–45; here 136.

19 September 1958: Douglas Sirk's *A Time to Love and a Time to Die* Tests Limits of Postwar Feeling

Jennifer M. Kapczynski

Thawing snow reveals the war dead on the Eastern Front.
A Time to Love and A Time to Die *(1958). DVD capture.*

WHEN DOUGLAS SIRK'S *A Time to Love and a Time to Die* opened commercially in West Germany on 19 September 1958 (under the German title *Zeit zu lieben, Zeit zu sterben*), it was something of a non-event: the first — and last — feature film Sirk shot in postwar Germany met with a skeptical press and a film-going public generally hostile to returning exiles. Although the film — a spectacular Cinemascope melodrama set in the fateful final year of the Second World War — received a Golden Bear nomination when it first showed at the Berlinale in July 1958, it enjoyed only a lackluster reception. Sirk found West German culture of the 1950s disturbingly "unreconstructed," "full of self-pity," and entirely unresponsive to his former émigré's vision of life under National Socialism, and he soon returned to Hollywood.[1] The emergent German culture of serious film criticism, embodied by the fledgling journal *Filmkritik*, bestowed only faint praise on the film. Its greatest endorsement came from elsewhere in Europe, when French New Wave director Jean-Luc Godard, writing for *Cahiers du Cinema* in 1959, effusively lauded the film for its realist rendering of wartime conflict: "I have never found wartime Germany so credible as in watching this American film made in peacetime.... Sirk can make things seem so close that we can touch them, that we can smell them."[2] Not until the early 1970s, when Sirk enjoyed his first European retrospective, and when New German Cinema's enfant terrible Rainer Werner Fassbinder extolled the director's films as some of the "most beautiful in the world,"[3] would his work find greater appreciation in West Germany, this time as a critic of American society and the Hollywood "happy end" — a "master of subversion" within the Hollywood system.[4]

And yet, the weak reception of *A Time to Love and a Time to Die* is what most succinctly captures its importance for German film history. The film's failure resulted not only from the fraught position of former exiles in postwar culture, but also from the ways it broke with the dominant conventions of 1950s West German popular cinema, particularly the generic formulae of the war film. Based on Erich Maria Remarque's 1954 novel *Zeit zu leben, Zeit zu sterben* (*A Time to Live and a Time to Die*), the film relates the developing romance between furloughed Wehrmacht conscript Ernst Graeber (John Gavin) and Elizabeth Kruse (Lieselotte Pulver). Childhood friends, the two are drawn together now by their shared search for their parents (Graeber's have been displaced by bombing, Kruse's father interned in a concentration camp for publicly doubting a German victory) and by their respective attraction to love as a respite from the horrors of war. Like the parsley seedlings that Elizabeth tends on her sill, their relationship appears tender, young, and fragile.

In typical Sirkian style, *A Time to Love and a Time to Die* stages highly emotional performances against a thoroughly flattened backdrop — in this case, the jagged ruins of a German cityscape (Berlin, although identified as Bremen) and an impossibly cerulean sky. Sirk's melodrama (as the trailer declares: "Their pounding hearts drowned out the sound of chaos thundering around them") further violated the unspoken rules of a cinema preoccupied with war but wary of feeling. As one contemporary critic seethed, "emigrant director" Sirk had staged a "lemonade-colored melodrama against the backdrop of a German collapse rendered in terms of an operatic bodice-ripper."[5] If Sirk's film drew criticism for its inflation of emotion, it also paradoxically came under attack for its mode of realism. Mainstream German reviewers wrote scathingly of the film's desire to "reconstruct" a ruined Berlin, accusing Sirk of attempting to reconstitute the "nightmares of our recent past" and "bury the woes of wartime love under a pile of rubble," while ignoring the extensive rebuilding that symbolized the beginnings of West German recovery.[6] In fact, the film was shot in the still-berubbled Tiergarten district. Cinephile publications were similarly unconvinced: writing for *Filmkritik*, Ulrich Gregor declared that Sirk's "reconstruction of the war" to be so consumed with "accurate naturalism ... that a convincing representation of the horror cannot emerge." Deeming the film just "acceptable," Gregor bemoaned the fact that the film's touted expenditure of "250 loads of dynamite and 800 pounds of smoke powder" produced "not chaos, but rather just a purely effect-laden arrangement of photogenic rubble."[7] In the end, Sirk's brand of distanced and highly stylized melodrama rendered his return to the German screen a missed connection rather than a homecoming.

The reception of Sirk's 1958 film is emblematic of his more generally vexed position within the larger field of film studies. Sirk, who was born Detlev Sierck but Americanized his name upon his arrival in Hollywood in 1939, had a career spanning three decades and two continents, from his early work in the Weimar German film industry, to a stint at Ufa (Universum Film A.G.) under National Socialism, and then to his years in Hollywood during the period from the Second World War to the McCarthy era. In scholarship, the director has occupied an alternately denigrated and privileged position — initially ignored as a director of emotionally overwrought works of populism, then celebrated as a brilliant manipulator of the American studio system, and, for his work during the Hitler years, held up as an example either of aesthetic resistance or collusion. His career serves as a veritable blueprint for exploring the possibilities and limits of artistic agency under political, institutional, and generic constraints.

A Time to Love and a Time to Die might have made the ideal vehicle for the émigré's triumphant return. While a number of Sirk's American films had played in West Germany, this new film represented a more direct form of homecoming. Sirk chose to shoot, edit, and print his film entirely in Germany, he employed an international cast of American and German-speaking actors, including up-and-coming Swiss ingénue Pulver, and the narrative, although it touches on a great deal of controversial material — from the atrocities of the concentration camps to the horrors of urban bombing — also takes an unusually generous view of its subjects, highlighting German resistance to National Socialism while reducing the scope of fascism to a select few sadists. As *New York Times* reviewer Bosley Crowther noted with scorn: "Most of the Germans are shown as sweet people — 'our kind.' They hate Nazism, which is represented by a few exaggerated perverts and brutes."[8] Perhaps inspired by Sirk's personal story — a son from his first marriage died serving in the Wehrmacht at the Eastern Front — the film's treatment of the military is similarly forgiving: Graeber fights alongside other war-weary German skeptics, the unit commander clearly cares for his men more than the regime, and the harmony of their battlefront community is threatened by just one lone fanatic, a roundly despised Gestapo plant. To anyone familiar with the generic conventions of the West German war film, these character types must seem intimately familiar. Indeed, part of what makes Sirk's film remarkable is the extent to which it hews to a portrait of the

German population and its military that was very much in vogue in 1950s West German film culture — begging the question, why did the film flop?

Undoubtedly, critics rejected Sirk's film in large part because they viewed his work as an unwelcome contribution to a war discourse considered off-limits for former exiles and Americans. Published reviews of *A Time to Love and a Time to Die* paint Sirk's perspective as false and foreign, his film "gray and flabby . . . colportage."[9] Certainly Sirk was not the only former exile to face such rejection: Peter Lorre and Fritz Lang, for example, never recaptured the prominence they enjoyed during the Weimar years, while Marlene Dietrich endured catcalls and accusations that she had "sullied the nest." The fact that Sirk's film was based on a novel by a fellow émigré and featured the author in the role of a persecuted former teacher probably also contributed to the film's weak reception. If Remarque had made his name in the 1930s as an antiwar novelist, by the 1950s he was, if the reviews of Sirk's film offer any indication, viewed as an irritating bad conscience.

Aside from its problematic provenance, the film provokes via its address of German crimes. It was commonplace for German war films to reference the concentration camps, but more as a means to certify the moral rectitude of their lead characters than to indict the National Socialist regime. This is a principle, however, that Sirk declines to follow on numerous occasions: the opening summary execution of partisans; the gleeful recounting by the local camp commandant of his favored method of prisoner torture and murder; Elizabeth's poignant indictment of the abusive local authority ("Murderers are never murderers twenty-four hours a day. Some adore their mothers, some cry when their dogs are dying, but it is enough if they are murderers for one minute a day."). *A Time to Love and a Time to Die* is perhaps most confrontational in a scene in which Ernst and Elizabeth discuss the honeymoon they would have liked to have: Paris and Rotterdam are off-limits because their citizens now hate the Germans for the destruction they wrought there. At a time when economic recovery had begun and West Germans began participating in intra-European tourism at high rates, the reminder of lasting antagonisms on the continent could only have been unwelcome.

A Time to Love and a Time to Die further tested the limits of a willingness to confront death as a central aspect of the German war experience. To be sure, Adenauer-era audiences flocked to war films: beginning with films such as *Canaris* (1954), the *08/15* trilogy (1954–55), and *Des Teufels General* (*The Devil's General*, 1955), domestic production of war films boomed in the mid-1950s. Yet while the tone of these films varied, particularly in their construction of heroic masculinity and the extent of their rejection of fascism, they were unified by a striking bloodlessness. When death did appear onscreen it was invariably clean, avoiding any display of agony or messiness and always respecting the integrity of the soldierly body. Sirk's film violates this unspoken dictum within its first few minutes, in the process challenging the limits of the expressible concerning the recent German past. In the opening scene set at the Eastern Front, a naïve new recruit, Hirschland (Dana J. Hutton), looks aghast as his fellow soldiers discover a blackened corpse buried in the snow, now partially revealed. "Sign of spring," one of them quips: the thaw unveils the landscape's gruesome history. Shortly thereafter, Hirschland, struggling with his conscience after being forced to help execute several Russian partisans, commits suicide atop their fresh grave. Both moments are startling for their frank treatments of guilt and death and their conscious melding of images of hope and despair. Sirk produces a similarly shocking image for an air raid scene: following the collapse of a shelter in a posh hotel, a woman runs shrieking from the building, her body a writhing column of flame. Whereas West German culture of the period found substantial legitimation in the narrative of German wartime suffering, it was uncommon, even radical to portray human agony in such direct terms. Sirk's film crosses a boundary when it shows (rather than simply tells) the vivid psychological and physical pain of war.

Indeed, *A Time to Love and a Time to Die* is a film haunted by death, refusing resolutely to offer redemption or relief from the horrors of war. It is clear from the outset that Elizabeth and Ernst's love, forged by the experience of the war, cannot outlive it, and although the circumstances of Ernst's death upon his return to the front are surprising, the fact of it is not. As Fassbinder noted approvingly in his 1972 reassessment of the film, Sirk falls short of endorsing love as an antidote to the coldness of war: "There is not a second which lets us think: if it were not for this lousy war everything would be so wonderful or something. . . . Sirk is saying that if it weren't for the war, this would not be love at all."[10] Sirk's world is one of loving *and* dying, not loving *or* dying. The opening credits offer ample indication of this dark trajectory: a borderline kitschy shot of a plum tree in full blossom against a characteristically Sirkian flat blue sky fades to gray, and as a snow storm sets in the tree turns barren and lifeless. The blooming branch introduces a symbolic correlative between the seasons and life cycle, but strikingly reverses their usual trajectory: were it to follow a natural course, it would go from bare to blooming. While this reinforces the film's delight in artifice — in fact, contemporary reviewers misjudge it entirely when they accuse it of naturalism — it also cues Sirk's preoccupation with death over life, with the icing over of German culture rather than its (putative postwar) thaw.

Sirk stages the tension between cooling and warming most succinctly in the opening scene, with the discovery of the corpse. As troops work to free the body from the tundra, the naïf Hirschland is astonished to observe that the fallen officer "looks like he's crying." A seasoned Graeber explains: "His eyeballs were frozen. They're thawing now." More than any other moment in the film, this instant — saturated with cinematic meaning for its emphasis upon vision — prompts questions about the German relationship to its recent past, and by extension, the progress of postwar recovery. Through the tears of a dead German soldier, Sirk at once weeps for war and, nearly a decade ahead of the famous Mitscherlich study on the "inability to mourn," casts suspicion on the country's capacity to grieve and atone for its dead. Although the film includes other scenes of crying, these cadaverous tears are its most vivid — false and yet surrogate, a liquid evocation of wartime's challenge to feeling and the imperative of its return.

See also:

- 4 March 1921: With *Das Floss der Toten*, the Dead Come Back to Town
- 22 March 1946: Screenings of *Die Todesmühlen* Spark Controversy over German Readiness to Confront Nazi Crimes
- 20 August 1981: R. W. Fassbinder's *Lola* Revisits Kracauer to Critique Adenauer Period

Notes

[1] Jon Halliday, *Sirk on Sirk* (New York: Viking, 1972), 139, 127.

[2] Jean-Luc Godard, "Of Tears and Speed," reprinted in *A Time to Love and a Time to Die*, DVD commentary, Masters of Cinema series, Eureka Entertainment 2009.

[3] Rainer Werner Fassbinder, "Six Films by Douglas Sirk," trans. Thomas Elsaesser, in *Douglas Sirk*, ed. Laura Mulvey and Jon Halliday (Edinburgh Film Festival Catalog 1972), 95–107; here 106.

[4] Eric Rentschler, "Douglas Sirk Revisited: The Limits and Possibilities of Artistic Agency," *New German Critique* 95 (2005): 149–61; here 151.

[5] "Zeit zu leben [*sic*] und Zeit zu sterben," *Spiegel* (1 October 1958): 69.

[6] Karena Niehoff, "Filme in Uniform," *Zeit* (1 September 1957): n.p.

[7] Ulrich Gregor, "Zeit zu leben [*sic*], Zeit zu sterben," *Filmkritik* 2, no. 9 (September 1958): 4–5.

[8] Bosley Crowther, "More Movie War," *New York Times* (13 July 1958): x1.

[9] "Zeit zu leben [*sic*], Zeit zu sterben," *Tageszeitung* (8 August 1958): n.p.

[10] Fassbinder, "Six Films," 104.

4 September 1959: *Der Frosch mit der Maske* Moves Popular Cinema from Idyllic Pastures to Crime-Infested City Streets

Tassilo Schneider

A night watchman runs afoul of the Frosch *gang.*
Der Frosch mit der Maske *(1959). DVD capture.*

In 1959, an era of German film history drew to a close that, "generically" speaking, had firmly been in the hands of the *Heimatfilm*. This uniquely German genre possessed an iconography marked by rural settings, alpine panoramas, and folk culture, and narratives that typically center around romantic entanglements, village festivals and the trials and tribulations of country life. Nearly one-third of German productions between 1950 and 1959 could be considered *Heimatfilme*, and the genre produced the decade's biggest blockbusters — among them *Schwarzwaldmädel* (*The Black Forest Girl*, 1950), *Grün ist die Heide* (*The Heath is Green*, 1951), and *Der Förster vom Silberwald* (The ranger from silver forest, 1954) — as well as its most popular and long-lived domestic stars. Remarkably, the successful run of the *Heimatfilm* was halted rather abruptly. By the end of the decade, the genre had all but disappeared from theater screens, replaced by a new series of domestic productions that easily rivaled its commercial success but in all other regards could hardly be more different.

To be sure, when *Der Frosch mit der Maske* (*Face of the Frog*) was released in September 1959, it was not immediately obvious that it marked a turning point in the history of German popular cinema. Based on a novel by British author Edgar Wallace, the film had limited commercial success at first (it placed twenty-first on the year-end box-office chart[1]). However, as a result of its tight budget it turned a sizeable profit and thus encouraged its producers to buy the rights to all of Wallace's novels. The ensuing cycle of thrillers came quickly: 1959 saw two, 1960 three, 1961 four, and 1963 five Wallace adaptations released within that year. By 1972, there would be a total of thirty-six films, which sold seventy-two million tickets and grossed 140 million marks in Germany alone.[2] Together with a series of German Westerns based on the novels of Karl May and starting with the release of *Der Schatz im Silbersee* (*The Treasure of Silver Lake*, 1962), the Wallace films dominated German box offices for much of the decade. At the end of 1963, of the five most successful domestic films of the year, three were Wallace thrillers and two were May Westerns. The following year, seven of the thirteen top-grossing films, including the first three, belonged to one of these two categories.[3]

By that time, the success of these crime films was significant enough to be noticed abroad: a 1963 *Films in Review* article speculated, "In the last three and a half years so many films have been made in West Germany from Edgar Wallace's stories and novels that some sort of sociological phenomenon seems to be in progress."[4] In the third Wallace adaptation, *Die Bande des Schreckens* (*The Terrible People*, 1960), this "sociological phenomenon" is inadvertently summed up by one of the film's own characters, police photographer Edwards, who talks of his resentment against having to take pictures of homicide victims: "I used to be an animal photographer. I took pictures of squirrels, of rabbits, and of deer roaming the forest. That was fun! But nowadays there is no demand for that kind of thing anymore. Corpses are what people want to see. Corpses!" Edwards's comment reflects the astonishing reversal in the taste of German audiences. Just a few years earlier, "animal photographers" had indeed been in high demand, filming countless squirrels, rabbits, deer, and other wildlife that populated the hundreds of *Heimatfilme*. Now it seemed that moviegoers' interests had shifted elsewhere — to deeds of sadistic violence and brutal murder at the hands of the deranged criminals that populated the new crime films.

Viewed against the background of the films of the 1950s, the Wallace thrillers marked a significant "escalation" of thematic, but also stylistic means. Unlike much of "classical" mystery fiction, their narratives show little concern with the work of crime detection and the figure of the detective and instead focus on the criminal and his or her crimes — objects both of loathing, and also of considerable fascination. In a Wallace film, murder victims regularly suffer slow, painful deaths, more often than not resulting from violence inflicted with bizarre, exotic weapons. They are impaled by arrows (*Der grüne Bogenschütze* [*The Green Archer*], 1960) or fishing harpoons (*Das Gasthaus an der Themse* [*The Inn on the River*], 1962), drowned in containers slowly filling with water (*Die toten Augen von London* [*Dead Eyes of London*], 1961), locked in cages to be killed by tigers (*Der Zinker* [*The Squeaker*], 1963), smashed by mill stones (*Die Gruft mit dem Rätselschloss* [*The Curse of the Hidden Vault*], 1964), strangled by whips (*Der unheimliche Mönch* [*The Mysterious Monk*], 1965), burnt with flamethrowers (*Der Bucklige von Soho* [*The Hunchback of Soho*], 1966), drowned in liquid gold (*Das Geheimnis der weißen Nonne* [*The Trygon Factor*], 1966), or perforated by iron hands (*Die blaue Hand* [*The Blue Hand*], 1967).

Most often, these crimes are committed by some deranged individual who invariably turns out to be merely the insanely devoted henchman of a master criminal. For much of the narrative, the latter remains out of reach because he or she appears to reside, alternately, outside and at the very center of social "normality." Bizarre masks and disguises are central elements of the films' iconography. The killer appears as a grotesquely clad scuba diver (*Der Frosch mit der Maske*), as a monk (*Der schwarze Abt* [*The Black Abbott*], 1963), and even as a corpse (*Im Banne des Unheimlichen* [*In the Spell of the Mysterious*], 1967). He leaves behind mysterious symbols: frog tattoos (*Der Frosch mit der Maske*), glass eyes (*Der Mann mit dem Glasauge* [*The Man with the Glass Eye*], 1968), or the heads of his victims (*Der Rächer* [*The Avenger*], 1960). And he is referred to as "The Frog" (*Der Frosch mit der Maske*), "The Shark" (*Das Gasthaus an der Themse*), or "The Blue Hand" (*Die blaue Hand*).

At the same time, the most elaborately grotesque disguises often turn out to have merely hidden the "other" identity of one of the films' most "respectable" characters: the reverend who runs a shelter for the homeless blind (*Die toten Augen von London*), the police pathologist (*Das Gasthaus an der Themse*), the detective's girlfriend (*Zimmer 13* [*Room 13*], 1963), even the private investigator himself (*Der Hund von Blackwood Castle* [*The Dog of Blackwood Castle*], 1967). What most delays the resolution of the narrative, however, is that the master criminal's identity remains obscured behind a virtually infinite number of "suspicious" characters. The police are regularly faced with a criminal abyss opening ever more widely to reveal an out of control world beyond, or rather below, social normality. The "overchallenged" detective finds his mirror image in the films' continuously mislead spectator who focuses attention on the most obviously suspicious character, only to regularly see this prime suspect be the next victim.

The narrative "chaos" and the resulting atmosphere of paranoid anxiety are reinforced by the films' production design, mise-en-scène, and sound. Indeterminate and claustrophobic spaces predominate: foggy streets and harbor piers, basements, cellars, windowless rooms, and subterranean corridors. Characters regularly wear masks or sunglasses, and there is a heavy reliance on nighttime footage (several films do not have a single daytime shot) which, together with the proliferation of fog, dark glasses, and disguises, emphasizes a preoccupation with problems of visibility and (mis)recognition. The impression of a threatening environment, pervaded by dementia, insanity, and violence is always present. Crosslights, backlighting, and underlighting distort settings and physiognomies while rapid pans and zooms generate a pervasive atmosphere of panic and paranoia, further reinforced by soundtracks in which gun shots and screams become part of the "music," and shrill brass arrangements battle with electronic sound effects and distorted voices. This mixing of disparate elements also reflects the iconography's synthesis of generic spaces. Heavily indebted to elements of gothic horror — the hidden vaults, secret passageways, and cavernous basements in ominous historic country mansions — the films' settings are nevertheless recognizably contemporary. This effect contributes to the overriding impression that below the surface of "normality," another, nightmarish space is threatening to erupt, ready to reveal that nothing is what it seems, and that nothing and nobody can be trusted.

What made German audiences so quickly lose interest in the formerly beloved village tales set in idyllic green pastures and become fascinated with accounts of violence and corruption in crime-infested city streets? What stood behind the allure to indulge in what appears to have been a monstrous "return of the repressed"? It is safe to assume that the narrative and stylistic "excesses" of the Wallace films are motivated in part by efforts to combat the threat of television in an area where the latter could not compete: constrained by the cultural and educational imperatives of its mandate under public law, German television in the 1960s could scarcely match the violent "sensations" offered by these crime films. Yet, those excesses might well also speak — symptomatically — of a cultural moment in which the social fabric of the immediate postwar era started tearing at the seams, before exploding into open social revolt and ultimately terrorism later in the decade.

At the onset of the 1960s, West Germany presented the image of a society marked by an increasingly visible deepening of divisions: between the profiteers of the *Wirtschaftswunder* (economic miracle) and the members of the working and middle classes for whom it became increasingly obvious that the promised level of status and consumption would remain out of reach; between the constraints of "traditional" models of social organization and the demands of a capitalist economy dependent on social mobility and mass consumption; and between a generation whose carefully reconstructed self-image relied on a sense of economic accomplishment and selective historical memory and their children who were more and more unwilling to play along.

Arguably, the "symptomatic" quality that the German crime films of this period exhibit in relation to these ideological conflicts surfaces most visibly in the radical reversals they represent, thematically and formally, with respect to the genre they displaced in the theaters. In *Heimatfilme*, few, if any, characters are beyond redemption, since the social fabric is sturdy enough to reintegrate all but its most violent offenders. The representatives of the social order are recognizable and trustworthy, the signifiers of ideological stability never ambiguous. Midway through any Wallace film, everybody and everything is suspicious, numerous characters become victims of blackmail because they have to fear some catastrophic "revelation" about their past, and the family in particular is, more often than not, a source of horror and violence, with the monstrous criminal organization and its murderous campaigns often rooted in familial hatred. Compositionally, the *Heimatfilm*'s landscape vistas with their reliance on horizontal lines and long takes are replaced in the Wallace thrillers by frantically rapid sequences of short oblique-angle shots. The *Heimatfilm* aesthetic is marked by bright colors and natural light, while the Wallace adaptations are primarily shot in black and white and characterized by low-key lighting. The *Heimatfilm* represents a directional movement outside (into the open landscape) and upwards (onto hills and mountains); in the Wallace films, everything moves inside and downward (underwater, into prisons, basements and cellars).

Seen within the context of the history of German popular cinema, the 1960s manifestation of the genre of the crime film, with its narrative and stylistic excesses, thus marks what might be called a "generic intervention." Of course, history cannot be "read off" a text or even a genre. And yet the popularity of the Wallace films can be considered symptomatic of their historical moment in that the modes of their narrative and formal expression bore a meaningful relationship to the terms and conventions through which audiences made sense of the social conditions and relations in which they found themselves. After a decade dominated by the *Heimatfilm*, the Wallace films charted a new terrain where specific social and cultural conflicts could be articulated and negotiated — a cinematic "parallel universe" in which a society striving to maintain an appearance of harmony, success, and stability met the projection of its most violent nightmares and contradictions.

See also:

- 29 November 1923: Karl Grune's *Die Straße* Inaugurates "Street Film," Foreshadows Film Noir
- 11 May 1931: With Premiere of *M*, a Gala Hit Becomes a Cultural Controversy
- 16 August 1949: Ilse Kubaschewski Founds Gloria-Filmverleih, Sets the Course of Popular West German Film

Notes

[1] *Film-Echo/Filmwoche* (31 December 1960): 1784/104.

[2] See Claudia Dillmann-Kühn, *Artur Brauner und die CCC: Filmgeschäft, Produktionsalltag, Studiogeschichte 1946–1990* (Frankfurt am Main: Deutsches Filmmuseum, 1990) and Joachim Kramp, *Hallo! Hier spricht Edgar Wallace: Die Geschichte der legendären deutschen Kriminalfilmserie von 1959–1972.* 3rd ed. (Berlin: Schwarzkopf und Schwarzkopf, 2005).

[3] See *Film-Echo/Filmwoche* (31 December 1964): 21, and (31 December 1965): 23, respectively.

[4] Jack Edmund Nolan, "West Germany's Edgar Wallace Wave," *Films in Review* 14, no. 6 (1963): 376.

Part V: 1962–1976

Begun as a provisional barbed wire fence in 1961, just one year later the Berlin Wall already represented a formidable structure, as GDR authorities solidified and expanded it to include the now-infamous "Death Strip." If this signaled the presumption that the division of the Germanys was permanent and thereby dampened the rhetoric of unification, the construction of the Wall also brought a measure of political stabilization, normalizing relations *between* the states even as both experienced substantial internal turmoil.

This shift in the relationship of the Germanys was due in no small part to political changes in the Federal Republic. In 1963, in the wake of what was called the Spiegel Scandal regarding government suppression of the free press, Adenauer stepped down as chancellor, bringing to a close an era of postwar leadership that had profoundly shaped West German development. Although Adenauer would be succeeded twice by members representing his own party, the age of CDU dominance was already beginning to wane. First came Ludwig Erhard, economic minister under Adenauer. Erhard had risen to prominence in the preceding decade as the champion of free-market economic policies that had ushered in unprecedented economic expansion. Although the *Wirtschaftswunder* (economic miracle) spread somewhat unevenly in West Germany, the nation's overall growth was nothing short of staggering. From the mid-1950s through the early 1960s, production and exports soared, and incomes and standards of living rose accordingly. West Germany's citizens — many of whom still recalled the privations of the war years — responded by embracing consumerism, participating in a *Kaufrausch* (buying frenzy) on a national scale. This translated into record sales of household goods, luxury items (including, after the country's surprise 1954 World Cup win, televisions), and automobiles — the latter, in turn, feeding a postwar travel boom. By 1961, unemployment had sunk to below 1 percent. In response to the period's labor shortage, West Germany began recruiting thousands of foreign laborers referred to as "guest workers," principally from Greece, Spain, and Turkey. In 1964, the federal government greeted the arrival of the millionth guest worker with a gesture that bespoke the era's preoccupations with modernization and mobilization: it gave him a moped.

By 1965, however, the West German economy had stalled in a recession. Following the dissolution of the CDU's coalition with the FDP in 1966, Erhard stepped down and was replaced by Kurt Georg Kiesinger.

Like Erhard, Kiesinger's chancellorship lasted merely three years — the result of his governance of a politically unwieldy "Grand Coalition" comprised of the CDU and SPD, as well as criticism of his past as a former Nazi Party member, which prompted protest from leading German intellectuals including an infamous public slap delivered by activist Beate Klarsfeld. Kiesinger also drew strong dissent from the student movement when his coalition passed the *Notstandsgesetze*, or German Emergency Acts. The APO (Extraparliamentary Opposition — a shorthand term for the student movement) organized to combat the laws, which enabled the activation of the German military in cases of war, natural disaster, or — the point most problematic for student protesters, who saw in it echoes of Weimar's troubled legacy — political emergency. Young leftists were also perturbed by West Germany's increasing ties to NATO, which promised to implicate the country ever more in an American foreign policy agenda — including, by the mid-1960s, the Vietnam War, which student movement leaders tended to view as act of US imperialism rather than anti-Communism. Matters came to a head in 1967–68 after police shot protester Benno Ohnesorg during a demonstration against the Shah of Iran, and then, just one year later, student movement leader Rudi Dutschke was gravely wounded in an attempted assassination by a right-wing laborer. Both events, coupled with the success of former Nazi Party members like Kiesinger and the passage of the emergency laws, as well as the general-consensus culture that emerged alongside West Germany's newfound economic growth, seemed to confirm the continued authoritarian character of West Germany's putatively democratic society.

The debates around Kiesinger's past and the *Notstandsgesetze* were the outgrowth of a decade of broader public struggle to work through the consequences of the Nazi period. The Auschwitz Trials of 1963 had represented the first key milestone, as the earliest example of West German (rather than Allied) prosecution of perpetrators. By 1965, when parliament again found cause to debate the statute of limitations for crimes of murder committed under National Socialism, both the SPD and moderates within the CDU argued successfully for an extension. Although the limitations on prosecutions for murder and genocide would not be lifted permanently until 1979, the debates of the '60s evidenced the beginnings of a profound shift in political attitudes toward the prosecution of Nazi crimes, as the process of "coming to terms with the past" came to be accepted as an integral component of West German democracy. This shift was the result of numerous factors, including international pressures on the FRG, which set as the price of reintegration the nation's conformity to political expectations such as support for Israel. Intellectuals within Germany, who decried postwar complacency and called for a thoroughgoing coming to terms with the past, provided further impetus. But the student movement also played an essential role in this transformation. Although largely restricted to the realm of German universities, the movement nevertheless helped to reshape West German public discourse — not only encouraging a new, critical stance toward the failures of the previous generation to adequately address the Nazi past, but also toward the postwar embrace of consumerism and the influence of American foreign policy.

When the SPD gained representatives in the 1969 elections, the rise of former Berlin mayor Willy Brandt to the position of chancellor signaled a new chapter in West German politics, as Germany's traditional left party took the helm for the first time since the end of the Second World War. Under the motto "Attempt more democracy!" Brandt's government, now allied with the FDP, sought to implement a wide range of domestic reforms in education policy, labor rights, family law, and penal law. In tackling the political extremism of the day, Brandt's coalition was less progressive, promoting stringent policies to stem the influence of student protestors and political extremists. In 1972, this resulted in the passage of the *Radikalenerlass* (Antiradical Decree) banning members of so-called fringe groups from employment in the civil service. The country's change in course was even more evident when it came to foreign relations, particularly in the relationship Brandt courted with the East. Brandt pursued a policy of *Ostpolitik* that fundamentally altered West German political relations with the Soviet bloc — deescalating tensions through rapprochement with the country's eastern neighbors, especially the GDR. This included fostering East-West trade, which Brandt argued would lead to change across the border, as well as a series of treaties of recognition that reestablished diplomatic ties with various Eastern European nations for the first time since the end of the Second World War. It was a marked change from the harsh Hallstein Doctrine of the 1950s, which had refused recognition to any state that acknowledged the sovereignty of the GDR. Yet Brandt's *Ostpolitik* was not only economic in nature, but also incorporated an attitude of public repentance for the crimes of National Socialism. Most famously, on a state visit to Warsaw in 1970, Brandt fell to his knees before a memorial to the victims of the Ghetto Uprising — a gesture that indicated a new style of official remorse, even if it also generated predictably ambivalent responses in the German public. For his efforts at East-West reconciliation, Brandt was awarded the Nobel Peace Prize in 1971. Then in 1972, East and West Germany signed the Basic Treaty establishing formal ties between the states. One year later, the treaty ratified, the United Nations recognized both Germanys for the first time. Brandt's policies were controversial among West German conservatives, who faulted him for appeasing the Communists and, in the case of expellee groups, for seeming to relinquish claims to lost territories in the East. Nevertheless, *Ostpolitik* took hold as the new West German policy toward the East, shaping foreign relations between the states long after Brandt stepped down in 1974 in the wake of an espionage scandal.

Brandt's successor, Helmut Schmidt, also of the SPD, served from 1974 to 1982. Schmidt faced a challenging array of domestic and international crises. The severe oil shortage following the 1973 Arab-Israeli war prompted gasoline rationing, while the subsequent world economic recession led to a rise in German unemployment and prompted a number of unpopular economic measures that reduced taxes but also raised the deficit. The new chancellor was also confronted with the growing problem of German domestic terrorism, as the student movement splintered and there emerged a new, militant wing: the Red Army Faction (RAF). Led by Andreas Baader, Gudrun Ensslin, and Ulrike Meinhof, the RAF engaged in increasingly violent attacks on governmental and commercial targets in an attempt both to combat a perceived residual fascist element in West German culture and to disrupt apathy regarding both the American-led Vietnam War and postwar consumerism. The RAF would test the mettle of the postwar democracy, as the West German government struggled to balance containing the movement with maintaining the system of justice. If older generations of West Germans generally viewed the RAF as deserving harsh punishment, for a generation of discontented students, the prison suicides of Meinhof in 1976 and then Ensslin, Baader, and coconspirator Jan Carl Raspe one year later only fueled their distrust of government and mainstream culture — laying the groundwork for the eventual emergence of oppositional movements such as the Green Party.

In the GDR, the erection of the Wall in 1961 marked the final closure of the border, isolating the country's citizens but also bringing on an era of greater stability that, by some measures, contributed to improved living conditions. With Nikita Khrushchev's assumption of power in the Soviet Union, the East German state, under the leadership of Walter Ulbricht, had already begun to move away from Stalinism. In a symbolic gesture signaling this shift, in 1961 the state renamed East Berlin's premiere boulevard, dropping Stalinallee in favor of Karl-Marx-Allee. In 1963, the GDR then implemented far-reaching economic reforms — known as the Neue Ökonomische System der Planung und Leitung (New Economic System of Planning and Management, NÖSPL). The program sought to increase efficiency in production through the application of scientific principles and to encourage quality over quantity, while also mitigating the effects of centralization by allowing for greater local control. That same year, East Germany, seeking to compensate for a depleted population and meet labor demands, entered into a series of international agreements to recruit workers from other Communist nations, including Poland, Hungary, Cuba, Albania, Angola, and Mozambique. It was also an age of great technological promise, perhaps best symbolized in the GDR by the construction from 1965–1969 of the famed Berlin Fernsehturm (television tower), which soared over the city skyline and served as an emblem of East German might. During this period the GDR also began to flex greater political muscle, in 1967 declaring its national independence and thereby doing away with a unified definition of German citizenship (although the first Western nation to acknowledge an exclusively East German citizenship was Austria in 1975). Indeed, the division looked ever more permanent, not least at the 1968 Olympics, when separate national teams competed for the first time. It was also a period of political repression: the GDR meted out harsh punishments for the so called *Mauerspringer* (wall jumpers) who tried to flee the country, and in 1968, as Soviet tanks violently suppressed the protestors of the "Prague Spring," Ulbricht applauded the brutal actions and ordered East German soldiers to stand ready at the Czech border.

In 1971, Ulbricht was forced from office on the grounds of health problems and replaced by Erich Honecker, a career politician who had overseen the planning of the Berlin Wall, and who would direct the East German state until its final days, only leaving office in October 1989 as the *Wende* (a term literally meaning "turn," but referencing the collapse of the GDR regime and onset of unification) was already underway. Honecker embodied elements both of reform and political dogmatism. Under his rule, East Germany attained the highest standard of living in the Eastern Bloc, as the state began to place greater emphasis on providing consumer goods and improving housing. In 1971, in response to the new mood of détente and following the signing of the Four Powers Agreement allowing the Germanys to regulate traffic between the states, the GDR and FRG ratified a transit agreement permitting greater travel to the East. Both trade and tourism increased between the states, and in this same spirit, in 1975, the GDR began permitting West German banks to open branches in the East. Yet that same year, as if to underscore the finality of the national partition, the state inaugurated a celebration of the anniversary of the country's founding. The celebration was marked by the signing of a twenty-five-year cooperation agreement with the Soviet Union that excluded all mention of a future German unification. Nor did the improvement in material existence correspond with a rise in political liberties for East German citizens: indeed, as pressures grew to allow greater civil rights, the regime responded by cracking down on dissenters. Thus 1975 also marked the commencement of construction of a secondary perimeter of the Wall that included a touch-sensitive sensor capable of automatic firing.

Although the precise nature of the unrest differed in each case, for both Germanys the years 1962–1976 were characterized by an air of cultural change and discontent. Under Ulbricht and then Honecker, GDR artists had to weather a climate that fluctuated regularly but unpredictably between phases of openness and ideological rigidity. This was in no case truer than with DEFA (Deutsche Film-Aktiengesellschaft, East Germany's state-owned film company). Following a relatively barren spell for East German filmmakers in the 1950s, as DEFA struggled to find a balance between artistry and political demands, the early 1960s seemed poised to usher in a renaissance of aesthetically edgy and critically constructive social dramas. Some, like Konrad Wolf's adaptation of the novel by Christa Wolf, *Der geteilte Himmel* (*Divided Heaven*, 1964), even touched on the sensitive issue of the Wall. This period of liberalization was cut short in 1965 by the Eleventh Plenum of the Central Committee of the SED: originally convened to discuss the New Economic System, it turned into a referendum on GDR youth and cultural policy. In a critique delivered by Erich Honecker, the SED railed against contemporary writers and filmmakers for undermining the socialist cause through purportedly "nihilistic" depictions of everyday life, particularly the country's disaffected youth. The results were nothing short of catastrophic for DEFA: numerous directors and executives saw their careers derailed, and the studio was forced to shelve the better part of its yearly production for 1965 and 1966, including Kurt Maetzig's *Das Kaninchen bin ich* (*The Rabbit is Me*), Frank Vogel's *Denk bloß nicht, ich heule* (*Just Don't Think I'll Cry*), Jürgen Böttcher's *Jahrgang '45* (*Born in '45*), and Frank Beyer's *Spur der Steine* (*The Trace of Stones*). In the void that followed, East German directors shied away from addressing contemporary matters and genre cinema like the Western flourished. The situation improved again briefly after Honecker rose to power in 1971. He declared no subject taboo for artistic representation, and a period of liberalization ensued along with the emergence a new generation of directors, resulting in landmark films like Heiner Carow's *Die Legende von Paul und Paula* (*The Legend of Paul and Paula*, 1973) and Frank Beyer's *Jakob der Lügner* (*Jacob the Liar*, 1974 — a film that broke barriers both as an exploration of Jewish persecution under National Socialism and as the only DEFA film ever nominated for an Oscar). But the atmosphere of openness had dissipated again by the mid-1970s in the face of SED discomfort with socially critical art, culminating infamously in 1976 in the expatriation of popular singer Wolf Biermann. The event inspired East Germany's most prominent intellectuals to draft a public letter of protest and, most disastrous for GDR film culture, subsequently prompted numerous DEFA luminaries to leave the country for the West.

West German cinema underwent its own revolution when, in 1962, a group of young directors gathered at a short-film festival in Oberhausen to demand fundamental change in the country's film culture. The document, known simply as the "Oberhausen Manifesto," called for changes in German subvention laws that would support emerging filmmakers and encourage formal innovation over formula. The signatories were forceful in their characterization of the existing climate: "The old cinema is dead. We believe in the new one." The federal government responded and on 1 February 1965 founded the *Kuratorium junger deutscher Film* (Committee for Young German Film), a fund designed to help finance young industry talent and thereby foster alternative productions. The manifesto, and more precisely its signatories — among them Alexander Kluge, Edgar Reitz, and Peter Schamoni — would go on to exert a profound influence on the art cinema of the FRG, forming the Young German Cinema movement, a loosely organized collaborative that sought to revolutionize West German cinema through aesthetic and narrative experimentation while also addressing the pressing political and social issues of the time. Kluge's *Abschied von gestern* (*Yesterday Girl*, 1966), a landmark film for its radical formal features and exploration of residual postwar antisemitism through the figure of the wayward Anita G., became the first work to receive Kuratorium support. By the early 1970s, the movement, now known as *Neuer Deutscher Film* (New German Cinema), had become a veritable international brand, garnering acclaim at international festivals with works by Volker Schlöndorff, Werner Herzog, and its most famous enfant terrible, Rainer Werner Fassbinder. Despite critical success, this new wave of West German art films never won big at the domestic box office. Far from expiring, popular genre cinema continued to thrive throughout the 1960s and 1970s in West Germany. Topping the charts were not the era's pensive, exploratory art films, but rather lighter fare: *Heimat* romances, Edgar Wallace crime dramas, and even the soft-core *Schulmädchen-Report* (Schoolgirl report) series. As it turned out, all declarations concerning the "death" of "Papa's Cinema" (as the preceding decades' film culture was derisively termed) proved rather premature.

Selected Bibliography • 1962–1976

Allan, Seán. "Revolutionary Aesthetics? Kleist, 1968, and the New German Cinema." *German Life and Letters* 64, no. 3 (2011): 472–87.

Alter, Nora M. *Projecting History: German Nonfiction Cinema, 1967–2000*. Ann Arbor: U of Michigan P, 2002.

Aurich, Rolf, Wolfgang Jacobsen, and Volker Noth, eds. *European 60s: Revolte, Phantasie & Utopie*. Munich: edition text + kritik, 2002.

Bergfelder, Tim. *International Adventures: German Popular Cinema and European Co-Productions in the 1960s*. New York: Berghahn Books, 2005.

Caprio, Temby. "Women's Film Culture in the Sixties: Stars and Anti-Stars from *Papas Kino* to the New German Wave." *Women in German Yearbook* 15 (1999): 201–25.

Corrigan, Timothy. *New German Film: The Displaced Image*. 2nd, revised edition. Bloomington: Indiana UP, 1994.

Davidson, John E., *Deterritorializing the New German Cinema*. Minneapolis: U of Minnesota P, 1999.

Elsaesser, Thomas. *New German Cinema: A History*. New Brunswick, NJ: Rutgers UP, 1989.

Falcon, Richard. "Cold Warriors." *Sight and Sound* 11, no. 11 (2001): 28–30.

Faulstich, Werner. "Vom Serienfilm über das Oberhausener Manifest zum jungen deutschen Film." In *Filmgeschichte*, 172–83. Paderborn: Fink, 2005.

Fay, Jennifer. "The Schoolgirl Reports and the Guilty Pleasure of History." In *Alternative Europe: Eurotrash and Exploitation Cinema since 1945*, edited by Ernest Mathijs and Xavier Mendik, 39–52. London: Wallflower, 2004.

Feinstein, Joshua. *The Triumph of the Ordinary: Depictions of Daily Life in the East German Cinema, 1949–1989*. Chapel Hill: U of North Carolina P, 2002.

Fischer, Robert, and Joe Hembus. *Der neue deutsche Film: 1960–1980*. Munich: Goldmann, 1981.

Flinn, Caryl. *The New German Cinema: Music, History, and the Matter of Style*. Berkeley: U of California P, 2004.

Hake, Sabine. "Political Affects: Antifascism and the Second World War in Frank Beyer and Konrad Wolf." In *Screening War: Perspectives on German Suffering*, edited by Paul Cooke and Marc Silberman, 102–22. Rochester, NY: Camden House, 2010.

Halle, Randall, and Margaret McCarthy. *Light Motives: German Popular Film in Perspective*. Detroit: Wayne State UP, 2003.

Harhausen, Ralf. *Alltagsfilm in der DDR: Die "Nouvelle Vague" der DEFA.* Marburg: Tectum, 2007.
Hoerschelmann, Olaf. "'Memoria dextera est': Film and Public Memory in Postwar Germany." *Cinema Journal* 40, no. 2 (2001): 78–97.
Knight, Julia. *New German Cinema: Images of a Generation.* London: Wallflower, 2004.
———. *Women and the New German Cinema.* London: Verso, 1992.
Kramp, Joachim. *Hallo! Hier spricht Edgar Wallace: Die Geschichte der deutschen Kriminalfilmserie von 1959–1972.* Berlin: Schwarzkopf & Schwarzkopf, 1998.
Langford, Michelle. *Allegorical Images: Tableau, Time and Gesture in the Cinema of Werner Schroeter.* Bristol, UK: Intellect, 2006.
Mathes, Bettina. *Die imaginierte Nation: Identität, Körper und Geschlecht in DEFA-Filmen.* Berlin: DEFA-Stiftung, 2007.
Miersch, Annette. *Schulmädchen-Report: Der deutsche Sexfilm der 70er Jahre.* Berlin: Bertz + Fischer, 2003.
Moeller, Hans-Berhard, and George Lellis. *Volker Schlöndorff's Cinema: Adaptation, Politics, and the "Movie-Appropriate."* Carbondale: Southern Illinois UP, 2002.
Paterson, Susanne F. "Fassbinder's *Ali: Fear East the Soul* and the Expropriation of a National Heim." *Post Script: Essays in Film and the Humanities* 18, no. 3 (1999): 46–57.
Petzel, Michael. *Der Weg zum Silbersee: Dreharbeiten und Drehorte der Karl-May-Filme.* Berlin: Schwarzkopf & Schwarzkopf, 2001.
Phillips, Klaus, ed. *New German Filmmakers: From Oberhausen through the 1970s.* New York: Ungar, 1984.
Prager, Brad. *The Cinema of Werner Herzog: Aesthetic Ecstasy and Truth.* London: Wallflower, 2007.
Reichmann, Hans-Peter, and Rudolf Worschech, eds. *Abschied vom Gestern: Bundesdeutscher Film der sechziger und siebziger Jahre.* Frankfurt am Main: Deutsches Filminstitut, 1991.
Rentschler, Eric. "A Cinema of Citation." *Artforum International* 47, no. 1 (2008): 416–84.
———, ed. *German Film and Literature: Adaptations and Transformations.* New York: Methuen, 1986.
———, ed. *West German Filmmakers on Film: Visions and Voices.* New York: Holmes & Meier, 1988.
Rinke, Andrea. *Images of Women in East German Cinema 1972–1982: Socialist Models, Private Dreamers and Rebels.* Lewiston: Edward Mellen, 2006.
Scharf, Inga. *Nation and Identity in the New German Cinema: Homeless at Home.* New York: Routledge, 2008.
Schneider, Tassilo. "Finding a New Heimat in the Wild West: Karl May and the German Western of the 1960s." In *Back in the Saddle Again: New Essays on the Western,* edited by Edward Buscombe and Roberta E. Pearson, 141–59. London: British Film Institute, 1998.

28 February 1962: Oberhausen Manifesto Creates Founding Myth for New German Cinema

Eric Rentschler

In the spring of 1962, the West German journal *Filmstudio* devoted a special issue to minor cinemas. Large letters, eccentric in their spelling and devoid of punctuation, covered a full page and proclaimed

> Papas cinema
> is dead mani
> festo of the young
> filmmakers 1962 ho
> pe or disaster

The reference, of course, was to the Oberhausen Manifesto of February 1962. It was well known to contemporary readers, who by then had heard and read much about the dramatic intervention of twenty-six brash filmmakers at the Oberhausen Film Festival. In an expression of Oedipal outrage, these angry young men spoke out against what they deemed to be a spiritually arid and intellectually bankrupt cinema, announcing their intention to bring creative redemption and intellectual renewal. Blending a harsh critique with a constructive resolve, the outspoken statement declared "the collapse of the conventional German film," reiterating this point in the closing ("The old film is dead") before expressing a hope ("We believe in the new one"). Moving from *Zusammenbruch* (collapse) to *Neubau* (new construction), the document demands a break with the past and offers a design for the future. In promising a fresh start, it unwittingly resembled the *Stunde Null* (Zero Hour) rhetoric that had circulated in Germany directly after the Second World War.

This legendary document would become the founding myth for the New German Cinema. Fifty years later, one does well to recall the energies that generated this outburst. The assault against "the conventional German film" was at once a response to established interests as well as to historical aporias. To decry the "conventional," above all, was to disdain the legacy of Ufa (Universum Film A.G.) and to applaud the postwar collapse of this famous (and infamous) studio and everything that it had stood for, especially the well-made German film with its staid tradition of quality that had dutifully and diligently served the National Socialist order. The young filmmakers rejected the cinema of their fathers (and grandfathers), particularly its *Geisteshaltung* (cultural perspective) — its collusion with the status quo and the establishment. In their virulent negativity inhered an equally ardent positivity, a belief that members of a younger generation might change the state of affairs if only they dared to stand up and seize the moment. In the words of film critic and fellow activist Enno Patalas, "Since the end of the war the state of the German film industry has never been so precarious. Which is to say it has never been so ready for an intellectual and artistic new beginning of German film."

Short films, maintained the activists (only a very few of whom had yet completed a feature), have made a splash at international festivals; these works have received the praise of foreign journalists and once again brought attention to German cinema. This gesture, to be sure, was prescient in its recognition of how powerful a bargaining chip foreign regard could be; indeed, in subsequent years, the New German filmmakers would become masters in the triangulation of desire, using their festival successes and triumphs abroad as a means to legitimate their endeavors at home and to secure funding for future productions. Beyond that, they asserted, these signs of life enact a new film language. (This point, it should be noted, is asserted without further elaboration.) The short film, in that way, has functioned as a school and a site of experiment for the feature film. If the feature of the future is to arise, however, dramatic changes need to take place: artists must be freed from outmoded conventions, commercial pressures, and external interventions. With great (if not altogether justified, given the lack of experience among them) certainty, the members of group asserted that they had "concrete intellectual, formal, and economic ideas" for future films. Likewise, the signatories acknowledged their willingness to bear financial burdens.

Surely an overdetermined document, the Oberhausen Manifesto looked back in anger and gazed forward with hope. As a historical reckoning, it reiterated well-known and longstanding concerns about the state of West German film culture, which was so dire that the government had not deemed any feature worthy of a State Film Prize in 1961. Journalists and critics in the FRG had, throughout the 1950s, made their dismay regarding the quality of domestic features abundantly clear and repeatedly had called for a renewal of the nation's film culture. Take, for instance, the January 1958 issue of the most significant film journal, *Filmkritik*, which enumerated the New Year's wishes of the editorial board that there be "no new films by Liebeneiner, Hansen, Ucicky, Braun (Harald as well as Alfred), Hächler, Maetzig and, of course, Harlan" — all of whom (except Hächler and Maetzig) had played prominent roles during the Nazi era — as well as "no new films about wise doctors and trusting patients, jovial estate owners and pious peasants, war heroes, invaders from outer space and other stand-ins for Bolsheviks, Russian subhumans (in films from the West) and American subhumans (in films from the East), hooligans and Marcelinos, drug addicts, hat thieves and other eccentrics."

In his polemical analysis with the caustic title, *Der deutsche Film kann gar nicht besser sein* (German film cannot be better, 1961), the publicist Joe Hembus summarized a nation's serious concerns about its dismal film culture: the country's productions lacked an international presence; its films did not circulate widely, and its best known directors (Käutner, Staudte, Hoffmann, Thiele) enjoyed little recognition abroad and did not possess a distinctive authorial signature. One looked in vain for formal masterpieces or cinematic hallmarks, for films that reckoned with the past or confronted the present in compelling ways, for endeavors that took formal risks or provided alternative designs. The features of the era, insisted Hembus, were impersonal and insipid, star-centered and genre-driven. Almost without exception, West German films of the 1950s were the work of casts and crews who had served in studios administered by Joseph Goebbels's Ministry of Propaganda. The French *nouvelle vague*, maintained Hembus, offered a valuable foreign example and a viable solution to the West German *misère*: here "a group of young people with something to say chose film as their medium and secured access to opportunities to say what they had to say."

Pulling the emergency brake in the speeding express train of history, the Oberhausen signatories demanded a change of course. The moment was right: West German film was, just about everyone agreed, a national embarrassment. The crisis of "Papa's cinema" coincided with the bitter end of the Adenauer administration and what was known as the "Spiegel affair" of 1962, a public scandal that ultimately led to the chancellor's resignation. Although there had been several attempts to foster renewal in the West German film scene, none of these previous endeavors (e.g., the "Memorandum Regarding a New German Film" of 1946 or the "DOC 59," a collective of documentarians, cinematographers, composers, and critics) had found success. The drafters of the Oberhausen Manifesto gathered on a January evening in a backroom of the Chinese restaurant Hongkong in Munich's Tengstraße. The impetus of Alexander Kluge, an author and a lawyer, very much influenced the shape and substance of the document. The new film would reflect the thoughts and energies of a younger Germany, a generation that had been doubly disfranchised, both as producers and spectators. Its proponents would seek dialogue with representatives of the other arts in order to free film from its intellectual isolation in the FRG. Cinema, argued Kluge, should embrace a more encompassing and expansive sense of reality and serve as a site of oppositional expression. It should dare to be different and militate against established interests and, in so doing, foster a more inclusive and dynamic public sphere. Any creative renewal, the Oberhauseners realized, could only take place if one transformed the means of production so that economic criteria did not remain the sole measure of success and quality.

The Oberhausen demonstration occasioned much critical comment. As one might expect, members of the film industry and the conservative press ridiculed the young men's presumptuousness, linking their inflated rhetoric to that of the liar of lore, Baron Münchhausen, and calling them "Obermünchhausener." Still, the initiative served as a valuable catalyst with significant and lasting results, including: the founding of film academies in Ulm, West Berlin, and Munich; the formation of a government funding agency, the Board of Curators of the Young German Film in February 1965, which would serve as a model for a large network of subsequent federal and regional funding agencies; and an initial wave of impressive films, all of which but one had received support from the Board of Curators, which appeared in 1966. *Es* (*It*, Ulrich Schamoni) and *Der junge Törless* (*Young Törless*, Volker Schlöndorff) premiered at the Cannes Film Festival where Schlöndorff received the International Critics' Prize. A few months later, *Schonzeit für Füchse* (*No Shooting Time for Foxes*, Peter Schamoni) garnered a Silver Bear at the Berlinale. And that fall Alexander Kluge's *Abschied von gestern* (*Yesterday Girl*) was awarded a Silver Lion at the Venice Film Festival. Critics from a host of countries celebrated a Young German Film. In the course of time auteurs from West Germany would gain a substantial profile as pliers of the New German Cinema, arguably the most significant national film movement of the 1970s. This success story would become well known and elaborated at length in a plethora of books and articles.

As a founding myth for a cinema of auteurs that would gain international prominence, the Oberhausen Manifesto provided a powerful legend. As a collective enterprise, it certainly marked a significant juncture where a number of creative and ambitious filmmakers came together and, for all their differences, spoke out in the name of a utopian vision. Their outspokenness was, given the historical moment, understandable and, in light of their marginal status, necessary; this outspokenness was above all contingent and, as such, warrants further scrutiny. Looking back at this foundational text from a different temporal perspective, we surely can note how it gave rise to a heroic narrative with some powerful and problematic consequences — a tale that deserves retelling in three crucial regards.

First, the Oberhausen activists occasioned criticism from various circles — and not merely the established film industry. They were strongly attacked by a number of independent filmmakers, individuals like Rudolf Thome, Roland Klick, and Klaus Lemke, as well as Jean-Marie Straub and Danièle Huillet, whose differences with the group ranged from formal reservations and political objections to discursive strategies. And the Oberhausen collective itself was never an uncontested and a united front, even if this gathering of filmmakers, most of whom operated out of Munich, deigned to speak for German film as a whole, overlooking and ignoring signs of life throughout the nation as well as a nascent alternative cinema that in fact existed in the 1950s. (Take, for instance, the work of Ottomar Domnick.) No mention is made of film production in the GDR; indeed, as was common at the time, one speaks of German film as if the FRG were the only Germany. In that regard, the Oberhausen Manifesto, for all its critical intent, remains a Cold War document. With its lack of female voices, it also reflected the patriarchal dispositions of the Adenauer era.

Second, Oberhausen's auteurist initiative, the antiauthoritarian impetus of 1968, and the programmatic resolve of the New German Cinema have played a strong, indeed predominant, role in how commentators have approached the films of the Adenauer era. We would, however, do well to reconsider the schematic and mythical narrative in which a limpid "Papas Kino" simply withered and vanished in response to an Oedipal uprising. In fact, this cinema and its proponents did not just disappear (several of its key figures are still prominent today). Fassbinder would not be the only one of his peers who would find a productive working relationship with representatives of the older generation. He would also not be the sole New German filmmaker to consider the Adenauer era and its mass culture with both fond and critical regard, and to acknowledge its influence on his own output. West German features of the fifties, for all their detractors, have had a remarkable staying power. Even today, various German filmmakers wonder how they might create a popular cinema and look back with envy at the Adenauer era. Others, to be sure, remain far less eager to let this sector of film history serve as a role model. It abides as a contested and a controversial cinema.

Finally, until recently scholars have gazed at West German films of the fifties mainly through the prism of the Oberhausen Manifesto and the New German Cinema, sharing the Manifesto's disdain for what the young filmmakers considered to be a compromised and bankrupt epoch. The ideological critiques of Siegfried Kracauer and Theodor Adorno had a strong influence on how West German film critics viewed the cinema of the 1950s as well as how the Oberhauseners assessed Adenauer-era productions. As pliers of distraction and effusions of a wannabe culture industry, the epoch's generic features found few progressive advocates. Moreover, as symptoms of a society ostensibly beset with collective amnesia, this fantasy ware, in keeping with Alexander and Margarete Mitscherlich's claim about West German culture at large, eluded the past and failed to engage the pressing concerns of the present. Recent scholars, returning to the cinema of the Adenauer era, are now coming to different conclusions. With renewed interest in the popular output of national cinemas has come a heightened regard for the multiple meanings (which include, but are not exhausted by, ideological operations) at work in genre films. It may well be, as Georg Seeßlen notes, more interesting to look for social truths in these films rather than to disclose their political falsehoods. No matter what conclusions we might reach, if we want to comprehend the shape and substance of West German dreams during the early postwar years, we can find no better resource. From this perspective, perhaps the cinema of the 1950s was neither as dead nor as moribund as the Oberhauseners maintained.

See also:

- 17 October 1930: Bertolt Brecht's *Threepenny Opera* Lawsuit Identifies Contradiction between Individual Creativity and Collective Production in Cinema
- 29 February 1972: With *Die Angst des Tormanns beim Elfmeter* New German Cinema Learns to Read
- 24 June 1974: Launching of *Frauen und Film* Creates Lasting Forum for Feminist Film Writing and Practice

1 February 1968: *Herstellung eines Molotow-Cocktails* Promotes Film as a Tool for Political Violence

Tilman Baumgärtel

As IN THE UNITED STATES and some other European countries, the month of May 1968 marked the climax of the *Studentenrevolte* (student rebellion) in Germany. The activities of the Außerparlamentarische Opposition (Extraparliamentary Opposition, APO) have become a canonized part of West Germany's postwar history. While incidents like the protests against the state visit of the Persian Shah Mohammad Reza Pahlavi, the assassination attempt on student leader Rudi Dutschke, or the blockade of the Berlin headquarters of the right-wing publishing house Springer have become the subject of history text books, the intimate connection that the student movement had with the film avant-garde of its time is less known.

These connections crystallized in the activities of the students of the Deutsche Film- und Fernsehakademie (German Film and Television Academy, DFFB) in Berlin. The short documentary and agitation films that the collective of politically interested students shot during their time at DFFB are documents of the German student movement that are almost forgotten today — probably due to the fact that these films typically are not mere documentary works on the student movement, but rather combine political radicalism and a stern filmic formalism in the spirit of the films of Jean-Luc Godard of the late 1960s.

Although largely gone from public memory, these films were important for the way that they debated — at first metaphorically, and eventually quite directly — whether one should remain an artist and political filmmaker or whether one should take the path to political violence. These alternatives became biographical reality for a good number of DFFB students: among the first batch of the DFFB were students who went on to become German film auteurs and proponents of *Neuer Deutscher Film* (New German Cinema) of the 1970s and 1980s, including Wolfgang Petersen, Wolf Gremm, Hartmut Bitomsky, Harun Farocki, Christian Ziewer, and Helke Sander. But two other students gave up on cinema completely and joined the Rote Armee Fraktion (Red Army Faction, RAF) and the Bewegung 2. Juni (Movement of the 2nd of June): Holger Meins and Philip Sauber, respectively. Both died in the mid-1970s as a consequence of their attachment to those terrorist groups: Meins died during a hunger strike in prison in 1975, while Sauber was shot in a police raid in 1975. These two possible paths for the DFFB students — artistic or militant — were already formulated in their school films.

The founding of the DFFB in 1966 was a relatively direct consequence of the Oberhausen Manifesto of 1962, one of a number of activities of the West German government intended to revive and support the local film industry. But almost from their first day at the film academy, the politically active students at DFFB were involved in a nonstop tug-of-war with the administration of the film school — a conflict that was observed with displeasure not only by the Berlin Senate, but also all the way up to the West German Ministry of the Interior, and almost lead to the shutdown of the school in the summer of 1968. The eighteen students behind the occupation of the school in May 1968 — including Farocki, Bitomsky, Ziewer, Petersen, Meins, Sauber — were eventually expelled from the school in November 1968.

The politicization of many students in West Berlin started in June 1967, when the Shah of Iran visited West Germany. This state visit and the television images of the *Jubelperser* — Iranians who cheered the Shah's visit to Germany, some of whom later turned out to be members of the Iranian secret police and who thrashed anti-Shah demonstrators with wooden slates and knuckle-dusters in Berlin — turned many German bohemians and liberals into radicals overnight. These included the students of the DFFB, many of which were on the streets on 2 June 1967. DFFB student Thomas Giefer filmed the violent clashes between police and protestors and, together with his fellow student Hans Rüdiger Minow, assembled the documentary *Berlin, 2. Juni 1967* (Berlin, 2 June 1967) from this footage.

In the evening of 2 June 1967, after a turbulent day of anti-Shah demonstrations in Berlin, the student Benno Ohnesorg was killed by shots from the service pistol of West Berlin police officer Karl-Heinz Kurras. Many of the former DFFB students are convinced still today that the shots were actually meant to hit Thomas Giefer and the camera that had documented police brutality during the anti-Shah demonstration in front of West Berlin's opera house. A court later decided that Ohnesorg had been the victim of an accident and, as Thomas Giefer puts it today, he does not want to "add to the mystification" of the incident. Yet the fact remains that Giefer and Ohnesorg looked similar, and both were at the Deutsche Oper at the same time, when the Berlin police quashed the demonstration. And Giefer was well known and unpopular with the Berlin police because he had used his 16-millimeter wind-up camera at earlier demonstrations.

In the following months the DFFB students grew politicized at a breathtaking pace. "In that year almost nobody finished a film," Harun Farocki remembered later, "Suddenly, many had much higher political demands on themselves and did not know how they should implement them in their films." The short films that came out of DFFB in 1967 and 1968 trace the radicalization among German students that would feed into the militant street actions of 1968 and, later, West German terrorism of the 1970s.

Harun Farocki's short film *Die Worte des Vorsitzenden* (The words of the chairman, 1967) was the first DFFB film that flirted, albeit subtly, with political violence. In it, pages from Mao's *Little Red Book* are folded into an arrow and then thrown at a figure bearing the facial features of the Shah of Persia, killing him. "The words of the chairman" must "become weapons in our hands, which hit the enemy out of the blue," intones the film's off-camera narrator.

The film is so stylized and so ironic that it still can be dismissed as a student prank. But this film suggests more than it actually says. Farocki's film shows words that turn into weapons. Thereby he foreshadows a discussion that became an increasingly important topic in other DFFB shorts as well as in the student movement proper: whether, instead of writing critical texts and giving speeches, instead of staging demonstrations or making films, one should turn to direct, militant action. This idea is worked through over and over again in the films made at the DFFB at the time, first still metaphorically and later in more concrete and intelligible terms.

In his next short film *Ihre Zeitungen* (Their newspapers, 1967), Farocki appears as a member of a "fighting collective" that wraps paving stones with pages taken from newspapers published by the right-wing Springer Verlag, which become one of the most important targets of the students in 1968 for its influence among the German working class as well as its biased and ultraconservative editorial style. "The paper gives the stone its direction," reads an intertitle at the end of the film, and the film ends with the sound of shattering glass. The message was plain: out of the cinema, comrades, and smash the windows of the class enemy! For those who still did not get it, Ulrich Knaudt's film *Unsere Steine* (Our stones), made a few months later, was even more obvious. It shows a young woman leafing through a Springer paper and carefully wrapping up cobblestones in the newsprint, followed by a cut to the high-rise office building of the Springer publishing house in the Kreuzberg neighborhood of Berlin partly concealed by eerie smoke. As a character in Jean Luc Godard's *One plus One* from the same year declares: "There is only one way of being a revolutionary intellectual: by ceasing to be an intellectual." For the DFFB students of that period, one could say: "There is only one way of being a revolutionary filmmaker: By ceasing to be a filmmaker."

Meanwhile, the flirtation with revolutionary violence slowly grew more serious. In early 1968 a film entitled *Herstellung eines Molotow-Cocktails* (The making of a Molotov cocktail) surfaced in West Berlin and was shown at teach-ins and at the Kommune 1. The film was anonymous, but it is now certain that Holger Meins made it. *Herstellung eines Molotow-Cocktails* demonstrates without any comment how to build a firebomb out of paper, gasoline, and an empty bottle. At the end of the film, there was, again, a long shot of the skyscraper of the Springer publishing offices. The paper from which the fuse was made was torn from Regis Debray's guerrilla manual. "Revolution in the revolution? Armed struggle and political struggle in Latin America."

Herbert Marcuse's "An Essay on Liberation," which appeared in 1969 in Germany and can be considered a kind of theory of the student movement after the fact, contended that the aesthetic should become a "productive force" and thus should lead to the "end of art through its realization." The politically active students at DFFB wanted to advance to the utopia that was expressed in art in just the same fashion. The films that emerged at the DFFB around 1968 give voice to the secret dream of the German student movement of the late 1960s. The sublimating cultural work of the intellectuals and the artists should for once turn into immediate emancipatory action: to throw a stone rather than making a political film, to plant a bomb instead of holding a speech.

When Farocki's *Die Worte des Vorsitzenden* declares that "the words of the chairman must become weapons in our hands that hit the enemy out of the blue," it was still possible to view the statement as a metaphor. With *Herstellung eines Molotow-Cocktails* such misunderstandings were no longer possible. The Meins film presented the two alternatives on the table at the DFFB and in the student movement at the time — political cinema or direct action — and demanded a decision. Do we want to keep on the sublimating production of culture or should we turn to militant action? Many student activists of that time decided to do the latter.

On 1 February 1968, a group including the Berlin lawyer Horst Mahler organized a teach-in at the Technische Universität in Berlin. An ultimatum was issued, and Springer was threatened with "direct action." Then 1500 students saw *Molotov-Cocktails*, with the long shot of the Springer skyscraper at the end, twice. The message was understood: in the wee hours of the next morning windowpanes at the offices of the Springer newspaper *Berliner Morgenpost* were smashed. Some of the stones were wrapped in leaflets, which demanded: "Expropriate Springer!"

"The paper gives the stone its direction," it says in Farocki's *Ihre Zeitungen*. On the morning of 2 February 1968, the stones started to fly in the specified direction. Art had turned into direct, revolutionary action and 1968 began in earnest. When a few weeks later student leader Rudi Dutschke was shot, it was the catalyst for riots that Germany had not experienced since the Weimar Republic. On Easter weekend students in West Berlin, who held the coverage by Springer's broadsheets responsible for the attempted murder, set fire to Springer delivery trucks. In Cologne, Munich, Hamburg, Frankfurt, and the Ruhr area Springer printing plants and offices were stormed or blocked as well.

The clashes at the DFFB gained momentum in the first half of 1968. In May, a group of students occupied the school, and renamed it "Dziga Vertow Academy." Not only in Berlin, but all across Europe cinephiles started to take to the revolutionary struggle of the summer of 1968. In Paris, filmmakers founded the "Estates-General of Film," a kind of revolutionary ad-hoc union of French film workers, that included even people like Roger Vadim and Claude Chabrol. Many of them made "Cine-Tracts," anonymous propaganda shorts that were shown at student demonstrations. Shortly after the founding of the Estates General of film, François Truffaut, Jean-Luc Godard, and a group of other cinema revolutionaries put an end to the Cannes Film Festival. A summer of interrupted festivals began: in Venice, where Pasolini lead the storming of the festival building, the army had to be called in to put an end to the uprising.

In November 1968, eighteen of the most rebellious students were expelled from the school after staging a "Go-In" in the office of DFFB Director Rathsack. Rector Erwin Leiser was forced to quit his post shortly after. In the years that followed, these former DFFB students continued to make films, but they now lacked the movement that had supported their productions. The movies that Christian Ziewer, Hartmut Bitomsky, Harun Farocki, Helke Sander, and other former DFFB students made in the following years were no longer revolutionary tracts, but rather socially conscious auteur films, and their activist films fell into oblivion. By the oppressive era of the mid-1970s, during what was called the *bleierne Zeit* (leaden time), it was no longer opportune to remind the public that they once were classmates of Holger Meins, the most famous of their ranks to choose the path to political violence over aesthetic sublimation.

See also:

- 4 September 1959: *Der Frosch mit der Maske* Moves Popular Cinema from Idyllic Pastures to Crime-Infested City Streets
- Fall 1968: Expulsion of Thomas Brasch from GDR Film School Signals Fate of East German '68ers
- 27 October 1977: *Deutschland Im Herbst* Equivocation on RAF Marks End Stage of Radical Filmmaking

1 February 1968: Konrad Wolf's *Ich war neunzehn* Evokes an East German Nation in Transition

Larson Powell

The grim image of an executed German deserter against an empty landscape evokes the boundaries of the GDR. Ich war neunzehn *(1968). DVD capture.*

THE LATE 1960s in the GDR marked the end of the Ulbricht era, with its brief period of economic liberalization (the New Economic System) and post-Wall openness to artistic experiment. The period after the Eleventh Plenum in 1965, which had put an abrupt end to that new freedom, was not only one in which DEFA (Deutsche Film-Aktiengesellschaft, East Germany's state-owned film company) was redefined, but also one in which the GDR state was refounded with a new constitution, first set out in 1968 and then revised in 1974. The first GDR constitution of 1949 was still seen as an "all-German compromise constitution," looking both backward to the end of the war in calling the GDR an "antifascist-parliamentary-democratic republic," and also forward to an imagined future where all of Germany, East and West, would be included in an "indivisible democratic republic."[1] By contrast, the 1968 version famously termed the GDR a "socialist state of German nationality" (*sozialistischer Staat deutscher Nation*) in its first article — a formulation that would be abandoned in 1974 in favor of "socialist state of workers and peasants."[2] Such formulations betray the paradoxical and contradictory nature of all such legal self-definitions of the GDR. Not only did the constitution as such have an insecure status within Marxist political thought, but the GDR could not close itself off as a legal identity without referring to nonexistent fictions, fictions born both of Marxist philosophy of history and of the German division. Such fictions were also built into the constitution of the FRG, which like that of the GDR acknowledged the unity of one German *Volk* that did not in fact exist. For GDR legal theorists, *nation* could not be the same as *nationality*. If the latter was ethnic and cultural, thus bound up to earlier German history, the former could be, like socialism itself, a developing and ongoing process — and one thus subject to the planned, rational social-engineering of socialist consciousness.

Film has always been one of the primary instruments of such social engineering, a technology of the social imaginary. It is thus not surprising to find some of the same paradoxes and tensions present in GDR legal thought at work in one of the most important DEFA films, Konrad Wolf's *Ich war neunzehn* (*I was nineteen*, 1968). *Ich war neunzehn* was not only a pivotal film in Wolf's oeuvre, an autobiographical testimony marked by the same personal authenticity sought by GDR writers like Christa Wolf, and a film that subtly combined documentary effects and fictional narrative with audiovisual montage (especially in its opening sequence) — it was also a film that helped put DEFA back on its feet after the collective trauma of the Eleventh Plenum. *Ich war neunzehn* premiered on 1 February 1968, the same day as the publication of the second GDR constitution, at a point almost exactly midway between the GDR's founding in 1949 and its collapse in 1989. It is thus appropriate that the film should itself retell the founding narration of the GDR's birth from the defeat of Nazi Germany in 1945, as seen from the perspective of nineteen-year-old Gregor Hecker, who has spent the years from 1933 to 1945 in exile in Moscow and only now returns to Germany from abroad — mirroring the experience of director Konrad Wolf, on whose wartime diaries the script was based.

We can find the tension between nation and nationality at work in the opening and closing sequences of this film. In accordance with a long German tradition, the opening gives sound preeminence over image, for we hear the voices of Gregor and his comrades in their propaganda truck before we see them. Gregor's voice on the microphone is not immediately identifiable as his. Nor is there any establishing shot showing us either the interior of the truck or the surrounding landscape. Instead of the usual spatial continuity, the viewer is given metaphors linking a hanged German deserter and Gregor, and several long shots of the Elbe valley, thus opposing the historical landscape of Germany's Eastern frontier to the Master's Voice of official antifascist discourse over the loudspeaker. We never see the Wehrmacht soldiers whom Gregor is addressing.

This split of sound and image — of silent natural frontier landscape and technologically mediated voice — may be related to one within the narrating subject position of Wolf's film. If Thomas Elsaesser found a split between seeing and being seen, exhibitionism and voyeurism in Fassbinder, and correlated it to the visual culture of Nazism as pleasurable spectacle, we may find here a split characteristic of DEFA cinema, marking the unstable position of a filmic narration divided between nation and nationality — state rationality and the irrational inheritance of German history — as represented in voice and image, respectively. The privileging of the voice bears a particular historical signature within the GDR's media landscape.[3] It is also the heir to a media politics of the voice defined by Nazi radio and the radio voice of exile writers, many of whom would return to Germany after 1945 to work for reeducation via broadcasting. In the film, however, the silent landscape and the invisible German soldiers appear unresponsive to this voice's insistent appeal.

Gregor's unease and uncertainty throughout the film is inseparable from his difficulties in learning to perform his own Germanness. We see his discomfort at having to speak German, his singing Soviet war-songs like "Katyusha" while on the road, and his imaginary dialogue with his reproachful mother when he is drunk during the victory celebrations at Sanssouci. As Jacobsen and Aurich noted in their discussion of the film, Gregor is "ein seltsam abwesendes Ich" (a strangely absent I).[4] This absence refers not only to his youth, or his double identity as German and Russian, but also his split between German nationality and a not-yet-existent GDR nation, for which Gregor's Russianness must temporarily stand in.

The opening scene is legible as an address to Germany Pale Mother, to a still-absent nation — a genre that has a long history in Germany (see Johann Gottlieb Fichte, *Reden an die deutsche Nation* [*Addresses to the German Nation*]). The appellative, imploring nature of Gregor's speech may be related to what, in legal terms, are called "*ordre-public*-formulas" (public policy formulas), which tend to be general in nature, appealing to larger overall principles or norms on which law is meant to be based; appeal to *ordre public* was one of the means by which GDR legal practice covered-over the rift between its stated principles and real practice, and attempted to compensate for the deliberate ambiguity of many of its statements.⁵ The split between nation and nationality defines the generic instability of *Ich war neunzehn* as an antifascist film as well. On the seam where image and sound cannot coincide, Gregor's voice falls out as voice-over, as confession of the ultimate impossibility of any closed, stable GDR identity.⁶ Like Christa Wolf, whose pursuit of personal authenticity he shared, Konrad Wolf then had to stylize this instability into the subjectivity of an art film.

The same split returns at the end of the film, thus creating a frame for the rest of the narrative. At the conclusion, we have another liminal situation at a frontier. As H.-J. Wulff has remarked, the historical origins of the GDR are here spatialized into a rite of passage from Nazism into socialism. Once more, we never see the viewpoint of the Wehrmacht soldiers (so that there is incomplete suturing in shot/countershot).⁷ Although the beginning of the scene is leisurely, Gregor's discovery that his friend Sasha has been shot provokes a passionate denunciation of the SS over the microphone. As Gregor yells angrily out over the landscape, the camera opens up the space while his voice acquires greater resonance. It is as if this voice had exploded the limits of filmic diegesis to address itself directly to the public.⁸ Finally, Gregor's voice quiets down again and retreats into the private and confessional sphere once more. In this muting of the appellative, Wolf comments on both the fragility of Gregor's position and that of the antifascist film genre.

Wolf's film gives André Bazin's notion that cinema should be a "dramaturgy of nature" a specific historical signature. For the frontier regions of this film have strong connotations. It was French historians who first showed how the idea of natural boundaries (*frontières naturelles*) arose from bourgeois nationalism's need to found itself in a natural order. Bazin's neorealist conception owed something to this as well; as a recent commentator has noted, "Geography is palpable not only in Bazin's ontology but also in his conception of the language of cinema."⁹ This presence of geography is also palpable in Wolf. *Ich war neunzehn* transposes the fluidity of the political (and medial) boundaries of the GDR onto the geographical openness of the East. The opening scene's shot of the hanged deserter recalls earlier revolutionary iconography. In 1790, Goethe — no friend of the Revolution — drew a picture of a *Freiheitsbaum* on the Mosel at the French border. The tree wore a Phrygian cap and the inscription, *Passans* [sic] *cette terre est libre*.¹⁰ Wolf's hanged deserter proclaims the opposite of this. Yet the empty openness of his Elbe landscapes also leaves open the possibility of historical change. The topographic flatness and emptiness of these spaces have the "heavy spell" Bazin saw in Welles's long takes, but they are given the signature of a specifically German view, at once mourning for the past and hesitantly hopeful for the future. The ambivalence of a nation's frontier landscape is one that is historically and legally coded. The continued openness of the "German question" — that is, of the relation between divided nation and united nationality — meant that until 1989, the concept of "Germany . . . as a diminished legal remnant of the 'Reich' still possessed . . . an indispensable function . . . for the occupying powers' legal questions and for an ultimate peaceful and contractual settlement in the future."[11]

The correlation between legal concepts and the national definition of the GDR sketched in here suggests that we need to complement the current habit of seeing communities as "imaginary" (à la Benedict Anderson) with a symbolic dimension. It does not make sense to marginalize questions of law and sovereignty in DEFA's redefinitions of Germanness. This is especially acute in the case of the GDR, whose instable "identity" was defined by a contradiction between nation and state. This contradiction has deep roots in Marxist theory. Marxist doctrine emphatically rejected any merely cultural idea of the nation, such as Otto Bauer's "community of fate" or, later, Willy Brandt's "feeling of belonging together" circa 1970. As Klaus Erdmann formulated it: "GDR theoreticians always saw the existence of the socialist state as an essential trait of socialist nations."[12] This became even more marked after the building of the Wall, as in 1968 when the new GDR constitution declared the GDR to be a "socialist state of the German nation." With this, GDR legal theorists reversed Marx's old idea of the withering away of the state (Erdmann, 116). It was as if they wanted to take seriously Brecht's suggestion, after the 1953 uprising, that "it would be better if the state would elect itself another people."

Even more problematic was that the concept of nation could not be abandoned either — meaning that in an age when film, with other forms of industry, was increasingly becoming globalized, DEFA remained tied to an older model of national production. Yet the GDR could not close its national boundaries without abandoning its claim to represent the entire German nation. This meant that "the GDR constitution . . . kept itself in a condition of territorial suspense" (Erdmann, 75). The tension between state and nation thus had to be deferred to an unspecified revolutionary future. The nation was seen as "being in transition" to some presumed higher synthesis — one it would however never reach. It is this openness of the GDR that is staged by *Ich war neunzehn*, and that makes it still fascinating today.

See also:

- 9 March 1954: *Ernst Thälmann — Sohn seiner Klasse* Marks High Point of Socialist Realism
- 20 June 1977: DEFA's Biggest Star, Manfred Krug, Leaves the GDR
- 2 February 1988: Last Generation of DEFA Directors Calls in Vain for Reform

Notes

[1] Herwig Roggemann, ed., *Die DDR-Verfassungen: Einführung in das Verfassungsrecht der DDR* (Berlin: Spitz-Verlag, 1989, 4th ed.), 23, 25, 64.

[2] Ibid., 16.

[3] See Jochen Hörisch, "Das Vergehen der Gegenwartsliteratur," *Merkur* 502 (1991): 89.

[4] Wolfgang Jakobsen and Ralf Aurich, *Der Sonnensucher* (Berlin: Aufbau, 2005), 316.

[5] Gerhard Dilcher, "Vom bürgerlichen Gesetzbuch zu den 'Rechtszweigen' — Sozialistische Modernisierung oder Entdifferenzierung des Rechts?," in *Rechtserfahrung DDR*, ed. Dilcher (Berlin: Spitz 1997), 118–19, 130. On the discrepancy between GDR legal theory and real existing political praxis, see Hermann Weber, *Die DDR 1945–1990* (Munich: Oldenbourg, 1993), 69–70. The deliberate unspecificity of these general formulae may also be related to the early GDR's reaching out to non-Communist intelligentsia through a tactical return to 1930s *Volksfront* policy.

[6] "Fall-out" is meant here in Lacan's sense, of an "object a" that falls out of the mismatch of symbolic language and subjectivity (see *Le Séminaire Livre XI: Les Quatre concepts fondamentaux de la psychoanalyse* [Paris: Seuil, 1973], chapter 6); here, however, this fall-out has a specifically historical East German index.

[7] Hans Jürgen Wulff, "Ein Brief zu *Ich war Neunzehn*," in *Konrad Wolf: Neue Sichten auf seine Filme; Ein Beitrag zur Film- und Fernsehwissenschaft*, ed. Renate Georgi and Peter Hoff (Berlin: Vistas, 1990), 133–45.

[8] Gregor's voice-over functions in the film both as first-person witness and also — from the viewpoint of historical retrospective, implied in the title's past tense — as what Sarah Kozloff has called a "frame narrator" (*Invisible Storytellers* [Berkeley: U California P, 1988], p. 42). Through "frame narrators," "the tale [of the film] is being deliberately addressed to us" (51).

[9] Ludovic Courtade, "Cinema across Fault Lines: Bazin and the French School of Geography," in *Opening Bazin: Postwar Film Theory and Its Afterlife*, ed. Dudley Andrew and Hervé Joubert-Laurencin (Oxford: Oxford UP, 2011), 13–31; here 18.

[10] See Daniel Nordman, "From the Boundaries of the State to National Borders" in *Rethinking France: Les Lieux de Mémoire*, ed. Pierre Nora, vol. 1, *The State* (Chicago: U of Chicago P, 2001), 105–32.

[11] Roggemann, *Die DDR-Verfassungen*, 85.

[12] Klaus Erdmann, *Der gescheiterte Nationalstaat: Die Interdependenz von Nations- und Geschichtsverständnis im politischen Bedingungsgefüge der DDR* (Frankfurt: Peter Lang 1996), 39. Hereafter cited in text.

7 April 1968: Straub, Huillet, and Fassbinder Share the Stage at Munich's Action-Theater

Barton Byg

O N 7 APRIL 1968, the stage was shared by two theatrical works that later became landmark films pointing forward to New German Cinema: Fassbinder's play, *Katzelmacher*, and Ferdinand Bruckner's 1926 expressionist drama, *Krankheit der Jugend* (*Pains of Youth*), directed by Jean-Marie Straub (credited alone, although he always rehearsed and directed in concert with Danièle Huillet). The date marks an important juncture in a history of productive intersection between theater and film that extended throughout New German Cinema, since it marks the origins of two key films: Straub/Huillet's *Der Bräutigam, die Komödiantin und der Zuhälter* (*The Bridegroom, the Comedienne, and the Pimp*, 1968) and Fassbinder's *Katzelmacher* (1969).

Both *Bräutigam* and *Katzelmacher* have at their core a stylized depiction — one might say a dissection — of constellations of sexual, social, and class relations, abruptly revealing the sometimes-violent dynamics of personal and political power. In addition to their presentation of gender dynamics via generic tropes, with the immigrant worker Jorgos in *Katzelmacher* and the Black character of James in *Bräutigam*, both films also touch upon issues of ethnic and national conflict. Equally significant, the cinematic fruits of this April evening offer among the most significant examples of "the Brechtian aspect of Radical cinema"[1] in the context of "political modernism."[2]

The collaboration represented a critical juncture in the work of Straub/Huillet as well as Fassbinder. *Krankheit der Jugend* soon formed the center panel of Straub/Huillet's "triptych" film *Bräutigam*, with Fassbinder in a central role — in the Bruckner drama as well as in the final "gangster" segment of the film. Fassbinder credited this experience, and Huillet's views on acting in particular, as a strong influence on his later work, though this is already evident in the film version of *Katzelmacher*. *Katzelmacher* was only Fassbinder's second film; *Bräutigam* was Straub/Huillet's fourth before leaving Germany for Rome, having also completed *Machorka-Muff* (1962), *Nicht versöhnt oder Es hilft nur Gewalt wo Gewalt herrscht* (*Not Reconciled or, Only Violence Helps Where Violence Rules,* 1965), and *Chronik der Anna Magdalena Bach* (*Chronicle of Anna Magdalena Bach,* 1967). Even in Italy they would soon return to German texts, however, with *Geschichtsunterricht* (*History Lessons*) in 1972, based on Bertolt Brecht's *Die Geschäfte des Herrn Julius Cäsar* (*The Business Affairs of Mr. Julius Caesar*).

The texts performed and the figures involved in this collaboration further reflect a number of key elements that make New German Cinema unique. Like the genre variations and homages to Weimar by other directors of New German Cinema, the Straub/Huillet film points back in some ways to early silent cinema, expressionism, and gangster films, as well as to the culture of the 1920s. Bruckner's diction, already compressed and violent in the telegram style of the era, is heightened by Straub's reduction of the entire three acts to eleven minutes. Fassbinder's film, too, has been compared to precursors, such as Dreyer's *La Passion de Jeanne d'Arc* (*The Passion of Joan of Arc,* 1928), but also points forward to his New German Cinema productions, which featured many of the same actors already present here. Appearing in both the Straub/Huillet and the Fassbinder film were Fassbinder himself, Hanna Schygulla, Harry Baer, Irm Hermann, and Lilith Ungerer (whom Straub considered the strongest actor of all). *Bräutigam* was Schygulla's very first film role, and the Bruckner play, according to Straub, her first stage performance. This overlapping of actors and reference to Weimar film history would become a hallmark of New German Cinema, resulting in a complex form of intertextuality that suggests links between films by one director or contemporaries, intergenerationally or internationally within the cinema, and between theater and film. Intergenerational references to Weimar are particularly poignant, for Straub/Huillet as well as for Rosa von Praunheim, Werner Schroeter, and Volker Schlöndorff, who have all cast or otherwise celebrated figures from Weimar cinema. And the reverence of Schlöndorff, Fassbinder, or Herzog for German film exiles from the 1930s is legendary. Syberberg and Fassbinder are unusual, on the other hand, for also connecting to the star culture of Ufa (Universum Film A.G.) in the Nazi era.

Brecht was another key common denominator between Fassbinder and Straub/Huillet, although no actual Brecht productions came about. Brecht's work was a central element in the political modernism of 1960s film, both for the French (such as Godard) and for the Germans, especially after the journal *Filmkritik* and others began an intensive critical engagement with both him and Walter Benjamin. Straub/Huillet's earlier film *Nicht versöhnt* signals this by beginning with a quotation from Brecht on acting that also applies to a self-reflexive, documentary-based approach to film fiction: "Instead of wanting to create the impression that he is improvising, the actor should rather show what the truth is: he is quoting." Fassbinder's initial invitation to Straub to direct at the Action-Theater had been for Brecht's *Die Massnahme* (*The Measures Taken*), but, according to Straub's recollections, Helene Weigel refused permission, saying: "That is a *Lehrstück*; it is not for the public." The "learning play" format, and its employment to experiment with cinematic and photographic representation, remained a touchstone for Straub/Huillet as it has been for much of German avant-garde cinema. To both Fassbinder and Straub/Huillet, Brecht was of crucial interest for political and formal reasons. They undertook what H. B. Moeller has called the "Brechtian attack . . . against the West German success story."[3] Although Fassbinder and Straub/Huillet maintained a distance from "movement" politics, their work reflects the period's bitter critique of West German society and its failure to come to terms with the Nazi past.

Elena del Rio and other critics rightly insist on the heterogenous range of influences on Fassbinder, as well as the wider theater and film scene in Munich at the time. They cite such figures as Andy Warhol, Antonin Artaud, Jean-Luc Godard, and the innovators of the Living Theater (Julian Beck and Judith Malina). Not only were expressionism and other historical avant-garde movements influential in the eclectic mix of 1960s film, the *Kritisches Volksstück* (the critical, realistic folk play) was also regaining currency at the time, hence Fassbinder's dedication of *Katzelmacher* to playwright Marieluise Fleißer. Parallel to Fassbinder's work, a film version of Martin Sperr's *Jagdszenen aus Niederbayern* (1965) was directed by Peter Fleischmann (*Hunting Scenes from Bavaria*, 1969). In contemporary innovations, the Living Theater represented another central influence on Munich's Action-Theater. Fassbinder's play *Preparadise Sorry Now* (1969), close in time to *Katzelmacher*, explicitly cites and parodies the 1960s counterculture mystique of Judith Malina and Julian Beck's *Paradise Now* (1968). But the influence of Brecht was never far away: Malina also authored one of the few English translations of Brecht's *Antigone*, and Straub/Huillet would much later turn this landmark of Brecht and Hölderlin into one of their most ambitious and significant films, *Die Antigone des Sophokles nach der hölderlinschen Übertragung für die Bühne bearbeitet von Brecht 1948 (Suhrkamp Verlag)* (Brecht's 1948 adaptation of Hölderlin's translation of Sophocles's *Antigone*, 1991–92).

If theater and opera have an unusually strong importance in Germany, both as cultural touchstones and as arenas for avant-garde experiment, their influences — and especially those of Brecht — are particularly crucial for New German Cinema. Many New German Cinema directors have worked in theater or opera, collaborated closely with playwrights, or are principally theater figures themselves. Ulrike Ottinger has collaborated with Elfriede Jelinek for the stage, and a range of theatrical elements is always present in her films. Opera productions have been directed by figures as diverse as Alexander Kluge, Werner Herzog, Hans-Jürgen Syberberg, and, much later, Andreas Dresen. Playwright Thomas Brasch ventured from theater to film with a number of remarkable works, while

Jutta Brückner has consistently returned both to Brecht and theater. Wim Wenders and playwright Peter Handke have collaborated, and Handke has also directed in his own right. Volker Schlöndorff worked with the British playwright Edward Bond early on in developing the script for *Michael Kohlhaas — Der Rebell* (*Man on Horseback*, 1969), and entitled a 2003 essay, "For me there was only one God, and that was Brecht."

For Fassbinder and Straub/Huillet in 1968, their Brechtian commonalities would include the distanciation of acting style and the avoidance of "psychological" realism or any attempt at emotional verisimilitude in the delivery of lines. The use of stylized gesture and static positioning ("gestus"), extended to formal composition and long takes in film, also is consistent with Brecht's modernist influence in cinema. The "social gestus," however, is not merely a formal example of distanciation, but is also meant to highlight and expose to criticism the power relations in society.[4] Indeed, Straub/Huillet's and Fassbinder's connections to Brecht, Artaud, and the larger world of contemporary theater are revealed most productively in the more experimental aspects of their theatrical and cinematic works, particularly their use of the body and the voice. For Fassbinder, the actor's body always is a bearer of social meaning, often trapped in restrictions of theatrical or cinematic nature, or suspended in quasi-expressionistic poses that convey power dynamics. For Straub/Huillet, the latter could also hold true, with a strong emphasis on landscape or framing (even if they place greater emphasis on the actor's body as a bearer of a voice that, in turn, serves as a bearer of a text). Several weeks of long and painstaking rehearsals for the eleven-minute version of *Krankheit der Jugend* (during which time Fassbinder was writing *Katzelmacher* with the same actors in mind) had for Straub/Huillet the primary goal of cementing the relationship between the speaker and the text, but in an intimate, physical and personal way.

In Straub/Huillet's films, the actor's cultural status and social gestus are documented with restrained dramatic techniques, while the physical aspect is also emphasized — what Peter Handke called the "athletic" quality of line delivery.[5] Past roles and a life of privilege resonate in the performances of Werner Rehm (cofounder of the *Schaubühne*) as Creon in *Antigone*, for instance, or of Mario Adorf as Uncle Jacob in *Klassenverhältnisse* (*Class Relations*, 1984). Laura Betti, famous for her roles with Fellini and Pasolini, provides an unforgettable cameo as Kafka's singer Brunelda, while Libgart Schwarz, also of the *Schaubühne*, delivers some of the most memorable speeches of stage or screen as Therese in *Klassenverhältnisse* and as the maid in *Antigone*. Lay actors' embodiment of literary texts is also crucial to the theatrical power of Straub/Huillet films, from the elder generation of Faehmels in *Nicht versöhnt* to the later works based on Vittorini and Pavese. Text and theatrical/cinematic composition are united by the diffused sunlight that falls on Lilith at the end of *Bräutigam*'s "gangster" segment, and the expressionistic lighting that illuminates the mother in *Sicilia!* (1999) (nonprofessional actor Angela Nugara) as she remembers her father on horseback — with both women gazing out a window toward an unseen, unrepresentable space.

From Munich in 1968, Fassbinder's attention eventually turned to Hollywood, as it did for other New German Cinema directors. But despite their adulation of Ford and Hawks and their parallel journey to the United States with Kafka's *Amerika*, Straub/Huillet returned to delve deeper into the European literary and dramatic tradition — culminating in landscape films based on Hölderlin, the mythological investigations of Pavese, and the political vignettes of Vittorini — with nonprofessional actors. Throughout the decades, Straub/Huillet continued to connect their film productions to theatrical practice. On the one hand, rehearsal with the actors over weeks and months remained a central tenet of their work, privileging both the text and the actor's performance with body and voice (never separated by cinematic rerecording technology). At the same time, Straub/Huillet have consistently linked their films to actual live performances, but without ever resorting to what would now be considered "multimedia." *Antigone* and *Moses and Aaron*, among others, were performed live for the residents of the regions in which they were filmed. The performers as well as the locations for Straub's latest works (both before and after Huillet's death) are closely tied to the theater community of Buti, Italy (Dante's *O Somma Luce* in 2009, Pavese's *L'Inconsabile/Orfeo* in 2010). With *Lukullus* (2010), the director has also returned to Brecht.

In the contemporary successors to Brechtian cinema and political, documentary-based fiction film, the influences described above remain productive. The 1968 encounter at the Action-Theater, the political aesthetic behind these works as they are transformed into film, their affinity to such contemporaries as Jean-Luc Godard, and the international nature of the artistic ferment of the 1960s provide a model for combining cultural and political content and innovative form. Straub has said that making *Bräutigam* in 1968 was his way of participating in the events of Paris, where he could not travel for political reasons. Straub/Huillet's vigorous exploration of one extreme in the spectrum of what could be called "Brechtian" in cinema has remained consistently visible in the juxtaposition of "theatrical" presentation and cinematic space — even documentary technique — in the works of such directors as Alexander Kluge, Harun Farocki, Pedro Costa, and Thomas Heise.

The latter two names in particular — one Portuguese, one from the former GDR — provide another contemporary link to the political internationalism of 1968. Straub/Huillet, like most of the New German Cinema of the West, had little to do with the GDR, despite its own direct legacy from Brecht and Weigel and its post-Brechtian theatrical innovations. Still, several locations from Straub/Huillet's Bach film were in the GDR, filmed with assistance from DEFA (Deutsche Film-Aktiengesellschaft, East Germany's state-owned film company), and indirect references to the East crop up in Fassbinder and Wenders, and even in Straub/Huillet's *Antigone*, where Albert Hetterle of the East Berlin Maxim Gorki Theater plays Tiresias. The 2003 "Brecht Dialog" *Brecht plus minus Film* provides an overview of the contemporary status of this Brechtian strain in theater, photography, and film. Here the New German Cinema is brought, via Brecht, into dialog with the GDR and with the international political modernist cinema as well. It is only fitting that this Brecht "learning play," which comes to us via the GDR playwright Heiner Müller and was recently filmed by Philippe Vincente, stands as a contemporary counterpoint to the emblematic encounter of film and theater that occurred in Munich in 1968.

See also:

- 27 May 1921: *Scherben* Seeks Cinematic Equivalent of Theatrical Intimacy
- 19 September 1958: Douglas Sirk's *A Time to Love and a Time to Die* Tests Limits of Postwar Feeling
- 20 August 1981: R. W. Fassbinder's *Lola* Revisits Kracauer to Critique Adenauer Period

Notes

[1] See Martin Walsh, *The Brechtian Aspect of Radical Cinema* (London: BFI, 1981).

[2] See David N. Rodowick, *The Crisis of Political Modernism: Criticism and Ideology in Contemporary Film Theory* (Berkeley: U of California P, 1994).

[3] Hans-Bernhard Moeller, "*The Marriage of Maria Braun — Veronika Voss — Lola*: Fassbinder's use of Brechtian aesthetics," *Jump Cut* 35 (April 1990): 102–7.

[4] See Elin Diamond, "Brechtian Theory/Feminist Theory: Toward a Gestic Feminist Criticism," *TDR* 32, no. 1 (Spring, 1988), 82–94.

[5] Barton Byg, *Landscapes of Resistance: The German Films of Danièle Huillet and Jean-Marie Straub* (Berkeley: U of California P, 1995), 223.

23 June 1968: Alexander Kluge Egged in Berlin, Months Later Awarded Gold Lion in Venice

Richard Langston

WEST GERMAN CINEMA was not unscathed by the rebellious ethos of 1968. In fact, the most radical fringes of film culture in 1968 left an indelible impression on the composition of West German film culture. Less than one semester into its existence, the state- and federally funded Deutsche Film- und Fernsehakademie Berlin (German Film and Television Academy, DFFB), the first of its kind, found itself caught up in the events unfolding in the streets of West Berlin. On the very evening that heated the entire West German student movement to a boil, film school students Thomas Giefer and Hans Rüdiger Minow captured enough footage of the violent clashes between students and police in front of the Deutsche Oper to make a powerful fifty-minute documentary simply titled *Berlin, 2. Juni 1967* (Berlin, 2 June 1967). Other first-year students quickly followed suit, shooting films in the service of the coming revolution. While some shorts, like Helke Sander's *Brecht die Macht der Manipulateure* (Crush the power of the manipulators, 1967/68), flirted with language of *cinéma vérité* and direct cinema, others like Harun Farocki's *Die Worte des Vorsitzenden* (The words of the chairman, 1967) and Ulrich Knaudt's *Unsere Steine* (Our stones, 1968) turned to allegory and thinly veiled allusion to convey their agit-prop. Attributed to DFFB student and later Baader-Meinhof accomplice Holger Meins, *Herstellung eines Molotow-Cocktails* (The making of a Molotov cocktail, 1968) sought to use the genre of instructional film as a tool to instigate urban guerilla warfare against the reactionary media monopoly of Springer Verlag. On 2 February 1968, a day after the film's screening at a mock tribunal against Springer held at the Technische Universität Berlin, windows of the Springer-owned *Berliner Morgenpost* were smashed.[1]

Aware of the likely reprisals from Berlin's police, Meins and fellow DFFB student Günther Peter Straschek traveled to Munich shortly thereafter with the hopes of enlisting support for their politicized filmmaking at the newly opened University of Television and Film Munich, but to no avail. They then turned to celebrated Munich-based filmmaker and lawyer

Alexander Kluge, who six months earlier had testified on behalf of Fritz Teufel and Rainer Langhans, both arraigned by Berlin police for inciting arson. Although Kluge did willingly downgrade the menace of the communards' May 1967 broadsides — one of which exclaimed "burn, warehouse, burn" — by characterizing their work in terms of politicized aesthetics not unlike Gerhard Hauptmann's nineteenth-century naturalism, he refrained from offering Meins and Straschek any such assistance.[2] After screening Meins's incendiary short, Kluge explained, "the Molotov cocktail is not dialectical enough."[3] Meins and Straschek's appeal to Kluge was surely an act of desperation. Exalted for his award-winning debut *Abschied von gestern* (*Yesterday Girl*, 1966) as the belated master of the Oberhausen Manifesto, Kluge would soon find himself, much like his philosophical mentor Theodor Adorno, in the crosshairs of the Federal Republic's rebellious students. At the fourteenth annual International Short Film Festival Oberhausen held in April 1968, for example, Hamburg filmmaker Hellmuth Costard lampooned with his pornographic *Besonders wertvoll* (Of special merit) the modest fruits of the Oberhauseners' media politics, the Young German Film Committee founded in 1965, and the Film Subsidies Act of 1967. Expelled from the DFFB along with Harun Farocki, Hans Rüdiger Minow, and seventeen others, Harmut Bitomsky drove Costard's point home: Kluge's advocacy for the public subvention of German film amounted to nothing more than a profit-motivated opportunism that sacrificed any and all aesthetic and political principles.[4] Only in a postcapitalist society, the offshoot "Culture and Revolution" of Berlin's Socialist German Students' Federation implored in an broadside from June 1968, can film ever assume a new form.[5] Kluge and, for that matter, his imprint on the Ulm Institute for Film Design and New German Cinema, both founded in 1962, were declared a failure.

A month after students occupied the DFFB and renamed it "Dziga Vertov Academy" after their Soviet constructivist patron, the attack on Kluge and his films turned personal. On 23 June 1968, in conjunction with the eighteenth-annual Berlin International Film festival, Kluge, Edgar Reitz, Christian Rischert, Johannes Schaaf, and Enno Patalas invited students from the DFFB to a dialogue about political action and filmmaking in the Audimax auditorium of the Technische Universität. Instead of meaningful exchange, students renounced their interlocutors' professed allegiance to leftist aesthetic politics and disqualified them altogether as "left-wing reactionaries."[6] Adding insult to injury, students then assaulted the five "lackeys of the capitalist film industry" with rotten eggs and then staged a show trial against DFFB directors Erwin Leiser and Heinz Rathsack.[7] The effects of the outburst were nothing less than devastating. Independent Munich documentarist Rischert was excoriated for advocating subsidy laws. Johannes Schaaf, 1968 recipient of the Filmband in Gold, quit his position as instructor at the DFFB; others quickly followed suit.

The viability of the DFFB was once again called into question. Director and cinematographer Reitz severed ties with both his longtime collaborator Kluge and the film program in Ulm he helped to establish. Film critic Patalas would soon question the resilience of Kluge's original cinematic principles. As for Kluge, he returned home to Munich, frustrated by the repeated dissolution of his and others' efforts to foster auteurism in West Germany. Shortly thereafter he packed up and moved back to Ulm, where in a few short months the School of Design — besieged in part by its own politicized student body — would close its doors permanently. A year later the semiautonomous Institute for Film Design would cast off its pedagogical mission entirely in order to turn exclusively to the more ascetic concerns of research and development.

It is this set of turbulent events — moments of contact between the Federal Republic's competing new film cultures based in Berlin, Ulm, Munich, and Hamburg — in which Kluge's pathbreaking film *Die Artisten in der Zirkuskuppel: ratlos* (*Artists under the Big Top: Perplexed*, 1968) came to fruition. In fact, seeds of the film may be thought to reach back to the "University Study," a funding proposal originally spearheaded by Kluge, Hans Dieter Müller, and Günther Hörmann that was intent on supporting an array of student films at the School of Design about the discrepancies between Wilhelm von Humboldt's Enlightenment idea of the university and the state of crisis German universities faced in the latter half of the sixties. Instead of contributing to Hörmann and Müller's numerous efforts to document student revolts (e.g., *Ruhestörung: Ereignisse in Berlin* [Disturbance of the peace: Events in Berlin], 1968), Kluge struck out in an allegorical and more grandiose direction. Initially conceptualized in 1967 as a science-fiction film about a female astronaut, the project quickly changed gears once filming began in July of that year. Struck by the historical link between the French Revolution and the advent of the modern circus, Kluge crafted with the assistance of his deft editor Beate Mainka-Jellinghaus a dizzying montage of a film about the ambivalences and paradoxes of the auteur film's utopian aspirations under late capitalism. Indeed, an artistic cinema's propensity to articulate utopia to mass audiences — "the imagination that something different could exist outside of the insufficient present moment" — is impossible under the eye of economic interests, Kluge insisted in an essay from late 1965.[8] And thus the metafilm *Die Artisten* spins the tale of Leni Peickert, a lover of the circus who attempts in three radically different financial situations to free it from the shackles of inauthentic entertainment. Neither as starving outsider artist, nor as entrepreneur, nor as millionaire can Leni successfully alter the fortunes of the circus. Ultimately convinced that "utopia always gets better when we wait for it," Leni abandons the circus, invests her remaining money, and shifts her energies to public television, which she hopes can one day serve the utopian potential of literature.

Over two months before the film won the Golden Lion at the Venice International Film Festival and three months before its German debut at the International Filmfestival Mannheim, the DFFB attack on Kluge was certainly a foreshadowing of imminent student contempt for the film's containment of politicized aesthetics.[9] Within Kluge's own camp, Patalas, one of New German Cinema's staunchest defenders, chided the director for paralyzing the sensibilities of his audience with the film's rapid and aleatory montage; others cited Kluge for succumbing to a defeatist, melancholy resignation.[10] Although *Die Artisten* was a curiosity at the box office, especially in those movie houses that allowed spectators to screen it twice for the price of a single admission, critique of Kluge and his film persisted. In April 1970, a mere three months before a renewed wave of domestic agitprop would again unsettle the Berlinale, Kluge found himself under attack on Hans-Geert Falkenberg's program *Ende offen* (Open ending), broadcast on the public television station Westdeutscher Rundfunk III. Unwilling to conform to the program's preconceived notion of *Die Artisten* and film's power to change society, Kluge was spectacularly charged on-air yet off-camera with manipulating the medium; once again, Kluge's elitism was, in effect, no better than the manipulation at work in the yellow press.

Amidst this torrent of critique, Kluge and his research associates in Ulm retreated entirely from reality by pouring themselves into the genre of science fiction. Although frequently thought of as a prophesy of Kluge's own shift from film to television in 1985, Leni's media work signaled only a generic shift for Kluge. Two low-budget science-fiction feature films and a science-fiction short later, Kluge returned from outer space in 1973 with a social-problem film that caused a furor among feminists, *Gelegenheitsarbeit einer Sklavin* (*Part-Time Work of a Female Slave*), about the gendered division of labor and illegal abortion.[11] His old recipe of fragmented narrative strands interrupted with seemingly extraneous montage material reemerged albeit in a somewhat milder form. (Not until his 1979 film *Die Patriotin* [*The Female Patriot*] would the frenetic montage characteristic of *Die Artisten* reemerge.) The attack on Kluge in the hot summer of 1968 and his ensuing foray into science fiction could distract him from the core issues subtending *Die Artisten* for only so long. In 1972 he and social philosopher Oskar Negt, whom Kluge met in late May 1968 while Hörmann worked on the "University Study," published their first of three volumes of theory. *Public Sphere and Experience*, a book about the possibility of social politics from below, grew out of their experiences in 1968 and became a must-read among the many new social movements that emerged in the wake of the student movement's demise.

One generation older than the primary actors of West Germany's student movement, Kluge is an unparalleled institution in postwar and contemporary film history. Since the Oberhausen Manifesto the decisive protagonist in the long fight for politically, economically, and pedagogically fostering a public German film culture committed to the idea of "utopia film," Kluge has devoted his filmmaking to the very same critique of capitalism that shaped the social philosophy of the Frankfurt School long before DFFB students and others insisted upon undialectical Marxian calls-to-arms. After fifteen feature films, sixteen shorts, nine volumes on policy, film history, and social theory, four volumes of fiction, and five expanded screenplays, Kluge finally followed the footsteps of utopian Leni Peickert and switched to the medium of cable television in order to forestall the complete foreclosure of the public idea of "utopia film" in this new dominant and private medium. After twenty years and more than 1,500 hours of programming broadcast on four separate television shows, Kluge has shifted gears once again. Since 2000 he has published another four volumes of prose and has filmed an eight-hour homage to Sergei Eisenstein's unrealized plans for a film adaptation of Marx's *Kapital*, as well as a follow-up film about the global recession that began in earnest in 2008. To present he has garnered practically every major film, literary, and cultural award in existence in Germany. Throughout his massive, celebrated oeuvre, the conundrum of 1968 reappears again and again. What, Kluge's work asks repeatedly, are the conditions of possibility of utopia? How can film (or any other medium, for that matter) contribute to the construction of a more harmonious and less violent community? What constitutes happiness? *Die Artisten* stands as the cornerstone of these fundamental queries. Looking back on the fortieth anniversary of the German student movement, Kluge recently confessed that the students had a legitimate claim with their disobedience practiced in the name of antifascism, antiauthoritarianism, anticolonialism, and pacifism.[12] And yet, Kluge has maintained over his lifetime, just as Leni explained at the close of *Die Artisten*, "You only make yourself look ridiculous with big steps, but with small steps I could become secretary in the state department." For better or worse, Kluge has positioned himself over the course of his fifty years in filmmaking as the minister of German cinema.

See also:

- 30 August 1936: Luis Trenker Tries but Fails to Sidestep Nazi *Filmpolitik*
- 30 June 1970: A Faltering Berlinale Founders on *o.k.* Controversy
- 6 August 1984: *Heimat* Celebrated as "European Requiem for the Little People"

Notes

[1] Tilman Baumgärtel, "'Ein Stück Kino, das mit Film nichts zu tun hatte': Terroristen und Filmemacher an der Deutschen Film- und Fernsehakademie Berlin (DFFB)," in *Deutschland im Herbst: Terrorismus im Film*, ed. Petra Kraus. (Munich: Münchner Filmzentrum, 1997), 40.

² Alexander Kluge, "Gutachtliche Äußerung," 4 June 1967, Institut für Sozialforschung, Hamburg, 2.

³ Baumgärtel, "'Ein Stück Kino,'" 44.

⁴ Hartmut Bitomsky, "Filmwirtschaft und Bewußtseins-Industrie," *Film* 7, no. 3 (Mar. 1969): 48; and Volker Pantenburg, "Die Rote Fahne: Deutsche Film- und Fernsehakademie, 1966–1968," in *Handbuch zur Kultur- und Mediengeschichte der Studentenbewegung*, ed. Martin Klimke and Joachim Scharloth (Stuttgart: Metzler, 2007), 199–206; here 199.

⁵ Quoted in Peter W. Jansen, "Ein Jahr Kinorebellion," *Merkur* 22 (December 1968): 1142.

⁶ Wolfgang Jacobsen ed., *50 Years Berlinale: Internationale Filmfestspiele Berlin*, trans. Catherine Kerkhoff-Saxon and Robin Benson (Berlin: Nicolaische Verlagsbuchhandlung, 2000), 155.

⁷ Jansen, "Ein Jahr Kinorebellion," 1142.

⁸ Alexander Kluge, "Die Utopia Film," *Merkur* 18 (December 1964): 1144.

⁹ Bitomsky, "Filmwirtschaft und Bewußtseins-Industrie," 46–49.

¹⁰ Enno Patalas, "Die toten Augen," *Filmkritik* 12 (December 1968): 826.

¹¹ Heide Schlüpmann, "'What Is Different Is Good': Women and Femininity in the Films of Alexander Kluge," *October* 46 (Fall 1988): 129–42. See also how Schlüpmann exempts *Die Artisten* from these critiques (142–50).

¹² Matthias Mattusek, "Mit dem Rücken zum Wahlkampf: Adorno, Kluge und Goethe," *Spiegel Online*. 21 September 2009, 21 October 2009, http://www.spiegel.de/video/video-1022695.html.

Fall 1968: Expulsion of Thomas Brasch from GDR Film School Signals Fate of East German '68ers

Katie Trumpener

IN 1968 ONE STUDENT PROTEST sparked another, leaping geographical divides as French, American, and West German students adapted rhetoric and tactics from China's Cultural Revolution. For Western leftists, 1968 was a year — like 1789, 1848, or 1918 — when worldwide revolution seemed imminent. For Eastern Europeans, however, 1968 became one in a very different sequence of years — 1956, 1981, 1989 — connoting political trauma and socialist disillusionment. As such asymmetries remind us, dates are not transparent. They resonate variously in different places, linked to different chains of historical causality, generating different afterlives. Thus, while film students in both East and West Germany turned to protest in the fall of 1968, their respective fates diverged significantly: the actions of the East German students had far more severe, often life-altering, consequences.

In August 1968, Warsaw Pact forces occupied Czechoslovakia, arrested First Secretary Alexander Dubček, and abruptly curtailed his socialist reforms. East Germany's media celebrated the invasion, and its Army mobilized to back it. Yet GDR intellectuals tacitly condemned it — and the Stasi (East German State Security Service) found anti-invasion graffiti and homemade protest leaflets across the GDR.

One tiny East Berlin protest created lasting ripples, subtly altering the course of GDR film and political history. Two groups of friends, mostly students from prominent families, left hand-written fliers — "Long Live Red Prague! Up with Dubček!" — in mailboxes and telephone booths. Florian Havemann, 16, hung a homemade Czech flag from his window; his brother Frank, 19, painted "Dubček" on fences and walls. The protesters were rapidly apprehended. Dramaturgy student Thomas Brasch, 23, and his girlfriend, rock singer Sanda Weigl, 20, spent a week in hiding before asking Brasch's father for help; instead, Horst Brasch, Deputy Minister of Culture, notified the authorities, a betrayal his son never forgave. The GDR's most prominent dissident, Robert Havemann, responded to *his* sons' arrests by alerting Western journalists. Bettina Wegener, a nineteen-year-old acting student and mother of Thomas Brasch's five-month-old baby, tried to continue the leafleting but was soon arrested. So was a friend of Florian Havemann's, after circulating a petition demanding Havemann's release.

In October, after weeks of investigative custody and interrogation in the secret Stasi high-security prison in Berlin-Hohenschönhausen, seven leafleters were publicly sentenced for subversive incitement (no small irony, given that up until 1961, East Berlin students repeatedly had been dispatched to West Berlin to distribute agitational leaflets). State prosecutors presented the leafleters' "criminal acts" as influenced by "enemy propaganda centers, radio and television stations."[1] The prosecution itself reflected the GDR government's fear of Western-style student protest — and of losing its own monopoly on media and information. Florian Havemann landed in juvenile detention. The others spent months in GDR prisons. Only personal intervention by Party Secretary Walter Ulbricht secured their early release — and even then they served many more months on parole, forced to labor in heavy industrial "production" in shifts sometimes lasting up to twelve hours.

Weigl's relative Helene Weigel rescued Brasch from production by employing him briefly at the Brecht Archive (nominally researching Brecht and film). Yet his own avant-garde plays remained banned, his stories refused (uncensored) publication. Expelled from university in 1965 for "existential opinions" and now expelled from the GDR film school, he remained unable to realize his plans for low-budget underground filmmaking.[2] His friends fared little better. For six years, Weigl was banned from giving concerts. Wegener, expelled from drama school, became a dissident singer-songwriter; her concerts, too, were eventually banned. Florian Havemann, barred from university, fled to West Germany in 1971. In "Enfant perdu," a protest song embedded within an East/West Berlin sound collage (including GDR radio coverage of the military parade marking GDR-Czech renormalization), family friend Wolf Biermann lamented Havemann's departure as political desertion, emblematic of a lost dissident generation.

In West Germany, there was a longer tradition of student dissent, stretching back almost 20 years before 1968. In 1950, Freiburg and Göttingen students had protested new films by Third Reich director Veit Harlan, picketing cinemas, disrupting shooting and screenings, and clashing with police.[3] In the 1950s and early 1960s, student film-clubs had tangled with government and university authorities over GDR films. Banned from West German release until 1958, Wolfgang Staudte's *Der Untertan* (*The Kaiser's Lackey*, GDR, 1951) was shown surreptitiously at Hamburg University — and openly at Frankfurt University (although University President Max Horkheimer feared campus unrest.)[4] In 1968, Frankfurt students protested the Vietnam War by picketing *The Green Berets* (Ray

Kellog and John Wayne, USA, 1968); West Berlin film students produced guerilla films, disrupted the Berlin Film Festival (pelting Alexander Kluge with eggs for suggesting alternative strategies), and — in the same month that the East Berlin students led their leafleting campaign, only a few miles away — occupied the West Berlin film school (renaming it the Dziga Vertov Academy). Although a quarter of the school's students were subsequently expelled,[5] many nonetheless became prominent filmmakers. The fates of the protesters in the GDR were necessarily different: there the state film school represented the main credentialing route for film and television careers, and there were no independent media.

Other differences separated the protests of the students in East and West Germany. While West Berlin's student occupiers used tactics pioneered by China's Red Guards, East Berlin's leafleters evoked the Third Reich resistance group, the White Rose. In 1943, the White Rose had leafleted Munich University, exhorting students and citizens to oppose Nazi genocide and fight for the restoration of human rights, including free speech. Nazi authorities quickly apprehended and guillotined the White Rose's tiny core (including university student Sophie Scholl), but its final leaflet was smuggled out of the country, mass-produced, and scattered over Germany by British airplanes. After 1945, Sophie Scholl, now admired as an antifascist martyr, was memorialized in the naming of many West German schools and Munich University held an annual ceremony marking the anniversary of her arrest. In February, 1968, however, radical students disrupted the commemoration, accusing university administrators of appropriating the White Rose.[6] Reanimating White Rose resistance tactics a few months later, the East Berlin leafleters similarly challenged self-legitimizing GDR claims to antifascism.

At the same time, GDR students' critique of Communist authoritarianism also diverged from Western students' revolutionary romanticism. Led by GDR émigré Rudi Dutschke, West Berlin's student movement identified with the New Left. Yet its film students borrowed Communist symbols, and championed the GDR against mainstream media. In one early action, film students thus filmed themselves at a West Berlin factory, handing workers leaflets endorsing diplomatic recognition of the GDR. West Berlin police immediately called the film school, wondering whether this was GDR agitation or a legitimate student project. In February 1968, seven West Berlin film students (including Harun Farocki, Holger Meins, and Helke Sander) filmed *Die rote Fahne* (*The Red Flag*), a provocative conceptual performance in which relay runners carried an enormous red flag through West Berlin's streets, then suspended it (illicitly) from Schöneberg's Red City Hall, site of John F. Kennedy's 1963 "I am a Berliner" speech.

West German student-movement critiques of capitalist media culture, as Sander documents in her Godardian student short *Brecht die Macht der Manipulateure* (Break the power of the manipulators, 1968) and retrospective feature *Der subjektive Faktor* (The subjective factor, 1981), catalyzed experiments with alternative media forms: activist leaflets and posters transformed university corridors and communal apartments into Vertovian wall-newspapers. Yet Western proponents of Marxist media forms generally ignored the neighboring realities of GDR media culture. East of the Berlin Wall, wall-newspapers had long lost any avant-garde edge — and often endangered their users. In Rolf Römer's *Hostess* (GDR, 1975), an East Berlin tour guide faces disciplinary action after posting a naked bottom on the collective wall-newspaper. In self-defense, she argues that media, like all aspects of GDR social life, has long been in socialist hands, rendering obsolete old forms of agitation: now only provocation can catalyze fresh thinking.

At the GDR film school, wall-newspaper postings repeatedly precipitated disciplinary action. In 1964, a camera student was expelled because his posting, citing Camus and Kafka, "raised critical questions." School officials promptly removed the piece, and when directing student Rainer Simon posted a note asking for the chance to read and judge for himself, he was almost expelled in turn.[7] In 1968, a student was expelled for her posting praising Egon Günther's soon-to-be-shelved *Abschied* (*Farewell*, 1968), its antimilitarism rendered inopportune by the Soviet invasion.[8]

West Germany's film-club movement peaked in the mid-1950s. Many GDR universities, in contrast, founded film clubs in 1956, inspired by the Eastern European New Waves and the political thaw inaugurated by Nikita Khrushchev. For the next three decades, club screenings repeatedly catalyzed public debate about political reform, drawing censure from university officials. After the 1956 Hungarian uprising, students accused of "misusing" film clubs for political debate were investigated or suspended. In the late 1960s, film-club leaders were pressured or removed for screening "counter-revolutionary" Czech films like Miloš Forman's *Lásky jedné plavovlásky* (*Loves of a Blonde*, 1965). During Poland's *Solidarnosc* crisis, Humboldt University officials disbanded the university's twenty-three-year-old film club, following screening/discussion of Krzysztof Zanussi's *Barwy Ochronne* (*Camoflage*, 1976); in the late 1980s, the Stasi targeted a design school student for programming Soviet Perestroika films.[9]

Meanwhile, a generation of filmmakers divided by the Wall belatedly found itself face-to-face. Banned for years from making records or giving concerts, in 1976 GDR dissident Wolf Biermann was allowed to hold a single, nationally televised concert in Cologne, West Germany — only to be refused reentry into the GDR after the concert. Many prominent GDR directors, actors, and artists petitioned the government to readmit him; not only did the government not relent, but most of these signatories (including Brasch and Wegener) also experienced such sustained reprisals that they themselves eventually emigrated.

Like Czechoslovakia's Charta 77, the Biermann support campaign built on 1968 precedents. Biermann's Cologne playlist itself had included "Enfant perdu." Yet as a result, Florian Havemann again endured West German leftists' reproaches for deserting the GDR.[10] Conversely, when first-year acting student Ulrich Mühe circulated his own pro-Biermann protest petition to Leipzig Drama School classmates, his department head warned him to withdraw it by citing the bitter experience of his own drama school cohort, whose anti-invasion protests in 1968 precipitated the forcible dissolution of the class and the relegation of students to army service or heavy industry.[11]

Imprisoned, exmatriculated and censored in the GDR after 1968, Brasch found himself forced out of the GDR after 1976. In West German emigration, Brasch was embraced by the local cultural establishment and began publishing stories, producing plays, and even (with the help of New German Cinema auteur Volker Schlöndorff) directing films. His first film, *Engel aus Eisen* (*Angels of Iron*, 1981), appeared years after his film school expulsion, yet Brasch described it, half-ironically, as his belated "thesis project." Shot in West Berlin, *Angels* cast Brasch's fellow émigrés (including his partner Katharina Thalbach) as the 1950s notorious Gladow Gang, who derived criminal advantage from Berlin's still-open borders. *Domino* (1982) and *Der Passagier — Welcome to Germany* (*The Passenger: Welcome to Germany*, 1988) meditated on recent German history, paternity, betrayal, competing aesthetics, and exile.

Brasch's films never played in the GDR — and had little impact on West Germany's New German Cinema. In 1977, Sander's *Die allseitig reduzierte Persönlichkeit* (*The All-Round Reduced Personality: REDUPERS*) quoted Brasch to plead for an artistic vision encompassing both Germanys. By 1980, however, Sander cited Brasch's acclaim to criticize a lack of support for West Germany's own artistic dissidents. When experimental and feminist filmmakers tackled controversial subjects, their films were not funded, hence never made. Banned or censored GDR filmmakers, Sander argued, got support simply by emigrating to the other Germany. "The question that poses itself is which country we could emigrate to."[12]

In 1981, *Angels of Iron* won the Bavarian Film Prize. West German leftists criticized Brasch for accepting it from Bavaria's ultraconservative premier, Franz Josef Strauss. The gala audience, conversely, booed Brasch's acceptance speech, because it thanked "the GDR film school for my training." Given Brasch's expulsion, this acknowledgement seemed largely ironic. Yet it was also a declaration of GDR roots, at a moment when West German conservatives reviled GDR dissidents as anarchists when they weren't embracing them as fellow anti-Communists. Small wonder, then, that his remark failed to find resonance, and instead met with trivialization: after the booing subsided, Strauss called Brasch a "living demonstration object."

See also:

- 1 February 1968: *Herstellung eines Molotow-Cocktails* Promotes Film as a Tool for Political Violence
- 20 June 1977: DEFA's Biggest Star, Manfred Krug, Leaves the GDR
- 27 October 1977: *Deutschland im Herbst* Equivocation on RAF Marks End Stage of Radical Filmmaking

Notes

[1] "Wegen staatsfeindliche Hetze bestraft," *Neues Deutschland* (29 October 1968), reprinted in *Arbeitsbuch Thomas Brasch*, ed. Margarete Häßel and Richard Weber (Frankfurt: Suhrkamp, 1987), 66–67; here: 66.

[2] Florian Havemann, *Havemann* (Frankfurt: Suhrkamp, 2007), 921–23.

[3] Gustav Meier, *Filmstadt Göttingen: Bilder für eine neue Welt? Zur Geschichte der Göttinger Spielfilmproduktion 1945 bis 1961* (Hannover: Reichold, 1996), 130, 140.

[4] Raimund Gerz, "Das 'andere' Kino: Filmclubs, Initiativen und Programmkinos in Frankfurt," in *Lebende Bilder einer Stadt: Kino und Film in Frankfurt am Main*, ed. Dieter Worschech (Frankfurt: Deutsches Filmmuseum Frankfurt, 1995), 226–51; here 230; Ulrich Gregor, "*Der Untertan*," *Film und Fernsehen* 19, no. 5 (May, 1991): 22; Erika Richter, "Zwischenzeiten: Fragmentarische Bemerkungen zum ost- und westdeutschen Film der 50er Jahre," *Film und Fernsehen* 27, nos. 3/4 (1999): 30–80.

[5] Thomas Brandlmeier, "Filmtheorie und Kinokultur: Zeitgeschichte und filmtheoretische Debatten," in *Kino-Fronten: 20 Jahre '68 und das Kino*, ed. Wolfgang Petermann and Ralph Thoms (Munich: Trickster, 1988), 50–74; here 70–71; Werner Kließ, "Berlin röchelt noch: Gegenwart und Zukunft der Berliner Filmfestspiele," *film* 6, no. 8 (January 1969): 1.

[6] Lutz von Rosenstiel, "Zum Geleit," *Die Weiße Rose und das Erbe des deutschen Widerstands: Münchener Gedächtnisvorlesungen* (Munich: C. H. Beck, 1993), 7–9: 8.

[7] Rainer Simon, "Kollektiv 63: Eine Spurensuche in Erinnerungen und Dokumenten," *apropos: Film 2001*, 29–34; here 32; Axel Geiss, *Repression und Freiheit: DEFA-Regisseure zwischen Fremd- und Selbtbestimmung* (Potsdam: Brandenburgische Landeszentrale für politische Bildung, 1997), 117.

[8] Egon Günther, "DEFA Spuren Fußabdrücke," *Film und Fernsehen* 26, nos. 5/6 (May/June 1996): 23–24.

[9] Wieland Becker and Volker Petzold, *Tarkowski trifft King Kong: Geschichte der Filmklubbewegung der DDR* (Berlin: Vistas, 2001), 78, 207–8.

[10] Havemann, *Havemann*, 375–81.

[11] Florian Henkel von Donnersmarck, "'Es hat schon viele Versuche gegeben, die DDR-Realität einzufangen': Ein Gespräch mit Ulrich Mühe," in *Das Leben der Anderen: Filmbuch* (Frankfurt: Suhrkamp, 2006), 182–204; here 199–200.

[12] Helke Sander, "Men Are Responsible That Women Become Their Enemies: Tales of Rejection" (1980), in *West German Filmmakers on Film: Visions and Voices*, ed. Eric Rentschler (New York: Holmes and Meier, 1988), 25–30; here 30.

30 June 1970: A Faltering Berlinale Founders on *o.k.* Controversy

Kris Vander Lugt

Sven (played by director Michael Verhoeven) objects to the brutal sexual murder of a young girl. o.k. *(1970). DVD capture.*

"Quo vadis, Berlinale?" Thus queries an article in *Die Welt* from 26 June 1970, just days before the twentieth annual International Film Festival in Berlin.[1] Even before the projectors started humming, journalists were reporting that the festival — with its "teenager years" behind it, now a "somewhat tired tween" — was "at a crossroads."[2] Ulrich Gregor, *Filmkritik* writer and cofounder of the Internationales Forum des Jungen Films (International Forum of New Cinema), later recalled the Berlinale circa 1970 as "a monument to antiquated conceptions of film," too mired in the vagaries of the still-struggling postwar film industry to produce real art.[3]

The festival had thus already been considered dysfunctional by the time it reached a critical stage in 1970, when a scandal erupted over Michael Verhoeven's anti-Vietnam War film *o.k.* As Gregor later recalled, the Verhoeven scandal was "the consequence of contradictions which in earlier times had become increasingly pronounced; thus these events possessed a certain logic."[4] The genealogy of that logic leads back to the very beginnings of the film festival. Initiated in 1950 largely by American occupation officer Oscar Martay, the festival was politically inflected from the outset. Precisely because of its location within the "divided city," the Berlinale was optimally situated to be a key player in both the construction of West German national identity and in the cultural politics of the Cold War. In an early letter to Martay requesting additional funds for the nascent festival, festival director Alfred Bauer emphasized its importance as a "cultural and political showcase for Western film vis-à-vis the East."[5] Festival organizers made special efforts before 1961 to entice visitors from the Eastern sector of Berlin, offering reduced ticket prices and screenings in the Soviet sector to ensure the broadest exposure in the East. At the same time, filmic contributions *from* the East were virtually nonexistent. Very early on, during one of the first organizational meetings in 1950, a committee had voted to deny admission to Eastern bloc countries. The snubbing of socialist countries became increasingly embarrassing once the festival reached "A-status" in 1956, making it an officially recognized international festival by the International Association of Film Producers Association (FIAPF). Attempts were later made to rectify this imbalance, including proposals to privatize the festival and associate it with other Berlin festivals, to "de-nationalize" it in a sense so that invitations to the East would come from a privately owned company rather than from the federal government in Bonn. These efforts mostly withered in the political freeze.

The film industry, for its part, was reticent to participate in the festival initially. The Spitzenorganisation der deutschen Filmwirtschaft (Executive Organization for German Film Economy, SPIO) declined to support the festival and expressed concerns that, "as a result of the film politics of the Allies," German film production would not be able to compete with "foreign" productions.[6] FIAPF, worried about an overcrowded market, was uncooperative from the outset and remained so for some time. Thus, the festival had the support of neither the largest industry representative nor the most important organization for international film festivals.

In 1954, FIAPF revised their regulations to include a stipulation that festivals would not be recognized if they included films that appeared too overtly political. This meant that the Berlinale, in order to be recognized by FIAPF, was prohibited from awarding its recently created prize for films that "best fulfilled the ideals of a world oriented toward freedom." In 1956, pressured by the German government and the French Ministry of Foreign Affairs, organizers withdrew from competition Alain Resnais's Holocaust documentary *Nuit et Brouillard* (*Night and Fog*, 1955) on the grounds that it was injurious to the feelings of Germans and threatened relations with France. Bauer later decided to show it in a special screening outside the official competition.

The quality of German films continued to disappoint for the most part throughout the late 1950s, and political tensions were rising toward irreconcilability. During the summer of the Wall in 1961, it became increasingly apparent that a storm would break. Objections to the selection procedure resurfaced, and critics complained that there was little appreciation for artistic films and new directions. That same year, no German feature film was deemed worthy of the German Film Prize and the Venice Film Festival rejected all West German entries.[7]

On 28 February 1962, the Oberhausen Manifesto exploded onto the scene. That June, in an already charged atmosphere, discussions over the impact of the manifesto ensued at the Berlinale. Stirrings of reform and innovation marked in more noticeable form the by-then-established fact that the Berlinale had become an important focal point and, increasingly, a forum for an emergent politics of cinema. Cineastes, inspired by talk of the "new film," eagerly awaited a festival renaissance.

Somewhat predictably perhaps, the following year brought no such renaissance, just more vague proposals and suggestions for reform that were postponed until the following year, when the Berlin Senate and the Senator for Sciences and the Arts finally deemed "far-reaching measures" necessary to reform the festival. Over the next several years, some changes were introduced, though to little avail. By 1966, a forum with several prominent directors, including Peter Schamoni and Volker Schlöndorff, was asking the question, "Does cinema have a future?" The crisis of German film continued unabated.

The revolution that could have followed the cancellation of the Cannes festival in 1968 did not take place in Berlin. Discussions among students led to little more than egg-throwing and further discussions. The festival chugged along for two more years before screeching to a halt in 1970 with the controversy surrounding Verhoeven's film. *o.k.* premiered at 3:00 P.M. on Tuesday, 30 June 1970 in the Zoo Palast, bringing to screen, in brutal detail, an historic incident from 1966 involving the rape and murder of a young Vietnamese girl by four American GIs that had been buried by the military until resurfacing in 1969. Verhoeven's film takes this incident and transfers it to Bavaria at Easter time (a "Vietnamese passion play," as Verhoeven called it). All the actors were rigorously coached to speak with perfect Bavarian accents. "I wanted to activate and increase the public's sympathy by transporting the film to our environment."[8] Contrary to Verhoeven's intentions, the majority of the international jury — including its two German members — was not sympathetic, viewing the film as an insult to an important political ally. While most viewers responded positively to the film's antiwar message, some protest erupted, including the early departure of German jury member Manfred Durniok, who later offered words of apology to the president of the Berlinale jury, American George Stevens. The focus of the scandal was neither the actual rape and murder of the young Vietnamese girl nor the film's highly explicit depiction of that brutal event, brought to screen by a sixteen-year-old, first-time actress (Eva Mattes). Rather, the real outrage was Verhoeven's implicit critique of American foreign policy and the fact that this film had been selected to represent Germany at an international festival.

Given that festival regulations indicated films should "contribute to the understanding and friendship between peoples of different nations," the jury asked the selection committee and the senator for Science and the Arts to "neutralize" the film until it could be reconfirmed that the film did indeed meet the regulations.[9] Rumors quickly surfaced that the film was being withdrawn from the competition. On 4 July, the *New York Times* ran the headline "War Film Dropped by Berlin Festival," and detailed Verhoeven's attempts to defend himself in the press against charges of anti-Americanism.[10]

The *Times* story appeared at the tail-end of several tense days of accusations and insinuations — numerous press conferences were called, rumor spread that Stevens had threatened to resign if the film weren't withdrawn, Verhoeven and producer Rob Houwer presented a notarized affidavit at a press conference claiming to have an informant on the jury who was crying "censorship," festival director Alfred Bauer and Berliner Festspiele head Walther Schmieding offered their resignations to the Berlin Senate, the jury was asked to step down but was swiftly reinstated only to then resign a day later, and finally the competition was cancelled. No prizes were awarded. On 9 July, the Berlin House of Representatives issued an urgent motion to request swift aid for the dying festival; hearings and consultations with various functionaries, experts, and officials followed.

As Gregor recalls, "The Berlinale days of the summer of 1970 were an historical hour, in which suddenly — with momentum, emotion and far-reaching consequences — conceptions of a cinematography, completely different from that which had previously existed, finally gathered steam and erupted, clearing away the obstacles in their path."[11] In August, festival organizers, working with the Senate, agreed to reforms. Amongst the most significant of these reforms was the creation of the parallel International Forum of New Cinema, designed to foster the work of up-and-coming filmmakers, a move that had begun in 1969 when the Friends of the German Cinematheque initiated an independent program of progressive and independent films that screened alongside the official festival.

In retrospect, the Verhoeven scandal proved to be an important turning point for the Berlinale and a significant impetus for reform and innovation in German film. The controversy over the film itself died out relatively quickly, though its effects were longer lasting. Despite being awarded two German Film Prizes in 1971 (honoring Verhoeven for best script and Eva Mattes for best young actress), *o.k.* was not screened on German television until 2001 and remains to this day commercially unavailable.[12]

The lasting impact of the controversy has been to help effect what Gregor later described as no less than a "renewal of the film medium in form and content."[13] The International Forum for New Cinema was integrated into the overall structure of the festival and remains a Berlinale mainstay, offering a venue for more innovative and independent films. While discussions continue to explore the tension between film's critical potential, its commercial appeal, and its political uses, the Berlinale remains the most important festival for showcasing, promoting, and rewarding German film, providing a network for filmmakers and film critics as well as a central space for interrogating the history, aesthetics, and politics of film.

See also:

- 28 February 1962: Oberhausen Manifesto Creates Founding Myth for New German Cinema
- 6 August 1984: *Heimat* Celebrated as "European Requiem for the Little People"
- 10 February 1999: Berlinale Premier of Four Turkish-German Films Signals New Chapter in Cinematic Diversity

Notes

[1] "Quo vadis, Berlinale?" *Die Welt* (26 June 1970), n.p.

[2] R.M., "Die Berlinale läuft: Das Fehlen sozialistischer Staaten bedauert," *Frankfurter Allgemeine* (29 June 1970), n.p.; Volker Baer, "Ein Festival im Wandel: Zwanzig Jahre Filmfestspiele in Berlin," *Tagesspiegel* (28 June 1970), n.p.; Hanns Lothar Schütz, "Berlinale am Scheideweg," *Welt am Sonntag* (28 June 1970), n.p.

[3] Ulrich Gregor, quoted in Wolfgang Jacobsen, ed., *50 Years Berlinale: Internationale Filmfestspiele Berlin*, trans. Catherine Kerkhoff-Saxon and Robin Benson (Berlin: Filmmuseum Berlin-Deutsche Kinemathek and Nicolaische Buchhandlung, 2000), 181.

[4] Ibid.

[5] Letter from Alfred Bauer to Oscar Martay (13 April 1951), reproduced in Jacobsen, 16 (my translation).

[6] SPIO statement quoted in Jacobsen, *50 Years Berlinale*, 18.

⁷ Thomas Elsaesser, *New German Cinema: A History* (New Brunswick, NJ: Rutgers UP, 1989), 20.

⁸ Verhoeven, quoted in Erich Kocian, "Vietnamkrieg in Bayern," *Abendzeitung* (26 May 1970), n.p.

⁹ Jacobsen, *50 Years Berlinale*, 166.

¹⁰ AP, "War Film Dropped by Berlin Festival," *New York Times* (4 July 1970): 7 (ProQuest Historical Newspapers).

¹¹ Gregor, quoted in Jacobsen, *50 Years Berlinale*, 183.

¹² Brigitte Bruns, Claudia Engelhardt, and Katja Kirste, eds., *Michael Verhoeven: Autor, Schauspieler, Regisseur, Produzent* (Munich: Münchner Filmzentrum, 2003), 38.

¹³ Gregor, quoted in Jacobsen, *50 Years Berlinale*, 180.

29 February 1972: With *Die Angst des Tormanns beim Elfmeter* New German Cinema Learns to Read

Brad Prager

FROM THE EARLIEST DAYS of New German Cinema, the entanglements that came of adapting literature into film were anchored to the question of legitimacy. Many cite Volker Schlöndorff's *Der Junge Törless* (*Young Törless*, 1966), an adaptation of Robert Musil's 1906 novel, as the dawn of New German Cinema. Although this has been contested as a point of origin, the question of whether the emerging auteurs of the German film would fetter themselves to the literature of the past remained an issue throughout the following years. Schlöndorff, a frequent adapter of literature, took up Heinrich von Kleist (*Michael Kohlhaas — Der Rebell* [*Man on Horseback*], 1969) and Bertolt Brecht (*Baal*, 1970); Werner Herzog turned to Achim von Arnim (*Lebenszeichen* [*Signs of Life*], 1968) and Georg Büchner (*Woyzeck*, 1979); and Fassbinder made use of Theodor Fontane (*Fontane Effi Briest*, 1974) and Alfred Döblin (*Berlin Alexanderplatz*, 1980). Herzog habitually used the term "legitimate" to describe the German cinema that emerged in the late 1960s and 1970s, and when speaking with the *New York Times*, he made explicit reference to literature, averring that he and other young German directors were "the exponents of 'legitimate' German culture — 'in the sense that Kleist, Büchner and Kafka are legitimate.'"[1] Cinema was, in this way, in the process of becoming as "legitimate" as canonical literature. This aspiration itself, however, was problematic insofar as the reliance on the weighty worth of German letters threatened to undermine cinema's own credentials as an art form. Some feared that German cinema was mired in this struggle for legitimacy and that a new form had erred in enchaining itself to an old one. The debate over whether there was too much adaptation and an over-reliance on literature led to the *Literaturverfilmungskrise* (literature adaptation crisis). Eric Rentschler points out, however, that many of New German Cinema's adaptations profoundly reconfigure their source material, expressing more about the filmmaker than about the original text, and that in some circumstances it may be more apt to speak of transformations instead of adaptations.[2]

Wim Wenders and Peter Handke met in the mid-1960s, and although Handke had begun to make a name for himself, he hardly carried the cachet of a Kleist or Büchner. Wenders chose Handke's 1970 novel, *Die Angst des Tormanns beim Elfmeter* (*The Goalie's Anxiety at the Penalty Kick*), as the basis for his first feature-length film, shot in 1971 in 35-millimeter with the support of Österreichische Telefilm Produktion, Westdeutscher Rundfunk, and the Filmverlag der Autoren. He was likely drawn to Handke's work because of its experimentation with narrative conventions. The story — in which an ex-goalkeeper picks up a cinema cashier, sleeps with her, murders her the next morning, and then sets off for the countryside — has the hallmarks of a thriller but is not one; it promises action but is laconic and refuses to deliver. Wenders had begun toying with narrative as early as *Same Player Shoots Again* (1968), a twelve-minute-long series of shots in which a man runs while carrying a machine gun. That film is only a fragment of a story; its protagonist — if there is one — becomes a pinball in cinema's repetitive machine. The ironic narrative of Handke's novel resonates along similar lines with experimental approaches of the French New Wave, particularly with Godard's *Breathless* (1960). Akin to Jean-Paul Belmondo's Michel Poiccard, Handke's Josef Bloch is a caricature of an action hero. He is a ladies' man (although his charms are difficult to fathom), and he makes no pretension of depth. He moves from action to action, from sequence to sequence, and appears to be composed of little more than an array of gestures imported from the worlds of cinema and sport. In *Breathless* the audience is aware that Poiccard enjoys playing the part of the gangster. However in both Handke's and Wenders's versions, it remains unclear what motivates Bloch.[3]

There is more than a merely narrative game being played in the pages of Handke's novel. It is also intended as a meditation on language. At its onset Bloch — who had been "ein bekannter Tormann" (a well-known goalie), but who is now working in construction — interprets a sudden disinterest on the part of his coworkers to mean that he has been fired.[4] The discovery that he has been "let go" from his job — "daß er entlassen sei" — sets in motion a displacement or a removal from language as well. Neither the novel nor the film are particularly concerned with presenting a psycho-biographical portrait, so it is hardly evident whether Bloch has been a sociopath prior to this point. As an outsider alienated from the German language, he shares something in common with Kaspar Hauser, a figure about whom Handke had written a play (*Kaspar*, 1967), and about whom Herzog would later make a film (*Jeder für sich und Gott gegen alle* [*The Enigma of Kaspar Hauser*], 1974). Bloch seems to be consciously or unconsciously seeking a space where he can be free from all language; he appears to find words burdensome insofar as they connect him with others, and this linguistic estrangement redoubles his misanthropy. His antipathy toward language is predicated on a sudden awareness of a problem familiar to the German Romantics as well as to Handke's fellow Austrian Ludwig Wittgenstein: language shapes reality, and the more we inspect it, the more aware we become that we are trapped in the echo chamber of our own fictions.[5] Wenders's adaptation connects its protagonist's predicament with a key problem of the New German Cinema: can one "see" the world without "reading" it? Is it possible for the camera to film objects without embedding them in language? Can Wenders have us look at the world through the eyes of Bloch, who, either willingly or unwillingly, has turned his back on words?

Bloch tries to interpret the world against its grain — to encounter its objects, for example, from right to left rather than from left to right. His efforts to perceive rather than read things in the terms provided result in knotty textual problems. At one point Handke dissolves his text into a series of pictograms. Wenders likely saw Handke's inclusion of images as an answer to those same questions that he and his contemporaries were confronting in cinema. Throughout his film Wenders's camera lingers on its objects, compelling us to look further and more deeply, yet this may not have been enough. In an effort to recreate the rebus into which Handke's novel falls, Wenders shows the illuminated letters "E-L" at the end of a hotel sign and then lets an elevated train — or an "el" — pass into the frame, as if to remind us that language is more than merely letters and that the boundaries of sign systems should be tested.

Reading the world in this way may be a symptom of Bloch's incipient schizophrenia, yet Wenders seems to suggest that his protagonist's problems are more semiotic than they are psychological. Bloch listens to wood cutters, border guards, and others as they reflect on various sign systems — on how one predicts the weather and on how to discern the presence of a hedgehog on a dimly lit road — and hardly seems to hear a word. He seeks out newspapers, yet seems unconcerned when reports about the murder he committed appear in them. A mute boy that goes missing and is sought in the last half of the story is a stand-in for Bloch's own inability to communicate. At points in the morning following his date with his victim Gloria — whose name Wenders changed from Gerda because he evidently liked the association with the 1964 song in which the name is loudly broken down ("G-L-O-R-I-A") into the letters that compose it — the conversation between the two seems quite normal. At other points, however, they seem to talk at cross-purposes in a way that indicates a complete failure to understand one another. She asks him, "Hast du noch einen anderen Beruf?" (do you have another career?), and he responds, making reference to the sound of a passing plane, "Das war aber keine Düsenmaschine" (that was no jet). She then lies on her bed toying with her necklace, apparently seeking to seduce him once more. After she twines her necklace flirtatiously around his throat, he strangles her in return. True to Handke's description, which resists offering the reader direct insight into his character's intentions — "Plötzlich würgte er sie" (suddenly he was choking her)[6] — Bloch's act comes upon him without contemplation and is completed with little sign of regret.

The main character's moral turpitude is a function of his hermeneutic disorientation. Following from Handke's novel, Wenders's adaptation — like many of the earliest works of the New German Cinema — becomes a means of calling into question our gaze and the terms in which we frame it. In this respect the film's long takes and its fascination with its camera's own images recalls the protracted shots of deserts and their dwellers in Herzog's *Fata Morgana* (1970), or Alexander Kluge's sustained fascination with elephants and circus performers in *Die Artisten in der Zirkuskuppel: ratlos* (*Artists Under the Big Top: Perplexed*, 1968). Wenders seems to reflect on how our brain fuses motion-picture frames along what the experimental German filmmaker Werner Nekes, in his programmatic lecture on the mechanics of cinematic vision, referred to as the "time axis."[7] In *Die Angst des Tormanns beim Elfmeter*, soccer spectatorship allegorizes the movement of the camera; as far as both the players and the fans are concerned, following the ball is the key. Like language, soccer is a game, and in neither arena will Bloch continue to play. The epigram of Handke's book, and the very point at which Wenders's film chooses to begin, is more or less an image of a man declining to participate. Handke writes: "Der Tormann sah zu, wie der Ball über die Linie rollte . . ." (The goalie watched as the ball rolled across the line). Yet attempts to terminate language games only beget new ones, and Wenders's film asks whether cinema can truly avoid yielding to the traps of conventional narrative. In the film's final scene Bloch sits in the stands and tries to read a soccer game differently — to watch against conventions — perhaps because he is tired of seeing things as they have been seen before, or of fusing time's "frames" in conventional ways. Seated next to a salesman, Bloch asks him whether he has ever tried to stay focused on the goalie rather than on the forwards. He observes that it is difficult to look away from the forwards and from the motion of the ball, remarking, "es ist etwas ganz und gar Unnatürliches" (it's utterly and completely unnatural). The salesman agrees that to do so makes you feel cross-eyed, and he then adds an observation that may explain Bloch's misanthropy and that resonates with the strangulation that has at that point been all but forgotten; the salesman notes that you can try to turn your focus from the ball, but your head begins to hurt and you cannot breathe properly.[8]

Though it first appeared on television, Wenders's film synthesizes a number of New German Cinema's questions about language and filmmaking. As an explicit comment on the traditional language of film, Wenders nods to Hitchcock's *North by Northwest* (1959).[9] A low-flying plane crosses the road just above Bloch, who thinks he may be pursued (although the film does not pay this particular tension much mind). The plane passes by him and crosses the road rather than flying along it, and the film thus arguably cuts straight across one of cinema's best known paths. As though the citation — and transformation — of Hitchcock's scene were not enough, Bloch, always willing to flirt, then asks two women who enter the frame why they are hurrying, to which one of them simply replies, "ins Kino" (we're going to the movies). Along similar lines, as a metareflection on cinema, one might charitably interpret a continuity error in the film: when a cinema is shown at the very beginning, the title on the marquee reads *Das Zittern des Fälschers* (*The Tremor of Forgery*), which we later see being replaced by Howard Hawks's *Rote Linie 7000* (*Red Line 7000*, 1965).[10] When Bloch subsequently returns to the movie-house, *Das Zittern des Fälschers* is playing again. Seen in the terms of the film, this is not a misstep but may instead be treated as a reflection on the overall falsity of signs symptomatic of New German Cinema's entanglement with the written word.

See also:

- 18 December 1913: *Atlantis* Triggers Controversy about Sinking of Culture
- 20 August 1981: R. W. Fassbinder's *Lola* Revisits Kracauer to Critique Adenauer Period
- 8 June 1986: Farocki's *Wie man sieht* Urges New Ways of Seeing

Notes

[1] See Leticia Kent, "Werner Herzog: 'Film Is Not the Art of Scholars, But of Illiterates,'" *New York Times* (11 September 1977): Arts 19, 30; here 19. The "legitimate" remark is often cited from "Tribute to Lotte Eisner (1982)" in *West German Filmmakers on Film: Visions and Voices*, ed. Eric Rentschler (New York: Holmes & Meier, 1988), 115–18; here 117.

[2] Eric Rentschler, *West German Filmmakers*, 141. Rentschler also provides a long list of filmed adaptations involved in the adaptation crisis, 131–34.

[3] Writing about Wenders's film *Die Angst des Tormanns beim Elfmeter*, Michael Covino notes: "The framework of the thriller, which was a skeleton for Godard to hang a different story on in *Breathless*, here dissolves into nothing. We are left not with a criminal but with a man quietly going mad." See Michael Covino, "Wim Wenders: A Worldwide Homesickness," *Film Quarterly* 31, no. 2 (1977–78): 9–19; here 11.

[4] Peter Handke, *Die Angst des Tormanns beim Elfmeter* (Frankfurt am Main: Suhrkamp, 1970), 7.

[5] This formulation is W. G. Sebald's. Writing about Peter Handke's novel, Sebald observes: "Das tautologische Verhältnis von Sprache und Realität, dessen der in sich Redende so inne wird, verrät, daß der Mensch an den ihn umgebenden Dingen

nicht mehr besitzt als das Echo seiner eigenen Fiktionen." See "Unterm Spiegel des Wassers: Peter Handkes Erzählung von der Angst des Tormanns," in *Die Beschreibung des Unglücks: Zur Österreichischen Literatur von Stifter bis Handke* (Frankfurt am Main: Fischer, 1994), 115–30; here 123.

[6] Handke, *Die Angst des Tormanns*, 23.

[7] See "Whatever happens between the pictures," *afterimage* 5, no. 5 (Nov 1977), 7–13; here 7–8. Parts of Nekes's 1975 lecture are included under the title "What Really Happens between the Frames," in *West German Filmmakers*, ed. Rentschler, 66–70.

[8] Handke, *Die Angst des Tormanns*, 124. The dialogue from the novel is fairly closely adhered to in this sequence.

[9] Wenders avows the citation in an interview with Tony Rayns. He notes: "The scene where the plane flies past was supposed to be more like *North by Northwest*, but the sun was already very low and so it's not that much like it." See Tony Rayns, "Forms of Address: Interviews with Three German Filmmakers," *Sight and Sound* 44, no. 1 (1974/75), 2–7; here 6.

[10] Wenders is aware of the continuity error: "Yes it's a big continuity slip. The other title is a novel by Patricia Highsmith, *The Tremor of Forgery*, which I like very much and always wanted to film. I was reading it when we made the film." See Rayns, "Forms of Address," 6. An adaptation of that work did not at the time exist, although Peter Goedel's *Trip nach Tunis* (1993) has since appeared.

A 1995 cover for Frauen und Film, *founded in 1974 and still the leading German-language journal for feminist film theory. Credit:* Frauen und Film.

24 June 1974: Launching of *Frauen und Film* Creates Lasting Forum for Feminist Film Writing and Practice

Annette Brauerhoch

THIS MUCH IS CERTAIN: *Frauen und Film* was first distributed at the 1974 Berlin film festival. But not even founder Helke Sander is certain whether the release was launched on Monday, 24 June, or Tuesday, 25 June. Gesine Strempel recalls: "I still own the first issue, produced single-handedly by Helke Sander, hand-typed and held together by two paper clips. The press didn't take much notice, but amongst those being present I remember Sabine Zurmühl, later editor of *Courage*, Erika Gregor, from *Forum des Jungen Films* and Magdalena Kemper (then and to this day radio correspondent at the *Sender Freies Berlin*, today called *Rundfunk Berlin-Brandenburg*)." The first issues were written on a typewriter at the *Deutsche Kinemathek* and generally designed and produced under conditions, "which would give our male colleagues nervous breakdowns."[1]

Improvisation has always been a feature — often out of necessity, later advanced to a credo. Sander's slogan was: "I like chaos, but I don't know whether chaos likes me." To this day *Frauen und Film* has neither office, editorial address, nor even official letterhead. It is published without academic or institutional affiliation, but has in 2012 established its own website. In the course of its existence, *Frauen und Film* has changed from a quarterly, to bi-annual, to annual, to a bi-yearly publication. The latest issue shows a line after the appearance date, stating laconically: irregular publication date. That's where it stands at the moment — but it is still standing strong. *Frauen und Film* was first distributed by the women's collective Brot und Rosen, went briefly on to the Orlando Women's Press, before Rotbuch Verlag, a leftist publisher, agreed at the time of the seventh issue to take on the project. Stroemfeld/Roter Stern started publishing *Frauen und Film* in 1983 and is to be credited for its continuing support and solidarity, as it continues to publish the journal to this day.

The journal's name is partly a tribute to a North American sister publication entitled *women & film*. More important in the German context, however, is the title's reference to history. In the 1950s, *Film und Frau* was an influential postwar West German women's magazine, considered a trendsetter. Founded in 1946 and running until 1967, it addressed fun-starved, luxury-deprived, and hard-working women as consumers with desires that went beyond food and home, even if in reality they often still worked for sheer survival. The journal's gold letters and depictions of style and glamour were intimately connected to the world of film stars. And yet the magazine's representation of female stardom only served to demonstrate that even actresses were "only women" working in film and private kitchen alike. The magazine's promotion of a return to housewifery after the emancipated war and immediate postwar years was thus sugarcoated with the icing of a stardom brought down to the level of "everywoman."[2] By ironically reversing the order of the original magazine's title to *Frauen und Film*, the founders of the new journal replaced the iconic imagery of "woman" with the collective many, and redirected the gaze from women to film.

Frauen und Film grew out of the first women's film seminar held in the Kino Arsenal in Berlin in 1973, a gathering of women working in film, radio, and television. Before developing a program to "examine the workings of a patriarchal culture in film, to recognize and define the beginnings of a feminist culture, to adopt its questions and develop them further,"[3] *Frauen und Film* sought to provide a platform to fight "sexism in the media," which was described as not just a topical matter: "It resides in image composition, framing, iconography" and is "present also in areas in which there are no women present, for instance in the way the news is organized."[4] From the beginning the concern was to recover history, a rewriting and reevaluation of women's contribution to film history, a reconsideration of working conditions of women in the industry, an analysis of current film productions, and a recognition of the social relevance of film. By calling attention to women involved in cinema — stars like Asta Nielsen, film sociologists like Emilie Altenloh, or film critics like Malwine Rennert — *Frauen und Film* made up for the failure of the first women's movement of the twentieth century to recognize the work of such female film pioneers and to acknowledge more generally cinema as a women's medium.

To this day the articles in *Frauen und Film* are sources of insight into early production conditions for women in the 1970s, examining the history of West Germany through its film culture. The journal's beginnings were fuelled by protest energy against male chauvinism in the student movement of 1968, exclusion and sexism in the otherwise leftist *Berliner Arbeiterfilme* (Berlin proletariat films), and by practices in film and television that paved the way for a New German Cinema by supporting male directors and often disregarding topics developed by female filmmakers. *Frauen und Film* took issue with film politics as well as the politics of the auteur. Hildegard Westbelt, founder of Chaos Film

(1979) — a distribution company for films by women and initiator of the first cinema for women in Berlin, Initiative Frauen im Kino, established in 1977 — recalls the impact the journal made upon its appearance: "I will never forget the press conference for the first issue of *Frauen und Film*. It was a hot day in June. I believe that those pages, hectographed on blue paper (and the + between *Frauen und Film* was, quite in the spirit of the times, represented by a Venus mirror) will remain the most important publication in my own personal library, . . . my initiation to being political."[5] And filmmaker Eva Heldmann remembers: "All of a sudden there was something concerning me. I was a student interested in film. But not before the appearance of *Frauen und Film* had I found a feminist perspective in print. It was electrifying." She continues: "It was visible, if only in leftist book stores. It had unusual covers, feminist collages by Sarah Schuman. Here I found opinions, reports, statements from filmmakers and film critics alike — more often than not all in one person. And a solidarity never experienced before. It was fresh, new, and present — and it was not Hollywood!"[6]

In the course of its over thirty-five years of existence, *Frauen und Film* has evolved from a hand-typed hectographed manifest to a journal of academic film theory. In the 1970s it introduced the perspective of female cinemagoers — and at first mainly documentary filmmakers — to a film-cultural scene that was then highly dominated by what was known as *Autorenfilm*. Heavily funded, *Autorenfilm* made inroads mainly for a male-dominated auteurist cinema by the likes of Schlöndorff, Wenders, Herzog, Kluge, and Fassbinder — names that to this day are seen as synonymous with New German Cinema, much more than Jutta Brückner or Ula Stöckl ever were. The journal pointed to inadequacies in funding policies, reported about film festivals, promoted experimental films by women, and introduced female filmmakers. The focus was on Germany and Europe, East and West. Unlike the writing of comparable North American publications, the analysis of patriarchy and representation in cinema in *Frauen und Film* did not focus primarily on Hollywood. The second issue was almost exclusively devoted to a popular film from the GDR, Heiner Carow's *Die Legende von Paul und Paula* (*The Legend of Paul and Paula*, 1973).[7]

Other issues examined the commercially successful new wave of male-directed "women's films" in the late 1970s, the situation of women editors in the industry, the practice of film funding, the question of feminist criticism (what is it and what is it good for?), and questions around pornography (particularly the discussion around *The Story of O*),[8] and the journal displayed an ongoing interest in the female spectator and cinema goer, actresses, and feminist countertraditions. Issue 28 in 1981 ("Trauer muß Sappho tragen?") presented an "avant-queer" approach to film studies and injected lesbian aspects into the feminist discussion.

For a long time, film criticism and the desire to make feminist films went hand in hand. The journal's profile was shaped by an exchange led by professionals examining the field of film production, history, and reception. When the Berlin editors pronounced *Frauen und Film* dead in 1983, convinced that, with its feminist goals, the journal had outlived its function in postfeminist times, the Frankfurt group — Gertrud Koch, Karola Gramann, and Heide Schlüpmann — believing that feminist criticism was far from obsolete, took over the journal with another goal in mind. In a specific inflection of Frankfurt School thought, the new group of editors focused greater attention on theory and the writing of theoretically inflected and motivated historiography. Feminist theory engaged not only with a male-dominated cinema, but a male-dominated theory, and even engaged critically with feminism itself. Long before German universities were ready to open themselves up to an academic engagement with film or women's studies, *Frauen und Film* devoted itself to the translation and dissemination of texts by Anglo-Saxon feminist film scholars for a critical audience. This in turn created a framework for locating *Frauen und Film*'s own theoretical position and it provided the groundwork for a future introduction of feminist film theory into course curricula in universities across the country.

In addition to its ongoing concern with recovering film history (issue 41, 1986), *Frauen und Film*'s approach to historiography concerned itself with the particular implications of Nazi legacies for the film culture of the 1950s (issue 35, 1983), and provided its own take on "fascinating fascism," including a very critical view in 1988 (double issue 44/45) on the film-historical renaissance of Leni Riefenstahl. In connection with their translations of British and American texts, the journal often focused on questions of genre (horror in issue 49, 1990; comedy in issue 53, 1992; and war films in issue 61, 2000), as well as topics such as masquerade (issue 38, 1985) and masochism (issue 39, 1985), which discussed social and psychological constellations through the perspective of film — always adding to the French-influenced Anglo-American theoretical perspective its particular inflection of a Frankfurt School tradition of thinking and (redemptive) criticism, above all insisting "upon the responsibility of the feminist critic to trace patterns of ideology even in her own fascination."[9] In the 1990s topics included issues on fathers and daughters (issue 48, 1990), aging (issue 50–51, 1991), ethnicity and gender (double issue, 54/55, 1994; and issue 60, 1997), and even medial aspects of color and music (double issue 58/59, 1996). The digital divide and its reverberations for the discipline of film and media studies as well as its implications for feminism and gender studies were elaborated upon in issues 64 ("The Old and the New," 2004) and 65 ("Celluloid & Co," 2006).

Frauen und Film became a widely read and internationally recognized film journal, particularly in the United States, but the journal has never had academic inclusion in Germany. The second Frankfurt generation of editors (Annette Brauerhoch, Heike Klippel, and Renate Lippert) maintain the journal alongside their academic positions, thereby providing a forum for critical views never integrated into the institutions of academic learning. Despite the general trend toward incorporating changing media landscapes and shifting relations between film and "the media" into institutional names, often substituting film with media, *Frauen and Film* cannot imagine changing its title to *Gender and Media*. The politics of naming persist in an insistence on material and sociological entities, and (female) spectatorship with its components of identification, fantasy, and history. That is why in 2000 *Frauen und Film* celebrated its twenty-fifth anniversary programmatically, not so much with a conference but with a film festival, in the conviction that no theory can live without its subject: film, cinema, and its audiences.[10]

See also:

- 10 January 1927: Brigitte Helm Embodies Ambivalence of the New Woman
- 2 February 1956: In Letter to Enno Patalas, Siegfried Kracauer Advocates a Socio-Aesthetic Approach to Film
- 16 May 1992: Marlene Dietrich's Berlin Burial Links Postunification Germany with Weimar Republic's Internationalism

Notes

[1] Julia Knight, "Institutional Initiatives," in *Women and the New German Cinema*, ed. Julia Knight (London: Verso, 1992), 102–21.

[2] Compare my very first contribution to *Frauen und Film*: Annette Brauerhoch, "Moral in Golddruck: Die Illustrierte 'Film und Frau,'" *Frauen und Film* 35 (1983): 48–57. Back issues of *Frauen and Film* can be accessed online at: http://www.frauenundfilm.de.

[3] *Frauen und Film* 6 (1975).

[4] *Frauen und Film* 1 (1974).

[5] *Frauen und Film* 62 (2000): 164.

[6] In a conversation with the author on 20 April 2010.

[7] *Die Legende von Paul und Paula* (*The Legend of Paul and Paula*) dir. Heiner Carow, perf. Angelica Domröse, Winfried Glatzleder, Heidemarie Wenzel, and Fred Delmare, DEFA, 1973.

[8] *Frauen und Film* 7 (1976) and *Frauen und Film* 30 (1981).

[9] Miriam Hansen, "Messages in a Bottle?," *Screen* 28, no. 4 (1987): 30–39; here 34.

[10] It is not by accident that the same year saw the founding of the *Kinothek Asta Nielsen* (mainly under the leadership of *Frauen und Film*'s former editor Karola Gramann, in cooperation with Heide Schlüpmann and others), which connected theory with archival work and continues to keep feminist film work alive not just in theory, but through practices such as cinema retrospectives.

Part VI: 1977–1989

In the annals of West German history, 1977 is most remembered as the year terrorist violence reached its bloody apex. The Rote Armee Fraktion (Red Army Faction, RAF) conducted a series of bold attacks, seeking to avenge the 1976 death of Ulrike Meinhof and secure the release of movement leaders Andreas Baader, Gudrun Ensslin, and Jan-Carl Raspe, found guilty in April 1977 by a Stuttgart court and sentenced to life in prison. That same month, RAF members shot State Attorney Siegfried Buback in broad daylight on a public street; in July, in the course of a kidnapping attempt, they murdered bank executive Jürgen Ponto; then in September, the RAF abducted businessman and industry representative Hanns-Martin Schleyer. On 18 October 1977, on the same day that a special operations unit successfully freed hostages on a Lufthansa flight hijacked to Mogadishu, Baader, Ensslin, and Raspe committed suicide in Stammheim Prison. In reply, Schleyer's captors executed him the following day. The exceptionally violent period became known simply as The German Autumn, and to contemporary observers seemed to symbolize the crisis of the leftist student movement, Helmut Schmidt's center-left coalition, and West German democracy more generally.

Although the years of his term were largely overshadowed by the struggle against domestic terrorism, Schmidt's coalition achieved a number of political successes. It implemented a series of progressive domestic reforms: vocational training aimed at bettering prospects for younger workers; antidiscrimination policies, including measures making it easier for married women and mothers to participate in the workforce; urban development projects; and improved benefits for families and the elderly. The Federal Republic also fared comparatively well during the world economic recession, seeing deficits rise but maintaining financial stability overall. As one consequence of these economic straits, in 1973 the West German government moved to limit the immigration of so-called guest workers, who by early that decade numbered approximately 2.6 million. In 1983, as the economy continued to stagnate, the Federal Republic went a step further, initiating a financial incentives program intended to encourage workers to return to their countries of origin. The program was unsuccessful, and immigrants continued the trend of settling long-term and bringing their families after them. It served as yet another marker of how the Federal Republic was increasingly becoming a "land of immigration," although official political rhetoric did not yet define the nation as such.

In the international arena, Schmidt fostered positive ties with Western Europe. In 1975, together with French President Valéry Giscard d'Estaing, Schmidt helped to inaugurate an annual economic summit of world leaders that would eventually become today's G8; then, four years later, Germany and France expanded the unification of Europe, first initiated in the 1950s, with the introduction of the European Currency System, forming the basis for the future euro. Toward the country's neighbors to the East, Schmidt continued the policies of *Ostpolitik* even as Cold War tensions rose with the ratcheting up of the arms race and the Soviet invasion of Afghanistan in 1979. Despite vociferous opposition from the West German peace movement, the Federal Republic joined NATO in signing on to the Double-Track Decision, an accord that called for a Soviet disarmament plan, but by way of deterrent arranged for the deployment of hundreds of midrange nuclear missiles on West German soil should the plan fail. Then in 1982, in the course of a growing rift in the SPD-FDP coalition, the FDP called a vote of no confidence. Schmidt lost, and in the shakeup CDU leader Helmut Kohl took the helm. The change would set the course for the final phase in West German political leadership before unification.

When the new coalition was confirmed in national elections in 1983, Kohl embarked on a conservative program that sought to bolster the economy and combat unemployment by fostering business growth, that promised to uphold West Germany's commitment to NATO, and that supported American interests in the final throes of the Cold War (for example, supporting a US plan to develop a controversial missile defense shield). Kohl faced new challenges, however, when the same elections gave the Green Party sufficient votes to enter parliament — proving the strength of the new peace and ecology movements, and introducing a four-party dynamic into the federal government for the first time since 1945. Regarding the GDR, Kohl maintained his party's traditional hard line against Communism while continuing to strengthen economic ties between the nations, even as relations with the Soviet Union grew ever more tense. In 1983–84, the FRG made extensive loans to the East, and in 1987 Kohl hosted a state visit by Erich Honecker, the first by an East German leader, during which the two reached accords on scientific collaboration and environmental protection. Under Kohl, the country also boosted relationships with its Western European Allies, most famously in 1984, when the German chancellor and French President François Mitterand joined hands during a joint commemoration at Verdun to remember the dead of both world wars — marking the culmination of a remarkable, three-decades long rapprochement between the former enemy nations. When it came to remembering the Second World War, however, Kohl also courted controversy. The chancellor — a self-declared member of the generation "graced by late birth" and hence excused of direct guilt for the Nazi past — raised an international outcry after he and US President Ronald Reagan laid a wreath in Bitburg Cemetery, even after it had been revealed as the burial site for a number of SS soldiers. The events of Bitburg, coupled with a wave of revisionist historical publications, culminated in a bitter public dispute known as the Historians' Debate — reviving intellectual discourse concerning the need for a national reckoning with the National Socialist past. FRG President Richard von Weizsäcker, elected in 1984, took a leading role in the reawakening of these discussions, calling upon his fellow citizens to accept the country's special burden to remember its terrible history. By the late 1980s, Kohl's government no longer enjoyed strong public support. But this would change with the dramatic events of October and November that year, as the Wall fell and plans to unite the two Germanys took shape. Kohl would ride the wave of unification enthusiasm to two more election victories, governing until 1998 — making him the longest serving chancellor in West German history.

Under Honecker, East Germans also experienced a period of extended political continuity. Elected SED General Secretary in 1976, Honecker sought to maintain a political hard line while appeasing the population's desire for material goods. Under his leadership, the state developed ever-stronger ties with West Germany, increasing trade and gradually easing travel and communication restrictions in exchange for cash infusions from the West. In 1978, the party reached an unprecedented agreement with the Protestant Church, allowing the organization greater freedom, and thereby inadvertently contributing to the creation of an alternate public sphere that would prove instrumental in bringing down the government in 1989. Under the auspices of the Church, the Swords to Ploughshares peace movement developed, which, together with other grassroots movements that emerged throughout the decades of the 1970s and '80s, increasingly called upon the state to permit greater civil liberties, foster peace, and improve its environmental policy. In response to growing pressure from citizen groups and the international community, the GDR increased its already tight state control — starkly limiting emigration, meting out strong punishment to those attempting to flee to the West, and amending the penal code in ways that made it easier to exact harsh sanctions against its critics. All the while, the GDR continued to press the West for full recognition of its sovereignty and the independent citizenship of its people. The high point in this effort came in 1987, when Honecker became the first GDR head of state to visit the Federal Republic — a moment that seemed to grant official validation to the socialist nation.

By the late 1980s, the East German state was beginning to look like a holdout against the reforms sweeping the Eastern bloc, as the country's ageing leadership declined to emulate the policies of perestroika and glasnost implemented by Soviet leader Mikhail Gorbachev. In January 1989, Honecker declared that the Wall would continue to stand for another hundred years, if the reasons for its existence were not removed. (In direct contradiction to this, Gorbachev would insist during a state visit to Bonn in June that the Wall *could* disappear, should there be a change in the conditions that *had led to* its creation.) But the cracks in the edifice were already evident. In May 1989, opposition leaders for the first time observed state elections and found widespread irregularities; public protests followed their revelation. Throughout that summer, increasing liberalization in other East Bloc countries placed new pressure on the East German regime. GDR citizens flooded embassies in Hungary and Czechoslovakia seeking asylum in the West; in August, Bavarian authorities began planning for a temporary refugee camp to accommodate the influx. Then in September, Leipzig marchers gathered for a peaceful protest, inaugurating the "Monday Demonstrations" that would spread to other GDR cities and offer visible evidence of widespread citizen discontent. With the motto "*Wir* sind das Volk" — "*We* are the people," and not the select few of the SED leadership — they demanded a voice in political reform. The situation escalated further in October, as East German leaders celebrated the fortieth anniversary of the German Democratic Republic with full pomp, while thousands of protesting citizens were met with police brutality and arrest. That same month, Honecker was forced from office and replaced by Egon Krenz. The complete collapse of the government was not far behind. On 9 November, at an international press conference, a GDR official bungled the announcement of a new travel policy, declaring an immediate lift on all restrictions. That night, thousands flocked to the Berlin Wall and crossed over freely for the first time since the border's closure in 1961. Within just weeks, despite calls by some intellectuals within the GDR to reform the state rather than allow it to be absorbed by the West, plans for German unification were underway.

The fall of the Wall would lead to a period of vigorous cultural revival in both halves of the country, coming on the heels of parallel periods of relative stagnation. In the late 1970s, a decade after changes in Federal Republic subvention policies had fostered a generation of new directors, West German cinema still seemed on solid footing. This was particularly true in the case of avant-garde film, as the directors of New German Cinema garnered ever more international attention for their aesthetically innovative and provocative explorations of national history and identity. Festivals regularly featured works by the likes of Volker Schlöndorff, Rainer Werner Fassbinder, Alexander Kluge, Hans-Jürgen Syberberg, Wim Wenders, and Werner Herzog. But the crisis of the Left that ensued following the violence in the fall of 1977 had left this emergent generation of cinematic talent shaken and a bit disoriented — a sentiment captured most poignantly in the collaborative New German Cinema opus

Deutschland im Herbst (*Germany in Autumn*, 1978). Pressure was also exerted by a wave of feminist filmmakers often excluded from the ranks of the largely male-dominated movement — directors such as Helma Sanders-Brahms, Helke Sander, Margarethe von Trotta, and Jutta Brückner. 1979 saw the founding of the Verband der Filmarbeiterinnen (Association of Women Film Workers), and weeks later feminists issued an amendment of sorts to the Oberhausen document of 1962. "The Manifesto of Women Film Workers" called for equality in funding, employment, and distribution. Then in 1984, New German Cinema's most visible representative, Fassbinder, died as the result of an accidental drug overdose, bringing his manic production to an abrupt and tragic conclusion, and effectively ushering in the end of an era. At the same time, a new generation of popular comedies emerged that, in contrast to New German Cinema, proved capable of drawing blockbuster audiences at home — from Doris Dörrie's breakthrough hit *Männer* (*Men*, 1985), to star vehicles for comedians Otto Waalkes (*Otto — Der Film* [Otto — the movie], 1985) and Loriot (*Ödipussi*, 1988). The New German Comedy became a dominant part of domestic production well into the nineties, but the local appeal of these films came at a price, often proving a tough sell abroad and thereby contributing to the isolation of an industry that only a few years earlier had earned international acclaim.

For DEFA (Deutsche Film-Aktiengesellschaft, East Germany's state-owned film company), the period of the late seventies and early eighties was one of contradictions. The studio was still reeling from the exodus of many of its most popular actors, including veritable stars like Manfred Krug and Angelica Domröse. The East German industry was also feeling the consequences of the political suppression of numerous directors whose careers might otherwise have been entering a mature artistic stage. Those filmmakers who did continue to attempt to work under these uncertain conditions faced difficult odds, confronted by a capricious censorship system, poor opportunities for the advancement of young talent, and attempts at studio reform that went unfulfilled. Yet these years would also yield some of the most successful works in DEFA history. A case in point is the cult classic *Solo Sunny* (1980). Created by two industry veterans — director Konrad Wolf and screenwriter Wolfgang Kohlhaase — the film explored the struggles of an East German pop star seeking to make her fortune in a languishing music scene. *Solo Sunny* was a huge hit with audiences, and lead actress Renate Krößner won the Silver Bear award at the Berlinale that year. As if to highlight the very problems and contradictions of the beleaguered studio, however, the film's preoccupation with the difficult lot of GDR performers took a real-world turn in 1985 when Krößner successfully petitioned to emigrate to the West. In 1988, a change in studio leadership was meant to revitalize production, and DEFA green-lighted a series of critical projects tackling the country's stifling conditions, most notably Peter Kahane's *Die Architekten* (*The Architects*, 1990), which foregrounded the dilemmas of East German artists forced to choose between battling a malevolent bureaucracy and abandoning their craft. But liberalization came too late. While the tumult of 1989 and the collapse of the German Democratic Republic gave rise to an unprecedented moment of creative freedom — from which arose a series of *Wende* films that, like Kahane's work, explored whether and how East German culture might be worth saving — DEFA's final productions were largely lost in the push toward unification. In 1992, the studio was formally dissolved and French conglomerate Compagnie Générale des Eaux purchased its holdings, thereby ending the era of East German cinema.

Selected Bibliography • 1977–1989

Bergfelder, Tim. "Popular Genres and Cultural Legitimacy: Fassbinder's *Lola* and the Legacy of 1950s West German Cinema." *Screen* 45, no. 1 (2004): 21–39.

Cook, Roger F., and Gerd Gemünden, eds. *The Cinema of Wim Wenders: Image, Narrative, and the Postmodern Condition*. Detroit: Wayne State UP, 1997.

Corrigan, Timothy. *New German Film: The Displaced Image*. 2nd, revised edition. Bloomington: Indiana UP, 1994.

Corrigan, Timothy, ed. *The Films of Werner Herzog: Between Mirage and History*. New York: Methuen, 1986.

Davidson, John E. *Deterritorializing the New German Cinema*. Minneapolis: U of Minnesota P, 1999.

Elsaesser, Thomas. *Fassbinder's Germany: History, Identity, Subject*. Amsterdam: Amsterdam UP, 1996.

———. *New German Cinema: A History*. New Brunswick, NJ: Rutgers UP, 1989.

Feinstein, Joshua. *The Triumph of the Ordinary: Depictions of Daily Life in the East German Cinema, 1949–1989*. Chapel Hill: U of North Carolina P, 2002.

Flinn, Caryl. *The New German Cinema: Music, History, and the Matter of Style*. Berkeley: U of California P, 2004.

Guder, Andrea. *Genosse Hauptmann auf Verbrecherjagd: Der Krimi in Film und Fernsehen der DDR*. Bonn: ARCult-Media, 2003.

Hillman, Roger. *Unsettling Scores: German Film, Music, and Ideology*. Bloomington: Indiana UP, 2005.

Indiana, Gary. "Germany inside Him: Rainer Fassbinder and the Spell of Dystopia." In *Utopia's Debris: Selected Essays*, 131–36. New York: Basic Books, 2008.

Kaes, Anton. *From Hitler to Heimat: The Return of History as Film*. Cambridge: Harvard UP, 1989.

Kinder, Marsha. "Ideological Parody in the New German Cinema Reading *The State of Things*, *The Desire of Veronika Voss*, and *Germany Pale Mother* as Postmodernist Rewritings of *The Searchers*, *Sunset Boulevard*, and *Blonde Venus*." *Quarterly Review of Film and Video* 12, nos. 1/2 (1990): 73–103.

Kligerman, Eric. "The Antigone Effect: Reinterring the Dead of *Night and Fog* in the German Autumn." *New German Critique* 38, no. 1 (2011): 9–38.

Klimek, Julia F. "Elusive Images of Women, Home, and History: Deconstructing the Use of Film and Photography in Edgar Reitz's *Heimat*." *Women in German Yearbook* 15 (1999): 228.

Knight, Julia. *New German Cinema: Images of a Generation*. London, New York: Wallflower, 2004.

———. *Women and the New German Cinema*. London: Verso, 1992.

Kolker, Robert P., and Peter Beicken. *The Films of Wim Wenders: Cinema as Vision and Desire*. Cambridge: Cambridge UP, 1993.

Langford, Michelle. "Film Figures: Rainer Werner Fassbinder's *The Marriage of Maria Braun* and Alexander Kluge's *The Female Patriot*." In *Kiss Me Deadly: Feminism and Cinema for the Moment*, edited by Laleen Jayamanne, 147–79. Sydney: Power Publications, 1995.

Linville, Susan E. *Feminism, Film, Fascism: Women's Auto/Biographical Film in Postwar Germany*. Austin: U of Texas P, 1998.

Lode, Imke. "Terrorism, Sadomasochism, and Utopia in Fassbinder's *The Third Generation*." In *Perspectives on German Cinema*, edited by Terri Ginsberg and Kirsten Moana Thompson, 415–34. New York: G. K. Hall, 1996.

Majer O'Sicky, Ingeborg. "Representing Blackness: Instrumentalizing Race and Gender in Rainer Werner Fassbinder's *The Marriage of Maria Braun*." *Women in German Yearbook: Feminist Studies in German Literature and Culture* 17 (2001): 15–29.

Majer O'Sickey, Ingeborg, and Ingeborg von Zadow, eds. *Triangulated Visions: Women in Recent German Cinema*. Albany: State U of New York P, 1998.

McGee, Laura G. "Revolution in the Studio? The DEFA's Fourth Generation of Film Directors and Their Reform Efforts in the Last Decade of the GDR." *Film History* 15, no. 4 (2003): 444–64.

Meurer, Hans Joachim. *Cinema and National Identity in a Divided Germany, 1979–1989: The Split Screen*. Lewiston: Edwin Mellen, 2000.

Moeller, Hans-Berhard, and George Lellis. *Volker Schlöndorff's Cinema: Adaptation, Politics, and the "Movie-Appropriate."* Carbondale: Southern Illinois UP, 2002.

Muckenberger, Christiane. "The Cold War in East German Feature Film." *Historical Journal of Film, Radio and Television* 13, no. 1 (1993): 49–58.

Rentschler, Eric, ed. *West German Filmmakers on Film: Visions and Voices*. New York: Holmes & Meier, 1988.

———. *German Film and Literature: Adaptations and Transformations*. New York: Methuen, 1986.

———. *West German Film in the Course of Time: Reflections on the Twenty Years since Oberhausen*. Bedford Hills: Redgrave, 1984.

Rinke, Andrea. *Images of Women in East German Cinema 1972–1982: Socialist Models, Private Dreamers and Rebels*. Lewiston: Edward Mellen, 2006.

Santner, Eric L. *Stranded Objects: Mourning, Memory, and Film in Postwar Germany*. Ithaca: Cornell UP, 1990.

Scharf, Inga. *Nation and Identity in the New German Cinema: Homeless at Home*. New York: Routledge, 2008.

Schönherr, Ulrich. "Out of Tune: Music, Postwar Politics, and Edgar Reitz's *Die zweite Heimat*." *New German Critique* 37, no. 2 (2010): 107–24.

Silberman, Marc. *German Cinema: Texts in Context*. Detroit: Wayne State UP, 1995.

Silverman, Kaja. "Fassbinder and Lacan: A Reconsideration of Gaze, Look, and Image." In *Visual Culture: Images and Interpretations*, edited by Norman Bryson, Michael Ann Holly, and Keith Moxey, 272–301. Hanover: UP of New England for Wesleyan UP, 1994.

Von Moltke, Johannes. "Camping in the Art Closet: The Politics of Camp and Nation in German Film." *New German Critique* 63 (Fall 1994): 77–106.

Williams, Bruce. "'Life is very precious, even right now': (Un)Happy Camping in the New German Cinema." *Post Script* 16, no. 3 (Summer 1997): 51–64.

20 June 1977: DEFA's Biggest Star, Manfred Krug, Leaves the GDR

John Griffith Urang

Manfred Krug in his most famous role as brigadier Hannes Balla. Spur der Steine *(1966). DVD capture.*

Geh doch mal ins Kino, da verfliegt die Wut.	Go out to a movie, Your rage will fly away
Koche mit Liebe, würze mit Bino!	Love cooked up nice with some Bitterfeld spice
Hin und wieder tut ein DEFA-Lustspiel gut.	A funny DEFA film would do you good today.
Stell die Sorgen in die Ecke, nimm dir deinen Hut!	Grab your coat and take your hat And put your cares away!
Spazier nur auf der Sonnenseite,	Just keep walking on the sunny side,
dann wird alles gut.	Everything'll be OK.

So urged the jaunty title song of Ralf Kirsten's 1962 musical comedy *Auf der Sonnenseite* (On the sunny side). Scarcely a year after the Berlin Wall had relieved East Germans of the choice whether or not to "keep walking on the sunny side," such cheery optimism may have seemed a tough sell. Still, *Auf der Sonnenseite* found an ideal salesman; the singer, backed by his aptly named "Jazz-Optimisten," was Manfred Krug, an impish young steelworker-turned-entertainer. In Kirsten's film, Krug plays Martin Hoff, a smelter whose charm and talent earns him a place in acting school and the affection of his love-interest, Ottilie (the real name of Krug's wife). This made-to-measure star vehicle was a runaway hit with audiences and critics alike. Film critic Renate Holland-Moritz quipped it was "a dangerous film," since it "robbed comic screenwriters and directors of their complacent excuses."[1]

Indeed, the struggles of the East German film studio DEFA (Deutsche Film-Aktiengessellschaft) to produce successful entertainment films, especially comedies, had been a matter of public consternation for more than a decade. The doctrine of socialist realism created a notoriously toxic environment for popular genre cinema, eschewing considerations of entertainment value in favor of ideological and didactic intelligibility. The opening scene of *Auf der Sonnenseite* pokes fun at the dreary, workaday plots encouraged by programmatic socialist realism. As the leader of his factory's lay theater troupe, Martin Hoff is putting on a play "in which steelworkers work on steel. I play the lead role," he explains in voiceover, "a steelworker." The play seems to be a straightforward rendition of daily life at the steelworks, complete with authentic costumes and tools. Disgusted, the audience whistles, heckles, and disappears, save one worker who is fast asleep.

The party might have been content to hitch its wagon indefinitely to the "boy meets tractor" school of drama, if not for the events of 17 June 1953. As workers across the GDR took to the streets to demand better working conditions, greater personal freedoms, and a higher quality of life, the party began to see the value of mass-cultural diversion. In a series of public editorials, East German cultural functionaries called DEFA on the carpet, soliciting movies with greater entertainment value — though without lifting the imperative of socialist realism. DEFA was caught between the devil of doctrine and the deep blue sea of public demand. How could it persuade East German moviegoers to watch what was good for them (ideologically speaking), especially when the alternative was only as far away as the nearest West German border cinema?

In the early years of Hollywood, the studios were faced with a similar conundrum, though with a bottom line of profits, not politics. As filmgoing shifted from a periodic novelty to an everyday activity, studios had to find a way to profit reliably from a product bought sight-unseen. Thus, writes film historian Richard Dyer, the star system was born: "Stars are made for profit. In terms of the market, stars are part of the way films are sold. The star's presence in a film is a promise of a certain kind of thing that you would see if you went to see the film."[2] Anthropologist Hortense Powdermaker makes a similar argument from the management side:

> The [star] system provides a formula easy to understand and has made the production of movies seem more like just another business. The

use of this formula may serve also to protect executives from talent and from having to pay much attention to such intangibles as the quality of story or of acting. Here is a standardized product which they can understand, which can be advertised and sold.[3]

Interestingly, Powdermaker's analysis can be directly reversed to apply to the GDR. East German cultural functionaries were concerned almost exclusively with the ideological "intangibles" of film production, combing scripts and rough cuts for political missteps or slips in tone and tenor. The more material question of box office receipts remained secondary — at least for a while.

Due in part to the ascendancy of politics over popularity and in part to the effort to avoid high-profile holdovers from Nazi productions, the fledgling DEFA was a studio without stars. As the political winds shifted in the summer of 1953, however, movie stars seemed ideal heralds of the New Course reforms, living proof of the glamour, prosperity, and enjoyment to be had in the GDR. Not yet existing, the East German movie star would have to be invented. Along these lines, an article in the April 1954 issue of the entertainment monthly *Das Magazin* argues for the creation of an East German star-system. Shuttling back and forth between the astronomical and colloquial definitions of "star" — or, in the article's tongue-in-cheek acronym, "ST-ate A-pproved entertaine-R" (*ST-aatlich A-nerkannter R-ahmenkulturarbeiter*) — the author ("Klaus") scolds DEFA for having reduced this important aspect of movie culture to a "black hole." "When you see a shooting star," he concludes, "you can wish for something. I wish for a star. Not an engineered, subsidized, dollar-made one, but a real one, a great and shining DEFA-star."[4]

In a belated push to address the desires of its audience, DEFA began to develop its own stable of screen idols.[5] East German audiences gradually came to recognize themselves in these only slightly larger-than-life heroes, lovers, workers, and even party secretaries. Stars lent spontaneity and humanity to overly ideological film scenarios, while at the same time legitimating the East German audience's participation in the dubious libidinal economy of silver-screen idolatry. It was acceptable to identify with *these* stars, since they were *volkseigen*, "people's-own."

More than any other, it was the cohort of actors who came of age in the mid-1960s that defined the distinctive look and feel of DEFA films, personifying the virtues and vices, fortes and foibles of East German society. Jutta Hoffmann and Marita Böhme portrayed poised, self-reliant, and beleaguered career-women, testifying both to the dramatic advances of East German women in the workplace and to lingering gender inequalities in jobs, relationships, and childrearing. Eberhard Esche, whose brainy, brooding characters lived the contradictions of modern socialism, seemed the very picture of the new class of "planner and leader" technocrats ushered in by the sixties' market-responsive New Economic System. Genre films had their stars as well. The brawny Yugoslavian Gojko Mitic fought cowboys and capitalists in the uniquely East German *Indianerfilme*, while Chris Doerk and Frank Schöbel became pop sensations after their rock-and-roll Baltic road-trip in the musical *Heißer Sommer* (*Hot Summer*, 1968).

Manfred Krug, as likely to burst into song as to sing the praises of the three-shift system, was perhaps the biggest DEFA star of all. Film historian Erika Richter calls Krug a "real star," one who has "such a charismatic personality that the viewer experiences him as the embodiment of his own desires."[6] To the apparatchiks, Krug was the second-generation steelworker who had voluntarily moved to East Germany and who, although he never joined the party, seemed genuinely committed to the socialist experiment. To his fans, he was one of their own, chock-a-block with proletarian authenticity.[7] In Krug's own words:

> [The] actor Krug and the person Krug were seen as identical. People saw an unusual aura of genuineness and independence, of impartiality. This was a person who didn't knuckle under. . . . Some of that came through in the movies, and the people said: look at that! . . . Right in the middle of the socialist flimflam, a person you can believe.[8]

The hallmark of Krug's characters — and by his account, of his off-screen self — was the trait that Oskar Negt and Alexander Kluge have dubbed "Eigensinn," a mixture of obstinacy and self-assertiveness characteristic of German proletarian culture.[9]

Manfred Krug's most quintessentially *eigensinnig* character was brigadier Hannes Balla in Frank Beyer's *Spur der Steine* (*The Trace of Stones*, 1966). Dressed like a gunslinger in a black vest and broad-brimmed hat, Balla first appears at the head of a flying wedge of carpenters, striding toward the camera and parting the crowd gathered for a political rally. Later, the brigade takes a drunken skinny-dip in the town duck pond and dunks a cop who tries to intervene. "We've always been a public nuisance," boasts the brigadier.

Spur der Steine reached only a tiny fraction of its potential audience. After deploying paid agents to stage protests against the film, the party pulled it from theaters within three days. *Spur der Steine* was not alone; at the Central Committee's Eleventh Plenum in December 1965, DEFA's entire production-run for that year was banned, as well as several projects still in development. By many accounts, the East German film industry never recovered from this ambush.

When folksinger and political gadfly Wolf Biermann was denied reentry to the GDR after a concert in Cologne in November 1976, East German cultural producers were given an opportunity to make amends for failing to stand up for themselves a decade before. Thirteen writers and actors — among them Manfred Krug — signed a collective letter protesting the expatriation. All of the signatories who refused to recant were effectively blacklisted; Krug, for instance, found all of his scheduled jazz concerts abruptly cancelled and film projects suddenly put on ice. After six months without employment, Krug submitted a request to leave the GDR. The party grudgingly approved his application and on 20 June 1977, Krug crossed the border into the West.

One border-crossing occasioned another; in West Germany, Krug the movie star squeezed his outsized personality onto the small screen. Whether as the long-haul trucker Franz Meersdonk in *Auf Achse* (On the road), the eccentric attorney Robert Liebling in *Liebling Kreuzberg* (Dear Kreuzberg), the gruff police investigator Paul Stoever in *Tatort* (Crime scene), or the avuncular Manfred in *Sesamstraße* (*Sesame Street*), Krug retained his formidable screen presence, his affable charm, and above all his distinctive — and perhaps distinctively East German — *Eigensinn*.

See also:

- 19 June 1935: Celebration of Lilian Harvey's Return Belies Ideological Incongruence in Nazi Entertainment Films
- 1 February 1968: Konrad Wolf's *Ich war neunzehn* Evokes an East German Nation in Transition
- 2 February 1988: Last Generation of DEFA Directors Calls in Vain for Reform

Notes

[1] Renate Holland-Moritz, *Die Eule im Kino* (Berlin: Eulenspiegel, 1983), 22, aqi Ralf Schenk, *Manfred Krug* (Berlin: Parthas, 1997), 43.

[2] Richard Dyer, *Heavenly Bodies* (New York: St. Martin's, 1986), 5.

[3] Hortense Powdermaker, *Hollywood, The Dream Factory* (Boston: Little, Brown, 1950), 229.

[4] Klaus Bartho, "Star Schnuppen," *Das Magazin* 1 no. 4 (1954): 36–37; here 36–37.

[5] Stefan Soldovieri reads stardom in the GDR as "an instructive example of the inherent tensions in DEFA's efforts to reconcile ideological pressures with the demand for genre films and popular entertainment." Stefan Soldovieri, "Managing Stars: Manfred Krug and the Politics of Entertainment in GDR Cinema," in *Moving Images of East Germany*, ed. Barton Byg and Betheny Moore (Washington, DC: American Institute for Contemporary German Studies and Johns Hopkins UP, 2002), 56–71; here 56.

[6] Erika Richter, "Zwischen Mauerbau und Kahlschlag," in *Das zweite Leben der Filmstadt Babelsberg*, ed. Christiane Mückenberger and Ralf Schenk (Berlin: Henschel, 1994), 185.

[7] Richard Dyer argues that the star system relies on a "rhetoric of authenticity" that mediates the complex relationship between the star's image and his or her "real self." "*A Star Is Born* and the Construction of Authenticity," in *Stardom: Industry of Desire,* ed. Christine Gledhill (London: Routledge, 1991), 132–140; here 137.

[8] Manfred Krug, *Abgehauen* (Düsseldorf: Econ, 1996), 143.

[9] The valences of *Eigensinn* are explored at length in Negt and Kluge's monumental *Geschichte und Eigensinn* (History and *Eigensinn,* 1981). Describing the behavior of German workers in the Taylorist factories of the Weimar Republic and under the dictatorship of the Nazis, historian Alf Lüdtke characterizes *Eigensinn* as a "third approach alongside the (rare) alternative of open opposition or the more widespread option of silent complaisance." Alf Lüdtke, "What Happened to the 'Fiery Red Glow'? Workers' Experiences and German Fascism," in *The History of Everyday Life,* ed. Alf Lüdtke, trans. William Templer (Princeton: Princeton UP, 1995), 198–251; here 226.

27 October 1977: *Deutschland im Herbst* Equivocates on RAF and Marks End Stage of Radical Filmmaking

Jennifer Marston William

Defiant sympathizers at the funeral of RAF leaders Gudrun Ensslin, Andreas Baader and Jan Carl Raspe. Deutschland im Herbst *(1978). DVD capture.*

RELEASED AT THE Berlinale International Film Festival on 3 March 1978, the collective montage film *Deutschland im Herbst* (*Germany in Autumn*) was nominated for the Golden Bear award, and won the German Film Award in Gold for "Outstanding Individual Achievement in Film Conception." It also achieved some measure of commercial success, attributed in great part to its timeliness, having appeared less than five months after the culmination of the 1977 German Autumn with the suicides of Andreas Baader, Gudrun Ensslin, and Jan-Carl Raspe in Stammheim prison. As the RAF persists as an object of fascination in the media and on the big screen more than three decades later, *Deutschland im Herbst* remains a milestone in German film history for its spontaneous representation of left-wing terrorism at a time of political and cinematic crisis.

The term "German Autumn" refers to a series of events in late 1977 involving the Rote Armee Fraktion (Red Army Faction, RAF) terrorist group and its efforts to force the German government to release its three leaders — Baader, Ensslin, and Raspe — who had been imprisoned since 1972. On 5 September 1977, RAF members kidnapped industrialist Hanns-Martin Schleyer, president of the German Employers' Association, and wrote the government demanding the release of the prisoners. The government refused to give in, and a month later, on 13 October, a group of four Arabs hijacked Lufthansa flight 181 from Palma de Mallorca to Frankfurt, and made similar demands. Less than a week later, while the plane was refueling in Mogadishu, a German GSG9 commando unit stormed the plane, killing three hijackers and rescuing the hostages. After reportedly hearing the news of the rescue in prison that night, Baader, Ensslin, and Raspe were found dead. That same day, Hanns-Martin Schleyer was executed and his body recovered the next day.

Deutschland im Herbst attempted to show the complexity of the German Autumn through an unconventional form that defies simple categorization. The film is framed by footage both of the heavily publicized funeral of kidnapped businessman Hanns-Martin Schleyer and of the contested public burial of the three RAF leaders in the Stuttgart-Dornhalden cemetery. This documentary technique was typical of many New German Cinema directors, especially those who were more interested in addressing domestic German audiences than ones abroad.[1] Yet documentary footage comprises only part of the film, which also features several fictionalized vignettes that attempt to encapsulate multifarious reactions to this time of political turbulence and media censorship. While some critics have described these fictional episodes as "embarrassing"[2] and as having "banal plots,"[3] it is largely during these scenes that the film "recreates the sense of disruption and fear"[4] experienced by many in West Germany at the time.

The fictional sketches were not the only aspect of the film to receive negative criticism. Although its list of filmmakers includes prominent leftist representatives of the New German Cinema such as Rainer Werner Fassbinder, Volker Schlöndorff, and Alexander Kluge, many on the left criticized *Deutschland im Herbst* at the time for not giving voice to the working class.[5] Feminist critics have noted the relative lack of women in the long list of contributors, and the "abstract nature of the key female figures in the film."[6] Another focal point of criticism over the years has been the film's perceived cinematographic weaknesses — poor lighting is a commonly cited example — as the filmmakers' sense of urgency and prioritizing of politics over aesthetics resulted in a hasty compilation and editing process. But given the media exposure that the RAF continues to receive even today, the film's ambivalent relationship to the terrorist group and its origins at a crossroads for radical German filmmaking deserve particular critical attention.

The Oberhausen Manifesto had declared the death of the old cinema in 1962, and by the time of the student protests of the late sixties, radical filmmaking had reached a pinnacle with, for example, political films from activist students at the Deutsche Film- und Fernsehakademie Berlin. After 1968, radical-revolutionary filmmaking already found itself in a decline — Ulrike Meinhof's own 1970 television movie *Bambule* was shelved until 1994 — and by the mid-1970s the New German Cinema had hit a crossroads. Many considered the deaths at Stammheim in 1977 to be an endpoint for the '68ers and the RAF (despite continued activities of next-generation urban guerillas), and with its closing scenes of the terrorists' burial, *Deutschland im Herbst* might be seen in turn as an endpoint for radical filmmaking in West Germany. Yet as the first response of filmmakers to the events of the German Autumn, it was indeed path breaking. With its experimental form and lack of state funding, it was "in many ways the ultimate fulfillment of the dream of a new, free, convention-breaking, economically independent, collective filmmaking proclaimed by the young German filmmakers in their well-known Oberhausen Manifesto in 1962."[7] However, while clearly a product of leftist politics, *Deutschland im Herbst* remained equivocal in its position on the RAF, which as a terrorist organization is referenced only indirectly in the film.

In various respects, the film implicitly supports the RAF's antiauthoritarian ideals. While the directors left their marks on the individual segments, the film as a whole lacks a controlling voice or vision — a fact that makes it as challenging as it is captivating. With its multitude of auteurs, the film denies a single presentation and interpretation of history and undermines the concept of authorial superiority. Further, the contemporary democracy is portrayed as a farce, most notably in Heinrich Böll and Volker Schlöndorff's pivotal *Antigone* segment, and at several points the postwar West German state is tied directly to the Nazi era. This perceived continuity is particularly palpable in Fassbinder's staged dialogue with his mother, actress Lilo Pempeit, who wishes for a benevolent dictator, as well as through the film's pointed use of music, visual arts, and mythic-folkloric allusion. The Mercedes-Benz banners in the vicinity of Schleyer's funeral are filmed from a low angle, appearing larger-than-life and remarkably similar to the Nazi flags in Riefenstahl's *Triumph des Willens* (*Triumph of the Will*, 1935), a silent allusion both to Schleyer's leadership of Daimler-Benz and to his complicity during Hitler's reign as an SS officer and Nazi Party functionary. At the same time, the opening voice-over of Alexander Kluge reading a letter from Schleyer to his son is likely to evoke sympathy in many viewers and, in that sense, can be read as an implicit criticism of the coldblooded violence that eventually led to the captive's murder.

Fassbinder's oft-cited proclamation that he does not throw bombs, but rather makes films, parallels the message that *Deutschland im Herbst* also puts forth: sympathy with the political aims of the RAF does not imply an endorsement of its violent means toward those ends. *Deutschland im Herbst* asserts its stance of antiviolence through the citation that appears both near the beginning and at the end of the film, attributed to Anna Wilde, mother of five, in reaction to an air raid in April 1945: "An einem bestimmten Punkt der Grausamkeit angekommen, ist es schon gleich, wer sie begangen hat: sie soll nur aufhören" (translated in the subtitles as: "When cruelty reaches a certain point, it's no longer important who initiated it — it should only stop"). The directors have commented that the viewers themselves must determine the connection of this quotation to 1977 West Germany,[8] emphasizing that they were not presenting an unequivocal political position as much as they were portraying the uncertainty of the time. Nonetheless, the quotation complicates the film's relationship to the RAF and its representation (indeed, its immortalization) through various media forms, as it suggests a defense neither of the actions of the RAF nor of the West German state. The filmmakers later stated explicitly that they were not the ultimate judges of the German Autumn events, yet they do appear to have applied the pacifist quote from one historical endpoint, April 1945, to their contemporary endpoint of Autumn 1977.[9] Their multifaceted and at times ambiguous position is neither surprising nor reproachable, as the complex circumstances and events of this period hardly called for a simplistic response.

Deutschland im Herbst was the earliest cinematic reaction to the specific events of Fall 1977, but it was not the first film to portray left-wing terrorism in the Federal Republic. It followed such works as Klaus Lemke's *Brandstifter* (Arsonists, 1969), based on the firebombing of a Frankfurt department store by Baader and Ensslin, and Volker Schlöndorff's adaptation of Böll's *Die verlorene Ehre der Katharina Blum* (*The Lost Honor of Katharina Blum*, 1975). In the decades following the release of *Deutschland im Herbst*, the RAF has captured the imaginations of filmmakers and other artists time and again. This phenomenon stems in part from the RAF's continued presence in the media over this time span, as some of its members have remained fugitives on the run, while others who were caught and sentenced to prison have been released. Thus even younger generations of Germans are well aware of the RAF and its activities, although they may have received more of a mythologized than wholly accurate image of them.

Fictionalized representations of terrorism produced after *Deutschland im Herbst* are numerous, and include Reinhard Hauff's *Messer im Kopf* (*Knife in the Head*, 1978), Fassbinder's black comedy *Die dritte Generation* (*The Third Generation*, 1979), Margarethe von Trotta's *Die bleierne Zeit* (*Marianne and Juliane*, 1981), and Volker Schlöndorff's *Die Stille nach dem Schuss* (*The Legend of Rita*, 2000). Docudramas specifically dealing with the German Autumn have also been popular, such as Reinhard Hauff's *Stammheim* (1986) and Heinrich Breloer's made-for-television *Todesspiel* (Death play, 1997), the latter of which focuses heavily on the perspective of then-chancellor Helmut Schmidt — a shift from *Deutschland im Herbst* that Thomas Elsaesser describes as "inverting" the earlier film.[10] As Ulrich Kriest notes, *Deutschland im Herbst* had tried to move away from the media's accounts of the events, whereas Breloer made liberal use of the public television station ARD's archive for *Todesspiel*.[11] Breloer's film thus followed the trend toward distinctly more authoritative versions of the German Autumn than what *Deutschland im Herbst* had offered in 1978.

The first decade of the twenty-first century has witnessed a continued interest in docudrama portrayals of the RAF and its victims — for example, Andres Veiel's documentary *Black Box BRD* (2001) (BRD refers to the German abbreviation of West Germany's name) and Christopher Roth's *Baader* biopic (2002), in which his protagonist is killed in a shoot-out with police rather than committing suicide in prison. Most recently, Uli Edel and Bernd Eichinger's film *Der Baader Meinhof Komplex* (*The Baader Meinhof Complex*, 2008), an adaptation of journalist Stefan Aust's 1985 book, has achieved critical and popular success. The film diverges significantly in both form and content from *Deutschland im Herbst* — for example, in its linear narrative structure and its graphic depictions of the RAF's utter brutality. While *Deutschland im Herbst* insinuates, particularly in Fassbinder's segment, that the Stammheim prison deaths were possible state-murder cases, *Der Baader Meinhof Komplex* is unambiguous in its presentation of the deaths as suicides. Overall, the film marks a clear effort to demythologize the RAF three decades after the ambivalence that had characterized *Deutschland im Herbst*.

The RAF has engaged not only writers and filmmakers but also other artists such as Gerhard Richter, whose 1988 series of paintings from well-known RAF photographs is on permanent exhibit at the Museum of Modern Art in New York. In January 2005, *Regarding Terror: The RAF-Exhibition* opened at the KW Institute for Contemporary Art in Berlin, following controversy over public funding for the project. The curators aimed "to present together the media echo of the Red Army Faction and artistic positions directly or indirectly addressing the history of the RAF."[12] By focusing on the press's role in shaping public perception, the exhibit accentuated the constructed nature of the RAF's image, which had been an intention of the *Deutschland im Herbst* filmmakers as well. The 1978 omnibus film thus stands out as the first in a long line of artistic attempts at making sense of divided public opinion and media frenzy surrounding the German Autumn. *Deutschland im Herbst* continues its legacy today, serving for instance as a model for the compilation film *Deutschland 09*, in which Fatih Akın, Wolfgang Becker, Tom Tykwer, and nine other filmmakers set out to document the sociopolitical climate of present-day Germany.

See also:

- 3 May 1925: French and German Avant-Garde Converge at *Der absolute Film*

- 28 February 1962: Oberhausen Manifesto Creates Founding Myth for New German Cinema
- 1 February 1968: *Herstellung eines Molotow-Cocktails* Promotes Film as a Tool for Political Violence

Notes

[1] Miriam Hansen, "Cooperative Auteur Cinema and Oppositional Public Sphere: Alexander Kluge's Contribution to *Germany in Autumn*," *New German Critique* 24, no. 25 (Autumn 1981–Winter 1982): 36–56; here 42.

[2] For example, Hansen describes Katja Rupé and Hans Peter Cloos's "Shadows of Fear" scene as "rather embarrassing" due to its echoes of the popular television crime series *Tatort* (46). In addition, Wolfgang Landgraeber wrote two decades after the German Autumn that Fassbinder's staged scenes "wirken heute nur noch peinlich." Wolfgang Landgraeber, "Das Thema 'Terrorismus' in deutschen Spielfilmen 1975–1985," in *Deutschland im Herbst: Terrorismus im Film*, ed. Petra Kraus. (Munich: Münchner Filmzentrum, 1997), 11–21; here 16.

[3] Ulrich Kriest, "Bilder aus 'bleiernen Jahren,'" in *Deutschland im Herbst: Terrorismus im Film*, 22–35; here 31.

[4] Gerd Bayer, "Images of Terror: Documentary Filmmaking and the RAF," in *Mediating Germany: Popular Culture between Tradition and Innovation*, ed. Gerd Bayer (Newcastle, UK: Cambridge Scholars P, 2006), 126–45; here 128.

[5] Hansen, "Cooperative Auteur Cinema," 54.

[6] Marc Silberman, "Introduction to *Germany in Autumn*," *Discourse: Journal for Theoretical Studies in Media and Culture* 6 (Fall 1983): 48–52; here 51.

[7] Helen Hughes, "Heinrich Böll's Contribution to the Film *Deutschland im Herbst*," *The University of Dayton Review* 24, no. 3 (Summer 1997): 173–81; here 173.

[8] Alfred Brustellin, Rainer Werner Fassbinder, Alexander Kluge, Volker Schlöndorff, and Bernhard Sinkel, "*Deutschland im Herbst*: Worin liegt die Parteilichkeit des Films?" in *Der alte Film war tot: 100 Texte zum westdeutschen Film 1962–1987*, ed. Hans Helmut Prinzler and Eric Rentschler (Frankfurt am Main: Verlag der Autoren, 2001), 287–88; here 288.

[9] Brustellin et al., "*Deutschland im Herbst*," 287. As Inga Scharf notes, the very title *Germany in Autumn* "invokes the image of a country close to its 'fall' or end of existence." Inga Scharf, *Nation and Identity in the New German Cinema* (New York: Routledge, 2008), 87.

[10] Thomas Elsaesser, "From Censorship to Over-Exposure: The Red Army Faction, *Germany in Autumn* and *Death Game*," in *I limita della rappresentazione. Censura, visible, modi di rappresentazione nel cinema*, ed. Leonardo Quaresima (Udine: Forum, 2000), 289–308; here 293.

[11] Kriest, "Bilder aus 'bleiernen Jahren,'" 34–35.

[12] Kunst-Werke Berlin E.V. — Institute for Contemporary Art, "News: Regarding Terror: The RAF Exhibition," http://www.kw-berlin.com/english/news_raf2.htm.

22 January 1979: West German Broadcast of *Holocaust* Draws Critical Fire and Record Audiences

Erin McGlothlin

BEGINNING ON 22 JANUARY 1979 and continuing on the evenings of the 23, 25, and 26 January, the American television miniseries *Holocaust: The Story of the Family Weiss* was broadcast in West Germany to an audience consisting of almost half the adult population of West Germany,[1] causing what has since been characterized as a media sensation, contributing to a new level of awareness about the Holocaust among Germans, and revolutionizing public perceptions of the Nazi genocide of European Jews even as the event met with a largely negative reception among critics and scholars. As an event and aesthetic object, *Holocaust* galvanized opinion about best representational practices, helping to shape subsequent televisual and cinematic representations of the Holocaust and their reception within and beyond Germany.

Written by Gerald Green, directed by Marvin J. Chomsky and produced by Robert Berger, *Holocaust* originally aired in the United States on the NBC television network in April 1978. Cast with such acclaimed actors as Sam Wanamaker, Rosemary Harris, Fritz Weaver, Meryl Streep, Michael Moriarty, and James Woods, *Holocaust* narrates the history of the Holocaust by focusing on the story of two fictional German families: the Jewish Weiss family, all but one of whose members perish in the Holocaust, and the non-Jewish Dorf family, whose male head joins the Nazi Party and gradually becomes a high-ranking officer directly involved in the development and implementation of genocidal policy. The series' impact in the United States was significant. Following on the heels of the immensely popular ABC miniseries *Roots* (1977), which earned an unprecedented audience share (66 percent), *Holocaust* was only slightly less popular, commanding a 49 percent share of the American viewing audience and earning 8 Emmy awards, including Outstanding Limited Series, Outstanding Directing in a Drama Series, and Outstanding Lead awards for actors Moriarty and Streep (Moriarty and Harris further won Golden Globe awards for Best Television Actor and Actress, respectively). Moreover, the series initiated a larger debate in the American press about the Holocaust in general and the appropriateness of television for mediating its history. According to Jeffrey Shandler, "Taking place over a period of months in a wide range of public forums, the discussion of *Holocaust* can be seen as constituting a 'big event' in American culture above and beyond the miniseries itself."[2] The critical response to the series, while generally positive, was not uniformly so; in particular, despite its popularity (or perhaps especially because of it), critics such as the Holocaust survivor Elie Wiesel excoriated the series for attempting "to show what cannot even be imagined" and for "transform[ing] an ontological event into soap-opera."[3]

After creating a critical and popular firestorm in the United States, *Holocaust* quickly became an international phenomenon, airing shortly after the American premiere in a number of countries, including Australia, the United Kingdom, Belgium, Israel, Japan, and Brazil. By the end of the 1978, it had been telecast by over a dozen countries. At this point, all eyes were on West Germany, waiting to see if and how it would broadcast the series. In April 1978, the regional public television station Westdeutscher Rundfunk (WDR) bought the series for DM 1.2 million, hoping to share the purchase and dubbing costs with the national public network, ARD, and through this partnership to broadcast the series nationally on either the first (ARD) or second (ZDF) nationwide public channels. However, the WDR purchase caused an immediate uproar within the West German television industry, prompting a series of debates in several newspapers among the heads of the various national and regional networks, some of whom initially refused to broadcast the series at all. Cultural critics from the West German press joined these contentious conversations, thus escalating the controversy; in what Andrei S. Markovits and Rebecca S. Hayden call a "'highbrow' debate among a select group of intellectuals," critics castigated the series for what they saw as its significant aesthetic, political, and pedagogical shortcomings, not the least of which was what they viewed as its crass commercialism, its employment of a kitschy aesthetic, and its blatant emotional manipulation of the viewer.[4] As a result, journalist Hans-Werner Hübner wrote in the *Süddeutsche Zeitung* in September 1978: "The American television film *Holocaust* . . . is, four months before its West German broadcast, already the most contentious film ever scheduled on German television."[5] In the end, *Holocaust* was broadcast on neither of the two national networks, but instead shown simultaneously on the third channel, the purview of the regional networks; some critics feared that, relegated to the regional channels, it would be unable to reach a wide audience. At the same time, the series was preceded or accompanied by a slate of other Holocaust-related programming on the various television networks and in other mass media, while federal agencies issued various viewing aids and surveys related to the series. According to Siegfried Zielinski: "Just because of the different tv magazines vying with each other and using superlatives, news of the [*sic*] 'Holocaust' must have reached over 80% of the West German adult population."[6] Both the largely negative public controversy and the promotional media blitz surrounding the series helped to pave the way for the astounding number of viewers logged during the four nights on which it was broadcast: nearly twenty million adult Germans saw at least one episode of the series. As gauged by the over ten thousand telephone calls received by *Anruf erwünscht* (Your call requested), a call-in show that aired immediately after the broadcast of each of the four episodes, *Holocaust* had an immediate impact on its viewing audience; according to Julius H. Schoeps, a professor of political science who was part of a panel of experts on *Anruf erwünscht*: "No one expected such a reaction to *Holocaust* . . . those who took note of the first telephone reactions to the film got the surprising impression that in the Federal Republic of Germany there had been as yet absolutely no sustained examination of the National Socialist past."[7]

Because of the large viewing audience and the intense immediate reaction to *Holocaust*, the series is often viewed as marking the decisive turning point in the West German public's acknowledgement of and relationship to Germany's genocide of the European Jews and crimes against other groups in the Second World War, even though, as scholars such as Michael E. Geisler and Wulf Kansteiner have shown, West German public discourse about the Holocaust (especially *televised* discourse, which included a number of popular documentary films and television movies) had been gaining steam throughout the 1960s and 1970s.[8] However, in the historical imagination, the story of *Holocaust* runs as follows: following the end of the Second World War, Germans were unable to relate personally to the crimes committed in the Third Reich and the Holocaust until a second-rate television miniseries (a low-cultural form imported from the hub of the capitalist culture industry, the United States) suddenly broke through the pervasive silence and brought about a collective emotional catharsis, thus achieving what decades of scholarly enlightenment and state-sponsored pedagogical projects had failed to accomplish. Importantly (as the narrative continues), this national purging of emotions and sudden mass acknowledgement of Germany's recent genocidal past took place in spite of the film's melodramatic plot structure, historical inaccuracy, and crude aesthetics. In short, according to this narrative, while *Holocaust* failed as a film, it was extraordinarily successful as a singular phenomenon of national, social, and historical import.

As with many widespread imagined historical narratives, this story of the effect that *Holocaust* has had on the German memory of and relationship to the Holocaust is not wholly inaccurate. Clearly the broadcast of *Holocaust* was a media event of remarkable proportions. Not only did it spark intense debate in the West German press in the period leading up to the broadcast, it attracted an unprecedented audience and provoked a great deal of postbroadcast commentary and analysis. Importantly, many of the discussions and responses to the television series took place not only among academics and public intellectuals but among the wider viewing audience, as evidenced by the large number of calls received by *Anruf erwünscht*. One can thus justifiably claim that the event precipitated a national conversation about the Holocaust, one that, by virtue of reaching viscerally into the West German living room, extended to the average West German viewer in an unprecedented way. At the same time, however, parts of the conventional narrative about *Holocaust* often exaggerate the effects that it had on West German consciousness of the Nazi genocide of the Jews. According to Geisler, neither was the series "the sole catalyst of a long-overdue nationwide consciousness-raising," nor can it be determined if the intense reactions displayed by West Germans during the period in which it was shown were due exclusively to the film itself: "we will never really know to what extent the quantity and quality of the responses were a direct reaction to the series' narrative and its particular modes of presentation and to what extent they were preconditioned by the perceived sociopolitical importance of the event."[9]

Moreover, while the director and producer of *Holocaust* concentrated on the whole on educating the public about the Holocaust and were less concerned with the aesthetic impact of the series, some scholarship disputes the conventional judgment that questions about the aesthetic dimensions of the film are "of secondary importance"[10] or somehow irrelevant to its reception by the West German public. First, the success of the series in facilitating a widespread discourse about the Holocaust among West Germans raises important issues about the conventional understanding of the relationship between aesthetics and historical education. According to Andreas Huyssen, it challenges the "false dichotomies of high versus low, avant-garde versus popular, political theater versus soap opera, truth versus ideology and manipulation" and calls into question "a specific type of Brechtian and post-Brechtian political aesthetic that has been taken granted on the Left" as the only viable vehicle for social and political enlightenment.[11] Critics who thus attacked *Holocaust* and its melodramatic appeal to spectators as a false or misguided method of educating them about the Holocaust failed to recognize the ways in which precisely the popular narrative and aesthetic aspects of the series that command audience identification allowed Germans to relate to the story it tells in a way not possible with more "objective" representations. Second, this possibility of viewer identification, which in large part contributed to the popular appeal of *Holocaust*, is directly tied to the medium in which the series was created — television. According to Michael Geisler, the aesthetics of television allow for a different type of experience than made possible by, for example, cinema; by virtue of the fact that the experience of television often takes place alongside and parallel to other daily activities, "television watching intersects with that reality-construct itself," creating a "discourse of everyday life."[12] For this reason, not only was the act of watching *Holocaust* one that was to some extent contiguous with the lives of its West German viewers, the series' concentration on the everyday lives of both a Jewish family and a Nazi family reinforced the connection and allowed for identification. Thus, according to Geisler, it "fuses the fictional reality of the narrative with the paramount reality of the viewer's everyday experience in a much more powerful and permanent way than does the single event of a one-hour documentary or even a regular feature. In a sense a miniseries, especially one with such a tremendous resonance in mainstream discourse as *Holocaust*, actually becomes part of the personal life experience and memory of the viewer."[13] In this view, the aesthetic medium in which *Holocaust* is presented was critical to its success as a West German national social phenomenon. Indeed, as this more recent scholarship suggests, the event of *Holocaust* was characterized by a profound intricacy of relationships between medium and message, between mass media events and social discourse, and between filmic representation and historical engagement with the past.

See also:

- 19 September 1958: Douglas Sirk's *A Time to Love and a Time to Die* Tests Limits of Postwar Feeling
- 6 August 1984: *Heimat* Celebrated as "European Requiem for the Little People"
- 31 December 1995: *Der bewegte Mann* Sells 6.5 Million Tickets to Mark Peak of New German Comedy

Notes

[1] According to Uwe Magnus, 48.1 percent of West Germans over the age of fourteen tuned in to at least one episode of *Holocaust*. "Die Einschaltquoten und Sehbeteiligungen," in *Im Kreuzfeuer: Der Fernsehfilm "Holocaust,"* ed. Peter Märthesheimer and Ivo Frenzel (Frankfurt am Main: Fischer Taschenbuch, 1979), 221–24; here 223.

[2] Jeffrey Shandler, *While America Watches: Televising the Holocaust* (New York: Oxford UP, 1999), 164.

[3] Elie Wiesel, "Trivializing the Holocaust: Semi-Fact and Semi-Fiction," *New York Times* (16 April 1978): 1, 29; here 1.

[4] Andrei S. Markovits and Rebecca S. Hayden, "'Holocaust' before and after the Event: Reactions in West Germany and Austria," *New German Critique* 19 (1980): 53–80; here 57.

⁵ Heinz Werner-Hübner, "Kein Lehrstück, sondern Lernstück: Der Fernsehdirektor des WDR begründet den Ankauf der Serie," in *Im Kreuzfeuer: Der Fernsehfilm "Holocaust,"* 56–58; here 56.

⁶ Siegfried Zielinski, "History as Entertainment and Provocation: The TV Series 'Holocaust' in West Germany," *New German Critique* 19 (1980): 81–96; here 88.

⁷ Julius H. Schoeps, "Angst vor der Vergangenheit? Notizen zu den Reaktion auf *Holocaust*," in *Im Kreuzfeuer: Der Fernsehfilm "Holocaust,"* 225–30; here 225, 226.

⁸ Michael Geisler, "The Disposal of Memory: Fascism and the Holocaust on West German Television," in *Framing the Past: The Historiography of German Cinema and Television*, ed. Bruce A. Murray and Christopher J. Wickham (Carbondale: Southern Illinois UP, 1992), 220–60; Wulf Kansteiner, "Entertaining Catastrophe: The Reinvention of the Holocaust in the Television of the Federal Republic of Germany," *New German Critique* 90 (2003): 135–62.

⁹ Geisler, "The Disposal of Memory," 222–23.

¹⁰ Ivo Frenzl, "Vorbemerkung der Herausgeber," in *Im Kreuzfeuer: Der Fernsehfilm "Holocaust,"* 11–22; here 19.

¹¹ Andreas Huyssen, "The Politics of Identification: 'Holocaust' and West German Drama," *New German Critique* 19 (1980): 117–36; here 118–19.

¹² Geisler, "The Disposal of Memory," 234–35.

¹³ Ibid., 236.

20 August 1981: R. W. Fassbinder's *Lola* Revisits Kracauer to Critique Adenauer Period

Brigitte Peucker

Lola's "sister act" alludes to Marlene Dietrich in Der blaue Engel. Lola *(1981). DVD capture.*

EVEN WHEN FASSBINDER'S FILMS are at their most political, they resort to theatricality and artifice. His paradigmatic *Lola*, a theatrical film set in 1957, is an oblique remake of Josef von Sternberg's *Der blaue Engel* (*The Blue Angel*, 1930), and the citational quality of Fassbinder's film is signaled in its opening images.[1] In the opening credit sequence, a black-and-white photograph of Konrad Adenauer (just elected to a third term as German chancellor) sitting near a radio and tape recorder provides a surface that is then slowly inscribed with the name of each participant in the film, the list written out in a brightly colored script that decorates the image. The indexical image of the photograph is covered over — veiled, embellished, prettified — by writing in shades of pink, lavender, red, and green. Even in its opening frames, then, the film has merged von Sternberg with Douglas Sirk, from whose films of the 1950s *Lola* derives its palette and lighting effects. The German flag is referenced by way of vertical ribbons of color, and while these obviously signify, the flag is reduced to a decorative edging that frames and obscures the photograph. Sound is brought into the picture both by way of the radio and tape recorder depicted in the photograph, as well as by an extradiegetic pop song of the 1950s, "A White Ship Sails to Hong Kong." Sung by pop icon Freddy Quinn, its lyrics articulate the complex attitude of avoidance and return that expresses the film's ambivalence toward the homeland, the *Heimat*: the lure of the exotic draws one away from home, claim the lyrics, but, once away, one is soon pulled back. Thus the credit sequence gives the effect of an interarts palimpsest — photograph, film image, the image of writing, music — that aligns Fassbinder with von Sternberg and Sirk, both émigrés, with a German art film tradition, and with Hollywood.

The initiating image of the filmic diegesis is Lola's red-lit hair. It is ensnaring and Medusan, perhaps, but more importantly it signifies the material substratum of the film, recalling the dialectic between surface appearance and "truth" that structures both the reading of the female body in representation.

This is the dialectic that prominently structures Siegfried Kracauer's scathing review of von Sternberg's film, likewise situated within the philosophical debate that interrogates the relation of surface to depth, illusion to reality. Not surprisingly, the review locates *Der blaue Engel* on the side of ornament and décor. Rather than focusing on its protagonist, Kracauer asserts, *Der blaue Engel* evades reality "like the painting on the theater curtain which gives the illusion of the play."[2] For Kracauer, ornament and décor are "stagy," not the province of film, which is the real — read: "sociopolitical" — world. To what use, Kracauer asks, does von Sternberg put "the legs, the effects, the technique, the gigantic theater?" (630). As Kracauer reads it, it is the aim of *Der blaue Engel* to cover over reality, to screen it from our view. Reality is "veiled" — Kracauer's term — in this film, its space hermetically sealed, its atmosphere so stifling that its characters lack the very air to breathe. That man's "interior" world rushes to fill the space left vacant by the denial of an exterior world is not surprising to Kracauer: it is this "interior" world that develops into the "ostentatious façade" that decoratively veils the "real" social world. Kracauer's metaphor for this inversion is the image of the inverted glove: "the inside becomes the outside so that the outside is made invisible" (630). In Kracauer's opinion, *Der blaue Engel* leaves itself open to "psychic invasion," and "spiritual events" take on a decorative function. It is as though Fassbinder's film were deliberately quoting Kracauer's review when it stages Lola's performance against the backdrop of a theater curtain upon which the "famous leg" — fetishistically cut off above the knee — appears. Here is the "painting on the theater curtain," as Kracauer puts it in his review, "which gives the illusion of" — but *is* not — "the play" (630). Lola as torch singer is nearly merged with this curtain — both the color and spangles of her dress match it, with theatrical lighting serving to blend human figure with setting. Under the sign of performance and spectacle, for one thing, woman as artifice and illusion, for another — and there is something more, for a second woman participates in the performance. Arrayed in black stockings, garters, and lingerie, she holds the phallic mike for Lola. It is a "sister act," imaging a lesbian sexuality while alluding to the gender-bending roles played by Marlene Dietrich. Thus the theatricality of the scene is also a clear reminder of the performative nature of gender and identity, a theme that forms both text and subtext of so many Fassbinder films.

"Authenticity" and interiority are constantly at odds with decor and performance in *Lola*, and the dialectic set up by Kracauer is scrambled if not totally undermined. The film's narrative stages a conflict between the "authenticity" of Building Commissioner von Bohm, and the charade that is city politics, especially insofar as von Bohm's new province, urban planning, is concerned. *Lola* reads von Bohm's "authenticity" in his old-fashioned conduct and demeanor, linking him to the Wilhelminian period in which the novel that formed the pre-text for von Sternberg, Heinrich Mann's *Professor Unrat*, is set. Von Bohm's "old-fashioned" ideas in the personal realm are linked to his vaguely haute bourgeois background and East Prussian heritage, yet insofar as von Bohm resembles a character out of a novel by Theodor Fontane (Fassbinder was his avid reader and filmed *Fontane Effi Briest*), he is displaced both spatially and temporally, a refugee from another era, a figure who obviously elides the Nazi past. In the postwar world of the economic miracle for which Adenauer paved the way, it will be von Bohm's fate — like that of von Sternberg's professor — to exchange his "authenticity" for marriage with the prostitute Lola. Typically in Fassbinder, desire triumphs over ideology, leading to the deeply ironic compromise by which von Bohm marries Lola, but the developer Schuckert (who has kept Lola for years and is purportedly the father of her child) continues his liaison with her. Von Bohm, whose defining characteristic had been that he was "not corrupt," will now look the other way not only when Schuckert has trysts with his wife, but he will close an eye to the violations of building codes by which Schuckert increases his profits. Here the film links sexual commerce and commercial interests metaphorically and literally through the agency of the body. The voraciousness of desire expresses itself both in the erotic realm and in the impulse to amass capital.

"This city isn't for you," Lola says to von Bohm, explaining that he is neither a fake nor a fraud — only his tweed walking suit is off-key. The tension between surface and depth — between "interior life" (*Innenleben*) and "exterior life" (*Außenleben*), as Lola puts it in dialogue with von Bohm — structures Fassbinder's tongue-in-cheek film in what could be viewed as a parody of Kracauer's review. Public life exists primarily in order to promote commerce, while its flipside, "interior life," plays itself out in a brothel that is the public world's mirror image. While Fassbinder's interest in Genet's metaphor of the world as brothel is expressed here, both Lola the character and *Lola* the film deliberately misappropriate the term *Innenleben*: used with reference to the brothel that is the open secret of the town, it does not refer to interiority, to the life of the spirit. Instead, its ultimate referent is the body. Once again Fassbinder is relentlessly material.

Insofar as authenticity and interiority exist in the film, music is integral to their representation. One of the film's more clichéd sequences occurs in a moment that signals interiority rather conventionally, as von Bohm plays the violin in his bedroom. Later on, interiority is subverted by physical desire as von Bohm's performance from the classical repertoire is eroded from within by Lola's signature song, "The Capri Fishermen," which he clumsily tries to reproduce on the violin. Similarly, the "authenticity" of the country chapel sequence is produced by the affective aural space of a folk song, a round jointly sung by Lola and von Bohm. In this acoustic space Lola and von Bohm find harmony: it is a utopian moment. If irony invades this scene, that is because nostalgia has opened up a space for feeling. As Lola puts it: "I haven't sung in such a long time" — pause — "so beautifully." Since Lola regularly performs as a torch singer in the brothel that is the setting of her "interior life," it has not been long since she has belted out a tune. The point is that only this song deserves the term "beautiful." The end of Lola's masquerade as a lady, her series of performances for von Bohm, is signaled when she sends him a telegram whose clichéd text reads: "Every song has an end." While music creates a special affective space, it is sequential, temporal, and finite, always moving toward a conclusion.

Although Fassbinder never portrays the countryside as "nature," the city of his film is even more centrally the space of artifice and illusion. Von Bohm's passage from a belief in the "exterior life" of the city to an understanding of its "interior life" takes place under the sign of an exposé staged by Esslin. Telling Schuckert that he is going to "rip that mask off" his face, Esslin takes von Bohm on a tour of the city that begins with Lola's brothel. Naturally Esslin is not motivated by political fervor, by a muckraking impulse to "clean up" the city, but by his jealousy of von Bohm and desire for revenge against Schuckert. By exposing Schuckert and the other town notables as speculators and the lady as a whore, Esslin reveals what lies beneath the façade of respectability: once again it is greed and the real of the body, the only genuine form of "authenticity." Even the melancholia that infuses the emotional lives of his characters derives from an awareness of the body's finitude, its undeniable course toward death, as Esslin reading Rilke makes clear. When the painted curtain is pulled up, it is the body that is revealed.

Lola's recourse to the dialectic of surface and depth, its emphasis on the metaphors of the mask and the "true face" that must be exposed, also suggest that G. W. Pabst's *Die freudlose Gasse* (*Joyless Streets*, 1925) resonates in Fassbinder's film. Pabst's film draws heavily on the trope that conflates the city (here Vienna) with the body of the woman: both are described as painted courtesans in the network of metaphors that structures the film. To expose the desiring, depraved body of the one is to expose that of the other. Like *Lola*, Pabst's film features a naïve male character whose friend wants to enlighten him concerning Vienna's "true face" — also by tearing off the city's "mask." Pabst's film, too, suggests that the substrate of representation is the body of a woman: in *Die freudlose Gasse*, a women's dress shop is the façade beyond which a brothel lies. Beyond the alluring clothing, in other words, there is the naked, desiring, commodified body. Here, too, the brothel is portrayed as a microcosm of sorts, a place where international investors conspire to fix the stock market to produce inflation. Here, too, commerce is sexual, economic, and almost always depraved. Like the brothel in *Lola*, Pabst's brothel features a performance space, a stage that is opened up at the end of the film, literally made continuous with the "real life" of the street.

Political activity is given a rather different spin in Fassbinder's film, however, where it, too, appears as performance, with two public ceremonies forming the set pieces in which political theater is staged. The first such moment involves the dedication of a memorial to the war dead of the Second World War and to the German Resistance — shockingly, the victims of the Holocaust are never mentioned. This sequence, too, is heavily aestheticized. Beginning almost as a still, framed by the arches of an arcade, the scene has the clichéd composition of a picture postcard. As Lola slowly walks across the town square in a black suit trimmed in fur and veiled hat, she seems a diva straight out of Fellini. But the scene actually cites a film more closely tied to Fassbinder's concerns: Rolf Thiele's *Das Mädchen Rosemarie* (*The Girl Rosemarie*, 1958), about Rosemarie Nitribitt, a real-life prostitute murdered in Frankfurt am Main, a film that evokes Fassbinder's personal vendetta against real estate speculation in Frankfurt, which may explain why he dedicated *Lola* to Alexander Kluge.[3] During the ceremony, Lola's appearance on this political stage consolidates the public expression of grief and the repression of violence as performances in themselves.

At the core of the film's take on politics is the insight that von Bohm's muckraking phase originates in his disillusionment in the brothel, when it is revealed that Lola is a whore who "belongs" to the speculator Schuckert. The mask has been removed from the face of the town's most prominent citizen; the wool removed from von Bohm's eyes. Fassbinder's cynicism concerning what motivates political activity is abundantly clear when von Bohm prevents the speculator's latest real estate project from getting underway. But once Schuckert is aware that it is desire for Lola that is troubling von Bohm, the way is paved for the two men's deeply ironic erotic compromise — one that leads to the film's second public ceremony, in which the city fathers dedicate Schuckert's new and lucrative housing development to the future. In this scene it is von Bohm — "quieter" now that he is married to Lola and totally co-opted — who breaks ground.

Schuckert, who is given the right of "first night" after Lola and von Bohm's wedding, presents Lola with a darkly ironic gift. It is the deed to the brothel — a counterpart to the marriage certificate — which the newly formed couple will hold in trust until Lola and Schuckert's illegitimate daughter, Marie, turns twenty-one. While the deed transforms Lola into the property owner and entrepreneur she has yearned to be, the document also asserts that the little girl is the "joint" daughter of the newly married couple. One of its functions, then, is to divest Schuckert of his embarrassing paternity. But the transformative properties of legal documents are questionable. In our final image of Marie she assumes the seductive pose in the hayloft her mother had assumed earlier, suggesting that little Marie is in every sense her mother's daughter. Fassbinder's dark view of inheritance is again grounded in the body.

The deed presented to Lola is a gift, of course, but it is also an advance payment that guarantees the continuation of Schuckert's sexual relationship with Lola. Removing her wedding gown, Lola asks, in what is only in part a parody of a prostitute-client interaction, whether Schuckert wants her naked, since that costs more. Yes, of course, Schuckert replies, "but please keep the veil on." If by this point the spectator's veil of illusion has been definitively torn, Schuckert's request signals what is undoubtedly a subtext of the film. Once again in Fassbinder, two men share a woman; once again the circuit of desire suggests a displaced erotic attraction between the men. Although the narrative itself never suggests an attraction between von Bohm and Schuckert, the structure the contract sets up is significant, complicating the question of identity that haunts the film, and implying that yet another man is affected by the terms of the contract. Like Schuckert and von Bohm, Lola's friend Esslin functions as a paternal presence in Marie's life — in fact, physically she resembles him, not Schuckert. Not only, then, does *Lola* undermine the philosophical tradition that posits the dialectic of inside and outside — the dialectic that structures Kracauer's review and on which the notion of identity is based — it posits a sliding identity that renders such questions moot.

See also:

- 2 February 1956: In Letter to Enno Patalas, Siegfried Kracauer Advocates a Socio-Aesthetic Approach to Film

- 7 April 1968: Straub, Huillet, and Fassbinder Share the Stage at Munich's Action-Theater
- 16 May 1992: Marlene Dietrich's Berlin Burial Links Postunification Germany with Weimar Republic's Internationalism

Notes

[1] *Lola* is third in the trilogy but was the second film produced.

[2] Siegfried Kracauer, "The Blue Angel," in *The Weimar Republic Sourcebook*, ed. Anton Kaes, Martin Jay, and Edward Dimendberg (Berkeley: U of California P, 1995), 630–31; here 630. Hereafter cited in text.

[3] Tim Bergfelder, "Popular Genres and the Issue of Cultural Legitimacy: Fassbinder's *Lola* and the Legacy of the West German Cinema of the 1950s," *Screen* 45, no. 1 (Spring 2004): 21–39; here 27. Mario Adorf, who plays Schuckert, had a central role in Thiele's film.

6 August 1984: *Heimat* Celebrated as "European Requiem for the Little People"

Rachel Palfreyman

In the opening shot of Heimat *(1984), a returning soldier surveys the landscape of his homeland. DVD capture.*

In the summer of 1984, Margarethe von Trotta, Wim Wenders, Volker Schlöndorff, Werner Herzog, and Alexander Kluge sent a telegram to Gian Luigi Rondi, the director of the Venice Biennale film festival, to support the screening in full of Edgar Reitz's epic *Heimat: eine deutsche Chronik* (*Heimat*), which had premiered on 30 June and 1 July that year at the Munich Film Festival. Concerned that a place might not be found in the schedule to accommodate such a project, they maintained that Reitz's film was a "European requiem for the little people," a film that reminds us "in this cosmopolitan age" of the "simple truth" that "the *Heimat*, the birthplace, is for every human being the center of the world."

Reitz's subsequent inclusion at the Venice festival played a part in the international success of *Heimat*, while the explicit support of these five respected German filmmakers and their extravagant assertions regarding *Heimat*'s significance as a requiem for the "little people" of the twentieth century was also significant in drawing attention to the film. Their intervention set the tone for a somewhat polarized and extraordinarily broad international reception for a German-language film weighing in at nearly sixteen hours, and bearing a title that is both difficult to translate (the term means alternately "homeland," "birthplace," and "regional roots," but often goes untranslated) and alludes to a specifically German film genre — and one that had become rather discredited at that.

Heimat was thus owned as part of the "quality mark" or brand, even, of the artistically ambitious cinema of the 1970s and 1980s that had grown from the 1962 Oberhausen Manifesto. Reitz and Kluge had both signed this declaration of renewal and aesthetic ambition. Along with a wider group of German filmmakers they had sought to escape the aesthetic banality that they saw as a feature of the existing industry. In the 1960s their call for new funding structures to support an uncompromising and artist-led German cinema had eventually contributed to the establishment of a cinema that attracted international respect and, in some cases, had considerable power to draw audiences, even if it never matched Hollywood's box office appeal.[1]

Reitz's own career had encompassed critical successes like the prize-winning 1966 film *Mahlzeiten* (*Lust for Love*), but also failures, such as *Der Schneider von Ulm* (*The Tailor from Ulm*, 1978), the commercial flop that immediately preceded his work on *Heimat*. In working on *Heimat*, however, Reitz embarked on a project of an entirely different scale, with a different approach to balancing funding, audience appeal, and artistic integrity. *Heimat* was to a large extent funded by the German public television companies WDR and SFB. And even after the success of *Heimat*, his second series *Die zweite Heimat* (*The Second Heimat*, 1992) was funded mainly by German and other European television companies such as the BBC, TVE, and Arte, to name but a few. Its landmark scale, which had Kluge and the other signatories of the telegram fearing for its acceptance at film festivals and for cinematic distribution, gives the film an "amphibian" quality: made for the cinema, and described by Reitz as a "film-novel" with epic ambitions, its widest audiences have nevertheless come from broadcasts in serial format on European television networks.[2] Indeed, though made before the digital age in television and cinema, *Heimat*, with its subsequent trilogy parts *Die zweite Heimat: Chronik einer Jugend* and *Heimat 3: Chronik einer Zeitenwende* (*Heimat 3: A Chronicle of Endings and Beginnings*, 2004), has slotted perfectly into the commercial and artistic climate of the box-set and Internet fan forum. It thus offers a different model in attempting to resolve the difficulty of an auteur cinema in a tricky funding climate: television, which might be perceived in some respects as an enemy of cinema, provided both resources and an audience. By the time he made *Heimat 3*, Reitz had become frustrated by the time constraints imposed by the television companies,[3] but at the moment of *Heimat*'s release, television seemed the answer to a difficult problem.

The amphibian nature of the project had its impact too on cinema screenings, which took on a different dimension and quality: a screening of *Heimat*, *Die zweite Heimat*, or *Heimat 3* is a veritable event, rather than just an everyday trip to the cinema. Cinemas have tended to treat screenings very much as a unique program, almost in the manner of a festival, with patrons invited to ancillary events such as wine receptions. At the premiere of *Die zweite Heimat*, moviegoers even received free branded cushions.[4] Much as with television scheduling, these screenings are programmed with special schedules, sometimes blocking the cinema out for a weekend or consecutive evenings of the week.

Although Reitz has been absolutely clear that he sees *Heimat* as a cinema film, the necessarily amphibian mode of distribution has tested the conventions of cinema and television viewing, and challenged spectators to undertake a different approach to the film. The film not only challenged convention in terms of length and structure, but attempted to fuse genres and styles in order to create a cinema of memory and experience. Famously critical of what he saw as the US "misappropriation" of German history in the TV miniseries *Holocaust* (1978), Reitz attempted to approach twentieth-century German history in a way that would dispense with a conventional identikit narrative of German history, which he saw as eliciting only "crocodile tears," rather than an honest critical reflection on individual experience that activated the faculty of memory.[5] His use of the rural *Heimat* genre to bypass urban centers of power and articulate layer upon layer of trivial personal experience was a provocative technique: on the one hand *Heimat* was spectacularly lauded by supporters like Wenders, Kluge, von Trotta, Schlöndorff, and Herzog as an elegiac evocation of memory and experience with a European resonance. On the other hand, the very wording of their telegram brought into sharp relief precisely the critical controversy over Reitz's film.

Heimat came under fire first and foremost for blurring notions of moral responsibility by constructing a German historical narrative that bypassed the Holocaust.[6] His emphasis on experience and memory appeared to be inadequate to tackle the most uncomfortable questions posed by Germany's history.[7] In addition, the return to the *Heimat* genre appeared calculated to exonerate characters (and, by extension, an audience identifying with them) by dint of their geographical distance from centers of Third Reich power and the sites of the concentration camps. The film appeared to invite audiences to "remember" a past unencumbered by the difficult questions of Germany's history. One of the film's fiercest critics, Gertrud Koch, felt that both the telegram and Reitz's own statements revealed dubious attitudes toward those Reitz had termed "Weggeher" (leavers), especially as he had identified Jews in particular as "'Weggeher' . . . since time immemorial."[8] Coupled with the skeptical use of the word "cosmopolitan" in the telegram (with its antisemitic connotations), *Heimat* appeared to be at best a naïve "sanctification of the German homeland," sidestepping discomfiting aspects of German history in favor of a relentless and myopic focus on the everyday and on the unreliable memories of ordinary people determined to cast themselves in the role of innocent bystanders.[9] Its tendency to mourn the passing of a contrived "simplicity" in its "requiem for the little people" also registered as a problematic manifestation of antimodern sentiment, a return to the cultural pessimism of earlier manifestations of the *Heimat* genre.

Many of the counterarguments and defenses of Reitz's project focused on its sophisticated appeal to spectators, the invitations to engage in a critical viewing process, and an appraisal of the role of film and television in supplying historical knowledge.[10] Seen in absolute isolation, Reitz's film offered a problematically partial reflection on German twentieth-century history. However, seen as one of a range of sources about German history, the possibilities for critical interaction emerge more clearly. As a study of repression, and of the apolitical ordinariness that coexisted with the atrocities of Nazi Germany, *Heimat* succeeded in provoking a thoughtful debate about the wider questions of perpetration, identity, and memory. In something of a contrast to other high-art cinema productions, Reitz was also spectacularly successful in attracting an audience.[11]

Indeed, the concern of the filmmakers to plead the case of *Heimat* as an important film that might struggle to find its place in the industry is itself indicative of the unusual audience relationships that Reitz's film has invited. The open telegram of support represents a kind of fan mail, in its enthusiastic, albeit articulate and sophisticated, praise of the film. It is a collective response, one that implies a communal engagement of the viewers with a film that appears to speak to and of them rather directly in its attempt to address memory and experience. The effort to engage with history in ways that relate to everyday experience, rather than presenting a narrative which can be viewed at a distance, with the viewer confident that s/he is not personally implicated in what is presented on screen, clearly runs the risk of eliding the atrocities of the period. Focusing on memories and experience with a narrative woven partly from testimony and autobiography, *Heimat* seeks to draw the viewer into recognition and emotional identification.

Poised between television and the Internet, Reitz's need to find a different way of funding a large-scale production and his desire to create a film that would engage a large number of "little" viewers prompted him to an amphibian film form, one that anticipated new digital communities, but also relied on an old-fashioned kind of state television. Indeed, the hybrid qualities that mark *Heimat* are not restricted to the territory it occupies in a changing media landscape. It is a film that operates between the celebratory and critical variants of the *Heimat* genre. Furthermore, as a historical narrative it largely ignores the "central" events of the period, but confines itself to the margins, allowing everyday experience, faulty memories, and the ironies of the audience's prior historical knowledge to collide in responses that invite sharing as well as reflection on personal experience.

The hybrid nature of the film leaves audiences in a complicated position. The telegram, for example, which was so important in branding *Heimat* part of the artistically ambitious and highly exportable New German Cinema, sees a group of respected filmmakers positioned not only as a sophisticated and privileged audience, a group of arbiters, but also as fans, petitioning a programmer on behalf of a beloved film, about which they are wildly enthusiastic. The telegram thus demonstrates a blurring of boundaries between the role of professional critic and supporter or champion of the film — anticipating the sorts of contemporary audience responses that have unfolded in the virtual realm of Internet sites and blogs. Such blurring of amateur and professional responses mirrors *Heimat*'s dependence on amateur actors performing roles that encompass fiction, biography, and oral testimony: Reitz calls his audience to participate in an ambitious historical project by including the audience in the project from its inception, and by deliberately allowing a dirty mix of history, memory, and autobiography to stimulate debate and discussion. The spectator is located neither quite inside nor quite outside the narrative.

Celebrating the ordinary, positioned between film and television, with porous borders between audience and performer, critic and fan, professional and amateur, and the national and universal, *Heimat* thus seemed to solve the problem of poor public engagement faced by many of the artistically ambitious films of Young and New German Cinema. At the same time, it opened itself up to fierce criticism with its contemplative pace and celebration of the ordinary and its fast-and-loose attitude to history and memory, which appeared to mark a turn away from 1960s and 1970s examinations of German culpability and Jewish suffering, and, in line with the most conservative expressions of the *Heimat* genre, even to exonerate or revere the rural German population. Nevertheless, what *Heimat* achieved was less a refusal to deal with the Holocaust than a risky new effort to encourage a critical reflection on historical complicity and responsibility by setting up a delicate balance of emotional engagement and identification, on the one hand, and a slow, meditative, and rather estranging pace, on the other. *Heimat* teetered between film and television, between critique and nostalgia, between reflection and celebration, and between history and memory in ways that encapsulated some of the key dilemmas of the postwar period and, indeed, later postunification cinema. Notwithstanding *Heimat*'s flaws and problematic omissions, the bold sincerity with which Reitz tackled his complex hybrid film and its unorthodox position within the marketplace have allowed a different and forward-looking relationship with audiences to emerge, enabling new developments in the national and international reflection on history, memory, and identity in the cinema.

See also:

- 22 December 1955: *Sissi* Trilogy Bridges Hapsburg to Hollywood through Hybrid Blend of Film Genres
- 23 June 1968: Alexander Kluge Egged in Berlin, Months Later Awarded Gold Lion in Venice
- 22 January 1979: West German Broadcast of *Holocaust* Draws Critical Fire and Record Audiences

Notes

[1] As one of the most successful of all New German Cinema films, *Die Ehe der Maria Braun* (*The Marriage of Maria Braun*, 1978), for example, made DM 4 million in West Germany. See Thomas Elsaesser, *Fassbinder's Germany: History, Identity, Subject* (Amsterdam: Amsterdam UP, 1996), 97. However, this still does not approach the German box office receipts of big American films from the same year such as *The Deer Hunter* or *Halloween*.

[2] Edgar Reitz, *Liebe zum Kino: Utopien und Gedanken zum Autorenfilm 1962–1983* (Cologne: Köln 78, 1984), 206–7.

[3] See interview with Edgar Reitz, "Ein Bruder ist ein Bruder," *Frankfurter Allgemeine Zeitung* (15 December 2004).

[4] Michael Kaiser, *Filmische Geschichts-Chroniken im Neuen Deutschen Film: Die Heimat-Reihen von Edgar Reitz und ihre Bedeutung für das deutsche Fernsehen*, http://repositorium.uni-osnabrueck.de/bitstream/urn:nbn:de:gbv:700-2004051012/2/E-Diss162_thesis.pdf, 355–56, accessed 23 July 2010.

[5] Reitz, *Liebe zum Kino*, 102.

[6] Jim Hoberman, "Once in a Reich Time," *Village Voice* (16 April 1985).

[7] Eric Santner, *Stranded Objects: Mourning, Memory and Film in Postwar Germany* (Ithaca, NY: Cornell UP, 1990), 57–102.

[8] Gertrud Koch, "Kann man naiv werden? Zum neuen Heimat-Gefühl," *Frauen und Film* 38 (1985): 107–9; here 108; Reitz, *Liebe zum Kino*, 146.

[9] Ruth Perlmutter, "German Revisionism: Edgar Reitz's *Heimat*," *Wide Angle* 9, no. 3 (1987): 21–37; here 21.

[10] Richard Kilborn, "Remembering and Retrieving the Past: Edgar Reitz's *Heimat* (1984)," *Forum for Modern Language Studies* 31, no. 1 (1995): 84–98; Christopher J. Wickham, "Representation and Mediation in Edgar Reitz's *Heimat*,"

German Quarterly 64, no. 1 (1991): 35–45; Johannes von Moltke, *No Place Like Home: Locations of Heimat in German Cinema* (Berkeley, U of California P, 2005); Rachel Palfreyman, *Edgar Reitz's "Heimat": Histories, Traditions, Fictions* (Oxford: Lang, 2000).

[11] According to ARD press releases, around twenty-five million viewers, or 54 percent of the viewing public, saw one or more episodes of *Heimat* on television in 1984 ("Kein Stammpublikum," *Tagesspiegel*, 20 November 1984). Between 2 and 3.3 million viewers watched in Britain in 1986, a far higher figure than one would normally expect for a subtitled film on BBC2 ("Das Ereignis des Frühlings: 'Heimat' in Großbritannien," Erstes Deutsches Fernsehen/ARD press release, 24/1986).

8 June 1986: Farocki's *Wie man sieht* Urges New Ways of Seeing

Michael Cowan

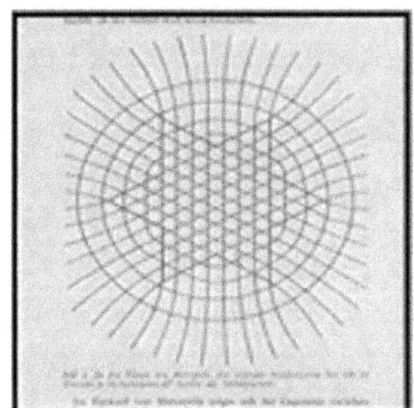 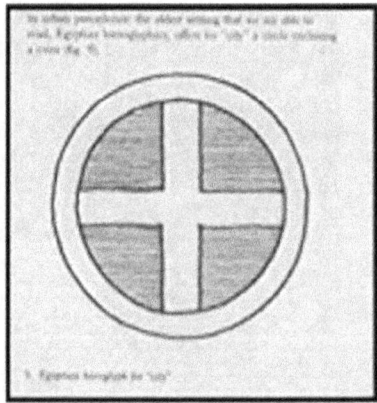

Two graphic images of the city: a representation of the city as rationalized ideal and an Egyptian hieroglyph, by Konrad Zuse. Wie man sieht *(1986). DVD captures.*

LIKE MOST OF HARUN FAROCKI's films and installations, *Wie man sieht* (As you see, 1986) defies easy summary. Consisting of still images overlain with narrative commentary and occasionally interrupted by live sequences, the film offers a meditation on the history of technology, the fate of human labor, and the imbrications between economic rationalization and mass warfare. No doubt, this description could apply to much of Farocki's work from the past four decades; from his agitational films of the 1960s through his "essay" films such as *Wie man sieht*, to his recent installations and meditations on war, prisons, and shopping centers, Farocki has consistently probed the links between capitalism, technology, and violence in the modern world.

But within this thematic constellation, Farocki's films also share a particular preoccupation with the role of *images*. As he notes in an interview with Thomas Elsaesser, "An image like a juncture, the way one speaks of a railway junction. I am looking for an image that is the concept for several sequences of movement." From the critique of press coverage of the Vietnam War in *Nicht löschbares Feuer* (*The Inextinguishable Fire*, 1969) to his most recent investigations of the "operative" images generated by the military and surveillance industries, nearly all of Farocki's work has sought to document the effects of modernity's image-making technologies. At the same time, his work attempts to use those technologies — whether film, video, or digital — to forge more critical images and make viewers see the world anew.[1] Whereas Farocki's early films sought to forge counterimages to those of the mass press (a strategy observable in *Nicht löschbares Feuer,* where he refuses to show burning napalm victims, training the camera instead on himself as he extinguishes a cigarette on the back of his hand), his later work adopts strategies of *détournement,* turning existing images against their instrumental functions.

Perhaps no single genre is more closely associated with this critical redeployment of images than the one for which Farocki is best known: the "essay" film. Replacing linear narrative with lateral montage, the essay film documents the *process* of thought, rather than its finished products, by continually recombining and reinterrogating images on the screen.[2] On account of this emphasis on provisional conclusions — underscored in Farocki by the frequent publication of multiple versions in different media formats[3] — the essay film genre has often been seen as part of a long tradition of essayistic writing, and Farocki's critics have compared his work in particular to that of Theodor Adorno, Robert Musil, and even the Jena romantics. But the open-ended quality of essayistic filmmaking resonates perhaps more specifically with the intellectual aspirations of an era marked by poststructuralist philosophy and the privileging of open forms of thought and representation. While one can certainly trace the influence of essayistic filmmaking on various domains of moving-image art today (e.g., the compilation films of Matthias Müller, the meditative documentaries of Nikolaus Geyrhalter or Michael Glawogger, or the multichannel museum installations of Farocki and others), the genre attained its greatest prominence in the 1970s and 1980s in the works of filmmakers such as Chris Marker, Jean-Luc Godard, Hartmut Bitomsky, Farocki, and Alexander Kluge, to name a few. As Farocki's first major essay film, *Wie man sieht* itself appeared at the height of poststructuralist debates in Germany, its release couched between the publications of Manfred Frank's *Was ist Neostrukturalismus?* (*What is Neostructuralism?*, 1984), Friedrich Kittler's *Aufschreibesysteme 1800/1900* (*Discourse Networks 1800/1900,* 1985), and Jürgen Habermas's *Der philosophische Diskurs der Moderne* (*The Philosophical Discourse of Modernity,* 1988).

Broaching questions about modernity, rationality, and the stability of meaning familiar from these debates, *Wie man sieht* brings them to bear specifically on the history of seeing. As the title suggests, the film is less about objects seen than about *modes* of vision, the how and why of image fabrication and consumption. The question appears in paradigmatic form at the beginning of the film, where Farocki introduces the Egyptian hieroglyph for "city"; consisting of two crossing lines inside a circle, the hieroglyph represents, according to the narrator, the mythical origin of cities at crossroads ("Often, a city arose at the point where two paths crossed").[4] The very invocation of the hieroglyph here is hardly neutral. If, as Thomas Elsaesser writes, "there is very little that Farocki cares about which is not also a reflection on cinema itself," the hieroglyph offers an obvious instance of such media-historical reflection;[5] few other metaphors were so bound up, in the writings of early film theorists, with the utopian view of cinematography as a new universal language, whose visual legibility would help to restore a sense of community to the modern world.[6] Coming after the demise of such modernist aspirations, Farocki shares little of the optimism of early film theorists. Accordingly, the hieroglyph at the beginning of *Wie man sieht* is characterized not by transparent legibility, but rather by an opacity that elicits a series of conflicting interpretations about the function of crossroads. As the narrator states, it all depends on who is looking: "The military seeks out the intersection to control two routes at once. The merchant uses it to serve travelers on two different routes. The traveler is forced to stop."

Of the three figures mentioned here, the first two — representing warfare and industry — embody the instrumental modes of looking and image-making that preoccupy so much of Farocki's work. The history of technology documented in *Wie man sieht* will consist largely in the ascendancy of military and economic rationality; Farocki's montage juxtapositions never cease to suggest a connection between the increasing efficiency of industrial production and that of war through continual rotation, the machine gun, perforated cards, and, eventually, informational technology. In every case, moreover, Farocki links this emphasis on efficiency to the increasing obsolescence of the human body: the demise of footwork still practiced in premodern societies, the replacement of the hand through mechanization, the increasing expendability of human bodies in mass warfare, and finally — in a theme Farocki will continue to pursue in his installations — the growing marginalization of the eye itself by a new regime of abstract informational technology.

But the modes of seeing espoused by the military and industry are also juxtaposed, in the initial shot of the hieroglyph, to a third mode, that of the lingering traveler who, forced to stop at the crossroads, might use this pause to contemplate or try out various paths and possibilities. Indeed, the hieroglyph sequence ends on an almost playful note about the possibility of a more experimental mode of vision. As a map of Europe appears overlain with migratory routes, the narrator states: "A nice thought: the traveler stops at the intersection in order to reflect on the other possible trajectories and destinations. The city arises from this act of pausing and reflecting." Imagining another history of European cities,

Farocki's "nice thought" attempts to imagine a public space structured not according to the logic of control or profit, but rather around an act of pausing that undoes instrumental, linear movement.

Precisely this rejection of linear trajectories describes Farocki's approach to the history of technology in *Wie man sieht*. "Technology history," we hear at one point in the film, "is all too eager to describe development as a path from point A to point B. It ought to describe other paths and determine who rejected them." Accordingly, another strand of *Wie man sieht* is concerned with these other possibilities of technological modernity alongside the story of automation and human obsolescence — alternative trajectories represented most prominently in the film by the famous workers' initiatives at Lucas Aerospace in Great Britain.[7]

But the gesture of pausing to consider alternative paths not only informs Farocki's history of technology; it is, more generally, a fundamental aesthetic gesture of the essay film, paradigmatically enacted in the very stilling of moving images.[8] Far from the logic of instrumental vision that Gilles Deleuze identified with the modernist "action image," Farocki's films demand a contemplative, experimental mode of viewing; before the essay film, spectators must trade in the habit of linear flow and narrative closure for a willingness to try out multiple paths and connections.

If the crossroads constitutes a metaphorical setting for such acts of experimental vision, it also — in conformity with the multiple significations and potentials inherent in any image — serves as a guiding metaphor in *Wie man sieht* for the history of rationalization itself, linking a whole series of efficient objects from highways to industrial fabric and even computer programs. The common denominator of technological modernity here appears precisely as the increasing rationalization of junctures. One sees this in the film's repeated thematization of highways and overpasses. The early cloverleaf junctions, the narrator states, allowed drivers to contemplate the various possibilities: "The pattern invites the driver to try out all four loops by continually veering to the right and thus playfully to imagine all the possible destinations." But in the accelerated development of postwar Germany, cloverleafs were replaced "turbine" systems with upper and lower entry and exit ramps, which enforce circulation and prevent any act of pausing: "It's impossible to imagine anyone stopping here to found a city."

But while the transformation of junctures characterizes the history of highways, it also marks the history of technology in general, represented most paradigmatically by the weaving industry. Like Dziga Vertov's *The Man with the Movie Camera* (itself recalling Marx), *Wie man sieht* presents weaving as a quintessential locus of technological automation, reminding viewers that the weaving industry was the first to be mechanized in the eighteenth century.[9] With the standardization of the bindings between threads, a new texture emerged, defined above all by its mechanical symmetry: "The regularity of the weave puts the unsteady hand of the worker to shame. The worker must be replaced." Precisely this type of regular weave comes to characterize thought and vision in the industrial age. Where Heidegger located the essence of technology in the framing and objectification of the world, Farocki finds it in a certain texture, a binding that both reflects and enforces an inhuman efficiency.

While this movement of rationalization rendered the feet and hands superfluous during the industrial phase, with the onset of informational technology it is entailing the obsolescence of the eye itself. Tracing the use of perforated cards from the Jacquard weaving looms of eighteenth-century France to the first computers of twentieth-century Germany, Farocki posits a continuity between industrial and digital technology, describing "the birth of the computer from weaving." The connection between the two, the film suggests, has everything to do with the rationalization of intersections: "A computer is also a traffic system. It contains a series of forks that demand a decision between yes and no, zero and one." Indeed, just how close a link exists between traffic systems and digital technology is suggested when Farocki reminds us that the inventor of the computer, Konrad Zuse, might well have become a city planner. Showing an abstract pattern composed of lines calculated to intersect at precise 60° angles, the narrator recounts that Zuse had composed the drawing after watching the film *Metropolis* to represent the streets of a rationalized and ideal city. While recalling the Egyptian hieroglyph in its abstract representation of the city, Zuse's geometric drawing gestures not toward the history of the film as picture writing, but rather toward the new phase of computer technology, in which images for human eyes are but a byproduct of abstract calculations.

Next to this new force of digital technology, Farocki suggests, images made for a human eye have already become obsolete. "Nothing has marginalized the image more than computing (das Rechnen)."[10] In another sequence on highway planning, the narrator argues that images no longer mean anything. "They simply serve to give the eye some exercise, as one exercises horses that don't work but are not free." Elaborating on this notion in an interview with Thomas Elsaesser, Farocki compared the production of film and television images to the practice of modern body culture, both functioning as a means of occupying human bodies and organs that have grown redundant. "Suddenly," he concluded, "I realized that this branch of working with images that I am in is about as modern as Muybridge's experiments with recording a galloping horse's movement."[11] If Farocki's reference to Muybridge seems to position the horse as an emblem of cinema technology, it also suggests a vision of that technology as one threatened with historical obsolescence: Muybridge filmed the horse at the very historical moment when horse-drawn transportation was disappearing. One is reminded of the recurring image, in

Wie man sieht, of a dead horse lying next to a tank on a battlefield; in an era of informational technologies, the celluloid medium itself is as superfluous as a horse in a technological war.

Nonetheless, the gamble of Farocki's essay films is to use this obsolete medium to critique the rationality underlying the technological production of images. Without ignoring the imbrications of the cinema itself in the ascension of modern instrumental rationality, *Wie man sieht* attempts to turn modernity's images against their instrumental function, to open them up, as it were, to a more experimental gaze that would linger over other connections and paths not taken. Like Vertov, Farocki compares filmmaking to an act of weaving, joining disparate images through montage. But where Vertov saw automated weaving as the metaphor for the superhuman vision of the KINO-Eye, Farocki asks what was lost through automation and attempts to find another texture — one that asks viewers to pause, like travelers at a crossroads, to consider alternative ways of seeing.

See also:

- 1 April 1921: Walter Ruttmann's *Lichtspiel: Opus 1* Shapes Culture of Abstract Filmmaking
- 30 April 1999: Werner Herzog's "Minnesota Declaration" Performs Critique of Documentary Cinema
- 11 February 2008: Ulrike Ottinger's *Prater* Wins German Critics' Award for Best Documentary Yet Highlights the Director's Ties to Both Fiction and Nonfiction Film

Notes

[1] Christa Blümlinger, "Harun Farocki: Critical Strategies," in *Harun Farocki: Working on the Sightlines*, ed. Thomas Elsaesser (Amsterdam: Amsterdam UP, 2004), 315–23; Volker Pantenburg, *Film als Theorie: Bildforschung bei Harun-Farocki und Jean-Luc Godard* (Bielefeld: transcript, 2006), 57–59.

[2] Jörg Becker, "In Bildern denken. Lektüren des Sichtbaren: Überlegungen zum Essayistischen in Filmen Harun Farockis," in *Der Ärger mit den Bildern: Die Filme von Harun Farocki*, ed. Rolf Aurich and Ulrich Kriest (Konstanz: Uvk, 1998), 73–93; Pantenburg 143–63.

[3] *Wie man sieht* was itself released almost simultaneously as film and illustrated text, each offering its own tentative arrangement of images and words. See Klaus Kreimeier, "Wie man sieht, was man sieht: Über einen Film von Harun Farocki," *epd Film* 8 (1987): 22–25; here 22.

[4] *Wie man sieht,* dir. Harun Farocki, Harun Farocki Filmproduktion, 1986. All translations from the German are mine.

[5] Thomas Elsaesser, "Harun Farocki: Filmmaker, Artist, Media Theorist," in *Harun Farocki: Working on the Sightlines*, 11–40; here 11.

⁶ Vachel Lindsay, *The Art of the Moving Picture* (New York: Liveright, 1970), 199–217.

⁷ In the Lucas workers' initiatives, unionized laborers threatened by layoffs protected human labor — and conceived another relation between humans and machines — by converting production from military technology to more socially useful products such as road-rail vehicles.

⁸ Elsaesser, "Harun Farocki," 24, 30.

⁹ On the connection between Vertov's representation of weaving and Marx, see Annette Michelson's preface to Vertov's writings in *Kino-Eye: The Writings of Dziga Vertov*, ed. Annette Michelson, trans. Kevin O'Brien (Berkeley: U of California P, 1984), xiii–lxi; here xxxviii–xl.

¹⁰ At this point, Farocki recounts how the first use of the Jacquard loom was, ironically, to weave a giant image of Jacquard himself, even as it was rendering images for human eyes obsolete. "Es verdient nachdrückliche Feststellung, dass die Rechenmaschine zu dem Zeitpunkt aus der Weberei entstand, als ein Bild gewebt werden sollte."

¹¹ Thomas Elsaesser and Harun Farocki, "Making the World Superfluous: An Interview with Harun Farocki," in *Harun Farocki: Working on the Sightlines*, 177–93; here 183.

2 February 1988: Last Generation of DEFA Directors Calls in Vain for Reform

Reinhild Steingröver

THE DATE 2 FEBRUARY 1988 points to an event that actually did not take place; more specifically, it dates an unread manifesto, the culmination of years of reform efforts, and written in preparation for the Fifth Congress of the Film and Television Workers Association (VFF) in the GDR. As required, all scheduled speeches were circulated beforehand among the hierarchy of the VFF for discussion and approval. The manifesto was the result of five years of discussion among the youngest generation of directors, producers, and cinematographers in the East German state-owned film studio DEFA (Deutsche Film-Aktiengesellschaft), the so-called Nachwuchsgruppe/Arbeitsgruppe 3, and signed by cameraman Tony Loeser, producer Thomas Wilkening, and director Peter Kahane. It was to be delivered by another representative from the fourth and last generation of DEFA-trained directors, Jörg Foth.

The manifesto critically analyzed the training and employment situation at DEFA film and demanded the abolition of all censorship and taboos, and asked for earlier opportunities for younger talents to realize their unique visions. The authors of the manifesto declared that DEFA films had become boring and irrelevant to their increasingly sparse audience. Instead, the younger generation demanded the formation of an alternative studio within DEFA for the production of experimental, low budget films, that would allow fresh talents to realize their creative potential quickly, without bureaucratic obstacles. The reaction by the leadership of the party, the studio, and the film workers association was swift: in a series of individual meetings with members of the younger group, they asked that the manifesto remain unread, in order to avoid unnecessary provocation, and to allow for a productive, internal discussion of the manifesto's content *after* the congress. In the hope that a less confrontational speech might indeed result in meaningful dialogue with the party and studio hierarchy, the group voted to agree to the demand, and withdrew the manifesto itself. Instead, Jörg Foth delivered the now famous speech "Our moment never came," lamenting the late start for directors in the

DEFA studio, the multiple layers of control in developing fresh material, and the climate of distrust toward the young directors. He stated, for example, that an average film underwent sixteen stages of examination, rejection, or alteration before it was approved, leaving no room for spontaneity and experimentation. In sum, he declared that his generation had been actively prevented from leaving its mark on East Germany's film culture, both aesthetically and substantively.

Cosignatory of the manifesto, Thomas Wilkening, who was to play an important role in the transition from the official DEFA studio to the free-market style economy after the fall of the Wall, reflected later on the willingness to compromise at this crucial moment in the work of the reform-minded group: "From today's perspective we were practically naïve. We believed in the possibility of educating the rulers (*Königserziehung*)."[1] As it turns out, trust in the leaders was misplaced and the promised dialogue did not take place. Reform was only belatedly implemented in the course of the gradually changing political landscape in the GDR in general. While the demand for an alternative studio for cheap productions was never met, funds for a new production group within DEFA were granted in the spring of 1989, and formally instituted on 1 January 1990. With a budget of 3.5 million marks for the first year, the production group DaDaeR (a play on DDR and Dada), under the leadership of twelve elected representatives of the youngest generation, headed by Wilkening, voted democratically to swiftly begin work on three unusual films: Jörg Foth's musical clowns program with GDR cabaret performers Steffen Mensching and Hans-Eckardt Wenzel, *Letztes aus der DaDaeR* (*Latest from the DaDaeR*, 1990); Peter Welz's directorial debut *Banale Tage* (Banal days, 1991); and enfant terrible Herwig Kipping's *Land hinter dem Regenbogen* (*The Land beyond the Rainbow*, 1991). None of these films could have passed the multiple levels of control in the traditional DEFA studio. Kipping's poetic and fragmentary film about the founding days of the GDR drew harsh reviews, chiefly from West German reviewers, but was honored with the German National Film Prize in Silver. This prize provided some of the funds that enabled Kipping to produce his next feature film, *Novalis* (1992), as one of the first releases of the now-privatized Wilkening production firm.

It is a sad irony of history that this fulfillment of years of reformatory efforts coincided with the end of the studio itself. The production group existed for only twenty-seven months, since its members, like all other DEFA employees, were terminated on 31 March 1992. Nevertheless, it did produce three important contributions to German film history that uniquely captured the historical mood of the collapse of the GDR and the unification period. These films should be considered today as foils against which later — and often West German-produced — films about unification or the Stasi (East German State Security Service), such as *Good*

Bye Lenin! (2003) or *Das Leben der Anderen* (*The Lives of Others*, 2006), respectively, may be read.

February 2, 1988 was not the first time the young film workers at DEFA sought dialogue and reforms with the studio hierarchy. During a casual conversation at the previous congress of the VFF in 1982 between Politburo member Kurt Hager and film students and recent graduates of the film academy Babelsberg (including Maxim Dessau and Helke Misselwitz), students complained about the poor training conditions and lack of opportunities in the academy and studio to Hager. Upon being invited to report more fully about their concerns to Hager, Misselwitz and Dessau organized the unprecedented meeting in the House of Hungarian Culture in Berlin on 28 October 1982. At this meeting, about seventy recent graduates of the film academy freely expressed their anger at being a highly qualified but superfluous work force, neither wanted nor entrusted with shaping new visions for the nation's movie theaters. Such open complaining in the presence of the entire film leadership was highly unusual in the studio — indeed, in the GDR. It marked the beginning of a cycle of hopeful initiatives and frustrated realizations that the studio was not interested in truly engaging criticism. Instead, the studio, party, and VFF leadership simply channeled the youthful energies with skillful procrastination maneuvers into controlled dead-ends.

As a result of the meeting in the House of Hungarian Culture, for example, the youngest generation expended considerable energy in producing a nearly fifty-page document that analyzed the training and employment situation for film artists in the GDR. This document, dated January 1983, was intended to serve as the basis for the hoped-for conversation with Kurt Hager himself. It detailed how even the smallest attempts at experimentation were suppressed, access to international films and artists was hampered, incompetence among faculty was rampant, and mistrust toward the young in the studio a given. The seventeen theses at the end of the document, which Hager claimed at the next VFF congress six years later never to have received, can be seen as a direct precursor to the manifesto of 1988. The party was skillful in keeping the group of young reformers busy: assigning them bureaucratic tasks, "losing" important documents, or refusing to participate in further gatherings under the pretext of time conflicts. Several times in the six years between the two VFF congresses, members of the reform group suggested dissolving because of their ineffectuality, but they always regrouped, ultimately drafting the 1988 manifesto and then subsequently founding the production group DaDaeR. The young GDR film artists were quite aware that the demand for a small studio for auteur-type, inexpensive films was being realized elsewhere in Eastern and Western Europe. In fact, in 1983 a party official forwarded a document regarding the founding of such an initiative in the Bulgarian film studio to the group, but recommended not distributing it further, as such a development was deemed unlikely for the GDR at that point.

Much of the time and energy spent during these years resulted in the irretrievable loss of valuable creative capital. Many of the most active organizers of the reformer group were only able to direct their first feature films after the fall of the Wall, such as Dessau (1990) and Misselwitz (1992). Foth, who had served for the majority of the time as spokesperson for the group, was allowed to direct and codirect several films during the 1980s, but never his own material. Viewing the three films that DaDaeR finally produced, one can still sense the eagerness to model their films after auteur idols like Fellini, Tarkovsky, and Fassbinder. Foth's *Letztes aus der DaDaeR* even stars Fassbinder actress Irm Hermann, in an obvious gesture toward the cult director of the West German New German Cinema. Foth's laconic summary regarding the efforts of those years points to the no-win situation of the youngest generation, which had hoped to reform unwieldy institutions (studio and academy) from within: "He who enters the apparatus gets lost in it. He who does not, loses."[2]

Instead of gaining more practical experience and applying their innovative ideas, the fourth and last generation of directors at DEFA had tilted at proverbial windmills. Their earnest hope and tenacious diligence may seem naïve or tame from today's perspective. But for aspiring, professional filmmakers in the GDR there were no alternative means to gain access to production than working in the DEFA studio. Claus Löser has documented the activities of the Super-8 experimental-film scene of the 1980s[3] and shown that for many artists (painters, writers, sculptors) the provisional quality of 8-millimeter cameras offered a liberating aesthetic force. But its character was self-consciously improvisational. They sought liberation from the state-controlled art scene and relished the immediacy of the cheap, readily available Soviet cameras, the amateurish editing on the kitchen table, and the private screenings in apartments.

Thomas Günther, son of prominent DEFA director Egon Günther, has described the importance of the unofficially published magazines and so-called artist books for the same time period. Even though this literature was produced in miniscule editions, often hand-copied and privately distributed (and Stasi-infiltrated, as later became clear), "the magazines were a kind of lifesaver for a generation of young artists that was otherwise condemned to silence."[4] In hindsight, neither the artistic merit nor the political impact of these small publications can be measured independently from considerations of the historical circumstances under which they were created. But Günther emphasized one particular aspect of the work of these unofficially published collections of drawings and poetry that resonates directly with the assessment that Cornelia Schleime had about her experiences with the Super-8 alternative film scene, and that Wilkening shared about his work in the young generation's reform group at DEFA: "The need for collectivity was the strongest motivation; it was about abolishing the isolation of the creative individual."[5] As such, the efforts by the youngest generation of DEFA-trained artists should not only be judged by the relatively small numbers of films they made, but also by their collective push for institutional change.

The unread manifesto may not have caused the scandal it could have in 1988, but it remains today as a testament to the idealism and commitment of DEFA's youngest generation to make films that could be aesthetically innovative, entertaining, and socially relevant. The transition of the DEFA production group DaDaeR into the independent production company Thomas Wilkening in 1992 shows that this commitment continued into the newly unified free-market economy. Despite some success, the Federal Republic has not been kind to its new film artists. Now "free" to direct whatever they wanted, the former DEFA artists once again found themselves idle. Only this time, they did not even have a studio hierarchy with which they might argue.

See also:

- 28 February 1962: Oberhausen Manifesto Creates Founding Myth for New German Cinema
- Fall 1968: Expulsion of Thomas Brasch from GDR Film School Signals Fate of East German '68ers
- 25 August 1992: *Ostalgie* Provides Pushback against Western Views on the East German Collapse

Notes

[1] Thomas Wilkening, internal document describing the background of the production group DaDaeR 16 February 1990, Wilkening estate, Film Museum Potsdam. All translations are mine.

[2] Jörg Foth, "Orangenmond im Niemandsland," in *Orangenmond im Niemandsland*, ed. Torsten Schulz (Berlin: Vistas, 2004), 21–25; here 25.

[3] Claus Löser, Karin Fritzsche, eds. *Gegenbilder: Filmische Subversion in der DDR 1976–1989* (Berlin: Janus, 1996). See also: Claus Löser, *Strategien der Verweigerung: Untersuchungen zum politisch-ästhetischen Gestus unangepasster filmischer Artikulationen in der Spätphase der DDR* (Berlin: DEFA Stiftung, 2011).

[4] Thomas Günther, "Die subkulturellen Zeitschriften in der DDR und ihre kulturgeschichtliche Bedeutung," in *Aus Politik und Zeitgeschichte: Beilage zur Wochenzeitung "Das Parlament"* 20 (8 May 1992): 27–36; here 36.

[5] Ibid., 27.

Part VII: 1990–2011

On 3 October 1990, Germans celebrated the official unification of East and West, as the two postwar nations formally ended half a century of division. The pace of transition from the fall of the Berlin Wall to the Day of Unity, as it was called, had been astonishing. Just weeks after the opening of the East German border, West German Chancellor Helmut Kohl had issued his "Ten Point Program for Overcoming the Division of Germany and Europe," and the rallying cry that had once unified East German demonstrators, "*Wir* sind das Volk" (*We* are the people — and not the ruling party) had been reframed as an assertion of national cohesion: "Wir sind *ein* Volk" (We are *one* people). A number of prominent East German intellectuals — among them novelist Christa Wolf and film director Frank Beyer — argued against an absorption by the West, calling for internal reforms rather than "selling out" the GDR's social and political values. But official and popular enthusiasm for unification far outweighed their objections, fed in no small part by Kohl's projections that financial support from the Federal Republic would transform the economically depressed state into a land of "blühende Landschaften" (blooming landscapes). Then, in January 1990, thousands of East German protesters stormed the offices of the infamous Stasi (State Security Service), revealing the vast extent of the country's domestic surveillance network and further fueling the public's desire to eliminate the last vestiges of the East German state. In May 1990, the countries agreed to unify their economic, monetary, and social systems, and by July negotiations regarding the terms of full political unification had begun. In September, the former Allied powers of the Second World War signed the final peace treaty of the war (a deed not possible earlier, since the Germany against which they had fought no longer existed as a political entity), clearing the final hurdle to ending the national division. Voters — a great number of them from the East, where the CDU experienced a meteoric rise in the wake of the *Wende* (the political turnaround of 1989) — rewarded Kohl in the first national elections in December 1990, making him the first head of state in the unified Germany and earning him the nickname the Unity Chancellor. In the months that followed, debate raged over the question of whether to relocate the capital to Berlin — a plan that hearkened to the city's heritage as the country's very first national seat of government, but that for some bore uncomfortable associations with Hitler's grandiose architectural plans to transform it into a Teutonic metropolis.

In June 1991, by a slim majority, parliament approved a phased transfer of government offices, signaling the start of a new era, the beginning of what has come to be known as the Berlin Republic.

The unified nation faced significant growing pains in its first years. The costs of merging two states were staggering, and on both sides the initial enthusiasm for unification was soon countered by new resentments. In the West, people grumbled about the high price paid to support and reinvigorate the infrastructure of the new states, and deemed their Eastern German compatriots insufficiently grateful for the benefits they received as the result of West German investment. In the East, the realities of a capitalist market economy proved difficult to navigate for a population used to a system of guaranteed employment, a problem that deepened as Western investment failed to produce the "blooming landscapes" that Kohl had foretold and unemployment rose sharply. In the phenomenon known as *Ostalgie* (nostalgia for the East), many East Germans also began to express a sense of profound loss at the disappearance of their former social systems and way of life, and the more general feeling that their history itself had been lost. Right-wing nationalism rose, particularly in the Eastern hinterlands, and a series of deadly attacks against immigrants and asylum seekers rattled public consciousness, not only fostering an image of the East as retrograde and racist, but also raising broader questions about how far the country had succeeded in overcoming the Nazi past and embracing its new reality as a nation with significant levels of migration.

In 1998, Helmut Kohl's CDU lost seats in the national election, ending the longest chancellorship in German history and for the first time bringing to power a "Red-Green" coalition, as SPD leader Gerhard Schröder rose to chancellor and Green Party candidate Joschka Fisher assumed the position of foreign minister. The shift not only signaled the growing strength of the relative newcomers the Greens, but also marked a generational transition, as for the first time former antiestablishment '68ers took on leading positions in government. Coming at the midpoint of the transition to the new capital, the change in power seemed to signal the first genuinely new phase of post-Wall politics. This was coupled with a decade of visible transformation for Berlin, which underwent an unprecedented construction boom: the renovated Reichstag reopened in 1999 and myriad new buildings sprang up in the former wasteland around Potsdamer Platz, as if to give a literal new shape to the national future. At the same time, Schröder's coalition began a series of deeply unpopular domestic reforms to the nation's vaunted benefits system, in particular to unemployment insurance. Although the government deemed the reforms necessary in order to sustain the system in the face of an ageing population, citizens protested the changes, which seemed to undermine the core principles of the postwar social welfare state.

Alongside these attempts at modernization, the first decade following unification brought with it a veritable avalanche of historical questioning, brought on by the need to craft a new national narrative out of two highly disparate accounts of the German past, and prompted further by the demographic shift occurring as the generation of the Second World War reached advanced age. A series of external provocations — like the 1994 premiere of Spielberg's *Schindler's List* and several publications by US historians concerning the participation of average German citizens in wartime atrocities — as well as internal events (the campaign to build a Holocaust memorial in Berlin, the 1998 opening of Daniel Libeskind's radically redesigned Jewish Museum, the controversial Wehrmacht exhibit about war crimes committed by German soldiers during the Second World War), as well as a nasty debate between author Martin Walser and German-Jewish leader Ignatz Bubis over Walser's claim that Auschwitz had been instrumentalized as a "moral cudgel," added fresh fuel to public discussions about the national confrontation with the legacy of National Socialism. Beginning in the late 1990s, a range of German intellectuals also discovered the putatively "lost" subject of German wartime suffering. Bestselling publications like W. G. Sebald's *Luftkrieg und Literatur* (*On the Natural History of Destruction*, 1999), Jörg Friedrich's *Der Brand* (*The Fire*, 2002), and Günter Grass's *Im Krebsgang* (*Crabwalk*, 2002) brought renewed attention to the terrible cost of Allied bombing campaigns and postwar expulsions from the East, fostering efforts to build a museum commemorating the history of German expellees, but also raising questions about whether the focus on the pain of average Germans would obscure the perspectives of those persecuted under the Nazi regime.

Parallel to this, heated debates in the late nineties about proposed changes to German citizenship laws, particularly concerning provisions that would have permitted immigrants to attain dual citizenship, brought to the forefront the challenges to expanding notions of national belonging even as they began to move the country away from its traditional reliance on the principle of "blood" as the prerequisite for inclusion. Following a popular petition campaign and objections by the CDU, the SPD-Green coalition sharply scaled back reform plans, but the controversy highlighted the period's renewed focus on questions of integration. Increasingly over the course of the years that followed, this discourse on integration would come to combine reflections on the work of confronting the legacies of both National Socialism and the GRD dictatorship, the need for unification of East and West, and the challenges to efforts to incorporate immigrant communities — with attitudes toward the integration of new populations serving as the litmus test of German success in overcoming a troubled history. This was never more evident than in 2010, when President Christian Wulff marked the twentieth anniversary of unification by declaring integration the "second German unification," and affirmatively declaring that Islam had a place within the nation — remarks that caused considerable controversy, not least because they were followed shortly thereafter by assertions by Merkel and other CDU leaders that the project of multiculturalism had "failed."

As German society seemed to look increasingly inward during the 1990s in a search for a cohesive narrative concerning its shared past, the country also strove to affirm its place within Europe, embracing a broader, continental identity. In part seeking to temper the anxieties of its neighbors about the state's newfound size and power, Germany forged ahead with plans to strengthen alliances with Europe, signing the Treaty of Maastricht in 1992 to create the European Union and lay the groundwork for the emergence of a common currency, the euro (implemented in 2002). The EU underwent a series of expansions in the years that followed — incorporating numerous new countries, including several from the former Eastern bloc, but also extending the very idea of Europe itself. Although the union's cohesion has faced numerous tests in subsequent years — from the failed effort to establish a shared constitution to the more recent fallout over weak economies of several member nations, which have strained commitment to the euro — contemporary Germany seems generally to have embraced a feeling of European cosmopolitanism. Part and parcel of this strengthened bond with the country's continental neighbors, along with a new confidence in international affairs, has been a shift in how German understands its NATO commitments. 1998 marked a sea change, when, in the course of the Kosovo crisis, German soldiers appeared in uniform beyond the nation's borders for the first time since 1945. While Germany remains extremely reluctant to send its soldiers into armed conflict, attitudes regarding the appropriateness of military engagement have clearly shifted since unification. Gerhard Schröder made his vocal opposition to the US invasion of Iraq a central part of his reelection campaign of 2002, and succeeded in large measure because his views enjoyed popular support. But the situation in Afghanistan evidences just how greatly German political attitudes have changed: while the country initially committed only humanitarian and postwar reconstruction support, the participation of German soldiers in Afghanistan has grown increasingly offensive in nature and from the standpoint of today looks ever more like conventional warfare. The recent decision to eliminate the system of mandatory military service in favor of establishing an all-volunteer army offers another indication of the transformation underway, as postwar fears about the potential risk posed by an independent military have abated.

In 2005, following a regional defeat for the SPD, Chancellor Gerhard Schröder deliberately called for and lost a parliamentary vote of confidence, leading to a dissolution of the Red-Green coalition and bringing to power the first woman chancellor, and the first raised in the former GDR: CDU leader Angela Merkel. For just the second time in its history, the country's two leading parties — the CDU and SPD — formed a Grand Coalition. Given their traditional opposition, the union proved unwieldy, and Merkel from the outset declared the intention to align with the centrist FDP — a restructuring accomplished following national elections in 2009. The leadership transition from Schröder to Merkel brought a number of discernible changes, particularly in the arena of foreign relations (e.g., when Merkel cultivated stronger ties with the United States). But in many respects, the course of the country has continued in a consistent vein since the late 1990s — in what observers both within and outside the nation have discerned as a pattern of "normalization." The shift was most visible during the 2006 World Cup celebration, as soccer fans waving and wearing the German flag provided an unprecedented display of national pride in a country that until then had tended to conflate patriotism with nationalism. Although talk of this "new normal" has faded somewhat in recent years, its results are still very much in evidence in the air of self-assurance that the country brings to its dealings domestically and abroad. For better or worse, contemporary Germany appears to have shed any residual fear of repeating its past and to be confident of its readiness to move forward into a different future.

The most recent history of German cinema also appears rather rosy. This was not entirely clear at the beginning of the 1990s. Following the sale and dismantling of DEFA (Deutsche Film-Aktiengesellschaft, East Germany's state-owned film company) in 1992 to French conglomerate Compagnie Générale des Eaux, East German filmmakers struggled largely in vain to find footing in the new terrain of post-Wall cultural scene. The studio's final output — a series of *Wende* films that addressed the immediate consequences of the fall of the GDR and the bitter disappointment felt by many artists burned by years of censorship but still faithful to the possibilities of socialism — went almost unnoticed, only recently rescued from their obscurity thanks to a traveling series organized by the DEFA Film Library at the University of Massachusetts Amherst with the support of the Wende Museum. The early years after unification did yield a number of successful topical comedies that traded on the novelty of the East, even as they often foregrounded the supposed peccadilloes of its citizens — titles like *Go Trabi Go* (1991), *Sonnenallee* (1999), or *Good Bye Lenin!* (2003). The early part of the decade was further dominated by the powerhouse of New German Comedy, which failed to translate into a strong export market and was generally viewed with disdain by scholars nostalgic for the aesthetically ambitious projects of New German Cinema, but which continued to attract strong domestic audiences. Nor has the New German Comedy left the scene — as evidenced by the recent success of Til Schweiger's *Keinohrhasen* (*Rabbit without Ears*, 2007) and its sequel, as well as a new cycle of popular spoofs by the likes of Bully Herbig. The 1990s also saw the rise of a new form of German historical drama — including works like *Comedian Harmonists* (*The Harmonists*, 1997) and *Aimée und Jaguar* (*Aimée and Jaguar*, 1999) — which borrowed from the successful model of British heritage cinema to produce glossy productions set during the most traumatic years of the German past. In particular, these films — with their faithful and imminently palatable reproduction of the look, if not always the factual details, of German history — found new footing for German film on the international market, symbolized not least by their disproportionate success at garnering nominations in the Best Foreign Film category at the US Academy Awards. This trend continues into the present, as evidenced by the strong reception of films like *Der Untergang* (*Downfall*, 2004) and *Das Leben der Anderen* (*The Lives of Others*, 2006). At the same, contemporary German cinema has grown ever more inclusive. In tandem with a changing awareness of contemporary Germany's cultural diversity and public debates about the terms of national belonging, a new generation of "hybrid" filmmakers emerged, like the Turkish-German Fatih Akın and Swiss-Jewish Dani Levy. While many erstwhile DEFA filmmakers never managed to reestablish substantial post-Wall careers, a select few, chief among them director Andreas Dresen, have succeeded in recent years in bringing to the screen subtle, nonsensational narratives that explore contemporary life in the former East. The spaces of the former GDR have also served as a favorite setting for the films of the so-called Berlin School, a loosely affiliated group of young directors who share a common dedication to producing aesthetically challenging depictions of life in postunification Germany. While these films have not achieved the sort of popular success, either domestically or internationally, of the more commercially oriented historical cinema being produced in Germany today, they have managed to capture the interest of festival organizers as well as film scholars, awakening new enthusiasm among cinephiles for the country's contemporary art-house productions. Taken as a whole, contemporary German cinema gives the impression of an industry emerging along numerous parallel tracks. Its multiple strands, in combination, afford cinemagoers a variety of offerings catering to both local and cosmopolitan tastes. While it is perhaps somewhat premature to prognosticate regarding the "history" of the German cinema still to come, from the vantage of today the twenty-first century looks to hold exciting promise — as a moment characterized by the sorts of diverse and mutually enriching trajectories that have marked German film history from its very inception.

Selected Bibliography • 1990–2011

Anderson, Susan C. "Outsiders, Foreigners, and Aliens in Cinematic or Literary Narratives by Boh, Dische, Dorrie, and Oren." *The German Quarterly* 75, no. 2 (Spring 2002): 144–59.

Bathrick, David. "Whose Hi/story Is It? The U.S. Reception of *Downfall*." *New German Critique* 102 (Fall 2007): 1–16.

Berghahn, Daniela. "Post-1990 Screen Memories: How East and West German Cinema Remembers the Third Reich and the Holocaust." *German Life and Letters* 59, no. 2 (2006): 294–308.

Burns, Rob. "On the Streets and on the Road: Identity in Transit in Turkish-German Travelogues on Screen." *New Cinemas: Journal of Contemporary Film* 7, no. 1 (2009): 11–26.

Clarke, David, ed. *German Cinema: Since Unification*. London: Continuum, 2006.

Cooke, Paul. *Representing East Germany since Unification: From Colonization to Nostalgia*. Oxford: Berg, 2005.

Cooke, Paul, and Chris Homewood, eds. *New Directions in German Cinema*. London: I. B. Tauris, 2011.

Costabile-Heming, Carol Anne, Rachel J. Halverson, and Kristie A. Foell, eds. *Textual Responses to German Unification: Processing Historical and Social Change in Literature and Film*. Berlin: Walter de Gruyter, 2001.

Dale, Gareth. "Heimat, 'Ostalgie' and the Stasi: The GDR in German Cinema, 1999–2006." *Debatte: Review of Contemporary German Affairs* 15, no. 2 (2007): 155–75.

Fiedler, Matthias. "German Crossroads: Visions of the Past in German Cinema after Reunification." In *German Memory Contests: The Quest for Identity in Literature, Film, and Discourse since 1990*, edited by Anne Fuchs, Mary Cosgrove, and Georg Grote, 127–46. Rochester, NY: Camden House, 2006.

Fisher, Jaimey, and Brad Prager, eds. *The Collapse of the Conventional: German Film and Its Politics at the Turn of the Twenty-First Century*. Detroit: Wayne State UP, 2010.

Göktürk, Deniz. "Turkish Women on German Streets: Closure and Exposure in Transnational Cinema." In *Spaces in European Cinema*, edited by Myrto Konstantarakos, 64–76. Exeter, UK: Intellect, 2000.

Gramling, David. "On the Other Side of Monolingualism: Fatih Akın's Linguistic Turn(s)." *German Quarterly* 83, no. 3 (Summer 2010): 353–72.

Halle, Randall. *German Film after Germany: Toward a Transnational Aesthetic*. Champaign: U of Illinois P, 2008.

———. "'Happy Ends' to Crises of Heterosexual Desire: Toward a Social Psychology of Recent German Comedies." *Camera Obscura* 44 (2000): 1–39.

Halle, Randall, and Reinhild Steingröver, eds. *After the Avant-Garde: Contemporary German and Austrian Experimental Film*. Rochester, NY: Camden House, 2008.

Hillman, Roger. "*Goodbye Lenin* (2003): History in the Subjunctive." *Rethinking History* 10, no. 2 (2006): 221–37.

Jesinghausen, Martin. "The Sky over Berlin as Transcendental Space: Wenders, Döblin and the 'Angel of History.'" In *Spaces in European Cinema*, edited by Myrto Konstantarakos, 77–93. Exeter, UK: Intellect, 2000.

Johnston, Ruth D. "The Jewish Closet in *Europa, Europa*." *Camera Obscura* 52 (2003): 1–33.

Kapczynski, Jennifer M. "Negotiating Nostalgia: The GDR Past in *Berlin Is in Germany* and *Good Bye Lenin!*" *Germanic Review* 82, no. 1 (2007): 78–100.

Karpf, Ernst, ed. *"Getürkte Bilder": Zur Inszenierung von Fremden im Film*. Marburg: Schüren, 1995.

Koepnick, Lutz. "Free Fallin': Tom Tykwer and the Aesthetics of Deceleration and Dislocation." *Germanic Review* 82, no. 1 (2007): 7–24.

———. "Reframing the Past: Heritage Cinema and Holocaust in the 1990s." *New German Critique* 87 (2002): 47–82.

———. "Consuming the Other: Identity, Alterity, and Contemporary German Cinema." *Camera Obscura* 44 (2000): 40–73.

Kopp, Kristin. "Reconfiguring the Border of Fortress Europe in Hans-Christian Schmid's *Lichter*." *Germanic Review* 82, no. 1 (2007): 31–53.

Linville, Susan E. "Agnieszka Holland's *Europa, Europa*: Deconstructive Humor in a Holocaust Film." *Film Criticism* 19, no. 3 (1995): 44–53.

Lornsen, Karin. "Where Have All the Guest Workers Gone? Transcultural Role-Play and Performative Identities in Fatih Akın's *Gegen die Wand* (2004)." In *Finding the Foreign*, edited by Robert Schechtman and Suin Roberts, 13–31. Newcastle: Cambridge Scholars Publishing, 2007.

Mennel, Barbara. "Local Funding and Global Movement: Minority Women's Filmmaking and the German Film Landscape of the Late 1990s." *Women in German Yearbook: Feminist Studies in German Literature & Culture* 18 (2002): 45–66.

———. "Political Nostalgia and Local Memory: The Kreuzberg of the 1980s in Contemporary German Film." *Germanic Review* 82, no. 1 (2007): 54–77.

Naughton, Leonie. *That Was the Wild East: Film Culture, Unification, and the "New" Germany*. Ann Arbor: U of Michigan P, 2002.

Paehler, Katrin. "Breaking the Post-War Goose-Step: Three Films by Michael Verhoeven." *Shofar: An Interdisciplinary Journal of Jewish Studies* 28, no. 4 (Summer 2010): 41–56.

Paver, Chloe. *Refractions of the Third Reich in German and Austrian Fiction and Film*. Oxford: Oxford UP, 2007.
Prager, Brad. "Passing Time Since the *Wende*: Recent German Film on Unification." *German Politics & Society* 28, no. 1 (2010): 95–110.
Rentschler, Eric. "From New German Cinema to the Post-Wall Cinema of Consensus." In *Cinema and Nation*, edited by Mette Hjort and Scott MacKenzie, 260–77. London: Routledge, 2000.
Schindler, Stephan K., and Lutz Koepnick, eds. *The Cosmopolitan Screen: German Cinema and the Global Imaginary, 1945 to the Present*. Ann Arbor: U of Michigan P, 2007.
Schlipphacke, Heidi. *Nostalgia after Nazism: History, Home, and Affect in German and Austrian Literature and Film*. Lewisburg, PA: Bucknell UP, 2010.
Schmidt, Gary. "Between Authors and Agents: Gender and Affirmative Culture in *Das Leben der Anderen*." *German Quarterly* 82, no. 2 (Spring 2009): 231–49.
Spector, Scott. "Wenders' Genders: From the End of the Wall to the End of the World." In *Triangulated Visions: Women in Recent German Cinema*, edited by Ingeborg Majer O'Sickey and Ingeborg von Zadow, 219–30. Albany: State U of New York P, 1998.
Taberner, Stuart. "Philo-Semitism in Recent German Film: *Aimée und Jaguar*, *Rosenstraße* and *Das Wunder von Bern*." *German Life & Letters* 58, no. 3 (2005): 357–72.
Twark, Jill E., ed. *Strategies of Humor in Post-Unification German Literature, Film, and Other Media*. Newcastle: Cambridge Scholars Publishing, 2011.
Uecker, Matthias. "Fractured Families — United Countries? Family, Nostalgia and Nation-Building in *Das Wunder von Bern* and *Good Bye Lenin!*" *New Cinemas: Journal of Contemporary Film* 5, no. 3 (2007): 189–200.
von Moltke, Johannes. "Sympathy for the Devil: Cinema, History, and the Politics of Emotion." *New German Critique* 34, no. 3 (2007): 17–44.
Wende, Waltraud "Wara," and Lars Koch, eds. *Krisenkino: Filmanalyse als Kulturanalyse; Zur Konstruktion von Normalität und Abweichung im Spielfilm*. Bielefeld: transcript, 2010.
Yeşilada, Karin. "Turkish-German Movies in Transition: The Filmmaker Fatih Akın." In *Belonging and Exclusion: Case Studies in Recent Australian and German Literature, Film and Theatre*, edited by Ulrike Garde and Anne-Rose Meyer, 75–93. Newcastle: Cambridge Scholars Publishing, 2009.

23 July 1991: ZDF Broadcast of *Ostkreuz* Initiates Darker Reckoning with the *Wende*

Mattias Frey

Hanna Flanders (Hannelore Elsner) *feels trapped in the new post-Wall Berlin*. Die Unberührbare *(2000). DVD capture.*

IN CONTEMPORARY GERMANY the most memorable visions of the Eastern past and the tumultuous events of 1989–90 — the movies used in schools to educate the young — are colorful *Ostalgie* pictures like *Sonnenallee* (1999) and *Good Bye Lenin!* (2003), or heroic epics such as *Das Versprechen* (*The Promise*, 1995) and *Das Leben der Anderen* (*The Lives of Others*, 2006).[1] The former assemble material objects as a cabinet of curiosity in order to rewrite a pan-German history; the latter invent comforting fairy tales of universal human values and hidden rebellion. Nevertheless, there exists a less well-known but crucial genealogy, which takes a subdued, strident, or otherwise unconventional attitude toward unification and its aftereffects. *Ostkreuz* (1991), the first major film in this vein, became the prototype for a series of idiosyncratic post-Wall projects that issued uncongenial images and narratives of intra-German relations and the course of unification.

Michael Klier's mood piece premiered at the Munich Film Festival on 27 June 1991 and aired on ZDF (Zweites Deutsches Fernsehen, Germany's second public television station) a month later. It begins with a pan across an icy mudscape in the winter of 1989/90. This is Potsdamer Platz, the center of Berlin, but might as well portray a suburb of Zagreb, Moscow, or Szczecin. Elfie trails her mother, who has just inspected an apartment: the DM 3000 deposit required is an impossible sum. They return to their trailer park, where they live with other refugees from the GDR and other Eastern Bloc countries. Makeshift offices, drafty mobile homes, portable toilets: this is the world that Elfie desires to escape. Her mother is a hairdresser, but finds no work in these post-Wall days; to get ahead, she beds Henry, a grubby schemer who promises to help out with money. Elfie quits school and earns pocket change with stolen Japanese car radios. Moonlighting as a window washer, she meets Darius, a petty criminal. The young Pole (played by Miroslaw Baka) offers her a cut on his business: she launders counterfeit notes and sells her grandfather's Meißner porcelain.

Elfie eventually musters the deposit. By this time, however, the goal has proved worthless: her mother hangs on Henry, her grandfather (a taxi driver who still lives in East Berlin) on the bottle. In a final confrontation, Elfie throws down her new leather jacket and leaves her mother. Forsaking her biological family, she searches out an alternative community in the company of Edmund, a homeless boy whose parents left the GDR but deserted him in the West.

Played by the sixteen-year-old Laura Tonke well before the actress's sultry turn as Gudrun Ensslin in *Baader* (2002), Elfie is neither girl nor young woman. A pale face framed by recalcitrant hair, she rehearses smoking and other gestures of adulthood in lonely patches of time lost to a restless ennui. Certainly, there is a simmering sexuality in these *temps morts*, when Elfie overhears her mother's pleasure through the delicate trailer walls. The elder woman's complex relationship with Henry — an association somewhere between prostitution and friendship — both baffles the teenager and excites her curiosity. Nevertheless (and despite Darius's lazy paw for a kiss), Elfie's Berlin is unglamorous and inhospitable even measured against *Christiane F.* — *Wir Kinder vom Bahnhof Zoo* (*Christiane F.*, 1981). Cinematographer Sophie Maintigneux's 16-millimeter captures a gray cityscape of grim peep shows, sullen bars, and dilapidated highrises. A single shot portrays the TV tower in the hazy sun, but mostly we witness muddy lots lined with leaky garages and carcasses of apartment blocks. This urban curiosity is evacuated of almost all people: remarkably absent are the energies of the *Volk* who took over the streets in these days, preparing to unite the land.

Ellipses punctuate the narrative rhythm, which moves through episodes without a center. Short, consecutive sequences depict the same place; the characters leave and enter the cramped trailer or the patch of dirt that makes up the front "garden." What has actually transpired in the meantime remains forthcoming. (The camera's stasis foregrounds exceptional kinetic flourishes in cinematography and editing: a decisive tracking shot in the Alexanderplatz station scene and anachronistic wipes.) When Elfie is stranded in Poland, the film's most dramatic action sequence (a shootout with Russian gangsters) adjourns abruptly; we never know how she returns. These, too, are empty spaces.

Klier's second feature, *Ostkreuz* continues the preoccupations of his first — *Überall ist es besser wo wir nicht sind* (*The Grass is Greener Everywhere Else*, 1989). In that film, Miroslaw Baka's character Jerzy follows his American dream from Warsaw to West Berlin, only to land in a New York that looks like Communist Poland. The post-Wall fates of Elfie and Edmund are similar: their Potsdamer Platz dwelling would be unrecognizable, were it not for the bombed-out Bundesrat building in the background. Is this the paradise for which they left the GDR? Even if the Kino Vorwärts plays *Pretty Woman* (1990), the pair can hardly afford tickets. They find themselves unwanted in this new order: their parents have left and in the restaurant they are only allowed to dine in the foyer. In these final scenes we understand that Elfie's forays into the gangster life somehow hoped to win her a bourgeois one. The last shot has Elfie looking out the window of the occupied flat, still waiting for a utopian future in the now-capitalist present.

For contemporary reviewers, Klier's vision hearkened back to older forms of cinematic realism. "Berlin in Year Zero," summarized *Der Tagesspiegel*; "*Ostkreuz* is," according to the *Frankfurter Allgemeine Zeitung*'s critic, "the paradigm of a new German neorealism, a new 'rubble film.'"[2] To be sure, the parallels to *Germania anno zero* (*Germany Year Zero*, 1948) are not to be missed. Klier and coscreenwriter Karin Åström allude to Roberto Rossellini's classic with the name Edmund; both projects share nonprofessional actors, dilapidated architectures, shadowy interiors, and a Berlin in historical upheaval. Like the rubble films, the 1991 production operates in border zones: between West and East, between yesterday and tomorrow. Nevertheless, *Ostkreuz* lacks the late 1940s' pathos and sensationalism. There are no monstrous pedophiles, no guilty consciences, nor absolute evils of any sort. Even Henry and Darius resist easy categorization. Elfie's story serves neither the sentiment of the viewer nor a larger pedagogical or statistical purpose; quite simply, it exists. In this way, the gritty prospect of post-Wall disorder draws inspiration from antecedents like Herrmann Zschoche's *Insel der Schwäne* (*Island of Swans*, 1983), which takes socialist urban planning in Berlin-Marzahn to task through the eyes of children. Klier, who grew up mostly in the GDR, recalls this pessimistic strand of DEFA (Deutsche Film-Aktiengesellschaft, East Germany's state-owned film company) across his oeuvre, including the later *Heidi M.* (2001).

Although lauded by critics and feted with prizes and festival distinctions, *Ostkreuz* never met the market success of contemporaneous, lighter approaches to East-West relations. Remembering that *Go Trabi Go* (1991), *Go Trabi Go 2* (1992), and *Wir können auch anders* (*No More Mr. Nice Guy*, 1993) bookended Klier's examination of dirty architectures and messy fates prevents us from dividing German film history into tidy periods of blithe and serious reckonings with the *Wende*. They existed in parallel. Synthesizing diverse traditions, *Ostkreuz* ushered in a series of formidable German-German accounts around the turn of the millennium, accounts that cut across the border in terms of their directors' origins but that are united by a common dark or uncongenial narrative mood. The most important of these was Oskar Roehler's *Die Unberührbare* (*No Place to Go*, 2000).

Even before this project, Roehler had imagined a contrarian narrative of the unification in two cowritten farces, Christoph Schlingensief's *Terror 2000 — Intensivstation Deutschland* (*Terror 2000*, 1992) and Niklaus Schilling's *Deutschfieber* (German Fever, 1992). His German Film Prize winner, however, would be much more personal. Based loosely on the events of his mother's life, *Die Unberührbare* tracks a West German writer named Hanna Flanders from the fall of the Berlin Wall to her suicide in early 1990. Although Hanna was an officially sanctioned success in the GDR, her Marxist novels have become too dogmatic for West German publishing houses. She senses, quite accurately, that the demise of real existing socialism bodes the end of her career as well. Desperate and broke, she embarks on an odyssey through the two Germanys. After visiting her son and a lover in Berlin, her parents in Nuremberg, and her ex-husband in Darmstadt, she lands in a Munich clinic, where she plunges from a window.

Roehler's confrontation with his mother's suicide plays out against a grim portrayal of November 1989. Like Klier, Roehler reroutes a problem of history into a dystopia of space: a woman seeks meaning in the GDR's ruins only to find the voids of lost promises. Interiors are minimalist: quadratic shapes and painterly frames delineate an algid domesticity. Compositions trap Hanna in the windows and doors of Munich condominiums and Marzahn high-rise blocks. More desperate than *Ostkreuz*'s Elfie, Hanna hastens alone across the empty fields in East Berlin boroughs envisioned by Communist city planners as a utopian antidote to the acute housing shortage. The nadir of Hanna's journey in East Germany takes place at the failure of socialist theory.

Roehler is serious about the past. According to the director, history "shouldn't be left to the Schlöndorffs and the other politically correct"; it is the "only source from which you can create, as a collective and as an individual."[3] Indeed, with an intertextual archive that includes allusions to *Sunset Blvd.* (1950), a wig straight out of *Naked Kiss* (1964), and the infamous robe in *Die Sehnsucht der Veronika Voss* (*Veronika Voss*, 1982), *Die Unberührbare* grapples with film history itself as material culture: the site of the *Ostalgie* pictures' blithe pastiche. Draining the period of its color, Roehler's monochromatic retrovision restores a discontent to the *Wende* and its aftereffects.

The turn of the millennium, fraught with dissatisfaction over unemployment, rising crime, and the "foreigner problem," saw other dark deliberations on ten years of unity. These included Andreas Kleinert's *Wege in die Nacht* (*Paths in the Night*, 1999), about a disgruntled Easterner who resorts to vigilante justice. More *Death Wish* (1974) than *Der Zimmerspringbrunnen* (The tabletop fountain, 2001) — a facile send-up of another *Ossi* loser — the seedy black-and-white nights of *Wege in die Nacht* belong to the murky tradition of *Ostkreuz* and *Die Unberührbare*. Director Andreas Dresen, on the other hand, has picked up on Klier's humanist realism more than his dingy aesthetic, offering sensitive portraits of post-Wall East German destinies in films like *Die Polizistin* (*Policewoman*, 2000), *Halbe Treppe* (*Grill Point*, 2002), *Sommer vorm Balkon* (*Summer in Berlin*, 2005), *Wolke Neun* (*Cloud Nine*, 2008), and others. Because Kleinert and Dresen came of age in the GDR and trained at DEFA, some commentators conclude that West Germans deliver simple *Ostalgie* whereas Easterners create more complex efforts. These categories fail to pass scrutiny. Leander Haußmann, of Quedlinburg, gave us *Sonnenallee*; Westerners like Christian Petzold have provided stunning prospects of the unification's legacy in the new *Länder*.

Indeed, Petzold and fellow colleagues of what came to be called the Berlin School remain the most important descendants of *Ostkreuz*'s paced milieu study. Their movement explicitly rejects representations of the past like *Good Bye Lenin!* (2003) and *Der Untergang* (*Downfall*, 2004) as "History-Porno." And yet despite these protests, the group's productions infect the present with the past. Miniature relationship dramas such as Valeska Grisebach's *Sehnsucht* (*Longing*, 2006) and Henner Winckler's *Lucy* (2006) yield laconic quotients of the former GDR. Petzold's *Yella* (2007) marries the low-budget American horror of *Carnival of Souls* (1962) with mentor Harun Farocki's antiglobalization documentary *Nicht ohne Risiko* (*Not Without Risk*, 2004). Addressing the pitfalls of unification, *Yella* features a woman eager to escape a stifling existence in a moribund East German town. Like Jerzy in *Überall ist es besser wo wir nicht sind*, her attempt to establish herself in the West reveals a nightmare lined with the ruins of capitalism: Hanover and the overbuilt landscape of the Expo 2000. Petzold's subsequent *Jerichow* (2008) adapts *The Postman Always Rings Twice* in Brandenburg to sketch a psychogram of Germany under Hartz IV (the social benefit reforms introduced by the former Social Democratic-Green coalition) that echoes Klier's *Wende*. Binding the roads of New Hollywood and the style of Antonioni to the specificity of Eastern Germany, 2009, Petzold creates a cinema of encounters. To be sure, the directors of the Berlin School owe their humanism to the Belgians Jean-Pierre and Luc Dardenne, just as their tranquil aesthetic compares to new Thai auteurs Apichatpong Weerasethakul and Aditya Assarat. Nevertheless, their haunted national prospects would be unthinkable without Elfie and Edmund: these too are excerpts from lives in which dreams are achieved only to be made futile by their very realization. Michael Klier's *Ostkreuz* began the film history of unification beyond nostalgia and déjà vu.

See also:

- 2 February 1988: Last Generation of DEFA Directors Calls in Vain for Reform
- 25 August 1992: *Ostalgie* Provides Pushback against Western Views on the East German Collapse
- 22 January 2007: Film Establishment Attacks "Berlin School" as Wrong Kind of National Cinema

Notes

[1] *Ostalgie* refers to a nostalgia for the GDR and especially an apolitical desire for the GDR's lost popular and material culture.

[2] Carla Rohde, "Berlin im Jahre Null," *Der Tagesspiegel* (2 January 1992); Wilfried Wiegand, "Anpassung als Katastrophe," *Frankfurter Allgemeine Zeitung* (25 July 1991).

[3] Quoted in Tilman Krause, "Geschichte ist die einzige Quelle," *Die Welt* (6 May 2000).

16 May 1992: Marlene Dietrich's Berlin Burial Links Postunification Germany with Weimar Republic's Internationalism

Barbara Kosta

Selling Dietrich at the KaDeWe in Berlin. Credit: Barbara Kosta.

TEN DAYS AFTER HER DEATH in Paris on 6 May 1992, Marlene Dietrich was laid to rest in Berlin, the city of her birth. The blue angel had finally come home, announced Hellmuth Karasek in the German weekly magazine *Der Spiegel*.[1] Dietrich's choice to be buried next to her mother, Josephine von Losch, marked a return to her hometown after a lavish Hollywood career that began with the success of *The Blue Angel*, and ended with life as a recluse in a Paris apartment on the Rue Montaigne. In tribute to her international stardom, her gravestone in the Friedenau Cemetery on the Stubenrauchstraße simply reads *Marlene*.

A few years after Dietrich's death, the city that received her remains without fanfare (an official gala event was cancelled) embraced her as its star and moral beacon and began to market her image. Her burial in Berlin was viewed as part of Germany's return to "normalcy" after German unification. Dietrich was celebrated as an ambassador of reconciliation, as an antifascist hero, and as an icon of Berlin's libertine Weimar past. Her image was to lend sex appeal and that certain something (*das gewisse Etwas*) to the newly unified Berlin, whose image-makers longed to be identified with the heyday of the Weimar Republic, when Berlin was considered the quintessential modern European city: a place of radical experimentation in the visual and performing arts, literature, architecture, and even politics, a place of wide-ranging gender performances and sexual liberation. In her aloof sex appeal and androgyny, Dietrich embodies the modern woman of the Weimar Republic in habit and appearance. Her name is synonymous with the edginess, glamour, and adventure of the roaring twenties, and with a sense of nostalgia that is retrospective as much as it is prospective.

At the same time, her biography offers Germany a narrative of resistance against Hitler's barbarous regime, and an intimate relationship with Hollywood's international film star. Even now, her star persona provides an imaginary space in which Berlin can invest and receive significant returns by marketing the city of her origin as the place that initially defined her. Dietrich continues to imbue the German capital with an aura of glamour and internationalism.

The purchase of Marlene Dietrich's estate for $5 million in 1993 finalized her return home. The proverbial suitcase of the famous song "Ein Koffer in Berlin" was now joined with a warehouse full of "Dietrichabilia." The inventory included 680 suitcases, 5,000 film stills and behind-the-scenes photographs, 1,000 private photographs, 3,000 textile items (including her wardrobe), 440 pairs of shoes, a plethora of written ephemera, and sound recordings, to name only a few of the items that now comprise the Marlene Dietrich Collection.[2] The sheer abundance of her effects speaks to the creation of the star spectacle. The acquisition of the Collection provided its curators with the opportunity to mine, catalogue, and exhibit every aspect of the film diva's life, including her childhood, her schooling as a violinist, her life as a modern woman of 1920s Berlin, her Weimar and Hollywood films, and her career as stage performer. For Berlin, this treasure trove still serves to advertise the city. Biographies, picture albums, and guides to Dietrich landmarks have flooded the market and solidified her identity as a Berliner. Today, the Marlene Dietrich Collection fills three rooms in the Film Museum on the Potsdamer Platz as part of a permanent collection. It makes Dietrich available to her fans and preserves her mythological stature. Significantly, possession of the Collection also facilitated the reclamation and appropriation of Dietrich for German cinema as Berlin's prodigy. Her Weimar films, long neglected and largely unknown, have since experienced a renaissance.

Marlene Dietrich's ambition to be an actress led her to Berlin's theaters and cabarets in the 1920s, after she had abandoned her initial plan of pursuing a musical career. She played minor roles in numerous plays; her most notable cabaret performance was "Wenn die beste Freundin" with Margo Lion in 1928, in which she wore a violet bouquet, as a coquettish nod toward lesbianism. After Dietrich's film debut in Georg Jacoby's *So sind die Männer* (*The Little Napoleon*, 1922), she appeared in seventeen more films during the 1920s — playing the lead role in at least five — all of which received little attention. Dietrich, however, made every effort to repress her earlier work so as not to invalidate the narrative of her legendary discovery for *Der blaue Engel* (*The Blue Angel*, 1930). Indeed, it was not until Austrian-born Paramount director Josef von Sternberg appeared on the scene to help Ufa (Universum Film A.G.) make the transition to sound film that Marlene Dietrich's feisty and tantalizing nonchalance were fully captured. The story of a reserved prep school teacher who strays when he falls in love with a sultry cabaret singer, Lola Lola, premiered on 1 April 1930 at the Gloria Palast. Mesmerized by Dietrich's detached, reserved, and cool acting style, critics enthused: "Miss Dietrich's performance is simply overwhelming."[3] The image of Dietrich wearing a top hat, sitting tilted slightly back on a barrel and seductively drawing up one leg to expose the flesh between her stocking and garter, while cooing the Friedrich Hollaender composition "Ich bin von Kopf bis Fuß" ("Falling In Love Again") has since gained iconic value in film history. The many shots of Dietrich's fetishized legs in *The Blue Angel* provoked Heinrich Mann, the author of the novel *Professor Unrat* on which the film was loosely based, to note famously: "the success of this film will be found in the naked thighs of Miss Dietrich!"

Dietrich departed for Hollywood on the night of the premiere of *The Blue Angel*, signing a five-year contract with Paramount and leaving behind her husband Rudi Siebert and six-year-old daughter Maria, with whom she would be reunited months later. Apprehensive about her reception as the risqué Lola, Paramount delayed the release of *The Blue Angel* in the United States until Dietrich secured her success with *Morocco* (1930), the first of her six Hollywood films directed by von Sternberg. His masterful use of lighting and fabrics and her alleged Prussian drive toward perfection turned these films into box office hits that sealed her stardom as Paramount's European star and Garbo's rival. More stylized in these films than in her role as Lola, Dietrich played seductive and cool femmes fatales who, driven by passion and determination, transcended boundaries. These films featured her erotic charisma and capitalized on her seductive relationship to the camera. In her Hollywood films, she would perfect her androgynous image as irresistible siren and sensuous, imperturbable aggressor. Her auratic power relied on the choreography of the surface and appearance. In *Shanghai Express* (1932), when her ex-lover regrets having ever left her, Shanghai Lily adds: "There's only one thing I wouldn't have done, Doc. I wouldn't have bobbed my hair." On screen as in life, Dietrich remained unreachable. She embodied the cosmopolitan, elegant seductress of ambiguous gender and sexuality, whose static sensuality, bravado, coolness, passion, and mystery captivated audiences. Her indeterminacy was the hallmark of her stardom in more ways than just her sexuality. Filmmakers capitalized on her "foreignness" to enhance her exotic/erotic allure and transience.

Not until the postwar years did filmmakers Billy Wilder (*A Foreign Affair*, 1947; *Witness for the Prosecution*, 1957) and Stanley Kramer (*Judgment at Nuremberg*, 1961) exploit her "Germanness" to reflect on Germany's fascist past. As someone who renounced her German citizenship in protest against Hitler's government and who became an American citizen in 1939, Dietrich initially rejected these roles. She was a committed anti-Nazi who spent the Second World War "fighting" Hitler's fascist regime in support of Allied troops. She toured with the USO (United Service Organization) to boost the morale of "her boys," as she called them, performing songs like "Lili Marleen" and "Let's See What the Boys in the Back Room Will Have." In addition to her approximately five hundred performances with the USO, she participated in the war-bonds drive and aired anti-Nazi broadcasts in German for Allied radio stations. Earlier, she refused Joseph Goebbels's invitation to return to Germany as Ufa's leading female star. In retaliation, the German press vilified Dietrich and her films were banned. They remained for the most part unavailable to German audiences even into the 1960s. And then, much in the same way as her image has been used postunification, the rerelease of *The Blue Angel* was framed within the discourse of postwar nation-building as proof of the defeat of German fascism and democratic renewal.

Dietrich's status in postwar Germany was precarious at best. News of her first German tour unleashed a maelstrom of criticism echoing the propaganda that had targeted Dietrich during the Third Reich. It was her first visit to Germany since arriving in Berlin with American troops in an American uniform. Scattered among her fans in 1960 were protesters who heckled her as a traitor, carrying exclamatory signs that demanded "Marlene Go Home!"[4] It appeared that Dietrich had been disowned by a city to which she had proclaimed her loyalties throughout her life. Her hostile reception resonated with Alexander and Margarete Mitscherlich's then-unpublished thesis of Germany's inability to mourn its defeat and the atrocities committed in its name.

Dietrich's persona, as well as her filmic image, have always been embroiled in and appropriated for a variety of complex political/cultural negotiations. Thus Dietrich's burial in Berlin thirty-two years later was held up as evidence that she had forgiven Germans for her reception in 1960 and that Germany had made steps toward addressing the legacy of National Socialism. Following her funeral, the Senator for Cultural Affairs eulogized in a press release:

> With this last gesture Marlene Dietrich showed the world that the fascist reign of terror and the unnatural division of the city of her birth has been surmounted. Berlin is starting to experience normalcy. In returning to Berlin, she is giving this city more than it ever was or is able to do for her.[5]

In discussions about her return, Dietrich's posthumous "presence" in Berlin was enlisted time and again as a call for a "new beginning for this [Berlin] city in the heart of a new Europe," with a vision toward the continued progress Germans had made in dealing with the past.[6] In stark contrast to her fraught initial reception, a decade after her death, on 16 May 2002, she was made an honorary citizen of Berlin.

Dietrich's persistent allegiance to her Germanness, and specifically to her identity as a Berliner, as expressed in her autobiography *Ich bin, Gott sei Dank, Berlinerin* (Thank God I am a Berliner), makes the selective exploitation of her image to promote national interests and feature Germany's own film industry all the more convenient. A plaque bearing her name on the Potsdamer Platz, in the heart of Berlin, reads: "Berlin's international star of film and chansons. Commitment to freedom and democracy for Berlin and Germany." In 2010, she became the first actor to be honored with a star on Berlin's Walk of Fame, and once a year the Berlin Film Festival draws international audiences to the Potsdamer Platz, who are reminded of Dietrich's origin. In many ways, Dietrich's symbolic "comeback" involves playing a new role as a central figure in German film history, which, through her, partakes in Hollywood fame. Her image has become a vehicle, in an advertiser's sense of the word, to promote Germany, and more specifically Berlin.

And yet, despite many efforts to repatriate and use Dietrich for a fantasy of national cohesion and a return to "normalcy," such efforts rely on disavowing the complexity and transgressive nature of her style and star persona. Her peripatetic lifestyle, serial affairs, friendships, and flirtations — in addition to the multiple roles she played — all defy locating and containing Dietrich both geographically and metaphorically within concepts of nation and normativity. On- and off-screen, she retains her status as an inimitable diva whose sexual ambiguity evokes a lasting fascination and desire — as her continued international fandom reveals. The lush excess of her performances and her perfection of provocative innuendo invite viewers to indulge in the enigma and openness of her persona. Her image transcends the confines of time and space. Marlene — cosmopolitan, trendsetter, cross-dresser, and femme fatale, the embodiment of glamour and self-invention, a figure of independence, individual empowerment, and subversion — remains unbound. It is this elusiveness that makes Dietrich a star and a legend.

See also:

- 10 January 1927: Brigitte Helm Embodies Ambivalence of the New Woman
- 19 June 1935: Celebration of Lilian Harvey's Return Belies Ideological Incongruence in Nazi Entertainment Films
- 20 June 1977: DEFA's Biggest Star, Manfred Krug, Leaves the GDR

Notes

[1] Hellmuth Karasek, "Filmhimmel ohne blauen Engel," *Der Spiegel* (11 May 1992) 222, 225.

[2] Werner Sudendorf, "'Is That Me?': The Marlene Dietrich Collection Berlin," *Dietrich Icon*, ed. Gerd Gemünden and Mary R. Desjardins (Durham, NC: Duke UP, 2007), 384.

[3] Quoted in Helma Sanders-Brahms, *Marlene und Jo: Recherche einer Leidenschaft* (Berlin: Argon, 2000), 74.

[4] Steven Bach, *Marlene Dietrich: Life and Legend* (New York: Da Capo, 1992), 399.

[5] Ulrich Roloff-Momin, Landespressedienst Berlin, *Aktuelles der Woche* (21 May 1992): 40–41.

[6] Ibid.

25 August 1992: *Ostalgie* Provides Pushback against Western Views on the East German Collapse

Roger F. Cook

A moment of youthful pleasure in a GDR disco, circa 1970. Sonnenallee (1999). DVD capture.

WHEN DEFA (DEUTSCHE FILM-AKTIENGESELLSCHAFT), East Germany's state-owned film company, was sold to the French company CGE and reorganized so as to meet the demands of the West German film industry this confirmed what was already a fait accompli. West German filmmakers who were familiar with the economic system in the Federal Republic would dominate German cinema's depiction of the history of the GDR and the effects of the *Wende* (the political changes leading up to the fall of the Berlin Wall) on its people and states. This meant, then, that in the founding years of unified Germany the most popular films about the East Germans' nostalgia for life in the GDR would also be made from the point of view of the West. However, *Ostalgie*, as this vibrant nostalgia for a lost cultural identity came to be known, developed in opposition to the West German tendency to dismiss the forty years of the GDR as a failed experiment. Films about *Ostalgie*, in turn, would present an opening for East Germans to inject an Eastern perspective into mainstream German cinema's narrative about the GDR.

In its early stages *Ostalgie* was directed mainly at East German consumer products that had quickly disappeared from the shelves after 1989. In a matter of a couple of years an entire segment of GDR material culture had been all but swept aside and replaced by that of the Federal Republic. The initial nostalgic reaction to this loss attached itself to the most tangible and familiar everyday commodities (such as the GDR brands featured in *Good Bye Lenin!* — Tempo-Bohnen, Globus grüne Erbsen, and Mocha-Fix Gold Kaffee) and to the most visible (and audible!) symbol of the GDR's inferior industrial production, the Trabant (Trabi). An unattractive, inefficient, obnoxiously loud car, it went overnight from being an object that many had waited years to purchase to an antiquated, undesired relic.

Two early box-office hits that capitalized on the first wave of *Ostalgie* featured the Trabi: *Go Trabi Go* (1991) and *Go Trabi Go 2 — Das war der wilde Osten* (Go Trabi Go! 2 — That was the Wild East, 1992). In these two films, as in Detlev Buck's 1993 film *Wir können auch anders* (*No More Mr. Nice Guy*), West German filmmakers concocted a mix of the newly popular *Beziehungskomödien* (situational comedies) of the 1980s and cinematic *Heimat* humor to produce successful films that presented the East's struggles to "catch up" with the West as an entertaining comedy of errors. At first the brunt of some of the earliest *Ossi* (the pejorative term for Easterner) jokes, the Trabi became in the wake of these films a symbol for East German resistance to the arrogant West German dismissal of all that was the GDR. As the scorn for everything associated with the GDR grew, some Easterners would defiantly choose to drive their Trabis to events attended by both East and West Germans and intentionally park them next to expensive Mercedes and BMWs. By the mid-1990s such isolated acts of resistance had burgeoned into the full-fledged countercultural movement of *Ostalgie*.

While former DEFA directors had little success in finding a foothold in the cinema of the Federal Republic, the newly established regional television channels in the "new" Eastern states offered the opportunity to make films for an almost exclusively East German audience. These films featured not only the consumer brands and material objects audiences knew, but also the lifestyles, language usage, and patterns of social interaction familiar from their GDR past. These regional broadcasts provided a sheltered outlet for cultural expression where East Germans could preserve memories of forty years of GDR life.[1] Directors such as Herrmann Zschoche (*Kurklinik Rosenau* [Spa clinic Rosenau], 1996/1997) and Marion Rasche had good success with their productions for the new television channels in the East.[2] As these filmmakers presented a nostalgic media image of the GDR they often poked fun at themselves for clinging to a bygone time to which they neither could nor wanted to return. These television films displayed derogatory Western stereotypes of the GDR citizen but parodied them in ways that offered critical distance and resistance. Their selective nostalgic remembering of past experiences also provided East Germans with a self-devised sphere of autonomy that enabled them to make sense of their lives in the New Federal States on their own terms.

But as long as this strategy was applied only in regional television films it did little to forge a collective German identity that included both Easterners and Westerners. This changed in a big way in 1999 with the resounding success of *Sonnenallee* (*Sun Alley*, 1999). It is a "rite of passage" film about a group of teenagers living on the East side of an avenue that was split in two by the Berlin Wall. Both the writers (Thomas Brussig and Leander Haußmann) and the director (Haußmann) grew up in the GDR and were able to capture effectively the attitudes and strategies that enabled the young people there to resist both the absurdities of their own authoritarian state and the disdain shown them by their arrogant fellow Germans on the other side of the Wall. The film's winning depiction of the resourcefulness of Sonnenallee's tight-knit community of teenage friends and rivals appealed to viewers in Germany from all different backgrounds. It was even intended, as Brussig declared in an interview at the time, to make the Westerner envious of this childhood in the GDR.[3] And its success as the biggest grossing German film of 1999 suggests that it may have indeed had this effect on some viewers.

Sonnenallee also had its share of detractors in the West. Some critics claimed that it glossed over the oppressive tactics and atrocities of the GDR state. There was even a lawsuit filed against Haußmann claiming insult against victims of state oppression. Since this opening volley of criticism German film scholars have offered a more balanced perspective on the film.[4] They have argued that it does not attempt to present a realistic portrayal of that life, but rather a performative spectacle. In stark contrast to films that lay claim to historical accuracy, such as *Das Leben der Anderen* (*The Lives of Others*, 2006), *Sonnenallee* steers away from passing judgment on the GDR. Rather it invites the viewer to evaluate critically the nostalgic (or *ostalgic*) remembering of GDR life that had become so widespread in the ten years since the fall of the Berlin Wall. But in doing so, Haußmann's film also counters the distorted Western perspective that focused on the GDR's authoritarian state, political corruption, and lagging economic output while ignoring everyday life.

As it cleverly satirizes the West's clichéd depiction of East Germans as malformed victims of an oppressive socialist regime, *Sonnenallee* stirs emotional responses to the past that are shared by Easterners and Westerners alike. The narrative focus on fond childhood memories transcends political realities and is able to resonate with viewers from different backgrounds. The film's final voiceover, "I was young and in love," reaffirms the universal nature of the nostalgic feelings stirred by the film story. Haußmann reinforces this sense of a shared past by employing cinematic idioms familiar to the Western viewer and incorporating popular rock and roll hits of the period into the film. He combines this appeal to the cultural memory of Westerners with prominently displayed popular objects of *Ostalgie*, such as the *Multifunktionstisch* (multipurpose table) in Micha's apartment. With this admixture of GDR and Western culture in a narrative about the happy experiences of youth, *Sonnenallee* fortifies the East German's sense of identity in the cultural context of unified Germany and normalizes views of life in the GDR. To the extent that the film resonates in this way with a broad audience of both Easterners and Westerners it points the way to a collective German memory in postunification Germany.

In 2003 the even more widely popular *Ostalgie* hit *Good Bye Lenin!* emulated *Sonnenallee*'s approach but to a much different ideological purpose with respect to the East-West divide. Made by the West German director Wolfgang Becker, who coauthored the script with Bernd Lichtenberg, also a West German, *Good Bye Lenin!* displays prominently many of the products and lifestyles popular among *Ostalgie* enthusiasts. The film works various aspects of everyday GDR culture — consumer goods, household furnishings, fashion design, television shows, youth clubs, government institutions — into a narrative in which its East German characters find the resiliency to withstand the post-*Wende* colonization by the Federal Republic. Like *Sonnenallee*, Becker's film invites the West German to share vicariously in the East Germans' nostalgic look back at their life in the GDR. But while Haußmann and Brussig's film helped East Germans carve out a new cultural identity in postunification Germany, the Westerner's identification with *Ostalgie* in *Good Bye Lenin!* serves to shore up a West German strategy for incorporating German history into a construct of national identity in the Federal Republic. This may have been one key element of the film's success. Becker's film was a major international hit, playing successfully in seventy countries and easily outdrawing other recent international hits *Nirgendwo in Afrika* (*Nowhere in Africa*, 2001) and *Lola rennt* (*Run Lola Run*, 1998). *Sonnenallee*, by contrast, had limited distribution outside Germany and has not been released as a DVD in the United States.

Despite all the attention to the process of "coming to terms with the [National Socialist] past" in the Federal Republic, the feeling of normalization that took hold after unification was still rooted in an incomplete confrontation with aspects of the nation's more recent history. As long as Germany had remained divided, this "provisional" arrangement enabled both sides to defer a comprehensive accounting of the past until national unity was complete. Each side could conveniently project the failure to come to terms with fascism onto the other. And only when the other half was pulled back into the fold could final redress occur. However, when the stasis of divided Germany ended, the total hegemony of the West enabled it to maintain its own one-sided narrative of national history. The West Germans' ability to fill in for their incomplete reckoning with the national past with a vilified history of East Germany remained largely intact.[5]

This construct was challenged by the success of *Sonnenallee*. Haußmann and Brussig's movie engaged Western viewers in the East German negotiation of their own self-critical narrative about life in East Germany and their nostalgia for it. *Good Bye Lenin!* instead offers the Western response to this cinematic deployment of *Ostalgie*. The film does not attempt to reverse the tide of positive feelings about everyday life in the GDR. Rather it invokes them to create a subtle allegorical account of unification that suggests all these positive experiences will now find their true home in the unified Federal Republic.

Good Bye Lenin! effectively employs material objects and consumer goods to tap into the emotional force of *Ostalgie*. Its strategy for constructing an alternative narrative draws primarily, however, on another, less tangible aspect of life in the GDR. At the heart of its positive depiction is the tendency of many East Germans to withdraw into private life with an intimate circle of friends and family, what became commonly known as the *Nischengesellschaft* (niche society). The nostalgic sense of community invoked in *Good Bye Lenin!* offers a postindustrial utopian vision that can be shared by all in the present-day context of unified Germany. The turning back of the clock to the crucial period of transition from divided to unified Germany enables both Easterners and Westerners to participate in an imaginary escape from a competitive free-market economy that promotes the continuous, spiraling growth of production and consumption as an end in itself.[6] This imaginary escape shelters the West from the GDR critique of West German society that had been swept away with the *Wende* but that threatened to resurface when more positive views of life in the GDR began to gain validity. In this regard the Western validation of *Ostalgie* in *Good Bye Lenin!* also serves as a hedge against confronting the Federal Republic's burdensome past more broadly. It diverts attention from the need to confront a debt of history that had been deferred while Germans awaited reunification, but then was simply wiped off the ledger of the Federal Republic and shifted over to that of a defunct GDR.[7]

See also:

- 2 February 1988: Last Generation of DEFA Directors Calls in Vain for Reform

- 23 July 1991: ZDF Broadcast of *Ostkreuz* Initiates Darker Reckoning with the *Wende*
- 25 February 2007: *Das Leben der Anderen* Follows Blueprint for Foreign-Language Oscar Success

Notes

[1] Thomas Elsaesser, *The BFI Companion to German Cinema* (London: British Film Institute, 1999), 14.

[2] See Werner Früh, *Ostdeutschland im Fernsehen* (Munich: Kopäd 1999).

[3] "*Sonnenallee* — Eine Mauerkomödie: Interview mit Leander Haußmann und Thomas Brussig, geführt von Sandra Maischberger," in *Sonnenallee: Das Buch zum Farbfilm*, ed. Leander Haußmann (Berlin: Quadriga, 1999), 22.

[4] For early defenders of the film, see Helen Cafferty, "*Sonnenallee*: Taking Comedy Seriously in Unified Germany," in *Textual Responses to German Unification: Processing Historical and Social Change in Literature and Film*, ed. Carol Anne Costabile-Heming, Rachel J. Halverson, and Kristie A. Foell (Berlin: de Gruyter, 2001), 253–71; and Paul Cooke, "Performing 'Ostalgie': Leander Haußmann's *Sonnenallee*," *German Life and Letters*, 56, no. 2 (April 2003): 156–67.

[5] See Roger F. Cook, "Re-charting the Skies above Berlin: Nostalgia East and West," *German Politics and Society* (Spring 2005): 39–59.

[6] See Roger F. Cook, "*Good Bye Lenin!*: Free-Market Nostalgia for Socialist Consumerism," *Seminar: A Journal of Germanic Studies*. Special Issue. Between Historization, Nostalgia and Mythmaking: Contemporary German Culture Looking back at the Two Germanies (Spring 2007): 25–42.

[7] See Dominic Boyer, "*Ostalgie* and the Politics of the Future in Eastern Germany," *Public Culture* 18, no. 2 (2006): 361–81.

10 August 1994: One Month after Founding of X-Filme, Filmboard Berlin-Brandenburg Paves Way for New Productions in the Capital

Brigitta B. Wagner

A publicity still for Lola rennt *(1998), starring Franka Potente and the city of Berlin. Credit: Deutsche Kinemathek.*

GERMAN UNIFICATION REQUIRED a broad reassessment not only of the country's "national image," but also of those "moving images" of it that would circulate at home and abroad. In particular, new films set in Berlin had the potential to represent the emerging, symbolic architectures of post–Cold War urban development, the process of East-West integration, and the unique social and cultural milieu of the city's all-German youth. 1994 was a crucial year for the alliance of urban and cinematic location politics (*Standortpolitik*). It marked not only the founding, in August, of the regional Filmboard Berlin-Brandenburg GmbH, which linked the concerns of all-German film subsidy within and beyond the city; in July, it also saw the establishment of the Berlin-based production company X-Filme Creative Pool, the boutique firm that produced three of the major Berlin hits of the post-Wall era: *Das Leben ist eine Baustelle* (*Life Is All You Get*, 1997), *Lola rennt* (*Run Lola Run*, 1998), and *Good Bye Lenin!* (2003). At a time when the German film industry and Berlin's planners, marketers, and cultural politicians were in need of new impulses, the converging interests of location-based film funding, urban marketing, and film production created opportune conditions for reimagining and *reimaging* Berlin cinematically.

In 1991, after the German Parliament's decision to establish the united capital in Berlin, that city of controversial monarchical, Weimar, National Socialist, and Cold War pasts became synonymous with projections of urban futures. As construction, preservation, and reconstruction projects promised to create architecture and skylines appropriate to the 1999 relocation of the government from Bonn to the "New" Berlin, the regional film industry was working to assure Berlin-Brandenburg's leading role in the national media landscape. When the statutes of the old (West) Berlin Film Funding Board (Berliner Filmförderung, BFF) expired at the end of 1993, it was clear that the BFF's successor, the Filmboard Berlin-Brandenburg, would not only have to create a new, integrated regional identity within existing film-industrial geographies (with strong competition, for example, from Bavaria and North Rhine-Westphalia) but also have to establish new funding criteria to ensure that films made in the region would reflect well on the service location. The Filmboard's notion of a successful film was thus, from the outset, one that would help to recruit new productions to Berlin-Brandenburg.

In the wake of popular discontent with the auteurist enterprise of New German Cinema, the Filmboard's appointment of managing director Klaus Keil, a professor of production and media economics at Munich's commercially oriented University of Television and Film, signaled a shift in the region's cinematic value system. Indeed, the German film industry was beset by a number of economic considerations that challenged notions of an art cinema grounded in formal experimentation and provocation of the spectator. These included: 1) the dependence of production budgets on ever more complex requirements from state, regional, and television funding boards; 2) the need to absorb the influx of East German film professionals (primarily based in and around Berlin) and to appeal to an East-West spectatorship; 3) poor market shares at the domestic box office; and 4) the 1990s' multiplex trend and the dominance of Hollywood features. The task for the Filmboard was twofold: to manage the quality of the films it subsidized (i.e., establishing a reliable location-based product), and to ensure that these films had economic potential (understood as strong regional investment during production and high domestic ticket sales during exhibition).

At the same time, a number of producers and filmmakers born in the 1950s and 1960s were disgruntled with the difficult conditions for getting films made in Germany, the "stigmatization" of German features at the box office, and the often uncinematic quality of film-television coproductions. Later dismissed by some observers as a "post-Wall cinema of consensus" — generic fodder for masses unwilling to confront the German "self-image" — much of 1990s German popular cinema targeted domestic audiences but did not aspire to international reception.[1] In response to this stagnation of talent, producer Stefan Arndt (Sputnik Film GmbH) and filmmakers Wolfgang Becker (*Kinderspiele* [*Child's Play*], 1992), Dani Levy (*Robbykallepaul*, 1989; *I Was on Mars*, 1992), and Tom Tykwer (*Die tödliche Maria* [*Deadly Maria*], 1993) founded the Berlin-based production company X-Filme Creative Pool. Claiming a continuity with the creative business partnership of Charlie Chaplin, Douglas Fairbanks, D. W. Griffith, and Mary Pickford's United Artists, X-Filme's members espoused a production concept that combined "an ambitious independent auteur cinema" with "authentic subject matter that takes place in Germany or has something to do with Germany but can also work internationally."[2]

Though X-Filme's appeal to "quality" through a revamped auteurism might at first glance seem to diverge from Keil's insistence on the financial "success" of the films funded by the Filmboard, the two approaches functioned symbiotically throughout the decade — particularly as an advertisement for the New Berlin. Like its predecessor the BFF, which was founded in 1978 as a defensive measure to keep all branches of West Berlin's troubled film industry active, the Filmboard was intent on achieving a "regional effect" by which a production's spending in the region would exceed the amount of the subvention. Known, however, for his slogans "No more support without an audience" and "Away with indiscriminate subsidies, no more shelved films,"[3] Keil was also concerned with the start-to-finish supervision of a range of development, production, distribution, marketing, and exhibition projects that both maximized a film's chances to be seen (regardless of its budget) and connected the "quality" of the final product to the Berlin-Brandenburg brand name. From screenwriting master classes to a requirement that producers raise 30 percent of the production budget themselves, have a distribution contract in hand, and repay the Filmboard from the film's profits within five years of its release, the Filmboard fostered a preproduction and production environment that favored screenwriters, directors, and producers with a strong orientation toward the market.[4]

As a Berlin company with plans to produce "x" films (which in German signals an indefinite number) and with a common financial interest in each member's productions, X-Filme was uniquely positioned to benefit from the Filmboard's financially and geographically circular policies.

Success in Keil's system served as a guarantee of future support. If a film generated enough profit to repay the Filmboard, these funds could be used toward a new project if this film, in turn, were produced in Berlin-Brandenburg. The revolving funds of this "reference principle" (*Referenzprinzip*) thus provided producers with an incentive to expand their business ties to the region. These returning customers and beneficiaries could also take advantage of "jump-start financing" (*Anschubfinanzierung*), designed to give a limited number of established production companies a chance to develop several new projects at once.[5]

During the 1995 Berlin International Film Festival, both X-Filme and Keil had the opportunity to comment on their business models and progress in critical interviews with the left-leaning *die tageszeitung*. Despite Levy's critique of a German film culture obsessed with ticket sales and Tykwer's partial defense of the legacy of Wim Wenders and Rainer Werner Fassbinder, the partners of X-Filme were quick to echo Klaus Keil's rhetoric when asked what they desired most from film subsidy boards, producers, and distributors: "We need enough money to develop films. That means that we need an understanding for development ... this is what Keil is advertising."[6] Not only was X-Filme applying for "jump-start financing" for 10–15 new projects, but the Filmboard had already cofinanced the production of Levy's *Stille Nacht* (*Silent Night*, 1996), the company's first feature, filmed at Babelsberg Studios. In Keil's general defensiveness about the Filmboard's initial preference for large-budget films, his decision to accept *Stille Nacht* (with DM 1.5 million) without a distribution contract and to support a new company of fledgling feature filmmakers served as a convenient example of the Filmboard director's flexibility and willingness to invest in the (lower-budget) oeuvres of specific artists ("Dani Levy is someone I'm betting on. He's already proven his quality.").[7] Though *Stille Nacht* sold little over 51,000 tickets, the film, which is set in Berlin and Paris, opened in the Competition of the 1996 Berlinale and thus could participate in the Filmboard's secondary category of success — a film's cultural effect — which included festival screenings and prizes. In addition, X-Filme's constant development of new projects assured the continual overlap of its films in various stages of production and exhibition throughout the 1990s.

If the ongoing collaboration between X-Filme and the Filmboard succeeded in promoting one brand through the other, it also contributed to a new catalogue of images of the German capital. Keil was quick to note Berlin's attractiveness as both a funding location and a location for shooting and also to claim that filmmakers required the "liveliness and excitement of a big city" for inspiration.[8] Beyond this concentration of talent and ideas in one place, however, the possibilities of filming in the rapidly changing city contributed to the very narratives and styles of the new regional productions.

A massive construction site in the decade following unification, Berlin's geographic center invited much speculation about the future cityscape. As print media, television, public displays, museum exhibitions, and new media applications mapped the urban spaces of the next millennium and promised the return of the city's Weimar cosmopolitanism, skeptics insisted on Berlin's inherent provincialism. In this vein, film critic Jan Gympel lamented in 1995 that the New Berlin was hardly a convincing urban locale, and that only "architecture . . . disseminated through moving images" could change the popular perception of the city. In the same year, Reinhard Hauff, the director of the German Academy for Film and Television Berlin, predicted that the conflicts of the unified city would soon begin to show in its films.[9] The importance of the cinema's contribution to the new "image" of the capital in this moment of transition should not be underestimated.

X-Filme's Berlin films — Becker's *Das Leben ist eine Baustelle* and *Good Bye Lenin!*, and Tykwer's *Lola rennt* — did not wait for a finished urban backdrop. Cowritten by Becker and Tykwer, *Das Leben ist eine Baustelle* (whose title alludes to Berlin's post-Wall construction boom) began production in November 1995 and premiered in competition at the 1997 Berlinale, where it received an Honorable Mention. Set in Berlin's historical present, the film explores the darker realities (the housing shortage, unemployment, AIDS) of a city in transition alongside the unique opportunities for self-actualization available to its younger generations. The film's love story between Jan (Jürgen Vogel) and Vera (Christiane Paul) offsets the dismal gray palette of its winter scenes, reminiscent of Cold War angst. With nearly 480,000 tickets sold during its theatrical run and distribution in several European countries, *Das Leben ist eine Baustelle* found an audience worthy of the Filmboard's investment of DM 500,000.[10]

Following the disappointing ticket sales of Tykwer's alpine thriller, *Winterschläfer* (*Winter Sleepers*, 1997), *Lola rennt* was a project that could be developed quickly and locally in order to secure "the survival" of X-Filme.[11] Its iconic central characters, Lola (Franka Potente) and Manni (Moritz Bleibtreu), countdown structure (the pair has three chances to produce DM 100,000 in twenty minutes), techno soundtrack, and virtuoso use of new digital editing technology imagined a "New Cinematic Berlin": a city of youth, dynamism, and forward motion. Running past sites evocative of the German past as well as the debris of new construction, Lola reinterprets the city's profilmic space for the post-Wall generation. Berlin, it would seem, might also provide the simple backdrop to an exciting kinesthetic experience. With over 2.2 million tickets sold in Germany, an international distribution deal with Sony Pictures Classics, more than $23 million in worldwide profits by the fall of 1999, and numerous awards, the film proved the successful formula of location politics, commerce, and art.[12]

In 1998, Keil proclaimed that the time had not yet come for "local stories for the global market" — those that would convey the continuing conflicts between Easterners and Westerners to the world at large.[13] By 2003, *Good Bye Lenin!*, X-Filme's tragicomic return to the events of 1989–90 and to the streets of East Berlin, was not only the highest grossing German film of the year; it also ranked third among all the films shown in Germany in 2003 after *Finding Nemo* (2003) and *The Lord of the Rings III: The Return of the King* (2003). With over 6.5 million tickets sold, a particularly large spectatorship in Berlin, a highly publicized and emotional screening for members of the Federal Assembly, and once again the international collaboration of Sony Pictures Classics, the film marketed an inclusive form of *Ostalgie* (nostalgia for the East) to local, national, and global audiences while also reintroducing the geographies of the GDR capital into the post-Wall cityscape.

By the time Keil stepped down from the Filmboard (which would reemerge as the Medienboard Berlin-Brandenburg) in 2004, the region had become a destination for countless international and domestic productions. X-Filme, which opened the distribution branch X-Verleih in 2000, was no longer a risky newcomer, but rather an internationally recognized guarantor of quality. If, in 1997, one headline expressed with skeptical surprise, "all at once, there's German film again," by 2006 another observer would muse: "There's hardly a German film these days that doesn't take place in Berlin."[14] While this emphasis on the capital region may reduce the "image" of Germany to an urban ideal or a recurring problematic that is not representative of the larger population and geography, the New Berlin has benefited from this exposure. After all, what technology can better sell a city than the cinema?

See also:

- 29 November 1923: Karl Grune's *Die Straße* Inaugurates "Street Film," Foreshadows Film Noir
- 21 June And 30 August 1957: *Jonas* and *Berlin — Ecke Schönhauser* Link Urban Reconstruction to National Cinema in Both West and East
- 25 August 1992: *Ostalgie* Provides Pushback against Western Views on the East German Collapse

Notes

[1] See Eric Rentschler, "From New German Cinema to the Post-Wall Cinema of Consensus," in *Cinema and Nation*, ed. Mette Hjort and Scott MacKenzie (London: Routledge, 2000), 260–77; and Jochen Brunow, "Bündnis für Film," in *Szenenwechsel*, ed. Michael Töteberg (Reinbek bei Hamburg: Rowohlt, 1999), 12.

[2] Stefan Arndt, quoted in X-Filme Creative Pool, "Eins, zwei, drei . . . x Filme," in *Szenenwechsel*, ed. Töteberg, 41.

[3] See, respectively, Benedikt Berg-Walz, "Die Filmboard Berlin-Brandenburg GmbH," in *Visuelle Politik*, ed. Wilhelm Hofmann (Baden-Baden: Nomos, 1998), 51; and Christiane Peitz, "Im Jahr des Produzenten," *die tageszeitung* (9 February 1995), 16.

[4] Dirk Lüneberg, *Filmförderung in Berlin & Brandenburg* (Berlin: Rubikon Verlag, 1999), 72–77. It should be noted that the repayment requirement ends five years after a film's premiere.

[5] Ibid., 71, 77.

[6] Christiane Peitz, "Filmemachen ist ein Hindernislauf," *die tageszeitung* (16 February 1995), 16–17.

[7] Peitz, "Im Jahr," 16.

[8] Ibid., 17.

[9] Jan Gympel, "Berlin — kein Schauplatz mehr für Filme?" in *Hauptstadt Berlin*, ed. Werner Süß, vol. 2 (Berlin: Berlin Verlag, 1995), 596; and Eric Hansen, "Berlin's Generation X," *Variety* (22–28 May 1995): 49.

[10] Lüneberg, *Filmförderung*, 86.

[11] See *Lola rennt* press kit (1998), 32, in Mappe 26631, Schriftgut, Deutsche Kinemathek.

[12] Liza Foreman, "X-Filme Eyes Distrib: *Run Lola Run* Producer Looking to Expand," *Daily Variety* (20 October 1999), 5.

[13] Klaus Keil quoted in Rolf Lautenschläger, "Geld und Erfolg für die Filme aus Berlin," *tageszeitung* (14 December 1998), 23.

[14] "Auf einmal gibt es wieder deutschen Film," *Frankfurter Allgemeine Sonntagszeitung* (6 July 1997); and Kai Ritzmann, "Good Bye, Fernsehturm!" *Welt Kompakt* (30 May 2006).

2 November 1995: *Neurosia* Embodies Seventy-Five Years of Queer Film History

Randall Halle

AT A PREMIER OF Rosa von Praunheim's latest film, as he is welcoming the audience with boastful remarks about the greatness of his films, a shot rings out and Rosa collapses. The murderer is able to flee without a trace, but in the following scene the trash-television investigative reporter Gesine Ganzman-Seipel (Désirée Nick) is assigned to shed some light on this assassination and perhaps find the gunman. She sets out to review Praunheim and his films from start to "finish." Thus begins Rosa von Praunheim's film *Neurosia: 50 Jahre Pervers* (*Neurosia: 50 Years of Perversion*, 1994). Designed as self-homage at age 50, the film offers a review of von Praunheim's oeuvre. While it may seem atypical in its form — relying on parody and self-satire — this critical self-persiflage actually takes up various strategies of production from his earlier films: underground, cult, low-budget, trash, camp, no-holds barred provocation, in your face politics, rebellious outing, and experimental engagements with popular culture. Moreover, against the broader backdrop of German film history, *Neurosia* reveals how von Praunheim's radical filmwork emerged out of a cinema landscape that has offered so many historical firsts: the first homosexual emancipation film, the first positive representation of lesbian desire, the first nude scene, the *Hosenrolle* genre of cross-dressing farces, and so on.[1] Yet the film does not simply recall this list, rather it shows that von Praunheim has extended it. Film historians Helga Belach and Wolfgang Jacobsen even credit von Praunheim with having reestablished an open public discourse around nonheteronormative sexualities that had existed in the Weimar Republic and were subsequently destroyed by the Third Reich.[2] If *Neurosia*'s narrative might parody such a claim, the overall film lends it credence.

Rosa von Praunheim was born Holger Radtke in 1942 in Riga in occupied Latvia, and grew up as Holger Mischwitzky in Frankfurt. As a young artist in the mid-1960s he took on the name Rosa von Praunheim, an indication of an early commitment to political provocation and scandal: Praunheim from the area of the city in which he grew up, and "Rosa" (pink) to commemorate the pink triangle that the Nazis forced homosexuals to wear. In 1967 Rosa produced his first film, *Von Rosa von Praunheim*. His early work relied on a form of operatic filming, miming, the display of emotion, tormented figures, full frontal and provocative nudity, and shock as confrontation with bourgeois morality that was more in line with the likes of Jack Smith, Andy Warhol, or Werner Schroeter than with the narrative form of "Papas Kino" (as mainstream cinema of the fifties and sixties was dismissively dubbed) or even with his own contemporaries in the emergent Young German Cinema. With a turn to narrative in his first feature-length film, *Die Bettwurst* (1971), von Praunheim achieved the status of cult director, a German John Waters.

The independent trash and camp narrative style developed in *Bettwurst* extended into von Praunheim's next film, *Nicht der Homosexuelle ist pervers, sondern die Situation in der er lebt* (*It Is Not the Homosexual Who Is Perverse, But the Society in Which He Lives*, 1971). The film tells a kind of gay *Bildungsroman* story of Daniel, a young man from the countryside who arrives in Berlin and begins to explore the various aspects of the gay scene. He loses his innocence and naïveté and descends ever more into a kind of sex addiction, requiring increasing perversions to excite him. In the end, however, he meets the members of a radical gay-rights commune, who enlighten him about the cause of his condition and politicize him to get "out of the toilet and into the street." The provocation of this *Schwulenfilm* (queer film) unleashed a scandal throughout Germany and the response effectively resulted in the kind of discursive shift that the film's final sequence promoted: a new radical gay-political emancipation movement.

If we accept that a strong historical knowledge offers the foundation to von Praunheim's work, *Neurosia* indicates at least three approaches to the past in his body of work. Early on in his documentaries, there is a sort of monumental revolutionary relation taken to the immediate past. Along with *Nicht der Homosexuelle*, documentaries about gay politics in the United States — such as *Armee der Liebenden* (*Army of Lovers*, 1979) or the later three-part documentary *AIDS-Trilogie* (*AIDS Trilogy*, 1990) — used recent history to steer and guide future action. Then, starting in 1992, he took up an antiquarian-archival approach to history. With *Ich bin meine eigene Frau* (*I Am My Own Woman*, 1992), *Schwuler Mut: 100 Jahre Schwulenbewegung* (*Gay Courage: 100 Years of the Gay Movement*, 1998), and *Der Einstein des Sex: Leben und Werk des Dr. Hirschfeld* (*The Einstein of Sex: Life and Work of Dr. M. Hirschfeld*, 1999), von Praunheim produced three of the most cogent docudramas to represent a century of sexual history. In their construction of narratives of transformation and development, these films give hope but not explicit political direction. Finally, we might identify a kind of critical transformative use of the past. *Horror Vacui* (1984), *Anita — Tänze des Lasters* (*Anita: Dances of Vice*, 1987), and *Affengeil*

(*Life is like a Cucumber*, 1990) develop Weimar expressionist aesthetics to make them useful for critical interventions in the present.

For a director whose work has been central to gay politics, *Neurosia* does not present von Praunheim as (only) a gay director. Critical-historical assessments of von Praunheim run into an immediate difficulty, confronting the questions of how to identify him and how to position his work. Part of this difficulty derives from the fact that gay directors who emerged after the premiere of *Nicht der Homosexuelle* predominantly made films that represented successful individual coming-out stories.[3] On the general market and especially among gay audiences, affirmation and positive role models dominated the political-aesthetic agenda; as a result, less historically important films by minor directors have had a longer market life than many of von Praunheim's works. It was not until the 1990s, within the rise of New Queer Cinema, that a rebellion took place against the "positive image aesthetic."[4] From the start, von Praunheim was one who eschewed positive images of characters with whom audiences could have an easy identification. In his second film, *Rosa Arbeiter* (Red Workers, 1968), Rainer Kranich, whose skin bears extensive burn scars, plays a boy who is the object of a woman's (Carla Aulaulu) desire. Both are naked together on a bed but Kranich's burn scars disrupt easy erotic investments in this scene. Central to his strategy of provocation, von Praunheim has generally played up negative and unsympathetic aspects of his characters: his self-portrayal in *Neurosia,* the Anita Berber figure in *Anita,* the entire class of homosexuals in *Nicht der Homosexuelle,* or even AIDS sufferers in *Ein Virus kennt keine Moral* (*A Virus Knows no Morals,* 1985).

In his classic work on gay and lesbian film studies, Richard Dyer makes an important distinction between films containing images of gay and lesbian people and films that are "from and for the movement."[5] He places works by von Praunheim like *Schwestern, Nicht der Homosexuelle,* and *Armee* as clearly at the core of a movement, locating Richard Oswald's Weimar film *Anders als die Andern* (*Different from the Others,* 1919) in contradistinction to these, as work that existed outside of a movement. Dyer argues that even the key shots of the great sexual reformer Magnus Hirschfeld in *Anders als die Andern* "addressing a meeting . . . are only moments in a conventional feature film that neither deals directly with the gay movement nor declares itself to be part of it" (Dyer, 211). Such a distinction proves problematic, because it extends a discourse of gay identity and subjectivity back onto an earlier period in which no Gay Liberation movement existed, let alone a population operating politically or socially in a mode of gay identity. In failing to distinguish between a Weimar discourse of homosexual emancipation and a 1970s discourse of gay liberation, Dyer fails to take into account how both films actually generated movement. They produced images and conveyed a discourse that was radically tangential to the existing debates within the public sphere.

A better distinction would be to acknowledge both films, *Anders als die Anderen* and *Nicht der Homosexuelle*, as films at once from and for a movement, and then to question the nature of the movement in which they participate. Indeed the significant differences between the two make clear the differences between the Homosexual Emancipation and Gay Liberation movements. While the 1919 film contained the first open and positive representations of homosexuals, it was directed at a heterosexual audience, offering enlightenment and pleading for tolerance. Praunheim's 1971 film was viewed by a broad audience but its goal was to motivate gay action and to depict same-sex desire as an agent for liberation that exceeded the individual. Von Praunheim's film broke with the homophile quest for acceptance that infused Oswald's work and that characterized the preceding half-century of homosexual emancipation, and instead it instigated a rebellion that propelled a new discourse of gay pride. Dyer describes the qualities of the new movement as "demonstrations and sit-ins, storming and disrupting meetings and conferences, sabotage and mainly symbolic terrorism [that] went hand in hand with a readiness for, and often an insistence on, analysis and theory" (Dyer, 215). Such qualities had nothing to do with the Homosexual Emancipation movement; it was quite literally unthinkable, outside the discourse of the period.

I want to return to the observation above, however, that both films within their respective historical moments offer representations that are tangential to or at odds with existing debates, because this is what the retrospective *Neurosia* can set in relief. Oswald and von Praunheim have each in their own right performed what we could describe as a queer discursive shift in the public sphere. While the Habermasian notion of the public sphere is based on a notion of debate resulting in consensus between two relatively equal sides, it is important to note that social movements around groups like the gay, lesbian, transgendered, or S/M communities do not engage in sexual and gender politics on a terrain of equals.[6] Like *Anders,* all of von Praunheim's films have emerged out of existing subcultures. These films have made their interventions in social arrangements by offering new images that transform the image of the subculture both within the dominant society and the subculture itself. The strength of von Praunheim's work over Oswald's, and ultimately the success of the gay and subsequent sexual liberation movements, was that it empowered people to a radical advocacy for their own interests that went beyond tolerance and ultimately beyond social movements as well.

Given that such an astute film critic and historian as Richard Dyer exhibits a propensity to extend gay discourse back onto an earlier understanding of sexuality, we should recognize how especially difficult this act of projection is to avoid. Praunheim offers a good test case, because identitarian labels do not stick to the director with any ease. Von Praunheim's career has not remained focused on gay politics; rather he has participated in and produced new significant movements around the question of sexuality. Film history must not force one discursive paradigm onto a previous era, and this is especially important when it comes to questions of gender and sexuality. In von Praunheim's case, he has made both gay and transgendered films, and yet it is difficult to designate him as a gay or a transgendered filmmaker. As a survey of his work, *Neurosia* is a visual act of film *and* sexual-political history. On a metalevel it attests not only to von Praunheim's central position in discursive transformations, but also to the ongoing shifts in the representation of same-sex desire, gender transgression, and sexual diversity.

See also:

- 16 March 1925: *Wege zu Kraft und Schönheit* Educates Audiences in the Art of Nudity
- 31 January 1929: Limits on Racial Border-Crossing Exposed in *Piccadilly*
- 22 October 2005: Winner of Hessian Film Award *Fremde Haut* Queers Dual Binaries of Sexual and National Identity

Notes

[1] See James Steakley, *"Anders als die Andern": Ein Film und seine Geschichte* (Hamburg: Männerschwarm, 2007); Alice Kuzniar, *The Queer German Cinema* (Stanford: Stanford UP, 2000); Heide Schlüpmann, *"Ich möchte kein Mann sein*: Ernst Lubitsch, Sigmund Freud und die frühe deutsche Komödie," *KINtop. Jahrbuch zur Erforschung des frühen Films* 1 (1993): 75–93; Wolfgang Theis, "Tanten, Tunten, Kesse Väter: 100 Jahre Travestie im Film," in *Rundbrief Film: Filme in lesbisch-schwulem Kontext* 3 (Dec 95/Jan 96): 187–90.

[2] Helga Belach and Wolfgang Jacobsen, *"Anders als die Andern* (1919); Dokumente zu einer Kontroverse," *Richard Oswald: Regisseur und Produzent* (Munich: Text und Kritik, 1990).

[3] See Les Wright, "The Genre Cycle of German Gay Coming-Out Films, 1970–1994," in *Queering the Canon: Defying Sights in German Literature and Culture*, ed. Christoph Lorey and John L. Plews (Rochester: Camden House, 1998): 311–40; and James W. Jones, "History and Homosexuality in Frank Ripploh's *Taxi to the Toilet*," also in *Queering the Canon*, 340–50.

[4] For a critical discussion of positive image aesthetics, see Martha Gever, Pratibha Parmar, and John Greyson, eds., *Queer Looks: Perspectives on Lesbian and Gay Film and Video* (New York: Routledge, 1993). For New Queer Cinema, see Michele Aaron, ed., *New Queer Cinema: A Critical Reader* (New Brunswick, NJ: Rutgers UP, 2004).

[5] Richard Dyer, *Now You See It: Studies in Lesbian and Gay Film* (New York: Routledge, 2001), 211. Hereafter cited in text.

[6] Jürgen Habermas, *The Structural Transformation of the Public Sphere: An Inquiry into a Category of Bourgeois Society* (Cambridge, MA: MIT Press, 1989). For an extended critique along these lines, see Nancy Fraser, *Rethinking the Public Sphere: A Contribution to the Critique of Actually Existing Democracy, Habermas and the Public Sphere* (Cambridge, MA: MIT Press, 1992).

31 December 1995: *Der bewegte Mann* Sells 6.5 Million Tickets to Mark Peak of New German Comedy

David N. Coury

IN 1994, SÖNKE WORTMANN'S comedy *Der bewegte Mann* (*Maybe, Maybe Not*) became the highest grossing German film and one of the ten highest grossing films of the year. After decades of low domestic box-office receipts, German cinema had finally produced a commercial success that could rival a Hollywood film in its popularity. By the close of 1995, *Der bewegte Mann* had sold 6.5 million tickets, making it one of the top domestic films of all time, and its success resulted in a wave of comedies — dubbed by critics the New German Comedy — unprecedented since the Weimar and NS period. While not always critically successful, these films contributed to the move toward what Stuart Taberner has termed the "normalization" of Germany in the post-Wall era. Taberner argues that the cultural production of the 1990s highlighted the "'ahistorical normality' of globalized consumerism."[1] Taberner traces this phenomenon in literary works and cultural debates in the 1990s, but it is equally present in the post-Wall cinema of that decade as well. While German film of the 1970s and 1980s was characterized by its self-critical nature, historical awareness, and critique of materialism, these new film comedies were modeled on the dominant Hollywood cinema with its finance system, its stable of popular stars (Katja Riemann, Til Schweiger, Jürgen Vogel) and directors (Wortmann, Detlev Buck, Rainer Kaufmann), and a transnational and globalized system of funding and production. Thematically, the New German Comedy echoed many of the preoccupations of the pop literature that arose in the 1990s, which focused on the fetishization of market capitalism and the lifestyles of young urban professionals who blossomed during the salad days of the New Economy. Together these young writers and directors worked toward creating a new iteration of German cultural production that collectively embraced Germany's renewed place on the globalized cultural stage and imagined a nation that was neither burdened by nor obsessed with the work of *Vergangenheitsbewältigung* that had been the signature of the postwar New German Cinema.

While the romantic comedy was a mainstay of German cinema during the Weimar Republic and even during the Third Reich, German national cinema after the Second World War was identified (at least internationally) by its exploration of specific German questions and themes — namely, the collective guilt of the Holocaust, the postwar division of Germany, and the quest for national identity. In particular, the Young German Cinema of the 1960s and the more successful New German Cinema of the 1970s and 1980s came to be synonymous not only with German national cinema, but also with postwar European art-house cinema. After the fall of the Berlin Wall in 1989 and the subsequent unification of East and West Germany, many cultural critics anticipated a resurgence of introspective films that would delve into the historical significance of united Germany and its place within the European Union. But renowned filmmakers of the New German Cinema — such as Wim Wenders and Volker Schlöndorff — initially failed to transform the *Autorenfilm* of the previous decades into a vehicle for exploring the realities of the post-Wall German society. Instead, a new generation of filmmakers rose to prominence, who like Wortmann were graduates of the same film schools as the New German filmmakers, yet began making works that were stylistically and narratologically modeled less on the *Autorenfilm* than on Hollywood cinema, and that shared Hollywood's interest in romance, economic success, and happy endings over politics and history. These comedies portrayed young Germans struggling to find happiness and success in a milieu that resonated with young urban professionals there. The Germany depicted in these romantic comedies was not one burdened by the past or trying to come to terms with its unique history (as so often portrayed in the films of R. W. Fassbinder or Wenders). Rather, the social issues reflected in these situational comedies were similar to those found in other West European societies — economic prosperity, generational and social conflicts, the search for fulfilling personal relationships — suggesting that post-Wall Germany had attained a level of normalcy, at least as reflected in its cultural production, comparable to that of most of its neighbors.

In many ways, then, these films constituted a rejection of the New German Cinema and in the process gave voice to a younger generation of filmmakers. While the origins of this new wave of comedies can be traced to Doris Dörrie's groundbreaking film comedies of the 1980s (in particular her enormously successful film *Männer* [*Men*], 1985), it was not until the 1990s that the new film comedies came into their own. In fact, many of these productions owe their success to pop culture and the comics upon which they were based, reflecting an embrace of such culture and the mixed visual media of music and television, rather than the older traditions rooted in classic literature or the European avant-garde. Rötger Feldmann's *Werner* comics, for instance, were the inspiration for some of the highest-grossing German films in the 1990s, while Ralf König's popular comics helped propel the success of *Der bewegte Mann*. Not only were these films made by a generation born after the counterculture movements of the 1960s, but they were clearly pitched to their peers, who grew up immersed in American-style mass culture. In an article from 2000, Eric Rentschler criticized this new wave of German filmmakers, arguing that they ignored many of the nation's social problems and political debates. These contemporary productions, he argued, "studiously and systematically skirt the 'large' topics and hot issues: the messy complications of post-Wall reality, thematics like right-wing radicalism, chronic unemployment, or the uneasy integration of the former GDR into the Federal Republic."[2] As a result, Rentschler termed this mainstream cinema of the 1990s a "cinema of consensus," in which filmmakers sought to transform cinema into a "site of mass diversion" instead of maintaining it as "a moral institution or a political forum."[3]

At the heart of his critique, one shared by many others, was a lament over the end of the *Autorenfilm* and the death of the European art film. Critics were torn between rejoicing in the revitalization of German cinema and denouncing what most saw as the commercialization of the German film industry. Gone were low budgets and small teams of filmmakers and actors making socially relevant films — in their place were wealthy producers, transnational distributors, and the cultivation of a "star" system concerned more with profit than social change. On the other hand, Andreas Kilb, who first coined the term New German Comedy in an influential 1996 article in *Die Zeit*, argued that the most successful of these films — Katja von Garnier's *Abgeschminkt* (*Making Up!*, 1993), Wortmann's *Der bewegte Mann*, and Rainer Kaufmann's *Stadtgespräch* (*Talk of the Town*, 1995) — had little to do with the classic production comedies of the past, but in fact could be considered *Autorenfilme*: "small, independently developed subjects, mostly produced for television and almost without exception blessed and subsidized by the federal film board."[4] The only difference, he notes, between these films and the classic art-house film is that the former are successful. Other critics were less kind in their assessment and labeled the genre the worst since the end of *Heimat* films. By the turn of the millennium in 2000, Helma Sanders-Brahms, one of the leading female voices of the New German Cinema, went so far as to declare that German cinema was a wasteland that no longer functioned. In particular she bemoaned the lack of cooperation between successive generations of filmmakers, maintaining instead that there lacked continuity from one generation to the next as younger filmmakers rejected all previous bodies of work.

What exactly was being rejected, and how that came to affect German cinematic identity, has been the subject of numerous studies in recent years. Early analyses of these films pointed to structural and narratological differences, whereby the reliance on features of the dominant narrative cinema — linear story lines, causality, and happy ends — separated them from the more traditional *Autorenfilme*. Other sociological studies have focused on the romantic relationships that are common in most of the comedies, with some scholars positing that these films represented a shift from the political *Frauenfilme* to more traditional heterosexual comedies that may or may not represent liberation from patriarchal society. What is clear is that the majority of these romantic comedies in the 1990s are rather conservative in their gender politics, not least in their propensity to employ gay characters, as Randall Halle has observed, to facilitate heterosexual couplings and thus bring about a "happy end."[5] This is particularly true in the case of *Der bewegte Mann*. The film's story revolves around Axel (Til Schweiger), a serial philanderer whose girlfriend Doro (Katja Riemann) finally throws him out of her apartment after he is caught cheating. Axel then moves in with a shy gay man, Norbert, and begins to question his own lifestyle. When Doro finds out that she is pregnant, she tries to lure Axel back, unsure whether he will stay with Norbert and his friends or finally embrace his responsibility as a parent and become a faithful partner. Despite the fact that — or perhaps precisely because — the film's humor relies extensively on homophobic and sexist stereotypes, it was enormously successful. What is striking about the film is that a short five years after unification, there is no mention either of the growing divide between the former East and West regions of Germany, nor any reference to history or Germany's past. Moreover, despite taking place in Cologne, one of Germany's largest and most diverse cities, all of the characters are from the dominant culture. Even the street scenes feature few if any minorities or any reference to the urban and socioeconomic problems that were commonplace at the time. In many ways, this film could have just as easily taken place in California as in Germany, and perhaps for this reason the American video release was dubbed instead of having the usual subtitles expected for most foreign films, thereby underscoring the transnational appeal of this romantic comedy.

Much has been written about the young protagonists of the New Comedies and their roles and positions in the media-based New Economy of that decade. These young, attractive stars not only fulfill the desire for normalcy, but also fulfill the desire of the average cinemagoer to take part in the success and wealth of the New Economy. As Jan-Christopher Horak noted: "At a time when all moral values are fluctuating and even German unification failed to bring about the desired peace of mind, the romantic comedies offer the certainty that life will go on well, even if the problems are simply covered with bandages."[6] In this way, Wortmann's film struck a chord with many Germans who were perhaps seeking both escapism as well as a new pride in the economic and political success of a unified Germany.

The success of *Der bewegte Mann* came at the peak of the comedy boom in the 1990s. Kilb speculated that these directors would either grow up and grow out of the genre, or else move to Hollywood to begin making big-budget blockbusters. While the latter did not happen, the former did, prompted in many ways by the events of September 11 and the subsequent collapse of the New Economy, which led most of these directors to sober up to the realities of the twenty-first century. Although the situation comedies continued into the first decade of the new millennium — Til Schweiger's 2007 hit *Keinohrhasen* (*Rabbit Without Ears*) being the most notable example — they also began to at least acknowledge (if not explore) the social and economic problems that faced most Germans of the period. Comedies like Wolfgang Becker's *Good Bye Lenin!* (2003) and Dani Levy's *Alles auf Zucker* (*Go for Zucker*, 2004) owe much to the comedy wave of the 1990s, even as both explore important social (German-Jewish relations) and political (*Ostalgie*) themes in contemporary Germany. Perhaps the most lasting legacy of the comedy wave was that it brought particularly young Germans back into the cinema to see domestic films, giving German cinema a new respectability among the so-called "Generation Golf."

See also:

- Spring 1911: At Munich's Frankfurter Hof a Comedy Team Is Born
- 21 January 1914: Premiere of *Die Firma heiratet* Inaugurates Fashion Farce
- 21 October 2001: Television Provides Platform for Record Box-Office Success of *Der Schuh des Manitu*

Notes

[1] Stuart Taberner, *German Literature of the 1990s and Beyond: Normalization and the Berlin Republic* (Rochester, NY: Camden House, 2005), 81.

[2] Eric Rentschler, "From New German Cinema to the Post-Wall Cinema of Consensus," in *Cinema and Nation*, ed. Mette Hjort and Scott MacKenzie (London: Routledge, 2000), 260–77.

[3] Ibid., 262, 264.

[4] Andreas Kilb, "Ein allerletzter Versuch, die neue deutsche Filmkomödie zu verstehen," *Die Zeit* 18 (26 April 1996): n.p. Accessed 20 May 2009 online.

[5] See Randall Halle, "'Happy Ends' to Crises of Heterosexual Desire: Toward a Social Psychology of Recent German Comedies," *Camera Obscura* 15, no. 2 (2000): 1–39.

[6] Jan-Christopher Horak, "Die Tradition des deutschen Films," in *Der bewegte Film: Aufbruch zu neuen deutschen Erfolgen*, ed. Heike Amend and Michael Bütow, 13–24. (Berlin: VISTAS Verlag, 1997), 13–24; here 23.

10 February 1999: Berlinale Premiere of Four Turkish-German Films Signals New Chapter in Cinematic Diversity

Andrea Reimann

THE COLLECTIVE APPEARANCE in the late 1990s of a body of films about Turkish youth growing up in urban post-Wall Germany, written and directed by members of Germany's Turkish immigrant population, not only signaled a return of socially and politically aware filmmaking, but was also the beginning of a hyphenated German cinema that marks the cultural diversity of contemporary Germany. The shift toward the theme of multiculturalism meant an explicit shift toward transnational cinema, one that also signified a break with the narrow perception of German postwar cinema as a "special case" within Western cinema — one that is locked in the reworking of national history — and thus offered a chance to place postwar German film within the broader context of global postcolonial structures.

The breakthrough of Turkish-German film production was made possible by several factors, including the presence of a new generation of filmmakers, a changing political climate, the state of the German film industry, and the German media. During the 1990s, several writer/directors with Turkish backgrounds worked on autobiographically inflected projects that dealt with the lives of second-generation Turks in urban Germany. They were encouraged and supported by independent producers (most notably the Berlin-based company, zero film, and the Hamburg-based Wüste Film) and programs in German public television — especially ZDF (Zweites Deutsches Fernsehen, Germany's second public television station), whose "das kleine Fernsehspiel" (the small television play) feature slot, first created in the 1970s as a forum for new filmmakers addressing contemporary issues, has since emerged as a main player in the support and financing of the German *Autorenfilm*.

The timing of the production and exhibition was a defining factor in the creation of the Turkish-German wave, as the films premiered at a key moment both in terms of politics and film production. At the 1999 Berlinale, audiences could see premieres of Fatih Akın's *Kurz und schmerzlos* (*Short Sharp Shock*, 1998), Thomas Arslan's *Dealer* (1999), and Yüksel

Yavuz's *Aprilkinder* (*April Children*, 1998). Alongside these screened a related fourth film, *Lola + Bilidikid* (*Lola and Billy the Kid*, 1998), which centers on the lives of a group of Turks living in Germany, although its creator, writer/director Kutlug Ataman, hails from Turkey, received his training in Paris and Los Angeles, and did not conceive the film from within the context of post-Wall Germany. The films were highly topical, appearing simultaneously with the peak of debates about German immigration politics, which centered on issues like proposed changes to citizenship laws, dual citizenship, and the concept of a German *Leitkultur* (guiding culture). As such, these films signaled an engagement with contemporary social and political realities similar to the kind of "new realism" that emerged in 1990s French cinema, which included a considerable number of *beur* and *banlieue* films.[1]

The Turkish-German films drew particular attention for the ways in which they seemed to break with the practices of mainstream post-Wall German feature-film production, which generally shunned historical and political issues, and aimed to please its audiences with mostly shallow entertainment — in the words of Eric Rentschler, a "cinema of consensus."[2] Granted, experimental film production in West and East Germany flourished during the 1980s — as Randall Halle and Reinhild Steingröver demonstrate with their recent anthology — and even in narrative filmmaking there were significant exceptions (e.g., the films by Ulrike Ottinger, Harun Farocki, Jan Schütte, Michael Klier, Monika Treut, Andreas Dresen, and Hans-Christian Schmid).[3] But overall, German film production had reached a low point in the 1990s, particularly compared to the previous international artistic acclaim of the New German Cinema of the 1960s to the 1980s, and to the national and international success that German film has had since the new millennium. Accordingly, the four Berlinale premieres sent positive waves through the German media. Critic Tunçay Kulaoğlu even surmised: "The [long-awaited] New German Cinema is Turkish."[4]

German cinema is no exception to the collaborative and transnational trajectory of global film. However, up until the 1990s films that dealt with the topic of ethnic minorities in Germany were made predominantly by film auteurs who did not share the migration background of their characters: Rainer Werner Fassbinder's *Katzelmacher* (1969) and *Angst essen Seele auf* (*Ali: Fear Eats the Soul*, 1973), Helma Sanders-Brahms's *Shirins Hochzeit* (*Shirin's Wedding*, 1976), and Hark Bohm's *Yasemin* (1988). There were some exceptions, including Tevfik Baser's *40 m2 Deutschland* (*40 m2 Germany*, 1986) and *Abschied vom falschen Paradies* (*Farewell to a False Paradise*, 1988). Moreover it is possible to state broadly that the majority of films that preceded the 1990s wave represented members of ethnic minority groups for the most part as single figures and marginalized victims of German xenophobia, rather than as people who can speak for themselves.

In the realm of politics, ethnic minorities lacked their own representatives as well: they were represented by German *Ausländerbeauftragte* (commissioners for foreigners). Germany's "guest-workers" had been the subject of national debates since the 1970s, had formed a considerable number of associations, and had contributed a wealth of *Gastarbeiterliteratur* (guest-worker literature) in the 1970s and 1980s that engaged with the social exclusion of guest-workers in Germany and their longing for their home countries. These efforts notwithstanding, though, immigrants did not achieve official political representation until the 1990s. Hence, the Turkish-German filmmakers had to cope with the burden of representation not only in the artistic sense but also, however informally, in the political sense.

In view of the stage that ethnic minority representation had reached by the late 1990s, the simultaneous appearance of a group of films that flagged ethnic *and* cultural difference constituted a milestone in German film history. These filmmakers and their films signaled that minorities in Germany were no longer a marginal phenomenon that could be subsumed by a few stereotypes, but rather a central one that consisted of multifaced groups. In fact, a salient feature of the films that premiered in the late 1990s is the diversity with which they represent the Turkish diaspora in Germany. For example, Akın's *Kurz und schmerzlos* features a range of Turkish, Serbian, Greek, and Albanian characters, including tolerant Turkish parents as well as a Turkish sister who co-owns a business with a German friend. Yüksel Yavuz's *Aprilkinder* tells the story of a young Kurdish Turk who lives with his parents and siblings, falls in love with a German prostitute, and finally opts for an arranged marriage with a Kurdish cousin. The characters in Kutlug Ataman's *Lola + Bilidikid* include a young gay Turk, his mother, his gay brother and his macho boyfriend, and a gay Turkish hustler who falls in love with the son of an elderly aristocratic German woman. These first-wave hyphenated German films are also notable for their refusal to tell an "integration story." Their plots evolve around male protagonists who reject victimization and actively struggle to make sense of their hyphenated identities, but they are not centrally preoccupied with becoming "properly integrated" members of German society. These writer/directors may be criticized for reversing the victim/perpetrator paradigm by reinforcing the media stereotype of the criminal, violent male foreigner and — by centering their stories around young men — for reducing important questions of immigrant subjectivity and identity to problematic concepts of male subjectivity and identity. But these low-budget productions were nevertheless pathbreaking insofar as they helped lay the groundwork for a multiethnic German cinema that depicts members of Germany's immigrant generations as permanent residents and/or citizens who demand recognition of their cultural difference.

Scholars have noted the shift from the margins to the center, and from cultural resistance against the national majority to a transnational orientation in recent Turkish-German film. This shift follows the global trend in postcolonial "accented cinema" (Hamid Naficy's umbrella term for mostly independent films about exile and diaspora).[5] Considering the representation of "new ethnicity" (a category that Stuart Hall created in the 1980s for the then-new phase of Black representation, which focused on the politics of representation and on diversity within a given minority group) in transnational comparison helps to illuminate more clearly the significance of similarly accented films within recent German film history.[6] Namely, they beg the question of how German national film fits in the larger discourses on colonial and postcolonial identity and recognition — a question further complicated by prevailing accounts of German postwar immigration and postwar cinema, and by the relative inattention granted by postcolonial theory to the German colonial experience.

Germany's refusal to present itself officially as a country of immigration until the end of the past century has been the subject of countless debates. However, public discussions of the problems related to immigration generally date the arrival of migrant workers in the late 1950s, thus omitting historical perspective on Germany's long tradition of recruiting foreign labor.[7] While postwar labor immigration from Mediterranean countries was not directly related to colonial (in)dependence, it nevertheless bears traces of the colonial logic of Imperial Germany's politics of work migration. This notwithstanding, the theme of colonial interdependence in West Germany's policy of labor migration has not been addressed in detail. A similar blind-spot can be observed in standard accounts of German postwar cinema — and most notably the periods of the Young and New German Cinema from the 1960s to 1980s, a time that was marked by the collapse of the official structures of European colonialism. As German film scholar John Davidson writes, New German Cinema, with its focus on the reworking of the national past, relied on a narrow and problematic concept of postwar German identity that postulated German difference within the West so as to reintegrate Germany into the West — thus resolidifying, rather than interrogating, Eurocentrism.[8]

Optimally, recent hyphenated German cinema continues to stimulate the ongoing transnational revision of German film history that addresses precisely the larger connections between German film and postcolonial struggles for recognition. In addition to Fatih Akın's acclaimed work, some smaller films have also been made since the new millennium that offer evidence of a maturation that has generated new perspectives, especially in terms of gender — for example, Yüksel Yavuz's *Kleine Freiheit* (*A Little Bit of Freedom*, 2003), Ayşe Polat's *En Garde* (2004), and Buket Alakus's *Eine andere Liga* (*In Another League*, 2005). While these small films may not suffice to disrupt the more dominant strains of earlier works, they do point toward a continued process of opening in contemporary German cinema, one that makes possible greater inclusiveness and multiplicity.

See also:

- 30 June 1970: A Faltering Berlinale Founders on *o.k.* Controversy
- 14 February 2004: Golden Bear for *Gegen die Wand* Affirms Fatih Akın as Germany's Preeminent Transnational Director
- 22 October 2005: Winner of Hessian Film Award *Fremde Haut* Queers Dual Binaries of Sexual and National Identity

Notes

[1] Phil Powrie, *French Cinema in the 1990s: Continuity and Difference* (New York: Oxford UP, 1999).

[2] Eric Rentschler, "From New German Cinema to the Post-Wall Cinema of Consensus," in *Cinema and Nation*, ed. Mette Hjort and Scott MacKenzie (New York: Routledge, 2000), 260–77.

[3] Randall Halle and Reinhild Steingröver, eds., *After the Avant-Garde: Contemporary German and Austrian Experimental Film* (Rochester, NY: Camden House, 2008).

[4] Tunçay Kulaoğlu, "Der neue 'deutsche' Film ist 'türkisch'?: Eine neue Generation bringt Leben in die Filmlandschaft," *Filmforum* (February/March 1999): 8–11.

[5] Hamid Naficy, *An Accented Cinema* (New Jersey: Princeton UP, 2001).

[6] Stuart Hall, "New Ethnicities," in *Stuart Hall: Critical Dialogues in Cultural Studies*, ed. Kuan-Hsing Chen and David Morley (New York: Routledge, 1996), 441–49.

[7] See Klaus Bade, *Vom Auswanderungsland zum Einwanderungsland: Deutschland 1880–1980* (Berlin: Colloquium, 1983); Kien Nghi Ha, "Die kolonialen Muster deutscher Arbeitsmigration," in *Spricht die subalterne Deutsch? Migration und postkoloniale Kritik*, ed. Hito Steyerl and Encarnacion Gutierrez-Rodriguez (Münster: Unrast-Verlag, 2003), 56–107; Ulrich Herbert, *A History of Foreign Labor in Germany, 1880–1980*, trans. William Templer (Ann Arbor: U of Michigan P, 1990).

[8] John E. Davidson, *Deterritorializing the New German Cinema* (Minneapolis: U of Minnesota P, 1999).

30 April 1999: Werner Herzog's "Minnesota Declaration" Performs Critique of Documentary Cinema

Eric Ames

ON 30 APRIL 1999, Werner Herzog visited the Walker Art Center in Minneapolis, Minnesota, for a public dialogue with American film critic Roger Ebert. After they had both been introduced, Herzog walked alone to center stage of the museum's theater and addressed the audience of more than three hundred people:

> Ladies and Gentlemen, before we start this dialogue, I would like to make a statement. It is something that I have reflected upon for many years in the frustration of seeing so many documentary films. When you look at television you probably have experienced a similar frustration. There's something ultimately and deeply wrong about the concept of what constitutes fact and what constitutes truth in documentaries in particular. And very recently, traveling around a lot, I was jetlagged, woke up a couple of times during the night, tried to switch on television — and it was all bad. Between 3:00 and 3:15 in the morning in Sicily, I wrote down quickly a manifesto, which I would like to read to you. I would like to call it the Minnesota Declaration.

The audience responded with laughter and applause, effectively setting the tone for Herzog, who went on to declaim the twelve-point manifesto, which is subtitled "Lessons of Darkness."[1] Here is the key point: "5. There are deeper strata of truth in cinema, and there is such a thing as poetic, ecstatic truth. It is mysterious and elusive, and can be reached only through fabrication and imagination and stylization." Whereas Herzog introduced the manifesto with a mix of narrative (one sleepless night in Sicily), exposition (generalizations about documentary cinema), and humor (emphatic seriousness), he concluded by dramatically claiming a minority position for himself, involving the audience in his performance, and soliciting their assent: "Ladies and Gentlemen, I've never had a majority on my side throughout my life. I wish you to adopt this as the Minnesota Declaration by acclamation." Cheers followed applause when, on Herzog's cue, theater ushers handed out signed copies of the manifesto "as a souvenir of this evening," which had only just begun.[2]

The turn of the twenty-first century marked a period in which the German-born director, long known for his "visionary classics" such as *Aguirre, der Zorn Gottes* (*Aguirre, the Wrath of God*, 1972) and *Fitzcarraldo* (1982), had been working intensively and primarily in the documentary mode. Some commentators interpreted this moment in terms of the filmmaker's decline and drift into irrelevance — an interpretation that says a great deal about the prejudice against documentaries in favor of narrative features, but very little (if anything) about Herzog or his work. In retrospect, however, the Minnesota Declaration obtains new significance. For one thing, it announces Herzog's bid for continued relevance in a rapidly changing media landscape. For another, it marks a period of redefinition for documentary cinema. Today, most scholars of documentary emphasize its status as a "blurred genre," in the sense that its boundaries are shifting and unstable. Issues of stylization, once regarded as extrinsic to documentary, are now regarded as intrinsic.[3] That Herzog was a principal harbinger of this development has only been acknowledged in recent years. Earlier, his penchant for staging and stylization had all but disqualified him from serious consideration by scholars of documentary; his work is nowhere discussed in standard histories of the genre. And yet, in 2008, he received the International Documentary Association's career achievement award, which recognized both the extent of his output and its decisive impact on the genre's evolution. That same year, *Encounters at the End of the World* (2007) was nominated for an Academy Award (another first for Herzog) in the category of best documentary. Finally, the Minnesota Declaration has certain implications for our historical understanding of German cinema. And what it suggests is the wide-scale diffusion (and unforeseen consequence) of the critical and innovative engagement with documentary that characterized the work of many young German filmmakers after Oberhausen.[4] However idiosyncratic his films may be, Herzog extends this engagement beyond the New German Cinema and into the present situation, which is increasingly discussed in terms of transnational cinema, media convergence, and the proliferation of hybrid forms.

Herzog's contemporary relevance is predicated on his work in documentary both despite and precisely because of his outspoken aversion to this tradition. Paradoxically, the resulting films suggest that documentary is for Herzog a repudiated mode of filmmaking in which he all the more actively intervenes and creatively participates. The Minnesota Declaration provides discursive back-up for this critical intervention in the form of a manifesto. Intentionally or not, its theatrical declamation also foregrounds the role of performance, which is absolutely central to his intervention. The effect can be as provocative as it is paradoxical. Herzog's documentaries are often scripted, staged, even blatantly theatrical, but they are also unscripted, improvised, and boldly exploratory. In some instances — *Die große Ekstase des Bildschnitzers Steiner* (*The Great Ecstasy of Woodcarver Steiner*, 1973), *La Soufrière* (1977), *Mein liebster Feind* (*My Best Fiend*, 1999), *The White Diamond* (2004), *Grizzly Man* (2005), and *Encounters at the End of the World* — Herzog literally acts out the role of a star director making a documentary film.

The Minnesota Declaration relies on a similar mix of scripting and performance, as do all manifestos, and indeed this is precisely what makes them powerful as means of intervention. Most manifestos also condemn the past, the commercial, and the superficial, while advocating an idealistic quest for truth that has no illusions. The manifesto is a genre the form of which exceeds its content, by definition. Herzog is obviously aware of the manifesto as a genre that has a history of its own. With its stage setting and mix of polemic and buffoonery, the Minnesota Declaration recalls so many manifestos of the historical avant-garde. For historians of German film, it brings to mind the role of manifestos and declarations in the emergence of New German Cinema, beginning with the Oberhausen Manifesto of 1962. In contrast to that document, however, the Minnesota Declaration has only one signature; it neither speaks for other filmmakers nor seeks to articulate a collective identity. Nevertheless, it still constructs a binary opposition between "us" and "them," aligning film audiences with Herzog in opposition to certain other filmmakers, who are unceremoniously lumped together and characterized as naïve fools.

Herzog's nemesis has a pretentious-sounding name, which practically invites opposition: *cinéma vérité*. By this term he means not the French movement of the 1950s associated with Jean Rouch (whose work he admires), but rather a mode of observational filmmaking known in the 1960s as "direct cinema," epitomized by the work of Robert Drew, Richard Leacock, the Maysles Brothers, D. A. Pennebaker, and Fred Wiseman. Enacting their own break with the past, these American filmmakers rejected then-standard methods of planning, scripting, staging, lighting, reenactment, and interviewing. Instead, they formulated an observational ideal that relied on an unobtrusive filmmaker and an active suppression of style. Their bold claims to truth were based on the "uncontrolled" nature of the resulting footage. Since the early 1960s, their epistemological claims have been vigorously attacked by numerous filmmakers — including Herzog. What follows in the Minnesota Declaration, then, is a polemical act of renaming. Speaking from a position of authority, he widens the scope of the term *cinéma vérité* and brings it into the present. With Herzog, *cinéma vérité* becomes a catchphrase for the default mode of documentary at large and its institutional status as a branch of journalism. This is the dominant order that the Minnesota Declaration challenges and seeks to change. What conventional documentaries call truth, Herzog would expose as mere fact; what conventional documentaries posit as "the real," "the authentic," and "the sober," Herzog counters with "the possible," "the staged," and "the ecstatic." Indeed, the very techniques of scripting, staging, interviewing, and reenactment that were once standard practice, and that proponents of direct cinema had rejected, Herzog would reinvent as insurgent. Rather than abolish these historical conventions of documentary, Herzog employs and pushes them to new extremes. The Walker performance was more than just "a rant against *cinéma vérité*."[5] It was also an occasion to promote his own approach to documentary, by enacting it on stage before an audience of admirers.

In many ways, Herzog's delivery of the manifesto corresponds to his staging of documentary film. The audience in each context is implicated in a process of testing generic conventions and the expectations they create. The numbering of theses, for example, is a rhetorical move designed to grab the audience's attention, while creating the impression of seriousness, practicality, and precision. The theses that follow, however, almost immediately digress into aphorism, exhortation, and absurd metaphysical conceit. The topic of discussion likewise ranges from filmmaking to "Life" and "the Universe." Instead of drawing on historical sources of power for manifesto writers (such as apocalyptic revelation or Enlightenment philosophy), Herzog trades on his authority as a filmmaker, while employing a mix of humor and gravitas to draw viewers into the orbit of his subjective vision. "There is something that we should work on," he states in the dialogue with Ebert, rallying the audience around the idea that film conveys various forms of imaginative knowledge. "And that's why the gauntlet is thrown down," he says, referring to point nine of the declaration. "That's why I go into such wild rambling statements like, '11. We ought to be grateful that the Universe out there knows no smile.' It has nothing to do with truth and fact in cinema, and yet it is connected, because there is a poetic truth." Here, as in his documentaries, Herzog's performance hinges on the act of making truth claims. Although such claims have historically served to distinguish documentary as a film genre, his are emphatically unorthodox truths.

The point can be made more explicit by comparison with the Dogma 95 manifesto, another intertext for the Minnesota Declaration.[6] Written and signed by Danish filmmakers Lars von Trier and Thomas Vinterberg, the Dogma 95 manifesto condemned the worldwide influence of Hollywood aesthetics and proposed a radical alternative. The "Vow of Chastity," as it was called, entailed a set of aesthetic rules — indeed, ten commandments — for directors to follow and voluntarily impose as self-restraints: "1. Shooting must be done on location . . . 2. The sound must never be produced apart from the images or vice versa . . . 3. The camera must be hand-held," and so on.[7] The sensational reception of the Dogma manifesto, the international publicity generated for its followers, and the critical attention enjoyed by their films, gave Herzog several reasons to stage his own version of a manifesto. Significantly, however, instead of designing a set of self-restraints and taking a vow of chastity, Herzog commits himself to the very project of stylistic excess that he had been pursuing for decades. Rather than outline an agenda for future work by other filmmakers, the Minnesota Declaration reflects and promotes his established practice. Like errant Dogma filmmakers, Herzog clearly revels in the public ritual of "confessing," admitting to what he deems a virtue (and not a sin). Regarding a staged scene from *Little Dieter Needs to Fly* (1997), Herzog had this to say at the Walker: "I have confessed to more educated audiences, and I will do it again.... Yes, it is a lie, it is a fabrication, it is forgery, but for the sake of a much deeper truth."

Since then, the Minnesota Declaration has enjoyed an extraordinary afterlife. Like other notable manifestos, it has been printed, circulated, and anthologized. In an interesting twist, however, part of this declaration, which is based on Herzog's previous work, would later be converted "back" into a film. In *Encounters at the End of the World*, his feature-length documentary filmed in Antarctica, an aging scientist named Sam Bowser contemplates the thought of making his final plunge into the subarctic sea, before "passing the ball off to the next generation" — a moment that clearly reflects Herzog's situation as a grizzled veteran filmmaker. The biologist proceeds to describe an undersea world of "horribly violent" conditions. Speaking with Herzog, whose voice can be heard off camera, Bowser rehearses almost verbatim the final point of the Minnesota Declaration, which reads: "Life in the oceans must be sheer hell. A vast, merciless hell of permanent and immediate danger. So much of a hell that during evolution some species — including man — crawled, fled onto some small continents of solid land, where the Lessons of Darkness continue." The scene is staged, the dialogue scripted but unmarked, its source unnamed. Herzog takes a point of the manifesto, one that encapsulates his characteristically grim vision of the natural world, reframes it as a point of biological fact, and puts it in the mouth of an expert witness. More than just a humorous scene that parodies the conventional use of scientific authority, it rehearses and restages a part of Herzog's own manifesto, now in the form of a documentary film.

See also:

- 28 February 1962: Oberhausen Manifesto Creates Founding Myth for New German Cinema
- 8 June 1986: Farocki's *Wie man sieht* Urges New Ways of Seeing
- 11 February 2008: Ulrike Ottinger's *Prater* Wins German Critics' Award for Best Documentary Yet Highlights the Director's Ties to Both Fiction and Nonfiction Film

Notes

[1] Part of this essay comes from my book, *Ferocious Reality: Documentary According to Werner Herzog* (Minneapolis: U of Minnesota P, 2012). The Minnesota Declaration is readily available on the filmmaker's website, wernerherzog.com.

[2] The dialogue with Ebert included a series of film clips, followed by questions from the audience. Unless otherwise noted, all quotations are my transcriptions of the event's audiotape recording (Regis Dialogue, 4/30/99, Walker Art Center). I am grateful to Dean Otto, Daniel Smith, and Jill Vuchetich at the Walker Art Center, and to Bruce Jenkins at the Art Institute of Chicago, for their assistance in reconstructing Herzog's visit.

[3] See Bill Nichols, *Blurred Boundaries: Questions of Meaning in Contemporary Culture* (Bloomington: Indiana UP, 1994).

[4] See Thomas Elsaesser, *New German Cinema: A History* (New Brunswick, NJ: Rutgers UP, 1989), 162–70.

[5] Paul Cronin, ed., *Herzog on Herzog* (London: Faber and Faber, 2002), 239.

[6] The Dogma connection stems from Herzog's acting role as the tyrannical father in Harmony Korine's *Julien Donkey-Boy* (1999), a film that was certified and promoted as "Dogma 6." Herzog discusses the Dogma manifesto in A. G. Basoli, "The Wrath of Klaus Kinski: An Interview with Werner Herzog," *Cineaste* 24, no. 4 (22 September 1999): 32–35.

[7] "Vow of Chastity," in "Appendix I: Dogma 95 Manifesto and Its Progeny," in *Purity and Provocation: Dogma 95*, ed. Mette Hjort and Scott MacKenzie (London: BFI, 2003), 199–200. The Minnesota Declaration is also anthologized here (200–201).

13 May 1999: Germany's Best Fiend, Klaus Kinski, Remembered at Cannes

Will Lehman

Klaus Kinski performs the role of Fitzcarraldo with characteristic madness. Fitzcarraldo *(1982). DVD capture.*

AT THE 1999 CANNES FILM FESTIVAL, the only German film to appear on the official program (albeit not in competition) was Werner Herzog's *Mein liebster Feind* (*My Best Fiend*), a stylized documentary and filmic eulogy to Klaus Kinski, an actor best known for his gripping performances in five of Herzog's most celebrated films. Appropriate to its year, this cinematic moment serves as an end point from which we can look back at Kinski's contribution to German and international cinema, above and beyond his work with Herzog.

Much of film scholarship champions directors as the creative geniuses behind the cinema, particularly in the case of so-called auteur filmmakers, whose air of independence tends to obfuscate the invaluable talents of the dozens, sometimes hundreds of others whose labor is fundamental to film production. Accordingly, there is a dearth of critical analysis of the performance of the actors who bring writers' and directors' ideas to life and give physical, human expression to the abstractions of the written script. This essay attempts to redress, albeit in a small way, this intellectual vacuum through an analysis of the career of Klaus Kinski, arguing that precisely his performances not only helped to invigorate postwar German national cinema, but also transgressed national and ethnic boundaries to challenge the popular notion that annihilatory ruthlessness, single-minded obsession, or even the stereotypical *Größenwahn* (delusions of grandeur) are somehow the exclusive domain of the German.

It must be noted that any discussion of German "national" characteristics, be they at the cinematic or personal levels, is fettered from the outset by the sheer impossibility of codifying what constitutes the German (or any other) nation. This problem is further complicated in the cases of Kinski and Herzog, whose original surnames (Nakszyński and Stipetić, respectively) reveal mixed German-Slavic heritage that, while relatively common in Germany, is often glossed over or simply ignored, particularly in the international press. Kinski was actually born outside Germany in the so-called "Free City of Danzig" (now Gdańsk, Poland), into a German-speaking family that only relocated to Berlin and took German citizenship in 1930. Therefore, my references to the actor's Germanness is meant as a reference to his cultural and linguistic affiliations and to the ways in which he is perceived and fancied outside of Germany, rather than as an ethnic or racial designation.

Kinski's early fame as an actor derived from his bizarre yet very successful one-man theatrical shows in the 1960s, which could fill an entire stadium with fans eager to watch him rant, curse, and hurl insults at them. By the time of his first Herzog collaboration in the early 1970s, Kinski already had an impressive filmography in which his particular talents and affinities had been established. His penchant for villainy had been demonstrated in his performances in several popular filmic adaptations of Edgar Wallace's crime novels, while his cruelty had come to the fore in *Kinder, Mütter, und ein General* (*Children, Mother, and the General*, 1955), a film that left a lasting impression on the young Werner Herzog. Kinski's talent for portraying mental instability and unpredictability was likewise underscored in *Ludwig II* (1955), where he plays the mentally disturbed brother of the eccentric Bavarian king; in Jess Franco's *Count Dracula* (1970), where he plays a deranged Renfield; and in Sergio Leone's *For a Few Dollars More* (1965), where his murderous, twitchy-faced, hunchback character makes the principle villain, El Indio, look tame by comparison. Thus, Kinski was a natural choice for the title role in Herzog's *Aguirre, der Zorn Gottes* (*Aguirre, the Wrath of God*, 1972), as a mutinous conquistador who violently and ruthlessly destroys everyone in his expedition, including himself, in an obsessive quest to find the fabled El Dorado. Kinski's performance is nothing short of terrifying, as the intense and raw physicality of his acting style reveals a barely suppressed violence in his personality that blurs any clear distinction between performer and role. Indeed, Herzog claims that Kinski nearly killed another actor at one point when the intense violence of the scene overpowered Kinski's ability to control it. There can be little doubt that it was Kinski's stellar performance as the conspicuously blond, blue-eyed Conquistador that carried his fame (and Herzog's) beyond Europe, where his typecasting as the quintessential German "bad boy" was most pervasive.

Despite Herzog's insistence that his story of Aguirre's rise and fall was in no way a veiled reference to recent German history, the films international reviews almost invariably made note of Kinski's perceived Germanness, drawing parallels that Herzog denied. In 1977, Israeli filmmaker Menachem Golan chose to cast Kinski as the real-life German terrorist and hijacker Wilfried Böse in *Entebbe: Operation Thunderbolt*, which depicts the Israeli mission to rescue the hostages from the hijacked Air France plane in Uganda. Despite the Germans' left-wing politics, Israelis viewed them as latter-day Nazis intent on murdering Jews, and Golan's selection of Klaus Kinski to portray Böse thus reflects Kinski's international image as a specifically German bogeyman.

In his next two collaborations with Kinski, Herzog sought to downplay the actor's explicit association with uncomfortable notions of Germanness, attempting instead to reconnect with the rich tradition of Weimar cinema that had seemingly been forgotten in the aftermath of the Nazi dictatorship. In 1979, *Nosferatu: Phantom der Nacht* (*Nosferatu the Vampyre*) and *Woyzeck* were both released amid much fanfare in Europe. In *Nosferatu*, a remake of F. W. Murnau's 1922 loose adaptation of Bram Stoker's *Dracula*, Kinski plays the title role of the vampire, to which he brings a heretofore unexplored pathos and even sympathy by powerfully evoking feelings of existential loneliness and unquenchable longing. Interestingly, the uncanny sympathy that Kinski is able to evoke for this character undermines Herzog's attempt to bridge the cinematic void of the Third Reich, inasmuch as Kinski's performance boldly suggests that even cold, murderous monsters are capable of human emotion — a message that inevitably resonates in disturbing ways with Germany's most recent past.

In his role as the title character in *Woyzeck*, it is again Kinski's hauntingly convincing physicality that links the film as much to questions of twentieth-century German history as it does to Büchner's 1837 text. In the opening scene, for example, the lowly soldier Woyzeck is shown being abused in various ways by his commanding officer. His movements are sudden and stiff, desperate and automatic, as if he were only responding to the tugging strings of a cruel puppeteer. Moreover, the expressions of despair on his aging face, his open mouth, oddly spaced teeth, and bulging, wildly darting eyes, reveal a character far more compelling than Büchner's text evokes on its own. Kinski's interpretation of the role even recalls Peter Lorre's performance of child murderer Hans Beckert in Fritz

Lang's *M* (1931), who, like Woyzeck, is driven by demonic voices in his head. Seen in this light, the moral implications of Woyzeck's murder of Marie are called into question, as traditional interpretations focusing on the destructive power of jealousy and the degradations of modernity are displaced by a suggestion that Woyzeck, like Beckert, is simply unable to do anything other than to "follow orders," murdering as directed by the powers that be. Kinski's performance thus opens connections to contemporary questions of the guilt of common German soldiers in the Nazi murder machine.

In *Fitzcarraldo* (1982), Herzog returns to telling a quasi-historical story of a non-German (yet nonetheless European) colonist seeking fame and fortune in the jungles of South America. This time, however, Kinski's role as the obsessive but likeable Irish entrepreneur Brian Sweeney Fitzgerald (which was originally played by Jason Robards, who had to be replaced due to sickness) is overshadowed by the raw physicality of the plot itself, which revolves around the monumental task of dragging an intact ship over a mountain, for which Herzog refused the use of special effects. This is one of the better-known Herzog/Kinski collaborations and it enjoyed a considerable budget and a healthy dose of controversy, meticulously documented in Les Blank's *Burden of Dreams*. Despite Kinski's starring role, however, the film's "Germanness" owes much more to Herzog's laboriously articulated fantasies about Bavarian-style dream chasing, typified by King Ludwig and rediscovered by a modern German filmmaker hell-bent on fulfilling his dream of getting (other people to haul) a ship over a mountain, no matter what the cost. Nonetheless, Herzog claims that the dreams that he is revealing through the film are universal: "It's not only my dreams. My belief is that these dreams are yours as well. And the only distinction between me and you is that I can articulate them." It is here that Kinski's role in the film again subverts the filmmaker's intentions by mitigating the latter's universalist assumptions. For in the now-internationally recognizable German person of the on-screen actor, Herzog's claims of universality are given a German face, which is then emphasized by Herzog's decision to retain Kinski's own heavily accented voice for the English-language version, rather than dub over it as he had done in *Aguirre*. Thus, Herzog's dream of speaking for all humanity is revealed as a specifically German fantasy.

By the time the last of the Kinski/Herzog collaborations was released in 1987, Kinski's typecasting as the definitive German badass was solidified. Thus, *Cobra Verde*, which tells the story of a petty crook and insatiable womanizer who is sent from Brazil to Africa on a hopeless mission to rescue the slave trade, was doomed even before its release to suffer an identity crisis. Kinski is utterly convincing as a raving mad man, but again his uncontrollable long blond hair and blue eyes, highlighted through constant close-up shots, make his casting as a Brazilian farmer less plausible. As in *Fitzcarraldo*, Kinski's inescapable Germanness challenges Herzog's own claims about the meaning of the film. In *Herzog on Herzog*, the director claims "*Cobra Verde* is about great fantasies and follies of the human spirit, not colonialism." Yet, specifically because of Kinski, the informed audience is unable to luxuriate obliviously in an ahistorical bath of universal truths about human nature, but is instead invited to draw parallels between this story and German colonial history in Africa.

Throughout their collaboration, Kinski's acting style and physical appearance have added an interpretive level on which Herzog's films become legible as veiled commentaries on twentieth-century German themes that the filmmaker himself has been reluctant to address directly. Kinski's work with other directors raises similarly interesting questions about the role of actors in confirming and challenging assumptions about national identity. In Tonino Ricci's *The Liberators* (1969), for example, Kinski plays an American soldier who is sentenced to death for murdering German civilians and who, after his escape, engages and kills several German soldiers before finally being killed by their replacements. In George Roy Hill's *The Little Drummer Girl* (1984), Kinski plays an Israeli Mossad agent who forcibly recruits an American actress (Diane Keaton) to help trap a Palestinian bomber, in effect reversing the role he had played in *Operation Thunderbolt* seven years earlier. Despite the seeming turnaround, however, there is some indication that Kinski's penchant for effectively portraying obsessive, single-minded determination is not misplaced here, and that his perceived Germanness actually increases his effectiveness in the role. For whereas *Operation Thunderbolt* was an explicitly anti-German (and anti-Palestinian) film in which Nazi enemies could be killed ex post facto, *The Little Drummer Girl* openly sympathizes with the Palestinian cause, which often portrays Zionism as an inherently racist, exterminationist movement not unlike Nazism. Thus, Kinski comes to represent both German and Jew, opening rich interpretive possibilities and raising questions that are normally reserved for discussions of filmmakers and their oeuvres, not of actors.

By the time Kinski died in 1991, he had been filmed in more than 150 roles, many financed and directed by non-German individuals, which accounts for the abundance of stereotypically German figures in his filmography, from the deviant doctor to the sociopathic scientist and the crazed Nazi. Not to be forgotten, however, are his roles that problematize the association of single-mindedness and obsession with specific notions of Germanness, from Mexican bandit to Turkish sultan, from bounty hunter on the American frontier to English gentleman with a nasty secret. What these roles share is their imminent proximity to madness, on which Germans certainly have no monopoly. With that in mind, it can be said that Kinski transcended the strictly national to became not just Herzog's, but Germany's and perhaps even the world's best fiend.

See also:

- 27 May 1911: Asta Nielsen Secures Unprecedented Artistic Control
- 14 February 1924: *Die Nibelungen* Premieres, Foregrounds "Germanness"
- 30 April 1999: Werner Herzog's "Minnesota Declaration" Performs Critique of Documentary Cinema

19 May 2000: With *Code Inconnu* Haneke Asserts Cinema's Centrality to Public Sphere

Monica Filimon

An awkward silence at the dinner table between Jean and his father. Code Inconnu *(2000). DVD capture.*

THE ADVENT OF CABLE and satellite television in West Germany at the end of the 1980s coincided with new CDU policies professing entertainment as *the* mission of film. As art cinema was being quietly expelled from its last stronghold — television — Alexander Kluge lamented the dominant influence of big business on the public arena of political, social, and cultural debates. He insisted that art should catalyze its audience into active involvement in public decision-making: "It is not only a question of art, but of its reception. The reception itself constitutes public life and experience."[1] Having worked in television for some time, Michael Haneke was also striving for a cinema of spectatorial engagement that forced viewers into self-reflection. "I violate spectators into autonomy," claims the filmmaker today.[2] Haneke's disturbing cinema, firmly centered on a critique of violence, has ensured his international recognition as a major European auteur, representative of the social and aesthetic interests of both the German-speaking world and postindustrial, Western society. Haneke's particular contribution to cinema is his professed faith in film as a type of shared experience of ethical potential.

Born in 1942 into an Austro-German family, Haneke grew up in Austria and studied psychology, philosophy, and theater before starting his career as a reviewer for Austrian newspapers. In the late 1960s, he was a playwright and editor for a German television station, but his stage productions in Berlin, Hamburg, Düsseldorf, and Vienna eventually propelled him into directing for television in the 1970s and 1980s. He never reached the high public exposure of New German Cinema, but Roy Grundmann suggests that Haneke's television work did contribute to the national heritage of both countries.[3]

Haneke's distinctive mark is his clinically precise, detached style intended to cut into the viewers' most intimate convictions about themselves. Dubbed "the trilogy of glaciation," his first theatrical releases — *Der siebente Kontinent* (*The Seventh Continent*, 1989), *Benny's Video* (1992), and *71 Fragmente einer Chronologie des Zufalls* (*71 Fragments of a Chronology of Chance*, 1994) — centered on contemporary Austrian society and were distributed mainly in Europe. With *Funny Games* (1997), Haneke reached out to global markets, but it was the Cannes Film Festival premiere of *Code inconnu: Récit incomplet de divers voyages* (*Code Unknown: Incomplete Tales of Several Journeys*) on 19 May 2000 that marked his breakthrough to broader worldwide audiences. Haneke's decision to make this film was motivated by his interest in the topic of immigration, but the promise of European funds and wide promotion associated with a star such as Juliette Binoche also encouraged his commitment to the project.[4] Haneke moved to France in search of more opportunities to explore his various interests and more viewers for his films.

Code inconnu, and the French productions that followed, did ensure Haneke's international recognition and triggered a reexamination of his work in relation to the preoccupations and sensibilities of the German-speaking world. He shares with his generation of German filmmakers the intention to transform cinema into an alternative public sphere open to debates about past guilt, memory, and the role of the media in reshaping the real. Like the directors of the Young German Cinema, Haneke is interested in modernist aesthetics, Brechtian effects, and a critical approach to mass media. With New German Cinema he has affinities for themes such as the disintegration of the middle-class family, generational and gender strife, and the reconfiguration of national identity. Haneke's novel mission, however, is to raise viewers' awareness of their own implication in the daily "war of carelessness and unkindness" caused by a generalized incapacity for communication in the modern world.[5] To dramatize this, one of the tropes he regularly employs is the discussion around the (family) table, a space that recalls the seventeenth-century *Tischgesellschaften* (table societies) at the root of the ideal bourgeois public sphere. In Haneke's films, "table debates" suggest the characters' inability to relate to others and to their inner selves. As a reaction against such societal numbing, violence becomes a last resort for emotion, so protagonists often hurt each other with minimal explanation.[6] Following in the footsteps of Brecht and Kluge, Haneke provokes his own "table debates" with viewers, forcing them to engage with his texts.

Code inconnu is structured as a compilation of sequences intertwining the lives of several characters; it explores themes and stylistic strategies essential to Haneke's oeuvre. Anne (Juliette Binoche), an actress, and Georges (Thierry Neuvic), a war reporter, are at an impasse as a couple. Jean (Alexandre Hamidi), Georges's brother, and his father (Josef Bierbichler), can no longer live together. Amadou (One Lu Yenke), a second-generation Malian immigrant, cannot accept a society that he perceives as still deeply suspicious of the racial and ethnic Other, while Maria (Luminita Gheorghiu), an illegal immigrant, endures daily humiliation on the Parisian streets to gather money for a new family house in Romania. While the themes of intergenerational dissension and dysfunctional couples as prerequisites for explosive violence also animated Haneke's earlier productions, *Code inconnu* adds the strife surrounding immigrants at the heart of a Europe that viewed them as a threat to national cohesion, identity, security, and privilege.

Several "table debates" in *Code inconnu* record instants of apparently inexplicable distress. Haneke's families — in *Der siebente Kontinent*, *Benny's Video*, or *Das weisse Band: Eine deutsche Kindergeschichte* (*The White Ribbon*, 2009) — tend to remain silent at dinner, their eyes wandering no further than their plates. In *Code inconnu*, nothing spectacularly violent marks Jean's return home after his attempt to "escape" to Paris. Opening with a medium shot of the father having a meager dinner alone while browsing through a newspaper, the scene depicts an awkward family moment. Jean gives no justification for his absence and the father does not ask for it. Without a word, the older man goes into a dark bathroom, ponders for a few seconds, and then hides his face away from the camera, possibly weeping.

The cause of this behavior is not immediately clear. Neglect, even brutalization of the younger generation characterized Haneke's earlier films: the rigid education of the 1950s and parental indifference in *Lemminge* (*Lemmings*, 1979), unconcerned brutality in *Der siebente Kontinent*, or self-preoccupied coldness in *Benny's Video*. Constant suppression of affect has monstrous results, such as Max's shooting spree in *71 Fragmente*, the son's possible implication in the scheme against his family in *Caché* (*Hidden*, 2005), or the murderous complicity of the children in

Das weisse Band. The repression of guilt crosses generations, whether it is historical guilt regarding the Nazi or colonial past in *Lemminge, Variation* (1983), and *Caché* respectively, or a more obscure, yet equally lethal, guilt in *Die Klavierspielerin* or *Das weisse Band*. Like the New German Cinema directors, Haneke focuses on tormented families whose past is the site of unexplored trauma and constant distrust between parents and children. In *Code inconnu*, father and son refuse to acknowledge each other's needs and desires. Silence and loneliness at the dinner table lead to suffering, encouraging viewers to speculate retrospectively on the causes and implications of such prolonged, menacing moments.

In addition to the rift between generations, Haneke also concentrates on the intense crisis of the couple as the effect of the ongoing, traumatizing tensions of modern civilization. In order to express such concerns, he often relates couples' failures to communicate to the spaces they inhabit. In *Code inconnu*, Georges and Anne rarely share the intimate space of their studio, and their "table debate" occurs, suggestively, in a supermarket, while they are busy "consuming" readily packaged goods. Anne demands Georges's involvement in her decisions and only receives it when she emotionally attacks him. Violence also characterizes private spaces: the house itself becomes the object of the parents' hate in *Der siebente Kontinent*, of rape in *Die Klavierspielerin*, or outright abuse in *Das weisse Band*. Furthermore, the director refuses any psychological insight into his characters' behavior. It is not clear why Georges acts distant or whether Anne had an abortion, as she pretends; both are equally victims and victimizers. Through them, Haneke exposes the enigmatic malaise affecting the middle class, urging his viewers to question individuals' motivations.

Racial or ethnic minorities do not fare any better than their Western counterparts. In the opening long take of *Code inconnu*, Amadou defends Maria against Jean's contemptuous gesture of throwing the remains of his snack into her lap. Fatima Naqvi suggests that this superficial coalition between minorities is formed on the basis of their shared experience of victimhood, but it does not preclude their becoming perpetrators of violence in turn.[7] Furthermore, the momentary bond between these individuals does not prevent the self-disintegration of their families. In the Malian "table debate," the children replace the adults, pushed to the side by their unyielding allegiance to tradition. Several simultaneous voices condemn, defend, or explain long-established gender roles, revealing a younger generation at odds with their parents' values. At first glance more emotionally cohesive, the Romanians endure humiliations abroad so that they may build a new life at home. Their new houses, however, are ghost-ridden, and their communities are gradually torn apart by the parents' prolonged absences and sibling rivalry for new "goods." Always on the run, they have replaced the family "table" with a circle of acquaintances gathered in abandoned buildings, which only augments their loneliness. As their failed "debates" suggest, these individuals are haunted by self-doubt, isolation, and generational trouble as much as their French counterparts.

In addition to his examination of violence, Haneke's contribution to the history of German and European film includes his critique of the media. In *Code inconnu*, the director explores the role of mass-disseminated images to create empathy with the victims. The proliferation of ghastly war photos in the news leads, as one of Georges's friends remarks, to spectators' insensitivity to the pain of others. Georges later concludes that an "ecology of images" may have a better chance to stir viewers' sympathy. Georges's second photomontage of random subway riders aggressed by his act of photographing them without their consent is doubled by his voice-over narration of his kidnapping in Kabul. This disjunction between image and sound produces what Catherine Wheatley terms "ethical spectatorship": viewers are moved not only to analyze the photos, the voice, and the traumatic experiences involved, but also to position themselves morally in relation to the act of displaying the resulting images.[8]

If Haneke's cinema reflects on contemporary anxieties as possible causes for violence, his formal treatment encourages viewers' detachment and analysis. Fragmentation, the use of long takes, and sound manipulation are the major means through which the director forces audiences' ethical positioning. *Code inconnu* brings together segments of disparate lives in order to underscore the incommunicability of daily interactions and the dearth of affect in the metropolis.[9] Brief blackouts interrupt the narrative, sometimes even in the middle of a sentence; furthermore, the still camera often truncates bodies and eliminates important actions. Long takes and the camera's visible detachment further frustrate viewers' search for immediate meaning. John David Rhodes suggests that Haneke's manipulation of sound during the long take enlarges the ethical field of each image, implicating viewers in the moral dilemmas posed by the narrative.[10] Furthermore, Naqvi notes that the absence of camera involvement mimics the generalized indifference that renders individuals invisible in the public sphere, pushing them to assault others in order to gain recognition.[11] The filmmaker declares: "I try to make the viewer feel provoked and forced to do something against what I am showing him/her."[12] Like Bresson or Antonioni, Haneke repeatedly employs complex structures, but, unlike his European counterparts, he makes spectators uncomfortable. One feels uncomfortable when Amadou and Maria are the only ones arrested by the police, or when Amadou behaves aggressively with a waiter. One is also disturbed when Anne hears the screams of a little girl and takes no action, but also when she is harassed on the subway. In searching for the source of such discomfort, viewers cannot but confront themselves.

Code inconnu occupies a central position in Haneke's work: it ensured his international recognition as an auteur and reflects his lifelong critique of violence and modernist aesthetics. The film also illustrates Haneke's specific contribution to cinema: a mix of disconcerting themes and a consistent reliance on distantiation, critical reflection, and emotional shock. Each failed "table debate" on screen represents Haneke's provocation to intense communication with his audience. In the process, film reception becomes one key practice for the ethical engagement in "public life and experience."

See also:

- 13 October 1922: Alexander Kolowrat-Krakowsky Sets Course of Austrian (Inter)National Film
- 23 December 1924: *Der letzte Mann* Explores Limits of Modern Community
- 22 December 1955: *Sissi* Trilogy Bridges Hapsburg to Hollywood through Hybrid Blend of Film Genres

Notes

[1] Stuart Liebman, "On New German Cinema, Art, Enlightenment, and the Public Sphere: An Interview with Alexander Kluge," *October* 46 (Autumn 1988): 23–59; here 41.

[2] Roy Grundmann, "Auteur de Force: Michael Haneke's 'Cinema of Glaciation,'" *Cineaste* 32, no. 2 (Spring 2007): 6–14; here 12.

[3] Roy Grundmann, "Introduction: Haneke's Anachronism," in *A Companion to Michael Haneke*, ed. Roy Grundmann (Malden, MA: Wiley-Blackwell, 2010), 1–51; here 3, 9–11.

[4] Michel Cieutat, "Entretien avec Michael Haneke," *Positif* 478 (December 2000): 25–31; here 25; Christopher Sharrett, "The World That Is Known: An Interview with Michael Haneke," in *A Companion to Michael Haneke*, 580–591; here 589.

[5] Franz Grabner, "'We Live in a Permanent State of War': An Interview with Michael Haneke," trans. James T. Koranyi, in *Fascinatingly Disturbing: Interdisciplinary Perspectives on Michael Haneke's Cinema*, ed. Alexander D. Ornella and Stefanie Knauss (Eugene, OR: Pickwick, 2010), 13–34; here 14.

[6] Fatima Naqvi explains that violence is the immediate effect of contempt, the emotional reaction to the individual's inability to gain recognition in the public sphere. Fatima Naqvi, "The Politics of Contempt and the Ecology of Images: Michael Haneke's *Code inconnu*," in *The Cosmopolitan Screen: German Cinema and the Global Imaginary, 1945 to the Present*, ed. Stephan K. Schindler and Lutz Koepnick (Ann Arbor: U of Michigan P, 2007), 235–53; here 236–38.

[7] Naqvi, "Politics of Contempt," 242–43.

[8] Catherine Wheatley, "Introduction," in *Michael Haneke's Cinema: The Ethic of the Image* (New York: Berghahn Books, 2009), 1–14; here 7.

[9] See Scott Durham, "Codes Unknown: Haneke's Serial Realism," in *On Michael Haneke*, ed. Brian Price and John David Rhodes (Detroit: Wayne State UP, 2010), 245–67; here 258.

[10] John David Rhodes, "The Spectacle of Skepticism: Haneke's Long Takes," in *On Michael Haneke*, 87–105; here 93–97.

[11] Naqvi, "Mediated Invisibility: Michael Haneke," in *The Literary and Cultural Rhetoric of Victimhood: Western Europe, 1970–2005* (New York: Palgrave Macmillan, 2007), 47–73; here 54–56.

[12] Franz Grabner, "'We Live in a Permanent State of War,'" in *Fascinatingly Disturbing*, 15.

21 October 2001: Television Provides Platform for Record Box-Office Success of *Der Schuh des Manitu*

Sebastian Heiduschke

The TV-tested humor of Abahachi and Ranger.
Der Schuh des Manitu *(2001). DVD capture.*

WHEN TELEVISION COMEDIAN Michael "Bully" Herbig released his Western spoof *Der Schuh des Manitu* (*Manitou's Shoe*) on 13 July 2001, its success surprised many. The film shot to the top of the German charts, and on 21 October 2001, surpassed the earlier mark of 8.8 million viewers held by Otto Waalkes's 1985 *Otto — Der Film* (Otto — The movie) to eventually set a domestic box office record for a German film with more than eleven million tickets sold.[1] What initially appeared to be one of many "trash comedies about the sexual frustrations of German men" proved to be an innovative way to modify the genre conventions of what Bernd Moeller has called the film comedy of the post-1968 generation, thereby creating a Hollywood-style blockbuster.[2] New to German film was the way Herbig combined conventions of the 1990s film comedy with German cultural tropes. Unlike previous comedy directors, Herbig tailored the film exclusively toward a German-speaking market by developing an ingenious way of test marketing his film: he created parodies of German-specific topics, such as Karl May's Winnetou novels, presented the results in his television comedy show *Bullyparade*, and brought the themes with the highest potential for success onto the big screen.[3]

According to numerous press interviews, Herbig modeled *Der Schuh des Manitu* after Harald Reinl's successful 1960s Winnetou film adaptations of Karl May's novels. Herbig's spoof traces the quest for hidden treasure by the dysfunctional duo Apache chief Abahachi (a combination of the onomatopoetic German *Hatschi* [sneezing] and the name of another Karl May protagonist, the half-Indian girl Apanatschi) and Ranger (Herbig's Bavarian interpretation of the well-known figure of "Lone Ranger"). They are confronted by Abahachi's homosexual twin brother Winnetouch (mocking the name Winnetou), their arch villain Santa Maria (a reference to the villain Santer from the Winnetou film adaptations and to German pop singer Roland Kaiser's 1980 hit song "Santa Maria"), the Greek tavern owner Dimitri (a popular figure in Herbig's *Bullyparade*), and Uschi (an homage to Uschi Glas, the actress who played Apanatschi in *Winnetou und das Halbblut Apanatschi* [*Half-Breed*], 1966). At first glance, the film appears to be a shallow Western parody, but the humor resonated with the majority of German cinemagoers — particularly male teenagers and young adults. The tremendous success of *Der Schuh des Manitu* thus marked a revival of the German film comedy.

In the early 1980s, West German cinema began to gradually shift away from what Ian Garwood termed the "artisanal mode of production" that characterized New German Cinema and toward a more genre-oriented, commercial cinema influenced by market demands. Perhaps because Rainer Werner Fassbinder was New German Cinema's foremost practitioner, his death in 1982 closed an era of sociocritical films. Simultaneously, there emerged a new "Hollywood connection" around German producer Bernd Eichinger, who brought an international, market-oriented perspective to German filmmaking. Eichinger relied on bestseller material and international stars for his films (Sean Connery in *The Name of the Rose*, 1986; Meryl Streep in *House of the Spirits*, 1983), while Roland Emmerich (*Independence Day*, 1996) and Wolfgang Petersen (*Air Force One*, 1997) crafted blockbuster action hits that contradicted the stereotype of the aesthetically important but commercially unviable German film. These developments were coupled with changes in federal funding schemes initiated by conservative Minister of the Interior Friedrich Zimmermann, who, in reaction to Herbert Achternbusch's allegedly blasphemous film

Das Gespenst (*The Ghost*, 1982), revised the subsidy structure to focus on more commercially oriented films.

Out of these policy changes emerged a wave of German cinema productions that included films by television comedians Otto Waalkes, Vicco von Bülow (better known as Loriot), and Dieter Hallervorden. A new form of auteur cinema also surfaced in the films of Doris Dörrie, whose productions were inspired by Hollywood's genre films yet who also paid close attention to German details, as in her film *Männer* (*Men*, 1985).[4] As Thomas Elsaesser has argued, this new style of filmmaking was a "cockily mainstream, brazenly commercial cinema that want[ed] to have no truck with the former quality label 'art cinema.'"[5] These new comedies with their German-specific stars and directors fared well with domestic audiences, pleasing them with mostly lighthearted stories and German cultural idiosyncrasies. Internationally, however, these German-centric films — termed a "cinema of consensus" by Eric Rentschler — failed to achieve the critical or popular success of New German Cinema.

The following two examples illustrate how *Der Schuh des Manitu* ventures away from the archetypical comedies in this cinema of consensus. First, Herbig's film parodies cultural tropes unique to the German film and television landscape of the 1960s and 1970s, while the *Beziehungskomödie* (comedy of relations) of the 1990s attempts to transplant universal genre characteristics of international comedies into German settings. Because of their generic character, many comedies of relations were exported and experienced modest success internationally. But understanding Herbig's film requires familiarity with the significance of the Wild West in German culture. German fascination with the Western genre began at the end of the nineteenth century with the novels of Karl May, who, although he had never visited the United States, wrote a series of novels set in the Wild West. These novels became timeless classics for generations of Germans. A number of film adaptations of May's novels in the early 1960s enjoyed tremendous success, first on the big screen, and later during continual reruns on television. West Germany's love for Karl May's main characters Winnetou and Old Shatterhand also paved the way for *Karl May Festspiele*, outdoor theater festivals that for a long time even featured the actor who played Winnetou in all films, Pierre Briece. Outside the German-speaking world, however, Karl May is largely unknown, so that while virtually any German acknowledges Winnetou as part of German culture, for non-Germans this enthrallment with the culture of American Indians is confusing.

When Herbig combined the Winnetou trope with his own affinity toward American Indian culture for the television skits, he did so not to spoof the Western genre, but to deliberately satirize a peculiarity of German culture. Common to Herbig's parodies of the German cultural tropes is also a clichéd, stereotyped treatment of sexuality, particularly homosexuality. This is true not only of the Winnetou spoof, but also other popular *Bullyparade* skits such as the homosexual crew of *Unser (T)Raumschiff* (Our dreamship/spaceship) — Herbig's take on the original *Star Trek* series, blended with one of the most watched German television series, *Das Traumschiff* (The dreamship) — which debuted in 1981 and is similar to the US series *The Love Boat*. Another audience favorite was the transformation of Ernst Marischka's highly successful film *Sissi: Schicksalsjahre einer Kaiserin* (*Sissi: The Fateful Years of the Empress*, 1957) into Herbig's *Sissi — Wechseljahre einer Kaiserin* (Sissi: menopause of an empress). Whereas the comedy of relations institutes patterns of heterosexual behavior as the norm, thus pandering to a German audience seeking affirmation of homosexuality as aberration, *Der Schuh des Manitu* satirizes variations of homosexuality, whether it be the dysfunctional buddy relationship of the blood brothers Ranger and Abahachi, or Ranger's latent homophobia that is fueled by Winnetouch's sexual innuendos.

Second, by departing from an established model of television stations acting as coproducers, Herbig redefined the already existing intermediality between German cinema and television. This film-financing procedure had previously ensured the survival of German productions in the decades following the large-scale introduction and expansion of Germany's television network in the 1950s and 1960s. As cinemas struggled to survive in a shrinking market, many smaller cinemas converted to porn theaters or were forced to close for good, while larger cinemas concentrated on lucrative Hollywood imports. In a small market that had become even more competitive and left little room for domestic productions, West Germany's network of regional public television stations offered a viable answer to directors seeking monies beyond scarce state subsidies and became producers of numerous films, including many of the German film comedies.

But Michael Herbig turned the table; he created a reciprocal model when he ingeniously utilized the popular comedy show *Bullyparade* as a platform to build a reliable fan base for his film. His presence on German television since 1997 allowed him to fine-tune his comedic model — a strategy that translated directly into the commercial success of *Der Schuh des Manitu*. When television audiences cheered boisterously once they recognized the title melody of Reinl's films in Herbig's Winnetou parodies, their reactions demonstrated in advance the popular potential of a full-length Western telling the "true story" of Winnetou. Herbig all but guaranteed the film's success before the first screening by capitalizing on a loyal audience, yet he also went further in his development of the cross-fertilization between the big screen and television. The success of the movie reverberated with his television show and increased the ratings to the highest ever. In 2002, Herbig decided to discontinue the show at the height of its success, only to launch a similar show, *Bully and Rick*, a few years later to profit even further from the synergies of television. The film continued to enjoy its popularity. Along with a merchandising campaign accompanying the film release and an award-winning website, the extended version of the film, *Der Schuh des Manitu XXL*, was released in German theaters on 11 July 2002, boosting ticket and DVD sales yet again. A musical version of the film was produced in 2009, and even today the film receives high audience ratings during television broadcasts.

Michael Herbig continued his "Bully-style" — the test-marketing of German-specific themes — in his subsequent projects. *(T)Raumschiff Surprise — Periode 1* (*Dreamship Surprise — Period 1*, 2004) won the *Bullyparade* audience vote. The runner up, the *Sissi* parody, was realized as animated film *Lissi und der wilde Kaiser* (Lissi and the wild emperor) in 2007. While his more recent *Wickie und die starken Männer* (*Vicky the Viking*, 2009, based on a 1974 Japanese animated series popular on German television) did not have a predecessor in the *Bullyparade*, Herbig once again found the means to test its big-screen potential on the small screen first by launching a talent casting show, *Bully sucht die starken Männer* (*Bully's Search for the Vikings*, 2008), to find lay actors for the project. Although public interest in Herbig's film projects has declined from *Der Schuh des Manitu* to *Lissi*, the casting show illustrates that Herbig continues his innovative approach of combining television and the big screen.

See also:

- 21 January 1914: Premiere of *Die Firma heiratet* Inaugurates Fashion Farce
- 22 January 1979: West German Broadcast of *Holocaust* Draws Critical Fire and Record Audiences
- 31 December 1995: *Der bewegte Mann* Sells 6.5 Million Tickets to Mark Peak of New German Comedy

Notes

[1] IMDB lists Wolfgang Staudte's DEFA film *Die Geschichte vom kleinen Muck* (*The Story of Little Mook*, 1953) as having more than 13 million viewers and claims 14 million viewers for *Otto — Der Film* (Otto Waalkes, 1985), including an audience of 5.7 million East Germans watching in the German Democratic Republic. Hans Deppe's *Grün ist die Heide* (*Green Is the Heath*, 1951), released before recording of such statistics, may have attracted more than twenty million viewers. Official statistics by SPIO (Executive Organization for German Film Economy) and FFA (German Federal Film Board) after 1980 were only kept for the Federal Republic of Germany and did not include the sometimes unreliable numbers from the German Democratic Republic.

² Jan-Christopher Horak, "German Film Comedy," in *The German Cinema Book*, ed. Tim Bergfelder, Erica Carter, and Deniz Göztürk (London: BFI, 2002), 29–38; here 37. Hans-Bernhard Moeller, "Zur deutschen Filmkomödie der Generation nach 1968," *Monatshefte* 93, no. 2 (2001): 196–208.

³ The Germanocentric character is probably the reason why the film flopped internationally. According to IMDB, the film grossed only €40,476 in Spain and $196,959 in Russia.

⁴ See Sabine Hake, *German National Cinema*, 2nd ed. (London: Routledge, 2008), 182.

⁵ Thomas Elsaesser, "Introduction: German Cinema in the 1990s," in *The BFI Companion to German Cinema*, ed. Elsaesser (London: BFI, 1999), 3–16; here 3.

16 October 2003: Chancellor Gerhard Schröder Sheds Tears — Again — at Premiere of *Das Wunder von Bern*

Cornelius Partsch

THE ASCENSION OF THE Social Democratic-Green coalition government in 1998 marked the arrival of the so-called '68ers at the heart of the political establishment and the consummation of what was regarded by some as a "second founding" based upon the values of that generation. Chancellor Gerhard Schröder proclaimed that the time for "normality" regarding Germany's view of its past had arrived, introducing a supposed "new uninhibitedness" into the discourse of the New Left. The phrase implied a reluctance to be restrained by memories of Nazi crimes and a confidence that there would be no return to the chauvinistic nationalism of old.[1] In a parallel development, the socioeconomic and political realities of the postunification era rendered problematic the issue of continuity with the liberal values and the stability that were seen as legacies of West Germany's "history of success." West Germans began to suspect that the disorienting developments they had observed in the East would soon affect them as well. To many, the World Trade Center attacks reinforced this creeping sense of loss and displacement and brought about a crisis in German-American relations and the dissolution of a Western "value consensus." The term "westalgia" came to be incorporated into discussions about national identity. Consisting of a mournful preoccupation with West Germanness, westalgic narratives served to forge a sense of community out of a rosy reinvention of the pre-1990 FRG while expressing a refusal to identify with the transformations necessitated by unification, Europeanization, and globalization.

Sönke Wortmann's *Das Wunder von Bern* (*The Miracle of Bern*, 2003) stood not only as a prominent example of a newly flourishing, often autobiographical engagement with the 1950s, but also as part of a wave of publications timed to coincide with the fiftieth anniversary of the 1954 World Cup. In this context, the film about West Germany's unexpected victory over Hungary in Bern was a key work of the westalgic imagination. Focusing on the formative years of the FRG held the advantage of predating the escalation of the Cold War embodied by the Berlin Wall and the traumatic upheavals of the 1960s and 1970s. Fully cognizant of the game's privileged place in German collective memory, Wortmann set out to make a Hollywood-style sports film about a triumphant underdog and to contribute unabashedly to the game's transfiguration into a West German Fourth of July. The build-up to the film's theatrical release on 16 October 2003 featured comprehensive merchandising and public relations campaigns that utilized many of the key actors and included tearful farewells for two deceased heroes of Bern, Fritz Walter (d. 17 June 2002) and Helmut Rahn (d. 13 August 2003). Wortmann maintained that 4 July 1954 and 9 November 1989 were the only postwar dates most Germans remembered vividly as moments of patriotic pride. He added that the soccer victory provided "an encouraging counter-image to the Third Reich" and that a central message he hoped the film would convey to audiences was a disposition for reconciliation with the war generation.

When Gerhard Schröder confessed to being moved to tears during a private screening in August 2003, and then again during the film's public premiere two months later, the film finally became annointed as an officially sanctioned work of memory. Like many politicians before him, Schröder sought out the company of legendary soccer figures and aligned himself eagerly with the admissible brand of patriotism afforded by the remembrance of 1954. After the old Wankdorf Stadium was razed in 2001 to make room for a more modern facility, he declared it a national memorial to be listed alongside the Berlin Wall and Weimar.[2] This statement speaks to the close connection between soccer and national sensibilities that constituted a further dimension of the film's reception. Since the 1950s, West Germany's unforgettable World Cup matches have often involved neighboring countries where memories of the war made for explosive subplots accompanying the sport. Some of these encounters are still known by distinctive epithets such as "game of the century" (a controversial loss to England in 1966), "game of the systems" (an embarrassing defeat at the hands of the GDR in 1974), "water battle of Frankfurt" (a 1974 victory over Poland), "shame of Córdoba" (a 1978 loss to Austria), and "non-aggression pact of Gijón" (a questionable 1982 victory over Austria). In addition, *Das Wunder von Bern* allowed viewers to return to an imagined golden age of amateurism, a time before the star culture and the commercialization that have characterized soccer in unified Germany and have had an especially detrimental impact on the teams from the East.

Central to the film's westalgic status is its positioning of the GDR as a reference culture in its construction of a foundation myth for West Germany and, by extension, its negotiation of the apparently contradictory purposes of installing a nostalgically inflected West German particularity and appealing to a postunification audience. Set primarily in Essen, the film unfolds the story of the fractured Lubanski family, whose patriarch has been held captive in Soviet labor camps since the end of the war. Young Matthias Lubanski idolizes local soccer star Rahn as a surrogate for his missing father. The film's other plot lines are set in Munich, featuring a humorous account of a young journalist and his progressive-minded wife, and in Switzerland, tracing the soccer team's progress under the leadership of coach Sepp Herberger. *Das Wunder von Bern* opens with the three lines that also grace the film's publicity poster: "Every child needs a father. Every human being needs a dream. Every country needs a legend." In establishing a linkage between the personal and the national, these dicta framing the film's reception indicate that the personages may be taken as psychological, generational, and social types.

The character who most embodies ideological difference and acts as a divisive agent at the family level is seventeen-year-old Bruno Lubanski. Bruno, whose interests do not include soccer, is the oldest male in the house because of his father's absence. He repeatedly violates two of the film's central motifs: work as a means to establishing identity, and the avoidance of politics in any discussion of the past. At the outset, this prototypical postwar family lives in a working-class neighborhood, where the streets and houses are blackened by soot, and tries to make ends meet. Bruno informs his mother Christa that he did not respond to a job announcement for political reasons: "I won't work for a man who supported the Nazis." His mother's request that he help out in the pub she has been running since her husband's deployment to the eastern front is met with similar obstinacy. After Richard Lubanski's return from captivity has been announced, the family is shown waiting anxiously at the local train station. Bruno takes issue with his mother's speculation of what "The Russian" might have done to Richard, stating the unwelcome truth that Nazi Germany had attacked the Soviet Union and been soundly defeated. The traumatized father's return provides cause for numerous confrontations with his wife and children, as Richard objects to Bruno's lifestyle, the American pop music he plays with his band, and his political convictions, labeling his son a "loud-mouth with communist nonsense in his head." The conflict escalates after it comes to light that Richard killed Matthias's pet rabbit in order to provide a festive meal for his family. Bruno not only accuses his father of having a fascistic mentality but also denigrates his father's suffering, earning himself a hard slap in the face. Still, the film depicts Bruno as a likeable, compassionate character deeply concerned for his family's welfare.

Exactly at the halfway mark of the film, Bruno leaves his family under cover of night. He entrusts a farewell letter to Matthias and explains his decision to go to East Berlin: "All men are equal over there . . . and everyone is allowed to speak freely." In contrast to Bruno's prior political insight, his opinions about the GDR are shown as highly naïve projections of a desired alternative to West Germany. The reaction to his disappearance, presumably a cataclysmic event in the Lubanski family, is strangely subdued, and the narrative shifts swiftly to the development of Matthias and Richard's reconciliation. The divisions in the family begin to heal immediately after Bruno's departure, and the success story is allowed to run its course. Having obtained spiritual advice from his priest, Richard is next seen juggling a ball and guiding it into an empty goal with a scissor kick, a difficult and dangerous maneuver. This moment, filmed in slow motion for dramatic effect, rekindles Richard's self-confidence and enables him to overcome his insistence on paternal authority and discipline. He begins to open up to Matthias about his years as a prisoner and his suffering — without mentioning the war itself — and then decides to realize his son's dream by taking him to Bern, where Matthias will eventually witness Rahn's late, magical goal to break the tie with Hungary. The film recalls Bruno to memory in a brief shot showing him, clad in the uniform of the Free German Youth, listening to the radio broadcast of the final. Two days later, Matthias and Richard manage to sneak onto the special train transporting the victorious soccer team back to Germany. A meeting of the two father figures takes place, with Rahn generously ceding the territory to Richard: "Looks as if we have to thank you for the victory." Father and son enjoy a moment of familial bliss when Matthias hands over Bruno's letter. Overwhelmed, Richard bursts into tears: "He writes that we can visit him any time." Parallel to the nation's triumphant rediscovery of a common identity, the scene marks the restitution of Richard's masculinity, the healing of his war trauma, and his reintegration into the social fabric of the FRG.[3]

According to the three layers of signification outlined earlier, *Das Wunder von Bern* charts a movement toward a miraculous climax, a moving coming-of-age-story in which the personal and the national are crisscrossed in a web of symbolic meaning. The film adds to its West German story the figure of Bruno as a means of addressing the issue of German division. Bruno is drawn as an idealist who rebels against the dominant work ethic underlying the Economic Miracle. As an outspoken proponent of a critical reckoning with the past, he is the only character in the film equipped with a political outlook and thus serves as a precursor to the generational conflict of the 1960s. By dismembering the family through Bruno's emigration, the film forms a window in time in which the West German success story can unfold without obstruction in the family and without confronting the Nazi past.[4] The rejoining of Bruno and the family is only approximated through the placement of the letter. At the end, while the train heads off into a glorious sunset, Bruno, and with him the GDR, remain outside of the frame, as distant relatives who have extended a standing invitation. Having introduced the GDR as a reference culture, the film performs a double removal, first from its main narrative and later, when it is brought back as quotation, as a visual absence. The establishment of a West German particularity necessitated by the film's nostalgic mode entails a retrospective distancing from the reference culture that stops short of reuniting the family and the nation, but the film's competing strategies of exclusion and inclusion also speak to its status as a commercial product. *Das Wunder von Bern*, which did in fact achieve box-office success in Germany, may be viewed as an engagement with the FRG past imbued with resentment toward an externally imposed postunification order. West German experience is valorized as a means of making sense of the present while this restored past is, at the same time, implicated as the norm against which the present has transgressed. As the final image appears to indulge in the restitution of an untainted *Heimat*, referring perhaps to Helmut Kohl's unification promise of a "blossoming landscape," the film withdraws from its restorative impetus with a sobering note: "The Bern Eleven never played together again." This sudden shift to what Svetlana Boym has called "reflective nostalgia" emphasizes the irrevocability of the past, suggesting the existence of a national past and future beyond the realm of mournful longing.[5]

See also:

- 15 October 1920: Ernst Lubitsch Fuels Debate over Tears in the Cinema
- 19 September 1958: Douglas Sirk's *A Time to Love and a Time to Die* Tests Limits of Postwar Feeling
- 8 September 2004: *Der Untergang* Offers Palatable Authenticity

Notes

[1] Bill Niven, *Facing the Nazi Past: United Germany and the Legacy of the Third Reich* (London: Routledge, 2002), 193. See also Roland Binz, "Wenn sogar der Kanzler weint. Die Berliner Republik und ihr 'Wunder von Bern,'" *Zeithistorische Forschungen/Studies in Contemporary History* 1, no. 2 (2004): 1–5; here 1.

[2] Norbert Seitz, "Was symbolisiert 'Das Wunder von Bern'?" *Aus Politik und Zeitgeschichte* 26 (21 June 2006): 3–6; here 3.

[3] For a reading on the connections between masculinity, family, and nation, see Matthias Uecker, "Fractured families — united countries? Family, nostalgia and nation-building in *Das Wunder von Bern* and *Good Bye Lenin!*," *New Cinemas: Journal of Contemporary Film* 5, no. 3 (2007): 189–200.

[4] On the film's strategies of circumventing the critical engagement with Nazi crimes associated with the '68ers, see Stuart Taberner, "Philo-Semitism in Recent German Film: 'Aimée und Jaguar,' 'Rosenstraße' and 'Das Wunder von Bern.'" *German Life and Letters* 58, no. 3 (2005): 357–72; here 371.

[5] Svetlana Boym, *The Future of Nostalgia* (New York: Basic Books, 2001), 49–50.

14 February 2004: Golden Bear for *Gegen die Wand* Affirms Fatih Akın as Germany's Preeminent Transnational Director

Barbara Mennel

A wedding portait of Sibel and Cahit. Gegen die Wand *(2004). DVD capture.*

THE GOLDEN BEAR AWARD for Fatih Akın's film *Gegen die Wand* (*Head-On*, 2004) at the 2004 Berlin Film Festival established the Turkish-German director as one of Germany's preeminent filmmakers and highlighted the importance of Turkish-German cinema in general and its status as German cinema in particular. The controversy around the film's main actress Sibel Kekilli's appearance in pornographic films mirrors the film's passionate portrayal of a younger generation of Turkish-Germans engaged in a radical break with conventional expectations about gender and national belonging. Akın's oeuvre intervenes in the tradition of sociologically motivated films about so-called Turkish guest-workers in Germany. *Gegen die Wand*, Akın's fourth feature-length narrative film, established his position as one of Germany's leading contemporary directors, which the selection of his 2007 film *Auf der anderen Seite* (*The Edge of Heaven*) as Germany's entry for the 2008 Oscars cemented for an international audience.

Akın's filmmaking is deeply influenced by different international film traditions, including Italian, French, Turkish, and American cinemas. His oeuvre repeatedly addresses configurations of Turkish-Germanness in the form of reworking and deconstructing stereotypes, the construction of Turkish-German national and transnational spaces, and the movement between Turkey and Germany. Akın belongs to a generation of Turkish-German directors who first made films in the late 1990s and who include Thomas Arslan, Aysun Bademsoy, Seyhan Derin, Ayşe Polat, and Yüksel Yavuz. Their films — such as Arslan's *Geschwister — Kardeşler* (*Brothers and Sisters*, 1995) and *Dealer* (1998), Yavuz's *Aprilkinder* (*April Children*, 1998), Derin's *Ich bin die Tochter meiner Mutter — Ben Annemin Kızıyım* (*I am the Daughter of My Mother*, 1996), and Ayşe Polat's *Auslandstournee* (*Tour Abroad*, 2000) — collectively offer images of a self-confident second generation of Turkish migrants in Germany, indicating a shift that Deniz Göktürk has characterized as a move away from a "cinema of duty" toward one that embraces the "pleasures of hybridity."[1] These filmmakers have been applauded for their "sustained attempt to dismantle rather than recycle cultural stereotypes," and are now firmly anchored in the German film landscape with several feature films made or underway.[2] Akın's career and work, however, have become singularly representative of a unique mix of narrative conventions of globally circulating genres articulated through an auteurist vision of German multicultural identity.

Akın's oeuvre consists of short and feature films. The latter include works of traditional but diverse genres, including documentaries (*Wir haben vergessen zurückzukehren* [We forgot to return], 2001, and *Crossing the Bridge — The Sound of Istanbul*, 2005), the road-movie (*Im Juli* [*In July*], 2000), the migration family drama (*Solino*, 2002), and the ghetto-gangster film (*Kurz und schmerzlos* [*Short Sharp Shock*], 1998). His most critically acclaimed films, however, such as *Gegen die Wand* and *Auf der anderen Seite*, reflect his auteurist vision. His emotionally intense cinema addresses love and death in beautiful images of urban and rural landscapes, and articulates an innovative political and cultural cosmopolitanism beyond the dogma of the leftist politics of the 1970s or the identity politics of the 1980s. In addition to versatility, extreme productivity and proliferation characterize his artistic work and persona. From his early years of flexibility, in which, presumably in an effort to ward off the typecasting that has troubled many minority directors, he moved between genres, themes, and styles, Akın has matured into a crafter of sophisticated narratives about the psychological effects of globalization. While the award of the Golden Bear acknowledges his importance for the German film landscape at that moment, a living director and his developing body of work ultimately exceed the containment of an encyclopedic entry.

Characters in Akın's films crisscross time and space across national borders; the settings of his films move between different nation-states; and his documentaries illustrate historical and contemporary processes of cultural exchange, hybridity, and glocalization — the local manifestation of global processes. His work dialogues with the themes and aesthetics of transnational cinemas within and beyond Germany's borders in films by other minority directors in Germany (such as Angelina Maccarone) and in Europe (such as Isaac Julien in Great Britain, and Merzak Allouache, Abdelkrim Bahloul, and Karim Dridi in France). However, narratives of migration and a multicultural Europe are not only the purview of minority directors anymore. The global success of films such as John Carney's *Once* (2006), in which the migration from Eastern Europe to Ireland centrally defines a character, and Sarah Gavron's *Brick Lane* (2007), which captures the migration story from Pakistan to London, is mirrored by successful films such as Mexican Alfonso Cuarón's *Children of Men* (2006) and Canadian David Cronenberg's *Eastern Promises* (2007). The global circulation of an image of a New Europe as a space defined by multiculturalism and migration, even in films by non-European directors, points to a new understanding of national and transnational belonging and cinematic representation.

This rewriting of the notion of belonging in terms of a reconfigured relationship between the national and transnational constitutes a thread throughout Akın's work. His early short film *Getürkt* (1996), which plays with the usage of the word *türken* (to "turk," or to fake) as trickery and with the stereotype of Turks as drug dealers, takes place entirely in Turkey, reflecting the social reality of many Turkish-Germans who divide their time between the two nations. The short film introduces Akın's preoccupation with intergenerational conflict and his tendency to act in his own films: he cast himself in the main role as a young Turkish-German on holiday in Turkey. *Getürkt* establishes some of Akın's typical stylistic and narrative conventions: a self-reflexive irony about Turkish-German identity, rooted in intimate familiarity and the deconstruction of stereotypes through exaggeration. Just such a stereotype — that of criminal ethnic youth — characterizes his first feature-length film *Kurz und schmerzlos*, which earned him the respect of audiences and critics alike and provoked the question of whether the New "German" Cinema might in fact be Turkish.[3] The film follows transnational ghetto film conventions, portraying the intertwined fate of three young small-time criminals in Hamburg caught in a tragic downward spiral of violence, drugs, and criminality.[4]

In contrast, Akın's next feature-length narrative film, *Im Juli*, combines the genre conventions of the lighthearted romantic comedy and the newly emergent European road movie. With post-Wall film stars such as Moritz Bleibtreu, Mehmet Kurtuluş, and Idil Üner, Akın portrays configurations of Turkishness and Germanness that further distance his filmmaking from the explicitly political European cinema that had addressed migration until the mid-1990s. The comedy of errors pairs two young couples, one ethnically German, one ethnically Turkish-German, on their way from Germany to Turkey through several European countries. The crossing of borders becomes a comedic adventure in a Europe characterized by the absurd play of linguistic and cultural differences. The film's concluding shots in Istanbul portray a romantic, postnational cosmopolitanism, embraced by a new generation of Germans and Turkish-Germans who cross European borders for love, desire, and family obligations.

Akın proved his mastery of genre cinema with his feature-length *Solino*, an immigration family drama. Typical for the genre, the film follows two generations of Italians who have moved to the industrial area of the Ruhrpott, the main industrial area of former West Germany. Contrasting the parents' Italian restaurant with one son's dream of becoming a filmmaker, the Italian family embodies the differentiation between the labor migration of the first generation and the possibilities and dreams of the second generation.

Akın's next feature-film, *Gegen die Wand*, which received the Golden Bear, appeared as the highpoint of Akın's oeuvre at that point, integrating an unapologetically confrontational audience address with a sophisticated narrative structure and striking aesthetic features. *Gegen die Wand* depicts the lifestyle of second-generation Turkish migrants in Germany who are as alienated from their parents' generation as from bourgeois German society. Instead of one-dimensional minority characters offered for identification or pity, the two main characters, Cahit and Sibel, are complex and contradictory. They defy their parents and disengage from their Turkish-German community. They cannot be assimilated into simplistic generic narrative conventions, particularly that of the exploited, suffering, and lonely minority figure that had dominated the socially conscious representations of immigrants in New German Cinema. Repeated suicide attempts create a reoccurring motif throughout the film, give the film its title, and drive the narrative forward with a gritty and tense realism. In an excess of violence, love-making, smoking, drugs, drinking, and music, the two figures fall in love with each other. But in a tragic turn of events, Cahit is incarcerated, and Sibel must flee a father and brother seeking to avenge her loss of honor. Leaving for Istanbul, she enters another downward spiral of drugs, rape, and violence. The film's conclusion refuses the conventional happy ending, instead representing a "highly ambiguous" "return of Turkish Germans to the 'homeland.'"[5] Like some of Akın's other films, *Gegen die Wand* reverses the movement of Turkish migration to Germany. The narrative is intercut with scenes of traditional Turkish music performed in front of a classical Istanbul backdrop, which creates a recurrent refrain throughout the film, a metatext that exceeds the film's temporality and locality.

Akın's next film again shifts genre, since *Crossing the Bridge: The Sound of Istanbul* is a music documentary in the tradition of Wim Wenders's *Buena Vista Social Club* (1999). In contrast to Wenders's film, which freezes exotic Cuban music in place and time, Akın offers a highly dynamic depiction of contemporary and traditional music in Istanbul. A traditional documentary, including talking heads and staged music performances, the film presents the cultural dynamics of Europe, particularly in its metropolitan cities. Alexander Hacke, of the German band *Einstürzende Neubauten*, functions as the interlocutor: he explains how his collaboration with Akın on the soundtrack for *Gegen die Wand* led to the return to Istanbul for the making of *Crossing the Bridge*. Hacke leads the audience from one concert to another, from one performer to another, and from one band to another. Istanbul appears as a cosmopolitan and transnational city where musical traditions like rock and hip-hop are reworked into "glocalized" Turkish variations. As the film progresses, it traces the historical development of Turkish music and reveals that the national tradition emerged from transnational influences. In contrast to the presentism of the standard accounts of contemporary globalization, Turkish national culture emerges as always already hybrid.

Returning to feature-length narrative film, Akın's next film, *Auf der anderen Seite* integrates two of the themes that dominate his oeuvre, the movement between Germany and Turkey and intergenerational conflicts. The second part of his Love, Death, and the Devil trilogy parallels different configurations of Turkish and German parents and children. The film advances a sophisticated narrative, putting in play multidimensional characters and complex relationships between national and transnational, collective and individual, love and death, with movement between Germany and Turkey. Akın's first explicitly political portrayal of repression in Turkey situates the film in the tradition of Turkish left cinema, created by such filmmakers as Yılmaz Güney. The narrative establishes a complex web of relationships between parents and children and between lovers, all organized around the occasions of two deaths. Beginning in Germany, the film crosscuts between Turkey and Germany before it ends in Turkey. Akın's maturity as a filmmaker finds its expression in the complexity of the narrative but also in the theme of death and forgiveness that extends to the parental generation. The deaths of certain characters enable new connections for others, whether between biological parents and their children or in surrogate families. These occur in both Turkish and German spaces and across lines of national belonging.

The Golden Bear marked a key moment in Akın's career, and his oeuvre has since matured and grown. His films constitute an important body of work, not only for the manner in which they capture the director's auteurist vision, but also for the way in which they insert Turkish-German cultural production into the German archive of cinematic images.[6] But

Akın is also one of the principle figures in an emerging European cinema, and with the prevalence of the cinematic negotiation of hybridity with national traditions, movement with spatial imaginaries, national boundaries with border-crossings, Akın also belongs to the growing number of important directors of a new global cinema. Thus, as one of the central filmmakers of contemporary German cinema, he is also one of the main innovators of German cinema as a transnational cinema.

See also:

- 6 March 1920: Chinese Students Raise Charges of Racism against *Die Herrin der Welt*
- 31 January 1929: Limits on Racial Border-Crossing Exposed in *Piccadilly*
- 10 February 1999: Berlinale Premier of Four Turkish-German Films Signals New Chapter in Cinematic Diversity

Notes

[1] Deniz Göktürk, "Turkish Delight — German Fright: Migrant Identities in Transnational Cinema," Working Paper, ESRC Transnational Communities Research Programme, www.transcomm.ox.ak.uk [accessed 2/18/2009].

[2] Rob Burns, "Towards a Cinema of Cultural Hybridity: Turkish-German Filmmakers and the Representation of Alterity," *Debatte: Journal of Contemporary Central and Eastern Europe* 15, no. 1 (April 2007): 3–24; here 7.

[3] Tunçay Kulaoğlu, "Der neue 'deutsche' Film ist 'türkisch'?: Eine neue Generation bringt Leben in die Filmlandschaft," *Filmforum* 16 (February/March 1999): 8–11.

[4] See also Barbara Mennel, "Bruce Lee in Kreuzberg and Scarface in Altona: Transnational *Auteurism* and Ghettocentrism in Thomas Arslan's *Brothers and Sisters* and Fatih Akın's *Short Sharp Shock*," *New German Critique* 87 (Fall 2002): 133–56.

[5] Petra Fachinger, "A New Kind of Creative Energy: Yadé Kara's *Selam Berlin* and Fatih Akın's *Kurz und Schmerzlos* and *Gegen die Wand*," *German Life and Letters* 60, no. 2 (April 2007): 243–60; here 250.

[6] For an extensive discussion of "the Turkish turn in German culture," see Leslie A. Adelson, *The Turkish Turn in Contemporary German Literature: Toward a New Critical Grammar of Migration* (New York: Palgrave, 2005), here 1.

8 September 2004: *Der Untergang* Offers Palatable Authenticity

Michael D. Richardson

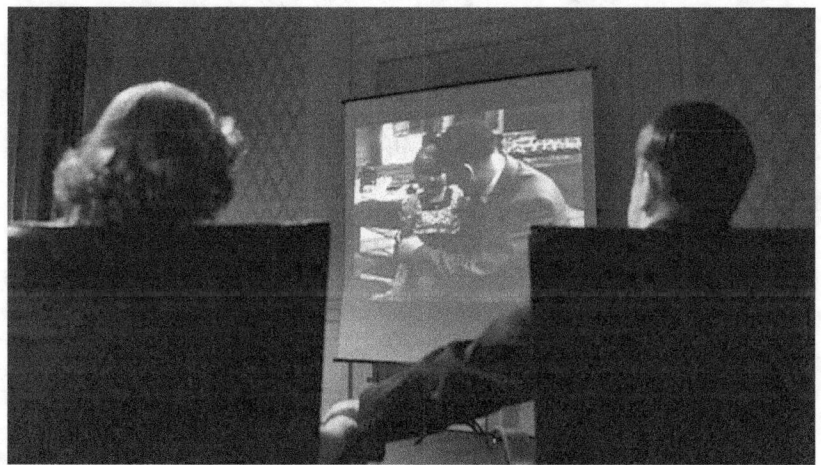

Hitler watches his own home movies. Mein Führer *(2007). DVD capture.*

THE 2004 PREMIERE of Oliver Hirschbiegel's epic account of the final days of the Nazi regime, *Der Untergang* (*Downfall*), generated a great deal of controversy for the centrality of its representation of Hitler by a German (actually Swiss) actor, the first since G. W. Pabst's *Der letzte Akt* (*The Last Ten Days*, 1955).[1] Primarily narrated from the perspective of Hitler's secretary Traudl Junge (the central figure in Andre Heller's 2002 documentary, *Im toten Winkel* [*Blind Spot*]), *Der Untergang* focuses on the last ten days of Hitler's life, alternating, like its predecessor, between scenes in the bunker and scenes above-ground in Berlin. Nearly three years later, a very different sort of film about the closing months of Hitler and the Third Reich, Dani Levy's 2007 *Mein Führer — Die wirklich wahrste Wahrheit über Adolf Hitler* (*Mein Führer: The Truly Truest Truth About Adolf Hitler*), was similarly met with a critical attack. What both films had in common was their perceived taboo-breaking status: both featured Hitler in a starring role, a rarity in German mainstream cinema, and both raised questions about the appropriateness of such a focus.

But it is there that their similarities ended. Although *Der Untergang*'s dramatic portrayal of a seemingly insane Hitler — debilitated by Parkinson's disease, ordering the movements of phantom armies, awarding medals to children conscripted to fight in the decimated German army, and engaging in compassionate exchanges with his subordinates — provoked controversy for its ostensible humanization and hence potential evocation of sympathy for Hitler, supporters and detractors alike generally concurred with Hirschbiegel's claim of historical accuracy, praising in particular Bruno Ganz's verisimilitudinous portrayal. Conceived as a satirical response to *Der Untergang*, Levy's film, a black comedy in which Goebbels rescues Hitler's old acting coach, the Jewish professor Adolph Grünbaum, from Sachsenhausen in order to help Hitler regain his killer instinct for an important speech, relishes in its own absurdity and, in the sheer implausibility of its premise and portrayal of Hitler, adheres little to principles of historical veracity.

The taboo these films purportedly broke had less to do with their mere existence and more to do with the fact that these were German-made films. Even this was less of a taboo than it was made out to be. While no dramatic fictional film made in Germany has afforded Hitler a central role since Pabst, during the Hitler-Welle of the 1970s, Hitler was the focus of both Joachim Fest's 1977 *Hitler — eine Karriere* (*Hitler, a Career*) and Hans-Jürgen Syberberg's 1978 7.5-hour epic *Hitler — ein Film aus Deutschland* (released in England as *Hitler: A Film from Germany*, and in the United States as *Our Hitler*). And this is not to mention the steady saturation of historical documentaries about Hitler that have been broadcast on German television — *Hitlers Krieger* (Hitler's warriors), *Hitlers Helfer* (Hitler's helpers), *Hitlers Frauen* (Hitler's women), *Hitlers Kinder* (Hitler's children) — spearheaded by Germany's most prominent television historian, Guido Knopp. In short, Hitler has never been far from sight on German television or in the German cinema. More significantly, this assertion makes a claim about the production of films about Hitler in Germany, but not their reception. There has certainly been no shortage of fictional representations of Hitler, both dramatic and comedic, in the past sixty years — nearly eighty actors have portrayed Hitler, ranging from bit players to major stars such as Anthony Hopkins and Alec Guiness. With few exceptions, these representations have found their way to a German public. Without discounting the variance in psychic significance of domestic and foreign representations of Hitler and the Nazis, given the tremendous impact that American productions such as the television miniseries *Holocaust* or Stephen Spielberg's *Schindler's List* have had on shaping German public consciousness about the Nazi era, it is clear that a film such as *Der Untergang*, with its "German sensibility," is nonetheless part of a much larger matrix of Hitler representations. Thus, while German filmmakers may have felt a taboo in depicting Hitler, no such taboo exists in Germany regarding the media exposure to representations of Hitler.

Whether or not *Untergang* or *Mein Führer* were indeed taboo-breaking in this sense was ultimately a moot point, and elides the larger issues at stake in their reception. Their real significance lay in how these films, particularly *Der Untergang*, reflected and impacted the contemporary terms of the discussion regarding the representability of the Nazi era and the relationship of the German populace to that era. In this regard, the differences in each film's box-office success are quite telling.[2] Although both films came under intense criticism, it was *Der Untergang* that managed to overcome critical qualms and achieve popular success both in Germany and abroad, while *Mein Führer* was marginalized as an ultimately unsuccessful comedic engagement with Hitler.

Seen by more than 4.6 million viewers in Germany and earning over $85 million worldwide, *Der Untergang* is one of the highest-grossing German films in history. The film shares with earlier Hitler representations an allegorical function and with earlier German representations an identificatory figure to counter Nazi evil. Pabst's film made similar claims regarding historical accuracy, but clearly functioned as a fantasy of resistance. When it was first released, the fictionalized documentary required a hero without a factual corollary — Captain Wüst, an officer driven by desperation and a recognition of Hitler's isolation from reality to speak for "the other Germany," pleading and even threatening Hitler.[3] As he lays dying, he gives voice to the moral of the film: "If you ever know peace, don't let them take it away. Don't say *Jawohl*. Don't ever say *Jawohl*." Though he may have been intended to serve as a sympathetic figure for an audience that wanted to think itself resisters, as Marc Silberman has noted, this direct confrontation with Hitler could not have been perceived as anything but pure fantasy in 1955. By 2004, the cultural climate regarding possible acts of resistance had shifted to such an extent that heroic acts of defiance, while still the standard for noble behavior during the war, were judged on a much more lenient scale.

Der Untergang appeared in the middle of a moment in which Germany was awash in reminiscences about the Nazi era and accounts of its end, beginning with a slew of productions that centered around the sixtieth anniversary of the 20 July 1944 attempt on Hitler's life, including Jo Baier's television-movie *Stauffenberg*. Dennis Gansel's *Napola — Elite für den Führer* (*Napola*) premiered in December 2004; the three-part docudrama *Speer und Er* (*Speer and Hitler: The Devil's Architect*) had just finished filming and would be broadcast on WDR, the public television station, in the spring of 2005; and Marc Rothemund's *Sophie Scholl — die letzten Tage* (*Sophie Scholl: The Final Days*) premiered at the Berlin Film Festival in 2005. Further, the film emerged in the larger cultural context of the *Luftkrieg* debate, prompted first by W. G. Sebald's *Luftkrieg und*

Literatur (*On the Natural History of Destruction*) and then more extensively with the 2002 publication of *Der Brand: Deutschland im Bombenkrieg 1940–45* (*The Fire: The Bombing of Germany, 1940–45*) by Jörg Friedrich, which incited a reassessment of German wartime suffering. If there was an uneasiness to the *Luftkrieg* discussion — since raising the specter of Germans as victims of allied attacks, however legitimate, risked sounded like self-justification — *Der Untergang* neatly sidestepped it by staging the conflict as a German-German one. Though it is the Soviet army that bombards the city and marches ever closer to the bunker, they remain an invisible enemy throughout nearly the entire film.

Given this context, the moment was ripe for an engagement with the Nazi past that allowed German audiences to condemn the Nazi regime and see itself as victims, without resorting to overt historical revisionism or to justifying German atrocities vis-à-vis Allied or Soviet actions (as with the *Historikerstreit*). But while the film asserts that it is based on events and conversations supported by documented eyewitness accounts, the fact that surviving eyewitnesses would be inclined to defend rather than condemn themselves means that we can hardly take as incontrovertible historical truth uncorroborated exculpatory accounts of private heroism and resistance — such as Albert Speer's claim to have defiantly confessed to Hitler that he did not sabotage needed civilian-supply lines. Further, the ostensible authenticity of Ganz's portrayal is entirely dependent upon these potentially self-serving recollections. Hitler's supposed humanity is mediated: based as it is on Junge's recollections, her accounts of his humanity serve to exculpate *her* — or at least explain how she was able to work for him — rather than make Hitler more sympathetic. That the critical acclaim of Bruno Ganz's portrayal hinges upon a notion of his "authentic" embodiment of Hitler's true personality is particularly problematic, not only given the film's source material, but also given the fact that it remains an open question as to whether an "authentic" Hitler can ever be known. The manner in which Ganz's portrayal has been praised is telling — he has been lauded both for his appearance and his uncanny mimicry of Hitler's voice and speech patterns. The inner Hitler remains inscrutable, however. Thus, to discuss the film in terms of its authenticity is to engage in a debate that has no absolute, for what constitutes the truth content of a particular Hitler incarnation depends not on its accuracy in drawing out an inner identity, but on its effectiveness in projecting a particular identity onto the dictator. Put somewhat differently, the success of Ganz's performance and the film more broadly hinges in large measure on its ability to confirm that which audiences already know.

Despite Hirschbiegel's claims that the film would provide a new *Blickwinkel* from which to view and engage in memory discourse in Germany surrounding the Second World War, *Der Untergang* owed its success to the fact that it avoided the more complex questions of guilt and responsibility. Its conclusion points toward an ending rather than a beginning of the discussion. The film's final shot of the reconstituted German family, the Aryan mother and son who bike out of the ruins of the city and into the lush countryside, serves as a counterweight to the perverted ideal of motherhood embodied by Magda Goebbels, who is shown poisoning her children rather than accepting the end of the Nazi regime, while the reappearance of the real Traudl Junge at the very end of the film (the footage excerpted from *Im toten Winkel*), ostensibly to ground the film in the present, instead reestablishes the audience's temporal distance from the events of the war.

By the time Levy's film had appeared, the cultural context had shifted, due in large part to the success of *Der Untergang*. The closure that the latter film had provided meant that the reception of *Mein Führer* was not about breaking any taboos; rather, the film came under the most criticism precisely because it was not deemed sufficiently generically pure, and therefore not funny. The problem, according to most critics, was that the film could not decide whether it was a comedy or a drama, and thus lacked a coherent identity or critical power. Though such comments are ostensibly directed toward the quality of the film, these criticisms are telling with respect to what critics and audiences could tolerate in a Hitler film, particularly a Hitler comedy, and raise questions regarding the newly comfortable German relationship with the Nazi era.

Though comedic moments abound, including scenes of Hitler playing with battleships in a bathtub and down on all fours, barking like a dog as his German shepherd Blondi tries to mount him from behind, the film is also largely driven by Grünbaum's attempts to protect his family, preserve his moral integrity, and leverage his sudden indispensability to force Goebbels to close Sachsenhausen. The film swings back and forth between two modes of representation — the traditional, realistic Nazi of documentary films, and the cartoonish Nazi of *Indiana Jones*.[4]

These two opposing models of representation employed in Hitler films — drama and comedy — each enmesh viewers in a process of identification that clearly delineates between good and evil, hero and villain, by defining the viewers' relationship with "the real" in a particular way, either by asserting its own authenticity, and thus engendering an emotional response such as pity or fear, or by positioning itself as decidedly fantastic and unreal, thus engendering an intellectual response, such as ridicule.[5] By alternating between comic and dramatic modes, Levy's film challenges the audience's level of engagement with the reality of the film and thus shares qualities with other Holocaust black comedies, most notably Radu Mihaileanu's film *Train de Vie* (*Train of Life*). Levy's film begins with an absurd premise, and, in its deliberate oscillation between genres, seeks to destabilize an ostensibly clear presupposition — in this case, the notion of authenticity — challenging both the role that authenticity plays in the current discussion of Hitler representations, as well as the nature of historical memory of the Holocaust in contemporary Germany.

The last scene of the film encapsulates its ongoing critique of the demand for closure. After Hitler loses his mustache and then his voice, Grünbaum is forced to give Hitler's speech for him. Hidden underneath Hitler's podium, Grünbaum orates while Hitler pantomimes. As with *The Great Dictator*, the masses are easily fooled by what should be an obvious artifice, and like Chaplin's impassioned plea, this speech has two addressees — the German crowd within the film, and the German audience in the movie theater. Unable to continue his charade, Grünbaum strays from his script, not to make a plea for tolerance, but instead to bitterly condemn his audience for following him despite his leading Germany into destruction, and condemns himself as a bed-wetting, drug-addicted, impotent, and unfeeling monster.

Grünbaum's final words to the cinematic audience, in the form of a voice-over, return to the problematic nature of his representation. In a moment that recalls the end of *Train de Vie*, Grünbaum states that "That was it — my history. It's 100% true, I can assure you of that," before quickly conceding that "Okay, maybe I exaggerated at a couple of points. That's possible. Don't you believe me?" This admission forces a reconsideration of the film: in challenging the very legitimacy of the narrative, even the moral status of Grünbaum may be questioned — further undermining any sense of closure.

What Levy's film shares with Hirschbiegel's — indeed with many of the recent films about Hitler — is that it is ultimately not about Hitler, but rather functions as an allegory for a German understanding and mastery of its Nazi past. But while *Der Untergang* allows Germans to reclaim a measure of victim status, while avoiding the more difficult questions of the cultural normativity of perpetrator behavior and the direct and indirect complicity of the German populace in the Holocaust and the extermination of the Jews, *Mein Führer* challenges the audience, refusing to offer an understanding of the dictator's true nature and even hinting that the very possibility of such an understanding is nothing more than absurd.

See also:

- 22 December 1955: *Sissi* Trilogy Bridges Hapsburg to Hollywood through Hybrid Blend of Film Genres
- 16 October 2003: Chancellor Gerhard Schröder Sheds Tears — Again — at Premiere of *Das Wunder von Bern*
- 25 February 2007: *Das Leben der Anderen* Follows Blueprint for Foreign-Language Oscar Success

Notes

[1] Some passages from this entry originally appeared in a longer essay on Levy's *Mein Führer*, entitled "Tragedy and farce: Dani Levy's *Mein Führer — Die wirklich wahrste Wahrheit über Adolf Hitler*," in *Hitler: Films from Germany; Myth, Memory, and History in German Cinema and Television since 1945*, ed. Karolin Machtans and Martin A. Ruehl (London: Palgrave, 2012).

[2] *Der Untergang* was an international success, grossing nearly $92 million worldwide, with less than half of that amount ($39 million) coming from Germany, and around $5 million from the United States. By contrast, *Mein Führer* was not only much more modest in its box office gross ($7.6 million), but nearly 90 percent of this amount ($6.8 million) came from the domestic box office.

[3] See Marc Silberman, *German Cinema: Texts in Context* (Detroit: Wayne State UP, 1995).

[4] Harald Martenstein, "Adolf auf der Couch," *Die Zeit* (4 January 2007). In an admittedly defensive response to criticisms of his film that was published in *Welt am Sonntag* and is available on the website for the film, Levy characterizes the genre discussion as "a German sickness... comedy and tragedy, serious theses and subversive laughter — why shouldn't that have a place in a film?"

[5] In his essay, "Holocaust *Laughter*?," Terrence Des Pres articulates the difference between drama and comedy in terms of a relationship to mimesis: "In its homage to fact, high seriousness is governed by a compulsion to reproduce, by the need to create a convincing likeness that never quite succeeds, never feels complete, just as earnestness feels inadequate to best intentions. Comic works, on the contrary, escape such liabilities; laughter is hostile to the world it depicts and subverts the respect on which representation depends." Terrence Des Pres, "Holocaust *Laughter*?," in *Writing and the Holocaust*, ed. Berel Lang (New York: Holmes and Meier, 1988), 216–33; here 219–20.

22 October 2005: Winner of Hessian Film Award *Fremde Haut* Queers Dual Binaries of Sexual and National Identity

Faye Stewart

Fariba prepares to return to Iran in the guise of the male refugee Simiak. Fremde Haut *(2005). DVD capture.*

GERMAN POLITICS AND SOCIETY of the late twentieth and early twenty-first centuries continue to be haunted by the multiculturalism question, which finds expression in a persistent obsession with the nation's physical and metaphorical borders. This preoccupation comes to life in representations of migrations, transnational identities, and hyphenated cultures in contemporary cinema, particularly in German-Turkish films. Fatih Akın's success both in Germany and internationally underlines the new status of hybrid filmmaking in the twenty-first century. Sharing a number of preoccupations with German-Turkish filmmaking in general and Akın's work in particular, Angelina Maccarone's *Fremde Haut* (*Unveiled*, 2005) won the Hessian Film Award for Best Feature Film, announced to the public on 22 October 2005, just two days after its German theatrical release.

Like Akın's oeuvre, *Fremde Haut* foregrounds the negotiation of identity in portrayals of exile, repatriation, and legality, while also exposing and critiquing the very boundaries of German society. *Fremde Haut*, however, is notable in that it is not a German-Turkish production; written and directed by the German-Italian Maccarone, it tells the story of a journey from Persia to Germany and back, and features a German-Iranian lead actress who experienced German immigration first-hand. Maccarone's representations of human rights, violence, sexuality, and belonging invite comparisons not only with Akın's films, but also with works as disparate as Kutluğ Ataman's *Lola + Bilidikid* (*Lola and Billy the Kid*, 1999), Rainer Werner Fassbinder's *Angst essen Seele auf* (*Ali: Fear Eats the Soul*, 1974), and Volker Schlöndorff's *Die Stille nach dem Schuss* (*The Legend of Rita*, 2000).

Since her television debut with the acclaimed *Kommt Mausi raus?!* (Is Mausi coming out?!, 1995), director and screenwriter Maccarone has created narratives that explore minority, hybridity, and in-betweenness through key categories of identity: gender, sexuality, ethnicity, race, class, and age. *Fremde Haut*, which critiques German multiculturalism and politics through the story of an Iranian woman who goes into exile because of a lesbian affair and is denied asylum in Germany, may represent Maccarone's first mainstream success, but it is not her first film to deploy the political dimensions of sexuality in confrontation with normative conceptions of Germanness. A number of these issues were articulated, albeit in different forms, in *Alles wird gut* (Everything will be fine, 1998), a made-for-television romantic comedy that won audience awards at two North American gay and lesbian festivals for its sympathetic portrayal of three Afro-German characters of different generations.

Although Maccarone has also written and directed episodes of the popular television series *Tatort* (Crime scene, for which she made three episodes between 2007 and 2009), critics and audiences have a tendency to pigeonhole her as a lesbian filmmaker because much of her work deals with sexual identity. In a discussion of subversive relationship comedies and post-1994 cinema in which "gay characters have been used repeatedly to evoke an atmosphere of sexual tolerance and worldly sophistication," film scholar Sabine Hake mentions both *Alles wird gut* and *Fremde Haut*, the latter of which "acknowledges both the power of love and the pervasiveness of homophobia, but without the didactic intentions that marred the first lesbian films from the early 1980s."[1] The film's success suggests, however, that it is noteworthy not only for its treatment of sexuality, but also for its engagement with contemporary issues that resonate with mainstream audiences both in Germany and abroad. Indeed, *Fremde Haut*'s central concern extends beyond the personal dimensions of desire and identification that function as its narrative axis; it also engages a nuanced consideration of their national and legal implications. Whereas words referencing sexual identity such as "lesbian" and "homosexual" are not articulated in the dialogue (at least not in German; large parts of the film dialogue and voiceover are in Farsi with German subtitles), geographical names and political terms such as "passport" and "asylum" abound, indicating that although sexual categories are a crucial narrative element, the national boundary is also of central thematic and structural significance.

In *Fremde Haut*, the German border organizes and regulates both the narrative and the articulation of its main character's gender and sexuality. Fariba Tabrizi (Jasmin Tabatabai), a lesbian refugee from Iran, is denied asylum in Germany because she closets her sexuality. During her short stay in a refugee detention center at the Frankfurt airport, she befriends fellow Iranian Siamak Mustafai (Navíd Akhavan), who commits suicide just before he is granted asylum on political grounds. Desperate to avoid repatriation to a homeland in which she faces persecution and perhaps even torture, imprisonment, or execution, Fariba seizes an opportunity to stay in Germany by taking Siamak's identity. Her new existence as Siamak in rural Swabia finds her living in an asylum home for men and working illegally in a sauerkraut factory, where the promise of a better life seems within reach: she makes contact with a forger of German passports and becomes romantically involved with coworker Anne (Anneke Kim Sarnau). But a number of obstacles threaten Fariba's freedom and survival, which rely on the successful concealment of her gender, identity, and illegal status. And Anne's small-town friends, who oppose her budding romance with a foreigner, will stop at nothing to keep them apart. Just as Fariba obtains her false documents and ceases to masquerade as Siamak, Anne's friends violently intervene, and the drama concludes with Fariba's deportation back to Iran.

This queer transnational film brings together the engagements of multicultural cinema with those of feminist and queer cinema. *Fremde Haut* might be assigned to a category that Gerd Gemünden calls "minority cinema" and Barbara Mennel describes as "new minority cinema," with which it shares the central themes of motion, space, and desire.[2] Examining the intersections of nation, ethnicity, gender, and sexuality, Maccarone's film enters into dialog with other cinematic narratives of migration since the mid-1990s, like *Lola + Bilidikid*, by interrogating the conditions of possibility for the safety and survival of the queer Other in contemporary Germany. *Fremde Haut* at once critiques the boundaries of German nationhood from its margins and investigates the possibilities that the performance of gender identity opens up for would-be immigrants who are denied legal protection. By foregrounding the perspective of asylum-seekers and their interactions with German political and cultural institutions, it responds to recent shifts in refugee policy. With the flow of refugees from Yugoslavian territories in the early 1990s, German asylum laws were revised in 1993, requiring asylum-seekers to provide documentation of their persecution. In 2005, a law recognizing *geschlechtsspezifische Asylgründe* (gender-specific grounds for asylum) went into effect. This category of refugee status fails to function in Maccarone's *Fremde Haut* because the main character enters the country with forged papers and is reluctant to label herself as homosexual — a choice the rationale of which is never explained in the film.

While politicians and artists tout the German nation as a bastion of *multikulti* (multicultural) tolerance and harmony, Maccarone constructs Germany's borderlands through cinematic geographies that insist on a resolutely monocultural society. Unlike Fatih Akın's depictions of German-Turkish identities as indelible and indispensable parts of the contemporary German cultural fabric, *Fremde Haut*'s would-be immigrant resonates with earlier cinematic representations of *Gastarbeiter* (guest workers) which are much more ambivalent. These include, for example, Fassbinder's *Angst essen Seele auf*, where there is little future for outsiders in mainstream German society, and German-Turkish films of the 1990s, such as those analyzed by Caryl Flinn, in which immigrants are figuratively likened to garbage: they are useless, disposable, and interchangeable.[3]

Fremde Haut articulates a feminist critique of the politics of immigration and asylum through its representation of the abject female body. Fariba disturbs the dominant order everywhere she goes: in Iran because of her sexuality, and in Germany primarily because of her gender and ethnicity. Fariba reenacts the terms of her oppression by negating her femininity through masquerade, during which her gender figures as a bodily excess that must be contained. Only in private does she remove her male disguise, but the violence of her masquerade remains inscribed on the body in the form of red welts on her chest. However convincingly she plays the male part, Fariba cannot exert full control over her body: menstruation presents a challenge to her masquerade and symbolically resists the terms of her oppression. After Fariba unveils herself as a woman in a single love scene with Anne, the consequences are devastating: Anne's friends perceive her queer sexuality as a threat to their community, and Fariba is deported from Germany. The abjection of the female body continues, however, when she discards all evidence of her identity and resumes her masquerade as Siamak on the return flight to Teheran — a gender performance that, however problematic, presumably offers a safer and brighter future than would entering Iran as a known lesbian.

The repeated negation and expulsion of the queer woman recalls Terry Castle's description of the "apparitional lesbian" in mainstream cinema.[4] However, there is a crucial distinction between the trend Castle identifies and the disappearance of the lesbian in *Fremde Haut*: although Fariba is invisible to other diegetic characters for much of the narrative, she is still visible to the spectator, even when she appears in male disguise. The spectator is aware of the deception, and evidence suggests that Anne is, too. For this reason, the film cannot be assigned to the genre that Chris Straayer identifies as the "temporary transvestite film," in which a straight love story is queered through gender masquerade.[5] Through its queer narrative, *Fremde Haut* examines the stakes of gender performance and passing, but unlike in Kimberly Peirce's *Boys Don't Cry* (1999), passing is not connected to transgender identification; rather, here it functions as a political maneuver. *Fremde Haut*'s identity constructions might therefore be compared to those of Agnieszka Holland's *Hitlerjunge Salomon* (*Europa Europa*, 1990), in which passing is a strategy for survival that is rendered intelligible within a specific German national context.

The repeated negation of femininity and homosexuality may lead spectators to read Maccarone's film as antifeminist, misogynistic, or even homophobic, for it suggests that there is no space for the woman who crosses sexual boundaries. But this is only one side of the story, in which the condition of possibility for Fariba's disappearance is the death of the male subject, which opens a door for the oppressed woman. And Fariba's life as a man has its own physical and social limitations: as Siamak, she must wear thick glasses and speak only rudimentary German, and her day-to-day existence is still subject to external control through oppression, violence, and policing.

Fremde Haut actively queers the binaries that permeate and regulate the institution of the nation. Fariba crosses visible and invisible borders, inhabiting an in-between space marked by oppression and resistance. Much of the narrative unfolds in transitional settings, emphasizing Fariba's liminal status while also underlining the challenges she faces in attempting to translate her identity into a politically legitimate existence. Multiple dichotomies that are commonly viewed as mutually exclusive — male or female, legal or illegal, asylee or deportee — are problematized through various aspects of Fariba's performances of identity, drawing attention to the gaps created in the processes of migration, translation, and interpretation. And this may well be the key to *Fremde Haut*'s success: ultimately, it celebrates the refusal to obey the mandates of binary identity through Fariba-as-Siamak's resolute inhabitation of both.

See also:

- 31 January 1929: Limits on Racial Border-Crossing Exposed in *Piccadilly*
- 2 November 1995: *Neurosia* Embodies Seventy-Five Years of Queer Film History
- 14 February 2004: Golden Bear for *Gegen die Wand* Affirms Fatih Akın as Germany's Preeminent Transnational Director

Notes

[1] Sabine Hake, *German National Cinema*. 2nd ed. (London: Routledge, 2008), 202.

[2] See Gerd Gemünden, "Hollywood in Altona: Minority Cinema and the Transnational Imagination" in *German Pop Culture: How "American" Is It?*, ed. Agnes C. Mueller (Ann Arbor: U of Michigan P, 2004), 180–90; and Barbara Mennel, "Masochism, Marginality, and the Metropolis: Kutlug Ataman's *Lola and Billy the Kid*," *Studies in Twentieth and Twenty-First Century Literature* 28, no. 1 (Winter 2004), 286–315.

[3] Caryl Flinn, "Somebody's Garbage: Depictions of Turkish Residents in 1990s German Film," in *The Cosmopolitan Screen: German Cinema and the Global Imaginary, 1945 to the Present*, ed. Stephan K. Schindler and Lutz Koepnick (Ann Arbor: U of Michigan P, 2007), 140–58.

[4] See Terry Castle, *The Apparitional Lesbian: Female Homosexuality and Modern Culture* (New York: Columbia UP, 1993).

[5] Chris Straayer, *Deviant Eyes, Deviant Bodies: Sexual Re-orientations in Film and Video* (New York: Columbia UP, 1996).

22 January 2007: Film Establishment Attacks "Berlin School" as Wrong Kind of National Cinema

Marco Abel

Markus and Ella share a tender moment by the lake.
Sehnsucht (2006). DVD capture.

AFTER A LONG LEAN PERIOD during which the German film industry had received little more than scorn by national and international observers, the new millennium rang in a new era for German films. The early 2000s brought this long-beleaguered cultural industry a remarkable series of success stories that manifested itself in box-office prowess and international award recognition. German-language film productions have displayed, for example, an astonishing dominance in the Best Foreign Language Film category at the Academy Awards since the turn of the millennium, winning the category three times and receiving an additional four nominations. During the same period the average annual share of German film productions at the German box office rose substantially; according to the German Federal Film Board (FFA), German films reached their best result since unification in 2009 when their share of the total annual box office amounted to 27.4 percent, besting the previous year's already stellar result of 26.6 percent.[1]

Coinciding with the emergence of a larger self-confident cultural discourse in Germany expressing a desire for *Normalisierung* — the desire to be treated as a "normal" nation just like any other democracy — the German film industry's unexpected renaissance soon expressed itself in a patriotic, indeed nationalistic, *wir sind wieder wer* (we're somebody again) rhetoric in the German mainstream press.[2] This attitude articulated the widespread sense of a newfound self-assurance among the industry's elites and the country's mass-market media. It is in this context that Günter Rohrbach's polemical, instantly controversial attack on German film critics, "Das Schmollen der Autisten" ("The Pouting of Autistics"), hit the German film world like a bombshell when it initially appeared in Germany's leading weekly news magazine *Der Spiegel* on 22 January 2007.[3]

In 2003 Rohrbach, an influential and successful film and television producer, assumed the presidency of the newly founded Deutsche Filmakademie, which in 2005 began awarding the country's most prestigious, and financially most lucrative, annual film award, the Deutscher Filmpreis (the LOLA). Modeled after the Academy of Motion Picture Arts and Sciences, the German Film Academy controversially replaced the previous, jury-based selection process for determining the award winners of the German Film Prize with a voting process in which each of the approximately 1,100 members of the Academy participate. Supporters of this new system point to its greater transparency and democratic process compared to the old system, which frequently stood accused of being too beholden to political interest groups; opponents, however, counter that the prize monies accompanying the awards (totaling 2.855 million euros in 2010) are *public*, that is, tax-based, monies, whereas the Academy is a *private* organization.

Furthermore, critics feared that as a direct consequence of what some characterized as a neoliberal privatization of public resources, smaller film productions, which often exhibit greater aesthetic adventurousness than more expensive mainstream productions, would lose additional ground in a national film culture that already showed little interest in home-grown films that neither cater to an audience's continued interest in the country's big historical issues (i.e., its fascist or socialist regimes, the RAF [Rote Armee Fraktion, or Red Army Faction] crisis) nor embrace a lowest-common-denominator entertainment aesthetic (as did those films Eric Rentschler dubbed "the cinema of consensus").[4] This institutional change, critics charged, would relinquish one of the best opportunities for promoting lesser-known German films to a larger audience. It would also effectively institute the redistribution of public funds that were originally meant to promote the diversity of German film culture; now, monies that used to support smaller production firms would end up subsidizing larger German film production companies, thus further hindering the former's ability to launch film projects off the ground that went against the aesthetic, narrative, and political grain of more mainstream cinema.

Indeed, Rohrbach conceived his attack on German film critics in direct response to their fear that the revamping of the selection and voting process for the Filmpreis would further disadvantage small-scale but artistically progressive film productions such as Valeska Grisebach's critically acclaimed *Sehnsucht* (*Longing*, 2006), which did not even make it through the first cut of the Academy's selection process in 2007. In his essay, he accuses German film critics of having "lost the trust of their readers" because they "sent [them] too often to the wrong films."[5] German film critics, says Rohrbach, have become "autistic" because they are more interested in proving their credentials as cineastes than in "providing assistance for potential viewers" (157). How much of Rohrbach's critique is issued from a position of newfound strength shines through in his appeal to the argument that "German film has in fact regained a large part of the audience it had thought to have lost to Hollywood" — a task, according to Rohrbach, that German film critics have yet to master (157).

In addition to Germany's professional film critics, however, Rohrbach's critical salvo has a second, more subtly expressed target. To establish what he considers the irrelevance of German film critics for the larger movie-going audience in the third millennium, Rohrbach points out that the same critics who lambasted Tom Tykwer's *Das Parfum — Die Geschichte eines Mörders* (*Perfume: The Story of a Murderer*, 2006), a mega-production produced by Bernd Eichinger's Constantin Film (for which Rohrbach serves as a board member), had showered Grisebach's low-budget film with effusive praise. The result of these critical efforts: the latter attracted a mere 26,000 German theatrical viewers whereas the former more than 5.5 million. Rohrbach could have certainly made the same point with different references, but his polemical intervention occurred at the very time when a larger debate in the German *Feuilletons* raged about the fact that the selection process for the short list of the Deutscher Filmpreis did not result in a single nomination for *Sehnsucht*, whereas *Das Parfum* received eight.

The fact that this most immediate context for Rohrbach's publication does not fully explain his choice of examples grows even clearer when Rohrbach concludes by referencing another low-budget German film that also enthused German film critics but failed to attract a larger audience at the box office: Christoph Hochhäusler's *Milchwald* (*This Very Moment*, 2003). Proffering his argument in the form of a rhetorical question, Rohrbach asks, "if, as one could read, *Milchwald* . . . was a masterpiece, then what is *Citizen Kane*?" (157). In his essay, Rohrbach does not mention that Hochhäusler was one of the most vocal critics among German filmmakers of the Film Academy's appropriation of the Deutscher Filmpreis.[6] It is therefore tempting to attribute this specific reference to the producer's desire for taking a cheap shot at one of his critics. Speculation aside, however, what remains undisputable is that both Hochhäusler and Grisebach are considered exponents of a new German filmmaking movement — the so-called Berlin School — that has received considerable acclaim not only from those German film critics who harbor low opinions of German mainstream films but also from a slowly but steadily growing group of cineastes and critics *outside* of Germany.

The Berlin School, which sometimes is also referred to as the *nouvelle vague Allemande* — a term French film critics coined in the mid-2000s upon seeing a number of German films that included, but were not limited to, films by directors associated with the Berlin School[7] — is a loosely configured group of filmmakers who share a desire to infuse German cinema with a new sense of reality. Displaying little interest in revisiting the well-trodden grounds of preunification history, these directors — Hochhäusler and Grisebach, who belong to the second generation of the Berlin School together with Ulrich Köhler, Benjamin Heisenberg, Maren Ade, Elke Hauck, Henner Winckler, and Maria Speth, as well as Christian Petzold, Angela Schanelec, and Thomas Arslan, who constitute the first generation — instead opt to find their smaller-scale stories in the present of post-Wall Germany. In so doing, films such as *Mein langsames Leben* (*Passing Summer*, 2001), *In den Tag hinein* (*The Days Between*, 2001), *Bungalow* (2002), *Falscher Bekenner* (*Low Profile*, 2005), *Yella* (2007), and *Karger* (2007) confront (German) audiences with new images of the country and its people that are narratively and aesthetically rendered so that they suspend viewers' ability immediately to recognize, and thus reduce to their own preconceived notions, what these films depict.

For example, these films generally refuse to provide establishing shots of locations, thus denying viewers the possibility of immediately reframing what they see through recourse to categories of recognition or knowledge; withholding such information requires the kind of encounter with images (and sounds) that enforces a suspension in the viewer of his or her desire for familiarity and pleasure, indeed that subjects the viewer to the images, rather than instilling a sense of control over them. Furthermore, most of these films abstain from psychologizing their characters; they do not allow audiences to identify with characters by providing us with easily legible signs by which we might be able to assess to what degree we should emotionally invest ourselves in the protagonists. However, perhaps most significant is many of these films' predilection for modulating the very language of "representational realism" to which most viewers have been habituated and, crucially, through which they tend to perceive the very *Realitätsnähe* (proximity to reality) that German viewers appreciate the most about home-grown productions.[8] In *Sehnsucht*, for instance, Grisebach initially subjects her viewers to images that appear as documentary-realist (with their attending codes of realism and veracity that affect viewers with the sensation of being "close to reality") only to subtly redistribute our sensations and perceptions of what we have seen by intensifying the degree of her images' "realism" to the point that we suddenly and unexpectedly find ourselves faced with melodramatic *tableaux vivants*, the very opposite of representational realism. The redistribution of the sensible effected by this aesthetic oscillation occurs repeatedly throughout the film, as if Grisebach were set on retraining our perceptive habits, our regard for reality: affecting her viewers more through the *force* of her images than through the detour of narrative, Grisebach confronts her viewers with the demand to resee — to resense and reperceive — the reality of the images themselves, rather than accepting the images as *realitätsnahe* representations of German reality.

If we can take this example as emblematic of the Berlin School at large, we might say that these filmmakers, who to date have collectively forty-some films to their credit, do not ask audiences to judge the representational veracity of what they show against a set of preformed images of Germany derived from standardized media representations that commonly count as *realitätsnah*; rather, the Berlin School films' affective intensification of the very sensation of alleged *Realitätsnähe* tends to force audiences to come to terms with the demand to resee that with which they assumed sufficient familiarity: Germany itself. What is ultimately at stake in Rohrbach's polemic is, then, the very perception of Germany — both within and without the country — that the Berlin School films might affect. Indeed, Rohrbach arguably singled out Grisebach's seemingly completely apolitical and commercially unsuccessful film as a major focus for his scathing critique of German film critics precisely because it marks the eruption into speech of those who otherwise find themselves merely spoken for, if not altogether ignored and frequently silenced in the German mediascape.

Judging from its critical reception, this eruption into discourse facilitated by *Sehnsucht* is itself defined by the film's particular mode of encounter with (German) reality — an aesthetic mode of encounter that simultaneously invokes the register of representational realism and its attendant truth claims, and affectively intensifies this register to such a degree that our *perception* of the reality (and truth) it seemingly represents is put at stake. In so doing it offers a counterprogram to what we might call the *Normalisierung* aesthetic of both the "cinema of consensus" films of the early to mid-1990s and post-"cinema of consensus" historical films such as Oliver Hirschbiegel's *Der Untergang* (*Downfall*, 2004), Florian Henckel von Donnersmarck's *Das Leben der Anderen*

(*The Lives of Others*, 2006), or Uli Edel's *Der Baader Meinhof Komplex* (*The Baader Meinhof Complex*, 2008) that the industry promotes as true representatives of contemporary German cinema and culture. The Berlin School contests such representational — indeed "state film" — claims, not by dialectically arguing against them on the level of content but by mobilizing a different mode of rendering reality sensible; as a result, films such as *Sehnsucht, Milchwald*, or, more recently, Petzold's *Jerichow* (2009) and Arslan's *Im Schatten* (*In the Shadows*, 2010), invite their viewers to reassess the self-serving, consensus-driven representational claims (to "normalcy") of "state films" precisely by virtue of the fact that the plane of the sensible itself is being affected — altered, reconfigured, redistributed — by the eruption into speech that Grisebach's unassuming film performatively marks.

In short, if one had to ascribe to the Berlin School something like a political program, then it would be that their interventions in German film history, and through that in the culture of Germany in the present, amount to the expression of a *countercinema* — a cinema consisting of an effort to counter the history of Germany manufactured by the mainstream film industry, by means of a recourse to a series of micro(hi)stories that cumulatively pose the question of who or what Germany (and thus a German *nation* as well as a *German* national cinema) is in the first place. Given this subtext of Rohrbach's attack on German film critics, we recognize the attempt by one of the central representatives of the German film establishment to defend its prerogative to determine who sets the definition of German national cinema and, implicitly, what images and stories end up representing Germany. The timing of this counterstrike by the establishment is significant, for it was at the very moment when the Berlin School experienced its long annus mirabilis (in the period demarcated by the 2005 Cannes Film Festival and the 2007 Berlin Film Festival, about a dozen of their films premiered), and when cineastes across the world slowly began taking note of this new German film movement, that one of the establishment's most prominent figures deployed significant rhetorical force against it — attempting, it would seem, to undermine the very legitimacy of any effort to provide a counterdefinition of German national cinema.

See also:

- 28 March 1933: Goebbels's Kaiserhof Speech Reveals Tension between National and International Aims of Nazi Cinema
- 23 June 1968: Alexander Kluge Egged in Berlin, Months Later Awarded Gold Lion in Venice
- 16 October 2003: Chancellor Gerhard Schröder Sheds Tears — Again — at Premiere of *Das Wunder von Bern*

Notes

[1] For German box office numbers, consult the biannual publications of the FFA at http://www.ffa.de/index.php?page=publikationsuebersicht.

[2] For a critique of this celebration's terms, see Katja Nicodemus, "Große Figuren, große Gefühle," *Die Zeit* (10 February 2005).

[3] Günter Rohrbach, "Das Schmollen der Autisten," *Der Spiegel* 04, no. 07 (22 January 2007): 156–57.

[4] Eric Rentschler, "From New German Cinema to the Post-Wall Cinema of Consensus," in *Cinema and Nation*, ed. Mette Hjort and Scott Mackenzie (New York: Routledge, 2000): 260–77.

[5] Rohrbach, "Das Schmollen," 157 (hereafter cited in text). The organization of German film critics offers a dossier, "Schwerpunkt 2: Rohrbach und die Folgen," featuring five responses to Rohrbach's essay at http://www.vdfk.de/122-notizen-zum-kino-3.

[6] Christoph Hochhäusler, "Klasse oder Masse: Ein paar Einwände gegen die Privatisierung des Deutschen Filmpreis durch die Bundesregierung," *Artechock* (09/08/2003), http://www.artechock.de/film/text/artikel/2003/09_17_filmpreis.htm.

[7] The term's earliest mention occurs possibly here: http://www.critikat.com/Nouvelle-Vague-Allemande-En-route.html.

[8] "Deutschen Filme werden im Vergleich zum amerikanischen Film — wie schon bei der ersten Befragung vor zwei Jahren — Realitätsnähe, inhaltliche Qualität und gute Dialoge attestiert." "Deutsche Filme immer populärer." http://www.ffa.de/downloads/publikationen/ffa_intern/ffa_info_1_2010.pdf.

25 February 2007: *Das Leben der Anderen* Follows Blueprint for Foreign-Language Oscar Success

Paul Cooke

A guilt-ridden Christa-Maria commits suicide.
Das Leben der Anderen *(2007). DVD capture.*

FLORIAN HENCKEL VON DONNERSMARCK'S *Das Leben der Anderen* (*The Lives of Others*, 2006) was something of a surprise choice by the American Academy of Motion Picture Arts and Sciences for an award. Set in 1984, the film offers the spectator a suitably Orwellian image of the East German state, in which the writer Georg Dreyman (Sebastian Koch) is placed under surveillance by the state's infamous security service, the Ministerium für Staatssicherheit (commonly referred to as the Stasi), on the advice of a corrupt party official, Minister Bruno Hempf (Thomas Thieme). During the surveillance operation, the controlling Stasi officer, Gerd Wiesler (Ulrich Mühe), a man initially wholly convinced of the GDR's status as the better postwar Germany and the need of his organization to protect the state against Western counterrevolutionary forces, begins to lose faith in the GDR's "socialist" project. He is attracted, instead, to the humanist artistic worldview to which he is introduced by spying on the writer and his actress partner Christa-Maria Sieland (Martina Gedeck), a woman who is, in turn, exploited with tragic consequences as an "Unofficial Collaborator" by the organization, and for sex by Hempf. As Wiesler is drawn ever closer to the couple, instead of relaying to his superiors Dreyman's gradual turn to dissidence, he protects the writer, producing innocuous reports and even removing an incriminating typewriter from the man's flat, which would have provided his Stasi colleagues with evidence that Dreyman was the author of an inflammatory essay published in the West.

That a German film should be nominated, or indeed win the Oscar for Best Foreign Language Film, the most prized of international accolades both in terms of national kudos and financial return to the production team, is no longer such a rare event. Since unification, German films have been a regular feature of the awards ceremony, from Michael Verhoeven's *Das schreckliche Mädchen* (*The Nasty Girl*) in 1990, to Uli Edel's *Der Baader Meinhof Komplex* (*The Baader Meinhof Complex*) in 2009, with a win in 2001 for Caroline Link's *Nirgendwo in Afrika* (*Nowhere in Africa*). This is not to mention the success of the Austrian-German coproduction *Die Fälscher* (*The Counterfeiters*, 2007), submitted under an Austrian flag in 2008, the nominations for best documentary of Wim Wenders's *Buena Vista Social Club* (1999) and Byambasuren Davaa and Luigi Falorni's *Die Geschichte vom weinenden Kamel* (*The Story of the Weeping Camel*, 2003), or the three wins for German Short Films, most recently Jochen Alexander Freydank's *Spielzeugland* (*Toyland*, 2007). If one includes the nine wins in the "Student Oscars" by a German production, or the thirteen Technical Oscars for the Munich-based film camera company ARRI, the magnitude of the nation's achievement becomes even clearer.

Nonetheless, *Das Leben der Anderen* was not the favorite to win. First, a film that cost only $2 million to produce would hardly seem to be in the Oscar-winning league. Compare this budget with the $19 million spent on Guillermo del Toro's *El Laberinto del fauno* (*Pan's Labyrinth*, 2006), which *was* tipped to win. Second, and perhaps more surprising, this was a film looking at life in the GDR, a topic that had never before attracted the attention of the Academy. During the existence of the East German state, only one film by DEFA (Deutsche Film-Aktiengesellschaft, East Germany's state-owned film company) secured a nomination: Frank Beyer's adaptation of Jurek Becker's depiction of life in a Jewish ghetto during the Second World War, *Jakob der Lügner* (*Jakob the Liar*, 1974). Since unification, the Export Union of German Cinema, which is responsible for selecting the German film to be put forward for nomination, has chosen a number of films dealing with GDR-related topics, including Margarethe von Trotta's story of a couple divided by the building of the Berlin Wall, *Das Versprechen* (*The Promise*, 1995), and Wolfgang Becker's comic engagement with *Ostalgie* (contemporary nostalgia for the GDR), *Good Bye Lenin!* (2003). None of these films gained even a final nomination by the Academy. As is clearly evidenced by Germany's two previous winners, Link's *Nirgendwo in Afrika* and Volker Schlöndorff's adaptation of Günter Grass's *Die Blechtrommel*

(*The Tin Drum*, 1979), National Socialism and the Second World War have historically provided the material with the best chances of Oscars success. That is not to say that other topics have not gained nominations: Link's first film, *Jenseits der Stille* (*Beyond Silence*, 1996), an account of a young woman's attempt to reconcile the needs of her deaf parents with her own musical ambitions, and Edel's depiction of 1970s West German urban terrorism, *Der Baader Meinhof Komplex* (*The Baader Meinhof Complex*), have both made the Academy's shortlist. Nevertheless, as Peter Zander puts it bluntly, "Nazi topics work best at the Oscars" — indeed, not only for German filmmakers, but across the whole range of awards, as the five nominations in 2008 for the US adaptation of Bernhard Schlink's *Der Vorleser* (*The Reader*) prove.[1]

Why, then, did *Das Leben der Anderen* win an Oscar, when all the other GDR-based narratives have failed? Of crucial importance was, without doubt, the extraordinarily well-orchestrated promotion campaign by the film's US distribution company Sony Pictures Classics. The film opened in Los Angeles for one week in December 2006 in order to qualify for the Los Angeles Film Critics Association Awards, an important event that often indicates subsequent Oscar success. This was then followed by special screenings for critics and other key opinion-makers, to create "buzz" around the film. It did not enter general release until February 2007, in the immediate run up to the ceremony, at which point Henckel von Donnersmarck was traveling the United States from coast to coast, giving up to twenty interviews a day, his confidence with the English language making him an easy guest for US talk-show hosts.

Moreover, while Henckel von Donnersmarck would seem to be bucking the trend with regard to the topic of the film, in other respects he would seem to assiduously follow the broader rules for winning the foreign-language Oscar. As Georg Seeßlen notes, in order to win in this category, first and foremost "the film has to be 'foreign enough,' but must also not flout the aesthetic codes of the dream factory too flagrantly."[2] This has, in fact, been a guiding principle of the German film industry since at least the days of Weimar, when Erich Pommer used the cachet of German expressionism amongst the American middle classes to market *Das Cabinet des Dr. Caligari* (*The Cabinet of Dr. Caligari*, 1920) in the United States, a film that *looks* avant-garde, but in many respects is simply a mainstream horror movie.[3] With regard to the foreign-language Oscar, recent winners have similarly mixed an exotic setting with a straightforward narrative that apes Hollywood genre conventions. One thinks, for example, of Gabriele Salvatores's pleasantly nostalgic Second World War comedy *Mediterraneo* (1991), or the French-Canadian *Les Invasions barbares* (*The Invasion of the Barbarians*, 2003), which although in a foreign language has the feel of an American "indie" in the style of cross-over hits such as Jason Reitman's Oscar-winning *Juno* (2007). In the case of

Das Leben der Anderen, the GDR serves as the backdrop to a universally understandable melodrama. In the tradition of Michael Curtiz (*Mildred Pierce*, 1945) or Douglas Sirk (*All That Heaven Allows*, 1955), the film follows the classic pattern of a female protagonist being punished for disloyalty to her lover. That said, for a number of critics it was less the way the film conformed to the genre conventions of melodrama that led to its success in the United States, than its resonance with the nation's growing mood of paranoia toward "global terrorism." Working, as Lars-Olav Beier suggests, in the tradition of "paranoia thrillers like Francis Ford Coppola's *The Conversation* (1974) or Alan J. Pakula's *All the President's Men* (1976)," which spoke to the Watergate generation, *Das Leben der Anderen* resonated, it was suggested, with an American public that could see its own dystopian future reflected in the film's portrayal of a government similarly obsessed with state security.[4]

Of course, while the foreign Oscar contender should be understandable to an American audience, it must, as already noted, still be "foreign enough" to give it a "Unique Selling Point" within the American market. As Seeßlen puts it, "a good 'foreign' film is one that shows an exotic, small secluded country. . . . A good foreign film is always like visiting a museum." The reference to a film as a museum is revealing here, and perhaps suggests why heritage films have always fared so well at the Oscars, since the genre first gained prominence in the 1980s with British films such as Hugh Hudson's *Chariots of Fire* (1981) and James Ivory's *A Room with a View* (1985). In such films the past becomes "another country," presented to the spectator as an exotic living museum, full of country houses and period dresses. In similar vein, *Das Leben der Anderen*, like many of the National Socialist-themed films that have garnered nominations and awards, can be seen as a German reworking of the British heritage genre, placing the nation's grisly history on display.[5] As he is at pains to make clear, Henckel von Donnersmarck put in a huge amount of effort to produce a chillingly authentic image of the GDR, augmented by cinematographer Hagen Bogdanski's use of a color palette of grey and brown tones familiar from old television footage of the time, which helps to transport the spectator back to the East Germany of the 1980s.[6] We learn how the Stasi insisted its victims sit on their hands, so that the interrogating officer could collect a sample of a prisoner's sweat, which would then be kept in store in case s/he escaped and needed to be tracked down by dogs. We see the devices the Stasi used to steam open the population's letters, and are granted a detailed tour of the room from where the surveillance operation against Dreyman is carried out. We are first introduced to the finished surveillance suite as Wiesler enters it. He walks in, flicks a switch, and the room is lit up in a flash of neon, revealing a GDR chamber of horrors where the Stasi officer can both listen to and influence life in the flat below. While we are left in no doubt as to the destructive capabilities of Wiesler in particular and the Stasi in general, the focus on original artifacts allows the spectator to indulge their fascination for the past. One is reminded here of Nazi heritage movies such as Oliver Hirschbiegel's Oscar-nominated film about the last days of Hitler, *Der Untergang* (*Downfall*, 2004), which similarly fed into Western society's perennial fascination with Nazi paraphernalia in its detailed visual presentation of the period, offering the spectator a virtual tour of Hitler's Bunker.

The notion of *Das Leben der Anderen* as a grisly reworking of the British heritage film, thereby linking it to films such as *Der Untergang*, leads us neatly to the final reason why Henckel von Donnersmarck's film was successful. While, on the face of it, this is a film about the GDR, *Das Leben der Anderen* ultimately has far more in common with recently nominated films that have depicted Germany's National Socialist history than with von Trotta's *Das Versprechen* or Becker's *Good Bye Lenin!* In this regard, it is revealing that Manfred Wilke should be the historical consultant for the film.[7] Wilke, a respected historian and sociologist, was also an expert witness on the Bundestag Commission into the nature and effects of the East German dictatorship, a commission that was seen by many to offer official sanction to a view of the GDR as nothing more than a totalitarian "Stasi State," and as such a continuation of the Nazi dictatorship in an another guise.[8] Such a view of the GDR past has led to a good deal of disquiet amongst citizens of the ex-GDR, many of whom feel it to be a misrepresentation of the everyday experience of the general population. Challenging a monochrome reading of the GDR as a totalitarian state — different from Nazi Germany only in the shift in color from brown to red — has been at the heart of many of the most successful films about East Germany of recent years, not least *Good Bye Lenin!* Although criticized by many as indulging contemporary *Ostalgie*, the film in fact explores the reasons behind the phenomenon, examining how nostalgia for aspects of GDR life reflects the population's need to acknowledge the continuing place of the former East German state as a lived experience in contemporary identity constructions.[9] In *Das Leben der Anderen* we see the return of the GDR as "Stasi State." This is an historical paradigm that remains deeply problematic for many who lived through this period of history, as the film's reception in Germany showed. However, for the Academy at least, it has allowed a further aspect of the nation's difficult past to be translated into Oscar gold.[10]

See also:

- 29 May 1929: Oscar for Emil Jannings Highlights Exchange between German and American Film Industries
- 23 July 1991: ZDF Broadcast of *Ostkreuz* Initiates Darker Reckoning with the *Wende*
- 8 September 2004: *Der Untergang* Offers Palatable Authenticity

Notes

[1] Peter Zander, "Nazi-Stoffe gehen bei den Oscars am besten," *Die Welt* (23 February 2009).

[2] Georg Seeßlen, "So gewinnt man einen Auslands-Oscar," *Die Zeit* (22 February 2007).

[3] For further discussion, see Mike Budd, "Moments of Caligari" in *The Cabinet of Dr. Caligari: Texts, Contexts, Histories*, ed. Mike Budd (New Brunswick, NJ: Rutgers UP, 1990), 7–118; here 64.

[4] Lars-Olav Beier, "On the Oscar Campaign Trail," *Spiegel Online International* (23 February 2007), http://www.spiegel.de/international/spiegel/0,1518,466450,00.html.

[5] For further discussion see Lutz Koepnick, "Reframing the Past: Heritage Cinema and Holocaust in the 1990s," *New German Critique* 87 (2002): 47–82.

[6] Sebastian Handke, "Die Wanzen sind echt: Kinodebatte über *Das Leben der Anderen*," *Tagesspiegel* (8 April 2006).

[7] See Manfred Wilke, "Fiktion oder erlebte Geschichte? Zur Frage der Glaubwürdigkeit des Films *Das Leben der Anderen*," *German Studies Review* 31, no. 3 (2008): 589–98.

[8] For further discussion, see my *Representing East Germany since Unification: From Colonization to Nostalgia* (Oxford: Berg, 2005), 27–60.

[9] See *Representing East Germany since Unification*, 128–40.

[10] For a discussion of the reception of the film in Germany, see Lu Seegers, "Das Leben der Anderen oder der 'richtige' Erinnerung an die DDR," in *Film und kulturelle Erinnerung: Plurimediale Konstellationen*, ed. Astrid Erll and Stephanie Wodianka, 21–52 (Berlin: Walter de Gruyter, 2008).

6 December 2007: Indie Film *Für den unbekannten Hund* Seeks Space for Marginalized Male Heroism

Patricia Anne Simpson

Bastian burns his companion's travel diary. Für den unbekannten Hund. (2007). Photo by Benjamin Reding. Credit: Dominik and Benjamin Reding.

WHEN TWIN DIRECTOR-SCREENWRITERS Dominik and Benjamin Reding released *Für den unbekannten Hund* (For the unknown dog, 2007) into the world of independent cinema, they contributed to a larger discourse about new models of heroism in a postnational context.[1] This film has a seemingly quirky choice of subject matter: a road movie about a *Wandergeselle* (journeyman) and his plight in the contemporary guild system. The Redings' focus on the characters who populate this marginal minority departs from their earlier work. Their film *Oi! Warning* (1999) revolves around conflict and conformity in a male-dominated subculture of skinhead-punk identities. In their 2007 film, the Redings effectively reimagine the genre of the road movie and its potentially, though not inevitably, redemptive qualities. Despite the apparent differences in the respective films, however, they share attention to marginalized masculine identities negotiating relationships to each other, to a topography, and to a code of ethical behavior that defines community.

In his work on deterritorializing the New German Cinema, John Davidson discusses the contrast between the open road and "home" as a sanctuary or refuge, one that "establishes a safe place within open space."[2] *Für den unbekannten Hund* stands in contrast to this generic model, for life on the road to redemption proves endless and treacherous, and the concept of home elusive. The Redings' version of the contemporary road eschews any recreation of home for the protagonist Bastian (Lukas Steltner), their incarnation of the modern tradesman-as-nomad. Throughout his journey, the fraternal bonds that are forged through work and mobility provide only a tenuous sense of community. Like their first film, *Für den unbekannten Hund* nonetheless follows a path to a new ethics of marginalized heroism instantiated in a journeyman's choice of a life on the road. In this way, the film also comments self-reflectively on the film industry, much like Wim Wenders's *Im Lauf der Zeit* (*Kings of the Road*, 1976), with its allegorization of a German film industry lacking adequate screening venues. In this tradition, *Für den unbekannten Hund* foregrounds the importance of the "artisanal" in independent filmmaking in a postnational and globalizing cultural context.[3]

The potential for allegory in this film is great; the role of the *Wandergeselle* owes its history to times of prosperity, rather than of poverty, though many references in this film recall the conditions of 1920s Germany, when, as the directors point out in the commentary, unemployment forced thousands to travel in pursuit of work. Bastian takes to the road in part to overcome guilt: he has committed a senseless murder during a gas station robbery, and the identity of his victim will shape his own fate. At first reluctant to live without motorized transportation and his cell phone, Bastian eventually embraces adherence to a code of honor established by the guild and its members. On the road, he learns his trade and internalizes the behavior and craft of the stonemasons who comprise his new community; he accomplishes this transformation through the intervention of Festus (Sascha Reimann), his mentor, friend, and fellow journeyman. In the course of the film, Bastian discovers that the homeless man killed in the inaugural crime was Festus's closest friend. For Festus, this friend had violated the guild's homosocial code of propriety, and we discover that Festus himself is capable of betrayal, of adhering to a code of honor at the expense of intersubjective relationships. The film portrays the bonds forged by work and wandering in this small, male-dominated community.

The Redings' treatment of the *Wandergeselle* is unique in contemporary cinema, yet haunting similarities nonetheless emerge between their portrayal of a postmodern journeymen and their previous film about subcultural loyalties and blood feuds. These films, when seen in the context of other cinematic dramas that focus on young men and group violence, among them *Kombat Sechzehn* (Combat sixteen, 2005), underwrite an ethics of marginalized heroism within postnational German film.[4] Randall Halle notes the audience potential for lamenting a lost "authenticity of the local and the specific" in current film production and consumption, but challenges this sense of demise on several levels.[5] The Redings' work attests to their ability to reassert the local without the arch politics of reclaiming the national as a primary category for organizing identity. These films disclose an alternative to the dislocated, deterritorialized identities characteristic of much contemporary German cinema. *Für den unbekannten Hund* represents a space in which marginalized masculinities can redefine their coming-of-age in a heroic register. The path is eccentric. The new hero commits violent acts, repudiates his crime, and seeks redemption on the road. In contrast to the nation as the key element of self-definition in the films from skinhead subcultures, *Für den unbekannten Hund* does not take recourse to the national as a constitutive model of contemporary identity, even though it inhabits the peculiarly national work-structure of the guild system.

In their earlier film *Oi! Warning*, the Redings portray the emotional and social dynamics of skinhead culture and its appeal to disaffected young men. Their stated intention is to portray "skinheads (nonpolitical Oi skins), squatters, modern-primitives and tribes" in ways that challenge prevailing media clichés.[6] Janosch (Sascha Backhaus) abandons his home and overly attentive mother in the Bodensee to seek out his friend, Koma (Simon Goerts), a Dortmund skinhead and kickboxer. Janosch moves from idyll to idol and himself shaves his head and becomes a member of the group. His allegiance to the skin collective is disrupted, however, when he meets and becomes sexually involved with Zottel (Jens Veith), a fire-eating punk who lives in a mobile home and literally revels in dirt. The hatred between skins and punks fuels Koma's urgent need to brutalize the punk, and Janosch's fear of his friend overwhelms his emotional and physical bond with Zottel. Rather than defend his punk partner, Janosch remains silent about their relationship, opting for acceptance from a tyrannical Koma. The voice-over at the end is full of regret: the audience learns a lesson in betrayal and remorse from Janosch's failure to acknowledge Zottel as an intimate friend. The film serves as a cautionary tale not to repeat the mistakes of its failed hero.

For better or worse, this film is often associated with more mainstream attempts to portray a young male subculture to a wider audience that expects nationalism to be an integral part of the skinhead story.

Mirko Borscht's *Kombat Sechzehn* also explores the psychodynamics of skinhead culture, but here the director complicates the sociopolitical context. Georg (Florian Bartholomäi) reluctantly moves with his father and sister from Frankfurt am Main to Frankfurt an der Oder. Again, the move represents a larger issue: the dislocation of identity symbolized by a territorial shift from the former West to East Germany. Borscht's film evokes issues of borderlands and political boundaries. Personal and political affiliations blur in this film. Georg's extensive training in Taekwondo and ability to prevail in street fighting make him an attractive recruit for a group of local kids. They all eventually fall under the influence of a larger, organized, ultra-right-wing movement. When the gang helps put up placards protesting plans for a new shopping mall, Georg claims that his objections are primarily personal — his father is involved in the project and this job precipitated the move that has derailed Georg's life. The right-wing organizer replies: "Germany is personal." Thomas (Ludwig Trepte) plays the scrappy leader of the local gang who first taunts and then befriends Georg. Yet Thomas shares the politics of the right-wing organizers. The audience learns late in the film that Thomas's vituperative hatred of Poles derives at least in part from his father's extramarital affair with a Polish woman. Thomas's nationalist politics reflect a need to police borders both geographic and personal: his father's affair destroyed his parents' relationship and ruined his family life. The interplay between personal disappointment and right-wing radicalism does not exculpate the film's protagonists from blame. Ultimately Thomas comes to Georg's defense in defiance of his public politics. Making decisions that return moral agency to the individual constitutes a critical moment in their friendship. That the characters act in defiance of the prevailing ethos generated by skinhead subculture redeems them and strengthens their bond. The film negotiates multiple affiliations in the attempt to stabilize a specific national identity within the maelstrom of post-Wall globalization, but returns loyalty to a personal level, at which adversarial relationships are channeled into martial-arts rivalries.

While films with a focus on male subcultures share common ground with a series of postunification "coming of age" films (such as *Sonnenallee*, *Herr Lehmann*, *Good Bye Lenin!*, and others), these works hail from socially marginalized spaces characterized most often by local codes, aggressive behavior, and acts of violence; these are predicated on conflict between dominant national and ethnic identities. In some ways, Bernd Schadewald's 1987 *Verlierer* (Losers) functions as a precursor to this generation of films about gang rivalry. His focus on the conflict between the Sharks and the Rats invites comparisons to *West Side Story*, but a friendship between Mücke and the young Turkish man he helps save from a beating by neo-Nazis replaces that film's love story. At first they are united by their flight from a common enemy, but gang politics overshadow their nascent friendship. Later films follow this paradigm, such as Yilmaz Arslan's riveting *Brudermord* (*Fratricide*, 2005), an allegory of hatred and revenge among Turkish and Kurdish immigrants in Germany. Such films reveal a sense of dislocation also legible in contemporary German cinema, but rewrite the role of the hero in an extremely bleak and leaden time precisely through recoding the meaning of ethical behavior, homosociality, and friendship. Violence becomes a constitutive element in overcoming what Barbara Mennel has discussed in terms of a radical politics that remains "immature."[7] Conversely, skinhead and punk narrative cinema reclaims an ethical high-ground through the experience of a radically local identity after it has been lived to the maximum, rejected, and exceeded. Few films manage to achieve realistic representation of contemporary "tribes" without moralizing. The Redings' film, *Oi! Warning*, shot in black and white, expresses a search for male identity, a journey fraught with violence and conflict. The film contributes to a new ethos of heroism, one based on courage that is not obvious, but rather embodied in a conscious choice to reject a code of violence — or, at least, to accept the guilt of adhering to that code. Knowledge provides a transition to a politics of maturity.

Für den unbekannten Hund explores the closed world of journeymen on the road through a screenplay that revolves around Bastian's journey and the murder in Mecklenburg that prompted it. Bastian aspires to a kind of personal redemption through becoming *zünftig* (proper, but in accordance with the dictates of the guild). The Redings unpack the complex story through snapshots, flashbacks, a whistled tune, and other subtle visual and audio clues that indicate the experience of nomadic work and emotional wandering for the audience. The camera work of Axel Henschel reflects this range with painterly frames, from the panoramic landscape that underscores isolation to the smallest detail of intimacy. The archaism of the uniforms, devotion to skilled handwork, and anachronistic travel stand in stark contrast with the sometimes-futuristic sets, alternately saturated and desaturated to paint the colors of the characters' interior states. Bastian's journey, from guilty flight to admission of guilt — he realizes eventually that his victim was Festus's friend — instills in him the guild ethics that ground him. In a key scene, Bastian and Festus are at an open-air concert when they meet two young women whose looks mirror each other: blond pigtails, dark shirts, ties, and dark red lipstick. The two perk up when they hear the journeymen address a fellow journeywoman as comrade. One blond insists: "You're just like us," and they define themselves as patriotic and national. Festus distances himself, repulsed by their chatter, and identifies himself and his cohort as members of a trade union. The bonds of skilled labor and training transcend any national identity represented in this film. The rockers organize around music and motorcycles, the journeymen around their skills. The Redings succeed in portraying a local identity that is predicated on its isolation from society. At the same time, the wanderers' code recapitulates a hierarchy based on strict measures of honor, dress, and personal discipline, with a goal defined by the acquisition of skills that harkens back to the fourteenth century. In both *Oi! Warning* and *Für den unbekannten Hund*, the Redings invoke radically nationalist politics only to have their protagonists reject those cultures. They make the point that local masculine identity is not necessarily grounded in excessive nationalism.

Though their journeyman film would seem to mark a radical departure from the skin-punk milieu of *Oi! Warning*, in point of fact their tale of the *Wandergeselle* shares common ground with the earlier work in its emphasis on the ethics and homosociality of contemporary subcultures. With *Für den unbekannten Hund*, the Redings reinvigorate the genre of the road movie, even as they resist any generic identification for this film, which has comic moments, an exploding gas station, and monologues of such dramatic intensity they invoke Shakespearean tragedy. Both films further share a concern with how masculine maturity, expressed through a learned ethics, may be achieved through fraternal bonding within the context of a larger community. With this film, the new heroism takes a step beyond the "immature politics" associated with other post-Wall youth dramas, coming-of-age genre films, and local rivalries. It instead reaches back into centuries of national history to chart an itinerary of ethical agency in a postviolent, postnational context.

See also:

- 23 December 1924: *Der letzte Mann* Explores Limits of Modern Community
- 10 January 1927: Brigitte Helm Embodies Ambivalence of the New Woman
- 16 October 2003: Chancellor Gerhard Schröder Sheds Tears — Again — at Premiere of *Das Wunder Von Bern*

Notes

[1] A more in-depth analysis of the film appears in my book, *Cultures of Violence in the New German Street* (Madison and Teaneck: Fairleigh Dickinson University Press, co-published with Rowman & Littlefield, 2012), esp. 105–31.

[2] John Davidson, *Deterritorializing the New German Cinema* (Minneapolis: U of Minnesota P, 1999), 75.

[3] This argument was inspired by Sabine Hake's characterization of contemporary European film production: "Just like the new models of film funding, film production remains divided between global ambitions and artisanal solutions." See Sabina Hake, *German National Cinema*, 2nd ed. (London: Routledge, 2008), 194.

⁴ In using the term "postnational," I intend both the means of production and the content of transnational and intercultural film.

⁵ Randall Halle, *German Film after Germany: Toward a Transnational Aesthetic* (Champaign: U of Illinois P, 2008), 19.

⁶ Dominik and Benjamin Reding, official website. http://www.oiwarning.de/new/english/udfilm/index.phtml.

⁷ Barbara Mennel, "Political Nostalgia and Local Memory: The Kreuzberg of the 1980s in Contemporary German Film," *Germanic Review* 82, no. 1 (2007): 54–78.

11 February 2008: Ulrike Ottinger's *Prater* Wins German Critics' Award for Best Documentary Yet Highlights the Director's Ties to Both Fiction and Nonfiction Film

Nora M. Alter

IN 1972, A 16-MILLIMETER CAMERA captures an extraordinary event performed in an empty field near the Berlin Wall. Nearly a hundred motor vehicles, ten per row, are driven slowly across the field maintaining as little distance between each other as possible. After thirty minutes, the drivers stop their cars, get out, and open their trunks 750 times, placing individual white dishes in and out of their trunks 375 times. A twelve-minute black-and-white documentary film — *Berlinfieber* (*Berlin Fever*) — of this Happening (staged by avant-garde German artist Wolf Vostell) was recorded by the relatively unknown (at that time) Ulrike Ottinger, who had been living in Berlin since 1969. The same year that she documented Vostell's action, Ottinger made another film, *Laokoon & Söhne* (*Laocoon & Sons*). The title references the plight of the mythical figure of Laocoon who, along with his sons, was strangled by sea serpents as punishment by the gods for exposing the ruse of the Trojan Horse. *Laokoon & Söhne* was as different from *Berlinfieber* as the Lumière Brothers' *Workers Leaving the Factory* was from George Méliès's *Voyage to the Moon*, the two films commonly viewed as dividing film history into nonfiction and fiction. Whereas *Berlinfieber* is a documentary short of a "real" event that took place one beautiful September day in Berlin involving "real" people and not actors, *Laokoon* is a fantastical narrative that follows an impossible quest for identity by a female protagonist (Tabea Blumenschein) who goes through a series of transformations into characters from other times, places, and genders.

Berlinfieber and *Laokoon & Söhne* bookend two types of filmmaking: in the former, film is used as a record, a testament to a "there was," its indexical nature being fully exploited, while in the latter, film is manipulated for its ability to manufacture illusions, for deception and sleight of hand — in short, for its magical qualities. And yet, despite apparent dissimilarities, one can unite the two projects. In the first instance, we are presented with a large-scale artistic Happening with a carefully crafted choreography of cars and humans rendered machine-like through their repetitive motions. In the second, there is the imaginary subjective performance of personal identity — an actor playing a character playing multiple roles. Ottinger's camera records this spectacle, staged against the backdrop of the banality of everyday life or embedded in the artifice of narrative fiction. *Laokoon* is thus structured intertextually by an imaginary story, a myth; conversely, *Berlinfieber* is framed by the documentary rubric — a cinematic frame of reality presenting an artistic work. In the decades that follow, what will gain Ottinger notoriety are her feature films like *Laokoon*, while her nonfictional excurses will be set aside.

Within the frame of New German Cinema, Ottinger represents a pioneer whose films defy and blur sexual desire and orientation, calling into question heteronormative spectatorship. It is precisely in her refusal to respect the rules of the cinematic game that Ottinger distinguishes herself from her counterparts, and we see unsettling figures emerge in several of her films: *Freak Orlando* (1981), *Usinimage* (1987), and her segment of the omnibus film *Seven Women, Seven Sins, Superbia — Der Stolz* (*Superbia — Pride*, 1986). She features a pair of lavishly costumed Siamese twins being hauled across a blighted barren field in a desolate urban landscape; a black and white painted, nude dwarf leading a giant Great Dane down a toneless city street. Their presence is difficult to accept, provoking lingering questions of exploitation and voyeurism. We are reminded of the films of Frederic Fellini whose cinematic worlds are similarly populated by markedly different figures, or by Diane Arbus's photographed portraitures of giants, twins, and other "freaks." Ottinger has been taking photographs of unusual and striking figures since the age of nine, when she encountered two "exotic" turbaned men on a ship. Her recent short *Still Moving* (2010) is composed primarily of still photographs from her archive, intercut with filmed images of statues, masks, and other ethnographic ephemera. In this respect, Ottinger is part of a larger art cinema, one that smoothly moves into the art world. Critics have noted that Ottinger's signature characteristic is precisely her hybrid style of film production and the intentional blurring of fact and fiction. At the beginning of *Johanna D'arc of Mongolia* (1989), Lady Windermere (Delphine Seyrig) poses the question: "Was it a confrontation with reality or with the imagination. . . . Must imagination shun the encounter with reality? Or are they enamored with each other? Can they form an alliance?" For the next four decades Ottinger's cinematic production will follow this double trajectory of fiction and documentary.

What is significant and unique is the manner in which Ottinger cinematically frames both individuals and their actions. The framing occurs in *Dorian Gray* (1984) when the characters perform on a theatrical set erected on a beach, or in *Johanna D'arc of Mongolia*, where the drone of the long train trip through Siberia is broken up by passengers' performances. In these instances, a documentary view takes over the fictional film as we observe the recorded spectacle — the attraction. But framing is also at play in Ottinger's cinematography — the way in which the subjects are centered in the mise-en-scène, the lighting, the colors, and the precise use of sound. All components are carefully orchestrated to draw the spectators' full attentions to the actor.

Whereas the above-mentioned performance spaces are situated within larger narrative contexts, Ottinger's 2007 *Prater* is a film about film, about the tradition or ritual of cinema and focusing on the art of performance, artifice, and illusion. The film opens with a close-up of a mechanical wooden doll whose mouth opens and shuts as its head turns from side to side. The amplified soundtrack, filled with the clickings and whirrings of its parts set in motion, provides an auditory correlative to the magnified image. Uncanny figures — automatons, dolls, puppets, animals, ghouls, and skeletons — dominate the film. These animated objects retain a museological function, returning the viewer to an earlier time of craftsmanship that recalls the haunting romantic figures of E. T. A. Hoffmann's Olympia or Carlo Collodi's Pinocchio. They remind us of other indicators of the mastery of machines — of the remarkable mechanized water gardens created for the Villa D'Este at Tivoli or Heilbrunn outside of Salzburg. They further remind us of the introduction in the eighteenth and nineteenth century of concepts of leisure and entertainment for the middle and lower classes. No longer was entertainment manufactured solely for the elite in the form of pleasure gardens, operas, and theater — rather, spaces were formally conceived and consecrated for popular use. The oldest such park, the Prater (1766), originated when Kaiser Joseph II decreed that the formerly private hunting park be opened to the public.

For the past two hundred and fifty years the Prater has been a permanent fairground functioning as a heterotopia in the Foucaldian sense, inspiring the creation of such places like Coney Island's Luna Park, similarly celebrated and marked by early cinema. In his 1967 text "Of Other Spaces," the theorist defined heterotopias as those real places in every culture, "which are something like counter-sites, a kind of effectively enacted utopia in which the real sites, all the other real sites that can be found within the culture, are simultaneously represented, contested, and inverted. Places of this kind are outside of all places, even though it may be possible to indicate their location in reality. Because these places are absolutely different from all the sites that they reflect and speak about, I shall call them, by way of contrast to utopias, heterotopias."[1] Many of the same inversions and possibilities that Mikhail Bakhtin theorizes for the carnival are at play in heterotopias, which similarly allow for the possibility of trying out alternative identities and performing new roles. As Ottinger observes, "although the Prater is in the immediate vicinity of the city center, it is an extraterritorial space. Here (almost) anything is possible. The poor encounter the rich, the country the city, foreigners Vienna natives."

Let us return to the opening sequences of *Prater*: following the shots of the wooden puppet, the music on the soundtrack gains momentum, becoming increasingly frantic and frenetic as it is played over images of the *Geisterhaus* (haunted house) — a voice calls out and commands "herein spazieren, herein spazieren!" (come on in!). And enter we do ... into a fantastic cinematic world composed of images and sounds chronicling the history of this most amazing amusement park. Earlier films by Ottinger have transported viewers to locations such as the plains of Mongolia, the markets of Shanghai, the steps of Odessa, and the underground of a divided Berlin. In each instance the journey is marked by the inclusion of performances that momentarily rupture the fictional or documentary frame that encases the narrative. And the journey into the Prater is no different; indeed it is all about performances, illusions, and rituals. As Ottinger notes, connecting modern amusements to age-old practices, "the ventriloquist, who seemingly makes his dummy talk, is here a imitator in the old sense, akin to the animal call imitators of nomadic and hunting societies."

The film offers a broad range of illusions, from phantom rides through the haunted house to the dizzying maze of mirrors and magicians' sleights of hand. The camera records performances of acrobats, musicians, and entertainers. We see how national and cultural identities are displayed and mounted for consumption, such as the nineteenth-century importation of African Ashantis, Fiji Islanders, and "wild men of Borneo." And alongside these "natives" are of course the "freaks," who earn their living displaying and exploiting their infirmities. *Prater*'s footage is a compilation from early films, photographs, and sound recordings, which Ottinger edits and mixes with her own images. The soundtrack includes texts from Joseph Roth, Elias Canetti, Erich Kästner, Elfriede Jelinek, and others. In this mise-en-abyme of illusions in the Prater, how does *Prater* move from being a mere cabinet of curiosities — a cinema of attractions — to a meaningful text?

This shift from attraction to text occurs through Ottinger's inclusion of history on multiple levels. Like Walter Benjamin's materialist historian, Ottinger restores lost narratives about the amusement park and its inhabitants. Thus, we learn about its origins and how some vestiges of its past linger — such as its metamorphosis from a hunting park for the nobility, to a park where until 1920 the average person was allowed to shoot game, to its recent inclusion of a game where people using facsimile rifles fire on mechanized figures that shoot back water. Or how the *Watschenmann* (slap man) used to be a real person who would endure the slaps and blows of customers, until he was replaced by an automaton. She traces the evolution of the park from rudimentary entertainment site to a place full of high-tech speed simulation rides.

Equally important to the official history are the stories of the everyday lives of those individuals who are intimately connected to the Prater; the performers, the freaks, the restaurateurs. Here Ottinger includes interviews with second and third generation Praterites. From the descendent of a man without arms or legs, we hear how his ancestor was compelled to go to Budapest to marry his fiancée since it was illegal for someone so handicapped to marry in Vienna. A Prater family tells the story of their grandfather's founding of the family business there, and a technician who fixes old machines laments their growing extinction, like the once popular dinosaurs buggies he nostalgically keeps in storage. Ottinger also includes footage shot during National Socialism and the fate of this heterotopia populated by "freaks," gypsies, and mixed races. Thus, through multiple interviews another history emerges, that of the private histories of the individuals who work to create the illusions. In *Prater* the voices and history of the Other are told as Ottinger uncovers the labor behind entertainment.

But there is another history that is being played out in *Prater*, and that is of film itself. Prater is a site for the making of films — most notably Carol Reed's *The Third Man*, with its fatal scene atop the Ferris wheel overlooking a war-devastated Vienna. Other films that feature the Prater include *Die kleine Veronika* (Little Veronica, 1929) and Erich von Stroheim's *Merry-Go-Round* (1923). Contemporary film references also abound, as when Veruschka appears in costume as Barbarella. But filmic references go further and exist on a metafilmic level. If, as Sander Gilman has argued, every text contains an autobiographical element, then *Prater* is an autobiographical gesture toward Ottinger's own filmic history. In addition to the insertion of Veruschka as Barbarella, Ottinger intercuts some of her own film footage from *Freak Orlando*. The link between Ottinger's "freaks" and those who inhabit the world of the Prater not only underscores the connection between the cinematic world and that of fairground amusements, but in *Prater*'s commentary and the material included it also points to the persecution of precisely those people considered different and "abnormal" during the Third Reich. Ottinger reminds us of the attempts to shut down the amusement park because it employed and provided a home for so many undesirables. *Prater* also engages with film's relationship to illusion, representation, and technology, metonymically staging a history of cinema. Cinema had its origins in fairgrounds, with films screened in large tents that, due to the fire hazards they posed, were replaced by the nickelodeon. Cinema was part of the many forms of entertainment and illusion promised by a visit to an amusement park. The Prater is above all a screening site — a huge theater distributing performances from all over the world.

The technical craftsmanship and innovativeness behind many of the seemingly banal mechanized automatons and amusements that surface throughout the film is extraordinary. Part of Ottinger's argument is precisely that "there was no technical innovation, no pathbreaking idea that did not immediately surface in the Prater as an amusement." The signifier par excellence for this side of the Prater is the Riesenrad, a huge spoked Ferris wheel that uncannily resembles a monstrous film reel. The Ferris wheel is an anachronistic machine of the nineteenth century, whose place in contemporary fairs and amusement parks is more for those in search of nostalgic experiences and great views rather than high-tech thrills. In his work on early cinema, Ian Christie argues that cinema is the last machine, a relic from the industrial age with all of its parts and components. *Prater* is a film about the archaic technology of filmmaking. As digital production replaces celluloid cinematic craft, just like new rides replace the old, cinema stands like the Ferris wheel — a giant overlooking a century and providing spectacular panoramic views.

Since the 1990s, nonfiction cinema has enjoyed a popularity and growth that has not occurred since its inception. What has been termed as a return to the "real" has dominated all major forms of audiovisual production, from blockbuster documentaries such as *Buena Vista Social Club*, to reality television shows and YouTube and Facebook postings. The genre of nonfiction that was once clearly positioned at the margins of filmmaking has now moved to the center. Ottinger's recent film work reflects part of that general shift. Films like *Prater* or *The Korean Wedding Chest* command as much attention as fictional narrative like *Twelve Chairs*. Perhaps today, more than ever, Ottinger's films, with their special hybrid mix of fact and fiction, hold a central place in the contemporary German filmic landscape.

See also:

- 24 June 1974: Launching of *Frauen und Film* Creates Lasting Forum for Feminist Film Writing and Practice
- 8 June 1986: Farocki's *Wie man sieht* Urges New Ways of Seeing
- 30 April 1999: Werner Herzog's "Minnesota Declaration" Performs Critique of Documentary Cinema

Notes

[1] Michel Foucault, "Of Other Spaces," *Diacritics* 16, no. 1 (Spring 1986): 22–27; here 24.

Epilogue: The Many Lives of Contemporary German Cinema

Jennifer M. Kapczynski & Michael D. Richardson

IN MANY WAYS, it seems an impossible task to write an epilogue for an event-based history such as this. How does one select a representative moment from the past several years that can adequately sum up the current state of German cinema, much less cap off a tradition that extends for more than a century? This challenge begs the question: what degree of hindsight is needed to reflect on the present and future of German-language film? Any scholar seeking to explore the implications and promise of current-day developments faces the challenge of a foreshortened perspective. As film critic Rüdiger Suchsland reflects, to write contemporary criticism requires a kind of "seismographic" perception — that is, an ability to register the smaller and larger shock waves that may run through a given cultural moment.[1] An exploration of the state of German filmmaking, however sensitive, must moreover bear within it a certain degree of uncertainty — that is, it offers less a diagnosis than a prognosis for the present. It is in this spirit that we write this epilogue — not as an effort to provide a totalizing view on the current state of German film, but rather to identify select currents coursing through it. These currents also run through this volume in patterns both convergent and divergent, and point, we believe, toward the future of German cinema.

The time is good for such a critical reassessment, as a recent resurgence in both independent and commercial filmmaking in German-speaking countries has fueled a rise in audience numbers and critical attention both domestically and abroad. Although interest in matters German rose sharply following the fall of the Berlin Wall and unification in 1990, as recently as ten years ago contemporary German-language film production was nearly invisible in international film festivals or critical discourse. We can trace the beginning of this absence back to the fading of New German Cinema in the mid-1980s, which brought a shift in German filmmaking practices, as directors turned their energies to creating works, many of them comedies, that would appeal to domestic audiences and that generally turned away from the formal innovation and critical investigative stance of the preceding generation of auteurist filmmakers. In 2000, film scholar Eric Rentschler identified this trend as a "cinema of consensus" — an insular, "unabashedly conventional" cinema that "consciously seeks ways of saying 'we' in its address to German audiences," in the process invoking troubling "fantasies of a German Film Empire and a national German tradition."[2] While certain films of the era — such as *Männer* (*Men*, 1986) and *Der bewegte Mann* (*Maybe, Maybe Not*, 1996) — did make it beyond the border, and other films, particularly the earliest wave of post-*Wende* films, attempted to grapple with serious domestic political and identity issues, German cinema of the 1990s could be described in broad terms as inward, even provincial in its outlook and reach.

The crisis that German cinema found itself facing at this moment was, in some ways, not new. One need only think of the protests voiced by the Oberhauseners in 1962 against what they saw as the tyranny of the conventional and the pressures of a marketplace that stifled formal experimentation and discouraged works that challenged audience preconceptions. Both moments, moreover, evoke a tension that has defined film from its very beginnings: between cinema as popular entertainment and cinema as an art form. By the 1990s, with films produced and distributed in a highly globalized environment, German cinema could not, if it was to thrive, merely cater to a domestic population. The increasing importance of the global market put pressure on films to appeal to a broader international audience, an appeal defined significantly though not entirely by expectations created and fostered by the conventions of Hollywood cinema. In order for German cinema to survive — to flourish — it would need to square the circle, to manage the tensions between these two impulses of the cinema. This is precisely what happened in Germany in the late 1990s. Those few examples of more challenging cinematic fare that managed to find both domestic success and break into the international market to earn both strong audiences and critical acclaim, such as Tom Tykwer's *Lola rennt* (*Run Lola Run*, 1998), achieved the greatest international success when they managed to speak to the popular narrative or generic conventions of Hollywood cinema, with its global impact on taste and style.

Yet what differentiated this most recent moment of renewal from similar such moments in German cinematic history was the fact that no single genre, no single movement (a là New German Cinema in the late 1960s and early 1970s) dominated. Rather, multiple currents emerged. To be sure, these currents had already existed in German film, but they now served to reinvigorate German cinema precisely by navigating the tensions that existed between the popular and the artistic, the national and the international impulses.

Taking a broad view of the currents that came to the fore at the end of the millenium and today stand out in the contemporary German film landscape, there are two essential trends we can identify. The first of these is a current of what we might dub "pastist" films. These are works that operate according to a basic faith in the particular value of history for the present. How these contemporary films construe that value, however, differs markedly according to their respective projects.

One strand in this pastist trend is embodied by historical dramas, which have continued almost unabated since their heyday in the 1990s and early 2000s, plumbing the depths of Germany's darkest history with aspirations to produce an authentic rendering of the past. The most successful exports of the 1990s and beyond, if we are to judge by such normative standards as box office numbers and industry awards like the Oscars, these films draw upon the history of National Socialism (including *Nirgendwo in Afrika* [*Nowhere in Africa*, 2001]), state abuses under East German socialism (such as *Das Leben der Anderen* [*The Lives of Others*, 2006]), and German terrorism (*Der Baader Meinhof Komplex* [*The Baader Meinhof Complex*, 2008]. These historical films, which Lutz Koepnick has productively identified as "heritage cinema," make hay by conjuring melodramatic tales set during the nation's most grim and tumultuous periods (most recently and controversially, in the case of *Jud Süß — Film ohne Gewissen* [*Jew Suss — Rise and Fall*, 2010], about the making of Nazi Germany's most infamous antisemitic propaganda film).[3] No less than the earlier wave of German "consensus" films, they have relied for their success upon both mainstream formal conventions and mainstream accounts of German history neatly cordoned off from the present. Unlike the earlier wave of comedies, however, these films appear to travel well across borders, and their production appears at present unabated, with a new crop released each summer. In these heritage films, the past is valued for pedagogical and commercial reasons.

A second and related, although aesthetically distinct, strand in the pastist trend is represented by a range of recent documentary films — among them, *Das Himmler Projekt* (*The Himmler Project*, 2000) and *2 oder 3 Dinge, die ich von ihm weiß* (*2 or 3 Things I Know About Him*, 2005) — that push at the boundaries of documentary form while also interrogating the relationship between the Nazi past and the present day. In some respects, these films might best be understood as the contemporary inheritors of New German Cinema, insofar as they explore the ways in which fascism and the Holocaust impact the present; in keeping with that tradition, and unlike recent examples of historical cinema, they resolutely refuse to segregate history, instead probing the blurred border between the past and today. Drawing upon archival footage and other realia from the Nazi period in provocative ways, these films challenge viewers to question a commonplace faith in the archive as the repository of knowledge about history. In the process, the German past opens up to reinterpretation and new processes of meaning-making in the present.

Still a third pastist strand in the contemporary German film landscape concerns not the production of new films, but the preservation and restoration of older ones. Given the landmark status of Fritz Lang's *Metropolis* (1927), its 2010 restoration was arguably the most significant such undertaking in German cinematic history. With a mere 10% of films from the silent era (1895–1930) and only 50% of films produced during the nitrate film sound era (1930–55) having survived, restoration is vital to providing film historians with access to the past and the material needed to develop an understanding of cinematic history. At the same time, film restorations reveal the ways in which film history — and film interpretation — is a subjective constructions, highly dependent upon the material available at any given time. As was the case with the 1998 restoration of *Die freudlose Gasse* (*The Joyless Street*, 1925), the inclusion of a significant amount of new material in *Metropolis* forced critics and film historians to re-evaluate existing interpretations of the work. A renewed focus on the preservation and restoration of early German cinema, spearheaded by the efforts of the Filmmuseum München, as well as the dissemination of restored works on DVD through publishers like Edition Filmmuseum, means that film historians will continue to reengage with and re-write the legacy of both seminal works and nearly-forgotten films.

The second major trend in contemporary German cinema we could identify as "presentist": it is a filmmaking first and foremost oriented toward contemporary questions, which, moreover, frequently questions what place, if any, the national past has in the present. While they have not achieved the same degree of audience success as their melodramatic pastist counterparts, these primarily independent films have drawn strong critical acclaim on the festival circuit and moreover have sparked renewed scholarly interest in contemporary productions. Austrian director Michael Haneke has earned myriad international accolades for films that subtly address conditions in the new Europe (such as *Caché* [*Hidden*, 2005]) or that confront lingering questions about the history of German violence (as in *Das weiße Band* [*The White Ribbon*, 2009]). Most recently, he received the top prize at the 2012 Cannes festival for *Amour* (*Love*, 2012). The so-called Berlin School, a loosely based group of young directors (among them Christian Petzold, Christoph Hochhäusler, Ulrich Köhler, Thomas Arslan, and Angela Schanelec) trained mainly, although not exclusively, at the DFFB film academy in the German capital, has made strong showings at the Berlinale and other international festivals with a body of aesthetically spare films that focuses attention on contemporary German society while also avoiding clichéd notions of German history or conventional sites of German national belonging. This trend is not limited to the Berlin School, but can be applied more broadly to films (many of them created by a generation of young directors) that appear dedicated not only to investigating those matters that shape life in German lands today, ranging from the dominance of global capital to debates on integration, but also to interrogating the role, once presumed by the crafters of New German Cinema, that history plays in the shaping of the present.[4] For this body of present-oriented films, German history — particularly the traumatic legacies of the Second World War or the brutalities of the East German dictatorship — no longer serves as the central orientation or starting point for investigations of contemporary life. This is not to say the past has no meaning for these films, but rather it is treated as only one, non-determinative node in a complex constellation of influences shaping the present day. A case in point is Robert Thalheim's *Am Ende kommen Touristen* (*And Along Come Tourists*, 2007), which, although set in the contemporary town of Oswiecim, Poland, site of the former Auschwitz concentration camp and now memorial, highlights the very inadequacy of today's pedagogical efforts to teach the lessons of the Holocaust to a youth distanced from that history by multiple decades and generations, and at the same time takes on new questions generated by such contemporary issues as economic disparities within the new Europe. While on the surface a film that addresses Auschwitz might appear to represent a classic example of a cinema oriented toward the past, the film ultimately highlights the insufficiency of understanding the present solely or even principally through the lens of history.

This presentist trend also runs through works by such transnationally focused directors as Fatih Akin, who have resituated German culture in a contemporary global context while also garnering extensive commercial and critical attention. Just as the definition of a national cinema has become blurred by globalization of the film industry, so, too, have the definitions of multicultural and transnational cinema become complicated. The urgencies of earlier films, which contended with the realities of immigrant communities and responded to the near complete absence of representations of racial and ethnic difference, particularly representations of Turkish-German identity, have given way to more nuanced and normalized representations of a multicultural Germany. From the sort of bleak portrayals of the lives of immigrants offered in earlier films such as Fassbinder's *Angst Essen Seele auf* (*Ali: Fears Eats the Soul*, 1974) or Helma Sanders's *Shirins Hochzeit* (*Shirin's Wedding*, 1975), we have seen a shift toward a new generation of films made by second-generation Turkish-Germans, such as Thomas Arslan's *Geschwister — Kardeşler* (*Brothers and Sisters*, 1997), which, although often unflinching in their portrayal of the challenges of assimilation, do not reduce Germans and Turks to irreconcilable antagonists. Just as films about migrant communities in Germany are no longer the sole province of minority directors (as this volume's entry on *Fremde Haut* has shown), moreover, Turkish-German directors have turned away from a principal focus on social problems. The best proof of this is Yasemin Şamdereli's 2011 film *Almanya — Willkommen in Deutschland*. Like other films by Turkish-German directors, *Almanya* takes as one of its central themes the navigation between multiple identities, the tension between assimilation and retaining one's cultural heritage that hyphenated Germans experience. But it does so with both a new lightness and a complexity: lightness because it couches its representation of serious issues in a humorous context, and complexity because it maps out a variety of relationships — national, ethnic, generational — that reveal identity formation as multidirectional, flowing between spaces and generations.

While it is impossible to find one key moment or text that might encompass all of these directions of German filmmaking, they do find their intersection in a particular cinematic institution. It should come as no surprise that the 2010 premiere of the restored version of *Metropolis* took place at the Friedrichspalast during the Berlinale. That same year marked the celebration of the Berlinale's sixtieth anniversary. Although the festival has had its share of contentious moments, today it stands as a significant event not just for German cinema, but world cinema as well. The European Film Market (EFM), one of the three largest movie markets in the world, is now held concurrently with the Berlinale, while the Berlinale Talent Campus allows young filmmakers to learn from and collaborate with seasoned film professionals. Here, too, however, the tension between art films and popular films, both international and domestic, often comes to the fore. As it has grown in size over the years, the festival has attempted to balance its traditional commitments to politically and socially conscious offerings and formally innovative works with attracting big-name directors and productions, leaving it with a slightly divided character. Films shown in the higher profile Competition section, ostensibly chosen for their broad appeal, have been more often critically disappointing and poorly received by audiences. Films more highly regarded by critics, such as the films from Berlin School directors, have appeared with some frequency — Angela Schanelec's *Orly*, Thomas Arslan's *Im Schatten* (*In the Shadows*), and Benjamin Heisenberg's *Der Räuber* (*The Robber*) all premiered at the 2010 Berlinale, for example — but they often get lost in the Forum or Panorama sections or are only given single screenings. Nonetheless, the Berlinale not only provides an important destination for contemporary filmmakers (both commercially minded and independent ones), but also a key bridge to film history in its Retrospective and Homage sections and, in the Perspektive Deutsches Kino section, a link to the future.

* * *

In this short and admittedly non-exhaustive summary of genres, trends, and institutions, we have attempted to elucidate the chief currents in contemporary German cinema. Which of these will have the most significant role in the future course of German film is difficult to predict, but if there is one thing that can be said with some degree of certainty about the current state of German cinema, it is that it is enjoying a particularly rich and productive moment. As evidenced by the breadth of scholarship contained in this volume, the same might be said about German film criticism. Much remains to be written about the various trajectories that German film history has taken, the moments that have sounded alarm, sparked debate, and encouraged innovation. We offer this volume in the hopes of similarly provoking thought and opening new horizons in the field of German film historiography.

Notes

[1] Rüdiger Suchsland, "Kann ein Seismograph utopisch sein? Gedanken zur Arbeit," *Revolver* 14 (2005) 95–101.

[2] Eric Rentschler, "From New German Cinema to the Post-Wall Cinema of Consensus," in *Cinema and Nation*, ed. Mette Hjort and Scott Makenzie (Routledge: London and New York, 2000), 260–77, here: 275.

[3] Lutz Koepnick, "Reframing the Past: Heritage Cinema and Holocaust in the 1990s," *New German Critique* 87 (Autumn, 2002): 47–82.

[4] Marco Abel, "Intensifying Life: The Cinema of the "Berlin School," *Cineaste* 33.4 (2008), http://www.cineaste.com/articles/the-berlin-school.htm.

Contributors

MARCO ABEL is Associate Professor of English and Film Studies at the University of Nebraska-Lincoln.

RUSSELL A. ALT is a PhD candidate in Germanic Languages and Literatures at Washington University in St. Louis.

NORA M. ALTER is Professor of Film and Media Arts at Temple University.

ERIC AMES is Associate Professor of Germanics and a member of the Cinema Studies faculty at the University of Washington.

ANTJE ASCHEID is Associate Professor of Film Studies at the University of Georgia.

HESTER BAER is Associate Professor of German and Women's & Gender Studies at the University of Oklahoma.

GARY L. BAKER is Professor of German at Denison University in Granville, Ohio.

DAVID BATHRICK is Jacob Gould Schurman Emeritus Professor of German Studies and of Theater, Film, and Dance at Cornell University.

TILMAN BAUMGÄRTEL is a visiting professor at the Department of Media and Communication at the Royal University of Phnom Penh in Cambodia.

HUNTER BIVENS is Assistant Professor of Literature and German Studies at the University of California, Santa Cruz.

JANELLE BLANKENSHIP is Assistant Professor of Film Studies at Western University Canada.

ANNETTE BRAUERHOCH is Professor of Cinema and Television Studies at the University of Paderborn, Germany.

BARTON BYG is a Professor in the German and Scandinavian Studies Program, Department of Languages, Literatures & Cultures, at the University of Massachusetts Amherst.

PAUL COATES is Professor of Film Studies at Western University Canada.

ROGER F. COOK is Professor of German and Director of the Film Studies Program at the University of Missouri.

PAUL COOKE is Professor of German Cultural Studies and executive member of the Centre for World Cinemas at the University of Leeds.

DAVID N. COURY is Associate Professor of Humanistic Studies (German) and Global Studies at the University of Wisconsin-Green Bay.

MICHAEL COWAN is Associate Professor of German Studies and World Cinemas at McGill University.

CAROLA DAFFNER is Assistant Professor of German at Southern Illinois University in Carbondale.

ROBERT VON DASSANOWSKY is Professor of German and Film Studies at the University of Colorado at Colorado Springs.

PAUL DOBRYDEN is a PhD candidate in the Department of German at the University of California, Berkeley.

MONICA FILIMON is Assistant Professor of English at Kingsborough Community College, CUNY (Brooklyn, NY).

JAIMEY FISHER is Associate Professor of German and Cinema and Technocultural Studies as well as director of Cinema and Technocultural Studies at the University of California, Davis.

MATTIAS FREY is Senior Lecturer in Film Studies and Co-Director of the Centre for the Interdisciplinary Study of Film and the Moving Image at the University of Kent, UK.

MILA GANEVA is Associate Professor of German at Miami University in Ohio.

GERD GEMÜNDEN is Sherman Fairchild Professor of the Humanities at Dartmouth College, where he teaches in the Departments of German Studies and Film and Media Studies.

DENIZ GÖKTÜRK is Associate Professor of German and Film & Media at the University of California, Berkeley.

CHRISTINE HAASE is Associate Professor of German in the Department of Germanic and Slavic Studies at the University of Georgia in Athens.

SARA F. HALL is Associate Professor of Germanic Studies at the University of Illinois at Chicago.

RANDALL HALLE is Klaus W. Jonas Professor of German Film and Cultural Studies at the University of Pittsburgh.

BRÍAN HANRAHAN is an ACLS New Faculty Fellow in the Department of Theatre, Film and Dance at Cornell University.

KAMAAL HAQUE is Assistant Professor of German at Dickinson College.

SEBASTIAN HEIDUSCHKE is Assistant Professor of German in the School of Language, Culture, and Society, and Affiliate Faculty in the School of Writing, Literature and Film at Oregon State University.

LAURA HEINS is Assistant Professor of German at University of Virginia, where she also teaches in the Department of Media Studies.

BASTIAN HEINSOHN is Assistant Professor of German in the Department of Modern Languages, Cultures, and Linguistics at Bucknell University.

DAYTON HENDERSON received his PhD in German and Film Studies from the University of California, Berkeley.

BRITTA HERDEGEN holds an MA in German Language and Literature from University of Florida.

NOAH ISENBERG is Director of Screen Studies at Eugene Lang College— The New School for Liberal Arts.

ANTON KAES is Class of 1939 Professor of German and Film & Media at the University of California, Berkeley.

JENNIFER M. KAPCZYNSKI is Associate Professor of German at Washington University in St. Louis.

LUTZ KOEPNICK is Professor of German, Film and Media Studies, and Comparative Literature at Washington University in St. Louis.

BARBARA KOSTA is Professor of German and Head of the Department of German Studies at the University of Arizona.

RICHARD LANGSTON is Associate Professor of German at the University of North Carolina at Chapel Hill.

WILL LEHMAN is Assistant Professor of German at Western Carolina University.

KATHARINA LOEW is Assistant Professor of German and Cinema at the University of Oregon.

MARTINA LÜKE is Assistant Professor In-Residence for German and Comparative Literature and Cultural Studies at the University of Connecticut.

DANIEL H. MAGILOW is Associate Professor of German at the University of Tennessee, Knoxville.

ERIN MCGLOTHLIN is Associate Professor of German and Jewish Studies and Director of Research and Grants at the Center for the Humanities at Washington University in St. Louis.

BARBARA MENNEL is Associate Professor of Film and Media Studies and German in the Departments of English and Languages, Literatures, and Cultures at the University of Florida, Gainesville.

ADELINE MUELLER is currently the Weston Junior Research Fellow in Music at New College, University of Oxford.

TOBIAS NAGL is Associate Professor of Film Studies at Western University Canada.

RACHEL PALFREYMAN is Associate Professor of German at the University of Nottingham.

CORNELIUS PARTSCH is Professor of German in the Department of Modern & Classical Languages at Western Washington University.

BRIGITTE PEUCKER is Elias Leavenworth Professor of German and Professor of Film Studies at Yale University.

LARSON POWELL is Associate Professor of German in the Department of Foreign Languages and Literatures at the University of Missouri–Kansas City.

BRAD PRAGER is Associate Professor of German and a member of the Program in Film Studies at the University of Missouri.

ANDREA REIMANN is a teacher of Deutsch, Gesellschaft and Englisch (German, Social Studies and English) at the Berufsfachschule Winterthur, Switzerland.

ERIC RENTSCHLER is Arthur Kingsley Porter Professor of Germanic Languages and Literatures and Chair of Film and Visual Studies at Harvard University.

MICHAEL D. RICHARDSON is Associate Professor of German and Chair of the Department of Modern Languages and Literatures at Ithaca College.

SIMON RICHTER is Professor of German at the University of Pennsylvania in Philadelphia.

MARTINA M. ROEPKE is Assistant Professor of Visual Culture at VU University Amsterdam, The Netherlands.

CHRISTIAN ROGOWSKI is Professor of German at Amherst College.

ROBERT SCHECHTMAN is an independent scholar.

HEIDE SCHLÜPMANN is Professor emerita of Cinema Studies at Goethe Universität Frankfurt am Main.

TASSILO SCHNEIDER holds a doctorate in Critical Studies from the School of Cinematic Arts at the University of Southern California and is currently working as an independent scholar in Frankfurt, Germany.

KAI SICKS is post-doctoral researcher at the International Graduate Centre for the Study of Culture (GCSC), Justus Liebig University Giessen.

MARC SILBERMAN is Professor of German at the University of Wisconsin in Madison.

PATRICIA ANN SIMPSON is Professor of German Studies at Montana State University.

JONATHAN SKOLNIK is Assistant Professor of German at the University of Massachusetts Amherst.

REINHILD STEINGRÖVER is Associate Professor of German and Film Studies and Chair of the Humanities Department at the Eastman School of Music, University of Rochester.

FAYE STEWART is Assistant Professor of German in the Department of Modern and Classical Languages and Affiliate Faculty in Women's Studies at Georgia State University.

PHILIPP STIASNY is a freelance film historian and editor of *Filmblatt* in Berlin, Germany.

KATIE TRUMPENER is Emily Sanford Professor of English and Comparative Literature at Yale, and a member of the graduate faculty in Film Studies.

JOHN GRIFFITH URANG is Assistant Professor of German at Worcester Polytechnic Institute (WPI).

KRIS VANDER LUGT is an independent German Studies researcher and language consultant. She teaches in the DC Metro area.

JOHANNES VON MOLTKE is Associate Professor for German Studies and Screen Arts & Cultures at the University of Michigan.

PATRICK VONDERAU is Associate Professor of Cinema Studies at Stockholm University, Sweden.

TAN WAELCHLI is Max Geldner Habilitations Fellow at the German Department, University of Basel.

BRIGITTA B. WAGNER is Assistant Professor of Germanic Studies and Film Studies and IU DEFA Project Director at Indiana University-Bloomington.

CYNTHIA WALK is Associate Professor Emerita of German and Film Studies at the University of California, San Diego.

ULRIKE WECKEL is Associate Professor of Modern History at the Ruhr University Bochum.

MICHAEL WEDEL is Professor of Media History at the University of Film and Television "Konrad Wolf" in Potsdam-Babelsberg and co-director of the Film Museum Potsdam.

VALERIE A. WEINSTEIN is Assistant Professor of German Studies at University of Cincinnati.

JOEL WESTERDALE is Assistant Professor in the Department of German Studies at Smith College, Northampton, Massachusetts.

JENNIFER MARSTON WILLIAM is Associate Professor and Chair of the Department of German and Russian at Purdue University.

WILFRIED WILMS is Associate Professor of German at the University of Denver.

GREGORY ZINMAN is Visiting Assistant Professor in the School of Literature, Communication and Culture at the Georgia Institute of Technology and Postdoctoral Fellow at the Smithsonian American Art Museum.

Index of Subjects

abstract cinema. *See* avant-garde cinema
acting, 24, 38, 41, 45–47, 52–53, 58, 67, 86–92, 107–8, 157, 169–70, 174, 186, 188, 191, 228, 357, 373, 407, 411–12, 414–15, 459–60, 477–78, 480, 487, 520–22, 554–55, 560–62, 563, 592, 598–600, 624–26
adaptation, 51, 55, 87, 95, 97, 106, 118, 120, 136, 138, 140, 150, 168, 178–79, 181–82, 213–15, 245, 283, 332, 338, 344, 375, 379, 382, 390, 413, 421, 436, 438–39, 440, 441, 467–68, 516, 560–61, 573–74, 610–11
advertising, 19, 24–25, 32, 41, 53, 61, 74, 82, 84, 101, 105, 145, 179, 188, 192–93, 203, 210, 222–23, 234, 280, 331, 366, 460, 519, 522, 533, 580
amateurism, 3, 4, 173–176, 202–4, 487, 500, 579
American cinema. *See* Hollywood
Amerikanismus (Americanism), 53, 55–56, 75, 168, 193, 264–65, 294, 545
antisemitism, 3, 120, 146, 157–58, 179, 180–83, 220, 234–35, 238, 252, 306, 391, 486
audience. *See* reception
Autorenfilm (author cinema), 47, 51, 106, 203, 445, 544–46, 548
avant-garde cinema, 1–2, 28–29, 67, 69, 81, 98–103, 160–65, 200, 203, 208–12, 283, 291–92, 300, 350, 367, 400, 413, 424, 426, 445, 452, 473, 494, 554–55, 611, 622
awards, 176, 191, 193, 269, 271–73, 291, 294, 309, 344, 371, 397, 418, 433–34, 453, 464, 470, 508, 534, 554, 583–84, 596–7, 602–3, 622, 631

Bergfilm (mountain film), 1, 67, 142–147, 246, 257, 269, 271
Berlinale. *See* festivals
biographical films, 121, 486–87, 548, 578, 626
British cinema. *See* European cinema

capitalism, 55, 59, 67, 79, 112, 118, 150–51, 169–70, 213–16, 245, 270, 282, 284, 289–90, 309, 382, 418–19, 421, 425, 461, 472, 478, 490, 504, 514, 516, 543, 575, 633
censorship, 18, 42, 76–78, 154–55, 162–63, 165, 173, 175, 186, 188, 219–20, 223–24, 227, 230, 238, 272, 291, 298, 309, 315, 331, 343–44, 349, 370, 424, 427, 433, 465, 497, 507
cinema of attractions, 24, 54, 62, 625
cinema of consensus, 532, 545, 549, 574, 603, 606–7, 630–31
cinemas. *See* exhibition
cinematography, 23, 52, 75, 92, 114, 156, 175, 198, 216, 294–95, 433, 465, 492, 514, 612, 624
city film. *See* urbanism
class, 13–14, 16–18, 52, 54, 59, 60–61, 63, 66–67, 105, 119–20, 126, 138, 145, 150, 168, 178, 186, 204, 214, 258, 302, 306, 309, 329, 350, 361, 368–69, 382, 402, 411, 414, 460, 465, 566, 568, 580, 597, 611, 624
colonialism, 14, 64, 75–76, 83, 93–94, 187, 189, 271, 273, 551, 563, 568

Index of Subjects

color, 3, 26, 100, 102–3, 122, 160, 162, 239, 294–98, 308–9, 350, 357, 373, 382, 446, 512, 516, 612

comedy, 37–42, 47–48, 57–62, 67, 100, 105, 118, 121–23, 175–76, 178–84, 238, 264, 266, 296, 337, 339, 341–42, 344, 446, 453, 458–59, 467, 507–8, 525, 543–47, 572–75, 585–96, 590–91, 593, 595, 597, 611, 629–30

consumerism, 58–59, 61, 66, 68, 83–84, 167, 179, 182, 204, 234, 257, 333, 367, 370, 382, 385, 387–89, 444, 525, 527–28, 543

coproductions, 120–23, 186, 208, 246, 332, 532, 575, 610

crime film, 126, 130, 132, 229–32, 378–83, 550, 560, 585, 597

distribution, 5, 17, 19, 44, 68, 74–77, 109, 119, 123, 175, 181, 200, 228, 237, 303, 328–33, 444–45, 453, 484–85, 527, 532–35, 545, 611, 630

documentary, 1, 2, 17, 45, 54, 117, 146, 153–59, 160, 174–75, 180, 203, 210, 216, 238, 256–57, 297, 315, 321–27, 362, 396, 406, 412, 415, 417–18, 432, 445, 465–69, 472, 474, 516, 538, 553–58, 559, 584–87, 589, 591, 593, 606, 610, 622–27, 631

Dogma 95, 206, 556–558

European cinema, 68, 98, 105, 109, 111, 113, 115, 189, 191–94, 220–22, 224, 247, 270, 282, 289, 343, 426, 483–84, 544–45, 566, 569, 585–86, 588, 620, 634; British cinema, 114, 122, 186, 188–89, 315, 322–23, 508, 612; French cinema, 19, 25, 51, 74, 120–22, 128, 160–65, 203, 206, 343, 359, 372, 396, 404, 412, 437, 446, 454, 524, 507, 549, 555, 566, 584, 605, 611; Italian cinema, 49, 122, 203, 244, 246–47; Scandinavian cinema, 19, 44, 48, 51, 55, 68, 75, 107, 122–23, 206, 556–558; Soviet cinema, 49, 68, 101, 164, 204, 244–45, 258, 292, 308, 350, 418, 421, 425–26, 493, 495–96, 500

exhibition, 5, 16–19, 25, 27, 44, 59, 67, 82, 168, 197, 199, 220–21, 227–28, 255–60, 321, 323, 328, 330, 519, 531–33, 575

exile and emigration, 2–3, 23, 54, 121, 123, 128, 149, 183, 185–86, 213, 235, 246, 263–64, 267, 282–87, 288–93306, 308–9, 334–40, 342, 359–61, 372–75, 406–7, 412, 425, 427, 451, 453, 477, 551, 581, 597

expressionism, 9, 49, 53, 67, 80–85, 91, 98–101, 105, 107, 109, 118, 120, 130–35, 149, 156, 197, 244–46, 411–15, 539, 611

feminism, 263, 420, 427, 442–48, 453, 465, 598–600

festivals, 294, 309, 326, 365–66, 372, 390–91, 394–95, 397, 404, 418, 420, 425, 430–35, 443, 445, 447, 452–53, 464, 483–84, 508, 513, 522, 533, 548–49, 556, 559, 583, 591, 597, 607, 629, 632, 634

film academies, 3, 9, 247, 397, 400–404, 417–20, 421, 423–26, 499, 534, 632

film criticism, 25, 58–59, 68, 76, 81, 83, 89, 125, 138, 143, 145, 152, 230, 238, 303, 308–9, 337, 359–64, 372–3, 395–96, 398, 412, 430, 443–48, 478–79, 481, 477, 605

film theory, 3, 31–32, 49, 68, 89, 119, 131, 133, 174, 198–200, 350, 359–64, 408, 442–48

French cinema. *See* European cinema

gender, 40–41, 53, 60, 96, 150, 168, 170–71, 176, 186, 238–39, 264–66, 279, 280, 328, 331, 341–42, 344, 375, 411, 420, 446–47, 478, 519, 521, 540–41, 546, 551, 566, 568, 581–82, 583, 597–600, 616–17, 620, 622

INDEX OF SUBJECTS ♦ 647

genre, 18, 38, 58, 60, 91, 95, 126–27, 145, 154, 238, 277, 279–80, 283, 328, 332, 337, 373–74, 378–79, 381–82, 390–91, 396, 408, 411, 417, 446, 459, 461–62, 484, 487, 545, 553–58, 573, 585–86, 587, 593, 595, 611, 616, 620, 630
Gleichschaltung (coordination), 233, 237, 258–59, 273, 295–96, 298
globalization, 6, 75, 14, 186, 188, 222, 244–45, 247, 409, 516, 535, 543, 548–49, 551, 566, 578, 584–88, 616, 618, 630, 632–34

Heimatfilm, 122, 238, 297–98, 308, 328–29, 332, 337, 341, 353–58, 359, 366, 368, 370, 378–79, 382, 391, 477, 483–89, 525, 545, 582
heritage cinema, 508, 612–13, 631
Hollywood, 2, 19, 23, 28, 55, 61, 68, 75, 103, 105, 108, 113, 115, 117–19, 120–23, 127–28, 133–34, 149–50, 154, 169, 185–86, 191–95, 200, 203, 220–224, 237–39, 244–47, 262–64, 282–83, 288–89, 291–92, 294, 297, 308, 315, 329–30, 335–36, 338–40, 343, 346, 353, 357, 359, 368, 372–74, 415, 445, 459, 477, 484, 488, 516, 518–20, 522, 531, 543–44, 547, 556, 573–75, 579, 584, 590, 604, 609, 611–12, 630
Holocaust, 180, 183, 234–37, 318, 321–27, 338–39, 432, 470–75, 480, 485, 487, 505, 544, 563, 589–95, 610, 633

internationalism, 52, 68, 188, 192, 195, 200, 243–48, 302, 341–46, 415, 518–23, 535, 574
Italian cinema. *See* European cinema

Kammerspielfilm (chamber play film), 67, 91, 105–110, 126, 149
Kinodebatte (cinema debate), 18, 51, 56
Kulturfilm (cultural film), 153–59, 160, 174, 176, 283

manifestos, 4, 101, 204, 309, 390, 401, 418, 420, 432, 453, 466, 484, 497–501, 553–58, 630
marketing. *See* advertising
Marxism, 118, 214, 349–351, 361, 406, 409, 421, 425–426, 493, 496, 515
mass culture, 16, 53, 55–56, 58–59, 66–67, 80–84, 98, 146, 154–55, 169, 179, 182, 193, 204–5, 245, 250–51, 257, 259, 284, 349, 361, 382, 398, 419, 459–60, 532, 537, 545, 569
mass media, 213, 215–16, 237, 250, 471–72, 474, 491, 566, 569, 603
mass ornament, 138, 247, 258, 477
melodrama, 67, 69, 75, 90–92, 96, 105, 121, 122, 126, 168, 181, 186–187, 243, 245, 247, 275–80, 281, 308, 356, 358, 372–374, 472, 473, 606, 612
mobilization, 15, 205, 252, 256, 258, 276–80, 336, 385
montage, 48, 68–69, 208–210, 257, 258, 350–51, 367, 406, 419, 420, 491–92, 495
movie theaters. *See* exhibition
multi-language films, 2, 68, 195, 200, 217, 220, 223, 289, 327, 341–46, 562
music and musicals, 39, 99, 100, 102, 103, 121–22, 123, 137, 139, 162–64, 165, 193, 198, 199–200 204, 205, 208, 209, 211, 212, 213, 238, 245, 258, 264–65, 276, 277, 279–80, 291–92, 296, 323, 332, 337, 339, 341, 348, 350, 355–56, 362, 368, 381, 407, 424, 438, 446, 453, 458–59, 461, 466, 477, 479, 498, 519, 520, 521, 544, 573, 576, 580, 586, 587, 611, 619, 624, 625

National Socialism, 1–3, 6, 23, 27–29, 42, 48, 66, 76, 103, 120, 121, 131, 138, 145–46, 157–58, 170–71, 175–76, 180–183, 192, 196, 205, 219, 230, 233–39, 243–48,

National Socialism—*(cont'd)* 249–53, 255–61, 262–67, 268–74, 275–277, 280, 282, 289, 290, 291, 294–298, 300–304, 305–9, 315, 316, 329, 335–37, 341, 344, 347–48, 321–27, 351, 357, 359, 360, 369, 372, 374, 375, 386, 387, 390, 395–96, 407, 408, 412, 413, 425, 446, 451, 466, 470–74, 478, 485–86, 504, 505–6, 521, 522, 527–28, 531, 538, 561, 562, 563, 568, 578–82, 589–95, 610–11, 612, 613, 618, 626, 631

nationalism, 2–3, 9, 13–16, 27–28, 68–69, 75–76, 78, 94, 114, 117–23, 125, 134–40, 169, 180, 199, 219–25, 234–35, 238–39, 243–48, 249–53, 255–61, 263, 284–86, 297–98, 300–304, 342, 354, 355, 365–71, 388–89, 405–10, 431, 483–88, 503–5, 507, 522, 544, 566–67, 578–82, 617–20

New German Cinema, 206, 370, 373, 390–91, 394–99, 400–401, 411–16, 417–21, 425, 427, 432, 436–41, 444, 445, 452–453, 464–69, 484, 486, 487, 488, 507–8, 531, 533, 534, 543–45, 549, 551, 554–55, 566, 568, 573, 574, 586, 616, 623, 629, 630, 631, 633

New Objectivity, 67, 120, 129, 131–133, 149, 203, 316

newsreels, 17, 19, 117, 145, 238, 256, 257, 291, 314–19, 321, 323, 325, 369

nouvelle vague (New Wave), 203, 206, 359, 372, 396, 437

Oberhausen. *See* manifestos

performance. *See* acting

photography, 25–26, 83, 99, 100, 142–143, 199, 203, 205, 210–11, 216, 228, 269, 295, 296, 360, 362, 379, 413, 416, 468, 476–77, 519, 569, 623, 625

politics, 1–3, 4, 5, 6, 9, 14–16, 19, 23, 29, 48, 64–66, 69, 76–77, 94, 107, 126, 136–37, 157, 168, 169, 176, 181, 182, 186, 189, 194, 200–201, 205–6, 214, 222–24, 230, 233–38, 244, 247, 249–51, 256–60, 263, 265, 268, 270, 272, 278, 282–87, 289–93, 294–98, 300, 302, 305–10, 316, 318, 325, 348–51, 355–58, 360, 361, 363, 366, 368, 374, 385–90, 398, 400–404, 408, 410, 411–16, 417–420, 423–28, 431–34, 444–45, 449–54, 459–62, 464–69, 471–73, 476–81, 497–501, 503–7, 515, 519, 521, 524, 526–27, 537–41, 544, 545, 546, 547, 548–51, 561, 565, 578–82, 584, 586, 587, 597–600, 603–4, 606–7, 618–20, 630, 634

popular cinema, 17–19, 38–39, 51–52, 57–62, 67, 74–76, 88–89, 98–99, 100, 107, 119–120, 123, 154, 160, 168, 175, 178–183, 185, 243, 245, 262–67, 275–80, 308–10, 328–33, 337–39, 341, 361, 366, 373, 378–83, 394–99, 445, 453, 459, 462, 470–74, 507–8, 524–28, 532, 537, 543–47, 560, 570–76, 630, 634

postcolonialism, 78, 548, 551

production companies: ARD, 468, 471, 489; Deutsche Film-Aktiengesellschaft (DEFA), 2, 115, 176, 308, 309–310. 338, 349, 359, 366, 367–368, 389–390, 405–9, 416, 453–54, 458–62, 497–501, 507, 508, 514, 516, 524, 525, 576, 610; Gloria, 4, 328–332; Nero, 203, 213–214, 217, 228, 231; Paramount Pictures, 68, 117, 119, 191, 193, 194, 195, 520; United Artists, 289, 532; Universal Pictures, 2, 114, 116, 223; Universum Film A.G. (Ufa), 2, 3, 19, 48, 67, 68, 74, 77–78, 95, 99, 100–101, 108–9, 114, 117, 120, 137, 149, 154, 160, 167, 171, 174, 193, 228, 238, 247, 258, 262–264, 297, 300, 308, 309, 329, 330, 374, 394–95, 412, 520, 521;

Westdeutscher Rundfunk (WDR), 420, 437, 471, 475; Zweites deutsches Fernsehen (ZDF), 9, 471, 512, 513, 529, 548, 613

propaganda, 1, 19, 23, 28, 69, 77, 117, 121, 145, 157, 175, 180, 181, 183, 192, 223, 234, 237, 238–39, 243–44, 246, 249–50, 251–53, 256–60, 263, 269–70, 271–72, 276, 294, 298, 300, 303, 307–8, 324, 348, 404, 406–7, 424, 521

publicity. *See* advertising

racism, 73, 76–78, 157–58, 187–88, 289, 504, 563

radio, 1, 37, 208–12, 245, 256, 257, 275–76, 279–80, 315, 319, 407, 424, 443, 444, 476, 477, 521, 581

reception, 5, 6, 31–35, 45–48, 51, 52–53, 55, 59, 60, 86–92, 105–10, 120, 137, 140, 149, 153–58, 163, 178–83, 188, 193, 198–200, 205, 215–16, 220, 227, 228, 231, 238–39, 258, 259, 272, 276–77, 292, 300–304, 308–9, 317, 321–26, 331–32, 337, 342, 357, 358, 372–74, 381–82, 419, 432–34, 446, 460, 470–75, 484, 487–88, 508, 520, 521, 525, 527, 532, 539–40, 549, 556, 565–70, 572–76, 579–80, 589–93, 604–6, 611–13, 614, 629–30

rubble film (*Trümmerfilm*), 308, 314–319, 336, 341, 514

Scandinavian cinema. *See* European cinema

screenwriting, 18–19, 51–52, 61, 74, 105–7, 109, 120, 121, 137–139, 187–88, 193, 194, 203, 213–17, 193, 227–229, 282–87, 249, 267, 288–93, 295, 309–10, 331, 337, 344, 353–54, 355, 368, 406, 414, 434, 453, 459, 460, 461–62, 514, 526, 527, 532, 548, 549, 550, 554–56, 560

sexuality, 40, 44, 45, 53, 56, 66, 76–77, 90, 94, 127, 128, 153–58, 167–71, 178, 187–88, 234, 283, 300, 302, 332, 341–46, 411, 478, 480, 513, 519, 521, 522, 537–41, 546, 572–75, 596–600, 623

silent cinema, 3, 18, 23, 24, 28, 38, 39, 40–41, 68–69, 75, 112, 115, 118, 120–21, 122, 125, 126, 127, 148, 179–80, 186, 188, 197–201, 202, 206, 247, 412, 632

sound cinema, 2, 3, 17, 26, 38–39, 41, 49, 67–69, 115, 121, 122, 138, 165, 170, 186, 188, 191, 193, 197–201, 208–212, 219–225, 228, 290, 343, 520, 632

Soviet cinema. *See* European cinema

special effects, 17, 24–25, 111–15, 117, 119, 124, 137, 164, 186, 203, 209–211, 296, 374, 381, 562

stars and star system, 3, 7, 18, 23, 38, 44–45, 59–60, 68, 88–89, 119, 123, 149, 168–69, 186, 191–95, 203, 206, 239, 246, 257–58, 262–64, 267, 270, 329, 331, 332, 335, 354, 357, 359, 368, 396, 412, 444, 453, 458–62, 463, 518–22, 543, 545, 546, 573, 574, 579, 590

talkies. *See* sound cinema

television, 122, 128, 206, 284, 309, 310, 325, 332, 338, 339, 354, 381, 385, 401, 419, 420, 421, 424, 425, 434, 439, 444, 466, 467, 468, 470–74, 484–85, 486–87, 489, 494, 513, 526, 527, 531, 532, 534, 544, 545, 548, 553, 565, 566, 572–76, 590, 591, 597, 603, 612, 627

theater, 18, 24, 25, 34, 41, 44, 47, 48, 52, 54, 58, 66, 67, 75, 81, 106–9, 118, 126, 154, 178–79, 181–82, 213–17, 245, 305, 339, 411–16, 459, 473, 477, 480, 566, 574, 624

transnationalism, 78, 121, 164, 246, 303, 328, 332, 543, 545, 548–549, 551–552, 554, 583–88, 596–98, 621, 633

unchained camera, 148–49, 175, 197
United States. *See* Hollywood
Urbanism, 16, 59, 125, 150–51, 167–68, 174, 186, 228, 503, 530; crime films/police films, 100, 126–28, 130–32, 195, 227–31, 308, 325, 335–36, 378–83, 391, 427, 462, 469, 550, 560, 585, 597; street film, 67, 124–28; as subject of film, 53–55, 81, 83–84, 120, 124–28, 148–52, 164, 175, 200, 203–4, 208–9, 211, 258, 271, 279, 283, 336, 341, 342, 365–70, 378–83, 480–81, 490–95, 513, 514, 530, 531, 533–35, 548, 569, 587, 624–25

war film, 19, 93–96, 117–18, 219–225, 238, 239, 249–253, 275–281, 328, 332, 338, 372–77, 405–9, 424–25, 431–434, 446, 505, 589–94, 611
Westerns, 270, 379, 390, 572–575
World War, First, 15–16, 19, 47, 52, 63–65, 67, 75–76, 80–84, 93–96, 98, 99, 106, 117–18, 121, 131, 133, 136–37, 150, 154, 192, 193, 194, 220, 259, 283, 450
World War, Second, 2, 29, 78, 128, 235–39, 244, 247, 252–53, 275–80, 282, 301, 305–7, 315–19, 321–327, 331, 335–339, 347–48, 354, 368, 372–77, 385, 387, 394, 405–9, 450, 472, 480, 503, 505, 521, 544, 579, 580–81, 589–94, 610–11, 633

Young German Cinema, 309, 390–391, 394–99, 432, 466, 484, 538, 544, 554, 566, 630

Index of Names

Aalten, Truus van, 40, 60
Abbot, John E., 28
Abraham, Karl, 31
Achternbusch, Herbert, 42, 573
Ade, Maren, 605
Adenauer, Konrad, 306, 307, 328, 375, 385, 396, 398, 476, 478
Adorf, Mario, 414, 482
Adorno, Theodor, 217, 245, 282, 284, 288, 291, 362, 398, 418, 491
Akhavan, Navíd, 598
Akın, Fatih, 468, 508, 548, 550, 551, 583–88, 596–97, 599, 633
Alaku, Buket, 551
Albers, Hans, 170
Alexander, Alexander, 228
Allen, Woody, 31
Allouache, Merzak, 585
Alsen, Ola, 61
Altenloh, Emilie, 89, 444
Amann, Betty, 168, 194
Ander, Charlotte, 60
Andra, Fern, 194
Angst, Richard, 2
Antel, Franz, 122
Antonioni, Michelangelo, 516, 569
Arbus, Diane, 623
Arndt, Ernst Moritz, 270, 271
Arndt, Stefan, 532
Arnheim, Rudolf, 3, 68, 163, 174, 198–200, 212, 230
Arnim, Achim von, 436
Arno, Siegfried (Sig), 38, 59, 180
Arslan, Thomas, 548, 584, 605, 607, 632, 633, 634
Arslan, Yilmaz, 619
Artaud, Antonin, 413, 414
Assarat, Aditya, 517
Åström, Karin, 514
Ataman, Kutlug, 549, 550, 597

Aust, Stefan, 468

Baader, Andreas, 388, 417, 449, 464–65, 467
Backhaus, Sascha, 617
Bacon, Lloyd, 197
Bademsoy, Aysun, 584
Baden, Max von, 63
Baer, Harry, 412
Bahloul, Abdelkrim, 585
Baier, Jo, 42, 591
Baka, Miroslaw, 513, 514
Baker, Josephine, 186
Bakhtin, Mikhail, 624
Báky, Josef von, 239, 297, 339
Balázs, Béla, 49, 68, 89, 119, 131, 133, 174, 198
Balzac, Honoré de, 94
Barnum, P. T. 82
Barry, Iris, 28
Bartholomäi, Florian, 618
Baser, Tevfik, 549
Bateson, Gregory, 300–304
Bauer, Alfred, 431, 432, 433
Bauer, Otto, 409
Bazin, André, 350, 361, 408
Beck, Julian, 413
Becker, Jurek, 610
Becker, Wolfgang, 468, 527, 532, 534, 547, 610, 613
Behrendt, Hans, 68
Behrens, Richard, 49
Belach, Helga, 537, 541
Belmondo, Jean-Paul, 437
Benedict, Ruth, 301
Benét, Stephen Vincent, 282, 283, 285, 286, 287
Benjamin, Walter, 66, 125, 133, 188, 189, 217, 412, 625
Bennett, Arnold, 187, 189

Berger, Ludwig, 191, 193, 194
Berger, Robert, 470
Berghahn, Winfried, 360
Bergmann-Michel, Ella, 2
Bergner, Elisabeth, 168
Bettauer, Hugo, 120
Betti, Laura, 414
Beyer, Frank, 3, 390, 392, 461, 503, 610
Bierbichler, Josef, 567
Biermann, Wolf, 390, 424, 426, 427, 461
Binoche, Juliette, 566, 567
Biró, Lajos, 194
Bismarck, Otto von, 13, 14, 252
Bitomsky, Hartmut, 400, 404, 418, 491
Blank, Les, 562
Blanke, Henry, 193
Bleibtreu, Moritz, 534, 585
Bloch, Ernst, 263
Blom, August, 52
Blumenschein, Tabea, 622
Boese, Carl, 93, 100
Bogdanski, Hagen, 612
Bohm, Hark, 549
Böhme, Marita, 460
Bohnen, Michael, 74
Bois, Curt, 38, 59
Böll, Heinrich, 466, 467
Bond, Edward, 414
Borscht, Mirko, 618
Borsody, Julius von, 119, 275
Bosse, Harriet, 106
Böttcher, Jürgen, 390
Brahm, John, 339
Brandes, Werner, 186
Brando, Marlon, 368
Brandt, Willy, 387, 388, 409
Brasch, Horst, 423
Brasch, Thomas, 9, 413, 423–28
Braun, Alfred, 395
Braun, Eva, 236–37
Braun, Harald, 317, 318, 395
Brauner, Artur, 328, 338–39
Brecht, Bertolt, 41, 66, 127, 213–18, 288–93, 350, 409, 412–16, 424, 436, 473, 566–67

Breen, Joseph, 282, 285
Brennan, Walter, 290
Breloer, Heinrich, 467–68
Breslauer, H. K. 120
Bresson, Robert, 569
Breuer, Josef, 34, 107
Brickner, Richard, 303
Briece, Pierre, 574
Brooks, Louise, 168, 194
Brückmann, Heinrich, 221
Bruckner, Ferdinand, 411–12
Brückner, Jutta, 414, 445, 453
Brüning, Heinrich, 66
Brussig, Thomas, 526, 527, 528
Buback, Siegfried, 449
Bubis, Ignatz, 505
Büchner, Georg, 436, 437, 561
Buchowetzki, Dimitri, 193
Buck, Detlev, 525, 543
Bülow, Bernhard von, 14
Bülow, Vicco von (Loriot), 42, 574
Buñuel, Luis, 134
Butting, Max, 100

Camerini, Mario, 246
Camus, Albert, 426
Canetti, Elias, 625
Capra, Frank, 264
Carney, John, 585
Carow, Heiner, 390, 445
Celan, Paul, 326
Chabrol, Claude, 404
Chamberlain, Arthur Neville, 235–36
Chaplin, Charlie, 38, 39, 286, 532, 594
Charcot, Jean-Martin, 34
Chion, Michel, 31
Chomsky, Marvin J. 470
Clair, René, 121, 160, 163–64
Clausen, Claus, 250
Clewing, Carl, 93
Colbert, Claudette, 264
Collodi, Carlo, 624
Connery, Sean, 573
Cooper, Gary, 264
Coppola, Francis Ford, 612
Coslow, Sam, 289, 292
Costa, Pedro, 415

Costard, Hellmuth, 418
Cronenberg, David, 585
Crowther, Bosley, 374
Cserépy, Arzén von, 68, 120, 250
Cuarón, Alfonso, 585
Curtiz, Michael (Mihály Kertész), 55, 118, 282, 291, 612

Dagover, Lil, 84, 194, 239
Dammann, Gerhard, 38
Dardenne, Jean-Pierre, 517
Dardenne, Luc, 517
Davaa, Byambasuren, 610
Davidson, Paul, 17, 44
Debray, Regis, 403
Degen, Michael Max, 3
Deleuze, Gilles, 493
DeMille, Cecil B. 119
Deppe, Hans, 41, 308, 337
Derin, Seyhan, 584
Dessau, Maxim, 499, 500
Deyers, Lien, 170
Diebold, Bernhard, 100, 102
Dieterle, Charlotte, 282
Dieterle, William, 282–87, 338, 339
Dietrich, Marlene, 2, 6, 23, 27, 69, 168, 170, 191, 195, 237, 339, 375, 476, 478, 518–23
Dreyer, Carl Theodor, 412
Dridi, Karim, 585
Döblin, Alfred, 127, 182, 436
Doerk, Chris, 461
Doesburg, Theo van, 101
Domnick, Ottomar, 308, 366–67, 369, 398
Domröse, Angelica, 453
Donlevy, Brian, 290
Donnersmarck, Florian Henckel von, 606, 609, 611–13
Dörrie, Doris, 453, 544, 574
Dreier, Hans, 194
Dresen, Andreas, 413, 508, 516, 549
Dressel, Roland, 3
Drew, Robert, 555
Dubček, Alexander, 423
Dudow, Slatan, 338, 349, 350
Duncan, Isadora, 53
Dupont, E. A. 92, 185–89, 191, 193

Durniok, Manfred, 433
Duskes, Alfred, 17
Dutschke, Rudi, 386, 400, 403, 425

Ebert, Friedrich, 63–64
Ebert, Roger, 553, 556
Edel, Alfred, 3
Edel, Uli, 468, 607, 610, 611
Edison, Thomas, 26
Eggeling, Viking, 99, 101–2, 160, 162–64, 165
Eibenschütz, Lia, 60
Eichberg, Richard, 188
Eichendorff, Joseph von, 156
Eichinger, Bernd, 328, 468, 573, 604
Eisenstein, Sergei, 68, 164, 204, 244, 350, 367, 421
Eisler, Hanns, 291–92, 350
Eisner, Kurt, 63, 64
Eisner, Lotte, 25, 68, 130, 138, 152, 337, 360
Elliot, Uschi, 60
Elsner, Hannelore, 512
Emmerich, Roland, 573
Engberg, Marguerite, 54
Engel, Erich, 41, 42
Ensslin, Gudrun, 388, 449, 464–65, 467, 513
Enzensberger, Hans-Magnus, 367
Erhard, Ludwig, 307, 385, 386
Erikson, Erik, 303
Esche, Eberhard, 460
Eva, Evi, 60
Eyck, Peter van, 323

Fairbanks, Douglas, 532
Falkenberg, Hans-Geert, 420
Falorni, Luigi, 610
Fanck, Arnold, 2, 143–46, 147, 271
Farocki, Harun, 400–404, 415, 417, 418, 425, 490–96, 516, 549
Fassbinder, Rainer Werner, 331, 373, 376, 391, 398, 407, 411–16, 436, 445, 452, 453, 465, 466, 467, 468, 469, 476–82, 500, 533, 544, 549, 573, 597, 599, 633
Feher, Friedrich, 120
Feldmann, Rötger, 544

Fellini, Frederic, 332, 414, 480, 500, 623
Ferdinand, Franz, 15
Fest, Joachim, 590
Fiedler, Werner, 296
Figdor, Karl von, 74
Fischer, Joschka, 504
Fischer, Samuel, 52
Fischinger, Oskar, 2, 99, 101, 102–3
Flaubert, Gustave, 53
Fleck, Jakob Julius, 117
Fleischmann, Peter, 413
Fleißer, Marieluise, 413
Fleming, Victor, 191
Flesch, Hans, 210
Flohr, Lilly, 60
Fønns, Olaf, 53
Fontane, Theodor, 436, 478
Ford, John, 415
Forman, Milos, 426
Forst, Willi, 119, 121, 123
Forster, Rudolf, 170
Foth, Jörg, 497–98, 500
Fox, William, 194
Franco, Francisco, 247
Franco, Jess, 560
Frank, Leonhard, 95
Frank, Manfred, 491
Freddi, Luigi, 246
Frederick the Great, 249–52
Frederick William I, 250–51
Frenz, Wilhelm, 27
Freud, Sigmund, 31–35, 40, 46, 95, 107, 134, 301
Freund, Karl, 148–49
Freydank, Jochen Alexander, 610
Friedrich, Jörg, 505
Fritsch, Willy, 239, 262, 264, 266
Froelich, Carl, 195
Fröhlich, Gustav, 95
Fromm, Erich, 303

Gable, Clark, 264
Gad, Urban, 44–45, 47
Gallone, Carmine, 246
Gansel, Dennis, 591
Ganz, Bruno, 590, 592
Garbari, Carlo, 144

Garbo, Greta, 27, 168, 243, 244, 245, 520
Garnett, Tay, 2
Garnier, Katja von, 545
Gavin, John, 373
Gavron, Sarah, 585
Gebühr, Otto, 93, 239, 251
Gedeck, Martina, 609
Geis, Jacob, 42
Genet, Jean, 479
Genina, Augusto, 246
Gerhardt, Karl, 73
Geyrhalter, Nikolaus, 491
Gheorghiu, Luminita, 567
Giefer, Thomas, 401, 417
Glas, Uschi, 573
Glässner, Erika, 180
Glawogger, Michael, 491
Gliese, Rochus, 202
Godard, Jean-Luc, 372, 400, 402, 404, 412, 413, 415, 437, 440, 491
Goebbels, Josef(ph), 27, 138, 180, 220, 231, 237–38, 239, 243–48, 249–50, 256, 263, 264, 265, 269–72, 275 276, 294–95, 296, 338, 396, 521, 590, 593
Goebbels, Magda, 237, 593
Goerts, Simon, 616
Goethe, Johann Wolfgang von, 33, 108, 156, 283, 408
Goetz, Curt, 337
Goetz, Ruth, 61
Golan, Menachem, 561
Goldwyn, Samuel, 31
Gompers, Samuel, 283
Gorbachev, Mikhail, 452
Goulding, Edmund, 244
Gralla, Dina, 60, 168
Gramann, Karola, 446, 448
Granach, Alexander, 290
Grass, Günter, 505, 610
Grassl, Erich, 259
Gray, Gilda, 187
Green, Gerald, 470
Gregor, Erika, 443
Gregor, Ulrich, 3, 360, 373–74, 430–31, 433–34

Gremm, Wolf, 400
Griem, Helmut, 3
Griffith, D. W. 118, 532
Grisebach, Valeska, 516, 604–7
Groener, Wilhelm, 63
Groll, Gunter, 366
Groschopp, Richard, 175, 176
Grossmann, Karl, 227
Grosz, George, 84, 100
Gründgens, Gustaf, 2, 170, 332
Grune, Karl, 2, 4, 124–25
Grynszpan, Herschel, 235
Guiness, Alec, 590
Güney, Yilmaz, 587
Günther, Egon, 426, 500
Günther, Thomas, 500
Gympel, Jan, 534

Haarmann, Fritz, 227
Haas, Willy, 89–90, 91
Haase, Hugo, 15
Habermas, Jürgen, 491, 540
Hächler, Horst, 395
Hacke, Alexander, 587
Hager, Kurt, 499
Haggard, H. Rider, 119
Haid, Grit, 60
Halbe, Max, 52
Hallervorden, Dieter, 574
Hamann, Evelyn, 42
Hamidi, Alexandre, 567
Handke, Peter, 414, 437–40
Haneke, Michael, 565–71, 632
Hansen, Rolf, 277, 395
Hanson, Lars, 95
Harbo, Thea von, 120, 136–40, 227, 229, 230, 231, 249
Hardy, Oliver, 38
Harlan, Veit, 3, 176, 238, 239, 252, 253, 265, 294–99, 395, 424
Harnack, Falk, 310
Harris, Rosemary, 470
Harvey, Lilian, 2, 262–67
Hasenclever, Walter, 34
Hauck, Elke, 605
Hauff, Reinhard, 467, 534
Hauptmann, Gerhart(d), 51–55, 107, 155, 418

Hauser, Kaspar, 437
Haußmann, Leander, 516, 526–28
Havemann, Florian, 423–24, 427
Havemann, Frank, 423
Havemann, Robert, 423
Hawks, Howard, 415, 440
Hays, William, 222, 224, 346
Hearst, William Randolph, 28
Heesters, Johannes, 342, 345
Heidegger, Martin, 494
Heise, Thomas, 415
Heisenberg, Benjamin, 605, 634
Heldmann, Eva, 445
Heller, Andre, 589
Heller, Leo, 229
Heller, Leonid, 350
Helm, Brigitte, 166, 167–72
Hembus, Joe, 396
Henschel, Axel, 619
Herbert, F. Hugh, 344
Herbig, Michael "Bully," 508, 572–76
Hermann, Irm, 412, 500
Herrmann, Bernhard, 283
Herrnfeld, Anton, 178, 182
Herrnfeld, David Donat, 178, 182
Herzberg, Georg, 180, 182, 183
Herzog, Werner (Stipetic), 146–47, 391, 412, 413, 436, 437, 439, 445, 452, 483, 485, 553–58, 559–63
Hetterle, Albert, 416
Heydrich, Reinhard, 289, 290, 291
Heym, Georg, 127
Hildenbrandt, Fred, 199
Hill, George Roy, 563
Himmler, Heinrich, 234, 269
Hindenburg, Paul von, 16, 66, 206, 233, 249, 251
Hinz, Werner, 249
Hippler, Fritz, 238
Hirsch, Leo, 229
Hirschbiegel, Oliver, 589, 590, 592, 594, 606, 613
Hirschfeld-Mack, Ludwig, 99, 102, 160, 162
Hitchcock, Alfred, 31, 114, 116, 149, 283, 439–40

Hitler, Adolf, 1, 65, 66, 69, 125, 138, 175, 217, 233–39, 244, 246, 249, 250, 251, 252, 253, 256, 257–58, 259, 264, 265, 269, 270, 271, 273, 284, 291, 295, 300, 303, 305, 323, 324, 335, 337, 351, 360, 361, 374, 466, 503, 519, 521, 589–95, 613
Hochhäusler, Christoph, 604–5, 632
Hoffmann, E. T. A. 624
Hoffmann, Josef, 119, 396
Hoffmann, Jutta, 460
Hofmannsthal, Hugo von, 120
Holden, William, 342, 345
Hölderlin, Friedrich, 413, 415
Holl, Gussy, 192
Hollaender, Friedrich, 2, 237, 520
Holland, Agnieszka, 600
Holland-Moritz, Renate, 459
Homer, 94
Honecker, Erich, 389, 390, 450, 451–52
Hopkins, Anthony, 590
Horkheimer, Max, 217, 245, 282–87, 288, 424
Hörmann, Günther, 419, 420
Horn, Camilla, 60, 194
Houwer, Rob, 433
Hübner, Hans-Werner, 471
Hudson, Hugh, 612
Hugenberg, Alfred, 68
Huillet, Danièle, 397, 411–16
Humboldt, Wilhelm von, 419
Huppertz, Gottfried, 139
Huston, Walter, 284
Hutton, Dana J. 376

Ibsen, Henrik, 107
Ihering, Herbert, 194
Ivory, James, 612

Jacoby, Georg, 520
Jacoby-Boy, Martin, 75
Jäger, Ernst, 200
Jannings, Emil, 68, 92, 148–52, 190–96, 250
Jaspers, Karl, 305
Jelinek, Elfriede, 413, 625

Jenbach, Ida, 120
Jerven, Walter, 40
Jessner, Leopold, 126
Jolson, Al, 197–98
Joseph II, 624
Julien, Isaac, 585
Junge, Alfred, 186
Junge, Traudl, 589, 592, 593

Kafka, Franz, 414, 415, 426, 436
Kahane, Peter, 454, 497
Kandinsky, Wassily, 100, 101
Kant, Immanuel, 251
Karasek, Hellmuth, 518
Karlstadt, Liesl (Elisabeth Wellano), 37–38, 40, 41, 42
Kastner, Bruno, 90
Kästner, Erich, 625
Kaufmann, Nicholas, 153, 154
Kaufmann, Rainer, 543, 545
Käutner, Helmut, 396
Keaton, Buster, 38
Keaton, Diane, 563
Keil, Klaus, 531, 532–33, 535
Kekilli, Sibel, 583
Keller, Gottfried, 150
Kellog, Ray, 424–25
Kemper, Magdalena, 443
Kennedy, John F. 307, 425
Kettelhut, Erich, 113
Keun, Irmgard, 170
Khrushchev, Nikita, 306, 307, 368, 388, 426
Kiesinger, Kurt Georg, 385–86
Kilb, Andreas, 545, 546
Kinski, Klaus (Nakszynski), 559–63
Kipping, Herwig, 498
Kirchner, Ernst Ludwig, 100
Kirsten, Ralf, 458–59
Kisch, Egon Erwin, 83
Kittler, Friedrich, 491
Klarsfeld, Beate, 386
Klein, Gerhard, 309, 366, 367, 368, 370
Klein-Rogge, Rudolf, 250
Kleinert, Andreas, 516
Kleist, Heinrich von, 436, 437
Klick, Roland, 397

Klier, Michael, 513–17, 549
Klimt, Gustav, 119
Klippel, Heike, 447
Kluge, Alexander, 3, 9, 309, 339, 391, 396, 397, 413, 415, 417–22, 425, 439, 445, 452, 461, 463, 465, 466, 480, 483, 484, 485, 491, 565, 567
Knaudt, Ulrich, 402, 417
Knef, Hildegard, 309, 317, 344, 359
Knopp, Guido, 590
Koch, Gertrud, 446, 486
Koch, Pyke, 49
Koch, Sebastian, 609
Kohl, Helmut, 450–51, 503, 504, 582
Köhler, Ulrich, 605, 632
Kohlhaase, Wolfgang, 368, 453
Köhn, C. M. 262
Kolm, Anton, 117
Kolowrat-Krakowsky, Alexander, 117–23
König, Ralf, 544
Korda, Alexander, 118, 119
Korda (Corda), Maria, 60, 119
Kortner, Fritz, 339
Kotulla, Theodor, 359, 360
Kracauer, Siegfried, 58, 59, 68, 76, 81, 83, 125, 138, 143, 145, 150, 181, 205, 303, 309, 359–64, 398, 476–77, 478, 479, 481
Krafft, Uwe Jens, 73
Kräly, Hanns, 193, 194
Kramer, Stanley, 521
Kranich, Rainer, 539
Krauss, Werner, 81, 106, 107
Kreisler, Fritz, 356
Krenz, Egon, 452
Krößner, Renate, 453
Krug, Manfred, 453, 458–59, 461–62
Krüger, Hardy, 342, 345
Kubaschewski, Hans, 329
Kubaschewski, Ilse (Kramp), 328–33, 383
Kulaoglu, Tunçay, 549
Kurras, Karl-Heinz, 401
Kürten, Peter, 227, 229, 230
Kurtuluş, Mehmet, 585

Lacan, Jacques, 31
Laemmle, Carl, 194, 223
Lamprecht, Gerhard, 251
Lang, Fritz, 23, 67, 68, 112, 120, 128, 130, 136–41, 163, 167, 169, 200, 227–32, 237, 244, 245–46, 282, 284, 285, 287, 288–93, 336, 338, 339, 354, 359, 375, 561–62, 632
Langhans, Rainer, 418
Lantschner, Guzzi, 330
Laurel, Stan, 38
Lázló, Alexander, 102–3
Leacock, Richard, 555
Leander, Zarah, 171, 239, 277, 329
Lee, Anna, 290
Léger, Fernand, 160, 163, 164
Leiser, Erwin, 404, 418
Lemke, Klaus, 397, 467
Leni, Paul, 193
Leone, Sergio, 560
Levy, Dani, 508, 532, 533, 547, 589–90, 593, 594, 595
Levy, David, 303
Lichtenberg, Bernd, 527
Libeskind, Daniel, 505
Liebeneiner, Wolfgang, 3, 395
Liebknecht, Karl, 63–64
Linde, Max, 77
Linder, Max, 38
Link, Caroline, 610–11
Lion, Margo, 520
Lippert, Renate, 447
Lissitzky, El, 101
Litvak, Anatole, 282
Loeser, Tony, 497
Lorentz, Pare, 326
Lorre, Peter, 23, 134, 237, 334–40, 375, 561
Losch, Josephine von, 518
Losey, Joseph, 228
Lubitsch, Ernst, 38, 48, 57–62, 67, 68, 86–87, 92, 182, 191, 192, 193–94, 282, 288
Ludendorff, Erich, 16, 19
Lumière, August, 17, 24, 25, 26, 622
Lumière, Louis, 17, 24, 25, 26, 622
Luxemburg, Rosa, 15, 64, 307

Lynch, David, 31

Maccarone, Angelina, 585, 596–600
Macheret, Alexander, 292
Maeterlinck, Maurice, 107
Maetzig, Kurt, 309, 347, 348, 349, 350, 390, 395
Mahler, Horst, 403
Mainka-Jellinghaus, Beate, 419
Maintigneux, Sophie, 513
Malina, Judith, 413
Mann, Heinrich, 478, 520
Mann, Thomas, 132
Mara, Lya, 60
Marcuse, Herbert, 403
Maris, Mona, 60
Marischka, Ernst, 122, 353–54, 355, 356, 575
Marischka, Hubert, 356
Marker, Chris, 491
Marr, Hans, 119
Martay, Oscar, 431
Martin, Paul, 262, 263, 264, 266
Maté, Rudolf, 237
Mattes, Eva, 433, 434
Matz, Johanna, 3, 342
Maupassant, Guy de, 337
May, Joe, 73, 74, 75, 78, 95, 127
May, Karl, 338, 379, 573, 574
May, Mia, 74, 77
Maybach, Christiane, 3
Mayer, Carl, 105, 106, 107, 108, 109, 126, 149, 164
Maysles, Albert, 555
Maysles, David, 555
McLuhan, Marshall, 217
McNamarra, Maggie, 342
Mead, Margaret, 301
Meinert, Rudolf, 3
Meinhof, Ulrike, 388, 417, 449, 466
Meins, Holger, 401, 403, 404, 417–18, 425
Méliès, Georges, 17, 45, 622
Melzer, Karl, 176
Mendelssohn, Moses, 251
Mensching, Steffen, 498
Merkel, Angela, 506, 507
Messner, Günther, 146

Messner, Reinhold, 146
Messter, Oskar, 3, 17, 19, 26, 28
Metz, Christian, 31
Meyer, Johannes, 170, 252
Mihaileanu, Radu, 593
Milestone, Lewis, 192, 223
Minetti, Hans-Peter, 351
Minow, Hans Rüdiger, 401, 417, 418
Misselwitz, Helke, 499, 500
Mitic, Gojko, 461
Mitterand, François, 450
Mix, Tom, 160
Moholy-Nagy, László, 99, 101–3, 163
Moja, Hella, 60
Molander, Helga, 60
Molo, Walter von, 250
Mondi, Bruno, 357
Morgen, Paul, 180
Moriarty, Michael, 470
Mühe, Ulrich, 427, 609
Mülleneisen, Christoph, 44
Müller, Hans Dieter, 419
Müller, Heiner, 416
Müller, Matthias, 491
Müller, Renate, 168
Müller-Lincke, Anna, 38
Muni, Paul, 282
Münsterberg, Hugo, 34
Murnau, F. W. 67, 68, 92, 108, 126, 127, 148, 149, 191, 193, 194, 197, 283, 561
Murphy, Dudley, 160
Musil, Robert, 35, 436, 491
Musser, Charles, 24
Mussolini, Benito, 247, 273
Mussolini, Vittorio, 247
Müthel, Lothar, 2
Muybridge, Eadweard, 494

Nebenzahl, Heinrich, 203
Nebenzahl, Seymour, 228, 231
Negri, Pola, 193, 194
Negt, Oskar, 420, 461, 463
Nekes, Werner, 439, 441
Neufeld, Max, 121
Neumann, Hans, 31
Neuvic, Thierry, 567
Nick, Désirée, 537

Nielsen, Asta, 3, 18, 44–49, 53, 86–92, 168, 444
Niemeyer, Erna, 162
Nietzsche, Friedrich, 53
Nissen, Aud Egede, 93
Niven, David, 342, 345
Noske, Gustav, 64
Nugara, Angela, 415

Ohnesorg, Benno, 386, 401
Ohrtmann, Richard, 27
Ophüls, Max, 3, 41
Orloff, Ida, 52
Osborne, Max, 155
Ostrovsky, Nikolai, 348
Oswald, Gerd, 339
Oswald, Richard, 339, 539, 540
Oswalda, Ossi, 160, 168
Ottinger, Ulrike, 413, 549, 622–27
Otto, Paul, 106

Pabst, G. W. 31, 67, 120, 126, 131, 144, 146, 168, 169, 200, 213, 214–15, 217, 231, 253, 480, 589, 590, 591
Pahlavi, Mohammad Reza, 400
Pakula, Alan J. 612
Papen, Franz von, 233
Parlo, Dita, 95
Parry, Lee, 60
Pasolini, Pier Paolo, 404, 414
Patalas, Enno, 359–64, 395, 418, 419, 420
Paul, Christiane, 534
Pavese, Cesare, 414, 415
Peirce, Kimberly, 600
Pempeit, Lilo, 466
Pennebaker, D. A. 555
Petersen, Wolfgang, 400, 401, 573
Petzold, Christian, 516–17, 605, 607, 632
Pewas, Peter, 2
Pick, Lupu, 105, 107, 108, 126
Pickford, Mary, 532
Pieck, Wilhelm, 306
Pinajeff, Elisabeth, 60
Pinthus, Kurt, 139
Plessner, Helmuth, 151, 152, 316

Plessow, Herbert, 176
Polanski, Roman, 31
Polat, Ayşe, 551, 584
Polt, Gerhard, 42
Pommer, Erich, 95, 127, 137, 149, 150, 193, 195, 328, 611
Ponto, Jürgen, 449
Porten, Henny, 3, 18, 60
Posca, Edith, 106
Potente, Franka, 530, 534
Pouctal, Henri, 74
Prack, Rudolf, 331
Prager, Wilhelm, 153, 154
Praunheim, Rosa von, 412, 537–41
Preminger, Otto, 339, 341–44, 346
Princip, Gavrilo, 15
Pudovkin, Vsevelod, 68, 244, 258
Pulver, Lieselotte, 373, 374
Putti, Lya de, 194

Quinn, Freddy, 477

Rahn, Bruno, 126
Rahn, Helmut, 579, 580, 581
Rasche, Marion, 525
Raspe, Jan Carl, 388, 449, 464, 465
Rath, Ernst vom, 235
Rathsack, Heinz, 404, 418
Reagan, Ronald, 451
Reding, Benjamin, 615–21
Reding, Dominik, 615–21
Reed, Carol, 626
Rehm, Werner, 414
Reimann, Sascha, 616
Reimann, Walter, 81
Reinecker, Herbert, 1
Reinhardt, Max, 58, 106, 126, 283
Reiniger, Lotte, 102
Reinl, Harald, 573, 575
Reisch, Walter, 121, 123
Reitman, Jason, 611
Reitz, Edgar, 3, 391, 418, 419, 483–89
Remarque, Erich Maria, 373, 375
Renard, Maurice, 134
Rennert, Malwine, 444
Resnais, Alain, 326, 432
Ricci, Tonino, 563

Richter, Erika, 461
Richter, Gerhard, 468
Richter, Hans, 2, 99, 101–3, 104, 160, 162–64, 165
Riefenstahl, Leni, 1, 27, 103, 145–46, 157, 176, 238, 244, 255–61, 330, 446, 466
Riemann, Katja, 543, 546
Rilke, Rainer Maria, 127, 479
Rippert, Otto, 60
Rischert, Christian, 418
Ritter, Karl, 265
Robards, Jason, 562
Robertson, Morgan, 51
Robeson, Paul, 186
Roehler, Oskar, 515–16
Röhm, Ernst, 234, 256, 258
Rohrbach, Günter, 603–4, 606, 607, 608
Röhrig, Walter, 81
Rökk, Marika, 329
Roller, Alfred, 120
Römer, Rolf, 426
Rondi, Gian Luigi, 483
Room, Abram, 204
Rossellini, Roberto, 514
Roth, Christopher, 468
Roth, Joseph, 625
Rothemund, Marc, 591
Rouch, Jean, 555
Royes, Gisela, 39
Rückert, Georg, 39
Rühmann, Heinz, 239
Ruttmann, Walter, 98–104, 155, 160 162–64, 165, 175, 203, 208–12, 244, 258, 295

Sachs, Hanns, 31
Sagan, Leonine, 2
Saharet (Clarine Campbell), 53
Saint-Denis, Ruth, 53
Salvatores, Gabriele, 611
Şamdereli, Yasmin, 633
Sander, August, 205
Sander, Helke, 400, 404, 417, 425, 427, 443, 453
Sanders-Brahms, Helma, 453, 545, 549, 633

Sandten, Thea, 60
Sarnau, Anneke Kim, 598
Sauber, Philip, 401
Schaaf, Johannes, 418
Schacht, Roland, 139
Schadewald, Bernd, 618
Schallert, Edwin, 192
Schamoni, Peter, 309, 391, 397, 432
Schamoni, Ulrich, 397
Schanelec, Angela, 605, 632, 634
Scheidemann, Philipp, 63
Schilling, Niklaus, 515
Schirach, Baldur von, 269
Schlaikjer, Erich, 55
Schleicher, Kurt von, 234
Schleyer, Hanns-Martin, 449, 465, 466
Schlingensief, Christoph, 515
Schlink, Bernhard, 611
Schlöndorff, Volker, 391, 397, 412, 414, 427, 432, 436, 445, 465, 466, 467, 469, 483, 485, 515, 544, 597, 610
Schmid, Hans-Christian, 549
Schmidt, Helmut, 388, 449–50, 467
Schmieding, Walther, 331, 433
Schneeberger, Gisela, 42
Schneider, Romy, 122, 353, 354, 357
Schnitzler, Arthur, 3, 52, 119
Schöbel, Frank, 461
Schoenberg, Arnold, 66
Schoeps, Julius H. 472
Scholl, Sophie, 425
Schröder, Gerhard, 504, 506–7, 578–79
Schroeder, Karl Ludwig, 52
Schroeter, Werner, 412, 538
Schubert, Franz, 121
Schüfftan, Eugen, 111, 113, 115, 203, 205
Schulberg, Stuart, 325
Schumacher, Kurt, 306
Schuman, Sarah, 445
Schünzel, Reinhold, 339
Schuschnigg, Kurt, 235
Schütte, Jan, 549
Schwarz, Hanns, 199, 200
Schwarz, Libgart, 414

Schweiger, Til, 508, 543, 546, 547
Schwerdtfeger, Kurt, 99, 102
Schygulla, Hanna, 412
Sebald, W. G. 440, 505, 591
Seeber, Guido, 26, 175
Seeler, Moriz, 203
Sennett, Mack, 39
Seyrig, Delphine, 623
Siebert, Rudi, 520
Siemsen, Hans, 49
Simmel, Ernst, 34
Simmel, Georg, 16
Simon, Günther, 348, 350, 351
Simon, Rainer, 426
Siodmak, Curt (Kurt), 203, 240
Siodmak, Robert, 128, 200, 202, 203, 338, 339, 359
Sirk, Douglas (Detlev Sierck), 4, 237, 338, 372–77, 476–77, 612
Sjöström, Victor, 107
Skladanowsky, Emil, 5, 16, 24–26
Skladanowsky, Erich, 29
Skladanowsky, Max, 5, 16, 22–30
Sklar, Robert, 7
Slezak, Leo, 119
Slezak, Walter, 119
Smith, Jack, 538
Söderbaum, Kristina, 3, 239
Speer, Albert, 256, 592
Spengler, Oswald, 150
Sperr, Martin, 413
Speth, Maria, 605
Spielberg, Steven, 505, 590
Staal, Viktor, 277
Stahlhelm, 1
Stalin, Joseph, 236, 306, 349, 368
Stark-Gstettenbaur, Gustl, 40
Staudte, Wolfgang, 308, 310, 315, 318, 360, 396, 424, 576
Steinhoff, Hans, 180–81, 183, 249, 250, 265, 302
Stella, Vittorio, 143
Steltner, Lukas, 616
Sternberg, Joseph von, 69, 126, 191, 194, 195, 476, 477, 478, 520
Stevens, George, 433
Stiller, Mauritz, 107, 192, 194
Stöckl, Ula, 266, 445

Stölzl, Philipp, 146
Straschek, Günter Peter, 417–18
Strasser, Alex, 175
Strasser, Gregor, 234
Straßmann-Witt, Hermine, 106
Straub, Jean-Marie, 397, 411–16 416
Strauss, Franz Josef, 427–28
Strauss, Richard, 120
Streep, Meryl, 470, 573
Strempel, Gesine, 443
Stresemann, Gustav, 65, 137
Strindberg, August, 48, 87, 106, 107
Stroheim, Erich von, 626
Stull, William, 113
Sutter, Johann August, 270, 271
Suttner, Bertha von, 52
Sybel, Heinrich von, 250
Syberberg, Hans-Jürgen, 412, 413, 452, 590
Szatmari, Eugen, 206
Sze, Henry, 74

Tabatabai, Jasmin, 598
Tarkovsky, Andrei, 500
Tati, Jacques, 332
Tennyson, Alfred, 95
Tergit, Gabriele, 230
Teufel, Fritz, 418
Thalbach, Katharina, 427
Thalheim, Robert, 633
Thälmann, Ernst, 347–52
Thiele, Hertha, 168
Thiele, Rolf, 396, 480, 482
Thiele, Wilhelm, 339
Thieme, Thomas, 609
Thimig, Hans, 119
Thomas, Jameson, 187, 189
Thome, Rudolf, 397
Tonke, Laura, 513
Tönnies, Ferdinand, 150–51
Toro, Guillermo del, 610
Totheroh, Dan, 283
Treitschke, Heinrich von, 250
Trenker, Florian, 272
Trenker, Luis (Luigi), 1, 146, 244, 246, 247, 268–74
Trepte, Ludwig, 618
Treut, Monika, 549

Trier, Lars von, 556
Trotta, Margarethe von, 453, 467, 483, 485, 610, 613
Truffaut, François, 404
Tse-Tung, Mao, 402
Tucholsky, Kurt, 82, 84, 206
Twardowski, Hans Heinrich von, 290
Tykwer, Tom, 468, 532, 533, 534, 604, 630

Ucicky, Gustav, 119, 121, 395
Ulbricht, Walter, 306, 307, 349, 388, 389, 405, 424
Ulmer, Edgar G. 202, 203
Ulrich, Kurt, 330
Üner, Idil, 585
Ungerer, Lilith, 412
Unthan, Carl, 54

Vadim, Roger, 404
Valentin, Karl (Karl Ludwig Fey), 37–43
Veidt, Conrad, 81, 82, 134, 194, 237
Veiel, Andres, 468
Veith, Jens, 617
Veltée, Louise (Luise), 117
Verhoeven, Michael, 430–35, 610
Vertov, Dziga, 244, 350, 418, 425, 493, 495, 496
Viebig, Clara, 52
Viertel, Hans, 289
Vincente, Philippe, 416
Vinterberg, Thomas, 556
Virchow, Rudolf, 83
Visconti, Luchino, 332
Vittorini, Elio, 414, 415
Vogel, Frank, 390
Vogel, Jürgen, 534, 543
Vostell, Wolf, 622

Waalkes, Otto, 453, 572, 574
Wagner, Richard, 120
Waldleitner, Luggi, 330, 333, 339
Wallace, Edgar, 379, 380, 381, 382, 383, 391, 560
Walser, Martin, 505
Walter, Fritz, 579

Wanamaker, Sam, 470
Wangenheim, Gustav von, 338
Warhol, Andy, 413, 538
Warm, Hermann, 81
Waters, John, 538
Wayne, John, 425
Weaver, Fritz, 470
Webster, Daniel, 283, 285
Wedekind, Frank, 107
Weerasethakul, Apichatpong, 517
Wegener, Bettina, 423–24, 427
Wegener, Paul, 32, 33, 34, 67, 88, 91, 92, 100, 163
Weigel, Helene, 413, 415, 424
Weigl, Sanda, 423, 424
Weill, Kurt, 213, 214, 217
Weizsäcker, Richard von, 451
Welles, Orson, 408
Welz, Peter, 498
Wenders, Wim, 414, 416, 437–41, 445, 452, 483, 485, 533, 544, 587, 610, 616
Wenzel, Hans-Eckardt, 498
Werner, Ilse, 239
Wessely, Paula, 119
Westbelt, Hildegard, 444
Wexley, John, 289
Wiene, Robert, 67, 81, 82, 83, 120, 129–30, 132, 134
Wiesel, Elie, 471
Wigman, Mary, 157
Wilder, Billy, 23, 128, 203, 205, 207, 237, 282, 288, 308, 315, 321, 338, 339, 521
Wilfred, Thomas, 102
Wilhelm, Carl, 57
Wilhelm II, 13, 14, 19, 63
Wilke, Manfred, 613
Wilkening, Thomas, 497, 498, 500, 501
Wilson, Woodrow, 63
Winckler, Henner, 516, 605
Wiseman, Fred, 555
Wittgenstein, Ludwig, 438
Wolf, Christa, 390, 406, 408, 503
Wolf, Konrad, 9, 338, 390, 392, 405–10, 453
Wong, Anna May, 186–89

Woods, James, 470
Wortmann, Sönke, 543, 544, 545, 546, 578, 579
Wulff, Christian, 505
Wulff, Hans Jürgen, 408
Wysbar, Frank, 245–46, 338, 359

Yavuz, Yüksel, 549, 550, 551, 584
Yenke, One Lu, 567

Zanussi, Krzysztof, 426

Zhdanov, Andrei, 349
Ziewer, Christian, 400, 401, 404
Zimmermann, Friedrich, 573
Zinnemann, Fred, 203, 339
Zischler, Willy, 175
Žižek, Slavoj, 31, 51, 88
Zschoche, Herrmann, 514, 525
Zuckmayer, Carl, 81, 344
Zukor, Adolph, 194
Zurmühl, Sabine, 443
Zuse, Konrad, 490, 494

Index of Film Titles

2 oder 3 Dinge, die ich von ihm weiß, 631
08/15, 328, 332, 375
40 m2 Deutschland, 549
71 Fragmente einer Chronologie des Zufalls, 566
437!! Ein Geiselfilm, 289
1000 Augen des Dr. Mabuse, Die, 354

Abenteuer des Prinzen Achmed, Die, 102
Abgeschminkt, 545
Abschied, 426
Abschied vom falschen Paradies, 549
Abschied von gestern, 391, 397, 418
absolute Film, Der, 99, 102, 160–65
Absturz, Der, 48
Abwege, 169
Acciaio/Steel, 244
Affengeil, 538
Afgrunden, 44, 46–47, 86, 90
Aguirre, der Zorn Gottes, 146, 554, 560–62
AIDS-Trilogie, 538
Aimée und Jaguar, 508
Air Force One, 573
All Quiet on the Western Front, 219–25
All That Heaven Allows, 612
All the President's Men, 612
Alles auf Zucker, 547
Alles wird gut, 597
allseitig reduzierte Persönlichkeit, Die, 427
Almanya — Willkommen in Deutschland, 633–34
alte Fritz (1896), Der, 250
alte Fritz (1928), Der, 251
alte und der junge König, Der, 249–54
Am Ende kommen Touristen, 633
andere Liga, Eine, 551

Anders als die Andern, 539, 540
Angelique, 332
Angels with Dirty Faces, 289
Angst des Tormanns beim Elfmeter, Die, 436–41
Angst Essen Seele auf, 549, 597, 599, 633
Anita — Tänze des Lasters, 538–39
Anruf erwünscht, 472–73
Anna Boleyn, 191, 192
Anna Karenina, 243, 244
Antigone, 413, 414–15, 416
Apfel ist ab, Der, 308
Aprilkinder, 549, 550, 584
Architekten, Die, 454
arme Jenny, Die, 47
Armee der Liebenden, 539
Arsenic and Old Lace, 337
Artisten in der Zirkuskuppel: ratlos, Die, 419–21, 439
Arzt von Stalingrad, Der, 328, 332
Asphalt, 127
Asphalt Jungle, 128
Atlantic, 186
Atlantis, 51–56
Auf Achse, 462
Auf der anderen Seite, 583, 584, 587
Auf der Sonnenseite, 458–59
Aus den Archiven des Erfinders Max Skladanowsky, 27
Auslandstournee, 584

Baader, 468, 513
Baader Meinhof Komplex, Der, 468, 607, 610, 611, 631
Ballet mécanique, 163, 165
Bambule, 466
Banale Tage, 498
Bande des Schreckens, Die, 379
Battleship Potemkin, 68, 164, 244

INDEX OF FILM TITLES ♦ 665

Beast with Five Fingers, The, 134, 337
Beil von Wandsbek, Das, 310
Benny's Video, 566, 567
Berg des Schicksals, Der, 142–47
Berg ruft, Der, 146
Berlin — 2. Juni 1967, 401, 417
Berlin Alexanderplatz, 436
Berlin. Die Sinfonie der Großstadt, 164, 175, 203, 208, 258
Berlin — Ecke Schönhauser, 309, 365–71
Berlinfieber, 622–23
Besonders wertvoll, 418
Betrayal, 192, 195
Bettwurst, Die, 538
bewegte Mann, Der, 4, 543–47, 630
Bierkampf, 42
Birth of a Nation, 118
Bismarck, 252
Black Box BRD, 468
The Black Dream, 47
Blackmail, 114
blaue Engel, Der, 6, 69, 126, 191, 195, 344, 476–77, 518, 520, 521
blaue Hand, Die, 380
blaue Licht, Das, 1, 146
Blechtrommel, Die, 610
bleierne Zeit, Die, 325, 326, 467
blonder Traum, Ein, 2
Bluebeard's Eighth Wife, 62
Blusenkönig, Der, 58
Blut und Boden, 258
Bommerli, 176
Börsenkönigin, Die, 47
Boys Don't Cry, 600
Brandstifter, 467
Bräutigam, die Komödiantin und der Zuhälter, Der, 411–12, 415
Breathless, 437, 440
Brecht die Macht der Manipulateure, 417, 425–26
Brick Lane, 585
Brüder, 97
Brudermord, 619
Büchse der Pandora, Die, 126
Bucklige von Soho, Der, 380
Buena Vista Social Club, 587, 610, 627

Bully and Rick, 575
Bullyparade, 573, 575–76
Bungalow, 605
Burden of Dreams, 562
Burgtheater, 121

Cabinet des Dr. Caligari, Das, 28, 31, 67, 80–85, 100, 105, 120, 129–30, 192, 194, 611
Caché, 567, 568, 632
Camoflage, 426
Canaris, 375
Capriccio, 265–66
Carnival of Souls, 516
Casablanca, 282
Cerro Torre: Schrei aus Stein, 146
Chariots of Fire, 612
Chien Andalou, Un, 134
Children of Men, 585
Choral von Leuthen, Der, 251, 253
Christiane F. — Wir Kinder vom Bahnhof Zoo, 513
Chronik der Anna Magdalena Bach, 412
Citizen Kane, 283, 604
Cobra Verde, 562–63
Code inconnu, 565–71
Comedian Harmonists, 508
Concentration Camp, 292
Condottieri, 246, 247, 273
Confessions of a Nazi Spy, 282, 289
Conversation, The, 612
Count Dracula, 560
Count of Monte Christo, The, 74
Crossing the Bridge, 584, 587

Dame, der Teufel und die Probiermamsell, Die, 57, 60
Danton (1921), 193
Danton (1931), 68
Dealer, 548, 584
Death Wish, 516
Deer Hunter, The, 488
The Defeat of Hannibal, 247
Denk bloß nicht, ich heule, 390
Der Leidensweg der Inge Krafft, 97
Der letzte Akt, 589
Der Rebell, 1, 244, 246, 269

Deutsche Himalaja-Expeditionen, 146
Deutschfieber, 515
Deutschland 09, 468
Deutschland im Herbst, 453, 464–69
Devil and Daniel Webster, The, 282–87
Diesel, 244
Dirnentragödie, 48, 90, 126
Doktor Bessels Verwandlung, 97
dolce vita, La, 332
Domino, 427
Donner, Blitz und Sonnenschein, 42
Dorian Gray, 623
Dr. Ehrlich's Magic Bullet, 282
Dr. Mabuse, der Spieler, 31, 34–35, 354
drei Mannequins, Die, 60
Drei von der Tankstelle, Die, 339
Dreigroschenoper, Die, 213–18
dritte Generation, Die, 456, 467
Dubarry von heute, Eine, 60

Eastern Promises, 585
Ehe der Maria Braun, Die, 331, 488
Einstein des Sex, Der, 538
elf Schillschen Offiziere, Die (1926), 251
elf Schill'schen Offiziere, Die (1932), 3
En Garde, 551
Encounters at the End of the World, 554–55, 557
Ende offen, 420
Engel aus Eisen, 427
Engelein, 47
Entlassung, Die, 196, 252
Entr'acte, 160, 163, 164, 165
Episode, 121
Erbschaft, Die, 42
Ernst Thälmann — Führer seiner Klasse, 309, 347–48, 350–51
Ernst Thälmann — Sohn seiner Klasse, 309, 347–52
Erzherzog Johanns große Liebe, 355
Es, 397
ewige Jude, Der, 180, 238
Experimente mit synthetischem Ton — Tönende Ornamente, 2
Exterminating Angel, The, 134

Fährmann Maria, 245
falsche Asta Nielsen, Die, 47
Fälscher, Die, 610
Falscher Bekenner, 605
Familientag im Hause Prellstein, 178–84
Fantasia, 103
Farbe-Licht-Musik, 102–3
Fata Morgana, 439
Faust (1926), 193, 194, 283
Faust (1960), 332
Feind im Blut, 155
Ferien vom Ich, 328
Feuerteufel, Der, 273
Film ist Rhythmus, 160, 162
Film von der Königin Luise, Der, 250
Filmprimadonna, Die, 45, 47
Filmstudie, 164
Finding Nemo, 535
Firma heiratet, Die, 57, 60
Fitzcarraldo, 147, 554, 559, 562–63
Floss der Toten, Das, 93–97
Flötenkonzert von Sanssouci, Das, 251
Fontane Effi Briest, 436, 438
For a Few Dollars More, 560
Foreign Affair, A, 315, 521
Förster vom Silberwald, Der, 379
Frau am Steuer, 263, 266–67
Frau im Mond, Die, 228
Frauenschicksale, 349
Fräulein Julie, 106, 107
Freak Orlando, 623, 626
Fremde Haut, 596–601, 633
fremde Vogel, Der, 47
freudlose Gasse, Die, 48, 126, 168, 480, 632
Freundin des gelben Mannes, Die, 77
Fridericus, 252, 253
Fridericus Rex, 68, 120, 246, 250
Frosch mit der Maske, Der, 378–83
Fuchsjagd auf Skiern durchs Engadin, Eine, 144
Funny Games, 566
Für den unbekannten Hund, 615–21
Fürst von Pappenheim, Der, 60
Fury, 282, 284, 287, 289

Gasthaus an der Themse, Das, 380

Gegen die Wand, 583–84, 586, 587
Geheimnis der weißen Nonne, Das, 380
Geheimnisse einer Seele, Die, 31
Gelbstern, 60
Gelegenheitsarbeit einer Sklavin, 420
Genuine, 130
Germanin, 273
Germany Year Zero, 514
Geschichte vom kleinen Muck, Die, 576
Geschichte vom weinenden Kamel, Die, 610
Geschichtsunterricht, 412
Geschlecht in Fesseln, 283
Geschwister — Kardeşler, 584, 633
Gespenst, Das, 42, 574
geteilte Himmel, Der, 390
Getürkt, 585
Glückskinder, 263–65
Go Trabi Go, 507, 515, 525
Go Trabi Go 2, 515, 525
Godfather, The, 354
Gold, 170–71
goldene Pest, Die, 339
goldene Stadt, Die, 294–99
Golem, Der (1915), 91
Golem, wie er in die Welt kam, Der (1920), 67, 91, 100, 156, 192
Gone With the Wind, 247
Good Bye Lenin!, 498–99, 507, 512, 516, 525, 527–28, 531, 534–35, 547, 610, 613, 618
Graf Chargon, 97
Gräfin von Monte Christo, Die, 166, 170
Great Dictator, The, 286, 594
Green Berets, The, 424–25
Grizzly Man, 555
große Ekstase des Bildschnitzers, Die, 555
große König, Der, 252–53
große Liebe, Die, 277–80
Großstadtschmetterling, 189
Gruft mit dem Rätselschloss, Die, 380
Grün ist die Heide, 328, 332, 337, 378, 576
grüne Bogenschütze, Der, 380

Hai-Tang, 189

Halbe Treppe, 516
Halloween, 488
Hamlet, 48
Hangmen also Die!, 288–93
Hauptmann von Köpenick, Der, 150
Haus des Dr. Gaudeamus, Das, 120
Haus in Montevideo, Das, 337
Heidi M., 514
heilige Berg, Der, 144–45
Heimat trilogy, 483–89; *Heimat — Eine deutsche Chronik,* 483–89; *Heimat 3 — Chronik einer Zeitenwende,* 484, 485; *Die zweite Heimat — Chronik einer Jugend,* 484, 485
Heimkehr (1928), 95–96
Heimkehr (1932), 2
Heimkehr des Odysseus, Die (1918), 97
Heimkehr des Odysseus, Die (1922), 97
Heißer Sommer, 461
Herr Lehmann, 618
Herrin der Welt, Die, 9, 73–79
Herrscher, Der, 176, 196, 244
Herstellung eines Molotow-Cocktails, 9, 400–404, 417
Himmler Projekt, Das, 631
Hintertreppe, 97, 105, 106, 126
Hitler — ein Film aus Deutschland, 590
Hitler — eine Karriere, 590
Hitlerjunge Quex, 6, 180, 249, 256, 300–304
Hitlerjunge Salomon, 600
Hitlers Frauen, 590
Hitlers Helfer, 590
Hitlers Kinder, 590
Hitlers Krieger, 590
Hoheit tanzt Walzer, 121
höhere Befehl, Der, 252
Holocaust, 470–75, 485, 590
Homunculus, 53, 75
Horror Vacui, 538
Hostess, 426
House of the Spirits, 573
How to Marry a Millionaire, 345
Hund von Blackwood Castle, Der, 380
Hunde, wollt ihr ewig leben, 338

I Was on Mars, 532
*Ich bin die Tochter meiner Mutter —
    Ben Annemin Kızıyım*, 584
Ich bin meine eigene Frau, 538
Ich geh' aus und du bleibst da, 60
Ich hatt' einen Kameraden, 97
Ich und die Kaiserin, 2
Ich war neunzehn, 9, 405–10
Ihre Zeitungen, 402, 403
Im Juli, 584, 585–86
Im Kampf mit dem Berge, 143
Im Lauf der Zeit, 616
Im Schatten, 607, 634
Im toten Winkel, 589, 593
Im Trommelfeuer der Westfront, 27
Immensee, 296–97
In den Tag hinein, 605
In jenen Tagen, 308
Independence Day, 573
Indiana Jones, 593
indische Grabmal, Das, 74
Inflation, 164
Inglorious Basterds, 146
innere Sicherheit, Die, 325–26
Insel der Schwäne, 514
Intolerance, 118
Invasion of the Barbarians, The, 611
Irgendwo in Berlin, 314, 318
It Happened One Night, 264

Jagd nach dem Tode, Die, 74
Jagdszenen aus Niederbayern, 413
Jahrgang '45, 390
Jakob der Lügner, 390, 610
Jazz Singer, The, 220
Jeder für sich und Gott gegen alle, 437
Jennys Bummel durch die Männer, 60
Jenseits der Stille, 611
Jerichow, 516, 607
Johanna D'arc of Mongolia, 623–24
Jonas, 308, 365–71
Juarez, 282
Jud Süß, 3, 238, 252, 294
Jud Süß — Film ohne Gewissen, 631
Juden ohne Maske, 180–81
Judgment at Nuremberg, 325, 521
Julien Donkey-Boy, 558
junge Medardus, Der, 119

junge Törless, Der, 397, 436
Jungfrau auf dem Dach, Die, 341–46
Juno, 611
Jurassic Park, 354

Kadetten, 252
Kaiser von Kalifornien, Der, 268–74
Kaiserball, 122
Kaisermanöver, 122
Kameraden, 106
Kampf um den Himalaja, 146
Kampf um Rom, 338
Kaninchen bin ich, Das, 390
Karger, 605
Karl Valentin, der Sonderling, 37, 40
Karl Valentins Hochzeit, 37, 39
Katzelmacher, 411, 413, 414, 549
Katzensteg, Der, 252
Keinohrhasen, 508, 547
Kinder, Mütter, und ein General, 560
Kinderspiele, 532
Kirschen in Nachbars Garten, 42
Klassenverhältnisse, 414
Klavierspielerin, Die, 568
Kleine aus der Konfektion, Die, 60, 61
Kleine Freiheit, 551
kleine Königstragödie, Eine, 175, 176
kleine Veronika, Die, 626
Kolberg, 239, 246, 252, 294, 298
Kombat Sechzehn, 617, 618
Kommt Mausi raus?!, 597
Königin Luise, 251
Korean Wedding Chest, The, 627
Krankheit der Jugend, 411, 414
Kuhle Wampe, 1, 289, 350
Kurklinik Rosenau, 525
Kurz und schmerzlos, 548, 550, 584, 585

Land hinter dem Regenbogen, 498
Laokoon & Söhne, 622–23
Last Command, The, 191, 195
Leben der Anderen, Das, 499, 508, 512, 526, 606, 609–14, 631
Leben ist eine Baustelle, Das, 531, 534
Lebende Buddhas, 74, 163
Lebenszeichen, 436

Legende von Paul und Paula, Die, 390, 445
Leise flehen meine Lieder, 121
Lemminge, 567–68
letzte Kompanie, Die, 251
letzte Mann, Der, 28, 92, 105, 106, 108, 126, 148–52, 191, 193, 194
Letztes aus der DaDaeR, 498, 500
Liberators, The, 563
Lichtspiel Opus 1, 98–104
Lichtspiel Opus 2, 160, 162
Liebe '47, 317
Liebe der Jeanne Ney, Die, 114, 169
Liebe, Tanz, und 1000 Schlager, 328
Liebelei, 3
Liebling Kreuzberg, 462
Liesl Karlstadt und Karl Valentin, 42
Life of Emile Zola, The, 282, 284, 287
Lissi und der wilde Kaiser, 576
Little Dieter Needs to Fly, 557
Little Drummer Girl, The, 563
Lola, 476–82
Lola + Bilidikid, 549, 550, 597, 598
Lola rennt, 527, 530, 531, 534, 630
Lord of the Rings 3: The Return of the King, The, 535
Love, 632
Love Boat, The, 575
Love Me and the World Is Mine, 185
Loves of a Blonde, 426
Lucrezia Borgia, 91
Lucy, 516
Ludwig, 332
Ludwig II, 355, 560
Luise, Königin von Preußen, 3, 251
Luxusweibchen, 60, 61

M, 128, 200, 226, 227–32, 287, 290, 336, 562
Machorka-Muff, 411
Mad Love, 134, 336
Madame DuBarry, 191, 192
Mädchen in Uniform, 2
Mädchen Rosemarie, Das, 480
Magnificent Ambersons, The, 283
Mahlzeiten, 484
Man Who Knew Too Much, The, 114
Man with the Movie Camera, The, 493

Mann aus dem Jenseits — Feldgrau, Der, 97
Mann mit dem Glasauge, Der, 380
Mann ohne Namen, Der, 74
Mann will nach Deutschland, Ein, 256
Männer, 453, 544, 574, 630
Maria Therese, 355
Marschall Vorwärts, 251
Maskerade, 121
Mediterraneo, 611
Medium, Das, 97
Mein Führer — Die wirklich wahrste Wahrheit über Adolf Hitler, 589, 591, 593, 594, 595
Mein langsames Leben, 605
Mein liebster Feind, 555, 559
Melodie der Welt, 208, 210
Melodie des Herzens, 69, 199, 200
Mensch ohne Namen, 97
Menschen am Sonntag, 202–7
Menschen ohne Vaterland, 27
Merry-Go-Round, 626
Messer im Kopf, 467
Metropolis, 111, 112, 114, 120, 130, 131, 167, 169, 228, 494, 632, 634
Michael Kohlhaas — Der Rebell, 414, 436
Milchwald, 604, 607
Mildred Pierce, 612
Miss Nobody, 75
Mobile Images, 160, 163, 164
Mon oncle, 332
Monna Vanna, 91
Moon Is Blue, The, 341–46
Mörder sind unter uns, Die, 308, 315, 317–18, 320, 336
Morgenrot, 246
Moritz macht sein Glück, 60
Morocco, 520
Moses and Aaron, 415
Mother, 68
Moulin Rouge, 186
Mozart, 355
müde Tod, Der, 246
Müller und sein Kind, Der, 117
Münchhausen, 239, 297
Mysterien eines Frisiersalons, 41

Nacht fiel über Gotenhafen, 338
Nachts, wenn der Teufel kam, 332, 338
Naked Kiss, 515
Naked Street, The, 128
Name of the Rose, The, 573
Nanga Parbat, 146
Napfkuchen, Der, 176
Napola, 591
neue Kunst: Raumlichtmusik, Eine, 103
neue Schreibtisch, Der, 41
Neurosia — 50 Jahre Pervers, 537–42
Nibelungen, Die, series, 68, 120, 136–41, 163, 245; *Kriemhilds Rache*, 138–39; *Siegfried*, 112, 137–40
Nicht der Homosexuelle ist pervers, sondern die Situation in der er lebt, 538–40
Nicht löschbares Feuer, 491
Nicht ohne Risiko, 516
Nicht versöhnt oder Es hilft nur Gewalt wo Gewalt herrscht, 411, 412, 414
Night and Fog, 326, 432
Ninotchka, 62
Nirgendwo in Afrika, 527, 610, 631
Nordwand, 146
North by Northwest, 439, 441
Nosferatu, 67, 70, 95, 131, 561
Nosferatu: Phantom der Nacht, 561
Novalis, 498

Oberst Chabert, 97
Ödipussi, 453
Ohm Krüger, 192, 196, 244, 249
Ohne Haupttitel, 162
Oi! Warning, 615, 617, 619–20
o.k., 430–35
Olympia, 145, 157, 244, 330
Once, 585
One plus One, 402
Operation Thunderbolt, 561, 563
Opfergang, 296–97
Orchesterprobe, 41
Orlacs Hände, 120, 129–35
Ostkreuz, 9, 512–17
Othello, 193
Otto — Der Film, 572, 576, 453

Pan's Labyrinth, 610
Paracelsus, 253
Parfum — Die Geschichte eines Mörders, Das, 604
Passagier — Welcome to Germany, Der, 427
Passion of Joan of Arc, The, 412
Patriot, The, 192, 193, 195
Patriotin, Die, 420
Peter der Große, 193
Piccadilly, 185–89
Polizistin, Die, 516
Postman Always Rings Twice, The, 516
Prater, 622, 624, 625, 626, 627
Pratermizzi, Die, 121
Pretty Woman, 514
Prinz und Bettelknabe, 118

R-1. Ein Formspiel, 103
Rabbi von Kuan-Fu, Der, 77
Rächer, Der, 380
Raskolnikow, 130
Rat der Götter, 309
Räuber, Der, 634
Rausch, 48, 87, 106
Red Line 7000, 440
Rennsymphonie, 164
Rhythmus 21, 101, 104, 162
Rhythmus 23, 162
Robbykallepaul, 532
Robert Koch, der Bekämpfer des Todes, 196
Room with a View, A, 612
Roots, 470
Rosa Arbeiter, 539
Rosenkavalier, Der, 120
rote Fahne, Die, 425
Ruf, Der, 339
Ruhestörung: Ereignisse in Berlin, 419
Ruttmann Opus 3, 101, 160, 163, 165
Ruttmann Opus 4, 160, 162, 163–64

SA Mann Brand, 256
Same Player Shoots Again, 437
Samson und Delila, 119
Scarface, 289
Scarlet Street, 182
Schatten, 131

Index of Film Titles ♦ 671

Schatz im Silbersee, Der, 379
Scherben, 4, 105–10, 126
Schindler's List, 505, 590
Schneider von Ulm, Der, 484
Schonzeit für Füchse, 397
schreckliche Mädchen, Das, 610
Schuh des Manitu, Der, 572–76
Schuhpalast Pinkus, 57–58
Schulmädchen-Report, 391
Schut, Der, 338
schwarze Abt, Der, 380
schwarze Husar, Der, 251
Schwarzwaldmädel, 308, 378
Schwestern der Revolution, 539
Schwuler Mut, 538
Sehnsucht, 516, 602, 604, 606–7
Sehnsucht der Veronika Voss, Die, 516
Sesamstraße, 462
Seven Women, Seven Sins, Superbia — Der Stolz, 623
Shanghai Express, 521
Shirins Hochzeit, 549, 633
Shop Around the Corner, The, 62
Sicilia!, 415
siebente Kontinent, Der, 566–68
Sieg des Glaubens, 256
Silhouetten, 121
Simpsons, The, 284
Singing Fool, The, 197–201, 220, 221, 224
Sins of the Fathers, 191, 195
Sissi trilogy, 122, 341, 353–58; *Sissi*, 353, 354, 356, 575; *Sissi, die junge Kaiserin*, 353–54, 356; *Sissi — Schicksalsjahre einer Kaiserin*, 353–56
Sissi — Wechseljahre einer Kaiserin, 575
Skladanowsky Primitives, 28–29
Sklavenkönigin, Die, 119
So sind die Männer, 520
Sodom und Gomorrha: Die Legende von Sünde und Strafe, 118
Solino, 584, 586
Solo Sunny, 453
Sommer vorm Balkon, 516
Song, 189
Sonnenallee, 507, 512, 516, 524–29, 618
Sophie Scholl — die letzten Tage, 591
Soufrière, La, 555
Speer und Er, 591
Spielzeug von Paris, Das, 121
Spielzeugland, 610
Spur der Steine, 390, 458, 461
Stadt ohne Juden, Die, 120
Stadtgespräch, 545
Stammheim, 467
Star Trek, 575
Star Wars, 354
Stauffenberg, 591
Steuermann Holk, 88
Still Moving, 623
Stille nach dem Schuss, Die, 467, 597
Stille Nacht, 533
Stolz der Firma, Der, 57
Stranger, The, 325
Straße, Die, 4, 124–28
Straßenmusik, 41
Street of Sin, 192, 195
Street with No Name, The, 128
Stuart Webbs, 75
Student von Prag, Der, 32–34, 91
subjektive Faktor, Der, 426
Sumurun, 62
Sünderin, Die, 309, 344
Sunrise, 127, 283
Sunset Blvd., 128, 515
Sylvester, 106, 126
Symphonie Diagonale, 160, 162–63

Tag der Freiheit, 244
Tag der Rosen im August, da hat die Garde fortgemusst, Ein, 97
Tagebuch einer Verlorenen, 126
Tänzerin von Sanssouci, Die, 251
Tartuffe, 193
Tatort, 462, 469, 597
Ten Commandments, The, 119
Terror 2000 — Intensivstation Deutschland, 515
Testament des Dr. Mabuse, Das, 245, 354
Teufels General, Des, 375
Theodor Körner, 250–51
Thief of Baghdad, The, 186
Third Man, The, 626

Tiger von Eschnapur, Der, 339
Time to Love and a Time to Die, A, 4, 372–77
Titanic, 146
Todesmühlen, Die, 321–27
Todesspiel, 467–68
tödliche Maria, Die, 532
Tönende Welle, 210
toten Augen von London, Die, 380
Toten kehren wieder — Enoch Arden, Die, 97
Totentanz, Der, 47
Train of Life, 593–94
Trapp-Familie, Die, 328, 332
Trapp-Familie in Amerika, Die, 328
Traumschiff, Das, 575
(T)Raumschiff Surprise — Periode 1, 576
Traumulus, 195
Trip nach Tunis, 441
Triumph des Willens, 27, 103, 145, 157, 238, 255–61, 466
Turm des Schweigens, Der, 97
Twelve Chairs, 627

Überall ist es besser wo wir nicht sind, 514, 516
Unberührbare, Die, 512, 515–16
... und über uns der Himmel, 317, 336
unheimliche Mönch, Der, 380
Unmögliche Liebe, 3, 49
Unser (T)Raumschiff, 575
Unsere Steine, 402, 417
Untergang, Der, 508, 516, 589–95, 606, 613
Untertan, Der, 424
Usinimage, 623

Vanina, 90–91
Variation, 568
Varieté, 92, 111, 114, 185, 186, 188, 191, 194
Verboten!, 325–26
verkaufte Braut, Die, 41
Verlierer, 618
Verlorene, Der, 334–40
verlorene Ehre der Katharina Blum, Die, 467

Versprechen, Das, 512, 610, 613
Versunkene Welten, 97
Virus kennt keine Moral, Ein, 539
Von Rosa von Praunheim, 538
von Uns, Eine, 170
Vordertreppe und Hintertreppe, 47
Vorleser, Der, 611
Vormittags-Spuk, 164
Voyage to the Moon, 622

Wachsfigurenkabinett, Das, 156
Wahlkampf 1932 (Letzte Wahl), 2
Warenhausprinzessin, Die, 60
Way of All Flesh, The, 191, 195
Weekend, 208–12
Wege in die Nacht, 516
Wege zu Kraft und Schönheit, 153–59, 160
weiße Band, Das, 567–68, 632
weiße Hölle vom Piz Palü, Die, 144, 146
weißen Rosen, Die, 47
Welt im Film, 315, 317, 323
West Side Story, 618
Westfront 1918, 231
White Diamond, The, 555
Wickie und die starken Männer, 576
Wie man sieht, 490–96
Winnetou und das Halbblut Apanatschi, 573
Winterschläfer, 534
Wir haben vergessen zurückzukehren, 584
Wir können auch anders, 515, 525
Wirkung der Hungerblockade auf die Volksgesundheit, Die, 155
Witness for the Prosecution, 521
Wizard of Oz, The, 134
Wolke Neun, 516
Workers Leaving the Factory, 622
Worte des Vorsitzenden, Die, 402, 403, 417
Woyzeck, 436, 561–62
Wunder des Schneeschuhs, Das, 143–44
Wunder von Bern, Das, 578–82
Wunschkonzert, 275–81

Yasemin, 549

Yella, 516, 605
Yvette, die Modeprinzessin, 60

Zapatas Bande, 47
Zimmer 13, 380

Zimmerspringbrunnen, Der, 516
Zinker, Der, 380
Zwischen Gestern und Morgen, 317, 318, 336

www.ingramcontent.com/pod-product-compliance
Lightning Source LLC
Chambersburg PA
CBHW070753300426
44111CB00014B/2392